Volume Two

HOUGHTON MIFFLIN COMPANY · BOSTON

Sociological Theories in Progress

JOSEPH BERGER
MORRIS ZELDITCH, JR.
BO ANDERSON

New York · Atlanta · Geneva, Illinois · Dallas · Palo Alto

Printed in the U.S.A.

Library of Congress Catalog Card Number: 66–4287

ISBN: 0–395–04179–1

This book is dedicated to three individuals who in their very different and distinctive ways have made major contributions to the development of rigorous theoretical work in our field: **George C. Homans, John G. Kemeny, and J. Laurie Snell.**

Acknowledgements

We would like to acknowledge the contribution made to this volume by the editorial staff of Houghton Mifflin; by Robert Z. Norman and J. Laurie Snell, of the Department of Mathematics of Dartmouth College who acted as mathematical editors, and Israel Adler, now of the Hebrew University in Jerusalem who assisted in reading several of the manuscripts; and by the secretarial staff of the Laboratory for Social Research, particularly Mika Koutsogyannis and Sue Poage, and the Department of Sociology, particularly Alison Wilson.

Contents

Introduction

Some sociologists want to know why Watts had a riot. Some want to understand the general process by which order and disorder are created: The nature of the process; its conditions, its consequences. Sometimes it is the same individual who asks both kinds of questions. Nevertheless, their character is different: The first is essentially *historical*: Not so much in the sense that it deals with something in the past, but rather in the sense that it is particular in time and place; for what matters is a particular effect to be explained. The second is *generalizing*: What matters is the formulation of abstract and general laws to be used in an indefinitely large number of such explanations. The difference between the two questions is not a matter of their formal structure. From a formal point of view their logic is the same, for in both cases one or more statements of fact are inferred from other statements of fact by means of general laws. The difference is rather one of purpose. But differences in purpose are important, and in this case give rise to fundamental differences in strategy: In what is seen to be an important problem, in what facts are seen to be relevant to that problem, in what sorts of criteria are used to define a problem as solved. The difference between a historical and a generalizing strategy is greater, in our opinion, than the difference between quantitative and qualitative research, or micro- and macro-sociology, or formal and informal theory. The papers in the present volume, despite great differences in subject and style, are all generalizing in orientation. They have, in consequence, certain characteristics in common. Our purpose in introducing them is to comment on the common characteristics of a generalizing strategy, on their status in contemporary sociology, and their proper relation to a historical strategy of research.

□ CHARACTER OF HISTORICAL AND GENERALIZING STRATEGIES

An explanation is a deductive argument in which some effect is inferred from one or more initial conditions and one or more general laws.[1] The structure of

---

[1] This does not distinguish deductive-nomological from probabilistic explanation. Although there are important differences between the two, particularly concerning the nature of inference, from our point of view what they have in common is more important, and our argument is not affected by their differences. Hence, we will discuss the simpler case here. For general discussions of the problem of explanation, see Hempel, 1942; Hempel and Oppenheim, 1948; Hempel, 1965, chapter 12; or Nagel, 1961.

such an argument is illustrated in the following example: In a 1925 paper on social distance, Bogardus reported that social distance was particularly emphasized in cities. The increased emphasis on social distance in cities, he argued, was caused by the short physical distances in cities, which made geographical mobility easy; the absence of any laws or customs that prevented individuals of different social status from living in the same neighborhood; and the assumption in large urban areas that common residence implies common status. Given these conditions, he reasoned, it was often the case that individuals of different status lived in the same neighborhood; the effect of this was to increase the status of status inferiors but decrease the status of status superiors; decreasing status causes status anxiety; but increased emphasis on social distance reduces status anxiety. In this argument the emphasis on social distance in cities is the *effect* to be explained; geographical and social mobility and the fact that common urban residence implies common social status are *initial conditions;* that decreasing status causes anxiety and increased emphasis on social distance reduces it are *general laws.* We accept such an explanation if we agree that the initial conditions are true of cities; if we accept the general laws used in it; and can show that the effect is validly deduced from its premises.

We have already said that historical and generalizing strategies do not differ in formal structure. The logical structure just described is common to both. What makes them different is the way in which this logic of explanation is used in research. In a historical strategy of research the primary focus of interest is on the particular effect to be explained. Given that this is so, the investigator's problem is solved when he has identified the causes, the initial conditions, that produced the effect. That France had a revolution in May 1968 was due (let us suppose) to overcrowding of the Sorbonne, the high rate at which students failed their exams, the high degree of centralization of the educational bureaucracy, the slow rate at which urban wages increased during a period of great economic growth, and the rapid change in the French occupational structure. The list could be made longer; but the point is that explaining the particular event focuses primary attention on its identifiable initial conditions.

Not that general laws play no part in this search. But their role is secondary, not primary; of instrumental, rather than intrinsic, significance. Logically they are required in order to deduce the effect from the causes; and they may play an important role in justifying why one rather than another list of causes is accepted. One might claim that rapid change of the French occupational structure was indeed one of the causes of the May revolution by arguing that universities prepare students for careers; that the French university had become less useful in this respect; and, in general, individuals become alienated from institutions that require performance of tasks not instrumental to their goals. But formulating concepts, laws, or theories is not the purpose of the investigation: The relation between goals, tasks, and commitment is not in itself the point; the investigator is not trying to formulate this process more generally, nor understand its conditions or consequences. He is trying to explain some aspect of the May revolution. His interest in more general processes may be so slight that they are left implicit; implying that the general principles are of the sort everyone knows and no one needs to state. Or if stated, they may be either common sense propositions or empirical generalizations of a very low level of generality.

In historical investigations the explanation of a particular effect is the main purpose and laws are largely instrumental to this purpose. In generalizing investigations laws are the primary focus of interest. In explaining student unrest in the May revolution we may have used the law that individuals become alienated from institutions that require performance of tasks not instrumental to their goals. A generalizing investigation would have as its purpose the abstract, general formulation of this process; would be interested in a study of its nature, its conditions, its consequences; would make its subject commitment, not the May revolution.

Because the focus of interest is the law itself, and not any particular one of its concrete instances, a generalizing investigation has a considerable degree of latitude in choosing the setting for its investigation. For the attitude towards particular causes and effects is purely instrumental, in the same way and to the same degree that in historical investigations it is general laws that are purely instrumental. The purpose of a generalizing investigation is to test, reformulate, refine, or extend an abstract, general theory. A large number of concretely quite different settings serve equally well as instances of the process, for no particular one of them has any special importance for the investigation. Which initial conditions and which effects are chosen for investigation depend on purely pragmatic considerations: Which are most sensitive? Which offer the best prospect of control over the process? Which are least obscured by other processes of no immediate interest to the investigation? Pragmatic considerations of this sort, for example, would be more important than considerations of social significance, historical relevance, or common occurrence.

For most sociologists the distinction just made between historical and generalizing strategies of research will be too sharp. It will fly in the face, too, of a widely accepted solution to the problem of making research theoretically relevant and theory empirically testable: A solution according to which the "gap" between theory and research must be closed by having theory provide researchers with ideas to guide them, while researchers provide theorists with leads that emerge from their explanations of particular events (Merton, 1957). We will argue that a sharper distinction is nevertheless necessary: A conclusion that follows if it is agreed that one of the goals of sociology is the accumulation of general knowledge of social behavior. For such knowledge accumulates only very slowly, if at all, from a purely historical strategy of research. Nor is it sufficient, in order to increase the rate at which it grows, to make the effects of a historical investigation also "theoretically relevant" if the aims, standards, and methods of such investigations remain in other respects historically-oriented; for the aims, standards, and methods of such research can often be at cross-purposes with the objective of accumulating general knowledge. Hence, not closing the gap, but a clearer distinction between historical and generalizing strategies is required.

☐ THE ROLE OF LAWS IN A HISTORICAL STRATEGY

Laws seldom emerge from a purely historical strategy: In the first place, laws are not the intrinsic interest of historical investigations; laws will therefore sometimes be left unstated; if stated, they will sometimes be either common sense propositions or empirical generalizations of a low degree of generality, sufficient to permit deduction of the effect to be explained but not much more; and even if they are general ideas, they will be suggested as leads for further investigation, but it will not be part of the purpose of the investigation to follow them up. In the second place, a particular effect is of intrinsic interest; it would therefore be irrelevant to follow up any theoretical leads it might suggest by choosing, on pragmatic grounds, some other effect, or some other set of initial conditions as the proper setting for an investigation; indeed, it would even be irrelevant to give the effect a highly abstract formulation. In the third place, a satisfactory explanation of a particular effect is defined as one that explains as much as possible of its variance; committing the investigation to criteria of "success" that assure complexity and holism rather than abstract, general formulation. In a sense, the pure historical investigation both demands less and insists on more than the formulation of abstract, general laws of behavior.

First: That laws are not of any intrinsic interest in a purely historical investigation makes it possible for the investigation to be content with a relatively unsystematic collection of relatively unformulated, relatively concrete, and relatively common sense propositions about social behavior. The difficulty is not so much in the fact that the purpose is atheoretical: For we will see that difficulties remain even if a socially important effect is also theoretically relevant. The difficulty is that it is an effect, not a law or set of laws, that is of central concern. For example: Sociologists have for a long time been interested in determinants of educational aspirations and in particular aspirations with respect to college. It is known that four variables determine these aspirations: Father's education, father's occupation, parental pressures for college, and family size. (See Rehberg and Westby, 1967 for bibliography.) Partial correlation methods, furthermore, permit the conclusion that, although these variables are correlated with each other, each has an independent effect on college aspirations (Rehberg and Westby, 1967). A causal model of this process may be formulated in which parental pressures are the most important determinant of the educational expectations of adolescent males. Parental pressures are determined by the father's education and occupation; the father's occupation is itself determined by the father's education. But the father's occupation and education have direct effects on the son's educational expectations over and above their effect on parental pressures; and family size reduces parental pressures on the son and independently of that, it also decreases the educational expectations of the son. (This model is taken from Rehberg and Westby, 1967.) While such a model may require the guidance of a theory, it does not itself formulate any abstract theoretical principles: The statement that parental pressures account for 25 per cent of the variance in the son's educational expectations is not a formulation of a principle of socialization. Furthermore, the independent effect of a father's education and occupation on a son's educational expectations is probably due to a process of role-modeling; but the analysis given here does not further our understanding of role-modeling as a general process. The effect of family size is presumably due both to a process of rational decision-making, having to do with allocation of resources, and to the part played by family size in decreasing the effectiveness of parental pressures on the son; but neither process is formulated by this model. The same argument can be multiplied, for several other processes are implied by the model; but the result of the argument is already sufficiently clear. What is important is the effect, educational aspirations. Educational aspirations might be explained by laws of role-modeling, decision-making, and other concepts, but the causal model of these aspirations does not formulate these laws, and could not, as a matter of fact, give a systematic and general analysis of them without being irrelevant to its main purpose. It would not make rational decision-making, role-modeling, or status maintenance processes the focus of the investigation; it would not make "status" or "resources" its principal concepts in place of "occupation" or "family size"; it would not even want to more abstractly formulate its narrowly limited scope: For the Rehberg-Westby model is a model of the aspirations of American male adolescents. It might be generalized, by more abstractly defining the kinds of occupational structures of which it is true. But for purposes of explaining the educational aspirations of American adolescent males there is no great need to do so.

Second: It does not serve the purpose of a historically-oriented investigation to take a pragmatic attitude to an effect that is intrinsically important: It does not serve its purpose to (a) formulate the effect in terms of a more abstract, general process, and (b) investigate that process in a situation chosen on purely instrumental grounds. It is doubtful, for example, that educational aspirations are the best situation in which to study rational decision-making, or role-modeling, or status maintenance processes. We might possibly study rational allocation of resources by studying the effect of family size on aspirations; but the process is obviously confounded by another in which either sheer size, or else the addition of older siblings as competing agents of socialization, also determines the effect. Perhaps experimental bargaining games are a better situation in which to study rational decision-making: Such games are simpler; they are more readily controlled, so that confounding factors can be more easily ruled out; their effects are more direct operational definitions of the outcome associated with the process, so that the data are more readily interpreted, at the same time that they are more easily and precisely measured. But from a historically-oriented point of view the simplicity of the situation makes it artificial; the manipulation of it, the fact that some of the conditions under which it is made to occur are uncommon, makes it unrealistic; and the effect, however revealing in other respects, is not educational aspirations and is therefore unrelated to the purposes of the original investigation. Not that experimental methods are the issue here: We are not arguing that a generalizing orientation requires experimentation. Comparative sociology has some equally abstract formulations, and its comparisons are sometimes made not for their intrinsic interest, but because they are most informative with respect to a general social process.[2] The argument, rather, is that whatever the choice of method one cannot formulate a process abstractly, and take towards any particular causes and effects of it an instrumental attitude, if the particular effect is itself intrinsically important.

Third: The degree to which a historical investigation is satisfactory is determined in part by the degree to which it takes every relevant factor into account. Hence, such investigations deal with quite complex processes. They are complex in at least two ways: They typically seek to explain quite a large number of different effects, and the effects themselves are often complex. For example, to understand the May Revolution in France, it would be necessary to know not only why the students were so ready to riot, but also why their professors encouraged them to do so, why the riot police were so excessively brutal, why the government was at first so unsure of itself, why the workers broke out in wildcat strikes at approximately that time, why the Communist party was at first so reluctant to bring down the government, why in the end the party "joined" the revolution, why the provinces were so frightened by unrest in Paris, why Marseilles was violent but Tours peaceful, why Pompidou, after so fumbling a beginning, ended by being so masterful, and a good deal more.

The difficulty this creates is well known: The more of this one revolution we try to understand, the less general is our knowledge of revolutions. No other revolution is quite like the May revolution and as long as we maintain a holistic interest in it we bar ourselves from any general study of such phenomena as the radicalization of middle-class students, or the wage comparisons of workers in expanding economies, or the instability of many-party states, or the psychology of political understudies, or whatever other processes one supposes to be going on in this particular revolution.

But not all historically-oriented investigations are holistic in this sense. Our notion of such an investigation encompasses not only the kind that explains many aspects of one situation, but also the kind that is concerned with one particular effect. It remains true that such an investigation is complex: Complex in the sense that it is made up of more than one process. For example, suppose the effect that concerns us is the alienation of French middle-class students. One source of this alienation may be the difference between the goals of the student and the goals for which the university prepares the student, a difference made increasingly wide by changes in the French occupational structure. This is a factor we have already mentioned. But some students come to the university for exactly the sort of preparation it gives, which is, essentially, access to elite status in the society. One may never use the technical training that the École Polytechnique provides, or the training that the École Normale provides, or even the training that the Sorbonne provides, and yet by passing their examinations

[2] For example, see Young's paper on the incest taboo (1967). Young shows the incest taboo to be only a special case of a more general kind of solidarity norm, and proposes investigating it in other kinds of solidary groups. But so far as we know, no one has yet done so.

one is prepared for such later statuses as, say, membership in the Conseille d'État. Historically, the university has controlled access to such elite statuses, and students have gone to the university to acquire them. The university is still an elite gate-keeper, and is therefore very strict about its examinations. As the number of students entering the university keeps increasing, the number who do not pass the exams keeps increasing. This number may be as high as 50 to 70 per cent of the total, depending on the faculty of the university in which the student is enrolled. One consequence is that French university education requires, among other things, a radical reconstruction of the self for large numbers of students. Already few students pass the Baccalaureate, which admits one to the university, and therefore admission to the university signifies that one is exceptional. But over half the students admitted must at some point come to terms with the fact that they are not good enough to complete a degree, which is no doubt a rather alienating experience. If this is true, the larger the number of students entering the university, the larger the pool of alienated intellectuals becomes. We do not insist that this explanation is true. But if it is true, the objectives of our investigation would require us to take it into account. For we would want to explain as high as possible a proportion of the variance in the effect.

Explaining more variance will usually mean complicating the process by which an effect is explained.[3] But complicating a process will lower its level of generality. This follows from the fact that invariance is a desirable property of any explanatory law. For complex processes are either not general or else not invariant. For example, we have just argued that alienation is a complex process in the sense that it is produced by at least two distinct, independent processes: One a utility process, having to do with the instrumental value of education for given goals; the other a self process, having to do with the radical reconstruction of the self required by failure. A law of alienation that does not distinguish the two is invariant if and only if they combine in other settings in the same way and to the same degree. Given a complex law of this sort, two strategies are possible: One is to confine its scope to those settings in which the utility and self processes do combine in the same way. The other is to analyze the process into its distinct parts, studying each component process independently of the other. Either strategy will render a law invariant; but the former will render the law invariant at the expense of generality.[4] Explaining a greater proportion of the variance is a strategy of the first type: Not that it is inappropriate to its purpose; it is precisely what is required by the explanation of a particular effect. But its purpose is not generalizing: Generalizing requires a quite different strategy; and that alternative strategy, analysis, is discouraged by adding more sources of variation to the explanation of an effect.

---

[3] Not every use of this criterion complicates by adding more processes. For example, one could use it also to add more conditions to the scope of a simpler process.

[4] It should be noted that whether or not a process is complex is an empirical issue; but given that it is complex, the argument that it is either not general or not invariant follows from the definition of the term *complex*.

It is important to observe that the difficulties of developing general explanatory propositions from historically-oriented investigations lie neither in any technical inferiority nor in the fact that there are not yet enough of them. Rehberg and Westby's investigation of educational aspirations is in no sense technically inferior; path analysis, which is likely to become the model for their kind of investigation in the future, is unquestionably a rigorous method — though its aims are basically historical (Duncan, 1966). Furthermore, in the case of educational aspirations it cannot be argued that if only there were more replications we would be in a position to develop general explanatory propositions from them. There were already 200 replications of the sort of research on which Rehberg and Westby's model was based, and still no formulation has emerged of any of the general principles required to explain their results. The research is good research, and there is enough of it. The results have been stable, the findings consistent; but no laws emerge. The difficulty is not in its quality nor in its quantity, but in its objectives, and in the strategy implied by those objectives.

□ IS THEORETICAL RELEVANCE SUFFICIENT?

There is an obvious objection to the argument just made: The "pure" historically-oriented investigation is pure fiction. There may once have been sociologists concerned only to explain particular effects; but more common today is the kind of strategy recommended by Rose in his presidential address to the American Sociological Association:

> "What often starts out as a trivial question in market research or the evaluation of the success or failure of some agency program can become restated as an intriguing question at the heart of sociological theory. The ascertaining of why a given product or program is a 'success' while another is a 'failure,' can lead to discoveries about basic aspects of human motivation and social structure — if such studies are carried on with sociological imagination." (Rose, 1969, p. 627)

In other words, a particular effect may also be seen as theoretically relevant: And if seen as theoretically relevant, the results of its investigation may suggest important questions for theorists to ask or even answers that have a more general significance.

This way of viewing the relevance of research to theory and of theory to research is in fact so widely accepted that good books on research method typically recognize theory as the mark of science's maturity: make accumulation of knowledge depend on the refinement, articulation, extension, or reformulation of theory rather than a linear increase in the number of sociology's discoveries of fact; and define problems as good to the degree that they are informative for some theory. All this is of course generalizing in orientation. It has as one of its consequences that pure historically-oriented research may be inhibited in its development; that some people may come to regard urban poverty research, for example, as poor stuff because it is seen as having little theoretical relevance. But this view not only seeks to make empirical research theoretically relevant, it also seeks to make theory construction empirically relevant: Cross-fertilization of theory and research is its primary objective; and it accomplishes this objective by "closing the gap" between the two.

The image of the gap is a common image among sociologists, and it provides sociology with a rather definite idea of who is ranged on either side of the gap, of what the gap itself consists, and what should be done to "close" it. On one side, is ranged those who

". . . seek above all to generalize, to find their way as rapidly as possible to the formulation of sociological laws." (Merton, 1957, p. 85)

On the other is ranged

". . . a hardy band who do not hunt too closely the implications of their research but who remain confident and assured that what they report is so." (Ibid.)

On this account, our troubles are due to the fact that hasty generalizers are much too indifferent to tests; the hardy empiricists are much too indifferent to explaining what they find. And the solution, obviously, is to bring them closer together· Theory must guide research, research must correct theory.

Gamberg has called this way of regarding the mutual relevance of theory and research the "neo-empiricist" tradition; and has argued, correctly we think, that instead of increasing the rate at which general knowledge of social behavior accumulates, it becomes a "justification of ongoing research" (Gamberg, 1969, p. 112). The neo-empiricist tradition tacitly assumes that it is sufficient to make a particular effect theoretically relevant for general knowledge to emerge from its investigation; but the research itself is essentially historical in strategy; there is no notion that the criteria by which such research is evaluated might defeat the purpose of generalization, or that a distinctive kind of research strategy might be necessary to effectively exploit the leads thus provided. Indeed, theorists in this view remain men who have great ideas; they think about the questions raised by historically-oriented research, and they provide hypotheses for such research; but they do not have a distinctive research strategy which is their own. Consequently, it is in fact true that neo-empiricist research provides suggestions about more general social processes; but these suggestions remain provocative leads: They are not followed up; the general process is not abstractly formulated, independent of its particular effects, nor are general questions about the nature of process, its conditions, or its consequences investigated.

Something like this is seen particularly clearly in the history of research on status crystallization. Lenski's first paper on status crystallization (1954) was an effort to explain political radicalism. It was from our point of view therefore a historically-oriented investigation. But his second was an effort to place these findings in the context of a process more general in its significance: A process, essentially, of status ambiguity (1956). Situations in which two or more people interact need to be defined; inconsistency in statuses makes such definitions ambiguous; ambiguity produces tensions, embarrassments, conflicts; such tensions motivate individuals in ambiguous situations to in some way reduce the ambiguity or withdraw from them.[5] Three "tests" were made of this formulation:

[5] Cf. Hughes, 1945.

First, Lenski in his 1956 paper sought to show that interaction was painful for inconsistents; second, I. Goffman, a student of Lenski's, improved his measure of radicalism (which had been the size of the Democratic vote in Detroit) and made an effort to show that inconsistents prefer a change in the power structure (1957); third, Jackson, another Lenski student, made an effort to show that inconsistents have more psychosomatic symptoms than consistents, implying they have more tensions (Jackson, 1962; Jackson and Burke, 1965). Nevertheless, only a small part of Lenski's 1956 paper is devoted to spelling out how the process he has in mind works; the question of the conditions under which it is found is not touched at all; its consequences remain very concrete in their formulation; and subsequent work has focused not on ambiguity as a general phenomenon, nor on its conditions and consequences, but rather on other particular effects that might be explained by such ambiguities. Of course, it is often argued that such investigations "test" theoretical formulations and can serve to suggest ways of reformulating them: But this is not so. Treiman, for example, has shown that inconsistency principles do not explain prejudice (1966). That inconsistency does not explain prejudice limits application of the theory: It does not suggest any reformulation of the way the process works, nor even of its conditions. It gives us no result that may be used in reformulating the general process by which statuses are defined. Even replications of Lenski's original work on radicalism, of which there have been several, do not do this. Kenkel (1956) has shown that Democratic voting in Columbus, Ohio, is not explained by the same principles as Democratic voting in Detroit. We may from this fact safely conclude that politics in Detroit are different from politics in Columbus; even that political radicalism is a complex as opposed to a unitary phenomenon; but not that inconsistency does not produce status ambiguity, nor even that status ambiguity does not produce tension and conflict, nor even that tension and conflict do not lead to some kind of resolution behavior. Various efforts by sociologists to test, apply, and in some cases even to reformulate Lenski's original formulation have in fact done little either to dispose of it or to improve on it.[6]

Thus, a neo-empiricist strategy of research produces some theoretical ideas and asks some important theoretical questions: But these leads are exploited largely by investigations that continue to be historically oriented in objectives and standards, which therefore can neither test them, revise them, nor answer fundamental questions about the nature of the process, its conditions, or its consequences. The difficulty that stands in the way of increasing our knowledge of the general process, and of discovering its conditions and consequences, is that the strategy of this subsequent research is at cross-purposes with the objective of studying status ambiguity as an abstract, general process. For general-

---

[6] Various methodological critiques have been made of this body of research, arguing that inconsistency effects cannot, for purely methodological reasons, be identified in survey data of the sort depended on by Lenski and his students, without additional *a priori* assumptions that would render the argument circular or beg the question. These arguments are sound, but they do not touch the central issue, for they tend to assume that historical investigations are the only source of empirical data relevant to the problem (Mitchell, 1964; Hyman, 1966; Blalock, 1966; Blalock, 1967).

izing and historical strategies are not only different; they are in some respects contradictory. Neo-empiricist claims for the theoretical relevance of a particular explanation do not alter this fundamental difference. What is purely an instrumental decision in a generalizing strategy is in a historical strategy intrinsically important; what is intrinsically important in a generalizing strategy is in a historical strategy largely instrumental. It remains true of the neo-empiricist tradition that it uses standards of "reality," of social importance, of historical relevance in choosing particular settings for investigation of general processes; and by its standards, a simpler, more readily controlled, more operationally clear investigation of an abstract, general process is still artificial, manipulated, and trivial. What is true with respect to choice of setting is true also with respect to criteria of solution: The explained variance criterion remains fundamental in neo-empiricist research, even theoretically relevant research. Instead of pursuing an analytic investigation, therefore, one looks for more sources of variation. The effect is to make the investigation complex; and therefore to defeat the purpose of generalizing from the investigation. If, as is required by generality, the investigation should be analytic, should focus on a unitary process, it will appear overly simplified and incomplete. What remains, therefore, from "theoretically relevant" historical research are some interesting suggestions, which might become the basis of a generalizing investigation, but suggestions that are typically not followed up because the aims, methods, and standards of the investigation remain in other respects historical in orientation. That it is obligatory to provide such leads in the neo-empiricist tradition is not the same as carrying out generalizing research.

□ WHAT IS TO BE DONE?

A historically-oriented strategy alone does not create a body of generalized knowledge about social behavior: Its focus is on particular effects; it uses laws, but their significance is purely instrumental; it searches for multiple causes, not the nature, conditions, and consequences of an analytically formulated abstract process. Making a particular effect theoretically relevant does not alter the situation: The aims, methods, and standards of work remain in other respects historically-oriented, and therefore in conflict with the purpose of generalizing from the research. Leads emerge; important questions are asked; but only very slowly, if at all, does general knowledge of social behavior accumulate.

If in fact sociology were a historically-oriented discipline, there would be no reason to complain of the slow rate at which its generalized knowledge accumulates. And it would of course be possible to make the discipline historically-oriented. No doubt there are some sociologists who view the discipline in this way, and if there are, there is no factual or logical rebuttal of their aims. The ultimate goals of a discipline are matters of value, not fact or·logic. Our argument, however, is based on the belief that many sociologists view their discipline differently: They remain committed to the view that whatever else sociology is, it is also a generalizing science. Strategies of research in sociology may more often be historical than generalizing; but the ultimate goal is general knowledge of social behavior.

If sociology is a generalizing science; if historically-oriented research alone will not create a body of general knowledge; if closing the gap between theory and research is insufficient remedy; it follows that sociologists require a distinctive research tradition the aims, methods, and standards of which are oriented to the accumulation of general knowledge. We emphasize that it is a tradition that is required; it is not enough simply to admire a few great men who have a few great ideas. Particular extraordinary men are not a tradition nor is having ideas enough. For some sociologists generalizing must be a customary, routine, ordinary way of work; individuals must be recruited, motivated, rewarded, trained for working in this way; and its practice must be seen as not the special province only of great men, but the distinctive strategy of those committed to explicitly developing general knowledge of social behavior.

This argument does not imply that less energy should be spent in historically-oriented research. There are good reasons for historically-oriented research, and this argument does not deny them. In fact, a clearer distinction between the two strategies, and a recognition of the cross-purposes at which they work, should free historically-oriented research of some of the inhibitions implied in the obligation always to be theoretically relevant. There are good reasons for urban poverty research that have nothing to do with theoretical relevance; good reasons for explaining race riots that have nothing to do with testing theories about rising expectations. In any case, it is difficult to see what purpose a generalizing strategy would have if there were no historically-oriented research. The purpose of a generalizing research orientation is to provide laws to be used in explanation, prediction, application. Of what point would the enterprise be if there were no explanation, prediction, or application? The two strategies are complementary; one could not supplant the other. All that we argue is that this complementary relation does not imply any similarity of aims, standards, or methods. The two strategies in fact work at cross-purposes: In our view, a clearer distinction between them contributes as much to the one as to the other.

We believe the aims, standards, and methods of a generalizing strategy are evident in the examples we have collected in this volume. The papers published here are for the most part concerned with the formulation of abstract, general processes rather than the investigation of particular effects: With reference group processes in decision-making, not voting; with exchange processes, not the economy or kinship. They are analytic, making no pretense of identifying all the sources of variation in any particular effect: While distributive justice may be a factor in riots, other obviously important factors in riots, such as community structure, access to political decision-making, and the behavior of police are neglected in the analysis given here in favor of a focus on the nature and conditions of the distributive justice process itself; while power has an obvious relation to authority, it is neglected here in a study focused on evaluational processes in authority structures. Where data are used, they are chosen because they are informative about the nature, conditions, and consequences of an abstract process, not for their intrinsic social or historical importance: Negotiations are studied in bargaining games, not international politics; decision-making in simple task-oriented dyads, not family or politics.

We publish these papers with two purposes in mind. One is didactic: In our view, training in the aims, methods, and standards of generalizing research lags far behind that of more conventional, more historically-oriented, research. If general knowledge of social behavior is to accumulate more rapidly, we believe students, whether they end by doing generalizing research or not, require a clearer understanding of the characteristics of a generalizing strategy. We hope that this collection of papers will contribute to their training in its methods, and to their understanding of its aims and standards. The other is scientific: These papers contribute to what we hope will be a growing body of research done from a generalizing point of view in sociology.

□ JOSEPH BERGER, MORRIS ZELDITCH, JR.
AND BO ANDERSON

□ REFERENCES

Blalock, H. M., "The Identification Problem and Theory Building: The Case of Status Inconsistency," *American Sociological Review* 31 (1966) pp. 52–61.

Blalock, H. M., "Tests of Status Inconsistency Theory: A Note of Caution," *Pacific Sociological Review* 10 (1967) pp. 69–74.

Bogardus, E. S., "Social Distance in The City," *Papers and Proceedings of the American Sociological Society* 20 (1925) pp. 40–46.

Duncan, O. D., "Path Analysis: Sociological Examples," *American Journal of Sociology* 72 (1966) pp. 1–16.

Gamberg, H., "Science and Scientism: The State of Sociology," *The American Sociologist* 4 (1969) pp. 111–116.

Goffman, I. W., "Status Consistency and Preference for Change in Power Distribution," *American Sociological Review* 22 (1957) pp. 275–281.

Hempel, C. G., "The Functions of General Laws in History," *Journal of Philosophy* 39 (1942) pp. 35–48.

Hempel, C. G., *Aspects of Scientific Explanation*, (New York: The Free Press, 1965).

Hempel, C. G., and P. Oppenheim, "Studies in the Logic of Explanation," *Philosophy of Science* 15 (1948) pp. 135–175.

Hughes, E. C., "Dilemmas and Contradictions of Status," *American Journal of Sociology* 50 (1945) pp. 353–359.

Hyman, M. D., "Determining the Effects of Status Inconsistency," *Public Opinion Quarterly* 30 (1966) pp. 120–129.

Jackson, E., "Status Consistency and Symptoms of Stress," *American Sociological Review* 27 (1962) pp. 469–480.

Jackson, E., and P. Burke, "Status and Symptoms of Stress: Additive and Interaction Effects," *American Sociological Review* 30 (1965) pp. 556–564.

Kenkel, W. F., "The Relationship Between Status Consistency and Politico-Economic Attitudes," *American Sociological Review* 21 (1956) pp. 365–369.

Lenski, G., "Status Crystallization: A Non-Vertical Dimension of Social Status," *American Sociological Review* 19 (1954) pp. 405–413.

Lenski, G., "Social Participation and Status Crystallization," *American Sociological Review* 21 (1956) pp. 458–464.

Merton, R. K., *Social Theory and Social Structure* (2nd Ed.), (Glencoe, Illinois: Free Press, 1957). Chapters 2 and 3.

Mitchell, R. E., "Methodological Notes on a Theory on Status Crystallization," *Public Opinion Quarterly* 28 (1964) pp. 315–325.

Nagel, E., The Structure of Science, (New York: Harcourt, Brace, and World, 1961).

Rehberg, R. A. and Westby, D. L., "Parental Encouragement, Occupation, Education and Family Size: Artifactual or Independent Determinants of Adolescent Educational Expectations?" *Social Forces* 45 (1967) pp. 362–374.

Rose, A., "Varieties of Sociological Imagination," *American Sociological Review* 34 (1969) pp. 623–630.

Treiman, D. J., "Status Discrepancy and Prejudice," *American Journal of Sociology* 71 (1966) pp. 651–664.

Young, F., "Incest Taboos and Social Solidarity," *American Journal of Sociology* 72 (1967) pp. 589–600.

One

**Decision-Making,
Exchange, and Interaction**

Chapter 1

Foundations for a Rational-Empirical Model of Negotiation*

■ OTOMAR J. BARTOS†

In a previous paper[1] we discussed a model of negotiation that may be termed a "causal" model: it was formally identical with the regression analysis model the dependent variable of which is the given negotiator's "present" demand, the independent variables, the same negotiator's "previous" demand and his opponents' "previous" offers. The main advantage of that model was that it allowed us to analyze a wealth of data gathered in experimental negotiations, and this analysis made it possible for us to inquire whether it is a good or a bad strategy to make concessions in our experimental negotiations.

Such an approach, fruitful as it was in many respects, still had some inherent limitations. Perhaps the most obvious of these was the implicit assumption that — for a given negotiator at least — there exists a *constant* tendency either to reciprocate concessions or to take advantage of them. Analysis of the data convinced us that, if there is indeed a constant tendency that characterizes a given negotiator, it is not as simple a one as that. It seemed that a negotiator's decision whether or not to reciprocate his opponent's concession depended not on a "blind" tendency to reciprocate, but rather on his *strategic* evaluation of the situation: if a concession was to his advantage, he made it; otherwise, he did not.

It would be impossible for us to point to any single feature of our data that convinced us of the limitations inherent in the causal model. Perhaps it was the generally low level of correlation between the concession-making of a negotiator and that of his opponents; perhaps it was the multiplicity of interpretations our findings allowed for.[2] In any case, we became interested in the

* The research on which this paper is based has been conducted under the Air Force Office of Scientific Research grant AFOSR 62–314.
† The author wishes to express his thanks for the cooperation and help given to him by the Social Science Research Institute at the University of Hawaii.
[1] Bartos (1966).
[2] See *ibid.*, "Discussion."

following problem: is it possible to formulate a model that takes into account the negotiators' *strategic* motivations and which, at the same time, utilizes the methods of *empirical* research to evaluate the plausibility of the model? This paper is a report on some preliminary solutions to this problem.

□ **GAME — THEORETICAL BACKGROUND**

Since it is our intention to inquire into the strategic aspects of negotiation, and since it is through negotiation that many social conflicts are resolved, it will be useful to preface the discussion of our model with a brief survey of an approach which has accomplished just that — applied the logic of strategy to social conflicts. This approach is, of course, the Theory of Games, originally codified by von Neumann and Morgenstern (1947). We shall discuss briefly two games which, in our opinion, are most directly relevant to the study of negotiation, as well as a recent theory of negotiation stemming from it.

Prisoner's Dilemma

One of the outstanding by-products of the Theory of Games is the formulation of a game having a rather disturbing property: if each player acts with "selfish" rationality — that is, if he is concerned only with maximizing his *own* utility — then the game ends in an outcome that is *less* satisfactory to each player than the outcome which results when all players ignore (selfish) rationality, and cooperate. This game is known as the Prisoner's Dilemma[3] and is exemplified by the following matrix:

Player 2

		C	D
Player 1	C	(2, 2)	(−2, 5)
	D	(5, −2)	(−1, −1)

Note that each player has two choices, C ("cooperate") and D ("defect"), and that each outcome has two payoffs: the first payoff of the pair shown in brackets is that of Player 1, the second, that of Player 2.

It can be shown that a player who wishes to be selfishly rational should play D; but if both play D, then both end up receiving −1 point. However, should both players choose C (a nonrational strategy), then each player receives +2 points. Thus the Prisoner's Dilemma game does indeed place the players in a dilemma: should one *trust* one's opponent and play cooperatively (note that violation of trust is both attractive to the opponent and punishing to the trusting player), thereby taking a chance at a large payoff, or should one play it safe and be satisfied with a low (negative) payoff?

[3] The name of the game as well as the game itself is attributed to A. W. Tucker.

The manner in which subjects (usually college students) in fact resolve this dilemma in *repeated plays* has been studied experimentally by several authors. The results to date seem to show that trust takes a long time to build — that at first the subjects tend to become "locked" in the "selfishly" rational solution DD, but that, as the play continues, the solution CC begins to predominate.[4]

The Theory of Walton and McKersie

The empirical approach to the problem embodied in the Prisoner's Dilemma is not the only one that can be employed. It is possible to inquire not only how this problem usually *is* resolved but also how it *should* be resolved. Since the Prisoner's Dilemma game is apparently unproductive in this respect, one may consider *expanding* the game by including variables which appear to be crucial in the plays of the game. The work of Walton and McKersie (1965) is quite instructive in this respect.

In its barest outlines, the argument presented by Walton and McKersie is as follows. A typical negotiation (their study was concerned primarily with labor-management negotiations) is not guided by a single motivating force (as is commonly assumed in the literature) but by no less than *four* distinct motivations:[5]

1. to maximize own payoffs;
2. to find a cooperative (jointly profitable) agreement;
3. to develop the most favorable attitudes;
4. to make a negotiator's behavior acceptable to the organization he represents.[6]

Not only are these four motivations distinct, but the behavior required to satisfy them is often conflicting. In the Prisoner's Dilemma, the first two motivations conflict; in different situations, other motivations can conflict as well. For example, mutual trust is needed if a cooperative solution is to be reached. However, an agreement is not completed by simply finding the solution with the largest joint payoff;[7] it is necessary to agree also on how the joint payoff is to be divided. And the struggle for determining this division tends to dissipate trust and may throw the participants back to a noncooperative solution, one which does *not* maximize joint payoff.

Bargaining Games

The Prisoner's Dilemma formalizes an important problem, one which confronts not only the student of negotiation, but also the student of most social conflicts. However, certain features of that game make it less than ideal as a basis for a

---

[4] For a good discussion of the Prisoner's Dilemma see, for example, Rapoport et al. (1965).
[5] We speak of four distinct motivations; the authors describe four "subprocesses."
[6] *Ibid.*
[7] Joint payoff from an outcome is simply the *sum* of the payoffs the outcome has for the individual participant.

study of negotiation: it presents the player with only two choices (to cooperate or to defect); it assumes that choices are made simultaneously, and it does not allow for making binding agreements. For these reasons, we shall consider another category of games which have gained some repute in the literature — those originally considered by Nash (1950). These games may be profitably termed "bargaining games."

A bargaining game may be represented by a $(n + 1)$xm matrix, the rows of which represent the $n + 1$ possible outcomes (the outcome "disagreement" and the n possible agreements on "proposals"), the columns representing the m negotiators participating in the game. For example, consider a negotiation game with three *proposals* (three possible agreements) and two negotiators:

$$
\begin{array}{cc}
 & \text{Neg. 1} \quad \text{Neg. 2} \\
\text{No agreement} & \begin{bmatrix} 0 & 0 \\ 2 & 7 \\ 3 & 5 \\ 0 & -3 \end{bmatrix}
\end{array}
\qquad (1)
$$

Agreement on: Proposal 1, Proposal 2, Proposal 3

Note that the "no agreement" outcome has *zero payoff* for both participants. This is a necessary ingredient of the so-called special bargaining games, and it allows for a particularly simple solution. However, Nash shows that if the game is in the same form as (1), and if the payoffs are *not* interpersonally comparable, and if rationality is defined in a plausible way,[8] then it is rational to agree on a joint strategy p^* that assigns a probability p^{*k} to each outcome and which maximizes the *product* of the expected payoffs. In other words, in order to obtain the Nash solution to (1), we first define the *expected payoff* w_i to negotiator i if he uses joint strategy $p_i = (p_{i0}, p_{i1}, p_{i2}, p_{i3})$ as

$$
w_i = p_i v_i = (p_{i0}, p_{i1}, p_{i2}, p_{i3}) \begin{bmatrix} v_{i0} \\ v_{i1} \\ v_{i2} \\ v_{i3} \end{bmatrix}
$$

The *Nash solution* of the game (1) is a joint strategy p^* that yields expected payoff $w_i^* = p^* v_i$ such that

$$
w_1^* w_2^* \geq w_1 w_2.
$$

It can be shown that for the game (1) the best joint strategy is one which chooses Proposal 1 with probability of $\frac{1}{4}$, Proposal 2 with probability of $\frac{3}{4}$. In other

---

[8] The most important of these assumptions is that, if the game is completely "symmetric," then it is rational to agree on an outcome that gives *equal* payoff to everybody. For a discussion of these assumptions see Bartos (1966).

words, it can be shown that $p^* = (0, \frac{1}{4}, \frac{3}{4}, 0)$ because the product

$$w_1{}^* w_2{}^* = (0, \tfrac{1}{4}, \tfrac{3}{4}, 0) \begin{bmatrix} 0 \\ 2 \\ 3 \\ 0 \end{bmatrix} \times (0, \tfrac{1}{4}, \tfrac{3}{4}, 0) \begin{bmatrix} 0 \\ 7 \\ 5 \\ -3 \end{bmatrix} = \tfrac{11}{4} \times \tfrac{22}{4} = 15.125$$

is larger than any other product $w_1 w_2$. Note that when p^* is used, Negotiator 1's expected payoff $w_1{}^*$ is $\frac{11}{4} = 2.75$, while Negotiator 2's expected payoff $w_2{}^*$ is $\frac{22}{4} = 5.50$. It is the product of these two expected payoffs,

$$2.75 \times 5.50 = 15.125,$$

that is the largest of all such products.[9]

We shall not be concerned here with the Nash solution as such. Of much greater interest to us is the concept underlying the solution, that is, the definition of bargaining games: the assumption that "no agreement" has zero payoff for everybody, the assumption that interpersonal comparisons of utility are not possible, the (implicit) assumption that a unanimous agreement is required.[10] We shall use these assumptions as a point of departure for our model.

Knowledge of Opponent's Payoffs

The work we have just discussed represents the mainstream of the current work that has bearing, directly or indirectly, on the theory of negotiation. The possibilities inherent in these approaches are many, and the results to date are gratifying. However, it is our opinion that one assumption common to these theories represents a stumbling block to further theoretical developments. This is the assumption that each negotiator knows the payoffs of his opponents.

We have both empirical and theoretical grounds for viewing this assumption as undesirable. On the empirical side, experiments by Fouraker and Siegel (1963) have shown that subjects who know the entire payoff matrix tend to reach a *different* solution than that reached by subjects who know only their own payoffs: full knowledge encourages diversity of solutions, with the "equal-split" cooperative[11] solution occupying a prominent place; ignorance of opponent's payoffs encourages "selfish" rationality and tends to lead to the noncooperative solution.

On the theoretical side, we offer two arguments. First, lengthy negotiation is much more necessary when opponents' payoffs are *not* known than when they are. When opponents' payoffs are not known, then negotiation is needed to establish not only what the opponent is willing to settle for, but also how *credible* are his protestations, "I will settle for nothing less than ..." The

---

[9] It can be shown that each bargaining game will have one and only one Nash solution.

[10] This last assumption is implicit in the very definition of joint strategy: it is the strategy that replaces the individual strategies of the players as one common strategy. Obviously, such a common strategy cannot be applied unless each player is willing to see it used instead of the individual strategies open to him.

[11] The "equal-split" solution is a solution in which each subject receives the *same* payoff.

fact that each negotiator knows reliably only his own payoffs makes it both mandatory for him to discover his opponents' payoffs (so he can evaluate his credibility) and possible to misrepresent his own payoffs (so his own protestations are more credible). If opponent's payoffs *are* known, then the credibility of a commitment is immediately obvious and thus there is no sense in making a commitment in the first place.[12]

In the second place, negotiators in real life are quite unlikely to know their opponent's payoffs and therefore usually are unable to determine what is and what is not an equal split of the joint payoff. Expressed in technical language, we believe that it is much more realistic to assume that "interpersonal comparisons of utility" *cannot* be made in real life than that they can. Such an assumption means that a negotiator never knows whether his opponent is earning a higher, the same, or a lower payoff than he is; he is able to tell only whether a particular outcome is more preferable or less preferable *to his opponent* than is another outcome.

This point has certain consequences for experimental investigation of negotiation. If one displays the entire payoff matrix, such as (1), then it is very difficult to convince the subjects that they should not engage in comparing each other's payoffs. As Fouraker and Siegel's experiments show, such comparisons will be made, the subjects will tend to agree on outcomes that give them equal payoff. In other words, the presentation of a matrix to the subjects biases the experiments toward the norm of equality — a norm which, in our opinion, is *seldom* applicable in real life negotiations, precisely because the payoffs of different participants *cannot* be compared.

□ BASIC ASSUMPTIONS

Our objective is to formulate a model that fits the negotiation process. In order to achieve this objective, we shall have to steer carefully between the difficulties of coping with negotiation in its full richness and complexity, and the sterility of oversimplification. Simplify we must. But we shall attempt to simplify only where it does the least damage.

The Rules of the Game

We believe that bargaining games provide a good starting point, one which strikes a workable balance between simplifying too much and too little. But we

---

[12] The uselessness of making commitments when all payoffs are known to all participants is predicated on the usual assumption that the payoff function describes fully *all* of a player's motivations. This means that the opponent knows precisely how valuable a particular outcome is to everybody. As a result, a particular alternative is *known* to be either advantageous or disadvantageous to a player. If it is not advantageous to him, the commitment to choose it will not be believed; if it is advantageous, he need not make the commitment. The only time commitment *does* make a difference under the condition of complete knowledge is when the rules of the game state that commitments are *binding*: then a commitment, once made, cannot be broken, hence it will be believed, no matter whether it is to the player's advantage or not.

shall make the game more realistic by assuming that a negotiator *does not know the payoff of his opponent "reliably."* Just what is meant by that assumption will be explained in some detail later.[13] At this point, we merely note that by making this assumption we introduce an entirely new motivation into the bargaining game, the motivation to discover opponents' payoffs.

To make our discussion simpler, we shall assume that the two negotiators speak in a sequence that does not vary throughout the session. Furthermore, we shall assume that each agreement is possible on only *one* proposal: to allow for agreement on several proposals is unnecessary,[14] and it introduces notational difficulties. We also assume that if an agreement is not reached by the time a deadline arrives, both players receive zero payoff. For easy reference, let us state these assumptions as the following *rules of the game*:

RULE 1: There are two negotiators $i = 1, 2$.

RULE 2: The negotiators speak in fixed order: 1, 2, 1, 2, 1, . . .

RULE 3: Each negotiator, when he speaks, has to endorse one and only one proposal f.

RULE 4: Each proposal has for each negotiator a constant payoff[15] v_{if}.

RULE 5: Throughout the session, each negotiator knows reliably only his own payoffs.

RULE 6: The session ends if two consecutive speeches endorse the same proposal, or if no agreement is reached before the deadline. The deadline occurs at a specific time which is known to both players.

RULE 7: If the negotiators agree on proposal f, each receives a payoff v_{if};[16] if they fail to agree before the deadline, each receives zero payoff. payoff.

[13] Basically, a player has a "reliable" knowledge of his opponents' payoffs if they are given by the rules of the game. Less abstractly, one can think of reliable knowledge as existing in situations when there is an *unimpeachable authority* which guarantees that the payoffs are those indicated in the matrix shown to the players.

[14] One can always view a combination of proposals as a "superproposal," hence, technically, restricting the discussion to single proposals does not decrease the generality of the discussion. However, some practical problems tend to be swept under the rug when the term "proposal" is used to apply both to single proposals and to combinations of proposals. The main problem is to determine the acceptability of a combination of proposals if the acceptability of *single* proposals only is given.

[15] The payoff v_{if} may be thought of profitably as *money* that is promised to the negotiator i if proposal f is unanimously agreed upon. This payoff is *constant* in the sense that the *only* thing that determines the payoff to negotiator i is the nature of the outcome: if proposal f is agreed upon unanimously, the payoff is v_{if}; if no agreement is reached, the payoff is zero.

[16] Clearly, the payoff actually received need *not* be the same for all negotiators.

The End-game

Of particular importance to the negotiation game defined by our rules are the last two[17] speeches delivered before an agreement is reached or the deadline arrives. Rule 6 states that these last two speeches will be the *sole* determinant of the payoff each negotiator receives: if both endorse the same proposal f, the payoff to negotiator i will be v_{if}; if they do not, his payoff will be zero. Given the importance of these last two speeches, we shall give that section of the game which they define a special name, the "end-game."

Among the two speeches that form the end-game, the first one stands out. It differs from the second in that the negotiator who makes this is the *only* negotiator who can choose which proposal to endorse. The one who speaks after him is reduced to either accepting or rejecting his choice because, as Rules 6 and 7 state, if he endorses a proposal different from that endorsed by the first speaker, the session ends in disagreement and everybody receives zero payoff. Thus we shall say that the negotiator who makes the first speech of the end-game plays a "dominant" role; the other plays a "passive" role.

Given the distinction between the dominant and the passive roles during the end-game, it is clear that any end-game can be represented by the following matrix:

$$
\begin{array}{cc}
 & \begin{array}{c} \text{Passive} \\ \text{Negotiator's Choice} \end{array} \\
\end{array}
$$

		Accept	Reject
	Proposal 1	(v_{11}, v_{21})	$(0, 0)$
Dominant	Proposal 2	(v_{12}, v_{22})	$(0, 0)$
Negotiator's	$\vdots$	$\vdots$	$\vdots$
Choices	Proposal f	(v_{1f}, v_{2f})	$(0, 0)$
	$\vdots$	$\vdots$	$\vdots$

We shall make the following basic assumption about the end-game:

ASSUMPTION 1: A rational player will accept, during the end-game, any proposal that has *positive* payoff for him.

One may object to this assumption on the grounds that some players may have a high level of aspiration and will not settle for anything below that level. Our answer is that this may be so, but in that case either of two circumstances will exist. First, the payoffs may not represent the true utilities of the players, the "no agreement" outcome may in fact have negative utility for the passive player — in which case it *is* rational for him to settle only for certain minimum payoff. However, we are assuming that "no agreement" has 0 utility for both players, and therefore such cases do not concern us. The second possibility is

---

[17] Because there are two negotiators who speak in an unchanging order.

that while "no agreement" may indeed have zero utility for the player, he is not rational, and hence he refuses to accept anything less than a certain minimum positive payoff. That case does not concern us either, since Assumption 1 refers to *rational* players only.[18]

Given assumption 1, it follows that the dominant player, being rational, will always attempt to endorse, during the end-game, only the proposal that has positive payoff for *everybody*. We shall thus distinguish among the set F of proposals f a subset of *universally acceptable* proposals g such that

$$v_{ig} > 0 \qquad \text{for } i = 1, 2 \tag{4}$$

It is obvious that the dominant player will limit his choice to the set G of acceptable proposals g: if he chooses a proposal having nonpositive payoff for his opponent, he will reject it, and he receives zero payoff; if he should choose a proposal that has nonpositive payoff for him, he would be non-rational since he can always get zero payoff from a nonagreement. However, there may be more than one proposal g in G. In that case it is clearly to his advantage to choose that proposal g which has the *highest* payoff for him. In other words, if he knew which proposals constitute the set G, he should choose g^* such that

$$v_{1g^*} \geq v_{1g} \qquad \begin{array}{l} \text{for all } g, \, i = 1 \text{ being the} \\ \textit{dominant negotiator.} \end{array} \tag{5}$$

If all negotiators knew all payoffs, then the *only* purpose of the negotiation preceding the end-game would be to determine who will be the dominant speaker during the end-game. The proposal g^* of (5) would then be the solution of our negotiation game. However, since our negotiators do not know their opponents' payoffs, the negotiation prior to the end-game can serve also to establish some plausible guesses about what is and what is not acceptable to the opponents. We shall now consider these guesses.

The Certainty Function

We shall assume that, while our negotiators do not know their opponents' payoffs reliably, nevertheless they can guess at them with varying degrees of *subjective certainty*. We thus associate with each player i a probability function p_{if} such that

$$0 \leq p_{if} \leq 1$$

The probability p_{if} is associated with the event that i's *opponent has positive payoff from proposal f*. This probability is subjective in the sense that it can be incorrect. In fact, this probability can be correct only if $p_{if} = 0, 1$, since the opponent either does or does not have positive payoff from a given proposal.

---

[18] An alternative interpretation of Assumption 1 is that it is in fact a *definition* of rationality: only those who satisfy that assumption will be called "rational."

Hence we can distinguish the following relationships between p_{if} and the true state of affairs:

    i. $p_{if} \neq 0, 1$; in this case p_{if} *cannot* be correct.
    ii. $p_{if} = 0$ or 1; in this case p_{if} *may, but need not,* be correct.

We shall refer to p_{if} as negotiator i's *certainty function*: p_{if} refers to his certainty that his opponent has positive payoff from f, $1 - p_{if}$ to his certainty that the opponent does *not* have positive payoff from f. Note that, since there are always two mutually exclusive events, the event "the opponent has positive payoff from f" and the event "the opponent does not have positive payoff from f," it does *not* hold true in general that $\sum_{f=1}^{n} p_{if} = 1$, the p_{if} do *not* form a probability distribution over the set of all proposals f in F.

The Main-Game

So far we have considered only the end-game, the last two speeches of a negotiation session. Ordinarily the end-game comprises only a minor part of the negotiation session, being preceded by a large number of speeches. Since the preceding part calls for a different analysis than does the end-game, and since it is usually much longer, we shall refer to it as the "main-game" of a negotiation session.

The basic strategic difference between the main-game and the end-game stems from the very fact that none of the speeches of the main-game is *final*: since the main-game is followed by the end-game, every speech of the main-game will be followed by at least one speech by each negotiator. Furthermore, only the final speeches — those of the end-game — determine the payoff for the negotiators; the speeches of the main-game have no payoff values attached to them. As a result, none of the speeches of the main-game can be viewed as an end in itself; each has to be viewed only with respect to its influence upon the end-game. Thus each negotiator should choose his speeches during the main-game with care; he should choose them in such a way that he will create for himself the most favorable end-game *conditions*. We now turn our attention to these conditions and their creation.

Optimal Conditions

We have pointed out that if our negotiators knew the entire matrix reliably, then the *only* question they would need to settle would be the choice of the dominant player for the end-game. But the situation changes drastically when we assume — as we do — that such knowledge is denied to them.

Note that Assumption 1 remains valid even when the negotiators do not know their opponents' payoffs; a rational passive player still should accept, during the end-game, *any* proposal that has positive payoff for him. But the usefulness of (5) is diminished: since the dominant player does not know his opponents' payoffs, he cannot identify the set of proposals g of (4), the proposals that have positive payoffs for his opponents.   As a result, he cannot decide on his own optimal choice, g^*, either.

But consider a dominant negotiator who, although not knowing his opponents' payoffs reliably, nevertheless is *subjectively certain* that he knows which proposals have positive payoffs for both of his opponents.   Would it not be rational for him to act on his subjective certainty as if it were objective truth? We believe it would, and make the following assumption:

> ASSUMPTION 2: If, at any point of the game, a player is *certain* about which proposals have and which do not have positive payoffs for his opponents, it is rational for him to act as if the proposals he believes to have positive payoff have such payoff *in fact*.

Given this assumption, it follows that the dominant negotiator $i = 1$ will endorse any proposal g if

$$v_{1g} > 0 \quad \text{and} \quad p_{1g} = 1. \tag{6}$$

The certainty function is (so far, implicitly) assumed to change as a result of the speeches of the negotiators during the main-game.   Two important consequences follow from this changeability of the certainty function and from (6):

i. the dominant player can make a rational choice during the end-game only if he is *certain* about all proposals, only if $p_{1f} = 0$ or 1.
ii. the passive player can influence the dominant players' final choice by causing the dominant player's certainty function to be *wrong*.

Let us turn our attention to ii. and consider just what would be the *optimal misinformation* that the passive negotiator ($i = 2$) should present to his opponent.   Since we know (and the passive negotiator presumably knows also) that the dominant negotiator will choose his final endorsement from the set G, the passive negotiator should focus upon this set.   Furthermore, he should somehow induce his opponent to endorse that proposal in G that has the highest payoff for the passive negotiator.   Thus we can distinguish two special proposals within G, g_1^* which has the highest payoff for the dominant negotiator and g_2^* which has the highest payoff for the passive negotiator.

There is only one way in which the passive negotiator can induce his opponent to choose g_2^*: since the dominant negotiator will always choose g_1^*, he will choose g_2^* only if $g_2^* = g_1^*$.   And we see immediately what strategy the passive negotiator should follow: he should try to convince his opponent that the set G consists of a single proposal, this proposal being g_2^*.   In other words, although there may be many proposals in G, he should try to convince his opponent that only one of them has positive payoff for the passive negotiator, the proposal which among all g has the highest payoff for the passive negotiator.

There is one flaw in this recommendation: the passive negotiator does not know the actual set G any more than the dominant negotiator does. To remedy this shortcoming, we apply Assumption 2 to the passive negotiator and substitute his beliefs for reality. We require that the passive negotiator be certain about which proposals have positive payoff for his opponent, that is, p_{2f} must be either 1 or 0. Once this requirement is met, he should strive to manipulate his opponent's certainty function p_{1f} in such a way that

$$p_{1f}p_{2f} = \begin{cases} 1 & \text{if } f = g_2{}^* \\ 0 & \text{otherwise} \end{cases} \tag{7}$$

Observe that we now use $g_2{}^*$ in a slightly different sense: $g_2{}^*$ is a member of the set of proposals the passive negotiator *believes* to have positive payoff for everybody.

To summarize, let us represent in tabular form what constitutes the optimal conditions during the end-game for both the dominant and the passive negotiators:

■ TABLE 1

Role	Prerequisite	Optimal Conditions
Dominant	—	$p_{1f} = \begin{cases} 1 & \text{if } v_{1f}, v_{2f} > 0 \\ 0 & \text{otherwise} \end{cases}$
Passive	$p_{2f} = \begin{cases} 1 & \text{if } v_{2f}, v_{1f} > 0 \\ 0 & \text{otherwise} \end{cases}$	$p_{1f} = \begin{cases} 1 & \text{if } f = g_2{}^* \\ 0 & \text{otherwise} \end{cases}$

Table 1 suggests several conclusions:

i. No matter which role our negotiator will play during the end-game, it is to his advantage to know *correctly* which proposals are acceptable to his opponents.

ii. However, there is an important difference between the two roles with respect to why such knowledge is desirable. For the dominant negotiator, such knowledge is necessary *and* sufficient for his final choice: once he knows which proposals are acceptable to his opponents, the optimal choice, $g_1{}^*$, follows *immediately*. For the passive negotiator such knowledge is necessary *but not sufficient*: it is merely the necessary prerequisite for determining the best misrepresentation of his own payoffs. To the extent to which it takes time to "mold" his opponents' beliefs p_{1f}, the optimal choice $g_2{}^*$ *does not follow immediately* after correct knowledge has been acquired.

iii. Thus the sufficient *and* necessary conditions differ for the dominant and the passive negotiators: for the dominant negotiator, it is correct knowledge alone; for the passive negotiator, it is correct knowledge *and* optimal misrepresentation of his own payoffs.

These conclusions, in turn, have a number of implications. First of all, note that our "rules of the game" leave unanswered the question of who will play the dominant role. Since the termination point of a session is either an agreement or the arrival of a deadline, none of the negotiators can expect with certainty to play the dominant role. Thus it seems reasonable that a negotiator should protect himself against the eventuality of ending up as a passive negotiator by satisfying *both* conditions of correct information and optimal misrepresentation. But in light of ii. above, such a negotiator will need to have correct information some time *before* he can hope to create optimum misrepresentation. Consequently, his negotiating behavior during the main-game can be divided roughly into two phases:

PHASE 1: Collecting *correct* information about which proposals are acceptable to his opponents.

PHASE 2: *Misrepresenting* own payoffs optimally [so that (7) is satisfied].

It is clear, since the availability of correct information is a prerequisite for optimum misrepresentation, that Phase 2 can start only *after* Phase 1 has been successful.[19]

A moment's reflection shows, however, that Phase 2 is possible only if it *coexists with Phase 1*, that is, only if Phase 1 is still in existence when Phase 2 begins, and both must continue. If this were not so — if Phase 1 ended the moment Phase 2 started — then any attempts to misrepresent own payoff (Phase 2) would be futile since the opponent is no longer collecting information (Phase 1 has ended).

But if Phases 1 and 2 coexist, then there is a feedback from one phase into the other:

a. Since each (rational) negotiator is trying to misrepresent his own payoffs optimally, each negotiator is gathering *wrong* information from his opponent.

b. Each new piece of wrong information may lead to a redefinition of own certainty function p_j and, as a result, to a redefinition of what is optimal misinformation q' and q''. Consequently, the behavior of the negotiators may become *erratic*; the opponents may be asked to believe different things at different times.

Thus we see what a typical negotiation session is like. It is characterized by a constant tug of war between the need to collect *correct* information and the need to give out *wrong* information. The main task of any theory of negotiation is to study the nature of this tension between the two motivations and to determine whether there is a rational solution.

[19] Phase 1 is successful if it makes the negotiator *certain*, if his certainty function contains only 1's and 0's.

Creating Favorable Conditions

We have been able to analyze our negotiation game with a minimum of arbitrary assumptions. In fact, we have made only two assumptions about our negotiators: one that a rational negotiator will accept any proposal with positive payoff; the other that, in the absence of reliable knowledge of which proposals are acceptable to his opponent, a rational player will substitute his beliefs for knowledge (provided he is certain about his estimates). With these two assumptions, we were able to identify the two basic — and conflicting — motivations a rational negotiator should have: to discover opponents' payoffs and to misrepresent his own.

But to identify *motivations* is not the same thing as determining how these motivations should be pursued. And, clearly, it is quite difficult to determine how a rational negotiator should behave: in order to do so, we have to make assumptions about:

i. the *actual* impact of the speeches delivered during the main-game upon the certainty functions, and
ii. the *believed* impact of the speeches upon the certainty functions.

Clearly, i. and ii. may be in fact false, and yet a negotiator can be guided only by what he believes to be true. The determination of the optimal strategies of negotiation, therefore, is very difficult when i. and ii. are unknown. All we can do is to make some plausible but nevertheless arbitrary assumptions about i. and ii., and proceed as if these assumptions were correct. The hope is that this procedure will ultimately shed some light upon ii. itself by suggesting what a rational negotiator *should* believe the impact of his speeches to be when certain assumptions are made. The validity of these assumptions about i. can then be examined by empirical research.

□ SUMMARY AND CONCLUSIONS

This paper is a preliminary attempt at building foundations on which a simple but sound theory of negotiation can be built. Therefore it is useful to state briefly the main features of the foundations we have laid as well as to describe briefly the structure that remains to be erected upon them.

Our Concept of Negotiation

Perhaps our most drastic departure from current practice is the emphasis on the fact that negotiators typically do not know (reliably) the payoffs of their opponents. While past theories either ignore this point or else fail to take it systematically into account, we introduced the concept of the *certainty function* and made it the most important variable of negotiation: each negotiator is concerned with and attempts to influence both his own and his opponents' beliefs as to which proposals are acceptable to everybody.

It should be emphasized that, in our conceptualization, the negotiator never tries to guess *how high* a payoff his opponent has from a particular proposal; he tries to decide only whether his payoff is or is not *positive*. This is a simplification that represents a departure from much of current thinking and from our own past work: the negotiator is expected only to be able to partition proposals into two subsets, those that are acceptable and those that are not.

This simplification has implications for our interpretation of an agreement that gives to one of the participants an exceptionally high payoff; how did this happen? Some theories of negotiation would explain it by reference to that participant's negotiating skills, perhaps pointing to the fact that he was tough, was slow to make a concession and quick to demand concessions from his opponents. Our explanation will *always* be in terms of the certainty function: the negotiator in question received the high payoff only if his beliefs about his opponent were nearly correct while his opponent believed (wrongly) that the payoff in question was our player's *lowest* positive payoff.[20]

Thus, indeed, the manipulation of the certainty functions becomes of central importance to a negotiator. However, as we have shown, to determine how one *should* manipulate his opponents' beliefs is far from easy — both for the negotiator and for the theoretician. There are two main reasons for this difficulty. First, before a negotiator can start manipulating his opponents' beliefs, his own beliefs have to be reliable; he has to be certain about which proposals are acceptable to his opponents. As a result he is motivated, early in the session, to gather all the information he can concerning what his opponents will accept; later in the session, he is motivated to misrepresent what is acceptable to *him*. Second, these motivations influence not just one of the negotiators, but both of them. As a result, everybody is gathering information early in the game; everybody attempts to misrepresent later.

This division into information-gathering phase and misrepresentation phase is the source of the difficulty. Ideally, one might wish to keep the two phases separate, so that the second would begin only after the first has ended.[21] However, such separation would result in the *disappearance* of the second phase. To say that the first phase has ended implies that the negotiators have finished collecting information about what is acceptable to their opponents; each has made up his mind on that score. But if that should happen, then misrepresentation of own payoffs could not occur, because any attempts at misrepresentation, after everybody has made up his mind, would fall on deaf ears. As a result, the negotiators will resist separation of the two phases. They will "contaminate" the first phase by realizing that whatever information they give to their opponents during the first phase will have a profound influence upon whatever misrepresentation they can "get away with" during the second phase. And the

---

[20] It follows from (6) that the dominant player will endorse a proposal f only if $p_{if} = 1$. Now, to say that a negotiator received "exceptionally high payoff" implies that the dominant negotiator received a low payoff. The only reason for him to choose the low payoff would be if his $p_{if} = 0$ for all proposals that have high payoff for him.

[21] This is the recommendation made by Walton and McKersie (1965).

second phase will be "contaminated" by information-gathering characteristic of the first phase: if it is possible to influence the certainty function during the second phase, then, by definition, information-gathering is still taking place.

It is clear that, if the two phases blend together — as we believe they will — then each negotiator finds himself continuously torn between two needs. On one hand, he has to *receive correct* information from his opponents (so that he can define his optimal strategy), on the other, he has to *give out wrong* information (so that he can implement his optimal strategy). These two needs are not logically contradictory — there is no *logical* reason why a negotiator could not receive correct information while he is giving wrong information — but there may be a *strategic* contradiction between them. It is possible that misrepresentation has a halo effect, that as soon as one negotiator starts misrepresenting, the others will also. And if that should be true, then it will be true that the more fully one need is satisfied, the more difficult it becomes to satisfy the other. In other words, the more incorrect the information one gives, the more incorrect is the information one receives.

It might seem that the only solution to this dilemma is for everybody to give completely truthful information. If everyone were truthful, one may argue, then agreement could be approached in truly rational fashion, in the search for an agreement that is truly fair to all parties.

It is our view that while truthfulness may be the best strategy, nothing in the above discussion proves that this is so. First of all, it is true that truthfulness would resolve our dilemma by requiring each negotiator to give up the weapon of misinformation. But it is not at all true that truthfulness will necessarily lead to a fair solution: when the certainty functions are absolutely correct, the dominant player has a definite advantage since he can choose the proposal that gives the passive player the lowest possible positive payoff.

Even if we assume that this problem can be resolved — perhaps through a set of norms which require the dominant negotiator not to take advantage of his strong position — the value of truthfulness still remains open to question. Since there is no way in which a negotiator can determine whether his opponent is truthful or not, his motivation to be truthful may be very weak indeed. It appears that such a motivation may nevertheless exist if one believes in the halo effect of truthfulness: the truthfulness of one negotiator leads inevitably to the truthfulness of the other.

Future Work

The variables which emerge at this stage of our work as the ones that will play crucial roles in future research are the variables of *truthfulness* and of *trust*. These two variables are considered crucial because they provide a link between the world of reality and the world of belief: the degree to which a negotiator is telling the truth represents the "distance" between reality and fiction; the extent to which a negotiator is willing to trust others represents his estimate of this "distance." The fundamental facts — in our conceptualization — concerning this "distance" and its estimate are that a negotiator

i. *has to* estimate it, he must always guess how truthful his opponent is, but he
ii. has *no empirical basis* for such estimates.

As a result, he has to substitute faith for reality testing.

Social scientists are familiar with situations that lack firm foundations from which group agreements can be built. For example, the famous experiments with the "autokinetic effect" have explored what happens when members of a group are asked to judge the length of a line under conditions that make realistic judgment impossible.[22] In some cases of such "unstructured situations" one encounters what has been termed "self-fulfilling prophecy": if the members of a group believe that X is true, then X actually becomes true.

Does trusting others in negotiation have the properties of a self-fulfilling prophecy? Can it be shown that when one member trusts his opponents, his trust will in fact be justified — that his opponents will stop misrepresenting their payoffs?

In order to answer this question — if indeed it is answerable at all — we shall have to link empirical research with logical analysis. Just how this can be done is hard to predict at this time, but it seems certain that the difficulties which lie ahead are considerable.

□ **POSTSCRIPT**

The paper "Foundations for a Rational-Empirical Model of Negotiation" describes a theoretical position that is truly "in progress," being tentative and concerned more with posing certain problems than with solving them. Since it was written, however, some progress has occurred.

The late 1960's witnessed some rigorous work on a new category of games, the games with "incomplete information."[23] While many of the results are quite formal — such as proving the existence of a solution — some are of more immediate interest. For example, one conclusion is that "putting all cards on the table may be a great disadvantage and has the tendency to create a feeling of expecting to gain more where, in fact, one would end up gaining less. The most important object is to keep both sides interested in negotiations so that they can approach each other . . . ."[24] At the same time, even the most rigorous approach does not appear to have been capable of resolving our problems

[22] See Sherif (1936).
[23] See Aumann and Maschler (1966), Harsanyi (1966), and Stearns (1967).
[24] Saaty (1968), pp. 129–30.

altogether. "The case of incomplete information for both sides appears very difficult"[25] is perhaps a fair description of the present state of affairs. Thus, in spite of some rather impressive recent developments, many problems remain unresolved and continue to pose a challenge.

□ **REFERENCES**

Aumann, R. J., and Maschler, M., Game Theoretic Aspects of Gradual Disarmament in "Development of Utility Theory for Arms Control and Disarmament," Contract No. ACDA/ST-80 and 116 with *Mathematica* (Princeton, New Jersey, 1966).

Bartos, O. J., "Concession-Making in Experimental Negotiations," in Berger, Zelditch, Anderson, eds., *Sociological Theories in Progress*, Vol. 1 (Boston: Houghton Mifflin, 1966), pp. 3–28.

Bartos, O. J., *Simple Models of Group Behavior* (New York: Columbia University Press, 1967).

Fouraker, L. E., and Siegel, S., *Bargaining Behavior* (New York: McGraw-Hill, 1963).

Harsanyi, J. C., "A Generalized Nash Solution for Two-Person Cooperative Games with Incomplete Information," prepared under *Mathematica*, Contract No. ACDA/ST-116 (September 1966).

Nash, J. F., "The Bargaining Problem," *Econometrica*, 18 (1950), pp. 155–162.

Rapoport, A., *Prisoner's Dilemma* (Ann Arbor: University of Michigan Press, 1965).

Saaty, T. L., *Mathematical Models of Arms Control and Disarmament* (New York: John Wiley and Sons, Inc., 1968).

Stearns, R., A Formal Information Concept for Games with Incomplete Information, Chapter IV in "Models of Gradual Reduction of Arms," Vol. II, *Mathematica*, Study ACDA/ST-116 for the Arms Control Agency (1967).

Sherif, M., *The Psychology of Social Norms* (New York: Harper, 1936).

von Neumann, J., and O. Morgenstern, *The Theory of Games and Economic Behavior* (Princeton: Princeton University Press, 1947).

Walton, R. E., and R. B. McKersie, *A Behavorial Theory of Labor Negotiations* (New York: McGraw-Hill, 1965).

[25] Ibid., p. 134.

Chapter 2

A Formal Theory of Decision-Making*

■ SANTO F. CAMILLERI, JOSEPH BERGER
& THOMAS L. CONNER

This paper presents a formalization and development of some ideas about choice behavior that have existed in the literature for some time and are currently to be found in the work of Festinger and Homans in particular. The theory is basically a utility formulation, but differs from most previous formal treatments of utility in that it describes actual choice behavior rather than normative choice behavior.

We shall first present a general form of the theory, then discuss some limitations on its generality and some issues connected with its application in empirical situations. Finally we will present in detail an application of the theory to one particular experimental situation.

□ THE THEORY

We intend that the theory will apply to a rather broad class of decision-making situations. We have in mind situations in which: (1) a person must choose one course of action from among several mutually exclusive courses available to him, wherein each course of action leads to particular outcomes; (2) he has preferences among these outcomes; (3) he is motivated to try to obtain preferred outcomes; and (4) no social or personal restrictions on his level of aspiration are present, that is, we assume that Actor is motivated to maximize personal gain and not bound by considerations such as "one must try to obtain only what is proper to one's position."

The usual representation of such a choice situation is a matrix like that given in Figure 1. The R's represent the set of responses available to Actor and the C's represent conditions that can affect the outcomes of his choice. The X's represent sets of outcomes. For example, if Actor selected response R_1 under condition C_1, he would receive the outcomes in the set X_{11}. We will represent elementary outcomes, members of some set X, by x's.

* This work was supported in large part by grants from the National Science Foundation (NSF G-13314, G-23990 and GS-1310) and by assistance from the Human Learning Research Institute and the Cooperation/Conflict Research Group of Michigan State University.

21

| | Conditions | | | | |
Responses	C_1	C_2	C_3	$\ldots$	C_n
R_1	X_{11}	X_{12}	X_{13}	$\ldots$	X_{1n}
R_2	X_{21}	X_{22}	X_{23}	$\ldots$	X_{2n}
R_3	X_{31}	X_{32}	X_{33}	$\ldots$	X_{3n}
$\vdots$	$\vdots$	$\vdots$	$\vdots$		$\vdots$
R_m	X_{m1}	X_{m2}	X_{m3}	$\ldots$	X_{mn}

■ FIGURE 1

General Probability and Utility Assumptions

We assume that Actor's choice will depend on the subjective value or utility he attributes to the outcomes and on the likelihood of the outcomes. Actor may be uncertain as to which condition holds true at the time of his decision. He may have no knowledge at all of which condition is true, or he may have some knowledge, for example, he may know that his choice of response alters which condition will be true. We assume that he acts as if he attributes a well-defined probability distribution to the conditions for each response. That is, we assume that the probabilities he attributes are real numbers lying between zero and one and that the sum of these probabilities over the entire set of conditions is unity. These probabilities are subjective and may or may not correspond to objective ones. We will not deal here in general with the complicated problem of the relationship of the subjective probabilities to the objective ones. Where required we will assume some simple connection between them.

The set of all possible outcomes in a given situation we will designate by O. For any x_i, $x_i \in O$ if and only if x_i is an elementary outcome. The outcome $x_o \in O$, where x_o corresponds to neither receiving nor losing any quantity or commodity.

We assume that the outcomes in O have some utility, or subjective value, for Actor. We designate by $u(x_i)$ the utility to Actor of certainly receiving outcome x_i compared to receiving x_o. The $u(x_i)$ are real numbers that can be positive, negative, or zero.

Most treatments of utility have assumed that utility is measured only at the interval level. We believe this is an error. Behaviorally, people do distinguish gains from losses in an absolute sense, and they do recognize the situation of having gained and lost nothing. An adequate utility theory must take account of this. So we assume the utility numbers form a ratio scale as follows:

(1.1) $u(x_o) \equiv 0$

(1.2) $u(x_i)/u(x_j) = k_{ij}$ where k_{ij} is a constant for each i and j not equal to zero.

(1.3) $u(x_i) > 0$ if x_i is an elementary gain.
        $u(x_i) < 0$ if x_i is an elementary loss.

An outcome x_i is an elementary gain if Actor prefers certainly obtaining x_i to certainly obtaining x_o. Similarly x_i is an elementary loss if Actor prefers x_o to x_i.

(1.4) $u(x_i) = u(x_j)$ if Actor prefers neither one of x_i and x_j to the other.

The matrix in Figure 1 involves sets of elementary outcomes, so we need a rule for assigning utility to sets of outcomes. If x_i is a subset of O, then we assume

$$(1.5)\quad u(X_i) = \sum_j u(x_j)\qquad \text{for all } x_j \in X_i.$$

We must be able to specify the utility scale values of the outcomes. This is both an analytical and empirical problem. It is analytical in that we must specify the theoretical relation that exists between the utility numbers and the possible responses. It is empirical in that the utility numbers assigned will depend on the values of empirical quantities specified by the theory. In the sections to follow we will display the required theory and indicate which empirical quantities will lead to the assignment of specific utility numbers.

The Expected Positive Utility Formula

Our basic conception is that Actor selects a response on the basis of the utilities he associates with that response. Clearly this process of selection must involve some comparison of the utilities of the outcomes of the different responses available to him. Actor might, for example, compare only the gains or only the losses of the outcomes, or he might look at the net gains (the gains less the losses) of the responses. Utility models that use the concept of expected utility are based on the conception of net gain. Our theory employs a combination of utilities different from any of the above.

The basic substantive idea of our theory is that, in considering which response to make, Actor is "pushed" toward selecting a particular response by the gains associated with that response and also by the losses associated with the remaining responses. Conversely, he is pushed away from a particular response by the losses associated with it and also by the gains associated with the remaining responses. Lewin's vector representation of forces acting on individuals is an historical antecedent of this conception. In his theory of cognitive dissonance, Festinger[1] explicitly states an identical conception in considering the pre-decision aspects of certain dissonance-producing situations. He writes, "Imagine a person who has two job offers. All the cognitive elements corresponding to

[1] Festinger, L., *A Theory of Cognitive Dissonance*. Stanford: Stanford University Press, 1957.

favorable characteristics of job A and unfavorable characteristics of job B (call this cognitive cluster A) steer him in the direction of taking job A. Cognitive cluster B, elements corresponding to favorable characteristics of B and unfavorable characteristics of A, steer him in the direction of taking job B."[2]

Many of Homans'[3] ideas in his theory of social exchange are suggestive of our formulation, in some instances quite strongly so. His basic conception, like ours, is that individuals are motivated to action by the rewards and punishments they associate with the action. In analyzing the punishments, or costs, as he calls them, of an action, he enunciates the principle that a cost is a reward (or gain) foregone. He also suggests the converse of this principle, that a cost foregone is a gain, or reward. For example, he writes, "... escape from or avoidance of punishment is rewarding ..."[4] Again, in paraphrase, he writes that a pigeon faced with the choice of acting and receiving food but also incurring fatigue from acting, or not acting and not receiving food, but not incurring fatigue, is faced with two alternative rewards, the food he would receive for acting, and the avoidance of fatigue by not acting. That is, the gain of one alternative and the avoidance of the loss associated with the other alternative are counterposed as rewards. He does not carry the analysis through to counterpose the complementary elements of the alternatives, but such an extension is compatible with the general character of his remarks.

We assume that the contribution any outcome makes to the push toward a response will vary also with the probability of that outcome's occurring. Combining this assumption with the reasoning above we may now define a quantity which we call the *expected positive utility* of a response.

The expected positive utility of a response is the sum of the values of the utilities of the positive elementary outcomes associated with the response *minus* the values of the utilities of the negative elementary outcomes associated with the remaining responses, each weighed by its subjective probability of occurrence.

This is the formal statement of one of the basic substantive ideas on which the theory is developed.

As an example, let us assume that in a two-response, two-condition situation, each of the sets of outcomes consists of one elementary outcome and that the utilities of the elementary outcomes are as given in Figure 2. Then, if α represents the probability of C_1 and $(1 - \alpha)$ the probability of C_2, the expected positive utility of R_1, denoted by G_1, is given by

$$G_1 = (1)(\alpha) - (-2)(\alpha) = 3\alpha.$$

[2] *Ibid.*, p. 40.
[3] Homans, G. C., *Social Behavior: Its Elementary Forms.* New York: Harcourt, Brace & World, 1961.
[4] *Ibid.*, pp. 57–58.

Similarly, the expected positive utility of R_2, denoted by G_2, is

$$G_2 = (3)(1 - \alpha) - (-1)(1 - \alpha) = 4(1 - \alpha).$$

The formulas for more complicated situations are arrived at in the same manner.

	C_1	C_2
R_1	1	-1
R_2	-2	3

■ FIGURE 2

Expected Positive Utility and Choice

Under the conditions stated, we believe that Actor will sometimes select one response and sometimes another. We interpret this to mean that there are probabilities associated with the selection of each response, and assume that the probabilities are a function of the expected positive utility of each response.

We might have stated any number of functions expressing the probabilities, and we investigated several which seemed on intuitive grounds to be acceptable. The one we selected is simple, generalizable to any number of responses, resembles solutions to similar problems adopted by Luce and others, and adequately represents all of the substantive properties we wanted the function to have. We will develop the function for the two-response example discussed earlier and then state its general form.

In the two-response situation, we reason that the magnitude of the probability that R_1 will be chosen compared with the magnitude of the probability that R_2 will be chosen will be the same as the magnitude of the expected positive utility of R_1 compared with the magnitude of the expected positive utility of R_2. That is, if P_1 = the probability that R_1 will be chosen and P_2 = the probability that R_2 will be chosen, then $P_1 : P_2 = G_1 : G_2$. Because P_1 and P_2 must sum to unity, we can write $P_1 = \dfrac{G_1}{G_1 + G_2}$, and $P_2 = \dfrac{G_2}{G_1 + G_2}$. That is, the probability of choosing a response is given by the expected positive utility of that response divided by the expected positive utility of all responses. For the example given in Figure 2 we find that $P_1 = 3/(4 - \alpha)$ and $P_2 = \dfrac{(4 - 4\alpha)}{4 - \alpha}$. If α were $\frac{1}{2}$, then P_1 would be approximately .43.

The general form of the function for m responses is given below as equation (1):

$$(1) \quad P_k = \frac{G_k}{\sum\limits_{j=1}^{m} G_j}$$

Equation (1) is a basic postulate of the theory.

Equivalent Responses and Equivalent Conditions

We now want to consider certain further restrictions on the application of the theory—restrictions that are more easily explicated now that the theory has been presented. The first of these restrictions concerns the criteria to be used in distinguishing responses from each other and in distinguishing conditions from each other. We will distinguish responses or conditions only in terms of the elementary outcomes associated with them. Two responses will be considered different or distinguishable if we examine their outcomes and find that for some condition one response leads to a set of outcomes different from the other. If, however, we find that two responses have the same outcomes for each condition, we will think of them as the same or equivalent responses and analyze the situation by calling the choice of either response the choice of a single, newly defined response. For example, in Figure 3, the outcomes for both R_1 and R_2 are X_1 if C_1 holds, and X_2 if C_2 holds. R_1 and R_2, then, are equivalent responses, and the matrix in Figure 3 should be collapsed to the matrix in Figure 4. If we interpreted R_1 to mean "purchase a new Ford" and R_2 to mean "purchase a new Plymouth" and if x_1 represented the price if power steering is available and x_2 the price if it isn't, then the matrix in Figure 3 would be read, "I will have to pay x_1 for either a new Ford or a new Plymouth if power steering is available and x_2 if it is not." The collapsed matrix would be read "I will have to pay x_1 for *my new car* if power steering is available and x_2 if it is not."

	C_1	C_2
R_1	X_1	X_2
R_2	X_1	X_2

	C_1	C_2
R	X_1	X_2

■ **FIGURE 3**   ■ **FIGURE 4**

For conditions a similar criterion is adopted. Two conditions are distinguishable if their outcomes for some response are different, and they are equivalent if they lead to the same set of outcomes for each response. A matrix containing equivalent conditions must be collapsed so that the equivalent conditions appear as only one condition. The definitions of equivalent responses and equivalent conditions restrict the application of the theory to only those matrixes from which equivalent conditions and equivalent responses have been eliminated.

Dominance

Suppose again our decision-maker is faced with a two-response, two-condition situation in which he receives either $1 or $2 for selecting R_1, and 50¢ or 25¢ for selecting R_2, depending upon whether C_1 or C_2 obtains. It seems unreasonable to us to believe that R_2 would ever be selected, although the theory as it stands specifies its selection at least some of the time.

It can be shown that, if one response has no probability of being selected over some other response, then the ordinary rules of conditional probability dictate that the former response will have no probability of being selected from any set that contains the latter response. The proof is found in Luce's[5] book on individual choice behavior. Thus, if we decide that some one response will never be chosen over a second, then the first can be eliminated entirely from the matrix. We must, then, develop a theoretically based rule that tells us when one response will never be selected over another.

We can describe one set of circumstances in which we are confident one response will never be selected over a second. If, for some two responses, the probabilities assigned to each of the conditions are identical, and if for each condition the set of outcomes from one response is always preferred to the set of outcomes from the other, we believe that the first response will always be chosen. An alternative phrasing, often found in the literature, is that, if the two responses and the conditions are *statistically independent* and if the first response *dominates* the second, then the second will not be chosen. The dominated response must be eliminated from the matrix. So, if we encountered the matrix shown in Figure 5, R_2 would be eliminated because R_1 dominates it. The new matrix would then look like the one in Figure 6.

	C_1	C_2
R_1	$1	$2
R_2	50¢	25¢
R_3	$2	10¢

	C_1	C_2
R_1	$1	$2
R_2	$2	10¢

■ FIGURE 5   ■ FIGURE 6

There are undoubtedly other circumstances in which some response will never be selected. We are unable at present to find a satisfactory rule that specifies what those circumstances might be. The issue may be resolved only after empirical investigations have been carried out.

□ A HYPOTHETICAL APPLICATION OF THE THEORY

Conner[6] has presented an analysis of classical non-zero-sum game situations

[5] Luce, D. R., *Individual Choice Behavior: A Theoretical Analysis.* New York: John Wiley & Sons, Inc., 1959, p. 6, Lemma 1. Our theory has many features in common with Luce's. Although we cannot review them here, several of the theorems Luce reports in Chapter 1 of his book are relevant to our work.

[6] Conner, T. L., "A Stochastic Model for Decision Making in Non-Cooperative Games," in Phillips, J. and Conner, T. L. (eds.) *Technical Report 70–1*, Cooperation/Conflict Research Group, Michigan State University, East Lansing, Michigan. This section and portions of the preceding sections are adapted from this work.

that make use of the theory presented here. Whenever the set of conditions in the decision situation is the set of responses by another Actor, we have what has been called a game. That is, the situation is one in which two decision-makers select from among a set of responses and the outcomes they receive are determined by the combination of their selections. The usual matrix representation of this kind of situation is shown in Figure 7. The two Actors are labelled A and B, and each has been restricted to two responses, α_1 and α_2, and β_1 and β_2. The sets of outcomes are written within parentheses, with the first set representing the outcomes to A and the second set the outcomes to B. Thus, for example, if A selects α_1 and B selects β_2, then A receives whatever is in the set X_2 and B receives whatever is in the set X_3.

B's responses

		β_1	β_2
A's responses	α_1	(x_1, x_1)	(x_2, x_3)
	α_2	(x_3, x_2)	(x_4, x_4)

■ **FIGURE 7**

Conner places four restrictions upon the situation which form part of the scope of the analysis. Two of the restrictions are a part of the more general formulation that there be no personal or social restrictions on A's and B's levels of aspiration and that dominated responses be eliminated. The other restrictions are, first, that the matrix be symmetric, and second, that A and B always be able to alter their own and each other's outcomes by selecting one response or another.

Conner asserts that there are in the situation four essential elements which affect selection of a response: the Actor's evaluation of the outcomes, his motivations for selecting a response, his judgment of the other Actor's evaluations of the outcomes, and his judgment of the other Actor's motivations. An Actor's judgment of the other Actor's evaluations and motivations is represented as the subjective probability he attributes to the possibility that the other Actor will select each of his own responses. For the matrix in Figure 7, as seen from A's perspective, those probabilities are written as $P(\beta_1)$ and $P(\beta_2)$.

Conner's analysis contains two axioms. The first is equivalent to our equation (1). The second, called the ignorance axiom, says that, given no information to the contrary, any Actor will assume any other Actor's motivations and evaluations are similar to his own. This allows us to equate $P(\alpha_1)$ and $P(\beta_1)$, within any Actor's perspective.

Using his two axioms, the first to arrive at an expression for $P(\alpha_1)$ from A's perspective, which involves $P(\beta_1)$, and the second to establish that $P(\alpha_1) = P(\beta_1)$, Conner derives quadratic equations that involve only utility numbers and $P(\alpha_1)$. For example, if all the outcomes are elementary gains, the appropriate equation is that shown below:

$$[u(x_1) - u(x_2) + u(x_3) - u(x_4)]P^2(\alpha_1)$$
$$- [u(x_1) - 2u(x_2) - u(x_4)]P(\alpha_1) - u(x_2) = 0.$$

A similar kind of analysis can be done for zero-sum games and for iterated versions of both zero-sum and non-zero-sum games.

□ **TESTING THE THEORY**

In order to test the theory empirically, we require an empirical situation that conforms to the scope restrictions of the theory and that provides sufficient information to permit us to apply equation (1). In general we must know (a) the number and identity of the alternatives permitted and the conditions involved, (b) the elementary outcomes associated with each response-condition combination, (c) the utility values of these elementary outcomes, and (d) the probabilities of occurrence of a subset of the conditions. These are all state conditions, the specification of which poses substantive and analytic problems.

Substantively, we must have prior knowledge of the decision situation that is logically independent of the theory. There is nothing in the theory that indicates to us what is at issue in any given situation, what the subjects expect to occur or what value they attach to these consequences. In specifying the numerical quantities involved, we can make use of analytic properties of the formulation to provide some of the necessary information, but some will have to be derived from considerations independent of the theory if we are to avoid sheer curve-fitting. The maximum number of independent quantities required would occur in the situation in which all the probabilities assigned to conditions were different for different responses. If the situation involves m responses and n conditions, there would be $m(n - 1)$ probability parameters. In addition, if there are k different elementary outcomes, there are k utility values. We require at most only the pairwise ratios of $k - 1$ of these utilities. In all, then, we would require at most $m(n - 1) + (k - 1)$ quantities. We must have an empirical situation and a rationale that permit us to estimate these quantities. If a sufficiently large number of subjects made choices in this situation, we would then have $m - 1$ independent equations to use in determining the quantities required. That is, $m - 1$ quantities can be obtained from these equations, but the rest must be estimated independently in some way.

There does not exist a routine procedure for accomplishing this analysis and specification for all decision situations. In any particular application of the theory, this information must be determined by an *ad hoc* application of appropriate substantive principles and procedures of estimation. The test then is necessarily confounded by this specification, for if we have made an incorrect substantive determination of either the state conditions or the numerical quantities, the theory will give incorrect predictions and thus be rejected. On the other hand, if the test succeeds, credibility is earned for the statement of state conditions, the estimation procedures, and the assertions of the theory.

We now present an application of the model to an experimental situation originally designed by Berger[8] to explore stochastic models relating performance expectations and performance evaluations to the acceptance of influence in decision-making.

Experimental Procedure

In the Berger experimental situation, a pair of subjects is asked to make binary choices in two steps. The subjects are shown slides presenting two alternatives. They are given the instruction to make a provisional, independent decision between the alternatives; then, after being told what the other has decided, each is to take this information into account as he sees fit in making a final decision on the trial. A subject's final choices are not communicated to his partner. Subjects are led to believe that final decisions are being evaluated as "correct" or "incorrect" and that such evaluations constitute their performance score in the task situation. These evaluations, however, are not communicated by the experimenter to the subjects during the series of trials.

The exchange of information about provisional decisions involves a deception — the communicated provisional choices are not necessarily the actual choices made but rather follow a schedule determined by the experimenter according to whether or not he wants to create a disagreement between the subjects. In the situations most studied, which are of interest to us here, the experimenter creates continuous or almost continuous disagreements between the subjects on their provisional choices. Whether a subject makes a final choice which is inconsistent with his provisional choice (an "other" response), or one which is consistent with his provisional choice (a "self" response) on any trial of the process is regarded as an indication of whether he accepts influence or not.

The subjects make these choices under various structural conditions. They are first induced in a manipulation phase to believe that each of them has a certain amount (not necessarily the same) of the ability needed to make the choices presented. Each subject is also made aware of the amount of ability possessed by his partner. These beliefs constitute the "expectation state" of a subject. Since each subject is induced to believe that he has either superior or below average ability, four expectation states are distinguished: high ability for self, low for other, which we denote by $[+ -]$; high self and high other $[+ +]$; low self and low other $[- -]$, and low self and high other $[- +]$.

[7] The remainder of the paper is adapted from an earlier report, Camilleri, S. F. and J. Berger, "Decision-Making and Social Influence: A Model and an Experimental Test." *Sociometry*, Vol. 30, No. 4, December, 1967.

[8] Berger, J. and T. L. Conner, "Performance Expectations and Behavior in Small Groups." *Acta Sociologica*, Vol. 12, No. 4, 1969.

The task conditions are typically so defined that the subjects are working as a team. They are told that performance scores based on their final decisions are being calculated for the team as a unit. Further, subjects may differ in their control over the team product: one of them may be given full control or they may each be given equal control. Where one subject has full control over the team product, only his final decisions contribute to the team performance. In this case, he is in the position of having final decision-making rights, and the other, without control, is in the position of an advisor. Where subjects have equal control, their final decisions are weighted equally in determining the team's performance. In this case, subjects are "equals" in their decision-making rights.

The specific experiments to which we apply our model were carried out during 1967–68 at Michigan State University on university undergraduates who were paid volunteers. The pair of subjects in an experiment were of the same sex and usually previously unacquainted with each other. In all cases subjects were randomly assigned to one of the four expectation states and to one of the three control conditions (full, equal, no control). After being induced into expectation states and assigned control positions, these subjects were asked to make provisional and final choices on twenty trials and found themselves in disagreement with their partners on all twenty trials.

Utility Assumptions

Our assumption in applying the model to this situation is that there are three sources of utility in the decision situation. The first utility, u_1, is derived from the subject's evaluation of his own choice behavior.[9] We assume that the subject values having the ability required by the task and being consistent in his exercise of it. If an individual makes a choice between alternatives and then is led to reverse his choice as a consequence of the behavior of another, he will devalue his initial behavior and will disapprove of himself, whether he believes his final choice is correct or not. Thus, we assume that this inconsistent act has negative utility for him. If on the other hand, he makes a choice between alternatives and is consistent in his behavior, whether or not he doubts his final choice, he avoids self-disapproval of his own behavior and this has positive utility for him. We assume that these utilities which arise from self-approval or disapproval have the same absolute magnitude but are opposite in sign. On any trial this utility is deterministic: it is a direct function of the subject's action.

The second utility, u_2, is derived from the approval or disapproval the subject expects from his partner. If a subject with control for the team's decision is correct in a choice, the other will also be rewarded, since a correct final decision will increase the value of the team product; therefore, an individual with control over the final decisions will expect approval from the other for this correct act. On the other hand, if an individual with control makes a final decision that is incorrect, the other will fail to be rewarded and the individual

---

[9] For the remainder of the paper we represent $u(x_1)$ as u_1, $u(x_2)$ as u_2, and $u(x_3)$ as u_3.

with control can expect disapproval from him for that incorrect act. The approval and disapproval have equal magnitudes of utility, but they differ in valence, the first being positive and the second negative. In general, we assume that in this situation, the greater the subject's control over the team's decision, the greater the value of u_2. By this line of reasoning, $u_2 = 0$ when a subject has no control over the team's product. For subjects with control this utility is contingent on the correctness or incorrectness of the choice made as judged by the experimenter: it is a probabilistic element. There is no feedback, however, so the subject cannot know whether his final choice was correct or incorrect. We assume that the individual's subjective probability of being correct acts as implicit feedback, so that if an individual believes that there is a high probability that his choice is correct, he will act as though he has received a proportion of the utilities involved equal to that probability.

The third source of utility, u_3, is derived from the experimenter. We conceptualize the experimenter as playing a social role which is significant to the behavior of the team. He is an external source of evaluation. From the standpoint of the members of the team, he is capable both of judging the correctness of their final decisions and of distributing approval and disapproval on the basis of these judgments. The approval and disapproval given by the experimenter are assumed to be equal in magnitude. Since the approval or disapproval is contingent upon the subject's giving a correct or incorrect response, it is a probabilistic element which enters into the subject's thinking in a manner similar to his partner's approval or disapproval.

Estimation Procedures

Denoting by S a final choice consistent with a preliminary choice, and by O one inconsistent with a preliminary choice, we can express the probability of an S or O decision as a function of four basic quantities: the subjective probability of being correct in a final choice (a); and the magnitudes of the three approval values, self, other, and experimenter (u_1, u_2, and u_3). The utility structure of the alternatives, whether to give a consistent (S) or inconsistent (O) final decision on a given trial, is:

$$S \rightarrow u_1 + a(u_2 + u_3) - \bar{a}(u_2 + u_3).$$
$$O \rightarrow u_1 + \bar{a}(u_2 + u_3) - a(u_2 + u_3)$$

where $\bar{a} = (1 - a)$. By the definitions given, the expected gains are:

$$G_s = [u_1 + a(u_2 + u_3)] - [-u_1 - a(u_2 + u_3)]$$
$$G_o = [\bar{a}(u_2 + u_3)] - [-\bar{a}(u_2 + u_3)]$$

and by our basic postulate,

$$P(S) = \frac{G_s}{G_s + G_o} = \frac{u_1 + a(u_2 + u_3)}{u_1 + u_2 + u_3}.$$

For the case where Actor's expectation state is [+ +] and Other is team representative, $u_2 = 0$. Then,

$$P(S) = \frac{u_1 + au_3}{u_1 + u_3}$$

and

$$\frac{u_1}{u_3} = \frac{P(S) - a}{1 - P(S)}.$$

Other cases may be expressed similarly.

We derive a specification of a from the following consideration: In the manipulation phase of the experiment the subjects are put through a number of trials, each involving a single decision. The subject's individual total scores, the number each had decided "correctly," are announced aloud and interpreted according to (fictitious) norms of superior, average, and below average ranges. We assume that each subject uses this information in forming his subjective probability of being correct in subsequent trials when they disagree. We assume, specifically, that the subject considers the ratio of the number he got right to the number his partner got right in the manipulation phase and places his and his partner's probabilities of being correct when they disagree in the same ratio. That is, given that they have disagreed on the preliminary decision,

$$\frac{a}{1 - a} = \frac{\text{number correct by Actor}}{\text{number correct by Other}}.$$

By imposing the condition that the sum of the subjective probabilities is unity, we derive:

$$a = \frac{\text{number correct by Actor}}{\text{number correct by both}}.$$

To induce subjects into the [+ +] state, each is told that he got as many correct as did the other and that their performances put them in the "superior" category. For the [− −] state, each is told that he got as many correct as did the other and that their performances put them in the "below average" category. Thus, in each case $a = .50$. For the [+ −] state, the high subject is told that he got twice (or approximately twice) as many correct as the low one. Therefore, $a = \frac{2}{3}$ and $1 - a = \frac{1}{3}$. It can thus be seen that in this situation a is a function of the subject's expectation state: that is, the higher the subject's expectations for self relative to his expectations for his partner, the higher the value of a.

Twelve experimental conditions are of interest to us, those resulting from distinguishing the four expectation states and the three degrees of control by Actor, full control, no control, and equal control. Of these twelve conditions we use three to provide the empirical estimates of the utility ratios required by our model. These empirical estimates then are used in the probability function to provide predictions for the remaining nine situations.

In the situation in which Actor's expectation state is $[+ +]$ and he has no control over the team decision, $a = .5$ and $u_2 = 0$. An empirical estimate of $P(S)$, based on 37 cases, is $P(S) = .71$. Thus,

$$\frac{u_1}{u_3} = \frac{.71 - .5}{1 - .71} = .72.$$

We proceed in a similar way to derive values for $u_1/(u_2 + u_3)$ in the full and equal control conditions. For the case where Actor's expectation state is $[+ +]$ and he has full control over the team decision, we use an empirical estimate $P(S) = .60$ based on 31 cases. We solve for $u_1/(u_2 + u_3)$ in

$$P(S) = \frac{u_1 + .5(u_2 + u_3)}{u_1 + u_2 + u_3} = .60.$$

The result is

$$u_1/(u_2 + u_3) = .28.$$

In line with our assumption relating an individual's decision-making control to u_2, we expect to find that the value of u_2 is less in the equal control than in the full control condition. We denote the value of approval or disapproval by partner in the equal control condition as u'_2, to distinguish it from the analogous component of the full control condition. To estimate the ratio $u_1/(u'_2 + u_3)$ in the equal control condition, we use the empirical estimate $P(S) = .67$, based on 31 cases, for the $[+ +]$, equal control condition. The computation yields $u_1/(u'_2 + u_3) = .52.$

■ **TABLE 1 / Means of Predicted and Observed Proportions of S Responses by Control and Expectation Conditions**

Expectation State	Full Control			Equal Control*			No Control		
	Pred.	Obs.	N	Pred.	Obs.	N	Pred.	Obs.	N
$[+ -]$	.75	.73	32	.77	.76	31	.80	.82	30
$[+ +]$	X	.60	31	X	.64	30	X	.71	37
$[- -]$	.60	.52	30	.64	.66	30	.71	.73	33
$[- +]$	.47	.24	31	.55	.42	30	.60	.43	35

* These data do not appear in the earlier reports. The experiments that generated them are replications at Michigan State University of the original experiments for the equal control conditions carried out at Stanford University.

Using these estimates of the ratios of the utilities to each other, on the assumption that the ratios are constant within control conditions, and the values of a derived from the manipulation phase in appropriate specifications of the probability function, we are able to predict the probability of an S response in nine experimental conditions. These predictions are entered in Table 1.

□ **RESULTS AND INTERPRETATION**

The data from these experiments permit us to make a provisional evaluation of the model. The empirical proportions of S responses found in these experiments are listed in Table 1. It is to be observed that in general the ordering implications of our model are consistent with the data. In terms of the substantive assumptions we have used to apply the model to this situation, we are able to predict that within each expectation state, the greater the subject's decision-making control, the greater the likelihood that he will be influenced by the decisions of his partner. This means that for each expectation condition, the mean proportion of S responses for the full control condition should be less than that for the equal control condition, which in turn should be less than that for the no control condition. Inspection of Table 1 reveals that the observed proportion of S responses do exhibit this ordering by control condition, except for one comparison, that between equal and no control for the [− +] expectation state.

Our model as applied to this situation also enables us to predict that within each control condition, the higher the subject's performance expectations for self relative to his expectations for his partner, the less the likelihood that he will be influenced by his partner's behavior. This means that for each control condition, the mean proportion of S responses for the [+ −] expectation state should be greater than that for the [+ +] and [− −] expectation states, and these in turn should be greater than that for the [− +] expectation state. It can be seen from Table 1 that these ordering predictions do indeed hold for all of the relevant comparisons. This second ordering prediction also implies that there should be no difference in the mean proportion of S responses for the [+ +] and the [− −] expectation states for each control condition. The results here are mixed: one clear inconsistency with our prediction is to be observed in the full control condition.

In addition to these ordering predictions, the model enables us to predict the actual mean proportion of S responses for nine of the twelve experimental conditions. In five of these nine experiments the predictions quite closely match the observed results. In four conditions the predictions are higher than the empirical results. Three of these four occur in the [− +] expectation state, and the fourth occurs in the [− −], full control condition.

The pattern of the differences from our predictions, particularly in the [− +] cases, suggests that, contrary to our assumption, the utility ratios may differ by expectation state. It is possible, for example, that where the subject's expectations for his partner are higher than those for himself, the value of his partner's approval (or disapproval) is correspondingly greater. While this may account for some of the discrepancy between the predicted and observed means, it cannot account for all of it. We can see by the basic equation that even if $(u_2 + u_3)$ were allowed to increase indefinitely, with u_1 constant, $P(S)$ would go to a as a limit. In terms of the assumption we have used to determine the value of a for this experimental situation, a for the $[- +]$ case is .33. This value is higher than the observed mean proportion of S responses for this case. It seems quite likely, therefore, that the actual value of a is lower than .33 for a subject in the $[- +]$ expectation state. This suggests that the assumption we have used to determine a may require modification. Our task now is to find independent theoretical grounds and experimental tests to determine what changes to make in our model.

□ SOME GENERAL IMPLICATIONS OF THE MODEL

It is interesting to pursue the implications of the model for the effects of changes in the relative values of the utilities in this decision-making situation. For example, if the value of u_1 were increased indefinitely, $P(S)$ would approach 1 as a limit. If u_2 were increased indefinitely, $P(S)$ would approach a as a limit. It would approach the same limit if u_3 were increased indefinitely. In the experimental situations reviewed above, $P(S)$ has generally been higher than a. Increases in external rewards associated with the team product should increase the relative value of u_2 and u_3 to u_1. The consequence of this should be to depress the probability of an S decision toward a, the probability that an S decision is correct. Under these conditions, our model predicts that the Actor behaves more objectively, as it were. On the other hand, increases in the importance of consistency will tend to increase the value of u_1 relative to u_2 and u_3 and thus increase the probability of S responses beyond their probability of correctness. The Actor becomes subjectively oriented and ignores the external demands upon him. He has, then, effectively left the social system.

Finally, it should be observed that our model specifies the probability of choice under specific values of the utilities and their associated subjective probabilities. As long as these quantities remain fixed, or more generally, as long as the ratios of the utilities remain constant, a specific probability value will result. Under these conditions, the process is one of independent trials. That is, if we imagine the subjects making a series of choices under exactly these conditions, the probability of choice of a given alternative is the same on every trial, regardless of which alternative was chosen on any previous trial or any combination of previous trials.

Both Homans and Festinger, however, have stressed the importance of postdecisional dynamics. These dynamics are expressed by Homans in propositions embodying principles of diminishing return and by Festinger in his theory of dissonance reduction. In the framework of our model such postdecisional dynamics must be conceptualized as changes in the componential structure of alternatives (the relative values of the utilities or the value of *a*) as a consequence of decisions which the Actor has previously made. Although we have already learned much about such postdecisional dynamics, the rigorous formulation of such processes within a model of the type we have presented here is a task still to be accomplished.

Chapter 3

Exchange Theory, Part I: A Psychological Basis for Social Exchange

■ RICHARD M. EMERSON

□ **A. INTRODUCTION: A GLANCE BEHIND EXCHANGE**

In recent years an exchange approach to social behavior has begun to form, notably through the writing of Thibaut and Kelley,[1] George Homans,[2] Alfred Kuhn,[3] and Peter Blau.[4] The fields of psychology, sociology, and economics are represented by these authors; yet, in the four very different volumes cited, a single approach can be discerned.[5] This convergence involves only the normal amount of influence between authors (Blau acknowledges heavy debt to Homans and Thibaut; Kuhn makes passing reference to Homans, but remains largely unaffected by his specific notions). While none of these works is representative of the field its author is primarily identified with, each clearly is anchored to the substance of that field; and some of them, notably Homans and Kuhn, attempt to tie their work to other fields as well. Thus, the exchange approach has a clear interdisciplinary flavor with no implied attempt to "integrate."[6]

Secord and Backman refer to this material (notably Homans and Thibaut) as exchange theory, and they attempt to use it as an explanatory tool.[7] Without pausing here to discuss the attributes of theory in general or exchange in particular, I feel this term gives premature dignity to exchange notions. I prefer to view it as an *approach*, characterized by the use of certain central concepts

[1] John W. Thibaut and Harold H. Kelley, *The Social Psychology of Groups*, New York: Wiley, 1959.

[2] George C. Homans, *Social Behavior: Its Elementary Forms*, New York: Harcourt, Brace and World, 1961.

[3] Alfred Kuhn, *The Study of Society: A Unified Approach*, Homewood, Ill.: Irwin-Dorsey, 1963.

[4] Peter M. Blau, *Exchange and Power*, New York: John Wiley and Sons, 1964.

[5] While additional work could be cited, we will identify the exchange approach with the four volumes cited here.

[6] Kuhn's work is an attempt to unify several fields within a new conceptual scheme. While the book is noteworthy for its measure of success in this respect, we are interested only in the exchange framework he develops.

[7] Paul Secord and Carl Backman, *Social Psychology*, New York: McGraw-Hill, 1964, p. 253.

(reward, cost, alternatives, transactions, etc.), which place observations into a frame of reference called *exchange*.

Judging from the work done within the exchange approach, a striking feature of the approach, per se, is the manner in which it directs attention to *social power* and related topics.[8] My initial reason for beginning the work set forth in these two chapters was to formulate a more encompassing (and hopefully enriching) framework around previous work on power-dependence relations.[9] However, as the title of Blau's volume suggests, exchange is more general and fundamental than power. As a result, I now am concerned with exchange theory in general, and I find several troublesome points therein which warrant concern.

Stemming partly from its reward-cost terminology and partly from its cross-disciplinary character, some ambiguities surround discussions of social exchange. These seem to center around (a) the role of rationality in social behavior,[10] (b) the possibly tautological character of what are meant to be basic propositions, and (c) strategic questions concerning "psychological reductionism." The question of tautology will illustrate my more general point. Homans' Proposition 2 reads: "The more often within a given period of time a man's activity rewards the activity of another, the more often the other will emit the activity."[11] Homans advocates the use of operant principles, and here he has offered one which, if reduced to Skinner's words, reads, "If the occurrence of an operant is followed by the presentation of a reinforcing stimulus, the strength is increased."[12] In operant theory, "strengthen" means "increase frequency

---

[8] In each of the four volumes cited above, "power," "influence," and "conformity" are major themes, or topics for extensive discussion. The natural affinity between exchange analysis and power analysis can be illustrated better in the work of Parsons. While Parsons would not be classified as an exchange theorist, when he focuses upon social power he adopts an exchange perspective. As he puts it, "Power is here conceived as a circulating medium, analogous to money. . . ." (See T. Parsons, "On the Concept of Political Power," *Proceedings of the American Philosophical Society*, Vol. 107, No. 3, June, 1963.)

[9] R. M. Emerson, "Power-Dependence Relations," *American Sociological Review*, Vol. 27, February, 1962, pp. 31–41; "Power-Dependence Relations: Two Experiments," *Sociometry*, Vol. 27, September, 1964, pp. 282–298. See also Thibaut and Kelley, *op. cit.*, on dependence; and R. H. Walters and R. D. Park, "Social Motivation, Dependency and Susceptibility to Influence," in L. Berkowitz (ed.), *Advances in Experimental Social Psychology*, New York and London: The Academic Press, 1964, pp. 232–272.

[10] In his review of Blau's *Exchange and Power*, Bierstedt paraphrases Blau as follows: "We decide, with conscious ratiocination, whether, as Julius Caesar put it, we want to be first in a little Iberian village or second in Rome. Once the decision is made we design our actions to support it, and our interactions with others thus involve calculations that will achieve our goal." Bierstedt continues: "The analysis is so complex that it is difficult to detect the flaw in it. It finally dawns upon the reader that the flaw is in the major premise — namely, that much human behavior is guided by considerations of exchange." (See *American Sociological Review*, 30, October, 1965, pp. 789–790.) In Blau's defense, we might observe that to offer a rational analysis of social behavior (exchange theory) is not to assert that behavior is guided by rationality. Clearly, some behavior is so guided, and exchange theory will accommodate it. Meanwhile, exchange theory a la Homans is said to be grounded in operant psychology which in turn is hardly restricted to "rational behavior."

[11] Homans, *op. cit.*, p. 54.

[12] B. F. Skinner, *The Behavior of Organisms*, New York: Appleton-Century-Crofts, 1938, p. 21.

or probability of occurrence" and "reinforce" means "strengthen." Thus, since Homans' "reward" means "reinforce," then both he and Skinner are saying that *if an action results in something which increases the frequence of that action, then the frequence of that action increases.*

We must be clear on this. I am *not* suggesting that either Homans or Skinner are talking in tautologies. In the above statements, both Homans and Skinner are assuming that we *know* from independent evidence which specific stimuli are rewarding or reinforcing to what men.[13] Homans anticipated such trouble and devoted several pages of discussion to it,[14] yet he is criticized on grounds of tautology.[15] But my purpose, for the moment, is to observe these ambiguities, not to resolve them. My contention is that this issue, along with rationality and reductionism, stems from an inadequate articulation between social exchange theory and an appropriate psychological basis. The question of tautology, at least in this case, arises concerning a psychological notion converted for social application. As a result, whether Homans' proposition is technically tautological or not, it appears to be *noninformative* to a sociologist (at least to this one). Thus, the question of tautology flows into strategy questions concerning psychological reductionism, whatever one's position on the latter topic might be.[16]

To suggest that some explanations couched in exchange theory are "noninformative" is difficult to justify. This reaction might stem from habituation to conventional concepts which already provide a "sense of comprehension," making translation into exchange terms seem unnecessary or noninformative. Indeed, it is my understanding that Homans would argue this to be the case concerning conventional concepts, and further, that they provide this sense of comprehension *because* we conventionally fall back upon simple exchange propositions without explicitly acknowledging them.[17] Conventional sociology does indeed take principles of learning for granted, and we seldom bother to articulate them and incorporate them into social theory. Hence, when these principles are brought to the fore in providing explanations, the explanations might well sound noninformative — unless, of course, they are augmented by other propositions which we would not have arrived at otherwise. Perhaps Homans' "distributive justice" approaches the latter point.

Related to tautology and reductionism, there is a dangerous pitfall which

[13] This is, of course, no problem at all for operant psychology in the laboratory. While it is a potential problem in nonlaboratory applications, as in child rearing, operant psychologists seem very alert to the need for evidence that a given stimulus is a reinforcer before using it to "explain."

[14] Homans, *Social Behavior, op. cit.*, pp. 42–43.

[15] See, for example, Morton Deutsch, "Homans in the Skinner Box," *Sociological Inquiry*, Spring, 1964, pp. 156–165.

[16] The position taken here can be simply stated: Whenever a class of social events or a sociological proposition *can* be readily reduced to or explained by a set of accepted psychological propositions, it *should* be reduced, and henceforth taken as nonproblematic in asking new (sociological) questions.

[17] George C. Homans, "Contemporary Theory in Sociology," in R. E. L. Faris (ed.), *Handbook of Modern Sociology*, Chicago: Rand McNally, 1964, p. 967.

psychological-reward approaches can easily drift into. Thibaut and Kelley, along with Kuhn, have avoided it. Talcott Parsons has identified the pitfall, and he argues that Homans has stumbled (rather, walked) into it: *descriptive historicism*, and *post*diction in the absence of *pre*diction.[18] If we are told that (a) society consists of behaving persons, and (b) behavior is governed by reinforcing stimulus conditions (i.e., "rewards," "costs," etc.), then society can be explained in terms of (c) the psychology of reinforcement, plus (d) knowledge of the reinforcing stimulus situations as "given conditions," either historical or contemporary. If this is the logical format for psychological reductionism, then another name for it is descriptive historicism. While there is nothing wrong with psychology or with history as such, sociological theory is not the history of societies, any more than psychological theory is the reinforcement history of individuals. While the logic of the above format is sound, it contains two obvious shortcomings: first, it conceives of society as the sum of individual behavior, or more accurately, it fails to offer a conception of society; and second, the overwhelming burden of "explanation" falls upon "given conditions." In short, it takes as "given" the very conditions sociology seeks to comprehend: the social structure surrounding "behaving persons," and lawlike changes in that structure.

My purpose in these chapters is to address "social structure" and structural change within the framework of exchange theory. However, the strategy adopted here warrants a final comment on history and psychology. As suggested above, social history is to social theory, as reinforcement history is to psychological theory. It is the relation of concrete data to a set of abstract organizing principles. As a result, there is an affinity between sociology and psychology which neither have with history, if the latter is taken in the narrow sense as a chronology of concrete events. It may well be that psychological *principles* can provide important building blocks for sociological *concepts* and principles. If this point smacks of "reductionism," then, to me, "antireductionism" has the flavor of defensive denial.

Part I in this discussion of exchange is an effort to formulate an explicit psychological basis for the social exchange theory, presented in Part II. It is my hope that some of the ambiguities mentioned above will be reduced in the process, while psychological points of substantive value are introduced. If *new* ambiguities replace the old, perhaps this can be taken as progress. Finally, formal theory construction is not taken as an end in itself in these two chapters, even though it might be a worthy end. At this stage of theory in progress, I have chosen to emphasize relatively broad substantive coverage at the expense of logical or mathematical rigor. Thus, in presenting "derivations," I will identify the previous assertions upon which they depend, but I provide no elaborate logical "proofs." If the general flow of the reasoning is clear, I will be content for the moment.

[18] Parsons was quite correct, on this point at least, in his criticism of Homans' position, and the best indication of Homans' historicism is contained in his reply. See *Sociological Inquiry*, Vol. 34, Spring, 1964.

Finally, in presenting the following theoretical assertions (both in Part I and Part II), I have chosen to make no explicit appeal for empirical validity *at this time*. While supporting or confounding studies might come to mind, a review of the relevant empirical literature is not provided. While existing studies could be selectively assembled and interpreted to provide a sense of empirical support, in the last analysis our formulations will stand, fall, or be revised in the light of subsequent research. Hence, attention is given to questions of operational feasibility rather than conceptual reinterpretation of existing data. The latter is left to the reader at this point in time.

□ B. EXCHANGE RELATIONS: AN OPERANT APPROACH[19]

Our purpose in Part I is to provide an explicit psychological underpinning as a basis for sociological theory construction in Part II. For coherence, we will look primarily to a single school of psychology, and operant theory seems to be the best candidate for several reasons.

First, operant concepts and principles are exceptionally operational — so much so that it might better be called a *method* for controlling behavior than a theory about behavior.[20] For example, Hilgard, after extolling the remarkable operant accomplishments in animal training (behavior "shaping"), closes his summary of the operant school with this appraisal: "From the point of view of a theoretical achievement this is really a pretty modest extension of Thorndike's law of effect ... the theory does not propose to predict."[21]   Partly because of its atheoretic character, the concepts it employs (operant, reinforcer, discriminative stimulus, etc.) are exceedingly general and just as applicable to human social behavior as to rat, pigeon, or chimpanzee behavior. We take the atheoretic character of operant psychology as a virtue for still another reason, given the purpose of this essay. While it has amassed a lot of information about empirical regularities, it is not committed, for example, to any theory of motivation, such as the (now very questionable) drive-reduction approach. As a result of its uncommitted theoretic import, operant psychology is sufficiently flexible to allow a sociologist to engage in considerable theoretical tampering.

Secondly, the operant school is chosen as our starting point for social exchange because operant behavior *is* behavior within a form of *exchange* process, otherwise called "feedback" or reinforcement. Hence, in examining operant notions in Part I, it is possible at the same time to establish our basic concepts

---

[19] In this section, I am particularly indebted to Professor Robert Burgess, who devoted a lot of time to long discussions on operant psychology while this section was being formulated.   Unfortunately, if operant psychology is misrepresented in any of the points which follow, I am solely responsible.

[20] B. F. Skinner, "Are Theories of Learning Necessary?" *Psychological Review*, Vol. 57, 1950, pp. 193–216.

[21] Ernest A. Hilgard, *Theories of Learning*, New York: Appleton-Century-Crofts, 1956, p. 119

for the analysis of social exchange carried out largely in Part II.

If there is any shortcoming to operant theory as a basis for social exchange theory, it is simply that (a) operant psychology contains few if any "cognitive" concepts, and (b) sociology has conventionally been tied most closely to cognitive psychology through such concepts as "expectation." However, while there is more to psychology than what the operant psychologist chooses to attend to or talk about, there is similarly more to sociology than what exchange theory attempts to organize. Even so, we shall find reason to weave some cognitive dimensions into the otherwise operant framework developed below.

1. Exchange Relations

We will begin by adopting four primitive or undefined terms, along with a simple notation, plus two expressions involving connected terms.

(a) *Actor;* A, B, C, etc.
(b) *Behavior;* of Type i on Occasion t: x_{it}
(c) *Situation;* of Type j on Occasion t: S_{jt}
(d) *Stimulus;* of Type k on Occasion t: y_{kt}
(e) Behavior x_i by Actor A on Occasion t: Ax_{it}
(f) Stimulus y_k *in or associated with* situation S_j: $S_j y_{kt}$

For simplicity, we will drop the subscripts when they can be taken as understood, and deal only with A, S, x, and y.

While these terms are taken as undefined, the environmental variables warrant comment. We proceed on the understanding that the *boundaries* defining types of situation, $S_1, S_2 \ldots S_n$, and types of stimuli, $y_1, y_2 \ldots y_n$, are governed by the psychology of stimulus differentiation and generalization on the part of the actor(s) involved. Furthermore, when the actors are human, we assume that stimulus differentiation and generalization are significantly determined by social or cultural "definitions of the situation." As a result, we are free to consider the case in which, for Actor A, the *situation* S_j is another Actor B, as a unique person or as a role-occupant, with stimulus y_k being the behavior of B. With this point understood, let us retreat momentarily into the simplified context of experimental operant psychology.

Consider a rat (A) who spends a lot of his time in a cage (S_1) and a portion of his time in a "Skinner Box" (S_2) which contains a lever. If the rat presses the lever (Ax) on any occasion he might receive a pellet in the Skinner Box $(S_2 y)$. To a lever press, the apparatus responds with a pellet; to a pellet, the rat responds with continued pressing. Such an experiment can be described as the study of an "exchange relation" between A and one segment of his environment, S_j, with x and y as the variable commodities exchanged. In this chapter we will attempt a step-by-step extension of this framework to accommodate the complex case in which A is a human actor engaged in many exchange relations with sets of other human actors. While complex social exchange involves more than operant principles from psychology, those principles are involved, and they will be used as a base to be built upon.

If we are to avoid the ambiguities referred to earlier, we must begin by stating basic operant concepts with unusual precision. Consider the following:

let $p_{y_k} = \text{prob}\,(y_k \mid Ax_i \wedge S_j)$;
let $p_a = \text{prob}\,(y_k \mid A\bar{x}_i \wedge S_j)$;
assume $p_{y_k} > p_a$, the probability that stimulus   (1)
   y_k will occur in situation S_j if A performs
   x_i is greater than if A does not perform x_i.
   (Or more simply, y is a "stimulus consequence"
   of x.)
Let $p_{x_i} = \text{prob}\,(Ax_i \mid S_j \wedge (1))$;
let $p_b = \text{prob}\,(Ax_i \mid S_j \wedge (\bar{1}))$;
assume $p_{x_i} > p_b$, the probability that A will   (2)
   perform x_i in situation S_j is greater if y_k
   is a "consequence" of x_i.

We resort to these symbolic expressions for two reasons. First, they define as clearly as possible our two main variables, p_{y_k} and p_{x_i}. Second, they portray the logical structure at the core of operant psychology.

Statements (1) and (2) are empirical conditions *assumed within the definitions* of basic operant concepts. When both (1) and (2) are known or assumed to be true, then operant psychologists call x_i an "operant," y_k is called a "positive reinforcer," and S_j is said to be or to contain a "discriminative stimulus."[22] These three concepts are thus defined in terms of each other through (1) and (2), thereby constituting a *single conceptual unit.* When this unit is broken, in an effort to "explain" behavior in terms of reinforcement, then we encounter the familiar tautology. We will carefully honor the integrity of this conceptual unit in the theory construction which follows. This unit is an organism-environment feedback system and we will call it an "exchange relation."

Meanwhile, statements (1) and (2) are introduced as empirical assumptions specifying the *domain of discourse* for this theory. The theory is meant to apply only when they are taken as true. The probability of performing an act sometimes depends upon the (actual or anticipated) consequences of the act. "Operant" behavior is a name for such instrumental action, whether Ax be a lever-press for food by a rat or a request for a raise by an employee. The probability p_{y_k} can be based upon frequencies of y (food) across a series of lever presses, or it can be "calculated" by an employee as a "subjective probability estimate" that a request will result in a pay increase.

Returning to our example, suppose a psychologist arranged a segment of A's environment so that it contains a lever, and a pellet (y_k) arrives in A's presence if and only if A presses the lever ($p_{y_k} = 1.0$; $p_a = 0.0$). Or suppose

---

[22] If $p_{x_i} < p_b$, then y_k is a "negative reinforcer"; if $p_{x_i} = p_b$, then y_k is a "neutral stimulus." We will deal only with positive reinforcers in this chapter. Hence, we understand that $p_{x_i} > p_b$

that without a psychologist's intervention, A's environment is so arranged that it sometimes contains Person B, (S_j), and B delivers "help" to A if and only if A behaves warmly toward B. If it then develops that A presses when levers are around or smiles warmly when B is around, then "pellet" and "help" are reinforcers for A. Note: In strict operant theory, A does not perform x *because* he finds y "rewarding." Rather, y is called rewarding or reinforcing because a name is needed for the empirical conditions in (1) and (2). If we choose the former wording, then we have stepped several miles outside operant psychology toward some implicit theory of motivation. It might be argued that if the pellet is known to be "food" or if A is known to "need" help, then we have learned nothing we did not already know in establishing that they are reinforcers. This is exactly the case! *In this chapter we will not presume to know the needs and motives of men.* We will see how far we can go on this skimpy basis.

A most prominent feature of operant psychology is its longitudinal study of single subjects in fairly stable interactive relations with the environment. If we are to *conceptualize* such research observations, the contingency in Statement (2) requires that we conceive behavior within a series of temporally linked transactions with the environment. Accordingly, we define:

> DEFINITION 1. Given (1) and (2), p_{y_k} and p_{x_i} jointly define an organism-environment *exchange relation* (symbolized $Ax_i;S_jy_k$, or simply $A;S_j$ with x and y understood) consisting of a series of temporally interspersed *opportunities* (S_{jt}), *initiations* ($S_{jt} \rightarrow Ax_{it}$) and *transactions* (($S_{jt} \rightarrow Ax_{it}) \rightarrow y_{kt}$); where $\rightarrow$ means "produces," "evokes," or "is accompanied by."[23]

With the exception of *exchange relation*, the terms introduced in this definition all have their equivalents in operant language. An *opportunity* is a stimulus situation which contains appropriate "discriminative stimuli" for evoking an initiation. An *initiation* is an "operant response" and a *transaction* is a "positively reinforced" initiation. Thus, Definition 1 is our principal coordinating definition, bridging operant psychology with the social exchange theory presented below. We introduced this shift in terminology for two reasons: (a) to facilitate more macroscopic analysis of behavior in contexts far removed from operant experiments; and (b) to accommodate special features of *social* exchange relations where S_j is B in which transactions are *reciprocally* reinforcing events which can be "initiated" from either end of the relation.

The concept of an exchange relation is hardly necessary in operant psychology, for it forms the outer boundary of most operant research. By contrast, for us it identifies the *smallest independently meaningful unit* in terms of which larger structures will be developed. A transaction, while fundamental as a

---

[23] Not all opportunities will evoke initiations, nor will all initiations result in transactions. Within any exchange relation there will be a ratio, Ax_i/S_j, of initiations per opportunity which approximates p_{x_i}, and a ratio y_k/Ax_i of transactions per initiation which approximates p_{y_k}, the "reinforcement schedule."

concept, is not a meaningful unit outside the exchange relation which contains it. This point will be clear if we recognize that a transaction is a feedback loop, constituting one empirical instance of an exchange relation as a feedback system regulating behavior across time (e.g., across recurring opportunities). The initiating behavior evokes stimulus feedback y, and while this stimulus consequence defines the temporal boundary of that transaction, *as feedback* it helps to regulate the *next* initiation, as Statements (1) and (2) clearly imply.

Finally, with the concept of an exchange relation we are in a position to move in a direction different from that taken by most economic theory, but required in social theory. The concept of a "market" makes the transaction the unit, with actors interchangeable, thereby emphasizing the $x;y$ relation. By contrast, our concept links each transaction to a history and a future for specified actors, emphasizing a more or less durable social relation between A and B (or S_j), with behavior x and y significantly modifiable across time. However, as we shall see below, market processes are included as well, with significant implications concerning social power and the character of role-relations.

Before proceeding into the theory proper, a word or two about its logical structure is in order. When a principle claims truth on solely empirical grounds it will be introduced as a numbered *proposition*. When a principle claims truth from its logical relation to a single previously numbered principle, it will assume that number and will be labeled a *corollary*. When a principle claims truth from its logical relation to two or more principles, it will be stated as a numbered *theorem*. While the proofs for theorems are not provided, reference is made to the previous points from which it might follow.

2. Formation and Change of Exchange Relations

The bulk of operant research concerns the formation and change of single exchange relations. Let us postulate a behavioral repertoire $x_1, x_2 \ldots x_n$, for Actor A in situation S_j, such that each item in the repertoire is (a) performable in S_j, (b) is a class of operants each with an associated value of p_{y_k} in S_j, and (c) has a value of $p_{x_i} > 0.0$.

> PROPOSITION 1. *Differential Reinforcement.* For any set of paired p_{x_i} and   (3)
> p_{y_k} values, if $p_{y_{k1}} \leq p_{y_{k2}} \leq \ldots p_{y_{km}} < p_{y_{kn}}$ then initiation behavior
> x_i will change across continuing transactions until $p_{x_1} \leq p_{x_2} \leq$
> $\ldots p_{x_m} < p_{x_n}$.

The reader should notice that a specific family of relationships will satisfy this proposition. For example:

(a) if $p_{y_{ki}}$ = .25 .50 .75 1.00
(b) then p_{x_i} = .10 .20 .30   .40
(c) or p_{x_i} = .00 .00 .00 1.00

will satisfy the proposition. While (c) might be the only terminal state if transactions are allowed to continue long enough, to my knowledge this is an unsettled empirical question. Meanwhile, we are interested in the x with the highest values of p_x and p_y. More than one x can have "high" values in a given exchange relation, and we consider the relation to have "formed around" those dominant behaviors. Thus, in a *formed* relation $Ax_i;S_jy_k$, the repertoire item x_i is the item with highest associated values of p_{x_i} and p_{y_k}.

> COROLLARY 1.1. *Behavior Change or "Exploration."* Given a formed   (4)
> relation, a decrease in p_{y_k} or m for x_i produces an increase in
> behavioral variation across items in the repertoire.

If the environmental contingencies governing p_y values are stable, the exchange relation will stabilize around relatively fixed behavioral content. If the environmental contingencies are fluid, behavior will be similarly variable or "exploratory." This point is of some importance in moving this operant approach from the laboratory to social exchange relations, in which B's behavior (the "environmental contingencies" mentioned above) is not experimentally standardized across occasions. We might note that one of the "functions" of socially standardized norms and role-expectations is the reduction of such behavioral variation and the consequent reduction of what Thibaut and Kelley, *op. cit.*, call "endogenous costs" in social interaction. In general, they render p_y values stable, thereby stabilizing exchange relations around highly predictable behavior.

> COROLLARY 1.2. *Extinction of the Exchange Relation.* Given as in (4), if   (5)
> p_{y_k} values reduce to 0.0 for all items in the repertoire, then initiations
> will decrease across recurring opportunities to the "operant level"
> (i.e., to p_b in (2)).

Principles (3), (4), and (5) are employed by operant conditioners in "shaping up" selected behavior and extinguishing other behavior in the subject. For our purpose, it is sufficient to note that they allow for and govern changes across time in the behavioral content x and y, while the relation $(A;S_j)$ maintains its identity.

3. The Timing of Initiations

Operant psychologists commonly present data and state relationships in terms of behavioral rates or frequencies, yet Proposition 1 makes no assertion about absolute frequencies. Rather, it specifies what behavior will predominate relative to other types of behavior. The occurrence of an initiation at a given time, and therefore rates or frequencies, is governed by two variables: one is the presence or absence of an opportunity; the other is the degree of "satiation-deprivation" for y_k on Occasion t.

PROPOSITION 2. Given $A;S_j$, and given S_{jt}, then $p_{x_{it}}$ varies inversely with (6) the number and magnitude of transactions during "some" time period immediately preceding t.[24]

DEFINITION 2. The frequency of transactions in (6) is called the level of *deprivation-satiation*.

We suggest that some form of Proposition 2 is true for all exchange relations, whether A be a rat and y water, or whether A be India and y wheat in international trade. Similarly, we argue that a professor's initiation of conferences with students can be predicted in part from (6), given that such exchange mediates some reinforcer for the professor.

An initiation will result in a transaction on each and every occasion if $p_{y_k} = 1.0$. Therefore, very high p_{y_k} promotes satiation, and:

COROLLARY 2.1. Given continuous opportunities, the frequency of initi- (7) ations decreases as p_{y_k} increases across high values toward 1.0.

THEOREM 1. Given continuous opportunities, the frequency of initiations (8) is a nonlinear function of p_{y_k}, with high frequency at intermediate values of p_{y_k}. (From Corollary 1.2 and 2.1)

4. Conditioned Reinforcement

Our main purpose in this chapter is to incorporate operant principles into a framework which can handle more complex situations than operant psychology normally confronts. Our first step in this direction involves the introduction of a feature operant analysis normally omits: behavior at *choice points*. Unlike maze experiments, the methodology of the Skinner Box blurs this notion. While the rat might respond to the left hand corner by smelling, to the right hand corner by standing and to the lever by "pressing," only the latter is recorded as data. However, if all were recorded, Proposition 1, as worded above, would describe such "choices" by the rat.

In terms of the concepts now at hand, A might confront a "choice" among two or more reinforcers $y_1, y_2 \ldots y_n$, or concerning a given reinforcer, y_k, he might confront a choice between two or more exchange relations, $A;S_1$, $A;S_2 \ldots A;S_n$. These two classes of choice points will be dealt with through the concepts of *value* and *alternative* relations, respectively, and in combined form through the concept of *dependence*. The operant principle which provides the basis for the first step in this elaboration is *conditioned* reinforcement:

PROPOSITION 3. Given the set of exchange relations, $Ax_i;S_jy_k$, $i, j = 1$ (9) to n, if y_k is contingent upon S_j to degree c_j, then S_j will become a

---

[24] The time period for which Proposition 2 holds is an empirical question for each class of reinforcers. While satiation-deprivation appears to be a very general phenomenon, it is difficult to formulate a general proposition which does justice to the complexities involved.

(conditioned) reinforcer with *strength* as a joint function of c_j and the strength and number of y_k in the $A;S_j$ relation.

While c_j is not explicitly defined here, this can be readily accomplished with considerable precision. For our purpose, it is sufficient to note that the contingency of y_k upon S_1 is *decreased* as additional relations $Ax_i;S_2y_k$, $Ax_i;S_3y_k$, etc., are added to the set of relations in (9).

Two major points will be developed out of Proposition 3. The first concerns the formation of large behavior sequences which can be taken as units of analysis (as single acts) in operationalizing the concept of "initiation." If S_j evokes x_i which produces and is reinforced by y_k, then to say that S_j has become a conditioned reinforcer implies (a) some prior action x'_i produced and was reinforced by S_j, and (b) some prior situation S'_j evoked x'_i. Thus, Proposition 3 implies a sequence $S''_j \rightarrow x''_i \rightarrow S'_j \rightarrow x'_i \rightarrow S_j \rightarrow x_i \rightarrow y_k$, wherein S's are conditioned reinforcers relative to y_k as a "primary" reinforcer. Can the action flow $x'' - x' - x$ be taken as a *bounded* unit act?

To illustrate, consider a rat's cage (S''_j) with three doors which open into tunnels (S'_1, S'_2, and S'_3), each of which empties into a separate Skinner Box (S_1, S_2, and S_3) with its own reinforcement schedule, p_{yk}. If y is a reinforcer for the rat, then by Proposition 3 we obtain behavioral series of the form $Ax''_i x'_i x_i, i = 1, 2,$ or 3. The rat will "choose" a door at x''_i and is then somewhat committed to the series i. The choice is determined by the relative strength of the doors S'_1, S'_2, S'_3, as conditioned reinforcers, which is in turn governed by the strength of y_k and the matrix of contingencies joining y to S_j and S_j to S'_j. Similarly, "choice points" and relatively "committed" paths unbroken by intervening choice points, can be rigorously defined in terms of such matrices of environmental-behavioral contingencies.

In operant language, the series $Ax''_i x'_i x_i$ is called a "chain." For Thibaut-Kelley, it is called a *behavior sequence* with internal continuity provided by a behavior "set" or "expectation" of y at the end of the chain. Now, given a complex chain or sequence *to start with*, how many elements does it contain? Thibaut and Kelley do not ask this question. They adopt the behavior sequence as their *unit*, and we will do likewise, calling upon Proposition 3 as the basis for collapsing $Ax''_i x'_i x_i$ back to Ax_i. Thus, for operational definitions, an initiation is a unit of behavior which begins at a choice point and ends when the *expectation* of reinforcement is either confirmed or refuted. We will examine the latter point further when we discuss reinforcement schedules. Meanwhile, this strategy has a theoretical basis. The operant psychologist can label the "components" of his chain only because he *built* the chain step-by-step, employing his own *arbitrarily* specified boundaries for stimulus and response units. *From A's point of view*, these boundaries are governed by the cognitive processes of stimulus differentiation-generalization. These are in turn governed by the environmental contingencies c_j and p_{yk}, the very contingencies which define choice points and reinforcements as boundaries of the unit initiation.

Thus, we are free to operationalize these concepts at whatever macro-level of behavior is suitable for the research in question, ranging, for example, from a "lever-press" to a "period of employment" measured in days, weeks, months, or years, as the empirical situation warrants or requires.

5. Dependence, Exchange Domains, and Alternative Relations

The second important feature of Proposition 3 is its implications concerning behavior at choice points, hence in "free" situations. Let us first define:

> DEFINITION 3. In any exchange relation, A is said to be *dependent* upon S_j for y_k (symbolized D_{AS_j}), and the magnitude of dependence is the strength of S_j as a conditioned reinforcer.

Thus, dependence is a joint function of c_j and the "strength" of y_k.[25] However, a conditioned reinforcer can be conditioned to more than one class of "unconditioned" reinforcers, $y_1, y_2 \ldots y_n$. In this case, S_j is called a "generalized reinforcer" (with generality of degree n) in operant language. Both questions of "strength" and "generality" force us to raise the problem of stimulus differentiation for classes of y.

An animal in its natural state, as distinct from the captive creature in a Skinner Box, can be conceived as a point, A, where many exchange relations, $A,S_1, A,S_2 \ldots A,S_n$ "connect." (Similarly, many actors can be "connected" at S_j.) During any period of time, A will initiate transactions temporally interspersed across many exchange relations connected at A. The temporal ecology of such initiation behavior across multiple exchange relations is governed by (a) available opportunities, (b) *dependence*, and (c) relative satiation-deprivation for $y_1, y_2 \ldots y_n$.

> DEFINITION 4. Given a set of exchange relations connected at A, and given the set T of all transactions A might initiate during an extended time period, in the same or different relations, an *exchange domain* is a subset d of T such that any transaction in the subset increases satiation for all other transactions in that subset.

The concept of an *exchange domain* employs the criterion of satiation as a behavioral basis for defining the boundaries between classes of reinforcers. Thus, d is a class of equivalent y. For simplicity, we will drop d and proceed on the understanding that y_k, a "type" of stimulus, is a domain. Domains may be thought of as points of articulation between A's "needs" or values and sectors of his environment.

> DEFINITION 5. Given an exchange relation $A;S_j$ in domain y_k, relation $A;S_a$ is an *alternative* to $A;S_j$ to the degree that it contains opportunities for transactions in y_k at comparable magnitudes of y.

---

[25] Glancing ahead, D_{AS_j} is identical with D_{AB}, the dependence of Actor A upon Actor B. See R. M. Emerson, "Power-Dependence Relations," *American Sociological Review*, December, 1962, pp. 31–41.

Since $A;S_a$ reduces c_j, the contingency of y upon S_j:

COROLLARY 3.1. D_{AS_j} varies inversely with the number and degree of   (10) alternatives to $A;S_j$.

DEFINITION 6. An exchange relation has *primacy* of degree n if it contains transactions in one or more domains, $y_1, y_2 \ldots y_n$.

We use the term "primacy" in recognition of the similarity with "primary social relations."

COROLLARY 3.2. An increase in the primacy of $A;S_j$ increases D_{AS_j} (11) (*both* through reducing the number of alternatives to $A; S_j$ and through increasing the number of domains contingent upon S_j).

While we have not yet confronted the "strength" of domains of reinforcement, employed in the above conceptions, we can summarize choice behavior as follows:

THEOREM 2. Given opportunities in a set of exchange relations in the   (12) same or different domain, the probability of initiation, p_{x_i}, varies directly with D_{AS_j} across this set. (From Propositions 1 and 3.)

6. Values and the Strength of Domains

Now that the concept of a domain has been introduced we can discuss "strength," in terms of both the magnitude of y and of "preference ordering" among y. Furthermore, if A has a generalized preference ordering for domains which transcends moment-to-moment states of deprivation, then we can speak of A's "values." But first, let us define the problem.

In basic operant psychology there appear to be two ways to approach the strength of an unconditioned reinforcer, y. One is to state that the strength of y is a function of deprivation for y (i.e., Proposition 2). The other is to measure its strength by determining its capacity to alter p_x, relative to some "other" reinforcer under standardized conditions. The latter approach will turn out to be a measure of relative deprivation anyway. It is like asking whether an animal needs water more than food, which will clearly depend upon thirst relative to hunger. In this sense, the "strength" of a reinforcer may have no meaning beyond quantity of it and deprivation for it. If an actor is an organic system with "needed inputs" such as food, water, and oxygen, it may be futile to search for a generalized ordering of them over and above his momentary deprivation in these domains. This seems to be Homans' position, for he equates "value" with deprivation.[26]

---

[26] For Homans, the measurement of *value* involves (a) determining that the object in question is a reinforcer, and (b) determining how long the person has gone without it. (G. C. Homans, *Social Behavior: Its Elementary Forms*, pp. 43–45.)

But we had best not let go of the problem so quickly. It is the same problem we encounter in social systems, and there we do find that the participants make differential *valuations* of "functional contributions," whether or not they "really" have different levels of functional importance in the social system. It might well be the case that the values humans hold are related to the history of deprivation for the valued objects, but sociology certainly does not conceive value as equivalent to current deprivation, nor as fully reducible to the history of deprivation. If we can find additional psychological bases for "values" we will be able to put psychology to some real use in social exchange theory. As it happens, operant research findings provide some very good clues. These are found in the work on intermittent reinforcement, notably as it relates to *conditioned* reinforcers.[27] Quite understandably, operant research has not raised the question of the relative strength of unconditioned reinforcers. It *has* investigated the strength of conditioned reinforcers, and this puts the question significantly into a *developmental* context, where any discussion of "values" might profitably reside.

The contingency p_{y_k} is called a "schedule of reinforcement" and an immense amount of research has explored a wide variety of schedules. Typical schedules used are *continuous* reinforcement ($p_y = 1.0$), *fixed ratio* schedules in which every n^{th} initiation is reinforced ($0.0 < p_y < 1.0$), *fixed interval* schedules in which reinforcements occur for the first initiation after the nth time unit has passed ($0.0 < p_y < 1.0$), *variable ratio* and *variable interval* schedules with reinforcements given randomly about a mean ratio or interval ($0.0 < p_y < 1.0$), and *extinction* schedules ($p_y = 0.0$).

Now, the p_{y_k} values corresponding to various intermittent (fixed or variable ratio and interval) schedules would appear to be $1/n$. Unfortunately, it is not that simple. First, *fixed* schedules are not probabilistic. Second, the boundaries defining a unit of behavior (an initiation), and therefore the value of n, are chosen by the psychologist to suit his convenience in recording a repeatable unit act, like one press of a bar which activates a counter. Thus in a fixed schedule with $n = 5$, if we define an initiation as "five presses" (and we have every right to do so) then $p_y = 1.0$ instead of 0.2, and we have a continuous reinforcement schedule instead of an FR-5 (Fixed Ratio 1/5) intermittent schedule. Since the operational definition of a unit act is completely arbitrary in such operant research, we are perfectly free to tamper with the definition. Furthermore, if we have a nonarbitrary basis for setting different boundaries for an initiation, then we are well advised to try them out. In the example above, concepts like expectation and confirmation would lead to five bar presses rather than one as the meaningful unit. Indeed, for any schedule in which (a) reinforcement occurs at a highly predictable point and (b) established well within the animal's performance or learning capacities, the occurrence of reinforcement (or the point in the pattern when it would be "predicted") fix the appropriate boundaries of an act.

[27] Morton Deutsch has criticized Homans for ignoring these particular findings in operant psychology. See Deutsch, *op. cit.*

On these grounds we suggest that, in most operant research, $0.0 < p_{y_k} < 1.0$ (i.e., the achievement of reinforcement is *problematic* for the subject) primarily when (a) *variable* schedules are in effect, or (b) when an established schedule is undergoing change, as during the onset of an extinction schedule. Related to this suggestion are the following facts: (1) the rate of behavior is high under variable schedules; (2) the onset of extinction is accompanied by a momentary increase in the rate and intensity of behavior; (3) extinction is slower from a variable schedule; and, most important, (4) conditioned reinforcers established under variable schedules are more effective ("stronger" reinforcers) in developing new behavior. In short, there is reason to suspect that the strength of a reinforcer is related to some nonlinear function of p_{y_k}, with high strength at intermediate levels of p_{y_k}.

On the surface, this finding should not surprise us, for we have provided a theoretical derivation for a similar pattern (see Theorem 1). However, that derivation is based entirely upon levels of deprivation-satiation as concomitants of p_y. But the empirical relation is obtainable with deprivation *held constant*.[28] We conclude that something is operating in the strength of reinforcers over and above moment-to-moment deprivation. That "something" is normally called a "value" (or "object cathexis" in psychoanalytic theory; or "valence" in Lewinian field theory), and it is related to a history of problematic or uncertain reinforcement outcome. Accordingly, we suggest the following formulation:

DEFINITION 7. The *value* (*V*) of a class of reinforcers is the strength of that class in evoking and reinforcing initiations, relative to other comparable classes, holding deprivation constant and greater than zero. (Note: If the class is a domain, other domains are comparable classes. If the class is a magnitude level within a domain, other magnitude levels are comparable classes.)

DEFINITION 8. For any class of reinforcers the corresponding class of initiations has *uncertain* (or "problematic") reinforcement outcomes to degree $U =$ "something like" $4(p_y q)$; where $q = 1 - p_y$.

PROPOSITION 4. The value of a class of reinforcers is a direct function of   (13) U across the recency weighted history of exchange.

COROLLARY 3.3. Given $Ax_i;S_jy_k$, D_{AS_j} varies directly with the value of   (14) y_k for A.

---

[28] As an example, Kelleher and Gallub summarize the findings of a 1957 experiment by Ferster and Skinner as follows: "These results suggest that when S_1 is paired with a fixed reinforcement frequency, it may be a less effective conditioned reinforcer than when it is paired with a variable reinforcement frequency with the same mean value." (Roger T. Kelleher and Lewis R. Gallub, "A Review of Positive Conditional Reinforcement," *Journal of Experimental Analysis of Behavior*, Vol. 5, October, 1962.)

THEOREM 3. Given $Ax_i;S_jy_k$, an increase (or decrease) in U for y_k pro-   (15)
duces a corresponding increase (or decrease) in D_{AS_j}. (From Corollary 3.3 and Proposition 4.)

Thus, if S_j is another Actor B in a social relation $Ax_i;By_k$, B can increase D_{AB}
by making y_k problematic (e.g., "playing hard to get"). As we will see in
Part II, this will increase B's power over A.

We suggest $U = 4(p_yq)$ only to convey the general meaning of a problematic
or uncertain outcome in exchange. So defined, U can assume values from 0.0
to 1.0, and its relation to p_y is nonlinear and symmetrical around $p_y = 0.5$.
Whether or not the function is symmetrical is an empirical question . . . and an
interesting question as well. A reasonable guess would be that *value* is *some*
nonlinear function of p_y for *all* actors, while for specific actors there may be
specific functions within this class. Thus, if there are personality traits such as
optimism or "need for achievement," — persons who tend to form and pursue
high levels of aspiration, etc. — we might find for such persons *value* functions
with maximum U at $0.0 < p_y < .5$; while for "pessimistic" or nonstriving or
"fear of failure" subjects, maximum U may correspond to $1.0 > p_y > .5$. If
this is the case, our exchange theory may be able to specify the kind of exchange
structures in socialization which produce such personality attributes. But,
meanwhile, we are interested in *all* actors and therefore committed only to *some*
nonlinear function of p_y as a determinant of emerging and changing value
orientations.[29]

The basic implications of Proposition 4 can be readily understood if we
return to the question posed above: if a system has "functional prerequisites"
or "needs" exchange in the domains of food, fluid, and oxygen, can these
reinforcers be arranged in a hierarchy of generalized strength or value? According to Proposition 4, if the environment is so arranged that obtaining food has
been more problematic than obtaining oxygen, then food will be "valued"
above oxygen. That both are "necessary" or equally "needed" is another
matter. As a result, efforts to obtain reinforcers with low relative value will be
governed more by Proposition 2, concerning deprivation, while highly valued
reinforcers are to that extent freed from deprivation as an impulse to initiations.

[29] The general theme involved in this formulation of *value* and *uncertainty* is hardly new.
It bears a resemblance, sometimes remote and sometimes very similar, to notions that have
been advanced in widely separated areas. For example, "Effectance motivation subsides
when a situation has been explored to the point that it no longer presents new possibilities."
(Robert W. White, "Motivation Reconsidered," in Donald Fiske and Salvatore Maddi
[eds.], *The Functions of Varied Experience*, Homewood, Ill.: The Dorsey Press, 1961, p. 315.)
Most of the contributions to Fiske and Maddi are relevant. See also D. E. Berlyne, *Conflict,
Arousal and Curiosity*, New York: McGraw-Hill, 1960, and John Atkinson, "Motivational
Determinants of Risk-Taking Behavior," *Psychological Review*, Vol. 64, 1957, pp. 359–372.
As Catton has observed, "Another plausible dimension (of value), that of *probability*, can be
traced back to the thinking of Jeremy Bentham. Probability . . . may be regarded as an aspect
of the valuer's *relation* to the desideratum. . . . Quite possibly the intensity of striving to
attain a goal will be *curvilinearly* related to perceived probability, with less striving for the
impossible and less striving for the automatic than for the goal of median likelihood."
(William R. Catton, Jr., *From Animistic to Naturalistic Sociology*, New York: McGraw-Hill,
1966, p. 148.)

But what if a domain is "necessary" and "nonproblematic" by virtue of $p_y = 0.0$ rather than 1.0? Will the *value* of the domain decline toward zero? According to Proposition 4 it will. The organism will either die or evolve, in one or another sense of these words; and in either case, what was considered "necessary" will diminish in value in the process. This question is of interest primarily because it points to the manner in which exchange theory can be converted into a theory of system "needs" and system change. Otherwise, it is academic, for most reinforcers are conditioned and these pose no problem concerning the plausibility of Proposition 4. For example, "human affection" might be a powerful conditioned reinforcer for a certain boy at age six. If obtaining affection then becomes too costly (see Corollary 4.1 below) or if p_y for affection approaches 0.0 in subsequent years, he will place little or no *value* on affection at age sixteen or so; that is, he will not initiate behavior resulting in affection. Whether or not he still "needs" it then becomes a clinical question anchored to society's values rather than to this boy's current state.

7. Reward, Cost, and Comparison Level

Our attention has been focused upon the value of domains, but Definitions 7 and 8 and Proposition 4 apply as well to magnitude levels within domains. If a man has a given salary, Y, which cannot be lowered but *might* be doubled if he works harder, we can conceive U as a curve beginning at $U = 0.0$ for Y, increasing to $U = 1.0$ at, say, salary $2Y$ and decreasing to 0.0 at very high salary $10Y$. Two questions can be asked. Will the man "try for" $2Y$ or for $10Y$? Which will be more reinforcing if obtained? The answer, of course, is $2Y$ (from Proposition 4) and $10Y$ (from Proposition 1), respectively. Thus, we are saying that this man who has Y dollars values $2Y$ dollars more than he values $10Y$ dollars. This is in accord with all we know about level of aspiration. If it seems to violate the common-sense notion of preference ordering, this is only because we are concerned with values in action as distinct from symbolic projections and verbalized ideals. If our subject is *really* offered a choice between $2Y$ and $10Y$, making $10Y$ truly possible, then U for $10Y$ is greater than U for $2Y$. Technically, A's *values* govern his *initiation* behavior. The difference between initiation and subsequent reinforcement is the difference between *value* and *reward*.

Let us assume that if y is quantitative it is measured on a scale from 0.0 to 1.0, and if it is nonquantitative it is either 0 or 1.

> DEFINITION 9. For any exchange relation $A;S_j$, if y is quantitative the magnitude level of y with $U = 1.0$ for recency weighted transactions in that relation is called the *comparison level* (CL_j) for that relation. If y is nonquantitative, $CL_j = p_{y_k}.$[30]

---

[30] This concept is taken from Thibaut and Kelley, *op. cit.*, and our formulation in terms of U is fully compatible with their treatment in most respects. Since we deal with alternative relations, their *CL* alt is represented here as well.

COROLLARY 3.4. D_{AS_j} varies directly with CL_j and inversely with the   (16) comparison levels for alternative relations.

DEFINITION 10. For any exchange relation, if y_{kt} occurs at magnitude level m in a given transaction, then y_{kt} is called a *reward* of magnitude $R = VD(m)$, where V is the value of the domain y_k and D is deprivation in that domain at time t.

DEFINITION 11. If A has a set of one or more opportunities, $S_{1t}, S_{2t} \ldots S_{nt}$, in the same or different domain, such that an initiation $(S_{jt} \rightarrow Ax_{it})$ removes other opportunities in the set, then the *cost* of that initiation is the largest associated value of $VD(CL)$ across this set. (Thus, cost is best conceived as "reward missed or foregone.")

COROLLARY 4.1. *Cost Reduction.* Given a set of exchange relations,   (17) $A;S_1, A;S_2 \ldots A;S_n$, in the same or different domains, if transactions in $A;S_j$ *preclude* transactions in one or more relations in the set, then cost first increases and then decreases across continuing transactions in $A;S_j$.

Corollary 4.1 involves an important process of value change or adaptation under conditions of value conflict . . . "What people can't get they stop wanting." If our concern were purely psychological, dealing only with a single actor in a passive nonsocial environment, this corollary would be trivial. However, in human social exchange, where one party (person or social group) takes action which *places A* in positions of value conflict (as when negative sanctions are applied), this principle assumes immense importance. In the entire area of power and social control, including the socialization process, this principle plays a large part in the stabilization of the social system.

□ C. SUMMARY: THE CENTRAL IMPORTANCE OF "DEPENDENCE"

We have been guided so far by a dual purpose: (a) to develop a set of basic concepts and principles to be used (in Part II) in the development of human social exchange theory; and (b) to make the psychological basis for our concepts fairly explicit. As a result, we began with terms employed or employable in the experimental analysis of behavior in a laboratory environment, and we have attempted a step-by-step elaboration of those terms to accommodate more complex behavior in a less restrictive environment. However, the concepts and principles developed above do not have equal importance in the scheme, nor equal relevance to our purpose in Part II. A sketchy summary will help to highlight the main points.

We defined an exchange relation as a temporal series containing *opportunities* which evoke *initiations* with probability p_{x_i}, which in turn produce or result in *transactions* with probability p_{y_k}. The latter probability was employed as the basis for a conception of *uncertainty* as the degree to which exchange is problematic. We suggest that the *value* of domain y_k, relative to other exchange domains, is a function of uncertainty across domains, and the *comparison level* within a given exchange relation was defined in terms of uncertainty within that relation. Thus, relations in the same domain (*alternative* relations) are comparable on *CL*, while relations in different domains are comparable on the value dimension, as a preference order. Both are derivatives of *uncertainty*, which is our way of utilizing the "reinforcement schedules" studied so extensively by operant psychologists. Meanwhile, since a given exchange relation can include transactions in more than one domain (i.e., mediate more than one type of valued outcome), we speak of the degree of *primacy* of a relation. The term is chosen because of the parallel with primary versus secondary relations in conventional sociology. Within the framework developed here, the most extreme secondary social relations would be exchange relations with primacy of Degree 1, and with many alternative relations (e.g., customer-sales clerk). By contrast, a highly primary exchange relation will (a) mediate a wide variety of valued reinforcers; and therefore (b) have few if any alternatives, while being (c) highly resistant to satiation.

Thus, an actor is conceived as a point where many exchange relations connect. Some of these relations are in the same domain, while others are in different exchange domains, and still others lie in two or more domains. What will govern behavior (initiations) in such complex networks of exchange? Each exchange relation is describable on several variables: *CL*; value; number of alternatives; and primacy. All these are *relatively enduring* though changeable states of the relation. They all converge, as independent variables, upon *dependence* D_{AS_j}, $j = 1$ to n. By Theorem 2, initiations are allocated across opportunities, $S_1, S_2 \ldots S_n$ as a direct function of dependence, holding relative deprivation across domains constant. Our theory makes no attempt to weight the variables contributing to dependence, for that is an empirical problem.

We now can move the discussion into human social exchange, as a special case. The concept of dependence will be one of our main tools.

Chapter 4

Exchange Theory, Part II: Exchange Relations and Network Structures*

■ RICHARD M. EMERSON

□ **A. INTRODUCTION**

The purpose of this essay is to begin construction of a theory of social exchange in which *social structure* is taken as the dependent variable. As Smelser points out, social structure "constitutes the chief conceptual focus of the discipline"; and structural concepts result from "progressions of conceptual abstraction" beginning at the level of behavioral data.[1] The conceptual progression presented below began with an analysis of experimental operant behavior in *Exchange Theory: Part I.*

While this essay assumes general familiarity with Part I, a sketchy review of salient concepts will help in making the transition. In Part I the analysis was purely psychological, involving a single actor in exchange with his environment. An exchange relation was symbolized $Ax_i;S_jy_k$, or simply $A;S_j$. Some Actor A "exchanges" behavior of type x_i for stimulus of Type y_k in Situation S_j. For example, suppose it is known that Mr. Jones (A) repeatedly visits Fish Lake (S_j), where he performs fishing behavior (x_i), which periodically results in a fish (y_k). In the language of operant psychology, the behavior might be called "operant" because it is increased or sustained by its consequence — a fish. Fish might be called a class of "reinforcers" (for Mr. Jones) because they increase or sustain his fish-gaining behavior. And the lake might be said to have Mr. Jones on an "intermittent reinforcement schedule." (If Jones caught a fish with every cast, the *value* he attaches to Fish Lake and to fishing would

---

* Since this paper was written there have been subsequent developments; see Richard M. Emerson, "Role-Theory and Diminishing Utility in Group Decision-Making," *Pacific Sociological Review*, vol. 11 (Fall), pp. 110–115; "Operant Psychology and Exchange Theory," in Burgess and Bushell (eds.), *Behavioral Sociology* (New York: Columbia University Press, 1969; "Exchange Theory: The Problem of Appropriate Data," unpublished technical report, Institute for Sociological Research, University of Washington (August 1971); "Power and Position in Exchange Networks," unpublished technical report, Institute for Sociological Research, University of Washington (August 1971).

[1] Neil J. Smelser (ed.), *Sociology: An Introduction*, New York: John Wiley and Sons, 1967, pp. 5–6.

□ B. SOCIAL EXCHANGE RELATIONS

In Part I the term "actor" was employed as an undefined term. We now stipulate that either or both actors in the $Ax;By$ relation can be (a) a person, (b) a role-occupant, or (c) a "collective" actor which confronts the other party as a single unit. In the interest of generality, we will attempt to formulate concepts and principles applicable to relations among actors in general.[6]

1. Reciprocity

In his critique of functionalism, Gouldner calls attention to the seemingly universal reciprocity in human affairs.[7] "Gifts," in virtually any land, are received with a sense of incurred obligation. Frequently, this appears as a moral restraint, sometimes, as an expedient recognition concerning subsequent gifts. In either case, it casts doubt on the altruistic nature of the gift despite any seemingly altruistic motive at the time of giving.

Stated differently, much gift-giving is operant behavior: it is therefore part of an interactive exchange; it is extinguishable; and it will extinguish if not reinforced (i.e., reciprocated). If A's behavior x_1 (which is rewarding to B) does not evoke rewarding behavior from B, then it will either (a) change to a form x_2 which *is* reciprocated (Corollary 1.1), or (b) the $A;B$ relation will extinguish (Corollary 1.2). What Gouldner calls the "norm" or reciprocity may be little more than a widespread human recognition of the contingencies intrinsic to all social exchange.[8]

A very important point now warrants restatement: Statements (1) and (2) in Part I are empirical conditions which define the boundaries of exchange theory. When these conditions are applied to both Actors A and B, reciprocity becomes an attribute of social exchange relations *by definition*. However, this does not define altruism or true gift-giving out of existence. If someone gives me an overcoat because I need one, with "no strings attached," this pure gift fails to meet the conditions of Statement (2). It is very likely that the coat and the time he spent giving it were of little value to him, thereby allowing his "concern for my welfare" to serve as sufficient incentive. The pure gift may occasionally occur, but it is not a *re*curring event in the relation and it lies outside exchange theory.

---

[6] Whether or not a simple principle will hold for the behavior of both individuals and groups as units is an empirical question. But it is also a matter of the level of abstraction employed in concept formation. The absence of reference to subjective states in operant concepts is a distinct advantage afforded by those concepts. If reward means reinforce, a group can be rewarded in the sense that a pattern of collective behavior (e.g., "cooperation") is maintained or increased by an event. Such language involves no "psychologizing" at the group level at all.

[7] Alvin Gouldner, "The Norm of Reciprocity," *American Sociological Review*, 25, 1960, pp. 161–178.

[8] Diffuse moral norms defining obligation to reciprocate can emerge over and above the contingencies inherent in exchange. Even so, I prefer to reserve the term "norm" for use in a more restricted way developed below.

2. Balance

Reciprocity as such is not a *variable* attribute of viable exchange relations, and, once recognized, it is of little theoretical interest. However, close examination of reciprocity in terms of principles presented in Part I leads to features which do have theoretical importance. To say that an exchange relation is reciprocal does not mean that *each* initiation evokes a transaction. To take an example from Blau,[9] a worker (*A*) might initiate by mixing admiration and deference into a request for help from an expert (*B*), only to be turned away on a given occasion. If this continues, *A*'s requests will extinguish; but if help is occasionally forthcoming from *B*, the *A*;*B* relation will become or remain viable. In operant terms, *B* could be said to have *A* on an intermittent reinforcement schedule, while *B*'s reinforcements are on a continuous schedule.[10] As a result, it is clear that variables developed in Part I can vary somewhat independently for the two actors involved in a relation. Since most of these variables are summarized in the concept of *dependence*, we will define:

DEFINITION 12. An exchange relation *A*;*B* is said to be balanced if $D_{AB} = D_{BA}$. Imbalance $= |D_{AB} - D_{BA}|$.

Since balance-imbalance will be a major variable describing exchange relations throughout this chapter, the problem of operational definition warrants discussion. The dependence of *A* upon *B* in the *Ax*;*By* relation is (a) a direct function of the *value* of *y* for *A*, and (b) an inverse function of the number of *alternative* relations, *Ax*;*Cy*, *Ax*;*Dy*, etc. Balance in the relation is therefore a function of four variables: *value* and *alternatives* for *A* and for *B*. If *A* and *B* value *y* and *x* to the same degree, then balance can be determined readily by examining the opportunity structure across their respective alternatives. This places the question of balance into the framework of positions occupied by *A* and *B* in the structure of exchange *networks*.

We will defer discussion of alternative relations to the next section on networks. Meanwhile, it will be instructive to discuss balance in the case of bilateral monopoly — the isolated exchange relation in which dependence is a function of *value* alone. Here we encounter the problem of *interpersonal utility comparisons*, often considered to be unsolvable.[11] As Kuhn points out in his discussion of bargaining transactions,[12] *if* a transaction takes place, *both* parties benefit, and it is meaningless to ask which got the "better deal." One party can be said to have come out second best in the transaction only if there is some external (social) standard specifying what he could have or should have gotten, but this implies a nonmonopolistic structure.

[9] Peter Blau, *Exchange and Power*, New York: Wiley, 1964, p. 177.

[10] As a result, the value attached to these activities by *A* and *B* will increase and decrease, respectively, if this situation continues. See Proposition 4, Part I.

[11] See, for example, Ilman Waldner, *Interpersonal Utility Comparisons*, unpublished dissertation, Stanford University, 1966.

[12] Alfred Kuhn, *The Study of Society: A Unified Approach*, Homewood, Illinois: Irwin-Dorsey, 1963, pp. 329–332.

If one attempts to measure balance-imbalance in the isolated $A;B$ relation through direct recourse to subjective values of A and B, he will encounter problems. Does Blau's expert value ego-inflation from the worker more or less than the worker values help and advice from the expert? Such a measure would require access to the entire preference order of each actor across their entire opportunity structure in the work situation, including *non*alternative relations. This problem would severely tax the methodology of questionnaire or interview techniques.

Fortunately, there is a direct behavioral solution to this measurement problem, implicitly developed in Part I. We have seen that dependence governs p_{x_i}, the probability of initiation in a given exchange relation. As a result, by Theorem 2, initiations are allocated across exchange relations as a function of dependence. Therefore, if $A;B$ is a balanced relation, initiations by A and by B are equally probable. If the relation is unbalanced, with B more dependent than A, B will be the more frequent initiator. We offer this formulation as a solution to the problem of inter-personal utility comparisons, a solution which does not require the direct comparison of two persons' values. Does A tend, over time, to offer ego-boosts to B in exchange for help, or does B tend to volunteer help in exchange for respect and deference? Measuring the balance-imbalance in a relation involves the assessment of two conditional probabilities: $p_A = p(Ax|B)$, the probability that A will initiate, given access to B (i.e., given the "opportunity"); and $p_B = p(By|A)$, the probability that B will initiate, given the opportunity. Thus, imbalance is conceptually defined as $|D_{AB} - D_{BA}|$, while for observational purposes it is defined as $|p_A - p_B|$. (Note that *both* p_A and p_B are identical to p_x in Part I.)

3. Cohesion

Now consider the viability of an exchange relation as a variable state of the relation. In operant terms, we have in mind something analogous to "resisting extinction." In developing a concept of relational *cohesion*, we can think of a relation as surviving unchanged, undergoing change, or extinguishing altogether under the impact of external events. These external events impinge upon the relation in the form of *cost* to one or both actors.

DEFINITION 13. For any exchange relation $A;B$, cohesion =
   $(D_{AB} + D_{BA})/2$.[13]

Cohesion comes into play whenever one or both actors in the relation encounter value conflict involving the relation. In the absence of conflict at a given time, it is an assessment of the level of potential conflict which the relation can absorb or survive.

[13] Since the *cost* of a transaction is *reward foregone* by that transaction dependence amounts to the level of cost an actor will accept in relation, before the relation extinguishes for him. As a result, it is tempting to define cohesion as the dependence of the less dependent party. However, as we will see, costs incurred by the less dependent party can be transferred to the more dependent member, by virtue of the concept of *power*.

4. Power

Perhaps the most widely used and quoted definition of power in sociology comes from Max Weber: "Power is the probability that one actor within a social relationship will be in a position to carry out his own will despite resistance."[14] In exchange terms, such definitions amount to the level of potential *cost* which one actor can induce another to "accept." Therefore, we define:

> DEFINITION 14. In any exchange relation $A;B$, the *power* of A over B (P_{AB}) is the level of potential cost which A can induce for B, and A's *power advantage* $= P_{AB} - P_{BA}$.

This definition is a fairly straightforward translation of Weber's definition of power. His "resistance" is our "cost," and our "potential" is his "in a position to." However, Weber's reference to "own will" is omitted intentionally in our definition. While power is often willfully exercised, the dynamics of power are not restricted to action with intent or awareness.

A moment's reflection upon our definitions of cost and dependence will show that dependence can be restated as the level of potential cost an actor will accept within a relation. Therefore:

> THEOREM 4. In any exchange relation $A \cdot B$, $P_{AB} = D_{BA}$ and power advantage equals imbalance. (From Propositions 1 and 3, and definitions of cost, dependence, and power.)

Skinner's power over his experimental subject, a rat or a pigeon, is that subject's dependence upon Skinner for food. The cost Skinner can impose is equal to the cost the subject encounters in the least costly avenue for food-getting. If Skinner provides the only avenue, the imposable cost is equal to the value of food. Thus, while our definition of power is very close to the most common sociological uses of the term, it is virtually synonymous with "the other's dependence." The concept of power could be redefined to remove this redundancy, either by removing its "potential" property or by reinstating the implicit voluntarism in Weber's definition. Either way, the next question becomes: under what conditions does an actor use power, and what factors limit or place ceilings on its use?

5. The "Use" of Power

Let us first acknowledge that *power* is redundant and unnecessary in this scheme, given our conception of dependence. We use it only as a shorthand substitute for a more complicated expression such as "B's dependence upon A,

[14] Max Weber, *The Theory of Social and Economic Organization*, New York: Oxford University Press, 1947, p. 152. A similar definition widely used is "A has power over B to the extent that he can get B to do something that B would not otherwise do," offered by Robert A. Dahl, "The Concept of Power," *Behavioral Science*, July, 1957, p. 202.

considered from A's point of view as a condition governing A's behavior." Viewed from A's position, B's dependence opens up a *range of possibilities* for increased reward or decreased cost for A, both obtainable through increased costs to B. When cognitive psychology is added to the operant psychology employed in this theory — that is, when A is a symbol-using, "role-taking" human actor — the "use of power" often becomes a phenomenologically distinct mode of action. Thus there is justification for the voluntarism implicit in Weber's definition. While our conception allows for the voluntary use of power, our approach is not voluntaristic. We will deal with the "use of power" in a more general way, and only as a step in arriving at other principles. Meanwhile, the main justification for introducing the term at all is to make explicit a point of exit from this exchange formulation into other sociological formulations.

Having defined B's power as a potential limited by the value of D_{AB}, the term directs our attention to a range of possibilities open to B. It will be useful to name these "additional possibilities" for B in a more generic way:

> DEFINITION 15. *Resources:* If A's behavioral repertoire contains items which can or do reinforce B (i.e., items valued by B), then those items are A's *resources* in the $A;B$ relation.

Thus, in $Ax_1;By_1$, x_1 and y_1 are resources of A and B, respectively, currently employed in exchange. However, each actor may have additional resources x_2, $x_3 \ldots x_n$ and $y_2, y_3 \ldots y_m$, as well as x_1 and y_1 above current CL. A's power is based upon his own resources and it gives him access to B's resources. Power is used in all social exchange if only to maintain the exchange relation at current levels of reward. But simple relational maintenance is a trivial and small part of power usage. Note, for example, that the cost of performing x_1 and y_1 decreases across time (Corollary 4.1). As a result there is typically a "power surplus," a potential to impose cost at levels higher than the current level. Our theoretical interest focuses upon increases in the use of power.

> DEFINITION 16. In any relation $A;B$, A's *use of power* is said to be *increasing* across a series of transactions if (a) B's costs increase through additional $y_1, y_2 \ldots y_m$ by B, or (b) if A's costs decrease through decreased x_1 by A without decreasing rewards to A.

To use power is to impose cost, but by "impose" we do not mean a willful act. Rather, we mean any recurring act by A in $A;B$ which has costly consequences for B, including decreased x_i by A.

The use of power, including increased use, is strictly governed by Proposition 1. Thus, in any exchange relation, if A's power is greater than B's current costs and if B has additional resources, A's *use of power will increase*, cutting further into B's resources, *until its use is offset by incurred or anticipated costs to A.*

6. Balancing

> The law of politics is almost as certain as the law of physics: power creates its own resistance.
>
> JAMES RESTON

The reader might feel that "cost incurred in the use of power" provides a dangerously sloppy catchall to explain away all instances of unused power. When employed in ad hoc interpretations of social behavior it tends to be just that. But our purpose here is theory construction, and we must conceptualize these costs-incurred-in-the-use-of-power a little further. If A has power over B, the costs incurred through its use fall into two main categories: (a) costs incurred in other relations, $A;C$, $A;D$, etc.; and (b) costs incurred within $A;B$. The former involves more complex exchange structures, as when A's behavior toward B evokes sanctions from C, and such analysis will be postponed. For the moment we are concerned with the dynamics of the unit exchange relation and therefore incurred costs of type (b). These have already been conceptualized as B's power. Thus, the principal limitation upon A's use of power in a relation is his *own dependence* in that relation. Applying Proposition 1 to the behavior of both parties:

> COROLLARY 1.3. In any exchange relation $A;B$, if A has a power advantage, then A's use of power will increase across continuing transactions as a function of power advantage. (In an unbalanced relation, the "exchange ratio" changes in favor of the party with a power advantage.)

> COROLLARY 1.4. In a balanced relation, increased use of power is unlikely; and increase in the use of power by A will be accompanied by an increase by B. (The "exchange ratio" is stable in a balanced relation.)

In our previous discussion we examined the meaning of balance and imbalance, concluding that initiations are more likely from the more dependent party. We now find that reward levels change in favor of the less dependent party. But most important, Corollaries 1.3 and 1.4 indicate that balance is a stable state, and that unbalanced relations change (toward balance?).

Having defined power as a potential, both *power* and its *use* can be taken as variables. The former is an attribute of the exchange relation,[15] while the latter is an attribute of transactions within that relation. We have seen that increased use of power is brought about by power advantage. What changes in the relation are produced by the increased use of power? The answer is fairly simple and extremely important: the use of a power advantage reduces the power advantage across time. In short, exchange relations tend to change toward balance.

---

[15] For a more extended discussion of this point see R. M. Emerson, Power-Dependence Relations, *American Sociological Review*, 27, February, 1962, pp. 31–41.

THEOREM 5. In any exchange relation $A;B$, if $D_{AB} > D_{BA}$ at time t_1, then D_{AB} decreases or D_{BA} increases across continuing transactions until $D_{AB} = D_{BA}$ at time t_n. (From Corollaries 1.1, 1.3, 3.1, 3.3, and Proposition 4.)

For example, as the advantaged party uses his power to gain increased rewards, his own dependence (and the other's power) increases. To have a power advantage is to *use* it; and to use it is to *lose* it. This assertion stands across all manners of power use, intentional or unintentional, subtle or obvious, on the suspicion that different types of behavior in the use of power only affect the value of t_n.

Blau's treatment of power differs significantly from the notions developed above (and below). Most importantly, he chooses to play down power-balancing processes.[16] In this regard it is well to point out that Theorem 5 *in no way* implies that actors strive for balanced power. Balance may come to be a valued state, but this is not required. On the contrary, if actors in general strive to maximize and maintain power advantage, the theorem still holds, for it is addressed to attributes of exchange relations, not to men's motives. In this respect it is a truly sociological assertion. It maintains that a balanced relation contains no internal basis for predicting a change in the state of the relation, while an unbalanced relation does change and toward balance. This does not mean that imbalance does not occur or cannot survive. It does mean that imbalance stems from events outside the relation, and its "survival" is a problem to be explained when it occurs. Meanwhile, having chosen to de-emphasize balancing process, Blau treats power only in terms of power advantage, based on one-way "exchange," and, by implication, a balanced state neutralizes or removes power. By contrast, in our conception power is fully operative in balanced relations — its use preserves the relation and makes the concept of *cohesion* possible. In a highly cohesive relation, both members are significantly controlled "by the relation."

7. Balancing Operations[17]

The state of balance-imbalance is governed by four variables operating jointly. If $D_{AB} > D_{BA}$, change in the $Ax;By$ relation toward balance can come about through any one or some combination of four operations:

OPERATION 1. A decrease in the *value* of y for A ("Withdrawal");

OPERATION 2. An increase in the number of *alternatives*, or CL for alternatives, open to A ("Network Extension");

[16] Blau, *op. cit.*, fn., p. 118.
[17] Emerson, *op. cit.*, fn., pp. 31–32

OPERATION 3. An increase in the *value* of *x* for *B* ("Status-Giving," from *A* to *B*); and

OPERATION 4. A reduction in alternatives, or *CL* for alternatives, open to *B* ("Coalition Formation" by *A*).

While these operations constitute the four logically generic balancing processes, we attach less generic descriptive labels (withdrawal, status-giving, etc.) to identify them in terms of more specific social processes they frequently entail.

Our theory might appear to be limited in that it cannot fully predict which one or what combination of these operations will take place, or when and how rapidly change will come about. However, this limitation is not severe. As with any theory, the addition of *given conditions* from knowledge of the concrete situation allows much more specific predictions. For example, if *B*'s power advantage over *A* is based upon alternative relations with *C*, *D*, etc., and if communication channels are open among *A*, *C*, *D*, etc., then Operation 4 is more likely than the others. Other specifiable conditions will favor other operations. "Other things being equal," a rationale can be advanced (the cost involved) for the ordering 2, 3, 4, 1. If all four are possible, Operation 2 is more likely than 3, etc., at least in short-range prediction. But more important, for long-range predictions concerning social structure, Operations 3 and 4 have a "survival advantage" for the following reason:

COROLLARY 3.5. Operations 1 and 2 decrease relational cohesion, and Operations 3 and 4 increase cohesion.

Operations 3 and 4 have a long-range advantage in terms of viable social structures, and we will give them more attention below.

8. Power in Bilateral Monopoly

Analysis of balancing processes requires discussion of larger structures. Meanwhile, they can be seen in their most simple form if we examine the case of "bilateral monopoly," a relation for which neither actor has alternative relations (i.e., *A* can obtain *y* only through *B*, and *B* can obtain *x* only from *A*). Let us re-examine Blau's worker-expert relation under these restrictions. Assume that Worker *A* does many things and receives many different rewards in the plant, one of which is advice about a task which only *B* (the "expert") can provide. Assume that *B* does many things for many different rewards, one of which is giving advice to *A* in exchange for deference which only *A* will give (because he alone needs advice). Finally, assume that *A* values advice more than *B* values deference from *A*. Thus, as the scene opens, $D_{AB} > D_{BA}$, and *B* has a power advantage.

This state of affairs between one worker and one expert will be short lived. The expert, with this power advantage, might be a nice guy who is not motivated to "exercise advantage," but unless he has valueless plant time on his hands, the advantage *will* get exercised: (a) the worker who needs and values help will be the principal initiator. However, (b) since what he has to offer in return for help is *low* in the expert's preference order, transactions will be more costly to the expert (see definitions of *value* and *cost*). While the expert might be inclined to accommodate, these recurring costs will undermine that inclination. His response to the worker's frequent initiations will change, assuming the flavor of "Don't call me — I'll call you." As this change occurs, (c) the worker's rewards decline and (by Corollary 1.1) adaptive changes take place on the worker's end of the relation. He will seek and possibly find help from other sources, breaking the monopoly and balancing the relation (through Operation 2, network extension). If other sources of help do not exist, then he must induce *B* to provide help by increasing *B*'s rewards. This also moves the relation toward balance through Operation 3, "status-giving." (He smiles, goes out of his way to carry coffee to *B*, confers praise, etc.) To confer status is to increase one's control over the recipient. However, the worker might have nothing additional to give which is valued by the expert. In this event, he will "learn to live without" the help he cannot get (Proposition 4). And this adjustment in his life-style also moves the relation toward balance through Operation 1, "withdrawal," the analogue to operant extinction.

By contrast, Blau says, "Since the workers in need of expert advice usually have nothing else to offer that the consultant needs, they must repay him for it by complying with his wishes. As they consult with him more and more, the cost in compliance and self-respect mounts for them."[18] Our theory takes issue with both assertions. First, if the worker *can* "comply" then he *does* have resources the expert values; and as the worker(s) comply, the expert's dependence increases. And second, while compliance will be costly to the worker, its cost will decrease rather than increase (see Corollary 4.1).

We conclude that, by virtue of balancing processes, the concept of *power advantage* has little importance in the case of bilateral monopoly. If the weaker member has additional resources to be exploited, their introduction balances the relation. If he has no added resources, the other's "advantage" is useless to him.

However, there is more wisdom in Blau's statement than our comments so far indicate, for he is speaking of a set of workers (two or more) in relation to a single expert. In such a structure (*uni*lateral monopoly) power advantage is based upon *position in the structure* in addition to the values being exchanged. Power advantage and its resolution through balancing operations must entail *structural change*, and the concept has utility for this reason.

□ **C. EXCHANGE NETWORKS**

Having developed some of the main features of the unit exchange relation, we turn now to more complex exchange structures incorporating that unit. A sharp distinction can be drawn between two types of exchange structure:

[18] Blau, *op. cit.*, fn., p. 177.

groups and exchange *networks*. In this section we will examine some of the properties of networks. For the moment, groups can be conceived as collective actors, while networks are sets of exchange relations among actors, either individual or collective. A more analytic distinction will be offered later. Meanwhile, we define:

> DEFINITION 17. An *exchange network* is a set of three or more actors each of whom provides opportunities for transactions with at least one other actor in the set. (Thus, a network can be considered an "opportunity structure" for each actor in the network.)

1. Connected Exchange Relations

Pairs of actors within a network may form an exchange relation, and some of these relations may be "connected" to form specific network structures.

> DEFINITION 18. Two exchange relations, $A;B$ and $A;C$, are *connected at A* if the frequency or magnitude of transactions in one relation is a function of transactions in the other relation.

Consider, as a simple example, a dating network in which A regularly dates B_1 and B_2 while having dating opportunities with B_3 as well. While B_3 is not participating behaviorally in the dating transactions during the time period in question, she is nonetheless part of the network, by Definition 17. If "dating" is an exchange *domain*, then A receives significantly similar reinforcements from B_1 and B_2, and potentially from B_3. As a result, $A;B_1$ and $A;B_2$ are alternative relations for A, and alternative relations are *connected*. In this case, the connection involves an inverse function: an increase in the frequency or "magnitude" of dating with B_1 produces or implies a decrease in dating with B_2, by virtue of the principle of satiation (Proposition 2).

The function referred to in Definition 18 can occur in many empirical forms, resulting in different types of connections. In this chapter we suggest a very simple 2 X 2 typology: positive or negative; and bilateral or unilateral. For example, if an increase in $A;B$ exchange produces or stimulates an increase in $A;C$ exchange but not vice versa, then we will call the connection *unilateral positive*. The dating network mentioned above is *bilateral negatively* connected. Obviously, this typology is a simplification which ignores many interesting empirical aspects of connections. The function might be strong or weak, providing the basis for assigning magnitude to connections; the function might be linear or nonlinear, with important threshold conditions involved; the function may involve time as a variable. But we are just getting started, and we will keep it simple.

It must be emphasized that connectedness can be taken either as a theoretical or an empirical question, depending upon our purpose and the adequacy of theory. For example, from the principle of satiation or diminishing utility we can deduce that mutually alternative relations are bilateral negatively connected.

If this is empirically not the case in a situation under observation, then we can infer the existence of a threshold state within this connection and direct our empirical work toward locating it if we so desire. Unquestionably, network connections entail very complex relationships, including possible shifts from positive to negative connections at different levels of exchange. Rather than probe into these complexities at this stage, we will proceed on this simple basis into network structures, to obtain some glimpse into the kind of theoretical payoff which intricate knowledge of connections might yield.

2. Graphic Representation

The study of exchange networks might be formalized through a set of coordinating definitions joining networks to graph theory,[19] thereby gaining access to the mathematical properties of that formal theory. Several coordinating strategies are possible, but we are not yet in a position to make an intelligent choice. In this chapter we will push toward further substantive understanding, and we will not attempt a complete formalization. Rather, we will employ di-graphs largely as representational devices, with occasional utilization of concepts from graph theory as a prelude to more thorough formalization. Figure 1 presents the coordination scheme adopted for this limited purpose.

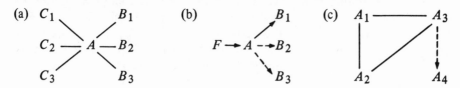

Coordinating Definitions:

Actor $A, B, C, --- N$:	Points $A, B, C, --- N$
Relation $A;B, A;C$, etc.:	$A—B, A \rightarrow C$, etc.
B opportunities for A:	$A \dashrightarrow B$
Bilateral Positive Connection:	$I—J—K$
Unilateral Positive Connection:	$I \rightarrow J \rightarrow K$ ($J—K$ contingent on $I—J$)
Bilateral Negative Connection:	$I_1—J—I_2$
Unilateral Negative Connection:	$I_1 \rightarrow J \rightarrow I_2$

■ **FIGURE 1.** Graphic Representation of Networks

In the notation established in Figure 1, bilateral and unilateral connections are represented through directionality. Thus, $A \rightarrow B \rightarrow C$ is a unilateral connection, with $B;C$ exchange contingent upon $A;B$ exchange, but not vice versa. The bilateral connection $A \rightleftarrows B \rightleftarrows C$ is represented $A—B—C$ for simplicity.

[19] F. Harary, R. Norman, and D. Cartwright, Structural Models, New York: John Wiley and Sons, 1965. Terms such as "cycle," "centrality," "distance," "reachability," and "connectedness" are used below approximately as defined by these authors.

In some cases, directionality can be understood as the direction of "resource flow." For example, in Figure 1(a) let A be a manager of a manufacturing concern, with employees B_1, B_2, and B_3 performing a given type of labor, and let C_i be a consumer of the product. Labor as a resource flows from B to C undergoing transformations in the process, while money flows from C to B (with some drained off en route). Similarly, in Figure 1(b) let F be a fraternity, A a member, and B_i, one of the girls he dates. If the dating relation is contingent upon the prestige A obtains in the fraternal relation, then a resource flows from F to B_i via A.

Finally, positive and negative connections are represented through categorizing actors into sets B_1, B_2, —B_n, etc., with each set homogeneous in terms of resources. Negative connections join an actor to two members of the same set, while positive connections join an actor to members of different sets. Thus, positive connections involve two resource inputs (exchange domains) at the point of connection, while negative connections involve only one. Note that Figure 1(c) portrays a network within one category of actors, and the structure contains *cycles*. For example, it might portray a visitation network among four families, or a marital exchange network among four family lines or clans.

The basis for this typology of network connections, and the structures it can generate, was established in Part I through the concept of an exchange *domain* as a set of reinforcing stimulus situations which are mutually satiating. For instance, if attending a theatrical performance on Monday night reduced the appeal of a symphony on Tuesday night for Mr. Jones, then both activities are considered to be instances of a single and more abstract kind (evening entertainment) and they lie in the same *domain* for Mr. Jones. Based upon this concept and others which spring from it, we can state certain rules applying to network connections:

RULE 1. Any two relations in the same domain and with comparable CL's for A are bilateral negatively connected at A.

RULE 2. Any two relations in the same domain with grossly different CL's are unilateral negatively connected at A.

RULE 3. Any two relations in the same domain with different degrees of primacy are unilateral negatively connected at A.

RULE 4. Any two relations positively connected at A lie in different domains for A and are therefore not alternative relations.

RULE 5. Any relation connected to $A;B$ is similarly connected to all alternatives to $A;B$.

3. Connections and Dependence

More important are the following derivations about the relationships between connection and the distribution of power and dependence among actors in the network.

> COROLLARY 3.1.1. Given A—B_1 at time t_1, if B_2—A—B_1 forms at time t_2, then D_{AB_1} will decrease from t_1 to t_2.

> COROLLARY 3.1.2. Given B_1—A—B_2 at time t_1, if B_1—A or (B_1, B_2)—A forms at time t_2, then D_{AB_1} is greater at t_2 than t_1. (The expression (B_1, B_2) is discussed below, as coalition formation.)

Concerning Corollary 3.1.1, if A—B_1 is balanced, then the formation of B_2—A—B_1 produces imbalance, placing A in a position of power advantage. Actor B_1 should not welcome B_2 into the network. By contrast, Corollary 3.1.2 describes structural changes through which balancing Operation 4 can come about: the removal of a competitor, or "cooperation among competitors" in the form of a coalition.

These two corollaries, simple as they are, can be applied and amplified in several ways and they warrant an illustrative digression. For example, consider the network

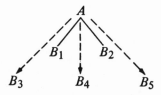

with power represented on the vertical axis. It might be a simple society or some segment of society, or some segment of an organization. It is the structural form we are concerned with, and in such a structure, all relations are unbalanced with A enjoying a structurally based power advantage. From Theorem 5 and Corollary 3.1.2 we predict that B_1—A—B_2 will change to A—(B_1, B_2), a process we will examine in more detail later (e.g., the collectivization of labor). Meanwhile, Corollary 3.1.1 raises questions about the possible conversion of $A \dashrightarrow B_i$ to A—B_i (e.g., the entry of "employable unemployed" into a labor category). *Hypothesis:* If resources are increasing across time at Position A, then "universalistic" standards will emerge governing entry into other positions. If resources are constant across time at Position A, then "particularistic" standards will emerge. Stated differently, status by achievement will emerge only in an expanding organization or in a society with an expanding economy, and only for as long as expansion continues.

But we can go much further with the aid of principles concerning the formation of positive network connections.

> THEOREM 6. Given A—B_1 or $B_2 \to A$—B_1 or B_2—A—B_1 at time t_1, if C—A—B forms at time t_2, where C and B are the same or "equivalent"

actors as B_2 and B_1 respectively, then D_{AB} and D_{AC} are greater than D_{AB_1} and D_{AB_2}. (From Proposition 1 and Corollaries 3.1 and 3.2)

This theorem relates to the emergence of new division of labor, or new roles in a role system. That is, B_2 develops a new skill or shifts to a different resource dimension which augments (is positively connected to) the behavior of B_1. Adding Theorem 5, in the unbalanced structure portrayed above, *increased division of labor* is predicted *as a balancing process*. We will examine this process further in a moment, but meanwhile it is hardly trivial to note that from Corollary 3.5 the cohesion of the system is increased as the division of labor increases. Thus, our concept of cohesion merges with Durkheim's organic solidarity.

The formation of positive connections is not the only way that division of labor can increase:

> THEOREM 7. Given B_1—A—B_2 at t_1, if B—A A—C forms at t_2, where B and C are the same or equivalent actors as B_1 and B_2, then D_{AB} and D_{AC} are greater than D_{AB_1} and D_{AB_2}, respectively. (From Proposition 1 and Corollary 3.1)

Theorems 6 and 7 distinguish between the connected network B—A—C and the unconnected network B—A A—C, as alternative balancing changes from B_1—A—B_2 as a prior unbalanced condition. In the connected case, the new resource introduced by C amplifies the value of B's resource. In the other case, the new resource satisfies a different and independent need for A.

Both forms of increased division of labor are predictable as *balancing processes* in Theorems 6 and 7, and both result in increased relational cohesion. But the difference between them remains important, for one points toward the ecology of communal division of labor and the other (the connected form) provides the basis for role differentiation in social organization. They can be compared through the following quaint example.

Let B_1 and B_2 be two blacksmiths with separate shops located by a stage station, and let A be the stage driver who brings his horses to either one of them to be shod in exchange for pay. Given these conditions, A has a power advantage in $A;B_i$ and B_i's level of living will go down over time, assuming that the two of them do not unite and act under a common policy as one actor (B_i, B_2). As the exchange ratio changes to B_i's disadvantage, B_i will be pressed to search for a new trade. Now, assume that a horse, in order to be of value to A, needs both nourishment and shoes, and assume that these need-states are correlated (i.e., at the end of a run, the horse is both hungry and poorly shod). Assume further, that a driver needs food, but this need is not correlated with the horse's needs. Then, if B_2 gives up his blacksmith shop and starts providing grain for horses, we have B_1—A—C, satisfying the conditions of Theorem 6. If B_2 starts cooking food for the driver, then we have B_1—A A—C, and Theorem 7 applies. However, in this "unconnected" case there might well develop a communal ecological connection between horseshoeing and driver feeding based upon the fact that horses are accompanied by the driver, and the driver sometimes needs food when his horses need new shoes. Thus, the cook might locate in a "community" containing a blacksmith. By contrast, if B_2 shifts to horse feeding, this division of labor has a more directly functional connection to horseshoeing. Indeed, the horse feeder and the blacksmith might well form a single organization (as distinct from a community) which produces serviced horses as a single product resulting from role-differentiation within that organization as a special form of divided labor.

Thus, Theorems 6 and 7 point up the difference between organizations and communities, conceived in exchange theory terms. They are both appropriately considered "ecosystems," for exchange theory directs attention to networks of resource flow and the manner in which resource inputs are sustained or discouraged by other resource inputs.

Finally, while both forms of divided labor increase relational cohesion, the connected form $B—A—C$ does so more than $B—A \ A—C$ does. In the latter case, D_{AB} and D_{AC} are increased only through the reduction of alternative relations for A. In the former case, dependence is increased both through reduced alternatives and increased value for A. Therefore:

> COROLLARY 3.2.1. Holding A's values constant in Theorems 6 and 7, D_{AB} and D_{AC} are greater in Theorem 6 than in Theorem 7.

Thus, it is to B_1 and B_2's advantage if B_3 starts feeding horses rather than cooking for the driver, while either change is better than the original state.

To complete this section, we must examine the main implication of *uni*lateral positive connections:

> COROLLARY 3.6. Given $A—B$ at t_1, if $A \rightarrow B \rightarrow C$ forms at t_2, then D_{BA} will increase from t_1 to t_2 and given no alternatives to $A;B$ for B, then $D_{BA} > D_{BC}$.

This type of connection resembles, at least superficially, most chains of command or hierarchical structures controlled from the top down, through successive levels of delegated power or transferred resources. But again, there are some subtleties in applying this notion. Within such hierarchies we tend to assume that "up" and "down" are obvious, but under what conditions will a person in the middle *in fact* be controlled more from above or more from below? The answer lies in part in a careful typing of the connection actually involved. If A's rewards from B are contingent upon C's performance, then the conditions in Corollary 3.6 are not fulfilled, even though the apparent organizational structure might superficially resemble those conditions. This is very often the case. Meanwhile, Corollary 3.6 can be understood through other examples. For instance, an employer should applaud the wedding of his employee, if marriage is contingent upon employment. While an employer might view a married man as more "reliable," in our terms he is more dependent, hence more controllable. In addition, the employer will have more power over the man than his wife does. She will tend to go where the employer sends her husband, or the husband will go without her.

In summary, we have argued that exchange networks change toward balance, with balance defined in terms of dependence. Having examined the relation between certain network connections and changes in the dependency of actors in the network, we can now examine structural change, as illustrated in the above discussion of the division of labor.

4. Unilateral Monopoly

The typology of network connections advanced here obviously can generate very complex network structures. A more complete formalization of our theory will facilitate analysis of change in complex structures. But for now we adopt the strategy of attempting to locate substantive principles governing change within a few fairly simple but basic structural components of larger networks.

Perhaps the most basic structural component is the set of relations $Ax_i;B_jy_k$, $j = 1$ to N, which can be graphed

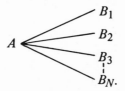

Since each B is a source of y_k for A they are alternative relations negatively connected at A, and B's are in effect competing with one another for access to x_i from A. If B's have no alternatives to A then the structure can be called *unilateral monopoly*. Furthermore, if the value of x_i to B_j is more than trivial, then the A—B_j relation is unbalanced and A enjoys a power advantage based upon his position in the network.

We choose this simple structure as our starting point for several reasons. First, it is empirically very common as a component in larger structures (organizational hierarchies, etc.). Second, it forms readily and frequently, notably when the number of actors in a system is increasing through population increase, member recruitment, etc. And third, it is unbalanced and therefore its existence or its formation is a stimulus to further change.

From unilateral monopoly a variety of structural changes can come about under different conditions. For example, under the impact of Corollary 1.3 (increasing cost or decreasing reward for B_j), exploratory behavior is set in motion (Corollary 1.1) which may uncover A_2 *if* such an actor exists in B_j's surroundings. This will weaken the monopoly and imbalance is reduced through Operation 2. Let us first consider the situation in which no structural change comes about because no A_2 exists, B's cannot communicate with each other or are prevented from doing so, etc.

COROLLARY 1.3.1. *"Exploitation" Type 1:* Given (a) a unilateral monopoly $Ax_i; B_j y_k, j = 1$ to N, (b) with additional resources $y_1, y_2 \ldots y_n$ uniformly distributed across $[B]$, (c) with x_i highly valued by B_j, and (d) given no structural change across time, then B_j's additional resources will enter exchange across continuing transactions, with A's resource utilization constant or diminishing.

Notice first that no reference is made to the value of $y_k, \ldots y_n$ for A, other than the fact that they are "resources" and therefore have value greater than zero. Even if y_k, the initial basis of exchange, has very high value for A at the outset, the assertion still holds. This structure makes the acquisition of y_k "nonproblematic" for A, and its value will decline. The same will happen to $y_1, y_2 \ldots y_n$ as they are introduced. (See the concept of "uncertainty" and Proposition 4.)

Will this exploitive process terminate or bottom-out at some definable point? In theory it will not do so, while it might appear to in practice. *It is to B_j's advantage to hide the fact that he has added resources if these resources are common across the set $[B]$.* Since these additional resources include capacities to develop new skills of value to A, it is then to B_j's advantage to be or to appear incompetent in A's eyes, as an adaptation to A's structural power advantage. But in principle this is a short-range adaptation, even though it might account for a sizable period of real time. Where does the system stand when B_j has no added resources, when he is, or appears to be, incompetent? Assuming that x_i is a *conditioned* reinforcer for B_j (i.e., assuming that B_j can biologically survive in its absence), then:

THEOREM 8. *"Exploitation" Type 2:* Given (a), (c), and (d) as above, and given no additional resources across $[B]$, then x_i will decrease and the value of x_i for B_j will decrease across continuing transactions. (From Corollary 1.3, Theorem 4 and Corollary 4.1)

The main feature of this assertion is a declining "level of living" and loss of aspiration as a value adaptation. It is a "balancing" process as well, through Operation 1 "withdrawal." A person stops wanting what he cannot get if he can get along without it. Meanwhile, if x_i is a condition for biological survival, B_j will be reduced to just that — biological survival. Slavery in North America and Negro adaptation to it provides a fair illustration of the above points.

Corollary 1.3.1 and Theorem 8 can work together, and the process need not look like anything one would call "exploitation." We are not concerned with the label, but with the structural type and the processes it entails. We need not turn to slavery or to feudal systems for our examples. To illustrate the generality of the principles, let us pick up the discussion of Blau's worker-expert relation where we left it. We found that if the more dependent worker *can* comply with the more powerful expert's desires, then he *does* have added resources, and the introduction of these resources (his own compliance) balances the relation — by definition. As a result, we concluded that power advantage is not a meaningful concept in analyzing bilateral monopoly. But unilateral monopoly gives the expert a structurally based power advantage which is more lasting, at least until the structure changes or until Theorem 8 runs its course to possible extinction. Suppose that several workers [B] have need for technical advice and only one person (A) can give it. Worker B_1 might approach the expert for advice (x_i) and get it, giving expressions of gratitude (y_k) in return. However, as $B_2, B_3 \ldots B_n$ start to do likewise, A, whose time is assumed to be of some value, will find advice-giving increasingly costly and gratitude decreasingly valuable (Proposition 4). Even if A is a "helpful fellow" B_j will find advice increasingly hard to obtain from A, and by Corollary 1.1 he will search his repertoire for added incentives to offer. Suppose B_1 brings coffee (y_1) to

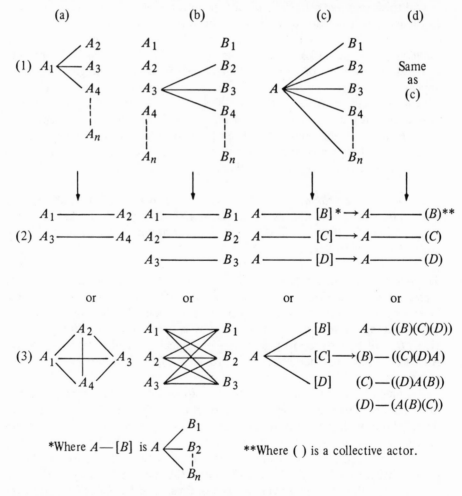

FIGURE 2. Structural Changes Stimulated by Unilateral Monopoly

A and while there asks for advice. This might work initially, but B_2 must now bring coffee or its equivalent. And so it will go, cutting into B_j's resources, until B_j finds another source of advice (Operation 2); finds a resource that other B's do not possess (division of labor through Operations 3 and 4); until B's unite under a single policy ("we" will not show respect for A unless each of us gets advice — Operation 4, coalition); or until B_j learns to live without advice (Operation 1). Each of these changes in the structure of the network is a balancing process, and Corollary 1.3.1 and Theorem 8 describe the impetus for such change starting with unilateral monopoly as a given condition. Figure 2 portrays several types of structural change emanating from unilateral monopoly, and we will discuss some of them as illustrative cases.

5. Division of Labor

Having mentioned this topic earlier, let us begin with the networks in Figure 2(c) which illustrate division of labor.

> THEOREM 9. *Division of Labor:* Given (a) a unilateral monopoly $A;B_j$, $j = 1$ to N, (b) in which balancing Operations 2 and 4 do not occur, and (c) given additional resources nonuniformly distributed across $[B]$, then the structure will change to one or a combination of the structures in Figure 2(2)(c) and 2(3)(c). (From Theorems 5, 6, 7, and Corollaries 1.1 and 1.3.1.)

The difference between Figures 2(2)(c) and 2(3)(c) has already been discussed in connection with Theorems 6 and 7 and the stage station. As a result, we understand that relations portrayed in 2(2)(c) can be considered connected at A in an ecological sense, if this is empirically the case. If it is the case, the network in 2(2)(c) portrays a simple "community." Meanwhile, for connections of the kind involved in 2(3)(c) to form the different resources available in $[B]$ must be complimentary in the sense that they interact in providing value to A. Such a network portrays "social organization."

Examples can be drawn at the societal level. Let A in Figure 2(1)(c) be a landlord, in feudal China at about 500 B.C., with $B_1, B_2 \ldots B_n$ taxed for the use of land. Woven through a matrix of unique (and therefore sociologically irrelevant) historical events, we can see our principles operating. Under the pressure of malevolent or *de facto* exploitation, the set of B's will subdivide through time toward a system approaching a combination of Figures 2(2)(c) and 2(3)(c). Some of the more robust sons of peasants will find employment as warriors, if the lord must protect his lands against encroachment. If warriors $[C]$ permit peasants to work unmolested and peasants feed armies, then we have the bilateral positive connection $[C]—A—[B]$. A's administrative tasks will multiply in the process, and the more literate sons of peasants and warriors $[D]$ will find positions in an emerging feudal government.

But the structure remains monopolistic in Figure 2(c), with such divisions in feudal labor only temporarily reducing the pressure of exploitation. Thus, further division will evolve. Some peasants will become carvers of jade [*E*], temporarily improving their position, and the position of peasants as well. If agriculture sustains jade carving but not vice versa, we have the connection [*B*] → *A* → [*E*], and during poor rice years the carvers will go before the soldiers do. Meanwhile, within the monopolistic structure of the court administration, labor will divide still further: a Confucius will emerge, specialized in giving advice to the prince specifically on matters concerning the maintenance of legitimacy in ruling over a restive peasantry. And the Confucian ethic will understandably emerge as the "official" religious philosophy specifically because it is a service rendered to the lord, legitimizing the established order.

Meanwhile, on the periphery of this monopolistic network, other balancing operations will be in motion, notably Operation 1, "withdrawal," along with the cultivated incompetence mentioned above as a subtle form of passive resistance. In short, Taoist teachings emerge in the form of parables, propagated by mystic recluses: "All we can guess about the authorship of these poems is that the main threads of their argument originated among recluses in remote valleys before Confucius' time and the result took (literate) form late in the third century B.C."[20] The form they took became a philosophy stated largely in parables, and quite alien to the Confucian ethic of deferential striving.[21] Taoism emerged at the bottom of the feudal system: renounce earthly social values and turn attention inward; renounce futile social striving, and find solace in harmony with nature. Keep your worth hidden and thereby gain freedom from paternalistic exploitation.[22] In its own way, the history of the American Negro illustrates the same "balancing" processes as an adaptation to power in unilateral monopoly.

6. Social Circles: The Principle of Closure

Networks of the form shown in Figure 2(b) involve cross-category exchange with no intra-category exchange. The categories might be the set of service station operators and the set of automobile owners. The former do not exchange gasoline for gasoline with one another and the latter do not exchange dollars for dollars. While such networks contain some important features more interesting to sociologists than to economists, they are nonetheless closer in form to economics than other networks in Figure 2, and we will forego discussion of such exchange at this time. We turn instead to intra-category ex-

[20] See R. B. Blakney, *The Way of Life: on Tzu*, a translation of the Ton Te Ching, New York: Mentor, 1955, pp. 26–27.

[21] *Ibid.*, pp. 32–33. Blakney begins: "Men do not flee civilized society and commit themselves to the rough embrace of mother nature unless their distress is deep. . . ." That is, balancing Operation 1 comes about as a last resort. We suggest that the rise of Taoism can be taken as an example.

[22] For example, see the parable of The Shang Mountain Tree ("The Works of Chuang Tze," in Robert O. Ballou (ed.), *The Bible of the World*, New York: The Viking Press, 1939, pp. 514–515.) In this parable, Tze Ch'i saw a tree of astonishing grandeur. On close inspection he found the branches "too crooked for rafters." " 'Ah,' said Tze Ch'i, 'this tree is good for nothing, and that is how it has attained this size. A wise man might well follow its example.' "

change and Figure 2(a). Such networks involve the same exchange domain(s) for all actors in the network. As a result, all network connections are negative. While a dating network is cross-category (assuming all actors are heterosexual), a friendship network is intra-category (assuming that friendship is an exchange domain, and friends are therefore significantly interchangeable).

The type of exchange structure in question was identified by George Simmel as a "social circle." Drawing upon Simmel, Kadushin describes social circles as involving three features: (a) indirect interaction among its members; (b) a common interest on the part of its members; and (c) "instituted to a relatively low degree."[23] Examples might include a set of tennis players or a set of theater-goers, who interact on the basis of a common interest in an activity, each helping to provide the other with rewarding access to that activity. A wide variety of networks can be examined in these terms, including families who visit in one another's homes, families eligible to exchange children in marriage, machinists who exchange shop-talk, etc. Within the exchange framework, the above three features listed by Kadushin can be restated: a social circle is (a) a network; based upon (b) intra-category exchange; and (c) it is not a group. While a social circle is not a group, both Simmel and Kadushin treat circles nonetheless as bounded social units. We will show that their boundary-forming and boundary-maintaining tendencies stem from specific features of intra-category exchange and balancing processes therein.

Several features of intra-category exchange networks follow by definition. First, all connections are negative. Second, in graph theory terms, connected relations can form *cycles* of *length* three or more. Furthermore, the *distance* between two points in a graph (or positions in a network) provides the basis for defining and measuring the relative *centrality* of each position in a network structure. Now, if a network is balanced to the extent that its relations are balanced, then: (a) imbalance is a function of differential centrality, with power advantage at more central positions; (b) cycle formation reduces differential centrality; and therefore (c) cycle formation is a balancing process (a special case of balancing Operation 2). But we can go one step further. Given a network like A_1—A_2—$A_3 \dashrightarrow A_4$, the formation of A_1—A_3 has two consequences. First, it completes the cycle A_1—A_2—A_3—A_1 balancing the previously unbalanced relations A_1—A_2 and A_2—A_3. And second, it reduces the likelihood that $A_3 \dashrightarrow A_4$ will convert to A_3—A_4, through increasing the cost to A_4 involved in this conversion. Thus, cycle-formation balances the network and also "closes" the network to entry by new actors. Cycle-formation is a boundary-forming process.

We can organize these points into more general statements if we define:

DEFINITION 19. A *component* of a graph (or of a network) is a set of mutually "reachable" points (or positions).

---

[23] Charles Kadushin, "The Friends and Supporters of Psychotherapy: On Social Circles in Urban Life," *American Sociological Review*, 31, 1966, pp. 786–802.

DEFINITION 20. A component is *closed* if all paths of length two or more (or all network connections) lie on cycles and all lines (or relations) lie on the same number of cycles. A network is closed if all its components are closed.

THEOREM 10. An intra-category exchange network tends to change until it is closed. (From Theorem 5; Corollary 1.3 and 1.1)

As a simple illustration, let [A] be a set of two or more tennis players. If the relation A_1—A_2 forms with no additional relations connected to it, we have a network with one component which is closed and the network is balanced. However, if A_3 arrives in A_2's surroundings and the A_2—A_3 tennis relation forms, it will form largely on A_2's terms, and we have A_1—A_2—A_3, a unilateral monopoly. It has one open component and therefore any A_i will have rather easy access to this tennis-playing-circle-in-the-making through A_1 or A_3 who are less centrally located. However, if A_1—A_2—A_3—A_i forms, the network remains unbalanced at A_1—A_2 and A_3—A_i while A_2—A_3 becomes balanced. Furthermore, the cohesion of A_2—A_3 is reduced in the process of balancing to a level lower than A_1—A_2 and A_3—A_i. As the network grows in a linear fashion, the network remains unbalanced, interior links are weakened, and "exploitation" is focused on actors at the ends of the chain. Being unbalanced it remains unstable. Thus, given A_1—A_2—A_3—A_i, then either

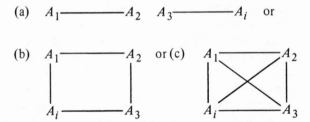

(a) A_1————A_2 A_3————A_i or

(b) A_1————A_2 or (c) A_1————A_2
          | | | |
         A_i————A_3 A_i————A_3

will form, all of which are closed networks. The networks (b) and (c) illustrate different degrees of connectedness.

In summary, what Simmel and Kadushin refer to as social circles can be taken as relatively closed components of intra-category networks. As social units they have "boundaries" to the extent that they are closed, and they tend to close as a balancing process. These boundaries can also be described (or felt) in terms of the ease or difficulty encountered when new members enter the network. As the closure and connectedness increases the *costs* of entry (for the entering party) increase. The new kid in a "closed" neighborhood must work hard at gaining friends. While there is more involved in the "rites of passage" into fraternal orders, brotherhoods, and so on, these network phenomena are clearly important conditions underlying such rites.

7. Stratified Networks

The notation established in Figure 1 and subsequent discussion of cross-category and intra-category exchange has provided an implicit definition of a category or set of actors [A]. Such a category is a set of actors classified together on the basis of some resource(s) and value(s) held in common. Thus, given the unilateral monopoly $Ax_i;B_jy_k$, $j = 1$ to N, [B] is a set of N actors each of whom values x_i in some degree and each of whom has resource y_k in some magnitude. Unilateral monopoly is the special case of cross-category exchange in which one category [A] has only one member. In the case of intra-category exchange ($A_hx_i;A_jx_i$, $h \neq j = 1$ to N) the category again is defined in terms of shared values and common resources. Each member of [A] has x_i as a resource and values x_i on the part of others. For Kadushin, x_i is the "common interest" which helps to define a social circle.

Now, one of the features of social circles Kadushin points out is their overlapping membership. Thus, a theater-going circle may also have a common interest in psychoanalysis and a preference for Scotch over beer. We then might speak of three social circles with nearly coincident boundaries, or one circle with a set of common interests. Let us treat x_i as a set of n values and resources shared by [A], in which case the $A_h;A_j$ exchange relation is a *primary* relation with primacy of degree n, as defined in Part I. (In operant terms, each party in the relation is now a generalized reinforcer for the other party.) This extension of intra-category exchange to include multiple resource dimensions does not change anything set forth in the above discussion of circles. It does raise the levels of dependence involved, and thereby it intensifies the closure or boundary-forming phenomenon. In addition, it points up an important empirical observation: virtually every example of intra-category exchange, or virtually every social circle, has the attributes normally associated with primary social interaction (as distinct from secondary); and primary relations occur largely within strata in a stratified system. Thus, intra-category exchange and the formation of bounded social circles may be intimately involved in the emergence of stratified social systems.

DEFINITION 21. An intra-category exchange network is *stratified* if it contains two or more components and the components are ordered on resource magnitude. A *social class* is a component or an unordered set of components in a stratified network.

THEOREM 11. Given an unstratified network in [A], with value equal and resource magnitude unequal across members of [A], then the network will tend to stratify, classes will tend to close, and value will become correlated with resource magnitude across continuing transactions in the network. (From Theorem 5, Propositions 1 and 4)

This assertion concerning the emergence of stratification is very gross and general, but it can be broken down into more refined statements, including stages in the process.

The process of stratification described here begins with some social category [A] defined in terms of a resource dimension x_i, where x_i is unequally represented in the repertoire of members of [A] yet valued by each member. Let each member value playing tennis, for example, while they differ in tennis ability (the ability to provide other players with rewarding tennis transactions). Any relation $A_h;A_j$ within this set of actors can be examined in terms of two pairs of probabilities which change over time: the probability of an *initiation* by A_h, and of initiation by A_j; and the probability of a *transaction*, given initiation by A_h or by A_j. Take, as a hypothetical start-up condition, a situation in which each player in the set extends and accepts tennis invitations to and from others indiscriminately, and examine departures from this state as exchange proceeds. If A_h has more ability than A_j, and if there are others with ability comparable to that of A_h, then the $A_h;A_j$ relation will have a predictable future in terms of the above probabilities. First, A_j will become the more likely initiator, but transactions will be more likely if A_h initiates (Stage 1). And second, if both have alternative relations at their own ability level, then the relation will approach or reach extinction (Stage 2).

Add to these simple operant principles the processes of structural change discussed in the closure of social circles, and we arrive at two stages in the process of stratification. In Stage 1 intra-class exchange predominates, and inter-class exchange has two features (in addition to being rare): initiations flow upward predominantly; and transactions are usually initiated from above. That is, the above pairs of probabilities are unequal in inter-class exchange and equal in intra-class exchange, which is another way of saying that some status aspiration (and by implication some status mobility) characterize Stage 1. In Stage 2 the paired probabilities are equal in all relations and equal to zero in inter-class exchange (e.g., families in different classes never exchange children in marriage, or dinner invitations, or what have you). In this formulation it is clear that resource distribution and acquisition is the independent variable governing stratification and passage from Stage 1 to Stage 2 or vice versa. Returning to an earlier hypothesis: in an "expanding" social system, stratification will form to Stage 1 and remain there until expansion stops, at which point it will move to Stage 2. Meanwhile, note Theorem 11 entails value change resulting in class-specific values.

A lot of space could be devoted to further elaboration on points relating to stratification, status aspiration and value changes, status consistency in terms of partially overlapping social circles, etc. We will point out only that x_i in the above analysis applies to any resource dimension (income, education, tennis skill, etc.) or cluster of dimensions. There has been much discussion in sociology on whether or not social classes are bounded social units or simply classificatory schemes imposed by the investigator as a classifier. The approach outlined here clearly provides a theoretical framework for treating this question in specific instances. Meanwhile, the main thrust of this approach treats the emergence and maintenance of stratification as a balancing process. Stage 2 in particular is a fully balanced and very stable state.

Finally, having conceived stratification in terms of intra-category exchange, with resource distribution as the independent variable, two points must be made: classes are tied together into one more complex exchange system through cross-category exchange (e.g., capital and labor); and the resource distribution involved as the independent variable in stratification is normally the result of such cross-category exchange.

8. Groups as Collective Actors: Norm Formation

We conclude this chapter with a very small beginning on two major topics: (a) groups as collective actors in a larger environment; and (b) the internal structure of groups as exchange systems. An important foothold is obtainable on both topics through an exchange approach to norm formation.

The network changes portrayed in Figure 2(d) depend upon the balancing process which is, by far, the most important — Operation 4 in the form of coalition formation, which turns out to be a special case of group formation and norm formation. When one party has a power advantage based upon alternative relations, this advantage can be reduced if these relations are condensed through coalition. Thus, the network

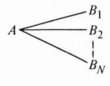

becomes the relation A ——————— (B) when the set $[B]$ coalesces. A's dependence (and B's power) is increased in the process.

Given that coalition formation is a balancing process, imbalance is a stimulus helping to generate the change; but it is not the only required condition. Clearly, communicative contact among members of $[B]$, as well as "mutual trust," etc., are facilitating factors; but in exchange terms we can specify such conditions more clearly. The ideal conditions for coalition formation are shown in Figure 3.

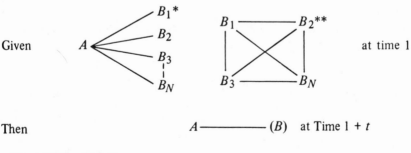

*Resources: $Ax_1; B_jy_1$

**Resources: $B_hz_1; B_jz_1$

■ **FIGURE 3.** Ideal Conditions for Coalition Formation

They consist of a two-component network with $N + 1$ actors, one component being an $N + 1$ actor *unilateral monopoly*, the other being an N actor *circle* with maximum connectedness. To say that (B) is a "collective actor" in the $A—(B)$ relation is to say that $B_1, B_2 \ldots B_N$ act on a common policy in their exchange with A. Thus, coalition formation is a special case of *norm* formation. If each B, in his relations with A, is effectively controlled by the set of other B's, then the set $[B]$ can be treated as a single unit. Such coalescence involves: (1) norm formation and sanctioning within the set $[B]$; (2) an increase in the power of $[B]$ over A; and (3) an increase in the *cohesion* of the $A—B_j$ relation. (As a result, it can be argued that the rise of organized labor has increased the viability of modern capitalism as an exchange system. Revolutionary Marxists should recognize organized labor as their main obstacle.)

Once coalition formation is seen for what it is — norm formation — the importance of intra-category exchange among $[B]$ becomes obvious, for it provides the needed basis for sanctioning. The period of Time t, in Figure 3, required for coalition to take place, will vary inversely with two main variables: (1) the value of z among $[B]$; and (2) the degree of connectedness among $[B]$.[24]

But if the coalition of B's in relation to A involves norm formation among B's, this in turn involves coalition processes within the set of B's. Thus, if B_j should violate the norm (work for less than x dollars; produce more than y units; be too friendly toward the teacher, or too sexually "loose" with boys) then

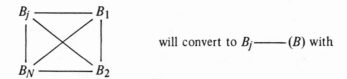

will convert to B_j———(B) with

reduced z for B_j (collective sanctioning).[25] As a result, the group (B) with N members can be analyzed in exchange theory as the set of N exchange relations $B_1—(B)$, $B_2—(B) \ldots B_N—(B)$, each of which has all the attributes examined above (reciprocity, balance, power, cohesion, and balancing processes). We leave the exchange interpretation of such intra-group structure, including role, status levels, and authority,[26] for later work.

---

[24] Throughout this discussion of coalition and norm formation we view intra-category exchange as providing the base for sanctions in the form of removed or reduced positive reinforcements. In the absence of intra-category exchange, negative reinforcers may be applied as negative sanctions. Thus, some "force" might emerge, as in some efforts to organize a segment of labor.

[25] John F. Scott has argued convincingly for a definition of norm in terms of sanction. See *A Theory of Moral Learning*, unpublished dissertation, University of California.

[26] The coalition of *all* $[A]$ against any one A_j, taken literally, has A_j in coalition with others against himself. The notions of internalized norms and legitimate sanctions are involved here. See Scott (*ibid.*) for an operant analysis of "internalization."

□ **D. SUMMARY**

A substantive summary seems futile. A statement of "where we might go from here" in theoretical directions would be more of the same rather than a summary. I will simply comment on the method of these two chapters.

Operant psychology appeared to be a fruitful point of departure for two reasons. First, it is nothing more than the study of *contingencies* relating an organism to its environment, and this is a sufficiently broad topic. Second, operant psychology looked to be useful precisely because it contains so little "psychology" in the form of concepts specifically anchored to a complex psychological theory. For psychologists this might be a drawback. For sociologists it is a lucky by-product of the atheoretical philosophy of many operant psychologists.

What we have done here might be called "reductionism" but "constructionism" is a better description of the strategy employed. We have taken psychological material as a *given* base to build upon. But the direction taken in the building process was partly predetermined, and it was not contained within that base. Conceptual distinctions were introduced selectively, guiding the analysis toward sociology. From the same base we could have moved into economics or into animal ecology.

One choice made repeatedly concerned the level of formality in theory construction. The theory is "formalized" only in a minimal sense: definitions and assertions are identified so that they can be located readily and re-examined; a notation scheme is used to identify the small set of basic concepts which are used repeatedly as the theory builds. Meanwhile, as indicated in the introduction to Part I, the logical structure was left rather loose, for two reasons. First was the interest in exploring the breadth of substantive questions approachable within a single framework. This seemed to require fairly coarse brush work. Second, this is a preliminary effort and tight theoretical structure seems premature. More rigorous logical structure will require much more precise conceptual work. However, every concept defined represents a decision made affecting the direction of subsequent development. These chapters have been addressed largely to exploring directions rather than making decisions. As a result, I have attempted to provide only a coarse outline of the logical structure of this theory. What it needs now is increased parsimony in its general structure, and increased detail in its subparts, the latter in preparation for empirical work. Both appear to be achievable.

Finally, this exchange approach is distinctly weak in treating all of those many facets of sociology which, implicitly or explicitly, tie to cognitive psychology. At this time I am not sure how serious a flaw this is.

Chapter 5

Reference Conflict

and Behavior[*]

■ RICHARD OFSHE

The importance of the social frame of reference which determines attitude formation and an individual's evaluation of his position in a social structure has long been recognized. Although one could doubtless unearth allusions to referential processes far earlier than Hyman's 1942 monograph, the fact that the concept of a *reference group* was first introduced in this work marks it as the starting point for any consideration of what is currently thought of as reference group theory. As coined by Hyman (1942), the concept denoted the group an individual used as a point of comparison for self-appraisal. The concept has, however, at least one additional generally recognized meaning. The second usage can be traced to Newcomb's (1943) study of attitude change. Newcomb considered a group to be a reference group for an individual if his attitudes were influenced by a set of norms that he assumed were shared with the group.

These two usages were recognized by both Kelley (1952) and Merton (1957). Kelley argued that there are two functions performed by reference groups, a comparative and a normative function. The normative function concerned the "setting and enforcing of standards for the person" while the comparative function was that of "serving as or being a standard or comparison point against which the person can evaluate himself and others." These distinctions are clearly in keeping with the Newcomb and Hyman usages of the concept. Kelley (1952) made a fundamental point concerning the need for identifying the different functions of reference groups. He proposed that the distinction between the two functions of reference groups is important because:

> ... it makes explicit the two main aspects of reference-group theory: the motivational and the perceptual. A more complete theory of reference groups must consist of at least two parts, one having to do with groups as sources and enforcers of standards and the other having to do with groups as the standard themselves. These two parts of reference-group theory should prove to be merely special cases of more general theories about the sources and nature of standards which, in turn, should ultimately derive from fundamental theories of motivation and perception.

* The research reported in this paper was conducted under grants from the National Science Foundation (GS-1368) and the Committee on Research of the University of California at Berkeley.

Kelley's recognition of the need to consider reference phenomena in terms of the basic processes of which they are constituted has by and large been ignored. Unfortunately, there has been no development of a coherent body of theory and research dealing with reference phenomena through their analysis in terms of more general theories. In 1952 it was possible for Kelley to write, "Although this theory [reference group theory] is still in the initial stages of development, because of the problems it formulates it promises to be of central importance to social psychology." Ten years later, Cohen's (1962) comment on the state of reference-group theory and research was as follows:

> What is termed "reference group theory" in the sociological literature is not sufficiently spelled out to be amenable to formal treatment. It seems to us that previous work on reference groups has attempted to isolate a phenomenon and argue for its importance as an object of research.

Despite the fact that with few exceptions there has been little theoretically significant research focusing directly on reference groups, there does exist a substantial body of research that bears upon the general topic of reference phenomena. Although the subject of this paper is the creation and test of a theory of behavior under conditions of normative reference conflict, it is necessary to distinguish between generically different types of referential processes in order to understand the paper's conceptual foundations. In the following sections three types of reference phenomena will be considered. They define three analytically distinct uses of an individual or group as a point of reference. The analytic distinctions rest upon differences in the motivational, functional and behavioral components which constitute the three processes. The distinctions that are introduced are made for the same reason that Kelley originally sought to identify the multiple functions of reference groups: major differences in the manner in which individuals employ social frames of reference necessitate separate theories of the phenomena.

□ **COMPARATIVE REFERENCE**

The comparative reference phenomenon centers around the type of behavior pattern considered by Hyman (1942) and Festinger (1954) in which an individual employs a person or a group as a point of reference for self-evaluation. Comparisons of this sort are not isolated events made for their own sake; they are attempts to evaluate the acceptability of one's position or the acceptability of some outcome. An individual who seeks to determine whether or not he is *successful* must compare his achievements against those of others. That his conclusion will be affected by the accomplishments of the referents he selects is borne out by the research of Hyman on the psychology of status and those of Stouffer et al. as reported in *The American Soldier* (1949).

There is considerable evidence demonstrating that a conclusion indicating that an individual is disadvantaged relative to his comparison figure leads to dissatisfaction and to attempts to bring about change. There is also evidence that conclusions indicating that an individual is relatively advantaged lead to cognitive reorganization and under some circumstances attempts to establish conditions of equity (cf. Adams 1965). The reactions to outcomes of instances of comparative reference have been studied under a variety of titles: relative deprivation, Stouffer et al. (1949), Davis (1959); rank balance, Benoit-Smullyan (1944), Homans (1953), Lenski (1956), Zelditch and Anderson (1966); and distributive justice and wage comparisons, Homans (1961), Patchen (1961), and Adams (1963, 1965).

The factors common to instances of comparative reference that will distinguish the comparative phenomenon from those to be discussed are as follows: (1) an individual's motivation to engage in comparisons follows from a desire to evaluate his position, achievements or rewards; (2) an individual need not have an interactive relationship with the referent. That is, persons may select as points of comparison individuals or groups with which they have only a symbolic contact or they may use social categories as in a comparison in which an individual evaluates his income against that of the *average* college graduate; and (3) individuals are self-sanctioning with regard to conclusions based upon comparisons. They are either satisfied or dissatisfied with their standing and apply appropriate sanctions to themselves.

When reference points are used for making social comparisons, it is usually the case that the individual is the initiator of the comparison, the judge of the outcome and the initiator of any resulting action. The comparative phenomenon is entirely intrapersonal and cognitive except in the event that subsequent attempts are made to change the status quo.

□ **NORMATIVE REFERENCE**

The normative reference phenomenon centers on the effect of acceptance of an individual or a group as a source of evaluations. Two classic examples of normative reference are found in the research of Newcomb and Stouffer et al. Newcomb (1943, 1958) demonstrated the evolution of attitudes as a consequence of reference to the opinions of positively valued *others*. In their discussion of data reported in *The American Soldier* Merton and Rossi (1957) interpreted the fact that inexperienced soldiers who were replacements in combat units showed greater similarity to combat veterans in their attitudes toward combat than to inexperienced soldiers in units composed solely of their own kind.

> [Our] hypothesis drawn from reference group theory would lead us to anticipate that the replacements, seeking affiliation with the authoritative and more prestigeful stratum of veterans will move from the civilian-like values towards the more tough-minded values of the veterans ... For replacements, the assumed function of assimilating the values of the veterans is to find more ready acceptance by the higher-status group, in a setting where the subordinate group of replacements does not have independent claims to legitimate prestige.

Additional work on normative reference may be found in the literature on social influence and group cohesiveness. In particular, the early research of Festinger and his associates, as reported in *Social Pressures in Informal Groups* (1950) and *Theory and Experiment in Social Communication* (1950), is significant since it examines the effects of variations in the importance of referents in the operation of influence. In addition the research on *cross-pressure* reported by Berelson et al. (1954) is quite important because it demonstrates the effects of conflict between the expectations of opposing normative reference groups on an individual's behavior.

Kelley (1952) points out the major differentiating factors between the comparative and normative reference process. "Implicit here [in normative reference] is the idea that the members of the reference group observe the person and evaluate him." In contrast to comparative reference, situations of normative reference require that sanctions be distributed by the referent. With regard to normative phenomena the referent is not simply an object of orientation but, rather, takes an active role in enforcing the individual's conformity to norms through the application of sanctions. The second major differentiating factor is such that when an *other* is used as a normative referent, the individual values his association or potential association with the referent and is concerned about both the referent's evaluations of and reactions to his behavior.[1] For example, the Merton and Rossi analysis of the assimilation of attitudes by replacements rests on the assumption that the replacements sought acceptance by the combat veterans. The third distinguishing feature of normative reference phenomena is that individuals rely upon referents to specify appropriate social definitions of situations and appropriate patterns of behavior rather than to assist in attempts to arrive at self-evaluations.

□ **INFORMATIONAL REFERENCE**

The third manner in which *others* may be used as referents is solely as an information source. An example of an informational use of a social reference is one in which an individual who is attempting to solve a problem receives advice from one or more *others* and therefore must decide the best manner in which to utilize the advice provided by the referents. He must decide whether to act on the basis of the *others*' advice or disregard it and rely on his own ability to solve the problem. His use of referents in this case is strictly instrumental since the individual is concerned with the extent to which the referents can contribute to attainment of the goal of achieving a correct solution to the problem. The individual is forced to evaluate the information provided by the referents if he is to make the correct decision. Evaluation of information in this type of situation is dependent upon the individual's evaluation of its source. That is, information relevant to a mathematical problem offered by a Ph.D. mathematician is likely to be more highly valued than information from a Ph.D. in English literature or a freshman majoring in mathematics.

This type of referential situation describes the classic social influence experi-

---

[1] The opposite would be the case for instances of negative or antireference. In this situation the individual would be concerned about the type of sanctions distributed by the referent since the receipt of positive sanctions from negative referents would be as disquieting as negative sanctions from positive referents.

ments of Asch (1951) and Sherif (1935). Consider, for example, Sherif's research on influence in the autokinetic situation. In this experiment subjects were simply asked to estimate how far a pin-point of light moved on each of a series of trials. Although the light was stationary, subjects perceived it to move under the conditions of room illumination employed by Sherif. The results of the experiment were that when two or more naive subjects participate together and make public estimates of the amount of movement, they tend to arrive, over time, at the same estimates. This result obtains in a situation in which a group decision is not a requirement of the experiment, there is no direct communication between subjects, no direct influence attempts are made, and subjects do not appear to differ in obvious characteristics (age, sex, social status, etc.) A reasonable explanation of the result is that when an individual is faced with a problem for which the correct answer is not obvious and finds that his estimate differs from those he hears, he is likely to assume that the *others* are as competent as he and hence modify his judgments such that the discrepancy is reduced. Since each subject in the experiment is faced with the same problem, the type of mutual convergence typically observed would be precisely the expected result.

Considerable work is available on this type of reference phenomenon. Papers by Berger, Cohen and Zelditch (1966) and Berger, Cohen, Conner and Zelditch (1966) present a theory of the manner in which actors utilize knowledge of the status characteristics and general and specific abilities of *others* in evaluating their potential contributions to group problem solving. The research of Torrence (1954), Strodtbeck, James and Hawkins (1957), Harvey (1953) and Sherif, White and Harvey (1955), and Moore (1968, 1969) provide empirical data relevant to the problem.

Informational reference may be distinguished from the other two types of referential behavior in that there is no valued association between the actor and the referent, no exchange of sanctions occurs and there is no general self-evaluation resulting from a comparison. In an informational situation an individual may be characterized as being task-oriented and concerned solely with the referents' potential contribution to his success at problem solving.

The three types of reference situations that have been discussed differ in numerous basic attributes. Although they are similar in that they all deal with the use of social frames of reference, differences in the functions of the frames of reference and in the major variables that determine behavior would seem to mediate against attempting to formulate a single theory of referential processes. An alternative strategy of pursuing theory construction by creating models of the various types of referential processes from propositions of more general theories would seem to have a greater likelihood of being rewarding.

□ NORMATIVE REFERENCE CONFLICT

The second strategy will be utilized in this paper in order to consider one facet of the normative reference phenomenon, that of behavior under conditions of normative reference conflict. The remainder of the paper will set to the task of developing a theory of behavior under conditions of normative reference conflict and reporting a series of basic experimental tests of the formulation. In the most general terms a situation of normative reference conflict is a social situation in which an individual is faced with the requirement of choosing one and only one action from a set of alternatives that represent the mutually exclusive performance expectations of at least two reference figures. It should be immediately obvious that when described in more concrete terms the occurrence of this type of choice dilemma is by no means a rare event. Consider as an illustration a case in which on a certain issue an adolescent discovers that his parents and peers hold mutually exclusive expectations for his performance and each group desires that he conform to their expectations. The adolescent's preference between alternatives modifies the nature of the choice dilemma to only a minimum degree. Even if the adolescent has a strong preference between alternatives that is independent of the referents' expectations, he is still confronted with the fact that his decision will be acceptable to one group and unacceptable to the other. In the case in which he has no independent preference between alternatives the social aspects of the choice dilemma are clearest. Under these circumstances his decision is a choice between competing reference groups, and the content of the decision (the particular response demanded by each group) is a relatively unimportant consideration. That is, his problem is really one of choosing which group's demands to accept and which group's demands to reject.

The theory proposed below represents an attempt to identify and interrelate the major variables that affect choice behavior in reference conflict situations. The task of the theory is to explain the sequential choice behavior of individuals faced with the necessity of making a series of choices between the mutually exclusive performance expectations of opposing reference figures.

Concepts and Definitions

Although there has been considerable utilization of the concepts of reference group and reference figure, there exist no generally accepted definitions for the terms that provide sufficient criteria for deciding whether some group or individual should or should not be considered to serve as a point of reference for a given individual.[2] The following definition of a reference figure is drawn in terms of the minimum properties of the relationship between an individual,

[2] In his paper "The Process of Choosing a Reference Group," Cohen (1962) treats the question of the vagueness of the concept of reference groups in some detail. He points out the need for explication of the concept and the problems which have arisen because of the failure to properly explicate the term. Examples of the vague use of the concept and allusions to "reference group or membership group theory" are frequent in the literature. For example, Siegel and Siegel (1957) in a paper entitled "Reference Groups, Membership Groups and Attitude Change" refer to the concept of reference group and "reference group theory" as if this theory were widely known and could easily be found in the literature. It is interesting to note that their article contains no reference to any paper which contains a theory of reference groups.

P, and some group or individual, *O*, that are necessary for *O* to be considered a reference point for *P* on a particular issue. The definition is minimal in the sense that it is intended to specify the relationship between an individual and a normative reference figure without any consideration of the properties that distinguish between relationships with normative, comparative and informational points of reference.

DEFINITION 1 — REFERENCE FIGURE. *O* is a reference figure for *P* if and only if *P* perceives a reference relation to exist between *P* and *O*.

DEFINITION 2 — REFERENCE RELATION. A reference relation is said to exist between *P* and *O* if and only if:

A. *P* positively values his association with *O*.
B. *P* believes that *O* has the right and/or ability to evaluate his performance of reference items.
C. *P* expects *O* to distribute sanctions on the basis of his evaluation of *P*'s performance of reference items.
D. *O*'s positive and negative sanctions are meaningful to *P*.

DEFINITION 3 — REFERENCE ITEM. A reference item is any unit of behavior for which a reference figure holds a performance expectation that is known to *P*.

There are several points concerning the above set of concepts which should be noted. As the definitions are presently constructed no distinction exists between a reference figure who is a single individual and one that represents a group since there is no reason to assume any difference in the characteristics of a reference relation between *P* and a single individual or a group of individuals. This is not to say, however, that all reference structures are to be treated as equal: there are several dimensions that serve to differentiate such structures. The differentiations will be made in terms of variations in the degree to which the association with the reference figure is valued and *P*'s perception of the importance to the reference figure of *P*'s conformity to expectations for performance of reference items.

A reference relation is independent of the property of group membership. That is, *P*'s *association* with *O* need not take the form of common membership in some group nor must *O* be a group in which *P* is a member. The term *association* is used broadly to denote the existence of a bond between *P* and *O* from *P*'s point of view. For example, *P* would be expected to perceive himself in *association* with the members of a group that he hopes to join in the future or the occupants of a status to which he aspires. *Association* alone, however, is not a sufficient criterion on which to judge whether or not some *O* is a reference figure for *P*. If, for example, *P* were formally the member of some group but did not value the sanctions distributed by its members, the *association* condition would be satisfied, but the group would not qualify as a reference figure for P.

The definition of a reference figure is restrictive since it is assumed that P positively values his association with O. The restriction of the definition of the concept to positively-valued normative reference figures is made on the grounds of expediency. Although the implications of negative reference relations could be outlined in the theory to be presented, it would unnecessarily complicate the present paper to attempt to do so. The current task is simply to specify the minimum properties of the relations between P and O needed for O to be considered a normative reference figure for P.

For a reference item (such as a political choice) P can have a predisposition toward a behavior (prefer one of at least two possible positions) or be indifferent to the possible alternatives. This condition represents a crucial variable in the analysis of P's choice dilemma since referents' expectations can reinforce or oppose an existing predisposition. In order to prevent confusion in future discussions it should be noted that unless otherwise specified only the simplest case of reference conflict shall be considered. That is, *it will be assumed that* P *has no preference among the behaviors that represent the expectations of the conflicting reference figures.*

Given that $O_{1\ldots n}$ are reference figures for P, an instance of reference conflict is said to exist given that:

DEFINITION 4 — REFERENCE CONFLICT. A reference conflict is said to exist for P if and only if at least two reference figures hold mutually exclusive expectations for P's performance of a reference item, and it is necessary that P choose to meet only one of these expectations.

A reference conflict situation is defined as follows:

DEFINITION 5 — REFERENCE CONFLICT SITUATION. If P is made to repeatedly choose between the mutually exclusive expectations of the same set of reference figures, a situation of reference conflict is said to exist.

For a conflict situation to exist it is sufficient that P choose between the mutually exclusive expectations of the same set of reference figures. The subject of their expectations (reference items) can vary provided that the condition of mutual exclusion is maintained. If reference figures O_1 and O_2 differ with regard to their expectations for P's performance concerning political issues, style of dress, choice of career, etc., there would exist only one reference conflict situation. The existence of the conflict situation and its continuity through time depend upon the maintenance of a condition of competition for P's conformity by the same opposing reference figures and not upon the concrete issues on which they disagree.

The social structure described in Definitions 1 through 5 specifies the structural aspects of a reference conflict situation. A concrete example of this type of social structure is apparent in the case in which P has two groups of friends who differ in political opinion and *put pressure* on him to vote for different candidates. He has no previous interest in the political campaign and/or cannot decide between the candidates on the basis of their qualifications, platforms or the parties they represent. As a consequence of a series of political discussions or through a series of self-induced attempts to decide on a candidate, P is repeatedly made to state his preference for one or the other candidate. Since he cannot discern a meaningful difference between candidates, substantive considerations are of no help to him in making his decision on any of the occasions on which one is necessary. The essence of the conflict is that P is torn between meeting the expectations of the two reference figures each time he states a preference.

There are two general phenomena that seem to be affecting behavior in the type of conflict situation described above: exchange and cognitive balance. The exchange aspects of the situation concern P's performance of reference items and the allocation of positive or negative sanctions by the reference figures. The balance aspect concerns the psychological effect on P of having a reference relation with O, knowing O's expectation for his performance and acting so as to conform or to not conform to this expectation. The theory to be developed here rests on the assumption that in any concrete instance of reference conflict an individual's behavior will be affected by both the social exchange and cognitive balance components of the situation. Therefore, the model of behavior under these conditions will incorporate propositions of both general theories. As a first step toward the construction of such a model it is desirable to specify the separate effects of the exchange and balance phenomena by analyzing the conflict situation through the application of each of the theories.

An Exchange Theoretic Analysis of Normative Reference Conflict

A normative reference situation is a social situation in which at least two reference figures distribute positive or negative sanctions on the basis of their evaluations of P's performance of a series of reference items. The sanctions available to P for the performance of a reference item constitute the social rewards in the situation and therefore determine an individual's profit or loss. In any exchange-theoretic analysis of behavior the crucial concept is that of profit. Homans (1961) defines profit as follows:

> Profit is the difference between the value of the reward a man gets by emitting a particular unit-activity [act] and the value of the reward obtainable by another unit foregone in emitting the first.

In the context of a conflict situation the elements of Homans' definition correspond to the available sanctions. If the act X_1 is a reference item, the payoff for its performance, $R(X_1)$, is defined as follows:

DEFINITION 6 — PAYOFF. The payoff for performance of a reference item, $R(X_1)$, is equal to the sum of the absolute values of the sanctions available for its performance

If P performs X_1, his payoff is equal to the sum of the values of the positive sanctions available for performance of X_1 and the value of avoidance of the punishments which would have been forthcoming had he failed to perform X_1. Defining payoff in terms of the absolute values of resulting positive and negative outcomes eliminates the conceptual and operational gymnastics necessary to consider the total payoff as the combination of a positive component plus the avoidance of a negative outcome.

The notion that there are two components to the payoff P receives for performance of a reference item is consistent with the basic conceptions of reference relations and reference items. If a reference relation exists between P and O, it is the case that:

> P expects O to distribute sanctions on the basis of his evaluation of P's performance of reference items.

Since O holds a definite expectation for P's performance, P expects some sort of positive reinforcement for conformity and punishment for failure to conform. This factor differentiates the exchange relationship between P and a referent from an exchange relationship between P and another non-referent individual. In the basic exchange relationship considered by Homans, acts are exchanged for positive sanctions. Failure to act simply means that no transaction takes place. The nature of a reference relation, however, is such that either the failure to act or the performance of a different act constitutes a failure to meet the referent's expectation and hence occasions the distribution of punishments. The avoidance of these negative sanctions should therefore be considered in any formulation which attempts to analyze the exchange elements in a normative reference situation. In terms of the conflict situation this is especially crucial since in the case in which two referents offer identical positive rewards for performance of reference items but threaten unequal punishments for non-performance, it is obvious that the payoffs for performance of alternative reference items must be treated as differing in value.

It is now possible to consider the costs of performance of the reference item X_1. The payoff for performance of an alternative act, X_2, can be considered to be the cost of performing X_1 provided that the following definition is satisfied:

> DEFINITION 7 — COST OF AN ACT. The payoff $R(X_2)$ for the act X_2 is the cost of performing act X_1 if and only if the performance of X_1 precludes the performance of X_2.

The cost to P of the performance of X_1 is therefore equal to the sum of the absolute value of the punishments received for failure to perform X_2 and the value of the positive reinforcements lost through failure to perform X_2.

It is clear that as the conflict situation is defined (Definition 4), there is a cost for the performance of a reference item. It is therefore possible to calculate P's profit for the performance of a given reference item. Profit for the performance of X_1 is defined as follows:

DEFINITION 8 — PROFIT

Profit = |Reward| − |Cost|

= |Payoff for X_1| − |Payoff for X_2|

= $R(X_1) - R(X_2)$.

Using Definitions 6, 7, and 8, it is possible to make three statements concerning the relations between the payoffs for various actions and P's profit. If P performs X_1 it is obviously true that:

1. Profit > 0 when $R(X_1) > R(X_2)$.
2. Profit < 0 when $R(X_1) < R(X_2)$.
3. Profit = 0 when $R(X_1) = R(X_2)$.

These three mutually exclusive and exhaustive possibilities are predicted to produce different behavioral consequences in P. As Homans (1961) asserts:

> The less a man's profit on a particular unit-activity [act], the more likely he is to change his next unit to the alternative.

Homans assumes an inverse relationship exists between profit and the probability of changing at the next occasion. Given this basic assumption the most reasonable expectation would be that when profit equals zero the probability of changing to the alternative act on the next occasion would equal one-half.

A somewhat more precise specification of the relationship between profit and choice is the first proposition of the conflict theory.

PROPOSITION I — PROFIT AND CHOICE. As the profit for conforming to the expectation of reference figure O_1 decreases, the probability of conforming to the expectation of reference figure O_2 on the next occasion increases. When profit equals zero, the probability of changing equals one-half.

Proposition I permits a prediction of P's behavior for any combination of payoffs for acts X_1 and X_2. Assume that initially P chooses X_1:

CASE 1. If $R(X_1) > R(X_2)$, then Profit > 0.
If Profit > 0, then the probability of changing on the next occasion will be < .5.

CASE 2. If $R(X_1) < R(X_2)$, then Profit < 0.
If Profit < 0, then the probability of changing on the next occasion will be > .5.

CASE 3. If $R(X_1) = R(X_2)$, then Profit = 0.
If Profit = 0, then the probability of changing on the next occasion will be = .5.

The analysis of behavior in situations of reference conflict will be focused primarily on Case 3 payoff conditions. It will serve as the context of the analysis because it affords the best structure in which to demonstrate the effects of states of cognitive balance and imbalance on P's behavior. In all other cases it is impossible to empirically separate the effects of exchange considerations from the effects of states of balance and imbalance.

The prediction for Case 3 is appropriate in situations in which two reference figures offer equal payoffs for conformity or non-conformity. The substantive prediction for P's behavior under these conditions would be a sequence of independent choices between the expectations of the competing reference figures with each decision being made with a probability of one-half of choosing either alternative. This type of choice behavior may be interpreted as indifference with regard to which reference figure is selected at any point in the process. The prediction for Case 3 constitutes the appropriate exchange theoretic prediction for behavior in a conflict situation in which the payoff for performance of act X_1 is equal to the payoff for performance of X_2 and no other variables are considered relevant.

The reward and cost variables in the conflict situation have been defined, and exchange theoretic predictions for behavior under various conditions have been advanced. Again, the situation of major concern is one in which competing reference figures offer equivalent payoffs for P's conformity to their expectations.

A Balance Theoretic Analysis of Normative Reference Conflict

Certain aspects of a normative reference conflict situation can be conceptualized as a problem in the relations between elements of sets of cognitions held by P and therefore fall within the scope of Heider's theory of cognitive balance.[3] Prior to proceeding with a balance theoretic analysis it is necessary to introduce a number of concepts and propositions.

Heider's theory of cognitive balance considers the relations between persons and objects and persons and persons and formulates the conditions of relations between entities (persons or objects) that generate change in cognitive structures. The theory defines the conditions that constitute states of balance and imbalance and specifies the effect of each state on cognitive structures. In balance theory entities may be related in two ways: by sentiment relations such as liking, disliking, admiring, loving or hating; or by unit relations such as causality, similarity, membership, ownership or proximity. In terms of a reference conflict situation the entities would consist of the actor P, the reference figures O_1 and O_2, and the reference items X_1 and X_2. The relations between elements are a sentiment relation between P and each referent and a unit relation between the referents and the reference items. P's selection of one of the

---

[3] The original balance papers are those by Heider (1944, 1946, 1958), and the formalization of the theory by Cartwright and Harary (1956). The form of concepts and propositions utilized in this paper is taken from the treatment of the theory by Berger et al. (1962).

reference items and rejection of the other can be treated as positive and negative unit formations.

The concepts of balance theory were first coordinated to the concepts of graph theory (Cartwright and Harary, 1956) such that an entity in balance theory was a point in a graph and a relation in balance theory was a line in graph theory. Given the translation into graph theory it was possible to define balance and imbalance in graph theoretic terms.

> DEFINITION 9 — BALANCE. A graph is balanced when all cycles are balanced. A cycle is balanced either when all relations between points are positive or there are an even number of negative relations.

A state of vacuous balance must also be defined.

> DEFINITION 10 — VACUOUS BALANCE. A graph is vacuously balanced when no path returns to its starting point.

Heider developed two propositions concerning reactions to imbalance; these are repeated as Propositions II and III of the conflict theory.

> PROPOSITION II — IMBALANCED STATES. If no balanced state exists, then forces toward this state will arise. Either the dynamic character of a relation will change or a unit relation will be changed through action or cognitive reorganization.

> PROPOSITION III — STRESS. If a change is not possible, the state of imbalance will produce psychological stress.

Given the above concepts and propositions it is possible to analyze the balance aspects of the conflict situation. Consider the graph presented in Figure 1. The graph represents relations among the cognitive elements that characterize a conflict situation prior to the performance of either act X_1 or X_2. The graph in Figure 1 has the property of vacuous balance, and therefore Propositions II and III do not apply.

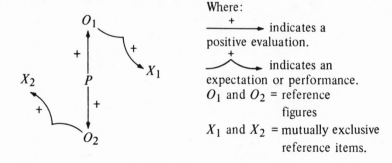

Where:
$\xrightarrow{+}$ indicates a positive evaluation.
$\overset{+}{\rightsquigarrow}$ indicates an expectation or performance.
O_1 and O_2 = reference figures
X_1 and X_2 = mutually exclusive reference items.

■ **FIGURE 1.** P's Cognitive Structure Prior to Conformity to Either Reference Figure's Expectation

Figure 2 represents relations among cognitive elements after P chooses between competing expectations for his performance. Since X_1 and X_2 are mutually exclusive alternatives, the selection of one necessitates the rejection of the other.

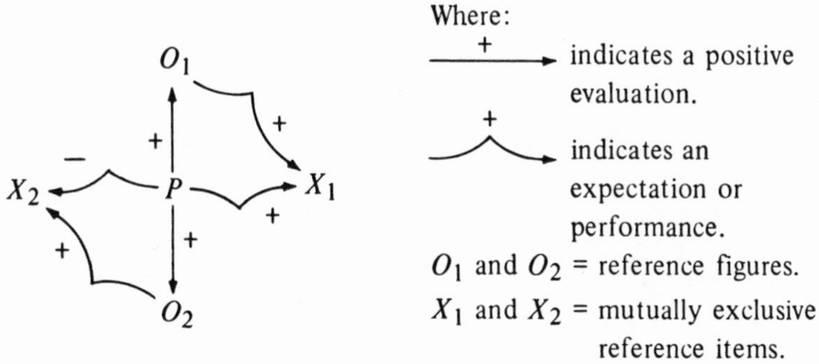

Where:

$\xrightarrow{\ +\ }$ indicates a positive evaluation.

$\overset{+}{\curvearrowright}$ indicates an expectation or performance.

O_1 and O_2 = reference figures.

X_1 and X_2 = mutually exclusive reference items.

■ **FIGURE 2.** P's Cognitive Structure after the Performance of Act X_1

The decision results in a graph that contains one balanced and one imbalanced cycle. If it is assumed that P cannot or does not change the unit relations or dynamic character of any relation, then, by Proposition III, psychological stress will result. The theory does not treat the conflict situation further and predicts only that as a consequence of failing to meet the expectation of a reference figure, P will experience psychological stress on each occasion on which he is forced to make a choice.

□ A THEORY OF BEHAVIOR UNDER CONDITIONS OF REFERENCE CONFLICT

Though definitions of the concepts of the theory as well as a specification of the structural aspects of the conflict situation have been presented, the task is to state those propositions from which predictions for P's sequential choice behavior can be derived. Toward this end three propositions have been introduced.

PROPOSITION I — PROFIT AND CHOICE. As the profit for conforming to the expectation of reference figure O_1 decreases, the probability of conforming to the expectation of reference figure O_2 on the next occasion increases. When profit equals zero, the probability of changing equals one-half.

PROPOSITION II — IMBALANCE STATES. If no balanced state exists, then forces toward this state will arise. Either the dynamic character of a relation will change or a unit relation will be changed through action or through cognitive reorganization.

PROPOSITION III — STRESS. If a change is not possible, the state of imbalance will produce psychological stress.

From Proposition III and the condition that P cannot change any relations it is predicted that he will experience stress as consequence of any performance which results in his failing to meet a reference figure's expectation.

In order to continue the analysis of P's profit or loss as a result of performance of a reference item it is necessary to introduce an additional concept at this point.

> DEFINITION 11 — SITUATIONAL COST. A situational cost is any structurally determined negative payoff resulting from a performance.

Given that it is reasonable to regard the discomfort that arises from failing to meet a reference figure's expectation as a negative payoff, it is possible to treat stress as a situational cost of P's decision. This assertion is introduced into the theory as Proposition IV.

> PROPOSITION IV — STRESS AS A SITUATIONAL COST. If stress results from failure to conform to a reference figure's expectation, P treats the stress as a situational cost of his action.

The analysis of P's profit for performance of a reference item under equal payoff conditions must be modified in order that situational costs may be considered. The new relations are:

$$\text{Profit} = \text{Reward} - (\text{Cost} + |\text{Situational Costs}|)$$
$$= R(X_1) - (R(X_2) + |\text{Value of Stress}|).$$

Under Case 3 conditions it is known that:

$$\text{Reward} = \text{Cost}$$

Therefore:

$$\text{Profit} = -|\text{Situational Costs}|$$
$$= -|\text{Value of Stress}|$$

The theory would therefore predict (by Propositions I, II, III and IV) that under conditions of a Case 3 conflict situation the probability of P's choosing to conform to the expectation of the reference figure not chosen on the previous occasion is greater than one-half on each occasion that he is forced to make a decision.[4]

According to this line of analysis, failure to conform to the expectation of any reference figure results in P's experiencing some degree of stress. The

---

[4] This prediction cannot be generated from either a strict exchange or balance analysis of the conflict process since each theory treats only a subset of the variables that determine behavior in the conflict situation.

factors which affect the magnitude of stress that P experiences due to a failure to conform to a reference figure's expectation and the effects of failure to conform over a series of decisions need to be considered.

Two additional propositions will be introduced. The first concerns the value of a cycle and the degree of stress generated in the event that it is imbalanced.

> PROPOSITION V — VALUE AND STRESS. The greater the value of the relations between points in a cycle, the greater the magnitude of stress experienced if the cycle is imbalanced.

The reference relation between P and O, O's expectation for performance of the reference item by P, and P's act of conformity or non-conformity to expectations are the bonds that relate points in a cycle. The value of a cycle is therefore a function of the importance of the reference relation to P, P's perception of the importance of his conformity to O, and the importance to P of performing the reference item.

In the case in which P perceives no differences in the desire for conformity to the expectations of two equally valued reference figures and is himself indifferent to the alternative reference items it follows that equal magnitudes of stress would result from imbalancing either reference cycle. It also follows that differences between cycles in the values of any of these relations should produce unequal magnitudes of stress when the cycles are imbalanced. If payoffs for conformity to either referent's expectation were equal, differences in the magnitudes of stress produced by failure to conform should produce predictable effects on an individual's sequential choice behavior.

The second new proposition concerns the effect on the magnitude of stress an individual experiences through a series of sequential rejections of the same reference figure. The proposition asserts that the stress an individual experiences increases as a function of the number of times he consecutively rejects the same reference figure. For the purposes of the conflict theory it is not necessary to attempt any specification of the cause of the change in the stress experienced. It might possibly be due to a change in the amount of stress generated through rejection of a reference figure for the Nth consecutive time or due to an accumulation of stress from the preceding acts of non-conformity.

> PROPOSITION VI — INCREASING STRESS. The magnitude of stress produced by an imbalance in a cycle monotonically increases with the length of the series of consecutive imbalancing decisions.

Each time P changes his choice of a reference figure he initiates a new series of imbalance producing actions related to the given cognitive cycle. The degree of stress generated by a cycle is therefore at its minimum at the start of each series and increases with the series length. Under Case 3 conditions the magnitude of stress generated by the first rejection of a reference figure in a potential series should be the same no matter which reference figure is rejected. Since there is no reason to assume that it is not the case, under conditions of conflict between the expectations of equally valued reference figures the rate of increase in the degree of stress resulting from sequential rejections of a reference figure should be the same for cycles relating P to each reference figure.

This yields a set of predictions that describe the sequential decision behavior of an individual involved in a conflict situation. To present the theory's predications straightforwardly, it is necessary to start with the description of the basic dilemma confronting an individual operating under conditions of reference conflict as a repetition of the problem of whether to choose to repeat the same conforming response made on the last occasion that a decision was required, or choose to alternate and conform to the expectation of the referent rejected on the last occasion. In order to provide all of the information about an individual's past performance that affects the theory's predictions under Case 3 conditions it suffices to know the length of the series of immediately preceding *consecutive* conforming responses to a referent's expectations that the individual made prior to the decision that is to be predicted. Since all of the action possibilities open to an individual can be described in terms of alternations between referents and lengths of series of consecutive conforming responses to the same referent and the theory yields predictions for choice behavior under any combination of these circumstances, it follows that the theory can completely describe an individual's sequential choice behavior.

Figure 3 presents a schematic representation of the actions open to P under Case 3 conflict conditions. When the usual Case 3 condition that the referents offer equal payoffs is combined with the assumption that P values his association with referents equally, all of the theoretically distinct action possibilities for P's behavior can be described by alternations between referents and series

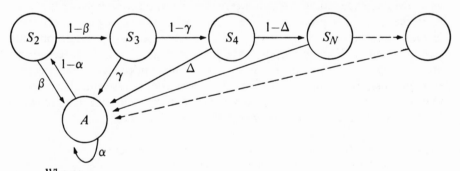

Where:

   →   = Paths between states.

   A = Alternation. Selection of the reference figure not chosen on the previous trial.

   S_2 = Choice of the same reference figure chosen on the previous trial.

   $S_3 \ldots S_N$ = Repetition of the choices made at $S_2 \ldots S_{N-1}$.

■ **FIGURE 3.** P's Action Possibilities and Transition Parameters under Conditions of Case 3 Conflict

of consecutive conforming responses. It is not necessary to distinguish between referents under these conditions, since the theory yields identical predictions for the probability of P's choosing to make an additional conforming response to either referent given the same number of immediately preceding conforming responses. If the referents offered unequal payoffs for conformity and non-conformity or were differentially valued by P, the theory would yield predictions of different probabilities of responses to each referent's expectations.

In Figure 3, the states identified as $S_2 \ldots S_n$ denote the length of a sequence of conforming responses to the same reference figure. For example, if P's situation can be characterized as an S_2 state, it means that he has made two consecutive conforming responses to the same reference figure, and his next decision is whether to choose either a third consecutive conforming response to that referent's expectation (an S_3 choice) or the expectation of the referent rejected on the previous occasion (an A choice). An A-state characterizes P's position after having ended a series of conforming responses to one referent through accordance with the other reference figure's expectation. On the next occasion P is confronted with the choice between making a second conforming response to the same reference figure's expectation (and moving to S_2) or alternating conforming acts by choosing to meet the expectation of the referent rejected on the immediately preceding occasion (and remaining in A).

The symbols associated with directed lines between states denote the probabilities of choosing the behaviors that determine P's transitions between the states represented in the figure. Although the theory does not generate predictions for the values of these parameters, it does yield predictions for their relative values and how they will be affected by changes in certain independent variables. For example, the assumption of Proposition VI is that the stress an individual experiences as a function of the rejection of a referent's expectation monotonically increases with the length of a series of consecutive rejections of that referent. Therefore, the theory yields the prediction that the probability of P's choosing to conform to the expectation of the reference figure chosen on the previous occasion decreases with the length of the series of consecutive conforming responses to that referent's expectations. It follows that the parameters that describe transitions between states should be ordered as follows:

$$(1 - \alpha) > (1 - \beta) > (1 - \gamma) > (1 - \Delta) \text{ and}$$

$$\alpha < \beta < \gamma < \Delta.$$

The theory is not limited to this basic description of the probabilities of alternative actions. Given changes in any one of a number of independent variables the model can be used to generate predictions for effects on the values of the parameters defined above. For example, under Case 3 conditions the relative values of transition parameters are determined primarily by the magnitude of tension resulting from the rejection of a referent. According to Proposition V, the magnitude of tension produced by an imbalanced cycle is a function of the value of the reference relation to P, P's perception of the strength of O's desire for his conformity, and the importance of performance of the reference item to P. Consider the following situations. In one instance P is involved in a Case 3 conflict situation in which the importance of the reference relations between P and each of the referents is minimal: a case in which referents O_1 and O_2 can be characterized as two *acquaintances* that P values equally. Assume that the symbols associated with transition parameters between states and the relations between parameters specified above denote the transition probabilities for P's behavior under these conditions. In a second Case 3 conflict situation in which the referents are equally valued by P but the value of the relationship with each is considerably greater than it was in the first instance (that is, the referents are both individuals with whom P has a *strong friendship*), by Proposition V the stress P experiences as a result of the rejection of a reference figure in the second instance will be greater than the stress generated by a similar rejection in the first instance. The gross result of the increase in stress between the two conditions should be a higher average probability of alternating conforming responses between reference figures in the second instance. Across the two conflict situations the parameters denoting the probabilities of moving to the A state should be related as follows:

Instance I: $\alpha < \beta < \gamma < \Delta$
Instance II: $\alpha' < \beta' < \gamma' < \Delta'$
Between Cases: $\alpha' > \alpha; \beta' > \beta; \gamma' > \gamma; \Delta' > \Delta.$

A second independent variable that can be manipulated under equal payoff conditions leading to predictions for behavior different from those in the basic conflict situation described above is the relative value of P's relationship with each of the referents. According to the conditions of these two instances of reference conflict, the only difference in P's expected behavior between the situations is in the probability of alternating conforming responses between referents. Since the referents offer equal payoffs and are equally valued by P, the theory yields the prediction that over the duration of the conflict the average probability of P's choosing either referent should be one-half. This prediction is independent of the absolute strength of the reference relation provided that relations with competing referents are equal. Consider a conflict situation in which P is faced with the choice between the expectations of two referents who offer equal payoffs for conformity and non-conformity but are differentially valued by P. If one referent is an acquaintance and the other is a friend, non-conformity to the acquaintance's expectation should produce less stress in P than failure to conform to the friend's expectation. According to the theory, a gross result of this difference should be different average probabilities of choosing each of the reference figures over the duration of the conflict. The theory predicts that under conditions of equal strength associations between P and competing referents the average probability of choosing either referent should be one-half. Under conditions of unequal strength associations between

P and competing referents the stress produced by non-conformity to the more valued referent's expectation should be greater than that generated by non-conformity to the less valued referent's expectation. This should result in a greater profit for conformity to the more valued referent's expectation, and therefore the average probability of choosing the more valued referent should be greater throughout the duration of the conflict.

□ **BASIC EXPERIMENTAL TESTS**

In reporting the results of experimental tests of the basic predictions of the theory, this section will present data relevant to the three predictions discussed at the close of the preceding section: 1) the probability of conforming to the expectation of the reference figure rejected on the previous occasion increases with the length of the sequence of consecutive conforming responses to the other referent's expectation; 2) the greater the value of the relationship between P and equally valued competing referents, the greater the probability of alternating conforming responses between referents; and 3) the greater the relative value of a relationship with a referent, the greater the average probability of choosing that referent. Since detailed reports of the research to be discussed here are available elsewhere (Ofshe, 1967, 1968), the description of the experimental program which generated the data will be brief, and only those aspects of the data directly relevant to the issues enumerated above will be considered.

The experiments were conducted in a standard experimental situation designed to permit the creation of sets of conditions necessary to evaluate various predictions of the theory. The experimental situation was designed such that it was possible to create a reference conflict situation in which P had to choose between the mutually exclusive expectations of two reference figures who desired his conformity in the performance of a series of reference items. The experimental situation was also intended to provide a conflict situation in which P had no independent preference between the alternatives that represented the referents' expectation.

In order to satisfy the condition of indifference between alternative reference items it was necessary to develop a binary choice problem such that in the absence of referents' expectations an individual's choice behavior could be described by a Bernoulli trials model with a parameter of one-half for the probability of selecting either alternative in each problem. A completely satisfactory problem was not developed. Although it was possible to develop a set of problems for which it was reasonable to characterize individuals as choosing each alternative with equal likelihood, the condition of independent decisions across the series of problems could not be attained.[5] This failure prevented attempts to evaluate possible formalizations of the theory but did not prevent tests of the predictions enumerated above.

[5] An analysis of the choice data on which the decision to use these stimuli was based together with a discussion of the dependence problem and its effects on experimental investigations of the theory are presented in Ofshe (1967).

The task that was developed called for subjects to be presented with a series of pairs of patterns and asked to indicate which one of the patterns in each pair they preferred. The final set of stimuli that were developed had the property that for each pair of patterns the probability of a subject's choosing either alternative was approximately one-half. In addition, it was found that if a pair of patterns were repeated at any point in the sequence, a subject was as likely to change his choice of preferred pattern as he was to select the initially chosen pattern a second time. Subjects were not, of course, aware that pairs of patterns were repeated. These results make it reasonable to conclude that subjects were indifferent between alternative patterns.

Given that the stimuli presented a binary choice problem on which subjects were indifferent to alternatives, the remaining problem was to design a social situation that created the conditions of a reference conflict situation and permitted the manipulation of certain independent variables. The standard experimental situation that was developed can be briefly described as follows:[6] Subjects were led to believe that they were participating in a study of the physiological reactions to social support or non-support of preferences for particular configurations of shapes and colors. They were informed that it had been discovered that on certain types of esthetic judgment individuals reacted with strong positive and negative feelings when they found that their preferences received social support or non-support if there was discensus with regard to which pattern was more pleasing. The topic of the study was purported to be an investigation of the nature of these physiological reactions and how they were affected by various social conditions.

When subjects were in the laboratory room in which the experiment was to be conducted, they were told that there were two other individuals in different rooms in the laboratory who were also taking part in the experiment. The reactions of these individuals to the subject's decisions were to be the focus of the investigation. The procedures of the hypothetical experiment called for the individuals in the other rooms to express their preferences between patterns presented as a series of pairs. In the event that these individuals disagreed, the pair of patterns was to be automatically shown to the subject, and he was asked to make a decision. The subject's decision was then automatically communicated to the other individuals and their physiological reactions were recorded. The experimental situation was one in which subjects believed that the other individuals were greatly concerned with their acts of conformity or non-conformity and reacted with strong emotional responses to each of the subject's choices. Over the course of the experiment the two reference figures appeared as if they disagreed on sixty occasions. During the experiment the two patterns were presented to the subject in fixed positions. The pattern that was supposedly preferred by *Individual One* was always shown in the upper

---

[6] Detailed descriptions of the procedures of the experiments are available in Ofshe (1967). The procedures used to manipulate the necessary cognitions were quite elaborate and placed considerable stress on the scientific interest in determining why these patterns should evoke such strong emotional reactions when individuals found that their preferences were supported or not supported.

half of a rear projection screen, and the pattern preferred by *Individual Two* appeared in the lower half of the screen.

The following procedures were used to create the various strengths of reference relations between P and each of the reference figures and to make certain that relations were equally valued in some cases and unequally valued in other cases. The creation of the necessary conditions required the use of a set of procedures that began more than one month prior to the time the subject entered the laboratory. Subjects were recruited from undergraduate sociology courses at another college. At the time subjects were recruited they were told that one of the other projects being conducted at the laboratory at which the recruiter worked was a study of friendship patterns on college campuses. All students in the class being addressed were asked to list the names of four other students of their own sex attending their institution whom they considered to be friends and who were believed to reciprocate the friendship relation. In order to make this request appear to be independent of volunteering for the experiments for which participants were being requested, students were asked to supply this information whether or not they agreed to take part in any experiments.

Approximately one month after being recruited, volunteers were contacted by telephone and appointments at the laboratory were arranged. At the time they were scheduled subjects were informed that it was important that they keep their appointments since two other individuals would be participating in the same study, and if anyone failed to show up, the session would have to be cancelled and rescheduled. This created the impression that there would be other participants in the research.

The procedures outlined above defined the basic research situation. The independent variable in the experiments was the strength of the reference relation between P and each of the referents. Depending on the condition desired, subjects were told that the *other* participants were either two friends, two students at their school whom they did not know, or one friend and one student. Since subjects had provided information about their friendships at the time they were recruited, it was not difficult to lead them to believe that their friends had been contacted, asked to participate, and asked not to inform the subject that they would be involved in the experiment.

Since subjects were not told which of their friends were participating, situations in which the referents were equally valued were straightforwardly created; subjects were simply told that both referents were friends and would be identified at the end of the experiment. In order to create conditions in which the strengths of the reference relations were equal and minimal, subjects were told that both other participants were students at their college whom they had never met. Informing subjects that one of the other participants was a friend and the other was a student at their college created conditions of unequal strength relations.

Experiment I

Experiment I sought to determine whether or not the model's prediction that the probability of an individual's conforming to the expectation of the reference figure rejected on the previous occasion increases with the length of a series of consecutive rejections of that referent. Under ideal circumstances it would be possible to determine whether or not this prediction holds by simply calculating the values of parameters α, β, γ, Δ, etc. Since it was not possible to create a set of individual problems on each of which subjects made completely independent decisions, simple calculations of these values were not satisfactory. It was, however, possible to obtain the necessary information and also control for effects introduced by properties of the stimuli by comparing the probabilities of ending a run of length N of consecutive selections of the patterns representing expectation of a given referent with the probability of ending a run of choices of patterns displayed in the same position under conditions in which the patterns did not represent the expectations of referents.[7] Since the stimulus set was identical under both conditions, the effects of associating the pattern with the expectations of reference figures can be ascertained by calculating the difference in choice probabilities between the two conditions.

One set of data was obtained under conditions in which subjects were simply requested to indicate a preference between patterns in each pair (the no-conflict condition), and a second set was obtained under conditions in which the patterns were associated with the expectations of reference figures. In both cases subjects made decisions on sixty pairs of patterns. Data were obtained from sixty subjects in the no-conflict condition and sixty-seven subjects in the conflict condition. Seven subjects in the conflict condition who became suspicious and reported in post-experiment interviews that they did not believe the manipulation were dropped from the analysis.

Rather than present a detailed analysis of the data generated in the two conditions (see Ofshe 1967 for a more complete analysis of the results), only the differences between conditions in the probabilities of ending runs of choices of the same pattern alternative will be considered. Table 1 presents these probabilities for runs of up to eight consecutive choices of patterns associated with the same referent's expectation. As indicated by the data reported in Table 1, the relationship between the length of a run and the increase in the probability of changing pattern choice is not precisely as the theory predicts: it does not show a strict monotonic increase. The distributions of runs of various lengths are, however, significantly different for the two sets of data, and there is a general difference in probabilities of the type predicted by the theory.

Experiment II

The second experiment tested the prediction that an increase in the strength of

---

[7] Note that in the conflict condition the stimuli were presented by projecting slide images and that the pattern preferred by Referent One was always presented in the top position while the pattern presented in the bottom position was the pattern supposedly preferred by the second referent. In the no-conflict condition subjects simply made choices between patterns in the top or bottom position. Naturally, the patterns that appeared in the top positions in the conflict condition also appeared in the top positions in the no-conflict condition.

■ TABLE 1 / **Change in the Probability of Ending a Run of Similar Responses Between No-Conflict and Conflict Conditions***

Run Length	Change (Conflict — No-Conflict)
1	.04
2	.07
3	.06
4	.15
5	.11
6	.07
7	.31
8	.25

* A chi-square test of the similarity of the distributions of frequencies of runs of various lengths in the two sets of data yields a value of p of less than .001.

P's relation with competing referents would result in an average increase in the probability of alternating conforming responses between referents. A third treatment condition was created in which relatively weak conflict conditions were manipulated was created for this experiment. In this case, the two referents were identified simply as students at the subject's college. Of the original twenty subjects in the weak conflict condition, two became suspicious and were subsequently dropped from the analysis. In Experiment II there were then three treatment conditions: no-conflict, weak conflict and strong conflict.

As the theory predicts, the three treatment conditions produced different average probabilities of alternating conforming responses between patterns in the top and bottom positions. In the no-conflict condition, .47 was the mean probability of alternating choices (selecting the pattern in the top position on trial N and the bottom pattern on trial $N + 1$ or the reverse). In the weak conflict condition this probability was .50. In the strong conflict treatment condition this probability was .55. Application of the Whitney (1951) extension of the Mann-Whitney U Test to three sample cases revealed that the probability that the subjects in the three samples were drawn from the same population was less than .05.

In addition to the result that the three treatment conditions produced average results that are statistically significant and ordered as the theory predicts, it is important to note that the effects of the experimental manipulations were consistent over the duration of the experiment. As indicated in Figure 4, the mean probabilities of alternations produced by the three groups of subjects are ordered as the theory predicts during the final three quarters of the experiment.

Experiment III

The final experiment to be reported in this paper concerns the effect on P's

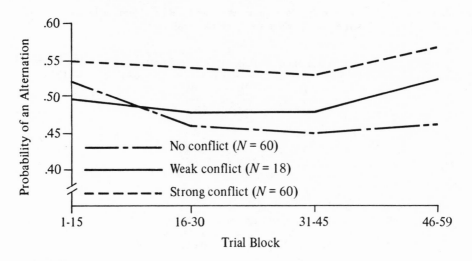

■ **FIGURE 4.** Probability of an Alternation through Time

sequential choice behavior of unequal strength reference relations between *P* and competing referents. The two treatment conditions that have already been mentioned were such that within the conflict situations created *P* had equally strong relations with competing referents, but the absolute strength of the relation with each referent differed between conditions. In one case the relationship between *P* and the referents was relatively weak (both referents were other students at *P*'s college), and in one case the relationship was relatively strong (both referents were individuals with whom *P* had friendships). The obvious manner in which to produce conditions in which the relations between *P* and competing referents are unequal would be to create a conflict situation in which one referent was a *friend* and the other was a *student*. In the unequal relation treatment condition the pattern preferred by the *friend* was always displayed in the upper portion of the screen. Twenty-two subjects were exposed to conditions of unequal relations with competing referents. Two subjects indicated suspicion and were dropped from the analysis.

The theory yields a clear prediction for the effect on *P*'s sequential choice behavior of equal or unequal strength reference relations: under the equal-strength relation conditions the probability of choosing the pattern presented in the *top* position should be approximately one-half while under the unequal relation condition this probability should be significantly increased.

Figure 5 presents graphs of the probabilities of a choice of the pattern presented in the top position for the combined data from the subjects in both equal strength relation conditions and the subjects in the unequal strength relation conditions. In the latter condition the pattern in the *top* position was preferred by the referent with whom the subject had the stronger relation. (The treatments produce differences throughout the entire duration of the experiment.) The mean probabilities of *top* pattern choices for subjects in the different conditions were: equal conditions = .49 and unequal conditions = .58. The

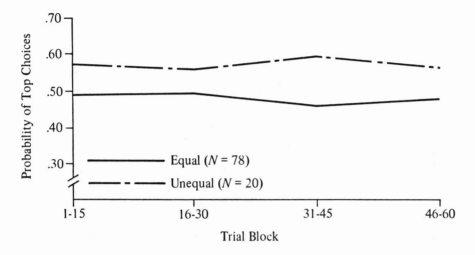

■ **FIGURE 5.** Regression of Top Choices through Time

difference between the means produced by the subject groups was significant at $p < .05$ (Mann-Whitney U).

□ **CONCLUSION**

This paper represents an attempt to re-introduce the argument that the investigation of the topic of the uses of reference groups or reference individuals should be approached by identifying distinct types of referential behavior and constructing predictive models through recourse to theories of basic social-psychological processes. At present there exists a no more coherent single body of reference group theory and research than existed when the works of Kelley (1952), Merton (1957), or Cohen (1962) appeared, and it does not appear that the emergence of a single reference group theory is imminent. There has, however, been considerable research directed at the creation of theories of the distinct types of reference phenomena; despite the lack of a conscious conceptual organization of the area along these lines, it seems that the behaviors of researchers concerned with the manner in which individuals utilize social frames of reference conform to the strategy originally advocated by Kelley.

The major portion of the paper has focused on the development of a theory of behavior under conditions of normative reference conflict and the presentation of the results of several basic tests of the formulation. In general, the results of the empirical tests of the theory were positive. Although the probability of alternating conforming responses and choosing the referent rejected on this last occasion does not increase in a strict monotonic fashion, the likelihood of an alternation generally increases with increased lengths of runs of sequential rejections.

This theory leads to certain conclusions about the basic nature of the conflict situation and yields certain suggestions for the direction of future research. It results in the realization that individuals involved in conflict situations adopt choice strategies through which they are able to maintain relations with competing referents even if they find the conflict situation generally noxious. The theory argues that if the structure of the conflict situation were to remain stable, P would indefinitely maintain the strategy of alternating between referents and would not act to resolve the conflict in any final manner.

Alternative formulations for behavior under conditions of reference conflict, notably Cohen's (1962) model, have led to the prediction that individuals will move toward conflict resolution through the rejection of one of the referents and complete conformity to the other. Since the Cohen formulation was never empirically tested, the only evidence that supports this point is the data reported in this paper and the previous papers concerned with this research program (Ofshe, 1967, 1968).

There is one prediction that discriminates between the two models. If, as the Cohen formulation predicts, there is a tendency toward conflict resolution, when data are considered for a group of individuals all of whom are operating under conditions of reference conflict, the mean probability of an alternation between opposing referents should decrease over time: as increasing numbers of individuals move to conflict resolution by choosing conformity to the expectations of a given referent, the number of individuals still attempting to maintain relations with both referents decreases. Therefore, the mean probability of an alternation for the group of individuals should decrease. If, as the theory developed in this paper predicts, individuals have adopted stable strategies for managing relations in the conflict situation and are attempting to retain relations with both referents, then the group data should reveal a relatively stable probability of alternation between opposing referents. Inspection of the data presented in Figure 4 indicates that there is no marked decrease in the probability of an alternation through time.

Given that it is reasonable to regard the behavior patterns that individuals adopt under conditions of reference conflict as stable (not necessarily leading toward conflict resolution), the area in which to search for variables that produce conflict resolution is that of the structural characteristics of the conflict situation. That is, what are the properties of conflict situations not included in the defining characteristics enumerated under definitions one through five of the theory that are related to conflict resolution? Clearly, one such variable is that of the individual's perception of future states of his social environment. The research reported by Berelson, et al. (1954) in *Voting* reveals that cross-pressured individuals arrive at final vote decisions somewhat later than non-cross-pressured voters but typically reach their decisions at a point prior to election day. That is, cross-pressured voters attain conflict resolution. The major theoretical difference between the social situation facing cross-pressured voters and those individuals operating under conditions of reference conflict in the experiments reported here is that the cross-pressured individuals can identify a future-point at which a final decision will be required. It is particularly interesting that cross-pressured voters delay their decisions relative to non-cross-pressured voters but make a final vote decision prior to election day. This suggests that cross-pressured individuals predicate their behaviors on both the conflicting expectations of referents as well as on projections for future states of affairs. The direction for future theoretical work on the reference conflict problem therefore seems to be that of how to incorporate such considerations into a model of behavior.

□ **REFERENCES**

Adams, J., "Toward an Understanding of Inequity," *Journal of Abnormal and Social Psychology*, 67 (1963), pp. 422–436.

Adams, J., "Inequity in Social Exchange," in L. Berkowitz (ed.), *Advances in Experimental Social Psychology* (New York: Academic Press, 1965).

Asch, S. E., "Effects of Group Pressure Upon the Modification and Distortion of Judgment," in H. Guetzkow (ed.), *Groups, Leadership and Men* (Pittsburgh: Carnegie Press, 1951).

Benoit-Smullyan, E., "Status Types and Status Interrelationships," *American Sociological Review*, 9 (1944), pp. 151–161.

Berelson, B., P. Lazarsfeld, and W. McPhee, *Voting: A Study of Opinion Formation in a Presidential Campaign* (Chicago: University of Chicago Press, 1954).

Berger, J., B. Cohen, J. Snell, and M. Zelditch, *Types of Formalization in Small Group Research* (Boston: Houghton Mifflin, 1962).

Berger, J., B. Cohen, and M. Zelditch, "Status Characteristics and Expectation States," in J. Berger, M. Zelditch, and B. Anderson (eds.), *Sociological Theories in Progress* (Boston: Houghton Mifflin, 1966).

Berger, J., B. Cohen, T. Conner, and M. Zelditch, "Status Characteristics and Expectation States: A Process Model," in J. Berger, M. Zelditch, and B. Anderson (eds.), *Sociological Theories in Progress* (Boston: Houghton Mifflin, 1966).

Cartwright, D. and F. Harary, "Structural Balance: A Generalization of Heider's Theory," *Psychological Review*, 63 (1956), pp. 277–293.

Cohen, B., "The Process of Choosing a Reference Group," in Criswell, J., H. Solomon, and P. Suppes (eds.), *Mathematical Methods in Small Group Processes* (Stanford: Stanford University Press, 1962).

Davis, J., "Structural Balance, Mechanical Solidarity and Interpersonal Relations," *American Journal of Sociology*, 68 (1963), pp. 444–462.

Festinger, L., K. Back, S. Schacter, H. Kelley, and J. Thibaut, *Theory and Experiment in Social Communication* (Ann Arbor: Research Center for Group Dynamics, Institute for Social Research, University of Michigan, 1950).

Festinger, L., S. Schacter, and K. Back, *Social Pressures in Informal Groups* (New York: Harper, 1950).

Festinger, L., "A Theory of Social Comparison Processes," *Human Relations*, 7 (1954), pp. 117–140.

Harvey, O., "An Experimental Approach to the Study of Status Relations in Informal Groups," *American Sociological Review*, 18 (1953), pp. 357–367.

Heider, F., "Social Perception and Phenomenal Causality," *Psychological Review*, 51 (1944), pp. 358–374.

Heider, F., "Attitudes and Cognitive Organization," *Journal of Psychology*, 21 (1946), pp. 107–112.

Heider, F., *The Psychology of Interpersonal Relations* (New York: Wiley, 1958).

Homans, G., "Status Among Clerical Workers," *Human Organization*, 12 (1951), pp. 5–10.

Homans, G., *Social Behavior: Its Elementary Forms* (New York: Harcourt, Brace and World, 1961).

Hyman, H., "The Psychology of Status," *Archives of Psychology*, No. 269 (1942).

Kelley, H., "Two Functions of Reference Groups," in G. Swanson, T. Newcomb, and E. Hartley (eds.), *Readings in Social Psychology* (rev. ed.) (New York: Holt, Rinehart and Winston, 1952).

Lenski, G., "Status Crystallization: A Non-Vertical Dimension of Social Status," *American Sociological Review*, 21 (1956), pp. 458–464.

Merton, R., *Social Theory and Social Structure*, rev. ed. (Glencoe: The Free Press, 1957).

Merton, R. and A. Rossi, "Contributions to the Theory of Reference Group Behavior," in R. Merton, *Social Theory and Social Structure*, rev. ed. (Glencoe: The Free Press, 1957).

Moore, J., "Status and Influence in Small Group Interactions," *Sociometry*, 31 (1968), pp. 47–63.

Moore, J., "Social Status and Social Influence: Process Considerations," *Sociometry*, 32 (1969), pp. 145–158.

Newcomb, T., *Personality and Social Change: Attitude Formation in a Student Community* (New York: Holt, Rinehart and Winston, 1943).

Newcomb, T., "Attitude Development as a Function of Reference Groups," in E. Maccoby, T. Newcomb, and E. Hartley (eds.), *Readings in Social Psychology* (New York: Holt, Rinehart and Winston, 1958).

Ofshe, R., *A Theory of Behavior Under Conditions of Reference Conflict*, unpublished Ph.D. dissertation (Stanford: Stanford University, 1967).

Ofshe, R., "A Laboratory Method for the Measurement of Identification," paper read at the meetings of the American Sociological Association (Boston: 1968).

Patchen, M., *The Choice of Wage Comparisons* (Englewood Cliffs, N. J.: Prentice-Hall, 1961).

Sherif, M., "A Study of Some Social Factors in Perception," *Archives of Psychology*, No. 187 (1935).

Sherif, M., B. White, and O. Harvey, "Status in Experimentally Produced Groups," *American Journal of Sociology*, 60 (1955), pp. 370–379.

Siegel, A. and S. Siegel, "Reference Groups, Membership Groups and Attitude Change," *Journal of Abnormal and Social Psychology*, 55 (1957), pp. 360–364.

Stouffer, S., E. Suchman, L. DeVinney, S. Star, and R. Williams, *The American Soldier: Adjustment During Army Life* (Princeton: Princeton University Press, 1949).

Strodtbeck, F., R. James, and C. Hawkins, "Social Status in Jury Deliberations," *American Sociological Review*, 22 (1957), pp. 713–719.

Torrance, E., "Some Consequences of Power Differences on Decision Making in Permanent and Temporary Three-Man Groups," *Research Studies*, State College of Washington, 22 (1954), pp. 130–140.

Whitney, D., "A Bivariate Extension of the U Statistic," *Annals of Mathematical Statistics*, 22 (1951), pp. 274–282.

Zelditch, M. and B. Anderson, "On the Balance of a Set of Ranks," in J. Berger, M. Zelditch, and B. Anderson (eds.), *Sociological Theories in Progress* (Boston: Houghton Mifflin, 1966).

Two

Authority, Evaluations, and Rewards

Chapter 6

Structural Aspects of Distributive Justice: A Status Value Formulation*

■ JOSEPH BERGER, MORRIS ZELDITCH, JR.,
BO ANDERSON & BERNARD P. COHEN

□ **INTRODUCTION**

The theory of distributive justice is concerned with the way in which socially valued rewards, such as salaries, promotions, or privileges, are allocated to members of social systems. Its basic notions are that: Rewards are allocated to actors on the basis of one or more socially defined and evaluated characteristics;[1] that a given level of reward is appropriate to a given state of a characteristic is determined by comparisons between kinds of actors; if two actors have similar states of similar characteristics they have a right to expect similar rewards as well; if similar actors have dissimilar rewards, or dissimilar actors have similar rewards, normative expectations are violated; violation of expectations about reward produce strain and some sort of pressure to change the situation. In the literature on the subject this violation of expectations has been variously called inequity, injustice, disequilibration, inconsistency, or imbalance.

The focus of the present paper is on the structural aspects of this process. By its *structural* aspects we mean the process by which, independently of the comparison of one individual with another, meaning is given to rewards and expectations are formed about their allocation. These aspects of the process are largely neglected in the currently most prominent formulations of distributive justice, which are exchange theories. These theories focus on comparisons between individuals and assume that the meaning of rewards and expectations about their distribution arise directly from such comparisons. Consequently,

* We gratefully acknowledge the support of NSF Grant GS 1170, for the study of status, power, and prestige structures, and ARPA contract DAHC 15–68–C–0215, for the study of distributive justice, that made the work reported in the present paper possible.

[1] Characteristics may be anything from age, sex, and occupation to specific capacities to perform particular kinds of tasks. Of course, rewards may also be given directly for particular performances; but what usually matters is the social definition of the performance as an instance of a given kind or amount of a capacity to perform.

119

empirical research on structural aspects of the process has been meagre. It has focused almost entirely on individual reactions to inequity, once defined, and not on the process through which the situation comes to *be* so defined.

In order to give an account of structural aspects of distributive justice we find it necessary in this paper to formulate the justice process in terms of the status significance of rewards instead of their exchange value. It might reasonably be objected that, in view of our meagre knowledge, a more sensible strategy would be conservative: What is called for is not a new theory, but only a modification of the most prominent existing formulations with a view to accounting for neglected features of the process. A study of what little we do know about justice suggests that such a modification would be insufficient to deal with structural aspects of the distributive justice process. We therefore propose to employ an alternative formulation, a theory of *status value*, which we believe provides a basis for understanding these aspects of the distributive justice process.

This paper is divided into three parts. Part 1 gives a history of the distributive justice problem, analyzes the exchange formulation of it, suggests why structural aspects of the problem are important, and argues that simple modifications of the exchange formulation are not sufficient to deal with the structural aspects of the justice process. Part 2 is a general theoretical statement of an alternative theory, the theory of status value. Part 3 applies that theory to an analysis of the structural aspects of distributive justice.

□ **1. EXCHANGE FORMULATIONS OF DISTRIBUTIVE JUSTICE**

Section 1 of this part reviews the history of the distributive justice problem and exchange formulations of it. Section 2 studies the problem of interindividual comparisons, which plays an important role in exchange formulations, and gives reasons why a structural analysis of the comparison process is necessary. Section 3 examines other objections to the exchange formulation of distributive justice, particularly those that suggest that a status-value formulation is necessary to account for the structural aspects of the process.

1. Formulations of the Justice Problem

The history of the justice problem has been closely connected with that of the status inconsistency problem. The earliest formulation was Weber's "Class, Status, and Party" (see Gerth and Mills, 1946), in which three basic dimensions of a stratification system are conceptually distinguished, but it is supposed that in time positions in the three tend to equilibrate. The Weberian formulation was restated in 1944 by Bénoit-Smullyan, whose paper became the point of departure for much of the later interest in the problem. Bénoit-Smullyan added to Weber's formulation the notion that if equilibrating tendencies were blocked, in some way there would be pressure for radical change. Why this should be so Bénoit-Smullyan did not attempt to explain. The first attempt at an explanation of the phenomenon, by Lenski in 1956, was based on Hughes' status ambiguity formulation (Hughes, 1945). Lenski claimed that inconsistent status creates status ambiguity, status ambiguity creates tension, and this tension is reduced by bringing statuses "into line."

In the process of constructing his formulation, Lenski to some degree simplified the process as Bénoit-Smullyan had understood it. In Bénoit-Smullyan, economic, power, and status processes were all treated as if they were one process obeying the same laws. Lenski, on the other hand, made no attempt to deal with power, which he treated as if it obeyed different principles.

In two respects, a marked advance over Lenski's formulation was made by Homans (whose earliest theoretical ideas about the equilibration phenomenon are found in Zaleznik, Christenson, and Roethlisberger, 1958). First, he saw for the first time that the equilibration phenomenon behaved like a relative deprivation process, and therefore made comparisons central to his theory. Second, he saw that status ambiguity and the allocation of rewards were two different processes. For Lenski, though he had simplified the problem by comparison with Bénoit-Smullyan, treated ambiguity and justice as if they were one process. It is in Homans that for the first time the justice problem *per se* emerges as a distinct theoretical concern.

In formulating status congruence, or ambiguity, Homans followed closely the Hughes conceptualization. But in formulating distributive justice, Homans used a new kind of explanation not previously seen in discussions of the equilibration phenomenon. This new explanation, in terms of social exchange, has become the most important focus of contemporary concern and research on the problem of justice.

Exchange formulations of justice are concerned with compensation for effort expended. Effort has a certain exchange value in the sense that its amount or quality will elicit reward from others. Reward, too, has a certain exchange value in the sense that it elicits effort from others. For an exchange of effort and reward to take place the reward must in some sense be enough, or appropriate to the effort. Whether or not a reward *is* enough is a relative matter: It is not a function of the absolute magnitude of reward but of the proportionality of reward to effort. To determine whether rewards are proportional to effort one must make a comparison between the ratio of reward to effort for two or more actors who are allocated rewards by the same source or are in some other way part of the same reward-allocation system. If the effort/reward ratios of the two are equal, their rewards are fair.

The two most important variants of the exchange formulation are Homans' own theory (1961) and Adams (1965). In Homans' theory an exchange is just if profits are in line with investments. Profit may be defined in the following manner: Let p be an individual who must choose between two alternatives, A or B. The consequence of choosing A has a certain positive value for p, its *reward*. But alternative B also has a certain positive value, and if p chooses alternative A he foregoes the reward he would otherwise obtain by choosing B. The reward foregone is the *cost* of choosing A. The *profit* associated with choosing A is the reward minus the cost of A. There is, of course, a profit associated with each of the two alternatives. It can be assumed that p will choose the more profitable alternative. If an *exchange* situation is one in which p's choice has consequences not only for himself but for another, say o, one may then imagine the interaction of p and o as a sequence of transactions each of which involves a profit to both p and o. Profits may be increased by increasing the value of the activities in a transaction. This could be done by making an *investment*, say in training or experience, which would raise the quality of p's contributions to o. A reward is *just* if profits are in line with investments. This can be determined by comparing p's profit/investment ratio to that of another actor in the system, such as o. The allocation of rewards is just if the higher profit goes to the higher investment.

Adams' theory (1963, 1965) differs in some respects, partly because it was originally a cognitive dissonance formulation. More recently, however (1965), it has clearly emerged as an exchange theory. In Adams, an exchange is equitable if outcomes are proportional to inputs. *Inputs* are any contributions made by p to an exchange. Energy, amount of effort, quality of effort, training to improve the quality of effort, would all be classed as inputs. *Outcomes* are any consequences that follow from the contributions made by p to the exchange. Approval, money, gifts, or respect would all be classed as outcomes. In Adams, as in Homans, satisfaction with outcomes is a relative matter: It is not a function of the absolute value of outcomes, but is determined by comparisons with others and behaves like a relative deprivation phenomenon. To determine if one deserves an outcome one compares the input/outcome ratios of two or more persons in the same reward-allocation system. An outcome is *equitable* if the two ratios are equal, and *inequitable* if they are not.

2. Comparisons

Exchange formulations make comparisons central to the analysis of distributive justice because the deprivations of injustice are quite evidently relative. But the conceptualization they give to the comparison process neglects what we regard as its structural features. As a consequence, necessary conditions of he distributive justice process are obscured; just and unjust states are incorrectly identified; and several different types of injustice, types of injustice that behave differently from each other, are not distinguished.

There are two basic ways to formulate comparisons. The first supposes, as exchange formulations do, that p compares himself with o. Comparisons in which one individual compares himself with another particular individual may be called *local*. The second supposes that p compares himself, not with any particular o, but with a *generalized* other. Thus, if p is an airline mechanic, instead of comparing himself with another particular person who is a mechanic, he might compare himself with "people who are highly skilled mechanics." Comparisons in which an individual compares himself with a generalized other may be called *referential*.

Current exchange theories formulate comparisons as local. But strictly local comparison is not sufficient to produce a distributive justice process. What unfolds if comparison *is* strictly local is a quite different process, best described as *anomie*. This is seen from examining the functions comparison is supposed to perform in distributive justice situations.

The purpose of comparison is to define the meaning that can be given to a particular reward. In example (1) there is no way to say whether

(1)   *P* is paid \$3.52 an hour.

\$3.52 is too much, too little, or the right wage for *p*; the meaning of the wage is undefined. In example (2) the problem appears to be solved, if *p* feels he is similar to *o*. *P* is underpaid.

(2)   *P* is paid \$3.52 an hour while *o* is paid \$4.33 an hour.

But why draw that conclusion? Why not draw the conclusion that *p* is paid an appropriate wage and *o* is overpaid? Or even that both are overpaid, but *o* more than *p*? There is no basis for the claim that local comparison, of which (2) is an example, defines the significance of a reward.

But suppose that, as in example (3), *p* believes that highly-skilled mechanics

	P is a skilled mechanic paid \$3.52 an hour.
(3)	Skilled mechanics typically make \$4.30 an hour.
	Unskilled mechanics typically make \$3.50 an hour.

make about \$4.30 an hour. Certainly there is no longer any doubt about how he defines the situation. He will believe he is underpaid. The difference between (3) and (2) lies in the use made by *p* of a stable frame of reference in terms of which local, particular comparisons are given their meaning. This frame of reference consists of generalized others, such as "skilled mechanics," and beliefs about the wage typically paid to them.

If comparisons have meaning only in terms of a frame of reference, what local comparison produces must be a process quite different from distributive justice. In distributive injustice *p* knows he has been unjustly rewarded; in local comparison he knows nothing of the sort. In fact, in local comparisons *p*'s problem is that he does not know how to define the situation in which he finds himself. His problem is to establish some standard. In other words, he is *anomic*. No doubt he is anxious and wants to change the situation. But his problem is not to protest injustice.

Hence, no justice phenomenon arises in the absence of a stable frame of reference. If accepted, this view has far-reaching consequences for the theory of distributive justice because both justice and injustice have different meanings in local as compared to referential comparison. A "just" state in local comparison sometimes is "unjust" viewed in terms of referential comparison, while some of the "unjust" states of local comparisons are "just" in referential comparisons. Even two states that are "unjust" in both views are seen as quite different *kinds* of injustice in referential as opposed to local comparison.

For example, when comparison is thought of only as local, (4) is always just, since similar individuals are paid similar wages. But (4) is not always just. If skilled mechanics typically make $4.30 an hour,

(4)
P is a skilled mechanic paid $3.52 an hour.
O is a skilled mechanic paid $3.52 an hour.

both p and o are unjustly rewarded, and instead of their being satisfied with their wage the foundation is established for a protest coalition. On the other hand, (5) may appear to involve injustice to both p and o in terms of local comparison. Is this reasonable?

(5)
P is a skilled mechanic paid $4.30 an hour.
O is a skilled mechanic paid $3.52 an hour.

Or is it more reasonable to say that as skilled mechanics typically earn $4.30, o is underpaid, but p is not. P may regard the *system* as unjust, and this may undermine its moral standing in his eyes, but it is not p himself who is unjustly rewarded.

Strictly local comparison confuses not only justice and injustice, but also different kinds of injustice. More accurately, in local comparison it is not possible to make distinctions that assume great importance in referential comparison. In (4) both p and o share the same injustice; in (5) only o is unjustly paid. Collective injustice should have different consequences than individual injustice, if for no other reason than the social support the sharing of injustice provides. Furthermore, in (5), while there is injustice in the system, p himself is not unjustly rewarded; his response will be a response to the moral injustice of there being others, unlike himself, who are unjustly treated. This situation, in which there is one individual injustice but it is the other who is rewarded unjustly, contrasts with (2) in which also there is one individual injustice, but p himself is unjustly rewarded.

Thus, the distributive justice process is obscured by formulating comparison as local. First, anomic states are confused with unjust states. Second, some states that are just are identified as unjust. Third, some states that are unjust are identified as just. Fourth, collective injustice cannot be distinguished from individual injustice. Fifth, situations in which it is oneself who is unjustly rewarded are not distinguished from those in which the other person is unjustly rewarded. Sixth, it is not even possible to always correctly distinguish situations of overreward from those of underreward.

If such distinctions make a difference to how p will respond to injustice, it is difficult to see how any lawful regularities in the behavior of distributive justice are to emerge if such distinctions are obscured. Thus, to make useful predictions about distributive justice, careful thought will have to be given to the nature and function of referential structures in comparisons.

3. Status Significance and Normative Expectations in Distributive Justice

If referential structures are important in defining states of justice and injustice, is it possible by some simple modifications to account for them in what remains basically an exchange formulation? Is it possible in such a theory to formulate their nature, their properties, and the process by which they come to define particular situations?

It seems reasonable to require that an analysis of referential structures satisfy three criteria: First, it should correctly account for the meanings given to rewards; second, it should account for the normative character of the expectations that emerge about the distribution of rewards; and third, it should yield a precise and unambiguous definition of states of justice and injustice. If these criteria are reasonable, then no simple modification of exchange theory will provide a satisfactory analysis of referential structures and the way in which they define local systems.

We consider first the meaning given rewards in exchange theory. An important clue to the nature of distributive justice situations, and one ignored in the exchange formulation of "rewards," is the special significance in defining injustice of small reward-differentials. Not uncommonly injustice occurs in situations such as example (6) in which the upshot is likely to be that Asst. Professor p demands another \$500 or so from his

(6) Asst. Professor p has been well thought of at University V for three years, receiving normal merit increases every year. This makes his salary equal to that of o, just hired by V, because the market price for new Ph.D's has increased each year at the same rate as V's raises.

chairman. Is it greater purchasing power that p is asking for? Is it the absolute size of the salary that is really important to p? Or is it not more important that there simply be *some* kind of reward-differential, and of a magnitude that has status significance to p?

The importance of small reward-differentials cannot be understood unless a distinction is firmly established between the *consummatory* and the *status* value of reward. The distinction we intend is of course Veblen's (1899). Veblen conceded that one aspect of rewards was the value to an actor of their use in consumption:

> The end of acquisition and accumulation is conventionally held to be the consumption of the goods accumulated ... Such consumption may of course be conceived to serve the consumer's physical wants—his physical comfort—or his so-called higher wants—spiritual, aesthetic, intellectual, or what not ... (Veblen, 1899, p. 25)

But, though one might want things in order to use them, consume them, and through consumption satisfy needs, Veblen felt that only among the poor did accumulation satisfy only a consummatory purpose. Among the more wealthy,

> ... it is only when taken in a sense far removed from its naive meaning that consumption of goods can be said to afford the incentive from which accumulation invariably proceeds. (Ibid.)

If the consummatory needs of the wealthy do not motivate accumulation, it does not follow that they have no motivation to accumulate. Indeed, they have a quite passionate acquisitive motive, because aside from their consummatory value,

> ... possession of wealth confers honor; it is an invidious distinction. (Ibid., p. 26)

Thus, objects possessed and objects consumed can stand for worth, respect, esteem, social standing: They have *status* significance. But in exchange formulations no account is taken of the important differences between consummatory and status value.

If the status significance of small reward-differentials is not accounted for in exchange formulations, neither is the significance of age, sex, ethnicity, race, or other status characteristics. All these characteristics, which sometimes form the basis on which rewards are allocated, are treated by analogy with the amount or quality of effort. In Homans, for example, they are all classified as investments. Investments are efforts to acquire a certain capacity to contribute to the accomplishment of some goal. Thus, education and seniority might be thought of as effort expended to acquire high skill, but it is hard to see that age, sex, race, or ethnicity can be looked at in the same way. Is effort expended to become thirty, male, and white? Is it for that effort that actors are compensated?

The significance of small differences in reward and the importance of status characteristics among what Homans calls investments both suggest that status significance is important in the theory of distributive justice. The definitions and assumptions of exchange theory are not easily modified to take this sort of significance into account. Perhaps they are more easily modified to deal with the other main structural feature of the justice process, the emergence of normative expectations about the distribution of rewards. Exchange formulations, of course, describe the emergence of some idea of a "fair" allocation of rewards; but proportionality of rewards has neither the shared nor the moral character such expectations evidently have in fact. The moral character of justice is one of its special peculiarities. It is seen in the fact, first, that underrewarded actors are not simply dissatisfied, they are morally indignant; and second, in the fact that overrewarded actors do not simply owe something to somebody, they are guilty. Accounts of injustice make it likely that even people who are neither over- nor underrewarded feel about injustice that disinterested outrage that sociologists associate with the violation of normative order. Even if the consequences do not touch them personally, such individuals apparently feel incensed at the shabby treatment of the underrewarded or the inexcusable favoritism shown the overrewarded.

The empirical investigations associated with exchange formulations have in fact pointed more clearly to the moral character of distributive justice than any other investigations; have pointed, that is, to the indignation of the underrewarded and the guilt of the overrewarded. But the theory itself has treated anger and guilt as individual reactions to injustice, not as aspects of the moral character of the process. To render these states moral in character is of course possible, in an exchange formulation, by deriving them from one all-embracing norm: The norm of reciprocity (Gouldner, 1960). One may suppose this norm to be shared and to be moral in character. Deviating from it will violate not only contractual calculations but also morally valid expectations. The expectations yielded by this simple assumption, however, are a little *too* all-embracing. What we require is an assumption that yields the expectations of specific situations and are nevertheless of a moral character. No simple modification of exchange theory yields a result that is at one and the same time shared, moral, and precise.

Having considered the meaning given to rewards and the problem of deriving the moral character of justice, it remains to consider how exchange theories define justice and injustice. In conceptualizing exchange in terms of effort and compensation for effort, exchange theories define distributive justice in terms of the proportionality of reward to amount or quality of effort. In Homans proportionality is not taken too seriously: It is the ordinal, rather than the interval or ratio properties of profits and investments that define justice and injustice (Homans, 1961, Chapter 12). What is required is that investments and profits be "in line," as in (7); the higher rewards go to the higher investments.

(7)
$$\$300/\text{month} < \$900/\text{month}$$
$$4 \text{ years training} < 12 \text{ years training}$$

The difficulty with this definition, of course, is that for the same two individuals (8) is quite as just as (7); so that the "in lineness" of profits and investments is a rather imprecise definition of justice.

(8)
$$\$100/\text{month} < \$1,000/\text{month}$$
$$4 \text{ years training} < 12 \text{ years training}$$

Nor, in this definition, does it make any difference how *far* rewards depart from proportionality. Adams' solution to this difficulty is to take proportionality seriously (Adams, 1965): He defines justice as the equality of two reward/effort ratios. Thus, if (7) is divided on both sides the rewards are just because both ratios equal 75. On the other hand, if (8) is divided on both sides, $25 \neq 83.3$ and the rewards are unjust. But this way of defining justice has its own difficulties: For in exchange formulations statuses such as age, sex, ethnicity, or race are among the things classified as inputs or investments. Therefore, it is possible to define injustice by ratios such as (9).

(9)
$$\frac{\$300/\text{month}}{\text{Female}} \neq \frac{\$900/\text{month}}{\text{Male}}$$

If we assume the importance of status, as status, in distributive justice, but do not conceive of dividing by denominators like male, or white, or Jewish, or middle-aged, we are left either with an imprecise definition of injustice or one that is meaningless for an important class of cases.

We conclude from this analysis that if our objectives are: (1) To conceptualize the frame of reference in terms of which status and rewards have their meaning; (2) to use the properties of this frame of reference to derive normative expectations about appropriate levels of rewards; (3) in doing so, to take into account the status significance of rewards; and (4) to give a precise and meaningful definition of states of justice and injustice for status significant situations; then we are committed to more than a reformulation of exchange theory. An alternative formulation that we believe satisfies the criteria we have in mind is offered in part 2.

□ 2. STATUS VALUE AND REFERENTIAL STRUCTURES

Section 1 introduces the main definitions and assumptions of the theory of status value, section 2 the nature and properties of referential structures. The theory in both sections is quite general: It can be applied not only to distributive justice situations, but more generally to situations in which status value is acquired, transferred, and modified. For example, it can also be used to analyze how awards, such as the Nobel prize, acquire their prestige, or how the assignment of statuses to the levels of a status hierarchy comes to be unstable.

1. Theory of Status Value

The theory of *status value* is concerned with evaluations of worth, esteem, or honor. "Status significance" in this usage means "honorific significance." Two kinds of elements may have status significance: States of characteristics and states of goal-objects. A *characteristic*, C, is any feature or aspect of a person that might be used to describe him, such as energy, height, or skin color. A state of a characteristic, C_x, might be, in the case of energy, high or low; in the case of height, tall or short; in the case of skin color, light or dark. In the present paper, all characteristics are treated as if they had only two states (hence the subscript x identifying states can take the values a or b only). A *goal-object*, GO, is any object, tangible or intangible, that an actor might want, or that might satisfy some need, such as shelter, income, or a title.[2] A *state* of a goal-object, GO_x ($x = a, b$), might be simple or elaborate shelter, a high or low income, a noble title or no title at all. A state of a characteristic or goal-object is distinct from its status value; for example, a state such as "great physical strength" might be given either positive or negative status value, might be good in some cultures, bad in others.

Every status situation is conceptualized from the point of view of some given

---

[2] In the more precise context of the theory of status value, we use the term "goal-object" instead of the term "reward" for three reasons: Reward often connotes only positive value, where we want to talk both of positive and negative values; reward often connotes various psychological notions about effects on p, such as reinforcement, that play no part in our formulation; and reward often connotes direct gratification of p, through consumption of the reward — exactly the wrong connotation for our theory. But suitably stripped of any such connotations, one could use the term "reward" in place of "goal-objects" and understand what we mean quite well.

actor, p; other actors and indeed p himself are treated as *objects* of p's orientation. That is, p is aware of and responds to other actors, but what is important in the theory is only p's awareness of and response to them. For example, the theory does not attempt to predict behavior of objects of orientation, except in the sense that other actors may of course also be treated as the actor p. Objects of orientation may include p as an object to himself (denoted p'), another particular actor, o, or such generalized objects as "airline mechanics" or "business executives"; all of which will be referred to as the "social" objects of the theory. (Generalized social objects will be distinguished from particular social objects, p' and o, by upper case Roman letters, such as Y and Z.)

It is sometimes useful to refer to general properties of *any* instance of an object of orientation, p', o, Y, or Z, in which case we designate objects as x. The corresponding notation for states of C and GO will be e_i.

The actor p may regard any social object, x, as possessing any element e_i, or p may *expect* that x possesses e_i. Our idea of possession is straightforward, but expectation here means both normative and cognitive expectation. We want to cover by the term somewhat more than "to anticipate," but we also do not want to exclude this meaning. Thus, we mean that p thinks x ought to possess e_i, but do not preclude his also predicting that x actually will possess e_i.

P may regard two distinct states of C or two distinct states of GO as *similar* or *dissimilar*. For example, an airline mechanic may compare himself to an automobile mechanic and believe that they have the same state (high) of the same characteristic (mechanical skill). Similarity involves both similarity with respect to characteristic or goal-object, and similarity with respect to the *state* of the characteristic or goal-object. The airline mechanic must believe both that the same sort of mechanical skills are common to airline and automobile mechanics and that they have the same degree of skill. Similarity, like any other aspect of a status situation, is seen from p's point of view: What matters is whether p regards two states as similar, not whether the sociologist regards them as similar.

Thus, there are two primitive relations between social objects and elements that have or acquire status significance, possession and expectation of possession, and one primitive relation on pairs of elements, similarity. We now use the ideas of possession and expectation of possession to define two fundamental relations in the theory of status value.[3]

DEFINITION 1. An element e_i is *associated* with an element e_j if it is the case that: If x possesses e_i, then x possesses e_j.

DEFINITION 2. An element e_i is *relevant* to an element e_j if it is the case that: If x possesses e_i, then x is expected to possess e_j.

---

[3] For readers of "The Stability of Organizational Status Systems" (Zelditch, Cohen, Berger, 1966), where an earlier formulation of the theory of status value was described, one of the major changes in the theory developed here is in the way *relevance*, which we are about to define, was treated in that paper. Relevance was in the prior formulation introduced as a primitive term. Here it is a defined term.

Certain important implications follow immediately from these two definitions. First note that:

If e_i is associated with e_j and e_j is associated with e_k, then e_i is associated with e_k.

For "e_i is associated with e_j" means that if x possesses e_i, then x possesses e_j; and "e_j is associated with e_k" means that if x possesses e_j, then x possesses e_k. From this it follows that if x possesses e_i, x possesses e_k. Hence, association is transitive.

Also note that:

If e_i is associated with e_j and e_j is relevant to e_k, then e_i is relevant to e_k.

This follows from definitions 1 and 2.[4]

Finally, note that association and relevance are not symmetrical relations. It is quite possible to say that C_x is associated with GO_x without claiming at the same time that GO_x is associated with C_x. Suppose that in p's eyes blacks are typically poor. It does not follow that p regards the poor as typically black. Therefore we distinguish the association of e_i to e_j from the association of e_j to e_i. The same is true of relevance.

We use the primitive idea of similarity and our defined concepts of association and relevance to study how status value spreads: How states that have no particular significance in and of themselves come to mean something important to p about the place occupied by p' and o in a status situation. We will not be concerned with how states acquire status-value *ab initio*. Though the problem is of obvious importance, it requires a theory of its own and one not relevant to the problem of distributive justice. But once at least one status-valued element is given in a status situation, S, other elements of the same situation come to be defined by their relations to the already valued elements of the situation. The general expression "related to," here, covers association, relevance, or similarity. Given such relations, status-value is acquired under the following conditions:

ASSUMPTION 1. (*Spread of Status Value*) Let e_i be a non-status-valued element of a status situation S, and let e_j, e_k, ... , be status-valued elements of S. If e_i is related to e_j, e_k, ... , or e_j, e_k, ... to e_i, then

  (1) e_i acquires the status value of e_j, e_k, ... , if e_j, e_k, ... , have the same status value.
  (2) e_i acquires no status value if e_j, e_k, ... , have different status values.

---

[4] Note that certain important ideas do *not* follow from definitions 1 and 2. For example, it does not follow that: If e_i is relevant to e_j and e_j is relevant to e_k, then e_i is relevant to e_k. Therefore, if we believe transitivity of relevance to be true, it must be made an independent assumption of the theory of status value. Because we do not need such an assumption for the problem of the present paper, we omit further discussion of it.

Thus, if executives use different washrooms from blue collar workers in a factory, the key to the executive washroom acquires status significance in the factory. For this to occur it is not necessary for there to be two or more status-valued elements in S, such as e_j, e_k, ... ; the process will take place if there is only one. But if there *are* two or more such elements, assumption 1 claims that status value spreads only if all those related to e_i have the *same* status value. If e_j, e_k, ..., do not have the same status value, no status value is transferred to e_i at all. Thus, in an organization with only one washroom, used by everyone regardless of their status, no status significance attaches to the washroom.[5]

Note that the assumption is mute on the subject of any change in status value that might be expected of e_i if it is *already* status-valued when it becomes similar to, associated with, or relevant to e_j and e_k. For example, the claim that e_i acquires no status value if e_j and e_k differ in value does not imply in any way that if e_i were already valued when it became attached to them, it would *decay* in status value. If a washroom is used indiscriminately, it will acquire no status significance. It does not follow that if it does have status significance and is *then* used indiscriminately, it will lose its significance. While in the long run this may be so, there will first be a protracted process of conflict and tension. (This view is developed below after the idea of balance is introduced.)

Prominent in many discussions of distributive justice is the idea that, like status value, relevance may spread along bonds created by similarity. For example: If p perceives that C'_x is similar to C_x and also that C_x is relevant to GO_x, then p will come to see C'_x as relevant to GO_x. This is the sort of process one must suppose when airline mechanics come to believe they should have the same wage as automobile mechanics because airline mechanics have skills similar to those of automobile mechanics. The underlying idea seems to be a natural one. Explicitly stated:

ASSUMPTION 2. (*Spread of Relevance*) If e_i is similar to e_j and e_j is associated with or relevant to e_k, then e_i will become relevant to e_k or to any element similar to e_k.

---

[5] A more general formulation of assumption 1 would permit spread of status-value among a larger number of non-status-valued elements simultaneously. If the several non-valued elements are themselves related, however, the assumption requires modification to avoid the undesirable consequence that under certain conditions the spread of status value through a status situation will depend on the order in which the assumption is applied to the elements. This occurs if non-status-valued element e_1 is related to two also non-valued elements e_2 and e_3, one of which is related to a positively status-valued element e_4, while the other is related to a negatively status-valued element e_5. Using $e_i R e_j$ to mean that e_i is related to e_j: If we start at e_4, e_1 acquires positive status value because $e_2 R e_4$ and $e_1 R e_2$. But at that point status value no longer spreads, because element e_3 is now related both to e_1, which is positive, and e_5, which is negative. On the other hand, if we start at e_5, then e_1 acquires negative status value and e_2 acquires no status value.

The required modification treats all the related status-valued elements as a single set, E, and all the non-valued elements, directly or indirectly related to E, as a distinct set, $\bar{E}$. Then all the elements of $\bar{E}$ acquire the status value of the elements of E if and only if all the elements of E have the same status value; otherwise, no elements of $\bar{E}$ acquire status value.

Note that what spreads is *relevance*, i.e. *expectations about* possession, not association. Thus, if e_i is similar to e_j, then either association or relevance of e_j to e_k leads p to *expect* any object that possesses e_i to possess e_k. Note also that unlike assumption 1, there is nothing that bars relevance from spreading between status elements that have different status value.

If the elements that come to be linked do have different status value, however, they are *imbalanced*. The idea of balance plays a key role in the theory of status value, because balance defines the conditions of stability of a status situation. (This formulation differs only slightly from that of two previous papers using the same notion. See Berger, Cohen, and Zelditch, 1966; or Zelditch, Berger, and Cohen, 1966.) Balance of a status situation may be defined in three steps:

DEFINITION 3.1. $[e_i, e_j]$ is a *relational unit* if there exists an e_i and e_j such that
(1) e_i is associated with e_j or e_j with e_i, or
(2) e_i is relevant to e_j or e_j to e_i, or
(3) e_i is similar to e_j.

Because we have limited ourselves to dichotomous characteristics and goal-objects, the status values of the states of a given C or GO may be treated as if they were either positive or negative evaluations. Thus, for occupational classes, the white collar class may be treated as if it were a positively-evaluated class while the blue collar class may be treated as if it were a negatively-evaluated class. From this perspective,

DEFINITION 3.2. A *relational unit* $[e_i, e_j]$ is *balanced* if and only if e_i and e_j are both status-valued and the sign of their evaluation is the same.

DEFINITION 3.3. *A status situation S is balanced* if and only if all its relational units are balanced.

The idea of balance is now identified with the stability of a status situation and with freedom from strain or tension. Imbalance, on the other hand, is identified with tension and pressures to change; and when pressures do arise, they will be pressures to change the situation from imbalance to balance.

ASSUMPTION 3. The status situation S is stable if and only if it is balanced.

By "stable" we mean that the status situation will not change as a result of any pressures within the situation itself. Thus, assumption 3 is *not* a definition of the terms "balance" or "stability"; the two terms are independently defined. "Balance" is a term having to do with the agreement in evaluation of two or more related status states in a status situation; "stability" is a term having to do with pressures towards change in a status situation.

ASSUMPTION 4. If a status situation S is imbalanced, there is tension generated within that status situation.

ASSUMPTION 5. If a status situation S is imbalanced, there will be pressures from within S to change in the direction of balance.

Note that all assumption 3 claims is that if a status situation is balanced, there are no pressures for change that arise from the way characteristics and goal-objects are related to each other. The assumption does not, of course, preclude the possibility that there are pressures on the system from some other factor or source. What the assumption implies, rather, is that if in some concrete setting there is tension or pressures for change, but the status situation is balanced, the source of tension and pressure must be from some other factor. Assumption 5, on the other hand, claims that, if imbalanced, the status situation is a source of pressures for change, but does not claim that any actual change will be observed. Again, the caution taken in this assumption is due to the fact that some factors outside the status process may have an opposite effect, inhibiting actual change.

2. Referential Structures

In part 1 a distinction was made between *local* and *referential* comparisons. What distinguishes local from referential comparison is the presence of a stable frame of reference providing a standard in terms of which local comparisons are given meaning. Of course there are many different kinds of "frames of reference" in sociology and psychology; they are important in many different kinds of problems. But in defining status situations the particular frame of reference used by p has the following four components:

(a) Generalized individuals,
(b) who possess given states of given characteristics,
(c) to which are associated given states of given goal-objects,
(d) where the characteristics and goal-objects are all status-valued.

A frame of reference having these four components will be called a *referential structure*.

A *generalized individual* is an individual such as "an airline mechanic" or "an automobile mechanic," as opposed to a particular, named individual like "Jones" or "Smith." The states of characteristics attributed to generalized individuals are those which they *typically* possess. Airline mechanics are typically highly skilled mechanics; apprentice automobile mechanics are typically unskilled. In the same way, goal-objects associated with the generalized individual are those typically allocated to the kind of people who have that much skill. It may be believed that skilled mechanics are typically paid $4.33 an hour. Finally, the states of each characteristic and the states of each goal-object associated with the generalized individual have status-value.

Given a referential structure, p sees his own characteristics and goal-objects as similar to or different from those of generalized social objects in it. It is in terms of such similarities and differences that his own characteristics and goal-objects acquire their status significance, and expectations emerge about which goal-objects he has a right to possess. Give p a job as sales clerk and he may see no significance in the fact that, like o who drives a delivery truck for the same firm, he is paid an hourly wage. But let him feel that he is similar to other white collar workers, and other white collar workers in the firm are paid a salary, and furthermore only blue collar workers are paid hourly: P will feel he has a right to expect a salary too and will define the method by which he is paid as degrading. The stage is set for a distributive justice process.

But for a distributive justice process to unfold, more is required than the simple existence of a referential structure. The referential structure must have three fundamental properties: (a) It must be unitary. (b) It must be differentiated. (c) It must be balanced.

By a *unitary* referential structure we mean one in which two goal-objects that differ significantly in status value are not both associated with the same generalized individual. In a unitary referential structure, Jones must suppose that skilled mechanics typically make around $4.60 while apprentices typically make around $3.50. Of course, there will be a range of wages around the typical value; not every skilled mechanic must make precisely $4.60. But the range must be well-defined, and must not contain values that overlap the range defined for the unskilled mechanic. If Jones hears of an exception, he must be able to explain it away, it must be something "atypical." For if some skilled mechanics made $4.60 but others made $3.50, there would be no fixed standard in terms of which local comparisons could acquire a definite meaning. Instead, Jones would develop *conflicting* expectations. Conflicting expectations are certainly common enough, but they are not the same as distributive justice.

A referential structure is *differentiated* when both the high and low states of a characteristic, and both the high and low states of a goal-object, are contained in it. For p to fully grasp the significance of an imbalanced goal-object in a local comparison, he must know not only that it is *not* the goal-object associated with his own state of a characteristic, but also that it *is* the goal-object associated with some other state. For the status significance of states and objects derives wholly from the *other* states and objects with which they are associated (by assumption 1). Thus, an airline mechanic must be aware not only that $3.52 is too little for a highly skilled mechanic, but also that it is the wage associated with unskilled mechanics, before $3.52 is fully interpreted.

A referential structure must be *balanced* because if it is not it is unstable. If it is unstable, the status values of the referential structure will change; and quite as much as in a strictly local comparison p will be unable to define the local situation. The process that unfolds is without question an important one to understand if we are to fully comprehend the dynamics of status. But it will not be a distributive justice process. Instead it will be a process of disintegration and decay of the status value of rewards, a disappearance of formerly important status distinctions, and a struggle to preserve the disintegrating status order by those to whom it meant much.

□ **3. DISTRIBUTIVE JUSTICE**

One application of the theory of status value is to the analysis of distributive justice. Section 1 below informally characterizes this process in terms of the theory of status value. The remaining sections are concerned with structural aspects of this process: Section 2, with the definition of the status significance of characteristics and goal-objects in local systems and the emergence of normative expectations about their relations; section 3, with the assessment of justice and injustice in local systems.

1. Informal Characterization of the Distributive Justice Process

The distributive justice process begins by p coming to see certain characteristics and goal-objects in a specific referential structure as similar to characteristics and goal-objects in a particular local system. Typically there is more than one referential structure in terms of which p might define a local system: A university professor of surgery, for example, might see himself as similar to surgeons in private practice, to surgeons in university medicine, or even to other university professors. As is widely recognized, the remaining stages of the process depend on which specific referential structure is chosen by p. (See, for example, Runciman, 1966; or Patchen, 1961a.) Given a specific referential structure, the status significance of characteristics and goal-objects in the local system is determined by their similarity to one or another of the characteristics and goal-objects in the referential structure. Thus, given private practice as a referential structure, a university surgeon might define his skills as worthy but his income as unworthy. From the same referential structure emerges some notion of what one has a legitimate right to expect in the way of income: One deserves, at any rate, a good deal more than the $25,000 that, though typical in the university, is about what an unsuccessful surgeon in practice might typically make. Given a specific definition of the status significance of characteristics and goal-objects in the local system, and specific beliefs about what one has a right to expect, the actual association of characteristics and goal-objects in the local system either coincides with expectations or it does not. If it does, it follows that (1) the status values actually associated in the local system are balanced and (2) the system is "moral" or "just," in the sense that it behaves in the way one has a legitimate right to expect. Thus, a surgeon whose referential structure is university medicine will expect to earn, say, an income of $25,000 and will define $25,000 as the income of a successful surgeon. If in fact he makes about $25,000, therefore, what he actually makes coincides with what he expects to make and a positively-valued state of a characteristic is associated with a positively-valued state of a goal-object, balancing the local system. If the actual association of characteristics and goal-objects in the local system does not coincide with expectations, it follows that (1) the status values associated in the local system are imbalanced and (2) the system is "immoral" or "unjust," in the sense that it does not behave in the way one has a legitimate right to expect. Thus, a successful surgeon who is affiliated with a university hospital but whose referential structure is private practice will expect to earn, say, an income of $75,000 or more and will define $25,000 as the income of a quite unsuccessful surgeon. If in fact he makes $25,000, therefore, what he actually makes is far from what he expects to make and a positively-valued state of a characteristic is associated with a negatively-valued state of a goal-object, imbalancing the local system. Note that he may have both a sense of unworth, because that is what his income signifies to him; and of moral outrage, because he has a moral *right* to expect more. It should be noticed, from this account, that in a local system balance and justice are equivalent: A system is just if and only if it is balanced. If balanced, the local system is stable—that is, there is no pressure to change its structure generated by the manner in which goal-objects are allocated in it. If imbalanced, the local system is unstable—that is, there is some pressure from within the system for change in the direction of balance. Just how the system will change appears to depend not only on the justice process, but also on the structure of the particular system: Among the paths to balance that have been identified are individual social mobility, collective protest, redefinition of one's self, and withdrawal from the situation; but probably a wide variety of resolution behaviors exist.

The entire process, as just described, is renewed with every change in *p*'s choice of a referential structure. Thus, the stability of any local system is dependent on the stability of the referential structures activated in it. It is obviously possible to conceive of a university-affiliated surgeon changing his referential structure from university medicine to private practice: The effect being to generate a new process of redefinition, formation of new expectations, and a reassessment of justice. What was a worthy income will come to be redefined as unworthy; the income one has a right to expect will be inflated substantially; a new assessment of the system will find it unjust. In most concrete situations, therefore, justice may be thought of as a recurrent process in which balance, tension, and resolution behavior fluctuate through time.

Our concern here is with the structural aspects of this process: That is, with the process by which the status significance of elements in the local system comes to be defined and redefined by their relation to an activated referential structure; with the process by which expectations emerge and change by virtue of the relations of status elements in the local system to the elements of the referential structure; and with the process by which, given the way in which the local system has come to be defined, together with the way in which goal-objects have actually been allocated, justice and injustice are assessed. In what follows, therefore, we neglect certain important aspects of the justice process: Specifically, how a specific referential structure comes to be seen by *p* as similar to his own situation and how imbalance is resolved. We neglect them for three reasons: First, they are the principal concern of most other investigations of justice, and therefore more studied, if not more understood, than structural aspects of the process. Second, they are complex processes, in which status value plays only a part. For example, activation of a specific referential structure may be due to processes of identity formation, or aspiration levels, or the way in which roles in the local system are institutionally defined, etc. Third, they are dependent on the structure of particular local systems. For example, the kind of resolution behavior one finds probably depends on opportunities for mobility, the power structure of the local system, its communication channels, etc. (In fact, it is probable that the most investigated aspects of the process are also its least general and invariant aspects.) For our present purpose, therefore, the process is assumed to begin at a point at which a specific referential structure has already been activated, and in section 2 we study the process by which status significance is defined and expectations emerge. Section 3 carries the analysis through to the point at which justice and injustice are assessed, stopping short of an analysis of what kinds of resolution might be observed if the local system is unjust.

2. Definition of Status Significance and Emergence of Expectations in the Local System

The status situation S with which we are here concerned consists of both a referential structure and a local system. The referential structure is made up of characteristics and goal-objects associated with generalized objects of orientation, to one of which p is similar. The local system is made up of characteristics and goal-objects possessed by individual objects of orientation, p' and o, together with associations among these elements. These associations represent the manner in which goal-objects have been allocated in the local system. We consider first the process by which status values in the referential structure determine those in the local system. In analyzing this process we neglect the interaction of any status values already formed in the local system back on the referential structure. If there are status values already formed in the local system, they will certainly have consequences for the process (Israel, 1960); but the behavior of this more complex process does not appear to pose any new theoretical problems, it merely complicates application of the theory. For the present purpose we ignore these complications. This means, in effect, that we regard status values in the local system as initially undefined.

We assume two conditions: First we take a balanced, differentiated, unitary referential structure as given, for reasons stated in part ii: In our view, for a distributive justice process to emerge at all, p must regard the referential structure as something unchallenged and unchallengeable either by himself or by people like himself. The structure, furthermore, must remain unchanged throughout the process. (Call this the *structure* condition.)

Second, our analysis is concerned with situations in which each state in the local system is similar to one and only one state in the referential structure. This condition rules out those cases in which, because an element of the local system is similar to two or more elements of a referential structure, no transfer of status value from referential structure to local system can occur. Because referential structures are differentiated, a one-many relation between local system and referential structure would permit the possibility of one element of the local system being similar to two *differently-valued* elements of a referential structure. Therefore, no transfer of status value would take place (according to assumption 1). On the other hand, the condition does not rule out the possibility that two or more states of the local system are similar to one state of the referential structure. (Call this the *similarity* condition.)

Given the similarity and structure conditions, states in the local system will acquire the status value of the states to which they are similar in the referential structure. This follows from assumption 1, the spread of value assumption. To see how this follows, let p' and o be objects in the local system, Y and Z be generalized objects in the referential structure, to one of which we assume p' to be similar; and let c_x and go_x be states in the local system and C_x and GO_x be states in the referential structure. We know, because it is given by the similarity condition that

(1) $\qquad\qquad c_x$ is similar to some state C_x.

Furthermore, if we neglect the status significance, if any, already possessed by c_x in the local system and we are given (again from the similarity condition) that

(2) c_x is not similar to, associated with, or relevant to any other state that is different from C_x in status value

it follows, given the structure condition, that

(3) $\qquad\qquad c_x$ acquires the status value of C_x,

from (1), (2), and assumption 1. In the same way it can be easily shown that, given the similarity of go_x to GO_x it follows that

(4) $\qquad\qquad go_x$ acquires the status value of GO_x,

again using assumption 1.

A more general result than (3) or (4) follows if in fact c_x and go_x did possess status value prior to their redefinition by the referential structure of S. For it is likely that such prior definitions are not as unitary, nor as sharply distinct, as those of the referential structure that accomplishes their redefinition. But if they are not unitary and sharply distinct in meaning before definition, they are likely to be after it: For meanings often become more accentuated by the process of redefinition. A not entirely bad salary becomes much more clearly bad by becoming more definitely the salary associated with that generalized object possessing negative states of C and GO. A not wholly good one may look better as it more clearly is defined as similar to goal-objects possessed by those people who possess positive states of C. For in general, the meanings taken on by characteristics and goal-objects in the local system reflect the balanced, unitary, differentiated properties of the referential structure.[6]

To account for the way in which normative expectations about the possession of goal-objects emerge in the local system we make use of assumption 2, the spread of relevance assumption. We know, from the similarity condition, that

(5) c_x is similar to some state C_x;

and from the definition of a referential structure that

(6) C_x is associated with GO_x;

and finally, again from the similarity condition, that

(7) go_x is similar to some state GO_x.

Therefore, given the structure condition,

(8) c_x becomes relevant to go_x,

which follows from (5), (6), (7), and assumption 2.

Note that (8) does not claim simply that p holds those expectations which are part of the referential structure which defines his situation; for there *are* no normative expectations among the relations in a referential structure. What the referential structure consists of are beliefs about what *is*. Only in the local system do we find beliefs about what *ought to be*. It is true that we often speak about revolutions of rising expectations, or about other sorts of changes in "expectations" taking place. For example, Runciman (1966, Ch. IV) argues that the depression reduced strike activity in England in the 30's in part because it altered expectations about the wages a worker could legitimately expect, hence reducing relative deprivation. But expressions of this sort are really statements about changes in referential structures, and on the present account are elliptical statements of a process involving both shifts in beliefs *and* formation of expectations based on them: "Changes in expectations" are based on changes in what people believe *is* the case. As a consequence of beliefs about what is typically the case, expectations in local systems come to be formed about what one can legitimately claim *ought* to be the case: For what (8) says, put less formally, is that p believes he *should* possess what he believes others like himself *do* possess; and, of course, o too should possess what others like o typically do possess.

----

[6] Note that the meanings are balanced even though associations created by actual allocations of goal-objects may or may not be balanced with them

The process we have just described, in which expectations are formed about the state of go_x one ought to possess, is the process usually at work in the typical investigation of distributive justice. The process has an inverse, however, which is of equal interest; that is, a process through which expectations are formed about the state of c_x one ought to possess. For under certain conditions the process we have just described works equally well to create expectations about the kinds of characteristics one ought to possess. Earlier we pointed out that association is not necessarily a symmetrical relation; that, for example, e_iRe_j need not imply e_jRe_i. Under certain conditions, however, symmetry does obtain; in which case we may speak of *unique* association, defined as e_iRe_j and e_jRe_i both true. If the status elements of the referential structure are uniquely associated, or more generally in any case that possessing GO_x implies that one possesses C_x, then expectations are created for the state c_x that one ought to possess in the local system, by an argument parallel to (5)–(7). From the similarity condition we are given that

(9) go_x is similar to some state GO_x

and by the condition just assumed

(10) GO_x is associated with C_x.

From the similarity condition

(11) c_x is similar to some state C_x

so that paralleling (8), we have

(12) go_x becomes relevant to c_x.

In other words, given (10), if p possesses go_x he comes to form expectations about the state c_x that he ought to possess. Further, if he does not possess c_x there will be both strain and pressures for resolution of imbalance, which, if concretely different in the kinds of strain felt or modes of resolution, in other respects parallel those that are more typically discovered in the case in which p does not possess an expected goal-object.

3. Assessment of Distributive Justice

Referential structures provide the basis for defining the meaning of characteristics and goal-objects in the local system and creating expectations about right ways of distributing them. The local system itself provides a third important set of conditions which determines the distributive justice process. By whatever allocation process functions within it, actual association relations have been established between characteristics and goal-objects. The stage is now set for the assessment of these association relations in terms of the expectations which have emerged in the process just described. All, some, or none of these association relations in the local system may coincide with relevance relations, or expectations, created by the referential structure. If all association and relevance relations coincide, then p' and o possess the goal-objects they deserve and the situation is "just" in the sense usually given that expression. If some or none of the associations in the local system coincide with expectations created by the referential structure, then p', or o, or both possess goal-objects they do not deserve, and the situation is "unjust" in the sense usually given that expression.

Thus, if S^* is a status situation in which status value and relevance relations have been defined, the states of justice and injustice may be defined by the relation between relevance relations and association relations in the local system:

DEFINITION 4. (Distributive Justice) A state of *distributive justice* exists in S^* if and only if all association relations between characteristics and goal-objects coincide with relevance relations in the local system. Otherwise a state of *injustice* exists in S^*.

If association and relevance relations coincide, the result is always a balanced status situation in the sense of definition 3. Furthermore, if they do not, the result is always an imbalanced status situation. Hence,

(13)   If a state of distributive justice exists in S^*, S^* is a balanced status situation. If a state of injustice exists in S^*, S^* is an imbalanced status situation.

The reason for (13) is perfectly straightforward. Relevance relations are determined by similarities between local and referential objects. Referential structures are always balanced (by the structure condition). Therefore, relevance relations in the local system always connect states that have the same status value, forming balanced relational units in the local system. Association relations connecting the same states will therefore also form balanced relational units. But associations formed between any other states will always connect states that have different status values, forming imbalanced relational units in the local system. It will always be the actual associations of characteristics and goal-objects that create imbalance, if imbalance exists, because the relevance relations are always balanced. On the other hand, it is important to note that *any* failure of an association bond to coincide with expectations will *always* create an imbalance.

From (13) and assumptions 3, 4, and 5 we immediately see that

(14)   If a state of distributive justice exists in S^*, the status situation S^* is stable. If a state of injustice exists in S^*, S^* is unstable.

(15)   If a state of injustice exists in S^*, there is tension generated within the status situation.

(16) If a state of injustice exists in S^*, there will be pressures from within S^* to change it in the direction of balance.

These particular results, of course, correspond closely to those derived from exchange formulations.

Definition 4 has the valuable property that there is always one and only one state of justice for any given local system, and we are always able to say what that state is.

(17)   For every S^* there is one and only one state of distributive justice.

Given the similarity and structure conditions we are always able to say what expectations p will develop for a given S^*. This will always identify which way of allocating goal-objects in S^* is just. Furthermore, the existence of a stable referential structure, and consequently of status values of local characteristics and goal-objects defined by it, makes it possible to identify which state x of c and which state x of go is positively or negatively evaluated. It is therefore possible to define precisely the nature of any discrepancy between relevance and association. If for the sake of simplicity we treat status values as dichotomies $(+, -)$, then for any given pattern of expectations there are only four ways of actually allocating goal-objects. (See Figure 1. The first two columns show the four possible patterns of expectations that can arise: Note that these are mutually exclusive and exhaustive. Each situation S^* also has its referential structure, not shown in this figure, which provides the basis for its status defini-tions $(+, -)$ and expectations. The next two columns show the four possible ways of allocating goal-objects for each pattern of expectations in S^*. There are 16 possible status situations in S^*. The fifth column identifies which are just and which unjust.) For any given structure of S^*, that is for any given pattern of expectations, only one of the possible ways of allocating goal-objects is just.

In part 1 we argued that over- vs. underreward, collective vs. individual im-balance, and self vs. other imbalance all made a difference to how people will respond to injustice. If such distinctions do make a difference, it is only by making them that we will be able to discover regularities in the justice phenome-non. The last three columns of Figure 1 show the types of imbalance that occur for each pattern of expectations that emerges in S^*.

What Figure 1 shows is that, first, by reference to the referential structure, one always clearly distinguishes over from underreward, and both from justice. For example, consider line (8) of Figure 1. A concrete instance of (8) might be the case, not uncommon during the period of greatest economic expansion of the academic profession, in which new Ph.D.'s were placed by university depart-ments in new jobs that paid as much or more than they were themselves paying their own assistant professors — owing to the fact that market-induced increases in salaries at least equaled raises given juniors by universities. Assume the assistant professor is p': Was the newer Ph.D. overpaid or was the older assistant professor underpaid? The referential structure in this case fairly clearly identi-

	Expected Allocation of Goal-Objects		Actual Allocation of Goal-Objects		Distributive Justice	Type of Imbalance, if Injustice Exists	Reward State	
	To p'	To o	To p'	To o			Of p'	Of o
(1)	+	+	+	+	yes	balanced	just	just
(2)	+	+	+	−	no	other	just	under
(3)	+	+	−	−	no	collective	under	under
(4)	+	+	−	+	no	self	under	just
(5)	+	−	+	−	yes	balanced	just	just
(6)	+	−	+	+	no	other	just	over
(7)	+	−	−	+	no	collective	under	over
(8)	+	−	−	−	no	self	under	just
(9)	−	+	−	+	yes	balanced	just	just
(10)	−	+	−	−	no	other	just	under
(11)	−	+	+	−	no	collective	over	under
(12)	−	+	+	+	no	self	over	just
(13)	−	−	−	−	yes	balanced	just	just
(14)	−	−	−	+	no	other	just	over
(15)	−	−	+	+	no	collective	over	over
(16)	−	−	+	−	no	self	over	just

■ **FIGURE 1. Types of Balanced and Imbalanced Status Situations.**

fied the salary, say $10,000 in about 1968, as a "beginning" salary. Hence fairly clearly the older assistant professor was underpaid, not the newer Ph.D. overpaid. Note that in actual cases such definitions are seldom in doubt, because in actual cases one does not treat such comparisons as interindividual comparisons of p' with o.

Second, one can always clearly distinguish collective from individual injustice. The collectively unjust system may be expected to show coalition behavior that is not open to the individually unjust. That such coalitions will result is shown by experiments such as the following: Three college students are required to perform a task in which more points are yielded by coalitions than by individual performance. One of the three students is a paid participant, the other two are naive subjects. The paid participant has sufficient knowledge of how the task is performed that on the first of five trials in the experiment he always earns more points than either of the other two students. In one condition this initial point advantage is made to appear just because the paid participant is defined as more able at the task (as shown by an initial test); in the other condition the paid participant is defined as having the same ability as the two naive subjects, so that the initial advantage is unjust. In the unjust condition, the two naive subjects will enter into more coalitions against the paid participant, and refuse more of his own coalition overtures, than in the just condition. In the just condition the naive subjects are more willing to enter into coalitions with the paid participant, and more willing to give him an advantage in points, instead of forming coalitions between themselves against him. (Cf. Hoffman, Festinger and Lawrence, 1954.)

Third, when it is only one member of a system who is imbalanced, self is always distinct from other imbalance. This makes it possible to clearly interpret the results of an experiment like the following: Female students compete in a contest requiring aesthetic ability. They compete in pairs for a prize perfume bottle. In each pair they are defined as almost identical in ability, though just one wins the prize — the one who has a negligibly greater number of points, such as 1 or 2 out of 100. In one condition, the system thus created is one in which both contestants are superior in ability, but one wins and one loses the prize. In the other condition, the system thus created is one in which both contestants are inferior in ability, but again one wins and one loses the prize. In each condition, though the system as a whole is imbalanced, one can clearly identify one subject as balanced and one as imbalanced, and their behavior is of course quite different. (Cf. Israel, 1960.)

□ **SUMMARY**

Distributive justice is concerned with the way rewards are allocated. In all formulations of this process, the essential idea is that actors who are similar in terms of socially defined and valued characteristics expect to be similar in their rewards. If not, normative expectations are violated. The violation of such expectations produces tension and pressures for change.

The most important current formulations of this process are in terms of social exchange. But these formulations fail to take into account the nature and importance of status value in distributive justice, typically give incomplete accounts of the comparison process by which actors define similarity or dissimilarity, fail to account for the distinctively normative character of the process, and fail to give meaningful and precise definitions of either justice or injustice.

An alternative way of conceptualizing distributive justice is in terms of status value. A theory of status value is concerned with evaluations of worth, honor, or any synonym of these (merit, esteem, prestige, etc.). It describes the way in which definitions of status significance and expectations spread. It also describes the conditions under which status situations are stable or unstable.

In the theory of status value, comparisons are formulated in terms of referential structures. A distinction is made between particular social objects, such as the actor himself or other actors with whom he actually interacts, and generalized objects of orientation, of whom an actor holds stereotyped, unitary conceptions. Among other things, referential structures contain information about rewards, or more exactly, goal-objects, typically associated with generalized objects.

Referential structures determine, first, the status significance of characteristics and goal-objects possessed by particular actors, and second, the expectations actors come to hold about the manner in which goal-objects may legitimately be allocated. In the context of the status significance and normative expectations created by the referential structure, actual allocations of goal-objects either coincide with expectations or do not. Those that coincide with expectations are defined as just; those that do not are unjust. A state of distributive justice is always a balanced status situation, while injustice is always an imbalanced status situation. Balanced status situations are stable, imbalanced status situations produce tensions and pressures for change.

The main results of formulating the process in terms of status value and referential structures are:

(1) A description is provided of the operation of two processes which are basic to understanding the structural features of the justice phenomenon: The process by which the status significance of elements in the local system comes to be defined and redefined by their relations to an activated referential structure; and the process by which expectations emerge and change by virtue of the relations of status elements in the local system to the elements of an activated referential structure. This description makes clear the necessary conditions of distributive justice because of the significance to it of a balanced referential structure. In the absence of this structure the process that develops is important but different from distributive justice.

(2) The definition of the state of distributive justice becomes meaningful and precise. There is always one and only one state of distributive justice for each status situation, and its meaning is always exact. The meaning of each state of injustice becomes equally precise, and important distinctions are made that are typically obscured, including the differences between: (a) Over- and under-reward, which cannot be distinguished in the absence of a referential structure; (b) collective vs. individual justice — some forms of collective injustice being typically confused with "just" situations; (c) self vs. other imbalance. This should improve the chances of finding and stating regularities in the behavior of people in unjust situations.

(3) Processes not formerly distinguished emerge as important for future investigation. These include: (a) The problem of *anomic* status situations, for which there is no referential structure; (b) the problem of imbalanced referential structures, for which there is a referential structure, but the structure is itself in the process of changing, either by devaluing goal-objects or breaking down status distinctions.

□ **REFERENCES**

Adams, J. S., "Inequity in Social Exchange," in L. Berkowitz (ed.), *Advances in Experimental Social Psychology*, Vol. 2 (New York: Academic Press, 1965), pp. 267-299

Adams, J. S., "Toward an Understanding of Inequity," *Journal of Abnormal and Social Psychology*, 67 (1963), pp. 422–436.

Bénoit-Smullyan, E., "Status Types and Status Interrelationships," *American Sociological Review*, 9 (1944), pp. 151–161.

Berger, J., B. P. Cohen, and M. Zelditch, Jr., "Status Characteristics and Expectation States," in J. Berger, M. Zelditch, Jr., and B. Anderson (eds.), *Sociological Theories in Progress*, Vol. 1 (Boston: Houghton Mifflin, 1966), pp. 29–46.

Blumstein, P., and E. H. Weinstein, "Redress of Distributive Justice," *American Journal of Sociology*, 74 (1969), pp. 408–418.

Gerth, H., and C. W. Mills (eds.), *From Max Weber* (New York: Oxford University Press, 1946), pp. 180–195.

Gouldner, A. W., "The Norm of Reciprocity," *American Sociological Review*, 25 (1960), pp. 161–178.

Hoffman, P., L. Festinger, and D. Lawrence, "Tendencies Toward Group Comparability in Competitive Bargaining," in Thrall, Coombs and Davis (eds.), *Decision Processes* (New York: Wiley & Sons, 1954), pp. 231–253.

Homans, G. C., *Social Behavior, Its Elementary Forms* (New York: Harcourt, Brace and World, 1961).

Homans, G. C., "Status Among Clerical Workers," *Human Organization*, 12 (1953), pp. 5–10.

Hughes, E. C., "Dilemmas and Contradictions of Status," *American Journal of Sociology*, 50 (1945), pp. 353–359.

Israel, J., "The Effect of Positive and Negative Self-Evaluation on the Attractiveness of a Goal," *Human Relations*, 13 (1960), pp. 33–47.

Lenski, G. E., "Social Participation and Status Crystallization," *American Sociological Review*, 21 (1956), pp. 458–464.

Patchen, M., *The Choice of Wage Comparisons* (Englewood Cliffs, N. J.: Prentice-Hall, 1961).

Patchen, M., "A Conceptual Framework and Some Empirical Data Regarding Comparisons of Social Rewards," *Sociometry*, 2 (1961), pp. 136–157.

Patchen, M., "The Effect of Reference Group Standards on Job Satisfactions," *Human Relations*, 11 (1958), pp. 303–314.

Runciman, W., *Relative Deprivation and Social Justice* (Berkeley: University of California Press, 1966), Ch. 4.

Veblen, T., *The Theory of the Leisure Class* (New York: Macmillan, 1899).

Zaleznik, A., C. R. Christenson, and F. J. Roethlisberger, *The Motivation, Productivity and Satisfaction of Workers* (Cambridge: Harvard University Press, 1958).

Zelditch, M., Jr., J. Berger, and B. P. Cohen, "Stability of Organizational Status Structures," in J. Berger, M. Zelditch, Jr., and B. Anderson (eds.), *Sociological Theories in Progress*, Vol. I (Boston: Houghton Mifflin, 1966), pp. 269–294.

Chapter 7

*Towards
A Theory of
Organizational
Change**

■ SHERMAN KRUPP

Any general theory of organization must deal not only with the total organization but also with its component parts. Traditional theories usually treat organizations as goal-achieving entities and examine the parts as they contribute to these goals. The organization is seen as an adaptive unit which survives and functions by adjusting to external circumstances. If the parts of the organization behave in a way that is not consistent with its collective goals they are dysfunctional to the organization and must be regarded as impediments. However, the relationship of each part to the whole has consequences for organizational behavior that cannot be described simply in terms of helping or hindering. This chapter discusses the complexity of the part-whole relationship and suggests a way in which the behavior of the parts can be made the basis for a more general explanation of organizations.

In traditional theories the component parts of an organization are functional units within a unified collectivity. The unity is attributed to the binding force of the collective goals of the total organization. This assumption does not encourage us to look for independent reactions on the part of the components or for divergence of interest among them. If we assume high interdependence among parts coordinated towards a single goal, we are led to believe that the environment acts on the components only insofar as they are part of the total system. In contrast, I suggest that the total organization is better understood as an aggregate than as a unitary system. I assume that the behavior of the parts must be explained in terms of their own environment, which includes other parts of the organization as well as the environment external to the organization as a whole. From this point of view, the goals of the organization become an

---

* For their criticisms and suggestions I am grateful to: Melvin Bers, Robert House, William Howton, Jo Carolyn Lewis, Charles Perrow, Martin Rein, Charles Smith.

element in the environment of the parts, and the adaptations of the total organization are a consequence of the aggregated reactions of the individual parts.

Since we are explaining the internal behavior of the organization as the result of relationships among the components, the organization's susceptibility to environmental influence is also interpreted differently. Environmental influences penetrate the organization by acting on the components, forcing readjustments and realignments among them. It is not only by the decisions of the upper administration or by the reaction of the system as an organic whole that the organization's adjustment to environment is explained. Environment affects all levels and components of organization. Nor need the various adjustments to the environment always be favorable to the survival of the organization as an entity. Since the parts may adjust in ways that do not contribute to the well-being of the organization, internal conflict is normally present in some degree. Such conflict becomes a part of the explanation of the total organization.

Stress on component behavior creates a basic shift of theoretical emphasis. Where collectivity is taken for granted, the individuation of the components is the phenomenon that requires explanation. The new emphasis takes differentiation for granted; unitary behavior is now what needs to be explained. In this way, power, conflict, and environment are integrated into the axioms of organizational analysis in a way that gives them fundamentally different meanings. Organizational survival, effectiveness, or goal maintenance become only particular kinds of adaptation. The presence of collective, unity-enhancing behavior among the components will depend not only on the activity of rational decision-makers and the diffusion of collective goals but also on the way the components group into larger wholes and respond to environmental influences.

Social organizations are traditionally divided into three interdependent subsystems: the division of work, authority, and the informal organization. These subsystems describe the arrangement and restriction of human action and choice within their respective domains. The following analysis deals with the division of work and the hierarchy of authority, but takes the distribution of organizational rewards (welfare) as the third basic analytical category. The informal system will not be dealt with directly because it is logically subsumed within my general framework. Each of my subsystems or sectors can be viewed as a domain of rules and roles that integrates the rational purposes of the organization with the values and beliefs of its participants. This integration need not function optimally for the achievement of organization goals nor need such integration be equally desirable from the points of view of the different participant groups. Thus, the rules that govern tasks, compliance, or the distribution of rewards can be regarded in terms of their effectiveness in the fulfillment of organization goals. They may also be regarded as the formal embodiment of constraints on the individuals and groups that make up the system.

□ **2. THE DIVISION OF WORK**

The work of an organization is normally divided into specialized activities.

Within an organization the attempt to arrange these activities rationally for the achievement of organization goals is usually taken to be the function of the administration or management. The division into specialized activities is under discussion whenever we speak of tasks, specific skills, or the distinction between labor and capital. However, the actual patterns and rules that emerge in an organization depend upon many factors, both internal and external. Internal factors affecting specialization include the size of the organization, on-the-job training of skills, or managerial styles of leadership; external factors include such considerations as technology, the educational levels of society, the class structure, or patterns of union power.

It is not always easy to decide whether a particular constraint on work specialization is internal or external. For example, an assembly line can permit great work simplification by requiring dexterity only in a highly simplified task. Within the assembly line operation the number of tasks and the complexity of each is initially indeterminate. It is often found that a work force with a low educational level requires the simplification of tasks, authoritarian management, and detailed rules. A more developed labor force frequently permits tasks of greater complexity, more individual discretion, and fewer rules. Once a particular pattern of work is established, a high degree of interdependence emerges among the activities and between activities and associated rules. Individual routines cannot be changed without reorganization of the total process. A pattern of work simplification that arose initially in response to a particular environmental condition, a low level of skills in the work force, is crystallized in rules and work patterns. The rules then establish a situation in which only a relatively low level of skills is employed. Once a style of work specialization has been established, the procedures become fixed costs within an organization. Originally introduced in the context of an external problem, these routinized procedures become anchored internally; indeed, they often become end-values in themselves. Alteration in any single procedure changes the patterns among the internal variables and may disturb the general pattern of established procedures. What was an externally determined variable in one context is transformed into an internal one in another.

The assignment of tasks is a solution to the problem of allocating a given supply of skills and physical resources. It is necessarily adjusted to social expectations as well. The extent to which work may be specialized is ultimately limited, for forces begin to work in the direction of diminishing returns. These forces may be either internal or external, social or physical. For example, work simplification may require additional supervisory personnel or an increase in the closeness of supervision. Fatigue, alienation, discontent, or a higher labor turnover can result from an increase in the degree of task specialization. Fatigue may arise from the repetitiveness of tasks; alienation may be the result of tasks excessively narrowed in scope; discontent could reflect the inability to use or extend personal skills. Turnover could increase as a result of any of the factors just mentioned, and it could increase if opportunities for internal advancement were low and external jobs were readily available. In all these ways, internally and externally, constraining conditions can reduce the technological effectiveness of work simplification and raise its costs.

The division of work is a vital element in organizational effectiveness, especially in a technologically-based industrial society. In American business the division of work is usually regarded as the crucial determinant of effectiveness. Here the managerial decision-maker treats the division of work as an independent variable and tries to adjust the hierarchy of authority and the distributive system to the priorities assigned to work specialization. Indeed, the argument that the division of work is fundamentally a technological consideration has often been advanced by management when its prerogatives in this area have been contested by unions. According to management, unions prevent the proper achievement of organizational efficiency by preventing development of an adequate division of work, and, consequently, distribution of organizational rewards and dispersion of power.

□ 3. HIERARCHY

A hierarchy consists of an orderly system of roles, authority flows, and jurisdictional rights arranged so that the occupants of higher positions determine the activities of those at lower levels. When A's preferences are formalized into a set of rules and regular expectations that act to bind B's behavior, A can predict the behavior of B. Although B can also affect the behavior of A, legitimate authority usually produces a basic asymmetry of influence because greater compliance can be demanded of B than of A. For example, A may initiate B's tasks, provide for his recruitment, control his rewards, construct his communication channels, formulate norms for his performance, judge his performance, decide on the continuance of his employment, and determine his successor. However, A's control over B is always limited to some designated range within any hierarchical order. This range is formalized by organizational rank and the assignment of tasks as well as by informal agreement.

The functional extent of authority is not determined by managerial fiat alone. B's compliance to A also depends upon the support, opposition, or neutrality B brings to A's directives. Consequently, the degree of authority exercised by A is partly determined by B's ability to resist where there is conflict of interest. His capacity to resist will depend upon such things as the degree to which he accepts A's goals and inducements, and the sanctions he can impose on A by varying the activities required of him. Normally there will be some areas in which B will oppose A and try to modify the situation to his advantage but as soon as B acknowledges a set of rules and expectations there is a range of undisputed activity he routinely performs.

Performance of expected activities implies neither support nor opposition. It does imply neutrality, but a neutrality that is always fluctuating. The quality of neutrality — its movement towards support or opposition — depends upon such things as morale, identification, satisfactions, rewards, reference group comparisons, organized opposition, ideology, and so on. A decline in the rewards offered by A or an increase in B's dissatisfaction can shift B's active support to neutral compliance or to active opposition that brings hierarchical rules into contest. Thus, the actual functioning of the hierarchy results from controlling forces, on the one hand, and the opposition to this control, on the other. This interplay creates shifting margins of legitimacy. The organizational hierarchy is itself bounded by environmental constraints that limit the patterns of inducement, the range of neutrality, and the opportunities for effective resistance. For example, the formation of a union might alter the range of neutrality and the opportunity for resistance by reinforcing differentially the values and claims of particular groups within the hierarchy.

In a highly authoritarian organization, the upper levels of the hierarchy will normally be the principal initiators of those changes which originate within the organization. This is partly because changes in the rules initiated at lower levels are usually seen as destructive of the legitimate authority of higher administration. The elaboration of formal rules of control, commonly referred to as "red tape," is one way in which upper administration protects itself from this erosion of control. It sharply constrains the prerogatives of participants. The participants, on the other hand, try to use the rules for their own purposes. An unusual illustration of this tendency occurred when the New York City policemen, protesting a decision of the higher political authority, threatened to undermine that authority by rigidly adhering to the rules of their organization.

The groups that support a given change and the groups that oppose it are often located at different levels of hierarchy and have unequal authority. If the authority of upper management is truly effective, a change in the rules that benefits higher administration will be easier to introduce than a change that benefits less powerful component groups. The more powerful groups can disregard losses sustained by weaker members. Therefore, the degree of centralization of authority is a crucial factor in explaining organizational response to change. Changes can be most effectively introduced when all groups gain and the more powerful decision-making groups gain the most.

The acceptance of change by the component groups depends upon how their welfare is affected. Where all participants benefit, even though their gain is not proportional, the resistance to change will be the lowest. Resistance will be slight if the change introduced yields large benefits to some powerful groups and leaves others either indifferent or likely to experience little dissatisfaction.

In instances in which the welfare of one group can improve only at the expense of the other, change is usually accompanied by conflict, but conflict usually does not occur over all matters. Conflict and bargaining are responses to change occurring beyond the area in which authority is accepted. The party in the stronger bargaining position is likely to gain the greater welfare position. When this happens, a change that improves the welfare position of the stronger party will be more readily accepted than one that benefits the weaker side. In short, the greater the relative bargaining power of one party, the greater will be the likelihood that further change in his favor will be instituted and that change unfavorable to him will be resisted.

What is the extent of hierarchical authority? We have seen that A's influence over B is not determined by managerial decision alone. The extent of authority is also established by the participants as groups that may support, oppose, or be neutral to hierarchical order. The range within which the hierarchical order is accepted, that is, where Group B routinely complies with Group A's rules, is the area of legitimate authority. Conflict and bargaining occur at the outer limits of this authority. The scope of hierarchical authority is marked by the number of rules acknowledged; its intensity, by the degree of compliance to any single rule.

An effective hierarchy insures the performance of tasks at some level of accomplishment. This level is flexible, but minimal fulfillment is essential for the organization's efficiency. Organizational inducements are maintained to support a reasonable level of accomplishment. The rules governing the distribution of sanction and reward, like the rules of authority, are normally arranged so that those at higher levels receive greater privileges than those beneath them. This reinforces hierarchic inequality, and it is usually assumed that unequal rewards and sanctions are necessary for control. Status, power, reduction of routine, personal freedom, and money are the chief rewards that vary with hierarchic levels. The question of how skewed this distribution of these rewards should be in order to achieve organizational effectiveness is continuously disputed. The distribution is resolved in practice by the interplay of three factors: the managerial need for control; the resistance of participants; and the constraints of environment.

□ 4. THE DISTRIBUTION OF REWARDS AND ORGANIZATIONAL WELFARE

As individuals and as groups, the participants in organization will find that their work meets their expectations in varying degrees. Some will derive personal satisfaction from the achievement of organization goals; others will differentiate between their personal goals and the goals of the organization, which usually serve the goals of higher administration. The kinds of satisfaction available must be found within the rules and informal norms generated by the division of work and authority. These rules define and limit the welfare that is attainable to participants. The expectations of groups may be altered by rule changes, and a change in expectations affects the way groups react to the organization rules. This is because any change in the rules is likely to alter the distribution of welfare, moving some groups into more favored positions.

Rule changes may benefit only a few participants in the organization or they may diffuse benefits widely throughout the system. A computer that is mainly capital-saving primarily benefits the managerial groups; an improvement in safety procedures benefits many groups in the organization. Ordinarily the computer will not be resisted unless its use shifts the established distribution of welfare. However, if the computer not only improves efficiency but also yields substantial increase in profits, there will probably be argument over how the additional profit ought to be shared. Similarly, changes in safety rules could shift the relative distribution of welfare to component groups if additional supervision is required to administer the new rules or if the productivity of some groups is reduced. In general, slight negative alterations in the balance of welfare distribution can be compensated for by an adjustment of rewards to affected groups.

Therefore, organizational welfare may be described as a complex of various states of value-fulfillment. Some groups, particularly managerial groups, consider the collective goals of organization as their own. They identify with the larger organization and achieve status or personal fulfillment when its goals are accomplished. They are usually the first to gain from organizational growth or improvements in the organization's status or power. By making managerial standards their own component groups assimilate their private values to the organization's collective goals. When the performance of specific tasks is not a result of such identification, the subordination of private values is usually necessary, so that the collective goals of organization are felt to provide a constraint.

Still, welfare is not a private matter, dependent upon private expectations. Individuals and groups may resemble each other in relation to their wages, in the type of work they do, or in their hierarchic position. When groups experience common constraints they often share expectations; large classes of participants often hold approximately identical welfare positions. The generalization of welfare states appears reasonable and normal if we contrast management and workers or officers and enlisted men, since welfare can then be treated as a common condition or as an aggregate of the positions of member groups.

Aggregation of this sort is not particularly useful where there are wide differences between groups and sharply varying systems of constraints. Also, from the point of view of the individual group, a welfare state may seem difficult to assess. When one group observes another closely, small differences often appear very large. Nevertheless, welfare states may be evaluated on several bases.

Welfare may be assessed for the organization as a whole, it may be proportionally determined among groups within the organization, or it may be related to welfare states outside the organization. In the first case, welfare is measured by an internal standard, for example, in relation to bases established by the highest and lowest levels of the organization. In the second case, we take into account the fact that groups are surrounded by other groups, and that contiguity within an organization often encourages comparison of welfare levels. The reference group can be in a similar hierarchic position. (One vice-president will keep a sharp eye on the quality of carpeting in another vice-president's office.) Or it may concern the preservation of differentials between one level and another. Finally, the welfare of one group can be compared externally with the level of welfare achieved by a similar group in another organization. Professional groups in one organization use professional groups in other organizations as their standard of comparison.

What factors enter into the evaluation of welfare? Such things as the extent of organizational democracy or authoritarianism, the degree of routinization, the opportunities for advancement, and the wage and salary structure must be taken into account. Turnover and absenteeism may be evidence of the dissatisfaction of individual groups. However, intra-organizational differences mean that the components' welfare states are not directly comparable. The assessment of welfare finally depends upon the scope and intensity of organizational rules in relation to the expectations of member groups.

The division of work, the authority system, and the distribution of rewards and sanctions supply values that affect the member groups. The member groups react to these values in terms of their preferences, which encompass such things as styles of leadership, morale, existing levels of satisfaction, group norms, communication patterns, level in the hierarchy, reference groups, ethnic heritage, or bargaining power. The relation between the actual rules and the preferred rules can help explain organizational resistance to change, providing a basis for the analysis of tensions and conflict. In principle, this relation can be systematically presented.

Designate the rules that act on an individual or member group in an organization by $[r_o]$ and the total supply of rules as $[R_O]$, where $R_O = \sum r_o$.[1] A desired arrangement of these rules for a member group will be $[r_o^*]$, while $[R_O^*]$ indicates the aggregation of member group preferences. It will be assumed that r_o and r_o^* can be given ordinal ranking and treated transitively. Characteristically, r_o^* is larger than r_o and $R_O^* > R_O$.

The rules that act on a member group can be broken down into three sub-sets: rules of work $[r_w]$, of authority $[r_a]$, and of distribution $[r_d]$. For any group, the rules that act on it, $[r_o]$, are the sum of r_w, r_a and r_d: $r_o = r_w + r_a + r_d$. The total collection of rules for any given sector will be R_W, R_A, or R_D, a summation in which $R_{W,A,D} = \sum r_{w,a,d}$.

Member groups will have preferences for a particular arrangement of rules r_o^*. The r_o^* for any member group can itself be decomposed into preferences for work r_w^*, for authority r_a^*, or for distribution r_d^*. Since an individual group might care a great deal about authority and little about material rewards (e.g., the military), the definition, $[r_o^* = ar_w^* + br_a^* + cr_d^*]$, requires coefficients a, b, and c which state the relative importance of the differential preference for the values of work, authority, or distribution. A preference pattern aggregating many individual groups could then be expressed as $R_O^* = aR_W^* + bR_A^* + cR_D^*$. R_O^* then clearly states two aspects of expectations. It expresses the expectations of member groups and it states a common pattern of values.

Such a summation is possible when the preferences of the groups being aggregated are comparable. A consensus among group members could then be achieved by voting; in practice, this is implied in the idea of representative government by unions. Questionnaire or other forms of testing (e.g., sociom-

---

[1] The connections among symbols are to be understood as composition rules and not as arithmetical statements.

etric devices) elicit member preferences. Collective patterns of belief can be stated in the norms, common values, and goals which come to characterize organizations and its sub-systems.

For an individual sector, the expression $[r^*_{w,a,d}] - [r_{w,a,d}]$ states the distance between the rules of work, authority, and distribution a group wants and the rules it faces. In turn, $\dfrac{r_o{}^* - r_o}{r_o{}^*}$ expresses the welfare position of any group as a relationship between the situation desired and the situation that exists.

Groups seeking to achieve their own goals try to move r_o toward $r_o{}^*$, and their success is measured by the reduction of distance between $r_o{}^*$ and r_o. If r_o must be taken as fixed, groups have three alternatives. They may adjust their preferences accordingly; they may retain their preferences but resign themselves to the given state of affairs; or they may leave the situation they cannot improve. In terms of power, a fixed r_o reflects the position of zero autonomy that obtains when other groups have set the rules and are in a position to demand compliance. Usually, r_o is not totally inflexible, but will show some sensitivity to groups acting to shift its values. The sensitivity of r_o is not a constant; the ability to alter the rules of work, authority, or distribution depends upon the relative power of the competing groups. (Nevertheless, as we will see, r_o is sensitive only within a range, since it is constrained by the limitations imposed by environmental conditions.)

The relative power among groups can be described in terms of expectations and rules. Consider a component group, A, to be constrained by the expectations and rules of Group B, ($r_B{}^*$ and r_B). If the fulfillment of $r_B{}^*$ or r_B reduces the capabilities of A to fulfill its own goals, then the power of A over B is defined as the ability to change $r_B{}^*$ or r_B in the direction of A's goals. This implies that other groups, such as B, try to maintain the initial, preferred values of r^* and r. Thus, a group at a lower level in an administrative structure has power over a higher level to the degree that it can induce the superior group to accept lower standards of performance than it would like. An administrative group has power over a lower one when it can induce the subordinate group to accept a lower welfare position. Therefore, power can be described by changes in r^* or r brought about by techniques of persuasion, influence, bargaining or coercion.

The change in welfare, that is, in $\dfrac{r_o{}^* - r_o}{r_o{}^*}$, suggests a measure of stress. A's ability to alter the expectations of B is also A's capability to resist the stress that arises as B's expectations remain unfulfilled. An increase in stress reflects effort on the part of the party whose welfare position is unfavorable (B) to improve the surrounding conditions. When the distance between $r_o{}^*$ and r_o is great, and the dissatisfied groups cannot by their own action reduce this stress, a power relation is evidenced. If the stress that results from the inability of the weaker party, B, to achieve a more satisfactory welfare position is acceptable to the stronger party, A, then B's high expectations and A's constraining rules can be simultaneously maintained in a context of high stress. Under this condition a group may satisfactorily fulfill the demands of authority, perform its assigned tasks, and function in a context of low satisfaction. Thus a system may be unresponsive to pressures by dissatisfied groups and tolerate a high degree of internal stress if power is significantly asymmetrical. This is a common feature of authoritarian structures.

□ 5. ENVIRONMENT AND THE ADJUSTMENT OF PARTS

An organization can respond to environment as an integrated whole or by adjustments among the individuated parts. Theories that deal with an organization and its environment usually assume the adjustment of the whole, analyzing the organization as though it were encased in a virtual boundary or skin that separates internal factors from the external influences acting on them. As a consequence, there is a break in the continuity between an organization and its external environment, a break determined by the thickness of the skin. In decision theories, for example, environment is discriminated as external to the organization and the rationally designed policies of the decision-maker become the instrument of organizational response to environment. Decision systems are seen as analogous to homeostatic mechanisms that keep the organization moving towards its goals by the continual formation of rational policy. In general, it is assumed that internal mechanisms create an integral response of the whole to environmental influences. Sometimes homeostatic mechanisms reduce the impact of environmental forces by preserving the initial state of the system. At other times they rapidly diffuse external influences within the organization. The character and rapidity of the organizational reaction to environmental influences is determined by the properties attributed to the internal mechanisms of response.

Organizational response may be analyzed as the result of individual adjustments of the parts as well as by holistic, homeostatic theories of response. By minimizing the integral response of homeostatic mechanisms, environmental effects on individual parts become highly visible. Organizational sensitivity and response to environment must then be explained by the behavior of the parts.

The sensitivity of an organization — which we have called the thickness of the skin — may also be formulated as the continuity of the organization with its environment. It is a relation between an environmental influence and the kind and degree of response that internal factors are permitted to express. In general, external influences penetrate the organizational system by providing limits on the range within which change in the parts can occur. An organizational factor, say, wages for a certain job, is internally determined insofar as it is the result of other internal variables — hierarchic level, working conditions, bargaining power, and the like. It is externally determined insofar as its value is determined by environmental factors — prevailing wages for that sort of job, availabilities of workers to fill it, occupational status, and so on. The difference between the internal and the external wage rate is normally produced by those factors that thicken the skin.

However, the desired sensitivity to particular environmental factors will vary with the organizational groups. Sometimes management wishes to increase the continuity with the environment. If other groups oppose, sensitivity may depend upon the organization's internal power structure. A strong central administration in a context of weakly organized groups with diffuse private goals can discount participant opposition to its policies. The more powerful group may bring about high conformity between internal and external conditions. Conversely, a weaker administrative authority in a context of well-formed and cohesive component groups may find itself unable to incorporate influences that are favorable to itself but not to the component groups.

How does environment affect organizational behavior? It influences the expectations of groups, the kinds of rules that can be made, and the amount of internal stress an organization must be prepared to sustain. An organization can also affect environmental factors directly.

First, the expectations of participants in organizations are formed by the values and opportunities present in the social environment. Participants compare the position, status, and well-being of their own group with those of other groups outside the organization and adjust their aspirations accordingly. Thus, r_o^* will be stated within limits suggested by the environment.

In an institution in which connection with the outside world has been removed by systematic techniques of indoctrination and coercive control, the participants' aspirations are determined by comparison with their peer groups within the structure, by reaction to the internal logic of authority and rewards, or by emergence of their own norms and status. In a total institution, a mental hospital or a prison, for example, individuals may prize such things as a bed near a window, occasional privileged relaxations of routine, or the status derived from having other inmates perform tasks assigned to them. In a closed system the r_o^* is almost totally a response to internally imposed conditions.

However, in highly open systems, r_o^* has important external determinants. Professionals such as scientists or engineers are often acutely aware of the material rewards and status achieved by their peers in other institutions. A physician will expect a hospital to fulfill minimum standards of cleanliness and to provide adequate equipment. More generally, competition may operate to make organizational conditions conform to social norms of the external world. People in organizations often take the market wage rate as their standard and adjust their expectations to this condition. The standards of other groups and organizations as well as market conditions in general limit the range of r_o^*. The extent to which the range has been narrowed depends upon the sensitivity of expectations to external influences.

Second, environment affects rules, which are formulated on the basis of the technological and social norms that relate to the assignment of work, authority, and rewards. We have pointed out that a shortage of skilled workers makes task simplification necessary. Skilled workers such as electricians cannot be assigned tasks that fall outside their craft. Unions often designate standards for job performance for its members, standards the business firm cannot significantly modify. The rapid promotion of college professors and the reduction in authoritarian line control in research and development organizations often are adjustments to environmental conditions. For instance, one would expect to find less authoritarian styles of administration among scientists than among general managers, not just because of the nature of scientific work but because of the high transferability of scientific skills. This mobility reduces the scientist's willingness to accept highly constraining work conditions. Thus we see that rules of work, authority, or distribution $(r_{w,a,d})$ receive many important modifying influences from the environment.

Third, environment affects the capability of the member groups to tolerate strain. Stress has been formulated as $\dfrac{r_o{}^* - r_o}{r_o{}^*}$ for individual groups, while $\dfrac{R_O{}^* - R_O}{R_O{}^*}$ summates this property over many groups. When stress focuses on a particular kind of rules, it may be expressed as: $\dfrac{r_{w,a,d}{}^* - r_{w,a,d}}{r_{w,a,d}{}^*}$.

Environment can act on the capacity for stress in a variety of ways. Stress may be general to a group and arise from the totality of the organizational situation, or it may focus on the scope and intensity of a subset of related rules. In wartime, soldiers accept stringent rules and unusually low welfare, conditions associated with high stress in the industrial world, because the total situation seems to make these conditions unavoidable. However, specific sources of high stress can be tolerated if the environment yields compensating advantages. Manual workers often accept highly constraining job routines because they see work as yielding only a small part of their total satisfactions; they often seek satisfaction in activities outside work. Stress that arises from a particular source, such as high routine, need not be felt equally by all groups. High stress that arises from a particular arrangement of rules may even be accompanied by high satisfaction with the rules as a whole. The fact that groups may have specific, rather than general, discontent helps explain why groups often do not act in concert. When the member groups of an organization exhibit sharp differences (in work, authority, reward), high stress among individual groups (or concerning a particular rule) may reduce their capability to consolidate for the kind of collective action that attempts to change the rules. Thus a balkanized system can sustain high stress without endangering the total organization's stability.

Finally, the organization can alter environmental factors directly. While small organizations cannot usually control their environment, some larger organizations can change the total setting in which they find themselves. Factors external to a small organization are often internal to a large one. For example, the business firm sees a market price as an external constraint. As the firm acquires monopoly power, however, its pricing policy increasingly becomes a matter of internal control. The increase in control over environment and the corresponding growth of internal discretionary power is accomplished by such familiar techniques as product differentiation, advertising, or restrictions on entry, that is, by exercising what the economist calls monopoly power. This is similar to the control over local politics that a large company frequently acquires in a small community.

The responsiveness of component parts to environmental factors describes the openness or sensitivity of the part. A group within an organization is normally sensitive to some set of environmental influences and insensitive to others, open to some internal forces and closed to others. Each group responds to those environmental factors according to the way its own capabilities for goal realization are affected. For instance, professional groups in organizations develop their own performance standards, which are often linked to external rather than to internal administrative criteria. Research physicians in a hospital would be highly sensitive to technological advances in medicine that occur externally. Should such a group decide that the hospital requires newly developed equipment, pressures would be put on the administration to make the necessary capital investment. In this way external conditions are introduced into organizations, initiating changes in expectations, rules, and welfare distribution.

Group preferences or organizational rules can show wide variations as a result of small changes in the environmental situation. Groups may react to the environment in ways that magnify or reduce this sensitivity. A university under external social pressure to admit students from disadvantaged groups may find the faculty unwilling to lower admission standards. The faculty is reacting to reduce the influence of the external social pressure. A magnification effect of the same pressures, on the other hand, may be evident in their willingness to give preferential treatment to Negro faculty members.

This transmission of external forces to the internal system need not occur deliberately, for groups inevitably develop mechanisms that tend to preserve their value-achieving capabilities. The loss in external status by a class of skilled workers can be reduced in its internal influence as workers support the symbols of their status (e.g., traditional craft ideals) or reinforce the rules that operate in their favor, (e.g., traditional craft methods). Such mechanisms are attempts to maintain the $(r_o{}^* - r_o)$ relation at a desired level. Mechanisms are defensive when they merely seek to prevent r_o from becoming less desirable; they are aggressive when they try to change the preferences or the rules of other groups.

When a group's sensitivity to environmental influences is reduced there is a complementary increase in the importance of internal forces. Behavior that was external is now internally determined. Many large corporations now finance their growth increasingly from internal capital sources rather than depend upon external capital markets. Some firms in the South have reduced racial discrimination more rapidly than has the local community. Policies that make this possible involve resisting influences from the local community and, occasionally, changing the external environment. These policies may alter the intensity of the rules of work, since compliance with the rules may have to be forced on prejudiced workers. When cafeteria and rest-room facilities formerly closed to Negroes are opened to them, the scope of the rules is also changed.

Groups enhance their control over environment by acting on group expectations (r_o*) or on rules (r_o), in general, by techniques that develop common goals, punish deviation from group standards, or enhance the group's bargaining power. Similarly, the organization as a whole reduces its sensitivity to environment by techniques such as indoctrination or the distribution of rewards and sanctions. Requiring a government official to sell his private property where there may be a conflict of interest, introducing pension plans that expire on leaving the organization, or maintaining an organization newspaper, are examples of the way organizations reduce sensitivity to environment.

The ability to limit the impact of an environmental factor is subject to diminishing returns. Groups cannot increasingly press for the achievement of their private goals, continuously improve their cohesiveness, or constantly better their bargaining position. The fulfillment of a goal usually requires the compromise or sacrifice of other goals. Participants may have competing demands from other groups or other roles and an increase in the efforts of one group often stimulates greater efforts on the part of other groups to maintain their initial positions. Nor can higher administration continuously increase the scope and effectiveness of its rules. The costs of rule enforcement rise as resistance to the new constraint increases.

Consider an organization in which the structure of rank and status is not consistent with standards prevailing elsewhere. The groups that desire change will exert pressure on other participants, who may be indifferent or in opposition to efforts to meet external standards. Opposition arises because change in a rank structure increases the relative deprivation of some groups. The initiators of change may be forced to compromise some goals as they make alliances with other groups. Goodwill can be exhausted, and resources of time, energy, or money can be drained. The status quo rarely goes undefended.

□ 6. CONCLUSION

I have presented a general explanation of organizations in which effectiveness, conflict, power, and environment appear not as separate problems but as part of a unified system of analysis. My starting point was the idea that member groups try to achieve their own ends while the larger goals of organization act to limit this achievement. In turn, organizational change is significantly determined by the interaction, conflict, and tension between member groups and systems of rules. However, I do not mean to say that conventional holistic and decision theories are erroneous points of departure. It is mainly that the axioms of individual difference implied in the independence of the parts permits systematic generalization of concepts that traditionally have eluded the main thrust of the theory. My belief is that theory drawn from micro-behavior axioms of individual and group difference could enormously sharpen our understanding of organizational behavior.

☐ BIBLIOGRAPHY

Barnard, Chester, *Functions of the Executive* (Cambridge: Harvard University Press, 1938).

Bertalanffy, Ludwig von, *Problems of Life* (New York: Harper, 1952, 1960).

Blau, Peter M., *Exchange and Power in Social Life* (New York:Wiley, 1964).

Boulding, Kenneth, *Conflict and Defense* (New York: Harper, 1962).

Boulding, Kenneth, *The Organizational Revolution* (New York: Harper, 1953).

Coser, Lewis, *Functions of Social Conflict* (Glencoe, Ill.: The Free Press, 1956).

Crozier, Michel, *The Bureaucratic Phenomenon* (Chicago: University of Chicago Press, 1964).

Caplow, Theodore, *Principles of Organization* (New York: Harcourt, Brace and World, 1964).

Dahl, Robert A., and Charles Lindblom, *Politics, Economics and Welfare* (New York: Harper, 1953).

Dahrendorf, Rolf, *Class and Class Conflict in Industrial Society* (Stanford: Stanford University Press, 1959).

Etzioni, Amitai, *A Comparative Analysis of Complex Organizations* (New York: The Free Press, 1961).

Friedmann, Georges, *Industrial Society* (New York: The Free Press, 1955).

Goffman, Erving, *Asylums* (New York: Doubleday, 1961).

Gouldner, Alvin W., *Patterns in Industrial Bureaucracy* (New York: The Free Press, 1954).

Gouldner, Alvin W., *Wildcat Strike* (Yellow Springs, Ohio: Antioch, 1954).

Krupp, Sherman, *Pattern in Organization Analysis* (New York: Holt, Rinehart and Winston, 1961).

Krupp, Sherman (ed.), *The Structure of Economic Science* (New York: Prentice-Hall, 1956).

Krupp, Sherman, "Equilibrium Theory in Economics and in Functional Analysis as Types of Explanation," *Functionalism in the Social Sciences*, Monograph No. 5 of the American Academy of Political and Social Science (Feb. 1965), pp. 65–83.

Krupp, Sherman with Eugene V. Schneider, "An Illustration of the Use of Analytical Theory in Sociology: The Application of the Economic Theory of Choice to Non-Economic Variables," *American Journal of Sociology*, Vol. XX, No. 6 (May 1965), pp. 695–703.

March, James and Herbert Simon, *Organizations* (New York: Wiley, 1958).

Olson, Mancur, *The Logic of Collective Action* (Cambridge: Harvard University Press, 1965).

Presthus, Robert, *The Organizational Society* (New York: Random House, 1962).

Rothernberg, Jerome, *The Measurement of Social Welfare* (New Jersey: Prentice-Hall, 1961).

Sayles, Leonard, *The Behavior of the Industrial Work Group* (New York: Wiley, 1958).

Selznick, Philip, *Leadership in Administration* (Evanston, Ill.: Row, Peterson, 1957).

Scott, William and Peter Blau, *Formal Organizations* (San Francisco: Chandler, 1962).

Simon, Herbert, *Administrative Behavior* (New York: Macmillan, 1945).

Suojanen, Waino, *The Dynamics of Management* (New York: Holt, Rinehart and Winston, 1966).

Thompson, Victor, *Modern Organization* (New York: Alfred Knopf, 1965).

Whyte, William Foote, *Money and Motivation* (New York: Harper, 1955).

Chapter 8

*Organizational Evaluation and Authority**

■ W. RICHARD SCOTT, SANFORD M. DORNBUSCH,
BRUCE C. BUSCHING & JAMES D. LAING

Authority systems in formal organizations are analyzed in terms of the process by which
the performance of organizational participants is evaluated. Authority is viewed as authorization to attempt to control the behavior of others, and rests in four different kinds of
authority rights, each of which is a component of the evaluation process. Authority
systems are defined in terms of the distribution of these rights among participants.

The theory specifies certain problems in the evaluation process, which make the
authority system incompatible with participants' achievement of evaluations acceptable
to them. Incompatible authority systems are postulated to be unstable and to remain so
until the incompatibility is resolved. A set of indices is developed for the identification of
unstable systems. This theory is the basis of a current study of authority systems in five
organizations.

This paper presents a conception of authority and authority systems, and a
theory predicting the instability of certain kinds of authority systems. Empirical
studies designed to explore the utility of the conception and to test hypotheses
derived from the theory are presently under way in a number of organizations.
In a forthcoming monograph and later papers, we shall discuss the operation-
alization of our concepts and report empirical findings.[1]

The conception of authority presented here is based on the process by which
performance evaluations of organizational participants are made. The conception is believed to be useful as a descriptive and analytic tool, independent
of the theory. Our intent has been to develop a formulation which is sufficiently
abstract to be applicable to a wide variety of concrete systems in many types of
organizations and specific enough to be useful in guiding the collection of
empirical data.

* This paper originally appeared in the *Administrative Science Quarterly* (June 1967).

[1] This research project is supported by National Science Foundation Grant G23990.
Collaborators on the project are Joseph Berger, Santo F. Camilleri, Bernard P. Cohen, and
Morris Zelditch, Jr. We are indebted for suggestions to Kathryn U. Barchas, Patricia Barchas,
Marjorie J. Seashore, James C. Moore, and Thomas R. Burns.

An early version of this paper, "Evaluation Processes and Authority Structures," was
read at the Annual Meetings of the American Sociological Association in Chicago, September,
1965.

162

The theory locates certain inconsistencies and deficiencies in the evaluation of the performance of an organizational participant that make the authority system incompatible with the participant's achievement of his personal goals. This incompatibility is predicted to be a sufficient condition for internal pressures for change in the authority system; i.e., for instability of the system.

Both conception and theory are limited in scope by the following conditions.

1. Organizational sanctions are distributed, at least in part, on the basis of evaluations made of participants.
2. Evaluators who influence the distribution of organizational sanctions attempt to base their evaluations, at least in part, on the performance of organizational tasks by participants.
3. Participants place some value on the evaluations of their task performance made by these evaluators.

The first and second conditions delimit the kind of organizations to which this conception of authority applies. The first condition excludes organizations in which sanctions are distributed independently of any evaluation of participants. (For example, where all rewards are distributed equally among participants.) The second condition excludes organizations in which, although sanctions may be distributed on the basis of evaluations, no attempt is made to base these evaluations even in part on how well or how poorly participants perform in organizational tasks. Thus, this condition excludes organizations in which evaluations are based entirely on status characteristics (such as ethnicity or seniority) or on other nonperformance criteria, even though in some cases these criteria may be related to performance. These conditions exclude very few organizations, however, at least in industrialized societies.

The third condition insures that the motivational basis of the theory is present by further delimiting the scope of the theory to those participants within the organization who place some value on the organizational sanctions themselves. It does require that they value the *performance evaluations* made of them by those who influence these sanctions. If performance evaluations were of no consequence to participants, they could ignore negative evaluations and could hardly be expected to become concerned about inadequacies in the way performance evaluations are made. (A rich boy working as a lark.) This condition, like the first two, is not very limiting. In an organizational context, most participants value their performance evaluations because at least some of the attendant sanctions are important to them. Furthermore, performance evaluations often possess symbolic value of their own, in part because of their importance to the development and maintenance of one's self-conception.[2]

Although based on the work of many predecessors, the conception described

[2] S. F. Miyamoto and Sanford M. Dornbusch, A Test of Interactionist Hypotheses in Self-Conception, *American Journal of Sociology*, 61 (1956), 399–403; L. G. Reeder, G. A. Donohue, and A. Biblarz, Conceptions of Self and Others, *American Journal of Sociology*, 66 (1960), 153–159.

here has some elements of novelty. Comparisons with previous perspectives are made after defining the concept, and then the theory is presented.

Authority as Authorized Control

In this paper the concept of authority is defined in terms of authorization to engage in certain attempts at control. One participant has authority over another to the extent that his control attempts are "authorized"; i.e., would be supported by superiors in the organization. A participant who is authorized to exercise a given control attempt over another is said to have an *authority right* over the other with regard to that attempt. Four different kinds of control attempts can be identified; when authorized, these constitute authority rights.

The process by which the performance of organizational participants is evaluated plays two major roles in this concept of authority. First, its importance is seen in the types of control attempts identified. These control attempts, and therefore the authority rights themselves, are chosen to embody the main components of the evaluation process: allocating, criteria setting, sampling, and appraising. These rights are identified in part because they are often assigned in various combinations to different participants. (The superintendent may allocate the job, engineers may set the criteria for acceptable tolerance limits, foremen may select the sample to be evaluated, and inspectors may be the appraisers.) Also, each of these rights can become a locus of problems in the authority system. Although other rights can be constructed within the general definition of an authority right, this set is sufficient for the analysis of most authority systems.

Second, the evaluation process is basic to this concept of authority since authorization stems from *significant evaluators* — those whose evaluations influence the distribution of organizational sanctions. By definition, *A* is said to be authorized to exercise a given control attempt over *B* with respect to a given task to the extent that:

1. the significant evaluators of *A*, if aware that *A* was attempting this kind of control over *B*, would not negatively evaluate *A* for making the attempt, and
2. the significant evaluators of all participants whose compliance is necessary for the success of *A*'s attempt to control *B*, if aware of noncompliance to the attempt, would negatively evaluate those not complying.

Note that this general definition allows for varying degrees of authorization. *A*'s authorization is incomplete if, for example, some evaluators require, while others prohibit, compliance with *A*'s control attempts. Problems arising from incomplete authorization are considered later.

Authority Rights

The four authority rights can now be defined by applying the general definition to each of the kinds of control attempts. The first criterion in this general definition of an authority right applies consistently to *A* for each of the authority rights. Under the second criterion, the participants whose compliance is necessary for the success of *A*'s control attempts vary according to the specific authority right under consideration and must be specified in defining each right. In these definitions, and throughout the rest of the paper, "evaluator" and "evaluation" refer only to *significant* evaluators and evaluations.

To assign a goal is simply to give an individual the task of attempting to achieve that goal. An *allocating right* is the right to assign an organizational goal to a participant. (For example, an employer assigns a typist the task of typing a manuscript.) *A* has the right to allocate to *B* to the extent that: (1) *A* would not be negatively evaluated for allocating, and (2) *B* would be negatively evaluated for noncompliance with *A*'s allocation.

Allocations vary in the amount of discretion they permit the recipient in performing the task. To facilitate the discussion, two polar types on this continuum are identified:

1. *Directive*, in which the particular operations to be performed are specified, leaving the performer minimal discretion in determining how to proceed. (For example, a typist is told to type a letter from dictation.)
2. *Delegation*, in which only the characteristics of the desired end result are specified, with the performer allowed to make the decisions on how to proceed. (For example, a typist is told to answer a letter.)

It is quite possible for occupants of a given position to have the right to allocate a given task only by directive or only by delegation. (Private physicians may be authorized to allocate to resident physicians in a hospital only by delegation, while the residents are authorized to allocate certain medical routines to clinical clerks only by directive.) Approximations of these two types of allocations can usually be distinguished empirically, but rarely are they perfectly represented. Directives cannot be detailed enough to specify all operations of the performance to be carried out; some decisions are always left to the performer. Thus, even the typist told to follow a standard format in the preparation of letters may still be allowed to determine which sheet of paper to use and the order in which the letters are to be prepared. Likewise, delegations do not usually allow the performer complete discretion, although, if genuine, they will allow him considerable latitude. Many allocations appear to be delegations to a naive observer, but because they occur in the context of an understood set of standard operating procedures, they are actually directives. For example, when an intern is told by a resident to "Bring this patient's fever down," he may know from past experience that he is to carry out a set of established procedures. Misunderstandings among participants can occur when directives are mistaken for delegations and vice versa, and can cause problems in the evaluation of performances.

A *criteria-setting right* is the right to specify those performance properties to be considered, their weights or relative importance, and the standards to be used in determining a performance evaluation. Those holding this right, therefore, are authorized to determine which properties of the performance of another will be considered and what evaluation is merited by any given level of performance. (For evaluating a manuscript typist, the criteria-setter may decide that, with no errors, a speed of at least forty words per minute is necessary for an evaluation of "good," and a minimum of sixty words per minute is required for "excellent.") A has the right to set criteria for B to the extent that: (1) A would not be negatively evaluated for setting criteria, and (2) B's appraiser would be negatively evaluated by his own evaluator for failure to use A's criteria in evaluating B.

The *outcome* of a task performance is the actual end result of a performance, in contrast to the desired end result, defined by the goal. A performance evaluation may be based on assessment of the characteristics of the performance of the task operations or on assessment of the characteristics of the task outcome. In either case, information on the actual performance or the outcome must be obtained. A *sampling right* is the right to select aspects of performances or outcomes that will be observed to provide information for an evaluation. (For sampling a manuscript typist's work, the sampler decides to inspect every fourth page.) A has the right to sample B's performance to the extent that: (1) A would not be negatively evaluated for sampling, (2.1) B would be negatively evaluated for not allowing the observations specified by A, and (2.2) the appraiser would be negatively evaluated if he did not use information from the sample specified by A in evaluating B.

An *appraising right* is the right to decide how the level of performance is to be inferred from the sample and to apply the criteria to arrive at a performance evaluation. (The appraiser judges the manuscript typist's work to be excellent on the basis of number of completed pages, a count of errors in the sample, and the criteria that accuracy is a primary and speed a secondary criterion of performance.) Since, as noted earlier, only significant evaluations are considered, participants holding the appraising right are authorized to make performance evaluations which are considered in the distribution of organizational sanctions. For this particular right, only the first criterion is applicable. A has the right to appraise B's performance of a given task to the extent that: A would not himself be negatively evaluated for appraising B's performance.

Authority Systems

An authority right that is regularly exercised by one participant over another is termed an *authority link* between the two. The sum of all authority links connecting two participants constitutes, by definition, an *authority relationship* between the two. The constellation of all authority relationships of a participant, both with others over whom he exercises rights and with those who exercise rights over him, with respect to a given task constitutes his *authority system* for that task. (The following relationships may constitute the authority system of a resident physician in a teaching hospital with respect to diagnoses of patients assigned to his service: his chief resident exercises the rights of allocating patients to him and of sampling and appraising his diagnostic performance; certain faculty members exercise their rights to set criteria, sample and appraise him; and the resident himself exercises all four rights over the interns, and also exercises the right to allocate tasks necessary to his diagnoses to nurses and laboratory technicians.)

The resident physician's authority system is a fairly complex one. Complexity of authority systems is a function of the total number of right holders and the extent to which there is differentiation among them. One source of differentiation involves the number of rights per right holder: in one system, one person may hold all four rights; in another, the four rights may be distributed among four or more individuals. Another kind of differentiation occurs when right holders only decide how their respective rights are to be exercised but do not themselves implement their decisions. For example, the person holding the right to decide how B's performance is to be sampled does not himself take the sample but directs another individual to do so.

In addition to examining an individual participant and his relevant authority system, authority can be analyzed as it is associated with positions. A *position* is a location within an organization whose occupants share a common organizational title and are members of the same organizational context. (Occupants of the position of quarterback on the first string of the varsity football team; nurses aides on the pediatrics ward, for example.)

An authority link is *structural* at a given position if the link is associated with the position itself, rather than with a particular occupant of the position. There need not be a complete correspondence between the relationships associated with a position and those associated with a particular occupant of that position. The exceptional competence, stupidity, or charm of a given occupant may produce discrepancies between his authority system and the system usually associated with the position. (A particular quarterback may not be authorized to allocate plays because of his inability to detect weaknesses in the opposition's defense, although other quarterbacks are not so restricted.) Authority relationships and systems are structural at a given position to the extent that the authority links comprising them are structural at that position. The set of structural links for a given position, i.e., that portion of occupants' authority systems which is structural, constitutes the *authority structure* at that position. Although more inclusive units of analysis can be constructed from these concepts, in this paper systems and structures are defined from the perspective of a focal position and task.[3]

---

[3] This conception has characteristics that can readily be modified for other analytic purposes: (1) As we have indicated, other authority rights can be identified (e.g., the right to select personnel for occupancy of a given position). (2) A similar authority system model could be based upon evaluators whose significance is defined in terms of perceived importance of their evaluations to participants, whatever their influence in the distribution of organizational sanctions. (3) Finally, more inclusive authority systems and structures can be identified across positions or tasks.

□ COMPARISONS WITH PREVIOUS CONCEPTIONS

At this point, it is appropriate to compare the concept of authority developed in this paper with some previous conceptions. Since for an authority right to exist those subordinate to its exercise are subject to negative evaluations, ultimately, negative sanctions for noncompliance, some may argue that we are studying power rather than authority. But our approach emphasizes the extent to which a participant is allowed by others in the organization to exercise control. *A* is authorized to exercise specified control attempts over *B* to the extent that significant evaluators permit him to attempt the control and require the compliance of others with the attempt. This definition makes it clear that we are concerned only with a particular kind of power: that which is authorized by other organizational participants. Authorized power, reflecting the interests of interdependent organizational members, tends to be circumscribed in its domain and regulated in its exercise. In short, we propose to study authority systems as the distribution of authorized power across persons or positions in organizations.

This view of authority can be compared with those of two influential organizational theorists, Max Weber and Chester I. Barnard. Weber[4] focused attention on the motivations of the subordinate group in his definition of an authority system as a legitimate power system: a system in which differences in power between *A* and *B* are justified by a set of beliefs that define the exercise of control by *A* and its acceptance by *B* as appropriate. Weber showed in his well-known typology how different systems of beliefs — traditional, charismatic, or legal — provide the bases for different kinds of authority structures.

Basing the definition of authority on the concept of legitimacy permits the investigator to explore the various kinds of "resources" upon which authority may rest. Many investigators have reported that perceived legitimacy may be a function of the technical competence or the interpersonal skills of an individual, as well as of his occupancy of an organizational position. One perhaps unanticipated consequence of interest in the resources upon which authority rests has been a tendency to take the formal authority structure as given and to focus attention exclusively on departures from it in informal arrangements. Approaching the study of authority from the perspective of authorized power facilitates consideration of both informal and formal authority, i.e., of both systems and structures.

From this point of view, legitimacy, if defined as the amount of congruence between the norms of subordinates and the distribution of power, is an important variable affecting the operation of an authority system. But legitimacy, in this sense, is not used as the defining criterion of authority. We wish to be able to speak of illegitimate authority systems as well as of legitimate ones. A subordinate may acknowledge that his superior exercises certain rights over him and is supported by the organization in their exercise, and yet believe

[4] Max Weber, *The Theory of Social and Economic Organization*, trans. A. M. Henderson and Talcott Parsons (New York: Oxford, 1947).

that his superior should not have been accorded those rights. That is, *B* may acknowledge *A*'s rights and still question their legitimacy. Empirically, our conception, if applied in terms of the perception of participants, places emphasis on the question, "Does *B* believe that *A has* authority rights over him?" but at the same time permits the question, "Does *B* believe that *A should have* authority rights over him?"

Some evidence for the utility of this distinction between legitimacy and authorization comes from two experimental studies of authority. In the first, Raven and French[5] reported that whether a superior was perceived as the legitimate occupant of his office (elected to office *vs.* usurping office) did not affect the degree of public conformity exhibited by his subordinates. In the second, Evan and Zelditch[6] found that variations in the perceived competence of the supervisor did not significantly affect subordinates' felt obligation to obey. The compliance reported in these experiments was little affected by the manipulation of perceived legitimacy and may be interpreted to rest on perceived authorization. In the Raven and French experiment, authorization could stem from the inaction of the experimenter, who did not attempt to control or remove the usurper,[7] and in the Evan and Zelditch study, from the presumed organizational support for the supervisor's decisions. This is not to argue that legitimacy is an unimportant variable in the study of authority. We suggest later that perceptions of legitimacy have an important effect on the ways in which subordinates attempt to resolve incompatibilities in the authority system.

In some respects, our concept of authority is similar to that developed by Barnard.[8] Barnard's view that authority resides in the authenticated "authorized communications" from an office appears to be consistent with our approach. Barnard recognizes the importance of sanctions to participants through his emphasis on orders being acceptable to subordinates only if they are consonant with their personal interests. We would only add that if the distribution of sanctions is perceived to be affected by the evaluation process, then this is an important reason why evaluations themselves can become important to participants. Barnard's view of authority differs from our approach, however, in that it contains elements of legitimacy that supplement his concern with authorization; his "zone of indifference" argument places emphasis on what orders subordinates will accept automatically. The two approaches are also put to a different use. Barnard uses the distribution of sanctions (incentives, in his terms) in order to explain the continued participa-

---

[5] Bertram H. Raven and John R. P. French, Jr., Legitimate Power, Coercive Power, and Observability in Social Influence, *Sociometry*, 21 (1958), 83–97.

[6] William Evan and Morris Zelditch, Jr., A Laboratory Experiment on Bureaucratic Authority, *American Sociological Review*, 26 (1961), 883–893.

[7] For a discussion of the unanalyzed effects on subject behavior of the role played by the experimenter, see Theodore M. Mills, A Sleeper Variable in Small Groups Research: The Experimenter, *Pacific Sociological Review*, 5 (Spring 1962) 21–28.

[8] Chester I. Barnard, *The Functions of the Executive* (Cambridge, Mass.: Harvard University, 1938).

tion of members in the organization. We also focus on the distribution of sanctions, as determined by the evaluation process. However, rather than emphasizing exclusively the decision to participate, we wish to account for one source of instability of authority systems which regulate the day-to-day behavior of participants.

An important feature of our view of authority, which differentiates it from previous conceptions, is its emphasis on the extent to which authority rights may be task-specific. *A*'s authority rights over *B* may be limited to a specific task. In complex organizations, it is possible for an individual to participate in a large number of authority systems. For example, the authority system in which an intern in a teaching hospital participates for the task of developing a therapeutic plan may depend on how the patient was admitted to the ward. For some patients, the intern reports to the patient's private physician; for others, he reports to an attending physician assigned to the ward. For other tasks, such as the clinical instruction of medical students, the intern may participate in still another authority system under the chief resident, and so forth. Concepts of authority which fail to recognize that authority may be limited in domain to a specific task encourage the investigator to oversimplify authority systems which are actually very complex.

The close relationship between the evaluation process and authority has been implicitly recognized by many students of organizations, although it has not been systematically examined. Some investigators have described evaluation systems designed to improve managerial control and have detailed how such systems can fail.[9] Others have examined the difficulty of establishing valid and reliable criteria for the evaluation of professionals. Vollmer[10] has investigated the difficulty in evaluating the performance of research and development personnel; and Freidson and Rhea[11] have studied problems in the evaluation of clinic physicians by their peers and the consequent difficulties in control by the professional group. Also of interest is the work of Jaques[12] who has empirically explored the idea that responsibility can be measured by the length of time between successive evaluations by a superior. These studies, together with many others, indicate that we are not alone in recognizing the importance of the evaluation process for the study of organizational behavior.

☐ **INCOMPATIBILITY AND INSTABILITY**

Incompatibility of Authority Systems

Given that participants attach some importance to the evaluations made of

[9] See Joseph S. Berliner, *Factory and Manager in the USSR* (Cambridge, Mass.: Harvard University, 1957); Peter M. Blau, *The Dynamics of Bureaucracy* (Chicago: University of Chicago, 1955); and Melville Dalton, *Men Who Manage* (New York: John Wiley, 1959).

[10] Howard M. Vollmer, *Applications of the Behavioral Sciences to Research Management: An Initial Study in the Office of Aerospace Research* (Menlo Park, Calif.: Stanford Research Institute, November, 1964). Mimeo.

[11] Eliot Freidson and Buford Rhea, Processes of Control in a Company of Equals, *Social Problems*, 11 (1963), 119–131.

[12] Elliot Jaques, *The Measurement of Responsibility* (Cambridge, Mass.: Harvard University, 1956)

their performance by evaluators who influence the distribution of organizational sanctions, we make the important assumption that the participant will attempt to maintain, i.e., both achieve in the present and insure for the future, evaluations of his performance at a level which is satisfactory to him.[13] The minimal level of a performance evaluation for a given task which is satisfactory to a participant is the participant's *acceptance level* with regard to that evaluation. The acceptance level for an individual may change over time and may differ among participants; some may be satisfied with a rating of "fair," while others are satisfied only with "excellent." Moreover, the level of evaluation that is satisfactory to the participant being evaluated may not be the same level that satisfies the evaluator. Some participants may have higher expectations for themselves than their evaluators, whereas others may be satisfied with low evaluations even though their evaluators are dissatisfied.

An authority system is here called *incompatible* if it prevents the participant from maintaining his evaluations at or above his acceptance level and *compatible* if it does not prevent the participant from maintaining evaluations of his performance at his acceptance level. Thus, an authority system is incompatible if the set of exercised rights is either incomplete or contains elements that conflict in a way which causes the system to prevent the participant from maintaining his evaluations at a level satisfactory to him. Systems may also be ranked by degrees of incompatibility. In general, the more frequently incompatibilities occur for the participant, and the more important to him are the evaluations that cannot be maintained at a level acceptable to him, the greater is the incompatibility of the authority system.

If a given authority system is structural, then the structure may be compatible for some occupants of the position and incompatible for others because, as noted, individuals may have different acceptance levels. For instance, a structure that prevents maintenance of evaluations at the level of "excellent," but allows maintenance at the level of "good" is incompatible only for individuals with a very high acceptance level, thus perhaps being incompatible for only a few occupants of the structure. An authority structure is incompatible to the extent that occupants of its focal position are subjected to incompatibility.

Sources of Incompatibility

Four sources of incompatibility are identified: (1) contradictory evaluations, (2) uncontrollable evaluations, (3) unpredictable evaluations, and (4) unattainable evaluations. These four sources are expressed as four types of incompatibility.

TYPE I — CONTRADICTORY EVALUATIONS. An authority system is incompatible if it places the participant in a situation in which the receipt of one performance evaluation at least equal to his acceptance level necessarily

[13] Alternative motivational assumptions could be considered in a similar theoretical framework. The participant's desire to have his evaluations be *appropriate*, i.e., accurately reflect the skill and effort he invests in his task performance, is an assumption which may be added in future formulations

entails the receipt of another performance evaluation below his acceptance level.

This type of incompatibility is produced by a contradiction between the evaluations of two different evaluators, or the inconsistency of two different evaluations by a single evaluator. The participant finds that doing the kind of work required to receive one evaluation high enough to satisfy him necessarily involves incurring another evaluation so low as to make him dissatisfied. This problem may occur during the evaluation of a single task or of two or more tasks. An individual may be negatively evaluated for not working fast enough; yet if he were to increase his speed, he would be negatively evaluated for not working carefully enough. Or, evaluators may expect a participant to perform mutually exclusive tasks simultaneously.

This type of incompatibility may also occur when an individual receives evaluations both on his performance leading to an outcome and on the outcome itself. In this case, the contradiction may occur between the kind of performances allowed and the kinds of outcomes expected. Such a contradiction frequently occurs when a participant is allocated a task by directive but evaluated on the basis of a sample of outcomes. An appraiser may expect results that are impossible to achieve by following the particular course the allocator has directed. For this reason, a participant who receives allocations by directive is more likely to be subjected to incompatibility of this type if outcomes of his performance are sampled rather than the performance itself. The more routine the task, the more likely that criteria-setters will understand and agree on what can be expected of participants, and also the easier it is for the sampler to decide on samples that are representative; thus, the probability of this type of incompatibility is reduced with more routine tasks.

Complexity of the system also increases the probability of this type of incompatibility. The more differentiated the authority system, i.e., the greater the extent to which each of the rights are separately held, and the greater the number of participants exercising rights in the system, the greater the chance of failure in coordination.[14] For example, different allocators may allocate conflicting tasks to a participant. If this conflict is not considered by the evaluators, the participant may not be able to avoid receiving an evaluation below his acceptance level.

TYPE II — UNCONTROLLABLE EVALUATIONS. An authority system is incompatible if it places the participant in a situation in which he receives evaluations below his acceptance level for performances or outcomes he does not control.

This type of incompatibility occurs when the outcomes that serve as a basis

[14] This reasoning provides a rationale for the unity of command principle of the traditional school of administrative management; type II and IV incompatibilities are relevant to the traditional responsibility and control principle.

for the evaluation of a participant are not a regular function of that participant's performances from task to task. Therefore, to the extent that these uncontrollable outcomes are used as a basis for the evaluation of the participant's performance, he will be unable to control his evaluations through his performance. If this lack of control results in the participant receiving evaluations below his acceptance level, an incompatibility results.

The most obvious and simple instance of this failure occurs when an unsatisfactory performance or outcome is noted and the evaluation is wrongly assigned to a participant who neither performed the task nor had authority rights over the participant who did. (A nurse's aide may be negatively evaluated for mistakes committed by an orderly.)

Interdependence may be another source of this type of incompatibility. *Interdependence* is present when more than one participant contributes to a common outcome, which is used as the basis for evaluation. If evaluated outcomes are produced interdependently, they may not be related to a particular participant's performance; therefore, that participant may not be able to maintain his evaluation at his acceptance level because he cannot control the outcomes on which it is based. A competent decision maker may be prevented from maintaining evaluations satisfactory to him because of incompetent implementation of his decisions by others over whom he lacks authority rights. (An automobile designer is negatively evaluated for the poor appearance of the automobile, which is, actually, the result of inferior workmanship.) Conversely, a participant who implements another's faulty decision may be blamed incorrectly for an unsatisfactory outcome. (The workmanship is blamed for poor appearance, although the design is at fault.) Interdependence does not produce incompatibility if the participant has sufficient authority rights over the other contributors to control their common outcome; or if the performance of others is of such quality that the participant is not prevented from maintaining evaluations satisfactory to him. Given interdependence, the probability of this type of incompatibility increases to the extent that evaluations are based on outcomes rather than performance, particularly for those participants who have no rights over those with whom they are interdependent.

Attributes of the task may also produce this type of incompatibility. All tasks may be considered to involve the overcoming of some type of resistance. The resistance may be offered by nature, or by another person or a group. (A problem must be solved. A tunnel must be dug through rock. A company must produce a better product than its competitors.) If the resistance to a given task is known to be relatively constant from performance to performance, then the task is said to be *inert*. (A mile is to be run along the school track. Bills are posted in a ledger.) If the resistance is known to vary from performance to performance, then that task is considered to be *active*. (The general must capture a city. An election must be won.)

To evaluate the outcome of a task, the evaluator might employ standards that criteria-setters have determined by examining outcomes achieved by other performers on similar tasks. In the case of inert tasks, a valid inference to the quality of the performance can be made directly from comparisons of the outcome achieved relative to outcomes obtained by others on similar tasks. Active tasks, however, are difficult to evaluate, because the variability of the resistance complicates the problem of inferring the quality of performance from the nature of the outcome.[15] The outcome of a good performance need not be success and often is failure. (The patient may die, even though the operation was performed well.)

Active tasks fall into two categories, based upon the degree of knowledge about the resistance to be overcome. First, even though the resistance is variable, it is sometimes possible to have specific knowledge about it for a particular task performance. (The strength of the opposition meeting the general in a given battle is known. A tunnel is dug through strata of known composition.) The evaluation of each task performance can thus validly be based on the assessment of the outcome, if one also considers the resistance encountered in that particular task. Secondly, if the resistance encountered in a single performance is unknown, there may yet be some knowledge of the distribution of resistance over a succession of performances. This knowledge permits appraisers to take a probabilistic approach to the evaluations of these active tasks. The proportion of successful outcomes can be compared to the results of other performances under like circumstances. (The death rate for all premature babies provides a valid measure of the performance of a pediatrics unit, but only if the sample and comparison group do not differ in the assignment of difficult cases.)

Thus, given active tasks, the probability of this type of incompatibility increases to the extent that evaluations are based on outcomes rather than on performances, unless the resistance is considered, or probabilistic interpretations are made. Professionals employed by organizations are usually allocated more active tasks than are nonprofessionals. The professional, therefore, seeks direct measures of the quality of performance; or, if results are used, he demands probabilistic approaches to comparable outcomes.[16]

TYPE III — UNPREDICTABLE EVALUATIONS. An authority system is incompatible if it places the participant in a situation in which he receives evaluations below his acceptance level because he is unable to predict the relationship between attributes of his performance and the quality of the evaluation.

This type of incompatibility occurs when the participant has insufficient or incorrect information about the properties, weights, and standards by which he is evaluated, and therefore is unable to adjust his performance to maintain evaluations at his acceptance level. Those being evaluated need not, of course, know all the details of the evaluation process, but only enough to be sufficiently

[15] Under type IV incompatibility, the effect of active tasks upon the setting of standards will be considered.

[16] Everett C. Hughes has noted the probabilistic orientation of professionals in *Men and Their Work* (Glencoe, Ill.: The Free Press, 1958), p. 91.

able to predict evaluations from their performance so that they can make the adjustments in their behavior necessary to produce acceptable evaluations. Occupants of a position acting upon false information about the criteria used in their evaluation is an extreme instance of this type of incompatibility. (University faculty may be told and may act on the belief that community service, teaching, and research are all taken into account in the evaluations made of them, when, in practice, community service is not considered at all.) All those conditions which impede communication between the participant and his evaluators tend to increase the probability of this type of incompatibility.

Unpredictable evaluations may also be produced by an irregular relationship between the participant's performance and the evaluations he receives. To the extent that the sampler takes samples which are not representative of performance, the relationship between a performance and the evaluation of that performance will be irregular. Thus, those organizational conditions which increase the probability of unrepresentative samples also increase the probability of this type of incompatibility; therefore, the more frequently a participant's performance is sampled, the less the probability of this type of incompatibility.

TYPE IV — UNATTAINABLE EVALUATIONS. An authority system is incompatible if it places the participant in a situation in which the standards used to evaluate him are so high that he cannot achieve evaluations at his acceptance level.

This type of incompatibility results when the participant lacks the facilities necessary to perform at a level that criteria-setters require if he is to achieve evaluations at his acceptance level; therefore, no matter how hard he tries, he cannot achieve evaluations acceptable to him. Facilities may consist of a certain level of skill or training (if a worker new to a job were expected to perform at the same level as more experienced workers, he would be subject to an incompatibility of this type) or physical equipment, such as tools. Facilities may also consist of authority rights themselves. If a participant is evaluated on his ability to control the performance of others, he must have sufficient rights and sufficient authorization to achieve the control; otherwise he may find it impossible to achieve the degree of control necessary to maintain evaluations at his acceptance level. (A university departmental chairman may be expected to ensure good teaching, but may lack important rights, such as the sampling right, over his faculty.) Thus, for a participant who is evaluated for his control over another, the greater the number of authority rights and the greater the degree of authorization of those rights, the less the chance of this type of incompatibility.

This type of incompatibility also may occur because the criteria setter has inadequate information about the task to select attainable standards. This is likely to occur if a task has been newly developed and if tasks similar to it have not been performed often enough to allow criteria setters to know what levels of performance can reasonably be expected. The variability of resistance encountered in performing an active task poses special problems to the criteria setter. If it is not possible to learn the nature of the resistance which occurred in a given performance of an active task, then it is necessary for the criteria setter to select standards on the basis of the frequency distribution of outcomes generated by past performances of the task in similar contexts. If such a comparison population is not available or is too small, then the criteria setter lacks information necessary for the selection of reasonable standards.

Incompatibility Produces Instability

Instability refers to the state of a system. A system is said to be *unstable* to the extent that it contains internal pressure for change. Highly unstable systems are, in short, in an "explosive" state and, as such, are highly susceptible to change. Stable systems do not contain internal pressures for change and, therefore, will change only as a result of external pressure.

We have assumed that participants will attempt to maintain their evaluations at or above their acceptance levels and have identified four ways in which an authority system can be incompatible with the focal participant's ability to succeed in this attempt. Participants so thwarted can be expected to be dissatisfied with the system and, therefore, are likely to engage in coping responses in an attempt to resolve the incompatibility. Some of these reactions to incompatibility represent internal pressures for change within the system. Thus the central proposition of the theory is that incompatible authority systems are unstable. The theory does not state that compatible systems are necessarily stable, for there are many other factors that may lead to system instability. For this reason, the theory cannot be advanced as a general explanation of the instability of authority systems; incompatibility is considered to be a sufficient but not necessary condition for instability.[17]

The instability of an authority system may become evident in various ways. The responses by the focal participant can be used to indicate pressures for change in the system; that is, as indices of instability. It is assumed that the set represents a sufficient variety of indices so that if a system is unstable, the instability will be indicated by the regular occurrence of at least one of them. The indices are: dissatisfaction with some component of the system or with the system as a whole, expression of dissatisfaction with the system to others in the organization, suggestion to others in the organization that the system be changed, and noncompliance with the exercise of any authority right as a consequence of dissatisfaction with the system.

The interrelation of these indices is complex. If instability is indicated by one index, the probability of its being indicated by another may be changed.

---

[17] It should also be clear that we are not studying effectiveness. Our empirical studies may uncover some degree of association between effectiveness, incompatibility, and instability, but effectiveness or productivity are not variables in the current theory. Indeed, a more effective structure may permit and encourage a higher level of certain behaviors indicative of instability, such as expression of dissatisfaction or suggestion of changes.

(The use of suggestions by the participant may reduce his use of noncompliance as a vehicle for effecting change in the system.) But aside from this interrelationship, it is expected that the greater the instability, the greater is the probability that each index is present and the greater its intensity. Thus, we make the empirical prediction that the greater the incompatibility of an authority system, the more likely participants are to be dissatisfied, and to express dissatisfaction, suggest changes, and fail to comply with the exercise of authority rights, and the more intense these responses will be.

There are a number of factors which influence the instability produced by incompatibility. One set of factors influences the form which instability will take in a particular system. For example, it is expected that occupants of positions with relatively high status in the organization will be more likely to respond to incompatibility by suggesting redefinition of the system components than will occupants of positions lower in status. Similarly, the absence of institutionalized mechanisms of appeal reduces the probability of suggestions for change. A second set of factors influences the amount of instability produced by incompatibility. For example, we expect there to be a "compositional effect"[18] in groups in which a large number of participants are subject to incompatibility. If a participant interacts with others who are subjected to incompatibility in systems similar to his own, he may begin to perceive a threat to his own ability to continue to maintain his evaluations above his acceptance level. Even though he is not thwarted by his system now, he comes to believe that he may be thwarted in the future, and is likely to begin reacting against his system. Also, in attempting to change his system, a participant subjected to incompatibility may succeed in enlisting the aid of others who are not themselves so subjected. Such compositional effects amplify the instability produced by a given amount of incompatibility.

Resolution of Incompatibility

The instability resulting from incompatibility can be expected to persist until the incompatibility is resolved. One resolution is for the participant to leave the system, either by moving to another system or by leaving the organization altogether, as would be indicated by high turnover rates. Another resolution is for him to reduce his acceptance level to that which can be maintained in the authority system as it is presently constituted. An incompatibility that produces an evaluation of "poor" may be resolved by the participant's reducing his acceptance level sufficiently that an evaluation of "poor" is satisfactory to him.

[18] James A. Davis, Joe L. Spaeth, and Carolyn Huson, A Technique for Analyzing the Effects of Group Composition, *American Sociological Review*, 26 (1961), 215–225. See also Peter M. Blau, Structural Effects, *American Sociological Review*, 25 (1960), 178–193; P. M. Blau and W. Richard Scott, *Formal Organizations: A Comparative Approach* (San Francisco: Chandler, 1962), p. 101; and Paul F. Lazarsfeld, and Herbert Menzel, "On the Relation between Individual and Collective Properties," in Amitai Etzioni (ed.), *Complex Organizations: A Sociological Reader* (New York: Holt, Rinehart, and Winston, 1961), chap. 16.

We are particularly interested in the resolution process which is activated by incompatibility when the participant neither leaves the organization nor lowers his acceptance level. In this case, resolution can be achieved only by reorganizing the system, either by changing the existing authorization or by changing the exercise of one or more of the existing rights. Thus, the theory would predict that newly emerging systems, and existing systems in which incompatibilities develop, continue to search through various distributions of regularly exercised rights until a compatible system is achieved.

This process is influenced by variables which affect the degree to which attempts to reorganize will be successful. For example, incompatible authority systems which are perceived as legitimate are expected to be less likely to provoke attack and to be more resistant to attacks that do occur than are systems perceived as illegitimate. It is also expected, however, that incompatible systems are more likely to become illegitimate than are compatible systems, therefore becoming more subject to attack and less resistant to change. The probability of success in attempts to change the authority system is also related to the degree to which the tactics utilized by participants succeed in causing others in the system to be subjected to incompatibility. If a participant resorts to noncompliance to resolve his own incompatibility, he places his superiors in an incompatible position to the extent that this noncompliance causes them to receive evaluations below their acceptance levels. These superiors can be expected to be more hospitable to negotiations aimed at reorganizing the authority system. In the final analysis, it may be possible to argue that, in an authority system which endangers one man's evaluations, no man is safe.

Empirical Studies

Empirical studies are under way which will make it possible to: (1) test the basic proposition that incompatible authority systems are unstable; (2) describe various types of authority systems and structures; and (3) explore some of the sources of incompatibility and some of the factors associated with types of instability and with the resolution of incompatibility. The major data-gathering instrument is an interview schedule which is used to elicit information from an organizational participant with respect to a selected task on: (1) the authority rights exercised over him and those exercised by him over others; (2) the kinds of incompatibilities to which he is exposed in this authority system and the frequency with which they have occurred; and (3) evidence of instability, such as his level of satisfaction with the authority system and the kinds of attempts he has made to attack or change the system.

At the present time, data have been gathered from the occupants of 16 positions in five organizations. Our intent was to select organizations differing along such basic organizational dimensions as size, technological development, complexity of division of labor and authority relations, and proportion of professional participants. The diversity achieved is suggested by the variety of organizations: a basic science research organization, an athletic team, a profit-making electronics firm, a teaching hospital, and a student newspaper staffed by volunteer workers. Within these organizations, the positions selected for study were also chosen for their variability. We attempted to maximize variation in degree of technical skills required, commitment to organizational goals, and importance attached to the evaluations received. Actual positions examined ranged from senior hospital residents and electronics engineers to assembly-line workers and nurses' aides.

Hypotheses

Six specific hypotheses have been derived from the basic incompatibility-instability proposition.

Hypotheses Predicting the Presence of Instability

1. An incompatible authority system is more likely to be unstable than a compatible system.
2. An authority system which contains more incompatibilities is more likely to be unstable than a system which contains fewer incompatibilities.
3. An authority system with more frequent incompatibility is more likely to be unstable than a system with less frequent incompatibility.

Hypotheses Predicting the Degree of Instability Present

4. An incompatible authority system is likely to be more unstable than a compatible system.
5. An authority system which contains more incompatibilities is likely to be more unstable than a system which contains fewer incompatibilities.
6. An authority system with more frequent incompatibility is likely to be more unstable than a system with less frequent incompatibility.

These hypotheses will be tested using data from occupants of the sixteen organizational positions.

Among the descriptive and exploratory objectives of the present series of studies, we would like to determine to what extent the authority systems associated with a given position are structurally defined; that is, how much consensus is exhibited among the occupants of a position as to the authority rights exercised over and by them for a given task. Furthermore, what are the relationships between the degree to which the authority system about a given position is structural and (1) consensus on the types of incompatibility present in the system and (2) the particular form in which system instability is expressed? Also, are some types of positions more likely to be associated with particular kinds of incompatibilities or behaviors indicative of instability? If so, can we begin to isolate the factors associated with these differences? Finally, are particular types of incompatibility more productive of instability or of a particular type of instability than other types? These questions are not definitive; they only illustrate the kinds of questions relevant to the development and extension of the theory to which answers will be sought in the data collected.

Three

**Status Structures
and Processes**

Chapter 9

Dynamics of Status Equilibration*

■ T. J. FARARO

<hr />

□ 1. INTRODUCTION

Recent theoretical work in the area of social status and mobility has emphasized the role of equilibrating efforts in the dynamics of status. From the standpoint of the theory of status characteristics and expectation states, for example, in certain situations the actor characterized at a high level on a "diffuse" status characteristic is expected to rank high on other dimensions (Berger, Cohen and Zelditch, 1966). From the standpoint of the principle of distributive justice (Homans, 1961) one or more of these statuses might represent investments and several of the others might represent various rewards: the principle says that actors expect rewards proportional to investments, so high-ranking "investment" statuses ought to be accompanied by high-ranking reward statuses. If not, according to Homans' application of behavior theory, the actor experiences emotional imbalance and presumably attempts to change the situation. An application of Heider's balance theory (Heider, 1958; Davis, 1966) to the triad consisting of the actor and two statuses shows imbalance when we have unit-forming connections of the actor to both statuses (they are *his* statuses) and a negative link between the statuses (one is high, the other low). Then the fundamental principle of balance asserts that psychological tension arises. Once again, we expect the actor to attempt to alter the situation (Zelditch and Anderson, 1966).

Focusing especially on this problem, Kimberly (1966) treats ability status and function status in a social system. Pressures to be upwardly mobile, or even downwardly mobile, are explicated in terms of a reward-cost analysis of such "imbalancing" status combinations as high ability and low position with respect to functions. Similarly, Galtung (1966) treats the problems of social integration and individual problems of rank disequilibrium using various postulates in reasonable accordance with those mentioned above. Galtung proposes two "axioms" for the behavior of the individual actor in a system of several statuses in which he may be confronted with equilibration problems:

* The research reported in this chapter was conducted with the support of research grants from the Social Science Research Council and the National Science Foundation (GS-2538). I would like to express special gratitude to Morris Zelditch for his extensive and useful critiques of drafts of this chapter and to Josephine Stagno for her patient and expert retyping of those drafts.

The "axiom of upward mobility" asserts that individuals seek to maximize total rank. The "axiom of rank equilibration" asserts that individuals try to equalize their statuses by moving the lower status upwards. In this formulation, some difficulty might seem to arise from a logical standpoint: the first axiom has the maximal status configuration as its only stationary status, while the second axiom has any status set with equal ranks stationary. (For a discussion of this point, see Robertson and Tudor, 1968.) The apparent inconsistency — stationarity for one axiom is nonstationarity for the other, yet both axioms are considered valid — is easily resolved in a mathematical treatment. This brings us to the approach of the present paper.

In this approach, we set up differential equations that define a model that can be termed a *Galtung Actor*. The defining properties of the Galtung Actor are that he *simultaneously* attempts to be upwardly mobile and to equilibrate. These motivational subsystems are conceptualized using feedback and related systems concepts. Having defined the Galtung Actor in this way, we then deduce the properties of such an actor, with a focus on questions related to equilibrium and stability.

In the Kimberly conception of the problem of status equilibration, an actor has a four-dimensional status profile consisting of function status, ability status, performance status, and loyalty status. We attempt to translate the substantive conceptions about the dynamics of this profile into a set of equations that define a model. (In this case, the attempt stops short of a definite mathematical model.) The fact that both models can be set up in a common systems framework, given by a more abstract mathematical formulation, means that we no longer have two isolated conceptions. The same techniques apply to the set-up and analysis of both models, and as will be shown, some of the same mechanisms are postulated using different terminological rubrics. In this way, the theoretical integration of the field of status dynamics is advanced through the use of mathematical language and techniques, guided by general systems concepts.

□ 2. DEFINITION AND MEASUREMENT

We begin by utilizing a familiar conception of status: We have a set of actors who are characterized in terms of a set of states forming a differentially evaluated social characteristic (Parsons, 1953; Barber, 1957; Berger, Cohen and Zelditch, 1966; Tumin, 1967).

A formal representation of this notion of status can be constructed (Fararo, 1968, 1970c). Let A be the set of actors, let C be the characteristic represented as a set of states, and let the differential evaluation be represented by a numerical scale defined over C. This scale may be ordinal or higher. To say that the actors are characterized in terms of C means that to each actor, say α, in A we assign a state, say $c(\alpha) = x$, in the set C. Here x represents an arbitrary member of C, and the assignment itself is denoted c. The differential evaluation, regarded in terms of the numerical scale, may be denoted v. Thus $v(x)$ is the scale value associated with state x of C. Since $c(\alpha) = x$, for some x in C, it follows that $v(x) = v(c(\alpha))$. The latter expression can be interpreted as assigning a number to each actor α in A under the rule: map α into a state $c(\alpha)$ and then map this state into a value $v(c(\alpha))$. Call this rule s. Then

$$s(\alpha) = v(c(\alpha)), \tag{1}$$

and we term $s(\alpha)$ the *status* of α (in terms of the characteristic C and the valuation v). The rule s defines a *status variable*.

In defining status variables, we do not restrict the characteristics in any way; they could be Galtung's "rank dimensions" (Galtung, 1966), or they could be the four abstract "substatuses" of Kimberly's theory of status equilibration (Kimberly, 1966). The representation problem here concerns the conceptualization and operational specification of the set C of states. For instance, for the educational characteristic in a given society, how should its various levels be demarcated as a preparation for the measurement of the valuation of these levels? How many and what types of "places to work" need to be specified prior to the valuation measurement of such places? We believe that for this problem there is no general theory, and only a detailed analysis of the particular characteristic can lead to a fruitful representation. (For a methodological discussion related to this problem, see Jackson and Curtis, 1968.)

In Freeman, et al. (1960) and Freeman (1968) assumed (but unmeasured) valuation scales served as the theoretical underpinning of tetrachoric correlations input to a factor analysis of status variables. However, it is more desirable to indicate a set of assumptions such that, when they are satisfied, the valuation exists, has a known measurement level, and can be empirically estimated. Further, it is desirable, as pointed out by Coleman (1964), to state this "measurement theory" such that it refers to the behavior which is the subject-matter of the theoretical system. In our case, the subject matter may be defined as "status movement," i.e., the dynamics of individual movement along one or more status variables. Given the definition of a status variable, this movement can occur in either of two ways: (a) the characterization of actor α shifts, or (b) the valuation of the characterizing state changes. We analytically relativize to systems in which (b) cannot occur, and say that we are theorizing relative to a *stationary value system*. This means that the dynamics of status movement stem from changes in state and not changes in the evaluation of these states.

Suppose an actor is in a certain position at a certain time. We interpret "in a certain position" to mean: the n-tuple of statuses of α. That is, the position of α is

$$(s_1(\alpha), s_2(\alpha), \ldots, s_n(\alpha)).$$

The requirement that the measurement theory refer to the theoretically relevant behavior can be interpreted as follows: At the given time, the actor faces an implicit decision consisting of a question of movement to one of a set of several *available states* in each variable. Included in the available set of states is the present state. An actor a short time later is in some position, either the same as earlier or different in one or more variables. The "choice" has been made. If an actor were free of all psychological or sociological constraints, a reasonable interpretation of what has occurred would be that on each variable the actor selected that state which he found *most desirable* in terms of a scale v and then shifted to this state. If this were the case, movement would always be "upward" along the several v-scales, which contradicts the existence of downward mobility in the world; further, a man faces psychological constraints (e.g., the problem of equilibration or balance). Also the social world is not so passive as to let our actor simply shift as he wishes. Nevertheless, this "vacuum" conception of movement suggests an interpretation of the v-scale as a construct whose meaning status movement *would reveal* as "going to the more desirable state" if there were no psycho-social obstacles to such movement. Instead of observing actual status movement, we revert to a standard sociological procedure: we ask a man to choose from a set of alternative states and attempt to "tune him" by experimental instructions to choose in abstraction from obstacles. Thus, although the actual construction of the proper instrument is no easy task (see, for instance, the discussion by Gusfield and Schwartz, 1963), let us assume that empirical research can realize the primitive idea of "more desirable than" as a relational predicate linking pairs of states of a characteristic, in which this predicate is realized apart from realistic conditions of side-effects, constraints, and the like.

In this sense, desirable places to live, or attend school; desirable occupations in which to engage; desirable things to own; and desirable personal appearance and forms of behavior are only a few of the ways to specify status variables.

Although other papers (cf. Fararo, 1970a) have used the term "preference" in this regard, a better rendition of the intuitive notion of differential evaluation is the above notion of desirability (as emphasized by Kluckhohn, 1951).[1]

Our next problem is to show how a theory of the choice behavior exhibited by the "subjects" in the measurement situation gives rise to the logical consequence that the valuation exists as a numerical scale formally representing the underlying empirical relationships. We follow the recent literature on measurement (see Suppes and Zinnes, 1963 and Pfanzagl, 1968) in placing an emphasis on the need for an explicit behavior theory leading to the scale. This distinguishes the measurement procedure to follow from related work like the NORC

---

[1] The mathematical relation representing preference satisfies some of the same basic conditions as that representing desirability, so that, in the abstract, often no harm is done by using these two concepts interchangeably. A view currently favored in mathematical psychology defines preference as a relation over the outcome space associated with a choice among a set of response alternatives. A man chooses a response, but he prefers outcomes: in this way one can explain why a man goes to a dentist when in a sense he would rather not (see Galanter, 1966). Desirability appears to be a more trans-situational notion, which in conjunction with the realistic aspects of definite situations, helps determine concrete preferences over possible outcomes. The general conceptual problem here is one of trying to formally link the basic value system of a society to the very construction of its stratification system, keeping in mind that lower-level values will be revealed in response processes depending upon position in the system.

scaling procedure. The concepts and assumptions of this measurement theory are now to be outlined. (Operational aspects are discussed in Fararo, 1970b.)

Let S be any nonempty, finite subset of C. For example, S could contain a sample of occupations, if C is the occupational characteristic. Our first assumption is that each actor α in A is associated with a system of probability functions denoted P_S^α such that for any x in S, with probability $P_S^\alpha(x)$ the actor α chooses x when his alternatives comprise S. A special case of importance is $S = \{x, y\}$, a set of two distinct states, and the actor must choose between them. In this case, we write

$$p^\alpha(x, y) = P_{\{x,y\}}^\alpha(x), \tag{2}$$

as an abbreviation for the cumbersome notation on the right. This is the probability that actor α prefers x to y in terms of "desirability." Because we assume a probability distribution, in the special case of two elements we have

$$p^\alpha(x, y) + p^\alpha(y, x) = 1, \tag{3}$$

which can be taken to restrict the empirical interpretations to cases in which the individual must make a selection. "Indifference" will be treated as probability one-half in pairwise choice.

Our next assumption is that, for any subset S of C,

$$P_S^\alpha(x) = P_S^\beta(x), \qquad \text{every } x \text{ in } S, \tag{4}$$

as α and β vary over A. That is, the probability functions are the same for all individuals in A. In contrast to the innocuous assertion that probability functions exist, this assumption requires some discussion, which will be presented subsequently. We can now drop the actor superscript and write $P_S(x)$ and $p(x, y)$ for various probabilities.

We postulate that our general choice principle is an axiom proposed by Luce (1959) which is also discussed in Fararo (1968) and more fully treated in Atkinson, Bower and Crothers (1965).

The context of job choice offers explication of this axiom. Let us state one version of the axiom in a formal way first: let T be a subset of S, which itself is contained in C; let x be an element of T. Imagine two different choice situations: in Situation One, the actor must choose an element of S; in Situation Two, the actor must choose an element of T. Let $P_S(x)$ be, as above, the probability that x is chosen from S. Let $P_T(x)$ be the probability that x is chosen from T. Let $P_S(x \mid T)$ be the conditional probability, in Situation One, that the actor chooses x, given he chooses an element of T. The axiom states that

$$P_T(x) = P_S(x \mid T). \tag{5}$$

An interpretation in terms of job choice is as follows: in Situation One, a man must choose a job from a certain set S of available jobs; in Situation Two, he must choose a job from a smaller available set T contained in S. The expression (5) says that the probability that in Situation Two he chooses job x is just the conditional probability, in Situation One, that he selects x, given he selects from T.

For a further intuitive interpretation, imagine N individuals in the same Situation One. Then $P_S(x \mid T)$ is estimated by the relative frequency of x-choices among those who selected from T. According to the axiom, if these individuals are constrained to select jobs from T in the first place, the expected relative frequency of x-choices is the same. The axiom is testable, as shown by the favorable results in Atkinson, Bower and Crothers (1965), although some psychologists have reservations about it (Restle, 1961; Galanter, 1966).

If Luce's axiom holds over a domain C of alternatives then there exists a ratio-level scale over C, denoted v, such that for *any* finite subset S of C,

$$P_S(x) = \frac{v(x)}{\sum\limits_{y \in S} v(y)}. \qquad (6)$$

That is, the probability that the individual chooses x from S is the "valuation" of x divided by the sum of the valuations of all alternatives in S. Since this is a ratio-scale, one can select some state of C, say a, and arbitrarily let $v(a) = 1$.

How can one actually estimate v and so s? Using pairwise choices, Luce showed that we have

$$v(x) = \frac{p(x, a)}{p(a, x)} \qquad \text{all } x \text{ in } C, \qquad (7)$$

where a is the state chosen for the unit. One use of formula (7) requires paired comparisons. This is a highly restricted type of situation. A more practical way of estimating $p(x, y)$ — and so v, and so s — from data of the kind readily obtained in sociological research is through rankings. Fortunately, Luce has done the axiomatic work, and the empirical tests confirm his ranking theory (again, see Atkinson, Bower and Crothers, 1965). Roughly speaking, the Luce Ranking Postulate states that the choice axiom applies at each level of choice to an ever-diminishing choice set S. The result is that $p(x, y)$, interpreted as the probability that x is preferred to y, *is equal to* the probability of a ranking of the set S in which x is placed ahead of y. The distinction here is that a ranking is a *context* of choice which is not empirically identical to a choice between two things; according to the Postulate and the confirming data, however, this context does not change the probability. Therefore, if we take the fraction of individuals placing x before y as an estimate of the probability that x is placed before y, then by the Ranking Postulate this estimates $p(x, y)$. Therefore, we can obtain estimated valuations $v(x)$ using formula (7) and estimates of the statuses of individuals by using expression (1).

The intuitive picture of the individual in such a ranking task (for the ranking of desirable places to work, for example) says: he first decides on the most desirable place, and formula (6) applies with S as the total set of places to give the probability for every place x that it ranks first; next, he chooses the most desirable of the remaining places where formula (6) applies with S suitably reduced; and so forth. In this way, for each possible ranking there is a corresponding probability in terms of the valuations. (A detailed calculation is shown in Atkinson, Bower and Crothers, 1965.)

To sum up, the basic assumptions of our ratio-level status measurement are as follows: individuals will be making choices from finite sets of alternatives on grounds of "desirability." They choose in accordance with Luce's axiom. This axiom applies to ranking situations. A homogeneous system of probabilities, as between individuals, is assumed. Given these assumptions, it is a logical consequence that a ratio-level scale representing the evaluations exists. Given a conception of status as a composition of characterization and valuation, we pass to its formal definition.

One problem associated with this theory concerns the assumption of identical probabilities for all actors in A. One interpretation of the assumption is that it specifies the set A as forming a culture relative to the existence of a homogeneous value system yielding a single scale v over C. This interpretation may help to identify a set A of actors for which the valuation over a given characteristic is homogeneous. But it also suggests, at least for complex social systems, that this set of actors is likely to be different for each characteristic: an arbitrarily selected set of actors is not likely to display homogeneity across the board. However, for those characteristics for which homogeneity obtains, just those characteristics form the basis of status differentiation (see Blau, 1964). The assumption of v-homogeneity, made for the sake of practical measurement, is conceptually acceptable in terms of how we consider the difference between characteristics that produce status differentiation and those that do not produce such differentiation in a collectivity. Nevertheless, the notion that v-homogeneity holds in A for a specified characteristic C is an assumption that could be wrong for the given set A. Therefore, we shall say that our theory is analytically relative, not only to a stationary value system, but also to a *homogeneous value system*. To apply the theory, one should choose just that set of characteristics for which the assumption of a homogeneous value system is reasonable. (For further comments and conjectures regarding the interpretation of v-homogeneity in A, see Fararo, 1968, 1970a, 1970b.)[2]

---

[2] Readers of these papers will see that the attempt to link the pragmatic condition of homogeneous probabilities to sociological thought has been a minor preoccupation of the author. The problem is subtle. It arises from the fact that the Luce theory is stochastic with respect to the individual. Luce is adamant that unless care is taken in applying the axiom, violence will be done to this basic idea. On the other hand, a man is not a coin; the opportunity arises seldom for independent identical trials permitting the estimation of these probabilities for a single individual. All applications that I have seen apply the theory to a set of individuals assumed to be identical in the probability sense. It is this inevitable pragmatic assumption that I wished to provide with sociological rationale.

□ **3. THE GENERAL FRAMEWORK**

A scientific theoretical system has many different aspects. First, there is a basis (for current purposes, measurement) for passing from observable things in the world to numerical scales or to other abstract objects representing these observable primitives. Second, there is an abstract system consisting of the space determined by a set of such measurement mappings and any general types of assumptions or definitions introduced. Third, there is an inexhaustible set of definite theoretical models of classes of actual systems, each model constructed by deploying the abstract framework and adding additional hypotheses. Finally, there is the set of auxiliary models (cf. Blalock, 1969) needed to make such abstract theoretical models concretely useful in the analysis of an actual system.

For example, in probabilistic work we have the "measurement" of probabilities by counting, the general axioms and definitions of probability theory, a vast supply of probabilistic models that are constructed for many purposes in many disciplines, and various techniques to solve parameter estimation problems. In Newtonian mechanics, we have the theoretical bases for the measurement of length, mass and time; Newton's axioms for motion; and the many mechanical models constructed to describe the motion of such diverse classes of actual systems as pendulums, vibrating strings and planetary systems.

In studying status-related phenomena, we think of the gradual evolution of such a scientific theoretical system. The first section of this paper attempted to make a small contribution to the evolution of an appropriate measurement basis. In this section we turn to the second aspect of such a theoretical system: a generic way of looking at the type of phenomenon of interest (random behavior, motion, status movements) which provides a framework within which a variety of models may be constructed. In the following sections such model constructions will be undertaken.

The starting point for our framework is given by writing definition (1) with time-dependence,

$$s(t, \alpha) = v_t(c_t(\alpha)), \tag{8}$$

where t is a time-index running over a time-domain, say T. This expression says that the status of actor α in A at time t in T is given by the valuation of the way in which he is characterized (on a characteristic C) at that time. The t-subscript on v indicates that the valuation itself may be nonstationary, but since we analytically relativize to a stationary value system, we have

$$s(t, \alpha) = v(c_t(\alpha)). \tag{9}$$

Advancing to the *position* of an actor, as a vector of statuses, we introduce notation for time-dependence in a stationary value system,

$$\vec{s}(t, \alpha) = (s_1(t, \alpha), s_2(t, \alpha), \ldots, s_n(t, \alpha)), \tag{10}$$

where

$$s_i(t, \alpha) = v_i(c_{it}(\alpha)),$$

for $i = 1, 2, \ldots, n$.

In studying individual status change, we hold the actor α fixed and let t vary. In this context, we can drop the notation for the actor to write the simpler form,

$$\vec{s}(t) = (s_1(t), s_2(t), \ldots, s_n(t)), \tag{11}$$

with a single actor understood.

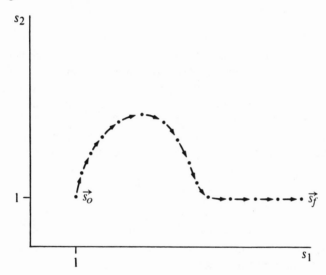

■ **FIGURE 1.** An Illustrative Status Trajectory

The path in n-dimensional space traced out by the vector $\vec{s}(t)$ as t varies is the *status trajectory*, the succession of positions held by an actor through time. When the vector has just two components, we have a geometric image of the trajectory as shown in Figure 1.

The individual at time t_o is at position $\vec{s}_o$ as shown in the figure; the arrows show the successive positions as time flows, culminating at $\vec{s}_f$. We see that initially this actor is upwardly mobile on both variables (arrows pointing upward and to the right); then he begins losing status on the second variable while still gaining on the first (arrows downward and to the right); finally, he remains fixed on the second variable while moving steadily upward on the first (arrows parallel to the s_1-axis and pointing to the right). A similar picture could be drawn for three variables; for higher dimensions we use intuitions obtained in the lower dimensions.

Our aim is to create models such that one has an intelligible explanatory basis for the movement shown by the arrows; the aim is to introduce mathematical representations of motivational and other processes *inducing* the shifts forming the status trajectory. Any such process, seen with regard to how it moves an individual in the space, is a *mechanism*. (This usage is essentially that of Parsons, 1951, p. 201.) As we shall see below, this dynamical viewpoint allows us to regard status inconsistency as a mechanism, a driving force for change in position.

Status dynamics may be regarded as the field in which we introduce functions of status and possibly of other variables, collectively denoted by the vector $\vec{u}$, in such a way that we have a system of the form,

$$\frac{d\vec{s}}{dt} = f(\vec{s}, \vec{u}). \tag{12}$$

This shows, on the left side, the rate of change of position, which (by standard mathematical definition) is just the derivative of each component of the vector. (Thus, this is a system of differential equations in vector form.) The right side shows a function of status and of "input" to the actor. This is the total mechanism, which depends on where the individual "is" and what is "happening" to him. To see how this form can generate a status trajectory, multiply both sides by dt (thought of as a small interval of time). This gives

$$d\vec{s} = f(\vec{s}, \vec{u})\, dt. \tag{13}$$

In looking at expression (13), we think of a movement, of magnitude and direction given by a "little vector" $d\vec{s}$, which is induced by the mechanism $f(\vec{s}, \vec{u})$ acting through an interval of time dt. For example, starting at $\vec{s}_o$ with input $\vec{u}_o$, the mechanism becomes, $f(\vec{s}_o, \vec{u}_o)$ which when multiplied by a suitable dt gives the first motion out of $\vec{s}_o$ as shown in Figure 1. By applying the mechanism again at this new location, we drive the system to its next location, and so forth. At point $\vec{s}_f$ we would find that the mechanism is still operative but induces no motion out of that position: this would be an equilibrium position.

This provides the interpretation that one would use in a numerical simulation. It is in greatest fidelity to the discrete "jumps" shown in an actual status trajectory. In analytical work reported here we idealize to methods which generate the trajectory as a smooth curve as in Figure 2, where we see the curve corresponding to the actual status trajectory of Figure 1. (The proper type of mathematics for dealing with the jumps, with stochastic elements built in, is the rather difficult field of "jump processes" described in Feller, 1966.)

In postulating mechanisms, we generally start from some substantive verbal basis which is translated into a system of differential equations using some general guidelines or principles. In particular, we can provisionally use the general principle that the displacement during any time interval is due to a sum of several positive and negative *mobilizers*, where the latter refers to some category of cause for changing characterization. There are two classes of mobilizers of general interest: the first will be termed the class of *natural mo*

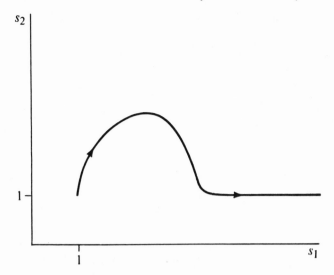

■ **FIGURE 2.** The Status Trajectory of Figure 1 as Generated by a Solution to a System of Differential Equations

bilizers, indicating what would happen if no extrinsic causal factors induced characterization stability or change. In particular, the characterizations $c_{jt}(\alpha)$ of actor α would then be valued by him as $v_j(c_{jt}(\alpha)) = s_{jt}(\alpha)$ according to our measurement theory, and it follows that if he were able, he would change $c_{jt}(\alpha)$ such that the value of his assigned profile would be higher. Thus, a natural mobilizer induces upward mobility. On the other hand, comparisons with *other* statuses form the class of equilibrational mobilizers. (Specific models to be constructed in later sections provide the best context for understanding these ideas.)

If $f(\vec{s}, \vec{u})$ is represented by a linear operator, we have a system of the form,

$$\frac{d\vec{s}}{dt} = A\vec{s} + B\vec{u},$$

where A and B are matrices. The matrix A is called the system matrix. Questions concerning equilibrium and stability are answered by an analysis of the system matrix, as will be clear in the following sections.

Should we not consider models with an output as well as input? In behavioral science, the output term of a behaving system is the observable response vector. Although the models to be constructed in the next section are deficient in this respect (they fail to include an explicit response process), we should be prepared to construct such models. The addition of a response term in a linear system means adding an equation of the form $\vec{r} = C\vec{s} + D\vec{u}$, so that the response of the system (actor) is a linear function of the present position and the input. For example, an actor in a certain position $\vec{s}$ at a given time who experiences a felt pressure $(\vec{u})$ to earn more money will respond $(\vec{r})$ in a certain way. In particular, suicide and other kinds of "extreme" responses may be conceived as joint functions of position (especially the degree of inconsistency among the statuses in that position, to be described later) and the input. It is not surprising that under identical pressures (inputs) actors in different social positions respond differently — in our framework it is almost definitional, with constancy a special case.

When the system may not be linear, the response will depend upon the position and the input according to some function, say $g(\vec{s}, \vec{u})$. Thus, the general system is of the form,

$$\frac{d\vec{s}}{dt} = f(\vec{s}, \vec{u})$$
$$\vec{r} = g(\vec{s}, \vec{u}). \tag{14}$$

Using a somewhat more general form,[3] engineers call this the "canonical form" of a dynamic system (see Schwartz and Friedland, 1965). For a first approach to the problem of status equilibration within this framework, however, we will rely only upon the first equation and postpone the explicit treatment of response processes.

□ **4. THE GALTUNG ACTOR**

In this section a model will be constructed in which the mechanism $f(\vec{s}, \vec{u})$ is proposed by reference to a recent substantive theory.

In his paper in the first volume of *Sociological Theories in Progress*, J. Galtung (1966) provides a comprehensive discussion of rank equilibration. In treating "intra-personal stability," he states two axioms referring to what I will call *natural mobility* and *equilibration*, respectively. Galtung's first axiom holds that an individual will attempt to maximize his "total rank." In our version, he is "oriented upwards" in each status dimension as a result of his valuation of the underlying states.[4] Galtung's second axiom states that an individual will

---

[3] For example, one can have time-varying coefficient terms, which abstractly introduce t as an argument of f or g. Also, one can generalize to a system of k actors. The same general system (14) holds but the vector $\vec{s}$, for example, now has nk components; also, the particular versions of (14) would be derived by using additional mechanisms, such as inter-actor comparisons.

[4] The idea of total rank seems to have no empirical basis corresponding to the addition of measurements across distinct status variables. One could suppose that some linear combination of all the statuses (as in Zelditch and Anderson, 1966) functions as a global status variable to be maximized subject to constraints. For present purposes, the idea of uncoupled positive feedback systems is the representation of the upward mobility mechanism. In that case, perhaps one should not use Galtung's name for this model. However, I urge that we think about defining a vast battery of families of models for possible systems of status movement: one such family, that using the particular positive and negative feedback mechanisms defined here, might be thought of as the Galtung family. Also, this is in agreement with Galtung's discussion, in the same paper, of sociology as the science of the socially possible. It is in this spirit that we later investigate a Kimberly Actor (Section 6).

try to equilibrate his various component statuses upwards. Galtung thus includes an axiomatic upward mobility bias even in respect to equilibration. However, we know that individuals sometimes equilibrate *downwards*. This point is emphasized in Kimberly's treatment of equilibration (Kimberly, 1966). Thus, in a slight alteration of Galtung's assumption, the system studied here will posit that equilibration can act in either direction; its basic motivational component is the "setting of things in balance." Basically, in this model the status trajectory is produced by a vector-addition of "virtual" movements induced by natural mobilizers inducing movement upwards, equilibrational mobilizers inducing upward or downward movements toward "balance," and external constraints. It will be shown that depending upon the relative importance of these mechanisms in a system, and his initial position, an actor can move unambiguously upwards (arrows up and to the right in the plane) or definitely downwards (arrows down and to the left in the plane), or experience a more ambiguous movement.

The system will be stated first in complete form, and then it will be derived in the sense of showing in detail how it arises from underlying mechanisms. In order to present the basic ideas with a minimum of mathematical complexity, the system will be defined in two dimensions.

Let

$$\frac{ds_1}{dt} = (a_1 - b_1)s_1 + b_1 s_2 - c_1$$
$$\frac{ds_2}{dt} = (a_2 - b_2)s_2 + b_2 s_1 - c_2 \tag{15}$$

where the parameters a_i, b_i and c_i ($i = 1, 2$) are positive.

Note that since

$$\frac{d\vec{s}}{dt} = \begin{pmatrix} \dfrac{ds_1}{dt} \\ \dfrac{ds_2}{dt} \end{pmatrix}$$

in vector form the system is given by

$$\frac{d\vec{s}}{dt} = A\vec{s} - \vec{c}, \tag{16}$$

where

$$\vec{c} = \begin{pmatrix} c_1 \\ c_2 \end{pmatrix}$$
$$\vec{s} = \begin{pmatrix} s_1 \\ s_2 \end{pmatrix} \tag{17}$$
$$A = \begin{pmatrix} a_1 - b_1 & b_1 \\ b_2 & a_2 - b_2 \end{pmatrix}$$

and so $f(\vec{s}, \vec{u}) = A\vec{s} - \vec{c}$, in this model. This is a linear model with constant input, $\vec{u} = -\vec{c}$.

The equations (15) arise as follows: if the actor were unconstrained by other actors or psychological factors, the mechanism $f(\vec{s}, \vec{u})$ could be taken as

$$\frac{ds_i}{dt} = a_i s_i \qquad (a_i > 0, i = 1, 2) \qquad (18)$$

with a_i thought of as some fraction. This implies ever-increasing status in each component. This is plausible because the actor acts in accordance with his values (measured in terms of choices based on desirability of state occupancy under these conditions), and there are no constraints on his manipulating his characterization to ever increase its value in each dimension: but this means ever-increasing status. For example, keeping in mind the analytical restriction to this single mechanism, a typical trajectory would be as in Figure 3, using $a_1 = a_2$ for illustrative purposes.

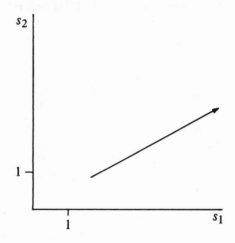

■ **FIGURE 3.** A Typical Trajectory Based on a Natural Mobilizer

In systems' terms, equations (18) define a pair of positive feedback subsystems which are uncoupled. That is, a gain in a given variable induces further gains (positive feedback), and neither facilitation nor blockage connects the two variables. (For a discussion of positive feedback, see Milsum, 1968; coupling is discussed in Ashby, 1956, and Lange, 1965.)

On the other hand, suppose our actor is a *pure equilibrator*; that is, the mechanism involves only *comparisons* "horizontally" along his statuses. When he finds agreement between his actual and expected statuses, he is satisfied with that characterization, while disagreement creates an imbalance he attempts to resolve by changing his characterization. We assume that the motivation to change characterization can be converted into change (e.g., the environment does not constrain the actor's movement).

To convert these ideas into an exact mechanism, let us assume that the equilibrated statuses all lie on an "expectation line" in the plane. (This can be generalized to a region.) For instance, if absolute equality is expected, then the 45°-line is the expectation line. (See Figure 4.) A more general expectation

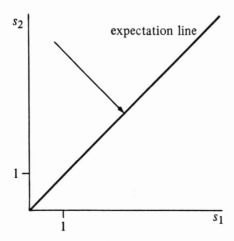

■ FIGURE 4. A Typical Trajectory Based on an Equilibrational Mobilizer

line model would be based on the assumption, "the higher I am here on s_1, the higher I ought to be there on s_2" which is any monotone-increasing curve in the plane. Taking a line through the origin as the model is an attempt to keep the mathematics simple. Analytically, the line is given by a function of the form,

$$e(s_1) = ks_1, \qquad (19)$$

with k positive. Positions on this line are equilibrated, other positions are not. At any time, when the actor is at status s_1, he expects to be at ks_1 on the second variable. The actor may be said to be s_2-balanced when $s_2 = ks_1$. The signed difference $ks_1 - s_2$ is the *degree of imbalance* at the given time, with respect to the second variable. It is reasonable to assume that the magnitude and direction of induced movement on this second variable will be proportional to the degree of imbalance:

$$\frac{ds_2}{dt} = b_2(ks_1 - s_2), \qquad (b_2 > 0). \qquad (20)$$

Thus, if at a particular time the individual's position is $\vec{s} = (s_1, s_2) = (s_1, ks_1)$, the mechanism does not induce change. If, however, s_2 is less than ks_1, then ds_2/dt is positive and he is induced to move upwards on s_2 to catch up to the expected status (based on where he is on s_1 at the time). If s_2 is above ks_1 so that he is above his expected place, the mechanism becomes negative, and he is induced downwards on the second variable.

Applying the same reasoning symmetrically to s_1 based on s_2, we merely traverse the expectation line from the s_2-axis horizontally to find the expected s_1-status, which will be $(1/k)s_2$. Thus the mechanism here will be of the form,

$$\frac{ds_1}{dt} = b_1(s_2/k - s_1), \qquad (b_1 > 0) \tag{21}$$

with identical reasoning as to the induced movement. The actor may be said to be s_1-balanced when $s_1 = s_2/k$. It follows that he is s_1-balanced if and only if he is s_2-balanced. The signed difference $s_2/k - s_1$ is the degree of imbalance at the given time, with respect to the first variable. Thus, equation (21) makes the direction and magnitude of induced status movement on the first variable proportional to the degree of imbalance on that variable. Relative to this mechanism only, the actor is in equilibrium if and only if the position lies on the expectation line, in which case he is both s_1-balanced and s_2-balanced. Any position on the expectation line is such an equilibrium position.

If we put $k = 1$ for the simplest model, we obtain from (20) and (21),

$$\begin{aligned} \frac{ds_1}{dt} &= b_1(s_2 - s_1) \\ \frac{ds_2}{dt} &= b_2(s_1 - s_2). \end{aligned} \tag{22}$$

Figure 4 shows a trajectory produced by this mechanism, taking $b_1 = b_2$. Note that when $s_1 = s_2$ we obtain zero derivatives, and the actor is not induced to move out of such a position.

Each of these two equations instantiates a general type of equation used in control systems theory under the label "negative feedback control." (See, for example, Bellman, 1961; Milsum, 1968.) The general equation is of the form,

$$\frac{dX}{dt} = b(D - X),$$

where X is some time-varying quantity (for example, temperature) and D is its desired level (for example, the thermostatic setting). The system is controlled in the sense that a disturbance produces a return to the state $X = D$, where the term dX/dt is zero, and the system is stationary. In the first equation of (22), s_1 plays the role of X and s_2 plays the role of the "thermostatic setting." In the second equation these roles are reversed. By this coupling of two subsystems, the "setting" for each subsystem varies dynamically. In equilibrium, the two statuses equilibrate each other. A disturbance produces a process of mutual correction whose precise nature depends upon the two parameters b_1 and b_2. This, of course, contrasts sharply with the positive feedback uncoupled subsystems representing the natural mobilizers.

To combine the facts that the actor is naturally driven upwards by acting in accordance with his valuation of the states of the characteristics and *also* is an equilibrator, one uses the additivity rule to combine the mobilizers of (18) and (22) to obtain

$$\frac{ds_1}{dt} = a_1s_1 + b_1(s_2 - s_1)$$
$$\frac{ds_2}{dt} = a_2s_2 + b_2(s_1 - s_2). \tag{23}$$

Finally, let us assume that *other* actors and the non-social environment constrain the actor's mobility. For simplicity, let us suppose this constraining input to the actor to be constant in time. Then the mechanism (23) with the negative inputs, $-c_1$ and $-c_2$, becomes the differential equation system (15). In the first equation of system (15), the coefficient of s_1 is negative if and only if a_1 is less than b_1. This means that the equilibrational mechanism "outweighs" the natural mobilizer in the determination of the qualitative character of the s_1 subsystem behavior. Similar remarks apply to the second equation.

To summarize, (15) represents on the left side the displacement or mobility rate of the actor; the actor's mobility rate is equal to the sum of certain mobilizers (inducing change in status). These mobilizers consist in, first, a natural upward movement because of the actor's values and his behavior in accordance with these values; second, an equilibrating effect due to a balance process connecting the two statuses; and, third, a constraining environment including other actors who act in such a way that we regard their combined effect on our actor as a constant input pushing his status downwards.

This model is but one among many possibilities. For example, with $c_i < 0$ the constraint terms now become pushes in the *upward* direction, and we have a model of a situation in which, aside from equilibration, the actor faces no block to his naturally upward mobility. Similarly, a "ceiling" on the statuses could be assumed. This leads to difficult nonlinear models, relative to which the present model can be regarded as an approximation. A brief discussion of the need for nonlinear models appears in Fararo (1970a). Another possibility involves closer attention to the object called the available set in the first section: the set of states accessible to the actor at a given time. Implicitly, the present model takes all states as available, and the constraints operate over the system as if the actor had been oriented toward a higher state and felt a contrary pressure, with the magnitude of the pressure independent of the state (constant inputs).

Consider the interpretation of the system parameters. The parameters a_i are like the constants in growth laws. Note that since from equation (18) for the natural mobilizers we obtain

$$\frac{ds_i}{s_i} = a_i dt, \tag{24}$$

integrating both sides, and letting $s_{io} = s_i(0)$, yields

$$s_i(t) = s_{io}e^{a_it}. \tag{25}$$

An examination of equation (24) shows that a_i has the dimension of the reciprocal of time, so we let T_i be the time such that $a_i = 1/T_i$. Then when $t = T_i$,
expression (25) yields

$$s_i(t) = s_{io}e, \tag{26}$$

and we can interpret T_i as the time that would be required to multiply the initial
status by $e \simeq 2.7$, were the natural mobilizer unconstrained. Since this time
varies inversely with the parameter a_i, we see that a large a_i implies a shorter
time to the point of exponential multiplication of the starting status. Let us
call a_i the *escapability* of a status variable s_i. Large escapability values imply
rapid dynamics of positive feedback, while low escapability means sluggish
positive feedback. The limiting case $a_i \rightarrow 0$ defines an approach to ascription.

Turning to the b_i parameters, we examine the equilibrational mobilizer.
This shows that the displacement ds_1 in variable s_1 introduced by the difference
$s_2 - s_1$ has a magnitude proportional to the parameter b_1. Thus b_1 measures
the *responsiveness* of the s_1 subsystem to the "thermostatic setting" operative
for it at any time due to an input from the s_2 subsystem. Similarly, the parameter b_2 measures the responsiveness of the s_2 variable to the equilibrating input
from s_1. A "symmetric" system ($a_1 = a_2, b_1 = b_2$) is symmetrically responsive
in the sense that neither variable dominates the "investment" role of the two
variable comparison. It can be shown that the dimension of the parameters
b_i is also that of a time reciprocal.

We turn now to the problem of equilibrium. (The analysis of the next few
pages is the same as that reported in Fararo, 1970a.) The meaning of a position
being an equilibrium position is this: *if* an actor is ever in this position, say $\vec{s}_e$,
then he stays there given the mechanisms of the system and unchanged parameter values. The point of this definition is that there is no assertion that the
actor will be in equilibrium or will gravitate toward it if he is not there. It is
purely a matter of what the mechanisms of the system imply concerning a
position. The stability or instability of this position is a separate question.
Correspondingly, the mathematical definition of an equilibrium point of a
system of the form,

$$\frac{d\vec{s}}{dt} = f(\vec{s}, \vec{u}),$$

is simply any solution of the system,

$$\frac{d\vec{s}}{dt} = \vec{0}.$$

Since for the Galtung Actor,

$$\frac{d\vec{s}}{dt} = A\vec{s} - \vec{c},$$

the equilibrium positions are the status vectors satisfying

$$A\vec{s} = \vec{c}. \tag{27}$$

Applying the inverse of A to both sides of (27), we obtain

$$\vec{s}_e = A^{-1}\vec{c}. \tag{28}$$

Computationally, we must have a nonvanishing determinant, denoted Δ. This, for the matrix in (17), is given by

$$\Delta = (a_1 - b_1)(a_2 - b_2) - b_1 b_2. \tag{29}$$

Summarizing:

PROPOSITION 1. If $\Delta \neq 0$, the status system has a unique equilibrium point given by (28).

Since the actor is an equilibrator, we ask: Is it the case that the components of $\vec{s}_e$ are at the same level, i.e., if $\vec{s}_e = (s_{1e}, s_{2e})$, must we have: $s_{1e} = s_{2e}$? By (28) we obtain

$$s_{1e} = \frac{1}{\Delta}[(a_2 - b_2)c_1 - b_1 c_2],$$
$$s_{2e} = \frac{1}{\Delta}[(a_1 - b_1)c_2 - b_2 c_1], \tag{30}$$

and, therefore, we can prove the following:

PROPOSITION 2. $s_{1e} = s_{2e}$ if, and only if, $a_2/a_1 = c_2/c_1$.

According to equations (30), $s_{1e} = s_{2e}$ if, and only if,

$$(a_2 - b_2)c_1 - b_1 c_2 = (a_1 - b_1)c_2 - b_2 c_1,$$

and, so, if, and only if,

$$a_2 c_1 - (b_2 c_1 + b_1 c_2) = a_1 c_2 - (b_1 c_2 + b_2 c_1).$$

Therefore, $s_{1e} = s_{2e}$ implies and is implied by $a_2 c_1 = a_1 c_2$.
The answer to our question is that an equilibrium point need *not* be one

which shows identity of components. Further, for an actor characterized with the ratio a_2/a_1, the condition of imbalanced equilibrium (i.e., $s_{1e} \neq s_{2e}$) is that the constraining inputs show a ratio $c_2/c_1 \neq a_2/a_1$. (But recall that an equilibrium may be unstable; a point to be developed later.)

To illustrate, consider the special system in which

$$a_1 = a_2, \quad \text{(call it } a\text{)}$$
$$b_1 = b_2, \quad \text{(call it } b\text{),}$$

previously termed *symmetric*. We have:

PROPOSITION 3. Provided that $b \neq a/2$, the symmetric system has a unique equilibrium point.

To see this, note that in the symmetric case,

$$\Delta = a^2 - 2ab,$$

and the condition $\Delta \neq 0$ of Proposition 1 becomes

$$a - 2b \neq 0.$$

By Proposition 2, only if the equilibrium of a symmetric system is exposed to symmetric inputs ($c_1 = c_2$) will it be a state of balance ($s_{1e} = s_{2e}$).

Since the reader may not find the proofs psychologically compelling — we are saying that the system is built around an equilibration toward the expectation line (identity of components in this model), and, yet, there may exist an equilibrium in which the statuses are unequal — let us consider one numerical example.

Let the system be symmetric and let

$$a = 1, \quad b = 3, \quad c_1 = 1, \quad c_2 = 2.$$

By Proposition 3, since $a \neq b/2$, we have an equilibrium position; by Proposition 2, since $c_2/c_1 \neq 1 = a/a$, the position will not be on the expectation line.

Numerically, we find that the system (15) becomes

$$\frac{ds_1}{dt} = 3s_2 - 2s_1 - 1,$$
$$\frac{ds_2}{dt} = 3s_1 - 2s_2 - 2.$$

The equilibrium condition of vanishing derivatives gives the algebraic system,

$$3s_2 - 2s_1 - 1 = 0,$$
$$3s_1 - 2s_2 - 2 = 0,$$

for which the solution is found to be $s_{1e} = \frac{8}{5}$, $s_{2e} = \frac{7}{5}$. Substitution of these values in the equations

$$ds_1 = (3s_{2e} - 2s_{1e} - 1)\, dt,$$
$$ds_2 = (3s_{1e} - 2s_{2e} - 2)\, dt,$$

shows no displacement, i.e., we get $ds_1 = 0$, $ds_2 = 0$, for any time interval dt. Thus the point $(\frac{8}{5}, \frac{7}{5})$ is an equilibrium point and is not on the expectation line: $s_{1e} \neq s_{2e}$. Yet, is it stable?

Stability means that if our actor finds himself at some time t_o in a position, say $\vec{s}(t_o)$, such that this is *not* the equilibrium $\vec{s}_e$, then

$$\vec{s}(t) \rightarrow \vec{s}_e$$

as $t \rightarrow \infty$: he gravitates toward the equilibrium. We could put this another way: suppose he is in equilibrium, and a random input throws our actor out of equilibrium $\vec{s}_e$; will he return to it or not? If yes, then we have a stable system; if not, we have an unstable system. Or, suppose we have a collection of actors who are identical in all parameter values but occupy differing initial positions. Then, if the equilibrium position exists and is stable, after a suitably long time interval all actors are near this equilibrium position. If the system is unstable, the initial differences translate through time into trajectories that do not proceed toward one and the same position. Our basic result is the following:

PROPOSITION 4. The equilibrium is unstable.

For a proof of this proposition, see Fararo (1970a). In the next section, it will be shown that this is a special case of a more general stability theorem.

A geometric picture of the system's behavior near equilibrium is provided in Figure 5 in order to illustrate the movement away from equilibrium characteristic of an unstable system. This is the previous example of the symmetric system with parameters $a_1 = a_2 = 1$, $b_1 = b_2 = 3$, $c_1 = 1$, $c_2 = 2$. As indicated earlier, the equilibrium position exists at $\vec{s}_e = (\frac{8}{5}, \frac{7}{5})$. We see, however, that if the Galtung Actor is deflected from this equilibrium or begins outside of it, he does not gravitate toward it. For four possible initial positions relative to the equilibrium, we have four different trajectories shown in Figure 5. Two of these trajectories are eventually "skid row" motions in which both statuses are steadily declining as time passes. The other two trajectories eventually are upwardly mobile movements on both variables, although the actor is not experiencing an entirely "happy" state of affairs because most of the time his position is not balanced (according to his own expectations).

To complete the mathematical analysis of the Galtung Actor, we should examine the case where $\Delta = 0$. Eliminating details, we simply note that even though in this case the entire s_1-axis forms a set of equilibrium solutions, they are unstable.

We now sum up the major analytical properties of the Galtung Actor. By

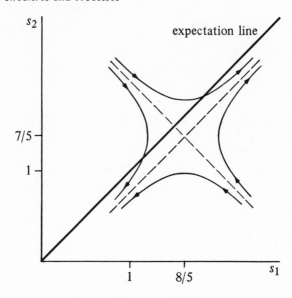

■ **FIGURE 5.** An Example of an Unstable System

definition, this actor experiences status movement as a result of the interplay of two major motivational mechanisms, natural upward mobility and equilibration, and a constraining environment. Under almost all conditions (values of parameters), the system possesses an equilibrium position (Proposition 1) uniquely defined under those conditions. *If* the actor were in such a position, he would stay there. However, the position is not likely to be one in which he is balanced (Proposition 2), and in any event, whether or not balance holds, it is unstable (Proposition 4) in the sense that he will not gravitate toward it if he is near it. The system possesses the property that under *all* conditions there is no stable equilibrium.

Sociologically, it is not intuitively appealing to have an actor who cannot possibly "settle in" to a position. Thus, this analysis makes the known tendency of people to "stay put" very problematic; surely, social life is not *that* fragile.[5] An examination of the deduced properties of this model leads to the search for reasons why it possesses this property of unconditional instability. We note that only two status variables were employed. In many situations this may be reasonable, but what of the effect of the fixed statuses? Are there not expectations for dynamical statuses based on ascribed statuses? (For example, an ascribed ethnic status sets up an expected level of achievement on dynamical variables.) These fixed statuses should play some definite role in the dynamics

---

[5] The same tendency appears problematic in Parsons' treatment of the position of the individual actor in *The Social System*, where this problem provides the analytical impetus to deal with mechanisms of socialization and social control. In the next section, our "controlled" actor has internalized certain expectations, based upon his ascribed statuses; relative to the present "uncontrolled" actor he can then be "kept in line."

of status equilibration over and above any role they may play in determining the initial conditions. These remarks lead to the conjecture that if the fixed status variables played a proper role in the model, it could be generalized to include the possibility of a stable equilibrium. In the next section we construct a model reflecting these considerations.

□ 5. THE CONTROLLABLE GALTUNG ACTOR

Our starting point is the Galtung Actor, with the introduction of one new mechanism. This mechanism links ascribed (time-invariant) states to dynamical elements via expectations. Deviations from expectations act as equilibrating forces. Suppose s_3 is a fixed status. That is, for all t in T, the time-domain of the model, we have

$$s_3 = s_3(t; \alpha) = v_3(c_3(\alpha)),$$

so that for the actor α not only the valuation but the characterization is time-invariant. We propose that this status, in the manner of the equilibration mobilizer of the prior section, acts as a negative feedback device vis-à-vis each dynamical status. For continuity with the prior section, suppose that, as in (19), we have

$$e(s_3) = Ks_3 \tag{31}$$

for the corresponding place on s_2 under the expectation based on s_3. Since s_3 is fixed, so is Ks_3, unlike the corresponding term of equation (19) which is a time-varying expected status. Call this expected s_2-status K_{32} to indicate that it is an expectation for s_2 based on s_3. (Similarly, we have K_{31} for the expected s_1 status based on the ascribed s_3.)

The equilibrational mechanism, as a negative feedback device, will follow the pattern of comparing the expected state (K_{3i}) with the current state of the dynamical variable s_i and then applying a multiplying coefficient to produce a displacement ds_i. That is,

$$\begin{aligned}
\frac{ds_1}{dt} &= b_{31}(K_{31} - s_1), \\
\frac{ds_2}{dt} &= b_{32}(K_{32} - s_2).
\end{aligned} \tag{32}$$

If this were the *only* motivational mechanism, then the equilibrium position for the position $\vec{s}$ would be (K_{31}, K_{32}) since these values make the right side of both members of (32) identically zero. However, our basic analytical principle is that status movement is the outcome of a linear combination of such mobilizers; further, we want to deal with the general case in which there is an arbitrary but finite number of fixed statuses as the dynamical elements of the situation unfold Thus, using the additivity principle, we write one equation such as (32) for each such fixed status s_j, and add to obtain

$$\frac{ds_1}{dt} = \sum_j b_{j1}(K_{j1} - s_1),$$
$$\frac{ds_2}{dt} = \sum_j b_{j2}(K_{j2} - s_2).$$
(33)

Equations (33) represent the induced status movement due to the combined effect of these "status thermostats" (with fixed settings). We let

$$w_i = \sum_j b_{ji}K_{ji}, \qquad z_i = \sum_j b_{ji},$$
(34)

for $i = 1, 2$. Substitution of (34) into equations (33) yields

$$\frac{ds_1}{dt} = w_1 - z_1 s_1,$$
$$\frac{ds_2}{dt} = w_2 - z_2 s_2.$$
(35)

Each b_{ji} has a responsiveness interpretation so that we can call the sum of these terms, which is z_i, the *external responsiveness* of s_i. The term "external" suggests the extent to which dynamical behavior within the system is controlled by statuses independent of the behavior of the system (as in Homans, 1950). High external responsiveness implies a rapid adjustment of the time-varying (situational) statuses. Were this mechanism the only one operative, the equilibrium would be that position such that

$$s_i = w_i/z_i, \qquad (i = 1, 2),$$

which by (34) means that each variable would equal a normalized weighted combination of the expected levels induced by the external variables, each weight having a responsiveness interpretation.

We now regard equations (35) as the third of the motivational mechanisms propelling our actor through various states. Equations (23) of the prior section defined the combined effect of the other two mobilizers. To avoid additional notation, the constant inputs can be regarded as part of the sum producing the w_i constants of equations (35) producing

$$\frac{ds_1}{dt} = (a_1 - b_1 - z_1)s_1 + b_1 s_2 + w_1,$$
$$\frac{ds_2}{dt} = (a_2 - b_2 - z_2)s_2 + b_2 s_1 + w_2.$$
(36)

Putting this in vector form, the system matrix becomes

$$A = \begin{pmatrix} a_1 - b_1 - z_1 & b_1 \\ b_2 & a_2 - b_2 - z_2 \end{pmatrix}, \tag{37}$$

and the input vector is (w_1, w_2).

A comparison of this matrix with the matrix shown in expression (17) indicates that the new system is a generalization of the earlier system; with $z_1 = z_2 = 0$, we recover the essential aspect of the earlier system given by its matrix. We can now interpret the Galtung Actor as an actor with no external responsiveness.

The analysis of the present system, which we might call the Controllable Galtung Actor, follows the pattern of the prior section.

Proposition 1 holds for the Controllable Galtung Actor with Δ given by

$$\Delta = (a_1 - b_1 - z_1)(a_2 - b_2 - z_2) - b_1 b_2. \tag{38}$$

By asking the same theoretical question that led to Proposition 2 for the uncontrolled Galtung Actor, we obtain the following general result by identical reasoning:

PROPOSITION 5. $s_{1e} = s_{2e}$ if and only if $w_2(z_1 - a_1) = w_1(z_2 - a_2)$.

This shows that only under strict conditions will the actor be in a *balanced* state of equilibrium. One sufficient condition is that $z_1 = a_1$ and $z_2 = a_2$, so that for each variable, the external responsiveness matches the escapability. In case the actor is not responsive to the ascribed statuses, the w_i terms become the inputs, denoted c_i in the previous section, the z_i vanish, and Proposition 5 becomes Proposition 2, a special case.

We now study in greater detail the question of stability of equilibrium for the Controllable Galtung Actor. The reader unconcerned with technical details will find our basic result in Proposition 7. We first move the origin of the coordinate system to the point $\vec{s}_e$ being investigated for stability by defining

$$\vec{r} = \vec{s} - \vec{s}_e. \tag{39}$$

In the new coordinate system, the origin $\vec{r} = \vec{0}$ corresponds to the point $\vec{s}_e$ of the original coordinate system. We differentiate both sides of (39)

$$\frac{d\vec{r}}{dt} = \frac{d\vec{s}}{dt} \quad \text{(since } \vec{s}_e \text{ is an equilibrium point)}$$

$$= A\vec{s} + \vec{w}$$

$$= A(\vec{r} + \vec{s}_e) + \vec{w}$$

$$= A\vec{r} + A\vec{s}_e + \vec{w}$$

$$= A\vec{r} + \frac{d\vec{s}_e}{dt}$$

$$= A\vec{r},$$

so that in the new coordinates we have the same system matrix but a so-called *homogeneous system* in which the input term is not present.

The qualitative theory of systems (see Brauer and Nohel, 1967; Rabenstein, 1966; Sanchez, 1968) investigates the stability of the origin of an arbitrary homogeneous system. By applying this theory we can determine the stability conditions for our equilibrium point $\vec{s}_e$. The origin of the homogeneous system is stable[6] if

$$\lim_{t \to \infty} \vec{r}(t) = \vec{0}$$

for any trajectory implied by the system. The status interpretation is that the origin represents the equilibrium position $\vec{s}_e$: if one were in this position at some time, one would remain there for given conditions represented by the parameters. But suppose one were subject to some random disturbance. Would a return to the equilibrium eventually take place? This is the stability question.

The basic proposition needed from the qualitative theory is that the origin of a homogeneous system is stable if and only if all eigenvalues of the system matrix A have negative real parts.

An eigenvalue is a number λ, such that for some nonzero vector $\vec{x}$, we have

$$A\vec{x} = \lambda\vec{x},$$

which is equivalent to

$$(A - \lambda I)\vec{x} = \vec{0},$$

where I is the identity matrix. For a nonzero $\vec{x}$ to make this true for some λ, the matrix operator $(A - \lambda I)$ must not be a one-to-one mapping and so must *not* have an inverse. Therefore, the necessary and sufficient condition that λ be an eigenvalue is that the determinant of $(A - \lambda I)$ be zero. Writing out this matrix for our system and obtaining the expression for the determinant shows that the eigenvalues of A are the solutions of the equation,

$$\lambda^2 - S\lambda + \Delta = 0, \tag{40}$$

where Δ is given by (38) and

$$S = (a_1 - b_1 - z_1) + (a_2 - b_2 - z_2). \tag{41}$$

Using the quadratic formula for the solutions of (40), one can show that the solutions have negative real parts if and only if $S < 0$ and $\Delta > 0$. These are

---

[6] Technically, this is asymptotic stability. Other kinds of stability become quite relevant in studying nonlinear systems. See Brauer and Nohel (1969).

the necessary and sufficient conditions for stability of equilibrium.
Let

$$Z_i = a_i - b_i - z_i \qquad (i = 1, 2)$$

so that one can write these two necessary and sufficient conditions for stability in the form,

$$\begin{align}
&\text{(a) } Z_1 < -Z_2, \\
&\text{(b) } Z_1 Z_2 > b_1 b_2.
\end{align} \tag{42}$$

To find the necessary conditions for stability in some readily interpretable form, suppose that the equilibrium is stable. Then both (42a) and (42b) hold. For various cases, depending upon signs, we have:

CASE 1. $Z_1 > 0$. Then,

$$\begin{align}
Z_1{}^2 &< -Z_1 Z_2 &&\text{(by 42a)} \\
&< -b_1 b_2 &&\text{(by 42b)} \\
&< 0, &&\text{(since } b_1 \text{ and } b_2 \text{ are positive)}
\end{align}$$

which is impossible since the square of any number is nonnegative.

CASE 2. $Z_1 < 0$.

SUBCASE 2a. $Z_2 > 0$. Then,

$$Z_1 Z_2 < 0 < b_1 b_2,$$

which contradicts (42b).

SUBCASE 2b. $Z_2 < 0$. Here we do not obtain any contradiction.

Thus, if the system is stable, then both Z_1 and Z_2 are negative. In terms of the original parameters, we have demonstrated the following:

PROPOSITION 6. If the system is stable, then for each status variable the escapability (a_i) is less than the total responsiveness $(b_i + z_i)$.

Briefly, the statuses must not be too easily escaped. Alternatively, the actor must not be too unresponsive to expectations.

From Proposition 6 we can prove Proposition 4. Suppose that the necessary conditions of Proposition 6 hold. The condition that $\Delta > 0$, which is (42b), may be written

$$(a_1 - z_1)Z_2 > b_1(a_2 - z_2). \tag{43}$$

This condition will fail if both $a_1 - z_1$ and $a_2 - z_2$ are positive because Z_2 is negative and b_1 is positive. Therefore, another necessary condition for stability is: it is not the case that both $a_1 > z_1$ and $a_2 > z_2$. However, for the Galtung Actor of the prior section, the $z_i = 0$, while the a_i are positive, so that this condition cannot be satisfied. Thus Proposition 4 follows.

This reasoning deals with necessary conditions for stability. That these conditions may obtain in the Controllable Galtung Actor induces us to seek a sufficient condition for stability. One conjecture is that the actor be controlled by the ascribed statuses to the extent that his responsiveness (z_i) to them exceeds the escapability in each dimension. That is: $a_i < z_i$, for $i = 1, 2$. To check this, we examine the conditions (42).

From the hypothesis that $a_i < z_i$ ($i = 1, 2$),

$$a_1 < b_1 + z_1 \quad \text{and} \quad a_2 < b_2 + z_2,$$

since the b_i are positive. Then $Z_1 < 0$ and $Z_2 < 0$, and condition (42a) is satisfied. To check if (42b) is satisfied, we use the equivalent condition (43). As the product of two negative quantities, the term $(a_1 - z_1)Z_2$ is positive. The term $b_1(a_2 - z_2)$ is a product of a positive and a negative quantity and so is negative. Therefore, the condition expressed in (43) is satisfied. Hence both conditions of (42) are satisfied: if an equilibrium exists, it is stable. But the second condition is the equivalent of $\Delta > 0$, which means $\Delta \neq 0$, and so a unique equilibrium exists. Therefore if the escapability in each variable is bounded above by the corresponding external responsiveness, a unique and stable equilibrium position exists. In summary:

PROPOSITION 7. If for each status variable the escapability is less than the external responsiveness (that is, $a_i < z_i$, for $i = 1, 2$), a unique stable equilibrium position exists.

Parallel to formula (30) for the Galtung Actor of the prior section, for the Controllable Galtung Actor we obtain

$$\begin{aligned}
s_{1e} &= \frac{1}{\Delta}[w_2 b_1 - w_1 Z_2], \\
s_{2e} &= \frac{1}{\Delta}[w_1 b_2 - w_2 Z_1].
\end{aligned} \tag{44}$$

To consider a concrete case, let the system be symmetric and drop subscripts on the parameters. Suppose $a = b = 1$, $z = 2$ and $w = 3$. Since $a < z$, it follows from Proposition 7 that a stable equilibrium exists and is computed by formula (44). Using the definitions of the quantities appearing in (44) and the illustrative numerical values, we compute the equilibrium position $(3, 3)$. To verify this, we enter equations (36) with $s_1 = 3$ and $s_2 = 3$ on the right side and find that both expressions become identically zero.

We now summarize the basic analytical properties of the Controllable Galtung Actor. By definition, this actor experiences status movement as a result of the interplay of three motivational mechanisms (natural upward mobility, equilibration between dynamical statuses, equilibration with respect to ascribed statuses) and a constraining environment. Under almost all conditions (values of parameters), the system possesses an equilibrium position (Proposition 1 with Δ given by formula 38) uniquely defined for those conditions. However, the position is not likely to be one in which he is balanced (Proposition 5), and, whether or not balance holds, a sufficient condition for stability is that the actor be sufficiently responsive to expectations based on ascribed statuses (Proposition 7). The system is controllable, in that there exist parametric conditions under which a stable equilibrium position can be achieved: the introduction of expectations based on ascribed statuses acts as a control system which stabilizes the actor's situational (dynamical) statuses provided that the actor is sufficiently responsive to these expectations. (For further discussion of this model, see Fararo 1970b.)

□ **6. THE KIMBERLY ACTOR**

In the introduction the claim was made that other theoretical conceptions of status equilibration could find a natural place within this framework. Let us now briefly illustrate the establishment of the four-dimensional system verbally specified by Kimberly (1966).

There are four "substatuses" in the Kimberly formulation of "the structure of status." Each substatus possesses its own unique variant of the measurement problem. For example, function substatus must be regarded as the valuation of a characterization depending upon functional uniqueness and centrality to the task. Bypassing these measurement problems, we have four status variables comprising the position of the Kimberly Actor, $\vec{s} = (s_1, s_2, s_3, s_4)$, where

s_1 is the valuation of the actor's special *functions* in the particular division of labor,

s_2 is the valuation of the actor's *performance* of these functions,

s_3 is the valuation of the actor's *ability* to perform these functions,

s_4 is the valuation of the actor's performance of universal functions, called his *loyalty*.

A general system for the dynamics of the Kimberly Actor is the four-dimensional version of the general system of equations (14) above. Now let us see how Kimberly's hypotheses can define éxplicit mechanisms that produce the dynamics of the system.

His first hypothesis states, "When function substatus is lower than ability substatus, there will be pressure on the individual to be upwardly mobile with respect to functions" (Kimberly, 1966, p. 225).

Though this sounds like a thermostat with ability providing the setting, it is one-way, whereas we would expect control upwards or downwards. This is the same as Kimberly's hypothesis 4 in which he states, "When function substatus is higher than ability substatus, there will be pressure on the individual to be downwardly mobile with respect to functions" (Kimberly, 1966, p. 225). Thus, these two hypotheses specify an equilibrational mobilizer, or negative feedback device, with ability as the source of the "expected state" and function status as the dynamical variable. This means an equation of the form,

$$\frac{ds_1}{dt} = b(s_3 - s_1), \quad (b > 0) \tag{45}$$

where, for the moment, s_3 is fixed and the mechanism produces equilibrium with respect to s_1 when s_1 agrees with s_3. (We assume that s_3 stands for the term ks_3, with $k = 1$, so that its dimension is that of s_1.) Multiply both sides of (45) by a small time interval, dt, and note that if s_1 is less than s_3, ds_1 will be positive in agreement with Kimberly's Hypothesis 1. If s_1 is greater than s_3, then ds_1 will be negative in agreement with Kimberly's Hypothesis 4. The "pressure" described by Kimberly is the contribution of this mobilizer to the total mechanism producing the actual status movement.

According to Kimberly's Hypothesis 2, there is "status aspiration" such that when it is strong, the actor is induced to move upwards on function status. This sounds like our natural mobilizer, as applied to function status. Thus, we can represent this hypothesis by the mechanism,

$$\frac{ds_1}{dt} = as_1, \quad (a > 0) \tag{46}$$

although any equation that implied an increasing function of time would do the job.

According to Kimberly, two "derivations" depend upon these hypotheses. Actually, as in most cases of verbal arguments, they are not logical consequences of the premises. Rather, they play the role of an additivity principle in the rule of combining mobilizers. Thus "Derivation A" which says, in part, "... the strength of the pressure ... to be ... mobile with respect to functions will be equal to the sum of the pressures resulting from status aspiration and status inconsistency," could be thought of as asserting,

$$\frac{ds_1}{dt} = as_1 + b(s_3 - s_1), \tag{47}$$

and "Derivation B" appears to be the same "derivation," with other sign combinations.

Perhaps Kimberly's treatment of reallocation of functions can be interpreted as a shift to a new set of parametric conditions. There seems no natural way of including this reallocation process in the system of equations for the dynamics of the Kimberly Actor. One reason may be that one should have $4k$ equations, 4 for each of k actors. In that case, the presence of new mechanisms linking the actors would be suggested, including, perhaps, allocation and reallocation.

In any case, this partial formalization of the Kimberly System shows that we have

$$\frac{ds_1}{dt} = as_1 + b(s_3 - s_1)$$

$$\frac{ds_2}{dt} = f_2(s_1, s_2, s_3, s_4)$$

$$\frac{ds_3}{dt} = 0 \tag{48}$$

$$\frac{ds_4}{dt} = f_4(s_1, s_2, s_3, s_4)$$

The first equation is (47). The second equation expresses the idea that performance status is a dynamical variable depending on the other variables. The third equation says that there is an assumption in the Kimberly model that the ability status is situationally fixed. Lastly, the equation for loyalty status expresses the fact that we need some mechanism depending upon the array of variables in the system. When f_2 and f_4 are specified, and the "reallocation of functions" representation is achieved, the mathematical model of Kimberly's work will be definite and analyzable.

Preliminary attempts to specify these functions (that is, f_2 and f_4) in reasonable accordance with the verbal theory have run into nonlinearities at an early stage. For example, f_2 becomes nonlinear if we assume that the natural mobilizer for performance status is constrained by an upper limit on performance given by the fixed ability variable. Thus, we must begin to study nonlinear systems.

What has been accomplished in this brief study of the Kimberly Actor? First, we see that the way in which Kimberly defines statuses and conceptualizes the phenomenon of status equilibration is compatible within our framework: we represent his system as a four-dimensional version of the general system. Second, the specific hypotheses proposed by Kimberly arise from reward-cost considerations not intrinsic to our framework and, yet, on analysis show themselves to be specifications of positive and negative feedback mechanisms of the type governing the Controllable Galtung Actor. Third, the attempt, however, to specify some of the detailed aspects of the system reveals nonlinear aspects are essential to its description.

Because nonlinear aspects appear essential to the Kimberly Actor, we cannot infer that the propositions that govern the Controllable Galtung Actor apply to the Kimberly Actor. This result provides a useful cautionary note to the unrestricted interpretation of status dynamics in linear terms and provides fresh motivation for the set-up and analysis of nonlinear models.

The reader attempting to keep track of the recent flood of formal work in social science may wonder how the approach presented here compares with other work. One mode of comparison is by type of mathematical model. Suppose we type along four dimensions: (1) dynamic or static; (2) continuous-time or discrete time; (3) continuous-variable or discrete-variable (state space); and (4) stochastic or deterministic. By this classification scheme, the work above is dynamic, continuous-time, continuous-variable, and deterministic although "position" has an intrinsically stochastic empirical meaning in terms of how we measure the valuations.

Most current dynamic models related to status movements treat this problem at the aggregate level using a discrete state space. They focus on the analysis of social mobility tables. (For a few examples, see White, 1963; Goodman, 1965; Bartholomew, 1967; Mayer, 1967; McGinnis, 1968; and McFarland, 1970.) Typically, this work attempts to subsume inter- and intra-generational mobility of an aggregate of units under a stochastic process which is analytically tractable.

The context of theoretical analysis gives rise to models somewhat different from those chosen within the context of data analysis. The empirical focus of mathematical sociology generates models which fit given forms of data and which *perhaps* may relate to some theoretical ideas. The theoretical focus of mathematical sociology gives rise to models which represent certain theories, and which *perhaps* may relate to some pre-existing forms of data.

The use of mathematics has an equilibrating effect in these two contexts. The model-builder, in the narrower sense, is induced to seek theoretical constructs and assumptions to make his formulation simpler and more cogent. For example, the Markov assumption is often unreasonable with respect to observable processes but is a matter of systematic meaning (Hempel, 1952) in the context of theoretical constructs (see Fararo, 1969a, b). On the other hand, the theoretician using mathematics is induced to seek definite linkages to observable processes. The difference, however, between the latter context and the first, is that the meaning of "data" may depend upon new theory. As sociology moves into more abstract modes of thinking, it can no longer be the case that readily available information must count as data. The theoretical work includes a component that governs the nature of the data that will be acceptable for that theory. When this is the case, "theory" and "data" are firmly coordinated.

To achieve this coordination within the present framework, the measurement theory of the second section must be activated. But this alone merely guarantees (assuming Luce's axiom is satisfied) that if observations over time are collected for a specified set of individuals, they can be translated into status data by applying the estimated valuation to the observed characterization successively over time. To test detailed models, a considerable amount of such data should be collected, which means close monitoring of the actors over time. In addition, the time scale must be chosen such that the stationary valuation assumption is plausible.

Taking an evolutionary point of view toward the development of a scientific theoretical system, the magnitude of work involved in this context should be no reason for alarm. Applied sociologists can continue to rely upon inexpensive indices and data-reduction systems; theoretical sociologists should seek to formulate more rigorously the foundations of our discipline.

□ **REFERENCES**

Ashby, W. R., *An Introduction to Cybernetics* (London: Chapman and Hall, 1956).

Atkinson, R. C., G. H. Bower, and E. J. Crothers, *An Introduction to Mathematical Learning Theory* (New York: Wiley, 1965) Chap. 4.

Barber, B., *Social Stratification* (New York: Harcourt, Brace and World, 1957).

Bartholomew, D. J., *Stochastic Models for Social Processes* (New York: Wiley, 1967).

Bellman, R., *Adaptive Control Processes: A Guided Tour* (Princeton: Princeton University Press, 1961).

Berger, J., B. P. Cohen, and M. Zelditch, Jr., "Status Characteristics and Expectation States," in J. Berger, M. Zelditch, Jr., and B. Anderson (eds.), *Sociological Theories in Progress*, Vol. I (New York: Houghton Mifflin, 1966).

Blalock, H. M., Jr., *Theory Construction* (Englewood Cliffs, N. J.: Prentice-Hall, 1969).

Blau, P. M., *Exchange and Power in Social Life* (New York: Wiley, 1964).

Brauer, F. and J. A. Nohel, *Ordinary Differential Equations, A First Course* (New York: Benjamin, 1967).

Brauer, F. and J. A. Nohel, *The Qualitative Theory of Ordinary Differential Equations* (New York: Benjamin, 1969).

Coleman, J. S., *Introduction to Mathematical Sociology* (New York: The Free Press, 1964).

Davis, J. A., "Structural Balance, Mechanical Solidarity, and Interpersonal Relations," in J. Berger, M. Zelditch, Jr., and B. Anderson (eds.), *Sociological Theories in Progress*, Vol. I (New York: Houghton Mifflin, 1966).

Fararo, T. J., "Theory of Status," *General Systems* 13 (1968), pp. 177–188.

Fararo, T. J., "Nature of Mathematical Sociology," *Social Research* 36 (1969), pp. 75–92.

Fararo, T. J., "Stochastic Processes," in E. Borgatta (ed.), *Sociological Methodology* (San Francisco: Jossey-Bass, 1969).

Fararo, T. J., "Status Dynamics," in E. Borgatta and G. Bohrnstedt (eds.), *Sociological Methodology* (San Francisco: Jossey-Bass, 1970).

Fararo, T. J., "Theoretical Studies in Status and Stratification," *General Systems* 15 (1970), pp. 71–101.

Fararo, T. J., "Strictly Stratified Systems," *Sociology* 4 (1970), pp. 85–104.

Feller, W., *An Introduction to Probability Theory and Its Applications*, Vol. II (New York: Wiley, 1966).

Freeman, L. C., *Patterns of Local Community Leadership* (Indianapolis: Bobbs-Merrill, 1968).

Freeman, L. C., W. Bloomberg, Jr., M. Sunshine, S. Koff, and T. J. Fararo, *Local*

Community Leadership (Syracuse: University College, 1960).

Galanter, E., *Textbook of Elementary Psychology* (San Francisco: Holden-Day, 1966).

Galtung, J., "Rank and Social Integration: A Multidimensional Approach," in J. Berger, M. Zelditch, Jr., and B. Anderson (eds.), *Sociological Theories in Progress*, Vol. I (New York: Houghton Mifflin, 1966).

Goodman, L. A., "On the Statistical Analysis of Mobility Tables," *American Journal of Sociology* 70 (1965), pp. 564–585.

Gusfield, J. and M. Schwartz, "The Meanings of Occupational Prestige," *American Sociological Review* 28 (1963), pp. 265–271.

Heider, F., *The Psychology of Interpersonal Relations* (New York: Wiley, 1958).

Hempel, C. G., *Fundamentals of Concept Formation in Empirical Science* (Chicago: University of Chicago Press, 1952).

Homans, G., *The Human Group* (New York: Harcourt, Brace and Co., 1950).

Homans, G., *Social Behavior: Its Elementary Forms* (New York: Harcourt, Brace and Co., 1961).

Jackson, E. F. and R. F. Curtis, "Conceptualization and Measurement in the Study of Social Stratification," in H. M. Blalock, Jr. and A. B. Blalock (eds.), *Methodology in Social Research* (New York: McGraw-Hill, 1968).

Kimberly, J. C., "A Theory of Status Equilibration," in J. Berger, M. Zelditch, Jr., and B. Anderson (eds.), *Sociological Theories in Progress*, Vol. I (New York: Houghton Mifflin, 1966).

Kluckhohn, C., "Values and Value-Orientations in the Theory of Action: An Exploration in Definition and Classification," in T. Parsons and E. A. Shils (eds.), *Toward a General Theory of Action* (New York: Harper, 1951).

Lange, O., *Wholes and Parts: A General Theory of Systems Behavior* (Oxford: Pergamon, 1965).

Luce, R. D., *Individual Choice Behavior* (New York: Wiley, 1959).

Mayer, T. F., "Birth and Death Process Models of Social Mobility." Unpublished manuscript. Michigan Studies in Mathematical Sociology, No. 2 (1967).

McFarland, D. D., "Intragenerational Social Mobility as a Markov Process," *American Sociological Review* 35 (1970), pp. 463–476.

McGinnis, R., "A Stochastic Model of Social Mobility," *American Sociological Review* 33 (1968), pp. 712–722.

Milsum, J. H. (ed.), *Positive Feedback: A General Systems Approach to Positive/Negative Feedback and Mutual Causality* (Oxford: Pergamon, 1968).

Parsons, T., *The Social System* (New York: The Free Press, 1951).

Parsons, T., "A Revised Analytical Approach to the Theory of Social Stratification," in R. Bendix and S. M. Lipset (eds.), *Class, Status and Power* (New York: The Free Press, 1953).

Pfanzagl, J., *Theory of Measurement* (New York: Wiley, 1968).

Rabenstein, A. L., *Introduction to Ordinary Differential Equations* (New York: Academic Press, 1966).

Restle, F., *Psychology of Judgment and Choice* (New York: Wiley, 1961).

Robertson, R. and A. Tudor, "The Third World and International Stratification," *Sociology* 2 (1968), pp. 47–64.

Sanchez, D. A., *Ordinary Differential Equations and Stability Theory: An Introduction* (San Francisco: Freeman, 1968).

Schwartz, R. J. and B. Friedland, *Linear Systems* (New York: McGraw-Hill, 1965).

Suppes, P. and J. Zinnes, "Basic Measurement Theory," in R. D. Luce, R. R. Bush, and E. Galanter (eds.), *Handbook of Mathematical Psychology*, Vol. I (New York: Wiley, 1963).

Tumin, M. M., *Social Stratification* (Englewood Cliffs, N. J.: Prentice-Hall, 1967).

White, H., "Cause and Effect in Social Mobility Tables," *Behavioral Science* 8 (1963), pp. 14–27.

Zelditch, M., Jr., and B. Anderson, "On the Balance of a Set of Ranks," in J. Berger, M. Zelditch, Jr., and B. Anderson (eds.), *Sociological Theories in Progress*, Vol. I (Boston: Houghton Mifflin, 1966).

Chapter 10

The Structure of Positive Interpersonal Relations in Small Groups*

■ JAMES A. DAVIS & SAMUEL LEINHARDT

□ **ABSTRACT**

The authors sought to test Homans's proposition that small groups inevitably generate a social structure which combines subgroups (cliques) and a ranking system. We present a graph theoretical model of such a structure and prove that a necessary and sufficient condition for its existence is the absence of seven particular triad types. Expected frequencies of the seven triad types in random graphs are deduced from elementary probability theory, and we suggest that a reasonable operational statement of Homans's theory is that in most groups the seven key triads are less frequent than the random model would predict. A data pool of sociograms and sociomatrices from 427 groups was collected from diverse published and unpublished studies. Random samples of thirty school and thirty adult groups were drawn from the pool and analyzed. Significant majorities of both samples showed deviations from chance in the directions predicted. As a check, sixty simulated groups with truly random relationships were analyzed and found to be close to the chance expectations and quite different from the real data samples. Overall, we claim support for Homans's theory.

In *The Human Group*[1] George Homans presents a set of closely linked propositions about subgroup formation and ranking. In paraphrase, his argument is this:

1. In any group the external system (loosely, the group's environment) makes it inevitable that frequencies of interaction will be unevenly distributed among the member pairs (p. 86).
2. Because differential frequencies of interaction, interpersonal liking, and

* This study was supported by NSF grant GS-1286, Public Health Service grant 7-F1-Ch-23, 346–01A2 and funds and facilities contributed by National Opinion Research Center and Dartmouth College. We wish to thank Zahava Blum, John Bramsen, and David Klassen for their contributions to the project.

[1] George C. Homans, *The Human Group* (New York: Harcourt, Brace and Co., 1950). All references in this paper not otherwise cited are to the same source. For a very similar view, see Roger Brown, *Social Psychology* (New York: The Free Press, 1965, pp. 51–100).

similarity in other sentiments and activities go together, pairs and larger subsets with initially higher rates of interaction come to be increasingly differentiated from the rest of the group, forming subgroups (cliques) characterized by high rates of voluntary interaction, positive interpersonal sentiments, and normative consensus (pp. 112, 118, 120).

3. Nevertheless, the members are more nearly alike in the norms they hold than in their conformity to these norms (p. 126), and since the closer a person's activities come to the norm, the higher his rank will be (p. 141), all groups develop systems of ranking.

It is hard to avoid the inference that if we examine voluntary interaction and sentiments in small groups, Homans expects us to find two sorts of structures, differentiation into cliques and elaboration into ranks, *and he expects us to find them in group after group after group.* Furthermore, he expects us to find both structures with the same variables. Not only do subgroup members have higher rates of interaction, but so do higher ranking members (p. 182). Not only do subgroup members have higher frequencies of liking, but higher ranking persons are better liked (p. 148).

These propositions are as well known as any in sociology, yet we have little systematic evidence for them. Homans himself says:

Let us be clear that it (the association between interaction and liking) is only a hypothesis, not a theorem. We have offered no proof, except what is provided by the behavior of the Bank Wiremen, and a statistician would say that a single instance is not nearly enough. Plenty of confirmatory evidence could be found in anthropological and sociological studies of small groups (p. 114).

This paper aims to test Homans's structural propositions, using simple statistical models developed from graph theory and applying them to a data pool of interpersonal relations measures (sociograms and sociomatrices) for 427 groups. To the extent that our model is plausible, our probabilistic reasoning is valid, and our 427 groups are representative, the results provide favorable evidence for the propositions.

□ A GRAPH THEORETICAL MODEL

While Homans's definitions are notoriously crisp, he nowhere defines the total structure which is implied by his twin principles. We take the liberty of sketching such a model, hoping that it does justice to the original.

We begin with the notion of a "positive relation" and say that person i has a positive relation to person j if he: (1) frequently interacts with j on a voluntary basis (formal authority is excluded from the hypotheses, pp. 244–248); (2) expresses a positive sentiment about j; (3) would prefer to interact with j on a voluntary basis; or (4) claims that j is his friend.

Note that the opposite of a positive relation, non-positive, may be neutral (indifferent) or negative (dislikes, avoids, etc.). Note further that positive relationships are not defined as symmetrical. If i has a positive relation to j, *j* may or may not reciprocate it. There are three logical possibilities, which we will call *M* for mutual positive relations, *A* for asymmetric relations in which there is a positive relation from *i* to *j* or *j* to *i* but not both, and *N* for mutual non-positive relations. In graphs, we may draw them as follows

$$(i \leftrightarrow j = M) \quad (i \rightarrow j \text{ or } i \leftarrow j = A) \quad (i \leftrightarrow j = N).$$

Having granted that pair relations may be symmetric or asymmetric, we should now turn to the triads produced by all possible combinations of members taken three at a time. The logical heart of our model will consist of a set of propositions about these triads. However, our discussion will be clearer, though less rigorous, if we skip ahead to the sort of group structure which is implied by our yet unstated triad propositions.

We begin by treating a group's ranking structure as a series of ordered levels, which is another way of saying that there may be more people than status distinctions in the group. It is useful to think of the levels as stories in a building, in the sense that people on a given floor do not differ in level, any two persons on different floors are unambiguously ordered by level, and the stories form a complete order.

The building analogy is useful, but misleading in one important sense. While floors and ceilings mark the levels in a building, in structural theory we seek to generate such features from the pattern of pair relations themselves. Indeed, one may think of social structure as those characteristics of a group which may be deduced from the characteristics of pair relations within the group. This leads us to one of the main ideas of the model: *Relations of the sort we have called A are assumed to connect persons in different levels, while M and N relations are assumed to connect persons in the same level. Further, we assume that in pairs connected by A relations, the recipient of the positive relationship is in the higher level.*

We are claiming that if you and I like each other or if neither of us likes the other we are probably in the same status level in our group, but if I like you and you do not like me, you are probably in a different and higher level. We may think of such *A* relations as "admiration" and summarize the whole business with the slogan, "admiration flows up levels."

The second major idea of the model is that within a level there may be disjoint subsets of people (cliques or subgroups) analogous to people in different rooms on a floor of a building. Again, these must be defined relationally. All intra-level relationships, of course, must be Type *M* or Type *N* if all *A* relations lie between levels, which leads us to the second main idea of the model: *M relations are assumed to connect persons in the same clique within a level. N relations are assumed to connect persons in different cliques within a level.*[2] Using our building analogy, we advance the slogan "*N* relations make partitions."

Putting both ideas together, the heart of the model is the notion that in

---

[2] The technical reader will note that this is the same definition of cliques used in the theory of structural balance.

small groups the members tend to be divided into levels by the pattern of their *A* relations, and within levels they tend to be divided into cliques by the pattern of their *M* and *N* relations. Figure 1 puts the idea in rough schematic form:

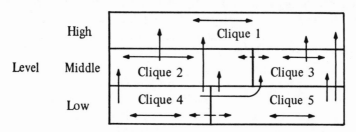

■ **FIGURE 1.** Levels, Cliques, and Relations

Remembering that we have not yet stated any principles which guarantee that such a structure must emerge and be consistent, let us examine Figure 1. We see that it has three levels and five cliques, though the number of cliques and levels is not fixed by the model. Within each clique all relationships are of the *M* type; where cliques differ in level there are always *A* relationships with the arrows pointing up; and between cliques at the same level there are *N* relationships. We further note that the top level has only one clique, which is to say that all cliques are assumed to lie within a level but it is not assumed that every level has a clique. None of the levels in Figure 1 has more than two cliques, but this is simply because the diagram would be too cluttered.

Let us now ask whether Figure 1 is a plausible translation of Homans's ideas. Considering cliques (subgroups) first, Homans defines them as follows:

> If we say that individuals A, B, C, D, E . . . form a group, this will mean that at least the following circumstances hold. Within a given period of time, A interacts more often with B, C, D, E . . . than he does with M, N, L, O, P . . . whom we choose to consider outsiders or members of other groups. B also interacts more often with A, C, D, E . . . than he does with outsiders, and so on for the other members of the group (p. 84).

In other words, cliques are subsets of individuals with higher rates of positive relationships among themselves than with outsiders. This, of course, is the definition of cliques in the theory of structural balance and clusterability.[3] Our cliques have this property since each pair within a clique has two positive relationships, while each inter-clique pair has either one positive relationship (if *i* and *j* are in different levels) or none (if *i* and *j* are in the same level).

Because Homans nowhere gives a formal definition of ranking it is harder to say that our version fits his second principle. However, the model has two properties which seem natural for a ranking.

First, people in higher levels receive more positive relations. Consider Person *i* in level *i* and Person *j* in some lower level, *j*. Mr. *j* receives positive

[3] Dorwin Cartwright and Frank Harary, "Structural Balance: A Generalization of Heider's Theory," *The Psychological Review*, (1956) 63: 277–93; James A. Davis, "Clustering and Structural Balance in Graphs," *Human Relations*, (1967) 20: 181–187.

relations from everyone in levels $1 \ldots j-1$ plus anyone in his own clique in level j. But lofty Mr. i receives all of these plus relations from everyone in level j whether or not they are in j's own clique, plus some from everyone in levels which might occur above j and below i, plus those from anyone in i's own clique. In the limiting case where i and j are the only members of adjacent levels, i still receives one more positive relation than j, the one from j to i, which is not, by definition, reciprocated. Thus, in general, if two persons differ in level, the one in the higher level will receive more positive relations. This property is not only consistent with Homans's statement that leaders are more popular, but when interpreted in terms of interaction, it squares with his proposition, "the higher a man's social rank, the larger will be the number of persons that originate interaction for him. Men that are not highly valued must seek others rather than be sought by them" (p. 182).

Second, positive relations are transitive. If i has a positive relation to j and j has a positive relation to k, then i will always have a positive relationship to k. The proof is simple, but tedious, and will not be presented in detail. One takes all the possible triads permitted under the triad propositions to be stated later, examines the six possible three-step paths in each (e.g., i to j to k, i to k to j, j to i to k . . . etc.) and sees that there are none in which the first two are positive and the third non-positive.

Since differential popularity and transitivity are the two most common definitions of ranking systems, we feel that the model has some plausibility. However, we have not successfully reflected every structural proposition in *The Human Group*. There is at least one near miss and one clear difference of opinion.

The near miss is the claim that all cliques are ranked (p. 139). In our model, the cliques are partially ordered (e.g., in Figure 1, the partial ordering is $1 > (2, 3) > (4, 5)$, but cliques within a level are not ordered.

The difference of opinion is worth some discussion. Homans states:

> The more nearly equal in social rank a number of men are, the more frequently they will interact with one another . . . if a person does originate interaction for a person of higher rank, a tendency will exist for him to do so with the member of his own subgroup who is nearest him in rank (p. 184).

In a group with three or more levels, this proposition implies N relationships between persons whose levels are not adjacent (Mr. Low seeks out Mr. Middle who seeks out Mr. High, but Messrs. High and Low do not seek out each other). Our model does not allow this. It does imply that the very highest rates of positive relations will be in the same level (intra-clique relations), but so will the lowest (inter-clique relations). Similarly, Homans implies that if i directs a positive relation to someone above him in rank, it will not go to everyone in that rank, while our model implies that everyone directs positive relations to everyone in every rank above him. The issue is of some interest because Homans uses it to argue, in effect, that interaction (and thus presumably sentiments) tend toward the structure graph theorists call a "tree from a point,"[4] the most common structural model for formal organizations.

[4] Frank Harary, Robert Z. Norman, and Dorwin Cartwright, *Structural Models* (New York: Wiley, 1965, p. 283).

Homans does go on to soften his proposition by saying that it is less true of smaller groups and those in less severe environments (p. 184). The question is an empirical one and the reader who is concerned about it should watch carefully in the data analysis for the results on what will be called "0-2-1-b" triads. For now, we merely note that our model assumes groups so small or in such benign environments that positive relations do not "go through channels."

We end our preliminary discussion of the model by noting its logical ties to some other models. It can be shown that by varying our assumptions about the presence of M, A, and N relations, the model can be changed into other well known structures.

1. If all pair relations are symmetrical, M or N, the structure consists of a single level and is equivalent to clusterability or structural balance.
2. If all pair relations are antisymmetrical, A, the structure consists of as many levels as people, all cliques are size one, and it is a transitive tournament.[5]
3. If all pair relations are M or A, there is only one clique at each level and the structure is what Hempel calls a "quasi-series."[6]

□ **TRIADS**

Having described the model in a non-rigorous fashion, it is time to state it more precisely. The procedure is this: we will list all the possible triads that could occur in a graph with M, A, and N pair relations, postulate that some of them do not exist, and then show that the structure discussed above is implied by the postulates.

We begin by counting the number of M, A, and N sides of a triad, using a three-digit code in which the first digit is the number of M edges, the second is the number of A edges, and the third is the number of N edges. Thus, a 3-0-0 triad has three M edges: a 1-1-1 triad has one M edge; one A edge; and one N edge. There are ten possibilities: 3-0-0; 2-0-1; 1-2-0; 1-1-1; 1-0-2; 0-1-2; 0-3-0; 0-2-1; 2-1-0; and 0-0-3. Within such types, triads may vary structurally if there are A relationships, depending on the "directions of the arrows." These subtypes will be defined later and identified by letters following the numerical code, e.g., 0-3-0-a, 0-3-0-b.

Figure 2 is a catalog of the possible triads in this classification.

Down the vertical axis we see the ten possible triad types when direction of A relations is ignored. In the middle of the list we see the four types (1-2-0, 0-2-1, 0-3-0, 1-1-1) where direction of the A lines makes a difference, and we further note that these have been subdivided into Subtypes "a" and "b". We also see a horizontal line below 0-3-0 and a vertical line between "a" and "b."

In a nutshell, the model states that *triads below the horizontal line and to the right of the vertical line never exist*, or rather that when they are absent, the

[5] *Ibid.*, pp. 289–317.
[6] Carl G. Hempel, *Fundamentals of Concept Formation in Empirical Science, International Encyclopedia of Unified Science*, Vol. II., No. 7, University of Chicago Press, 1952, pp. 58–62.

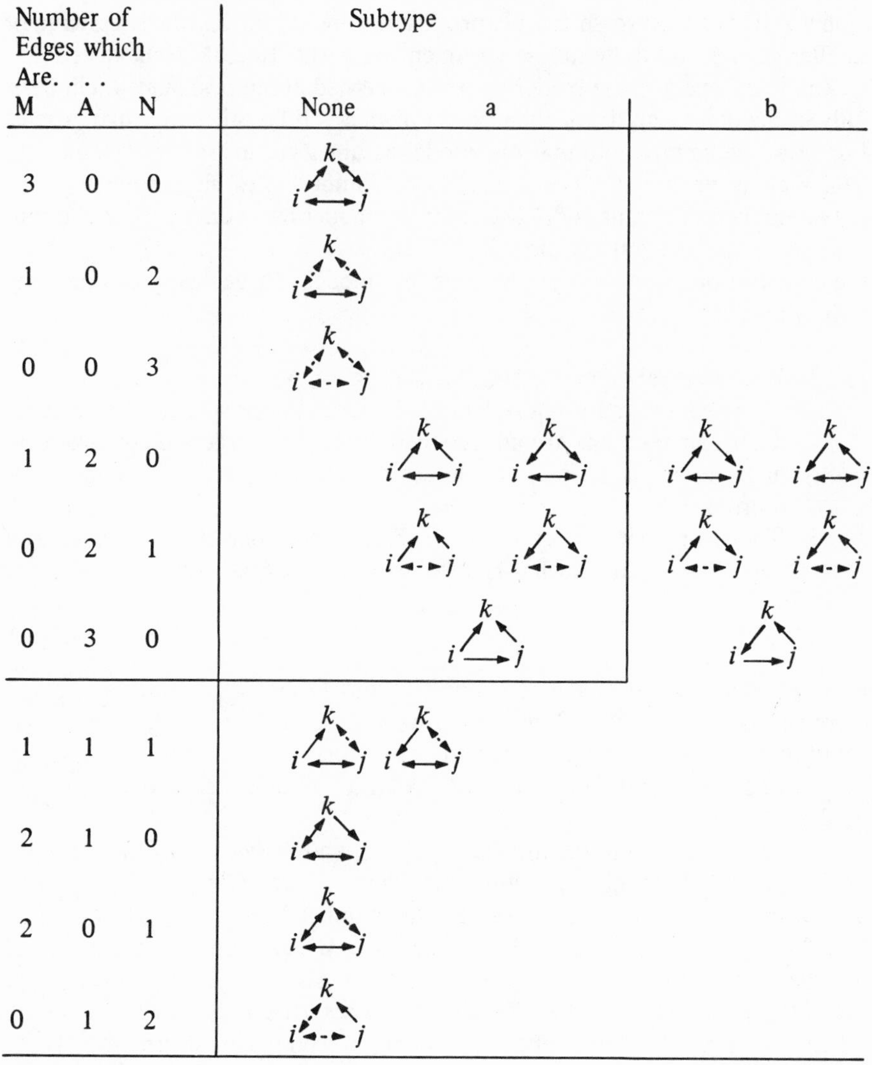

Number of Edges which Are....			Subtype		
M	A	N	None	a	b
3	0	0	(triad diagram)		
1	0	2	(triad diagram)		
0	0	3	(triad diagram)		
1	2	0		(two triad diagrams)	(two triad diagrams)
0	2	1		(two triad diagrams)	(two triad diagrams)
0	3	0		(triad diagram)	(triad diagram)
1	1	1	(two triad diagrams)		
2	1	0	(triad diagram)		
2	0	1	(triad diagram)		
0	1	2	(triad diagram)		

■ **FIGURE 2.** Classification of Triads

total structure will have all of the marvelous properties discussed above.

Let us examine each triad type, beginning with the permissible cases. Again, we are not giving formal proofs but we will soon.

Triads of Type 3-0-0 are certainly permissible as they must be three persons in the same clique at the same level.

Triads of Type 1-0-2 consist of two persons, i and j, in the same clique at one level, and a third, k, in a different clique at that level.

Triads of Type 0-0-3 consist of persons from three different cliques at the same level.

Triads of Type 1-2-0-a consist of two persons, i and j, in the same clique at the same level, and a third person, k, in a higher or lower level.

Triads of Type 0-2-1-a consist of two persons, i and j, in different cliques at the same level, and a third person, k, in a higher or lower level.

Triads of Type 0-3-0-a consist of persons from three different levels such that k is the highest, i is the lowest, and j is intermediate.

We now explain why none of the remaining triads can be assigned to cliques and levels without some contradiction.

In 1-2-0-b triads i and j are in the same clique at the same level, but k is above one and below the other, a contradiction.

In 0-2-1-b triads, i and j are from different cliques at the same level, but k is above one and below the other, a contradiction.

In 0-3-0-b triads, we see the notorious "cyclic triads"[7] that cannot be ordered. The arrow from k to i, for example, implies that i is above k, but the directed path i to j to k implies the opposite.

In 1-1-1 triads (regardless of the direction of the A relation), i and j must be placed in the same clique at the same level, but the directed line between i and k implies that k is in a different level while the N relationship implies that k is in the same level, a contradiction.

Having seen that any of the permissible triads can be assigned to levels and cliques without a contradiction but none of the other triads can, we are ready to show that if all the triads are consistent, the entire graph must be consistent.

We want to prove the following:

In a graph with M, A, and N relationships, the points can be arranged simultaneously into disjoint subsets called levels and disjoint sub-subsets called cliques, such that: (a) points are in different levels if and only if they are connected by A relationships (and consequently in the same level if they are connected by M or N relations); (b) points are in the same clique [and at the same level as a consequence of (a)] if and only if they are connected by M relations (and consequently in different cliques at the same level if they are connected by N relations); and (c) the levels form a complete order . . . if and only if the graph has no triads of Types 2-1-0, 0-1-2, 1-1-1, 2-0-1, 1-2-0-b, 0-2-1-b, or 0-3-0-b.

The argument draws heavily upon the theorem of clusterability[8] and is influenced by the notion of duo-balance.[9]

We begin by altering the notation of the lines (edges) so that M and N relations are "positive" and A relations are "negative." Inspection of Figure 2 reveals that there are no permissible triads with two "positive" and one "negative" line (i.e., 2-1-0, 0-1-2, and 1-1-1 triads are not permitted). From the clusterability theorem it follows that the points can be arranged in unique disjoint subsets such that all lines within subsets are "positive" (M or N) and

[7] Harary, Norman, and Cartwright, pp. 296–304.

[8] Davis, *op. cit.*

[9] John G. Kemeny and J. Laurie Snell, *Mathematical Models in the Social Sciences* (Boston: Ginn and Co., 1962, p. 107).

all lines between subsets are "negative" (*A*). We call these subsets levels and note that we have satisfied (a) above.

Next we consider points and lines within a level. Each level is a graph consisting of points connected by *M* or *N* lines. The clusterability theorem tells us that unique disjoint subsets will emerge if and only if there are no triads with two "positive" and one "negative" line. If we call *M* positive and *N* negative, the fact that 2-0-1 triads are not permissible implies that levels are internally clusterable, which satisfies (b) above.

Finally, we note in Figure 2 that any pair of points connected by an *M* or *N* line (i.e., points within the same level) and connected to a third point by an *A* relation have *A* relations identical in direction (see 1-2-0-a and 0-2-1-a in Figure 2). This enables us to condense the graph so that each level becomes a single point. That is, anything we show for the condensed graph must be true for each point within a given level. The condensed graph is complete, directed, and a-cyclic, i.e., a transitive tournament. This satisfies (c) above and completes the proof.

□ **A PROBABILISTIC MODEL**

The discussion so far is of some interest as a logical exegesis of Homans's propositions and because it reveals a bridge between tournaments and structural balance. Nevertheless, it is of little scientific use because it is stated in a strong deterministic fashion. The validity of the propositions requires that each and every triad meet the assumptions. Thus, a graph of, say, thirty people, which has 4060 triads, only one of which was not permissible, is just plain "wrong" by the arguments above; yet intuition tells us that such a graph is "pretty near" the model.

In order to make these ideas useful in empirical research we must develop a probabilistic version that claims forbidden triads are relatively rare, rather than totally absent. As a standard for "relatively rare" we will use the triad frequencies to be expected in a "random graph" — a graph with the same frequencies of *M*, *A*, and *N* pair relations but where particular pair relations are assigned by some chance mechanism.

The gain is enormous. In the relatively large collection of data to be discussed later there are few if any sociograms which meet the graph theoretical conditions, but quite a number which show the predicted probabilistic trends. We must remember, though, to qualify our interpretations, since the results, while fairly consistent, are statistical. Putting it another way, while we can seldom demonstrate the unequivocal existence of these structures, we can often demonstrate tendencies in the direction of these structures.

The probability argument is elementary. We simply say that if *m* proportion of the pair relations are of Type *M*, *a* proportion are of Type *A*, and *n* proportion of Type *N* and lines are assigned at random, then the expected proportions for triads of various types are obtained by multiplying these independent probabilities.

We give as an example, Type 2-1-0. Consider an arbitrary triad with edges I, II, and III. If I and II are M and III is A, then it is Type 2-1-0 and the expectation for this event is $(m)(m)(a) = m^2a$. However, there are two other ways a 2-1-0 triad might occur (I $= A$, II $= M$, III $= M$ and also I $= M$, II $= A$, and III $= M$), each of which has the same probability m^2a. The three expectations sum to $3m^2a$, the expected proportion of 2-1-0 triads in a random graph.

Expectations for each of the remaining nine triad types in the rows of Figure 2 are easily calculated in a similar fashion.

For those triads with both "a" and "b" subtypes (1-2-0, 0-2-1, 0-3-0) it is necessary to take one further step. We see in Figure 2 that for 1-2-0 and 0-2-1 there are four equiprobable outcomes within each, two of which are permissible and two of which are not. Thus, for 1-2-0-b and 0-2-1-b we halve the expectations for the general type. In the case of 0-3-0-b, it is well known[10] that the expected proportion of cyclic triads in a random tournament is .250. Thus the expectation for 0-3-0 triads is multiplied by .250 to give the expectation for 0-3-0-b.

Table 1 gives the results.

■ TABLE 1 / Expected Triad Proportions in a Random Graph with *m, a,* and *n* Proportions of *M, A,* and *N* Pair Relations

Triad Type M A N				Expectation			
Not Permissible							
2	1	0		3	m^2	a	
0	1	2		3		a	n^2
1	1	1		6	m	a	n
2	0	1		3	m^2		n
1	2	0	*b*	1.5	m	a^2	
0	2	1	*b*	1.5		a^2	n
0	3	0	*b*	.25		a^3	
Permissible							
3	0	0			m^3		
1	0	2		3	m		n^2
0	0	3					n^3
1	2	0	*a*	1.5	m	a^2	
0	2	1	*a*	1.5		a^2	n
0	3	0	*a*	.75		a^3	

It is straightforward but tedious to count all the triads in a graph (sociomatrix or sociogram) and to calculate the expectations from the observed frequencies of *M, A,* and *N* pair relations. It is easier and much more accurate to have the work done by an electronic computer. The junior author has written a program which calculates the number of observed and expected triad types and the neces-

[10] Harary, Norman, and Cartwright, p. 303.

sary pair data so that a complete analysis of a graph emerges in a few seconds on a single sheet of paper.[11]

In the next section we will report results from a number of groups, but it may be useful to present a few detailed examples now to make the procedure clear.

Let us examine data from Theodore Newcomb's study, *The Acquaintance Process*.[12] Newcomb established an experimental dormitory at the University of Michigan where new transfer students participated in two studies testing his "ABX" theory, a set of principles about interpersonal relations and attitudes closely related to balance theory. Newcomb's theory gives special attention to the effects of similarity in values on pair relations. However, in Chapters 8, 9, and 10 of his book he provides a richly detailed analysis of sociometric structures, that, taken as a whole, suggests his data might fit our model. We shall not attempt a detailed re-analysis of his week-by-week data, but merely report the results for the fifteenth week of each year. The raw sociometric data are complete rankings of the seventeen men in the study, the first year's criterion being "how much you like each man," the second year's being, "favorableness of feeling." We dichotomized ranks at the median.

The model requires that non-permissible triads be rare, not that each type of permissible triad be disproportionately common. Therefore, we will report the results only for the seven types at issue even though the program prints results for all triad types. Table 2 gives the results for the two experimental groups.

■ **TABLE 2 / Triad Results in *The Acquaintance Process***

Triad	Year I Week 15			Year II Week 15		
M A N	expected	observed	difference	expected	observed	difference
2 1 0	75.4	68	−7.4	72.7	66	−6.7
0 1 2	75.4	76	+0.6	72.7	62	−10.7
1 1 1	150.7	163	+12.3	145.3	157	+11.7
2 0 1	69.1	54	−15.1	51.9	25	−26.9
1 2 0 *b*	41.1	39	−2.1	50.9	27	−23.9
0 2 1 *b*	41.1	37	−4.1	50.9	31	−19.9
0 3 0 *b*	7.5	3	−4.5	11.9	4	−7.9
Total	460.3	440	−20.3	456.3	372	−84.3

[11] The program has an additional feature, not discussed here. If the members (points) can be dichotomized, e.g., by sex, it will present a subanalysis within each half of the dichotomy and for all triads which are heterogeneous in terms of the dichotomy.

[12] Theodore M. Newcomb, *The Acquaintance Process* (New York: Holt, Rinehart and Winston, 1961). Professor Newcomb was extraordinarily helpful in providing us with the new data from his study, in a set of circumstances in which most men would have been considerably less cooperative.

The results may be viewed in three ways.

First, we may ask how many predictions are successful. In Year I five out of seven triads show the predicted negative value and in Year II, six out of seven. In both groups a majority of the predictions are correct.

Second, we may ask whether there are fewer non-permissible triads in total than one would expect in a random graph. The bottom row of the table shows that in Year I there is a cumulative deficit of -20.3 and in Year II -84.3. As a rough index we will divide these cumulated differences by the cumulated expectations (460.3, 456.3), giving values of $-.044$ in Year I and $-.185$ in Year II. Both results support the hypothesis: in Year I there are 4 per cent fewer non-permissible triads than in a random graph with the same pair relationship frequencies, while in Year II there are 18 per cent fewer.

Third, treating the two groups as a sample, we may ask the fates of particular hypotheses. For what it is worth, we note that both groups support the predictions for 2-1-0, 2-0-1, 1-2-0-b, 0-2-1-b, and 0-3-0-b; neither group supports the hypothesis for 1-1-1; while we get one confirmation and one disconfirmation for 0-1-2. In a sample of two groups, this approach is not very revealing, but we present it to set the stage for later analysis of larger samples.

In general we conclude that the two *Acquaintance Process* groups tend toward Homans's clique and level theory of social structure.

The data in Table 2, like most sociometric data, contain both A relations and mutual M and N relations. However, the same approach may be taken where the data are perfectly symmetrical, in which case we are making a statistical test for clusterability alone. The men in the Bank Wiring Room (p. 69) are a good example, as well they might be, since they were the impetus for this whole business. Data on friendship among these men are reported as perfectly symmetrical, and since 2-0-1 triads are the only non-permissible ones with no A relations, to test for clusterability one merely examines the results for this triad type. Computer analysis gives a total of 19.1 expected, 10 observed, a difference of -9.1, and an index value of $-.476$. There are 48 per cent fewer 2-0-1 triads in the Bank Wiring Room than backers of a chance model would anticipate. We conclude, as we already knew from reading *The Human Group*, that the men in this famous work group tended to form cliques.

When dealing with perfectly symmetrical data, we can ask a question which is irrelevant in the larger model: does the group tend toward balance? The clusterability theorem states that a group that can be divided into cliques (one with no 2-0-1 triads) will have exactly two cliques when there are no 0-0-3 triads, but will have three or more cliques when 0-0-3 triads are present. This suggests that we use the observed and expected proportions of 0-0-3 triads as a probabilistic measure of tendencies toward structural balance (division into exactly two cliques) in data which have been shown to be relatively clusterable. In the Bank Wiring Room data we observe 230 0-0-3 triads, expect 229.2, find a difference of $+0.8$, compute an index of $+.004$, and infer no tendency toward balance.

Our third example is the opposite case, completely anti-symmetrical pair relationships, known in graph theory as a tournament. Anti-symmetric pair relationships are rare in human data[13] but in the form of "dominance relationships" they are common among other animals.[14] A typical example appears in an essay by Phyllis Jay on the Indian langur, a small monkey.[15] She counted dominance interactions in a group of six adult and two subadult males and reported 138 such interactions in an eight-by-eight matrix. Coding a frequency of one or more as positive, the data can be handled by our program. The results appear in Table 3.

■ TABLE 3 / Triad Results in Dominance Relations in Indian Langur Data

Triad M A N	Expected	Observed	Difference
2 1 0	0.7	0.0	−0.7
0 1 2	1.6	1.0	−0.6
1 1 1	2.1	2.0	−0.1
2 0 1	0.1	0.0	−0.1
1 2 0 *b*	4.0	0.0	−4.0
0 2 1 *b*	6.1	3.0	−3.1
0 3 0 *b*	7.8	0.0	−7.8
Total	22.4	6.0	−16.4

All seven deviations are negative and the index (−16.4/22.4) of −.732 is healthily negative. Indeed this "inhuman group" fits the model better than do the vast majority of the human groups we have examined. Furthermore, because more than half the negative deviations comes from Type 0-3-0-b we see that these data, while not perfectly anti-symmetrical, tend toward the tournament model.

[13] In the two samples to be analyzed below, fifty-five out of sixty groups show a greater tendency toward reciprocation of positive relations than chance would predict. Cf. Renato Tagiuri, "Social Preference and its Perception," in R. Tagiuri and L. Petrullo, eds., *Person Perception and Interpersonal Behavior* (Stanford: Stanford University Press, 1958, pp. 316–336).
[14] Cf. William Etkin, *Social Behavior and Organization Among Vertebrates.* (Chicago: University of Chicago Press, 1964, pp. 256–295). For a more detailed review of dominance per se, cf. N. E. Collias, "Aggressive Behavior Among Vertebrate Animals," *Physiol. Zool.*, 1944, 17: 83–123, or V. C. Wynne-Edwards, *Animal Dispersion in Relation to Social Behavior* (New York: Hafner Publishing Co., 1962, pp. 127–144). Two older essays of considerable interest to sociologists are, Thorleif Schjelderup-Ebbe, "Social Behavior of Birds," in Carl Murchison, ed., *A Handbook of Social Psychology* (New York: Clark University Press, 1935, pp. 947–972) and W. C. Allee, *The Social Life of Animals* (New York: W. W. Norton & Co., Inc., 1938, pp. 175–208). For a verbal description, but alas no data, of a system with cliques and levels, cf. Konrad Z. Lorenz, *King Solomon's Ring* (New York: Thomas Y. Crowell Co., 1952, p. 151).
[15] Phyllis Jay, "The Common Langur of North India," in Irven DeVore, ed., *Primate Behavior* (New York: Holt, Rinehart and Winston, 1965, p. 245).

Examples which tend to support the model are encouraging, but we must not confuse "for instance" with "generally." Further, while we have no frame of reference for making the judgment, intuition tells us that some of the discrepancies (e.g., the index value of $-.044$ for Year I in Table 2) seem tiny. We have not dared to enter the combinatorial thicket to answer the question of whether a particular graph is significantly different from the chance expectations. We believe that evidence for our hypotheses is best obtained by analysis of a large and heterogeneous set of sociomatrices. If we find that more than half of them depart from the chance model in the directions we predicted, we will consider our results "significant," regardless of the size of the particular discrepancies. We would be delighted to find social science generalizations which always produced whopping effects, but they are in short supply. We must settle for an attempt to show that the hypotheses hold in a large number of groups, although in many of the groups they may be holding by the skin of their teeth.

In the next section we will seek evidence on the model by analyzing two random samples of thirty groups each from a data bank of 427 groups.

☐ **THE DATA**

We propose to assay our hypotheses by examining the results in a large set of sociograms. Strictly speaking, a test is impossible because a truly representative sample of groups would consist of a probability sample from all possible subsets of humanity. Practically speaking, it is possible to collect and analyze data from a reasonable number of diverse groups through the secondary analysis of a data pool of sociograms. If we obtain consistent results in diverse groups with assorted sociometric items collected by numerous independent investigators, we believe that a prima facie case will be established.

The authors spent most of a calendar year collecting sociograms and sociomatrices to form a data pool. Our aim was simply to collect as many matrices as we could from as many different studies as possible. No a priori standards of quality or content were imposed save that we excluded a handful of matrices where no information was available on the group or the content of the items, e.g., where an author of a methods text wrote, "here is a sociogram" and gave no further information.

The final pool consists of 1092 sociograms from 549 groups, collected from 162 sources.

In terms of sources, seventy-one were journal articles, of which, as one might expect, forty-seven were from *Sociometry* or *Sociometry Monographs*, the next highest count being a mere three from *The American Sociological Review*. An additional thirty-one books provided sources, along with thirteen pamphlets, yearbooks, agricultural experiment station bulletins, etc., and four unpublished theses. Most important, perhaps, are the forty-three individual investigators who graciously provided us with raw, unpublished data in response to personal inquiries and letters to the editor in selected social science journals. Many of these people went to considerable trouble to help us and we regret that space limitations preclude detailed acknowledgments beyond listing their names:

William Bezdek, University of Chicago
Carolyn Block, University of Chicago
R. Darell Bock, University of Chicago
Merl E. Bonney, North Texas State University
Richard Boyle, University of California, Los Angeles
Julia S. Brown, University of Iowa
Edson Caldwell, Sacramento State College, California
Donald Campbell, Northwestern University
Theodore Caplow, Columbia University
Kathleen Evans, University College of South Wales and Monmouthshire
Fred Fiedler, University of Illinois
Bruce Frisbie, University of Chicago
John Gagnon, University of Indiana
Richard Gilman, University of Chicago
Harold Goldhammer, University of Chicago
Robert Graebler, Niles Township High School, Skokie, Ill.
Eleanor Hall, University of Chicago
Paul Hurewitz, Hunter College
John James, Portland State University
Richard Jessor, University of Colorado
Donald L. Lantz, Educational Testing Service
Robert A. LeVine, University of Chicago
William H. Lyle, United States Bureau of Prisons
Raymond Maurice, Columbia University
David Moment, Harvard University
Nicholas Mullins, Vanderbilt University
Theodore M. Newcomb, University of Michigan
Mary L. Northway, University of Toronto
Gordon O'Brien, University of Illinois
James Peterson, University of Chicago
Charles H. Proctor, North Carolina State University
Kullervo Rainio, Helsinki University
Anatol Rapoport, University of Michigan
Jack Sawyer, University of Chicago
Maria D. Simon, Institute for Advanced Studies, Vienna
Ralph M. Stogdill, The Ohio State University
Hilda Taba, San Francisco State College
Eugene Talbot, Austen Riggs Hospital
Herbert Thelen, University of Chicago
Michael G. Weinstein, Harvard University
Milo E. Whitson, California State Polytechnic College
Thomas Wilson, Dartmouth College
Leslie D. Zeleny, The American University in Cairo

■ **TABLE 4 / Characteristics of Group in the Data Pool**

(A) *Group Type*

(1) Students

			Setting			
Level	Class Room	Dormitory	Summer Camp	Institution	Voluntary Association	Total
Pre-School	17					17
Grades 1–6	137				5	142
Grades 7–12	104		10	8*	17	139
College	17	11				28
Total	275	11	10	8	22	326

(2) Adults

Neighbors, villages	54
Civilian employees	54
Military units	34
Prisoners, mental patients	24
Voluntary associations	11
"Classes"†	15
Other	12
	204

(B) *Number of Persons*

40 or more	93
30–39	80
20–29	168
10–19	150
3–9	58
	549

(C) *Location*

United States and Canada	478
Latin America	31
England and Europe	19
All other	19
Unknown	2
	549

(D) *Sex Composition*

All male	155
Mixed	191
All female	124
Not applicable‡	79
	549

* mostly correctional institutions
† defined as persons falling into a logical class, not *necessarily* members of an interacting group, e.g., all the doctors in a community or all truck farmers in a county
‡ e.g., whole families

The 162 sources provided data on 549 groups. The majority are students, but there are also work groups, military units, and neighborhoods, and there are a few esoteric tidbits such as employees of the Costa Rican Census Bureau, [16] German Olympic rowing teams, [17] woodcutters in a Bulgarian village, [18] and all the employees of a large woolen mill; [19] along with such old favorites as the Bank Wiring Room, the girls at Hudson, [20] MIT's Westgate student housing project, [21] and the Rattlers, Eagles, Bulldogs and Red Devils. [22]

Table 4 gives a summary of selected group characteristics in the pool.

The 549 groups provided 1092 different matrices, roughly two apiece. It is quite difficult to classify them in terms of content, but Table 5 will perhaps convey the flavor.

■ TABLE 5 / Contents of 1092 Sociomatrices in the Data Pool

Content	N
Prefer for task interaction (e.g., prefer to serve with on committee)	164
Prefer for socio-emotional interaction (e.g., invite to a party, play with at recess)	160
"Friend," actual or preferred	160
Prefer for generalized interaction (e.g., prefer to sit next to in school, prefer as roommate)	103
Valued trait (e.g., named as leader, rated as a good dancer, preferred as class president)	99
"Like" or "Like best"	81
High rate of voluntary interaction (e.g., visit frequently, see frequently)	56
All other, including combinations of the above	269
Total	1092

[16] Charles H. Proctor, unpublished data.

[17] Hans Lenk, "Conflict and Achievement in High Performance Sports Teams," *Soziale Welt* (1964) 15: 307–343.

[18] Irwin T. Sanders, "Sociometric Work with a Bulgarian Woodcutting Group," *Sociometry* (1939) 2: 58–68.

[19] John James, unpublished data.

[20] Jacob L. Moreno, *Who Shall Survive?* (New York: Beacon House, 1953).

[21] Leon Festinger, Stanley Schachter and Kurt Back, *Social Pressures in Informal Groups* (Stanford: Stanford University Press, 1950).

[22] Muzafer Sherif, O. J. Harvey, B. Jack White, William R. Hood, and Carolyn W. Sherif, *Intergroup Conflict and Cooperation* (Norman, Oklahoma: Institute of Group Relations, University of Oklahoma, 1961); Muzafer Sherif, "Experiments in Group Conflict," *Scientific American* (November, 1956), pp. 2–6.

While every matrix in the pool was catalogued and an IBM card describing its major characteristics was punched, financial limitations made it impossible to code, punch, and analyze each one. Instead, we drew two random samples of groups, one of thirty school-age youngsters, the other of thirty adult groups. Each is a simple random sample (where more than one matrix was available on a group, one was chosen through a random number) of groups, so that the findings may be used to estimate characteristics of the total data pool.

Certain restrictions were placed on the sample so that all groups or matrices were not eligible. The four restrictions are: (1) size was limited to eight through eighty, the upper limit being chosen so that the data could be punched on a single IBM card, the lower set arbitrarily so that every group would have more than fifty triads; (2) data where the distribution of M, A, and N pair relations was forced by the investigator (e.g., where only mutual positive choices were presented) were excluded[23]; (3) a handful of cases where the respondents were not people or families (e.g., nations, tribes, Indian castes) were excluded; and (4) three content codes were excluded as outside the scope of Homans's hypotheses: (a) sheer kinship, (b) formal authority, and (c) "relational analysis" items where individuals are asked to guess the choices of others in the group.

The result of these restrictions is that the generalizations from the sample apply to 279 out of 326 school groups and 148 out of 204 adult groups, a total universe of 427 groups.

The statistical procedure used is sequential analysis,[24] i.e., we treated each sample as a cumulative set of random samples steadily increasing in size from 1 to 30. Since each hypothesis tested has an unequivocal answer in each matrix,[25] we used tables for the sign test[26] to assess the results. That is, we made a sequential test of the null hypothesis that 50 per cent of the groups show negative deviations from the expectations of the random graph model.

We also possess results on some 200 matrices which had been coded as the data were acquisitioned and before financial exigencies forced us to shift to sampling. They are not technically representative of the data pool; but for what it is worth, the results in this convenience sample are essentially the same as those in the two random samples.

Table 6 and Table 7 describe the sixty groups in the two samples.

[23] For the Bank Wiring Room, Adult Group Number 21, the data already presented were not eligible. This explains why the results for that group differ from those we have already seen.

[24] For an introductory discussion, see Irwin D. J. Bross, *Design for Decision* (New York: The MacMillan Company, 1953, pp. 130–1444).

[25] Since computers calculate expectations to a large number of decimals, it is very rare for observed and expected values to be exactly equal. Such rare cases are counted against the hypothesis.

[26] William J. MacKinnon, "Table for Both the Sign Test and Distribution Free Confidence Intervals of the Median for Sample Sizes to 1,000," *Journal of the American Statistical Association* (1964) 59: 935–960.

■ TABLE 6 / Sample of School Groups

	Size	Sex Composition	Type of Group	Criterion	Source
1.	14	All male	Boys in 7th-grade class, Greendale School, Greendale, Wisc.	Three best friends in this group	Arthur Singer, "Certain Aspects of Personality and Their Relation to Certain Group Modes and Constancy of Friendship Choices," *Journ. Educ. Res.*, 1951, 45: 33–42
2.	24	Mixed	6th-grade class, Univ. of Chicago Laboratory school	Three best friends	Herbert Thelen, unpublished data
3.	24	Mixed	6th grade class "in a small city"	Best friend	Beverly Grossman and Joyce Wrighter, "The Relationship Between Selection-Rejection and Intelligence. Social Status and Personality Amongst Sixth Grade Children," *Sociometry*, 1948, 11: 346–55
4.	17	All male	Boys in all-Negro 5th grade in Tampa, Fla.	"With whom you would like to work"	Donald Lantz, unpublished data
5.	16	Mixed	3rd grade in Univ. of Michigan Laboratory School	"I get along best with these children in doing work in school"	Willard C. Olson, "The Improvement of Human Relations in the Class Room," Childhood Education, 1945–46, 22: 317–25
6.	16	Unknown	Graduate student class at American University in Cairo	Preferred to join small discussion group	Leslie D. Zeleny, unpublished data

236

Table 6 (continued)

Group	Size	Sex Composition	Type of Group	Criterion	Source
7.	18	Mixed	2nd grade in Univ. of Toronto Laboratory school	"Who would you like best to have sitting near you in the classroom?"	Mary L. Northway, unpublished data
8.	25	All female	Inmates in Park Cottage at New York Training School for Girls, Hudson, N.Y.	Preference to eat at same table	Helen Jennings, "Structure of Leadership — Development and Sphere of Influence," *Sociometry*, 1937, I: 99–143
9.	16	All female	Girls from 5th-grade class in Tampa, Fla.	"… with whom you would like to play"	Same as Group 4
10.	35	Mixed	"A second grade"	"Who would you like to work with on our science project?"	Merl E. Bonney, unpublished data
11.	22	Mixed	6th-grade class, Univ. of Chicago Laboratory school	Same as Group 2	Same as Group 2
12.	17	All male	Boys from a 5th-grade class in Tampa, Fla.	Same as Group 4	Same as Group 4
13.	15	All female	Girls from "a fourth grade class room"	Best friends	Commission on Teacher Education, *Helping Teachers Understand Children*, American Council on Education, 1945
14.	27	All female	Inmates in Cottage C3 at New York Training School	Preference for sharing the same house	J. L. Moreno, *Who Shall Survive?* Beacon House, Beacon, N.Y., 1953

237

Table 6 (continued)

Group	Size	Sex Composition	Type of Group	Criterion	Source
15.	24	Mixed	5th-grade class, Univ. of Chicago Laboratory School	Same as Group 2	Same as Group 2
16.	25	Mixed	"A third grade"	Prefer to work with on the Christmas play	Same as Group 10
17.	14	All male	8-year-olds attending a settlement house in Boston	Prefer to sit next to	Sumner Cohen, "Group Structural Changes as Affected by Age of Members and Passage of Time," unpublished undergraduate honors thesis. Harvard University, 1952
18.	25	Mixed	"A first grade"	Prefer to sit next to	Milo E. Whitson, unpublished data
19.	27	All female	Inmates in Cottage C15 at New York Training School for Girls, Hudson, N.Y.	Same as Group 14	Same as Group 14
20.	18	All male	Boys from a 5th grade in New York City	"... whom you would like to sit beside you"	Joan Henning Criswell, "A Sociometric Study of Race Cleavage in the Classroom," Archives of Psychol., 1939, No. 235
21.	10	Mixed	Class at experimental nursery school for welfare families	Good friend	Eleanor Hall, unpublished data
22.	26	All female	Inmates in Cottage C4 at New York Training School for Girls, Hudson, N.Y.	Same as Group 14	Same as Group 14

Table 6 (continued)

Group	Size	Sex Composition	Type of Group	Criterion	Source
23.	15	All male	Boys from a 5th grade in Tampa, Fla.	Same as Group 8	Same as Group 4
24.	25	Mixed	"A third grade class"	Prefer to sit next to	Paul Hurewitz, unpublished data
25.	22	All female	Students in a teacher preparation college in Wales	Preference as companion for practice teaching	Kathleen Evans, unpublished data
26.	18	All female	Junior high school home economics class	Preference for working on the same committee	Helen H. Jennings, "Sociometric Grouping in Relation to Child Development," in Caroline Tryon, ed., *Fostering Mental Health in Our Schools*, National Education Association, 1950
27.	40	Mixed	7th-8th-9th grades in a Protestant church Sunday school	Like to have on committee to plan party	Same as Group 10
28.	28	Mixed	12th-grade class in a Texas high school	"... whom would you like to work with on research for our next oral discussions"	Same as Group 10
29.	29	Mixed	5th- & 6th-grade class in Wilmington, Del.	Prefer to sit with	Hilda Taba, unpublished data
30.	16	All male	Boys from a 5th grade in Tampa, Fla.	Same as Group 23	Same as Group 4

239

■ TABLE 7 / Sample of Adult Groups

Group	Size	Sex Composition	Type of Group	Criterion	Source
1.	32	All male(?)	Physicians in a Midwestern city	"Who are the three or four physicians with whom you most often find yourself discussing cases or therapy . . ."	James S. Coleman, Elihu Katz and Herbert Menzel, *Medical Innovation*, Bobbs-Merrill, 1966
2.	20	Mixed	Random sample of names in North Carolina State faculty directory	"Have you ever spoken with this person?"	C. H. Proctor, unpublished data
3.	16	All male	Executives in a manufacturing firm	"Do any of your personal friends work (here)?"	Harrison White, *Research & Development as a Pattern in Industrial Management*, unpublished Ph.D. thesis, Princeton Univ., 1960
4.	20	Families	Families in a neighborhood in San Juan, Puerto Rico, Barrio #25	Report mutual aid or mutual visiting and entertaining	Theodore Caplow, unpublished data from study reported in Caplow, et al., *The Urban Ambience*, The Bedminster Press, 1964
5.	41	Mixed	Medical corps trainees at a naval base	"Like"	William Bezdek, unpublished data
6.	56	All male	Squadron of Naval aviators	"What two men would you most like to fly wing with in combat?"	John G. Jenkins, "The Nominating Technique as a Method of Evaluating Air Group Morale," *Journ. Aviation Med.*, (1954) 19: 12–19
7.	20	Families	Same as Group 4 — Barrio #11	Same as Group 4	Same as Group 4

Table 7 (continued)

Group	Size	Sex Composition	Type of Group	Criterion	Source
8.	13	All male	Maintenance department workers in a woolen mill	"Who are your friends here — the persons you like best?"	John James, unpublished data from study reported in "Clique Organization in a Small Industrial Plant," *Research Studies, State College of Washington*, 1951, 19: 125–130
9.	13	All female	Night shift in weaving department of woolen mill	Same as Group 8	Same as Group 8
10.	11	All male	Salesmen in a steel corporation	"Friends"	Abraham Zalesnik and David Moment, *Casebook on Interpersonal Behavior in Organizations*, Wiley, 1964
11.	28	All male	Truck farmers	"from whom they secured advice and information about vegetable growing innovations"	Everett Rogers, *Diffusion of Innovations*, Free Press, 1962
12.	20	Families	Same as Group 4 — Barrio #12	Same as Group 4	Same as Group 4
13.	23	All male	Night shift in finishing department of woolen mill	Same as Group 8	Same as Group 8
14.	8	All male	Warehouse workers in a woolen mill	Same as Group 8	Same as Group 8

241

Table 7 (continued)

Group	Size	Sex Composition	Type of Group	Criterion	Source
15.	37	Mixed	Engineering department in a large firm	Named as "being supportive" (in interpersonal relations)	David Moment, unpublished data from David Moment and Abraham Zaleznik, *Role Development and Interpersonal Competence*, Harvard University Graduate School of Business, 1963
16.	13	Men	Day shift in picking room of woolen mill	Same as Group 8	Same as Group 8
17.	30	Mixed	Teachers at a guidance and counseling institute	Preference for working together	Merl E. Bonney, unpublished data
18.	13	All male	Executives in a woolen mill	Same as Group 8	Same as Group 8
19.	8	All male	German 8-man amateur rowing team	"With which two rowers would you like best to sit in the same boat?"	Hans Lenk, "Conflict and Achievement in High Performance Sports Teams," *Soz. Welt*, 1964, 15:307–343
20.	42	All male	Same as Group 5	Same as Group 5	Same as Group 5
21.	14	All male	Workers in the Bank Wiring Room at the Western Electric Company	Observed to help one another	F. J. Roethlisberger & W. J. Dickson, *Management and the Worker*, Harvard University Press, 1946
22.	14	All female	Night shift in spinning department of a woolen mill	Same as Group 8	Same as Group 8

Table 7 (continued)

Group	Size	Sex Composition	Type of Group	Criterion	Source
23.	45	Families	Rural neighborhood in Peru	Visiting relationship	Charles P. Loomis and J. Allan Beegle, *Rural Social Systems*, Prentice Hall, 1950
24.	8	All male	Same as Group 19	Like best to have as a room mate during a trip	Same as Group 19
25.	20	Families	Same as Group 4 — Barrio #14	Same as Group 4	Same as Group 4
26.	50	All male	Same as Group 5	Same as Group 5	Same as Group 5
27.	14	All male	Night shift in weaving department of a woolen mill	Same as Group 8	Same as Group 8
28.	45	All female	"Women in an adult education center in a poverty stricken district"	"With whom would you like to work on a committee?"	Rose Cologne, "Experimentation with Sociometric Procedures in a Self-Help Community Center," *Sociometry*, 1943, 6: 27–67
29.	17	All male	American naval aviation squadron	With whom they would wish to go on a mission	Paul H. Maucorps, *Psychologie des Mouvements Sociaux*, Presses Universitaires de France, 1950
30.	45	Mixed	Employees in research & development department of a large firm	Frequently spend free time (such as coffee breaks) together	Richard Gilman, unpublished data

243

□ RESULTS

We will first report the global results for the model as a whole and then turn to the results for the seven specific hypotheses. Tables 8 and 9 give the global results for the two samples.

■ TABLE 8 / Global Results for School Room Sample

Group	(1) Sum of Deviations	(2) Sum of Expectations	(3) (1)/(2)	(4) Cum.	(5) Predictions Right	(6) Wrong	(7) Cum.
1.	−6.1	278.0	−.022	1	4	3	1
2.	+3.6	570.3	+.006	1	5	2	2
3.	−8.6	529.6	−.016	2	4	3	3
4.	−122.5	398.5	−.307	3	5	2	4
5.	−14.3	250.3	−.057	4	5	2	5
6.	−53.6	363.4	−.147	5	6	1	6
7.	−16.4	323.5	−.051	6	4	3	7*
8.	−31.6	723.6	−.044	7	6	1	8*
9.	−150.8	357.9	−.421	8	6	1	9*
10.	−181.9	3140.8	−.057	9	5	2	10*
11.	−11.8	469.9	−.025	10*	5	2	11*
12.	−54.7	407.6	−.134	11*	5	2	12*
13.	−12.4	230.5	−.054	12*	6	1	13*
14.	−68.4	765.4	−.089	13*	5	2	14*
15.	+12.4	610.5	+.020	13*	4	3	15*
16.	−72.0	1322.9	−.054	14*	5	2	16*
17.	−24.0	183.8	−.131	15*	6	1	17*
18.	−33.3	1230.3	−.027	16*	6	1	18*
19.	−55.9	998.0	−.056	17*	6	1	19*
20.	+6.5	284.5	+.023	17*	4	3	20*
21.	+5.2	45.9	+.113	17*	4	3	21*
22.	−124.1	1128.0	−.110	18*	7	0	22*
23.	−67.0	284.0	−.236	19*	5	2	23*
24.	−11.4	925.5	−.012	20*	4	3	24*
25.	−5.5	597.6	−.009	21*	5	2	25*
26.	−24.3	300.4	−.081	22*	4	3	26*
27.	+6.3	2839.6	+.002	22*	4	3	27*
28.	−116.7	1714.6	−.068	23*	5	2	28*
29.	−14.1	1011.2	−.014	24*	4	3	29*
30.	−49.8	317.8	−.157	25*	5	2	30
Per Cent Correct				83%			100%

* = cumulative frequency of correct predictions is significant at .01 level for sign test

The seven columns in each table may be read as follows, using Group 5 in the school sample as an example. The entry in Column one, "−14.3," tells us that there is a total of 14.3 fewer triads of the seven-types-predicted-to-be-rare than the chance model would lead us to expect. The entry in the second column, "250.3," is the total number of "bad" triads expected under chance. The entry in the third column, "—.051," is our index of the degree of discrepancy (—14.3/250.3), and it tells us that there are roughly 5 per cent fewer "bad" triads than we would find in a random graph with the same frequencies of pair relations. The entry in Column four, "4," tells us that of the first five groups drawn in the random sample, four had negative deviations in Column 1 (and hence, Column 3); the entries in Columns five and six, "5" and "2," tell us

■ **TABLE 9 / Results for Adult Sample**

Group	(1) Sum of Deviations	(2) Sum of Expectations	(3) (1)/(2)	(4) Cum.	(5) Right	(6) Wrong	(7) Cum.
					Predictions		
1.	—56.5	1357.5	—.042	1	5	2	1
2.	+0.3	225.7	+.001	1	2	5	1
3.	—5.4	129.4	—.042	2	5	2	2
4.	—405.9	698.9	—.581	3	6	1	3
5.	+15.1	1073.0	+.014	3	6	1	4
6.	—236.6	3433.5	—.069	4	5	2	5
7.	—108.2	584.1	—.185	5	5	2	6
8.	—22.1	138.1	—.160	6	5	2	7
9.	—17.2	139.1	—.123	7	6	1	8
10.	—10.1	82.1	—.123	8	6	1	9
11.	—10.1	458.1	—.022	9	6	1	10*
12.	—59.0	556.0	—.106	10	5	2	11*
13.	—25.6	392.6	—.065	11	5	2	12*
14.	+1.8	23.2	+.078	11	5	2	13*
15.	—456.2	3884.1	—.117	12	6	1	14*
16.	—2.8	76.9	—.036	13	5	2	15*
17.	—229.5	2256.5	—.102	14*	7	0	16*
18.	—47.8	178.8	—.267	15*	6	1	17*
19.	—7.6	33.6	—.226	16*	6	1	18*
20.	—47.7	920.7	—.052	17*	6	1	19*
21.	+3.5	117.6	+.030	17*	3	4	19*
22.	+0.7	168.3	+.004	17*	4	3	20*
23.	—54.1	2257.1	—.024	18*	4	3	21*
24.	+2.8	30.3	+.092	18	3	4	21*
25.	—21.3	357.3	—.060	19*	2	5	21*
26.	—53.7	1432.7	—.037	20*	6	1	22*
27.	+1.7	94.7	+.018	20*	5	2	23*
28.	—266.3	2668.5	—.100	21*	2	5	23*
29.	+0.1	24.9	+.004	21	3	1+	24*
30.	—1524.1	9442.1	—.161	22*	5	2	25*

| Per Cent Correct | | | | 73% | | | 83% |

* = cumulative frequency of correct predictions is significant at .01 level for sign test
+ = only 4 predictions possible because extreme symmetry of data made expectations of 0.0000 for three triad types

■ TABLE 10 / Results for Specific Hypotheses in the School Sample Triad Type

Group	210	Cum.	012	Cum.	111	Cum.	201	Cum.	120-b	Cum.	021-b	Cum.	030-b	Cum.
1.	+	0	+	0	—	1	—	1	—	1	—	1	+	0
2.	+	0	+	0	—	2	—	2	—	2	—	2	—	1
3.	+	0	+	0	+	3	—	3	—	3	—	3	+	1
4.	—	1	+	0	+	3	+	4	—	4	—	4	—	2
5.	—	2	—	1	—	3	—	4	—	5	—	5	—	3
6.	—	3	+	1	—	4	—	5	+	6	—	6	—	4
7.	+	3	+	1	—	5	—	6	—	7	—	7*	—	5
8.	—	4	+	2	+	6	—	7	—	8	—	8*	—	6
9.	—	5	—	2	—	6	—	8	—	9	—	9*	—	7
10.	+	5	+	2	—	7	—	9	—	10*	—	10*	—	8
11.	—	6	+	2	—	8	+	10*	—	11*	—	11*	—	9
12.	—	7	+	3	—	9	+	10	—	12*	—	12*	—	10
13.	+	7	+	3	—	10	—	11*	—	13*	—	13*	—	11*
14.	+	7	—	3	—	11	—	11	+	13*	—	14*	—	12*
15.	+	7	+	4	—	12	+	12	—	14*	—	15*	—	13*
16.	+	7	+	5	—	13	—	13	—	15*	—	16*	—	14*
17.	+	7	+	6	—	14*	—	14*	—	16*	—	17*	—	15*
18.	+	7	—	6	—	15*	—	15*	—	17*	—	18*	—	16*
19.	+	7	—	6	—	16*	—	16*	—	18*	—	19*	—	17*
20.	+	7	+	7	—	17*	—	17*	—	19*	—	20*	+	17*
21.	—	8	+	7	+	17*	—	18*	—	20*	+	20*	—	18*
22.	—	9	+	7	—	18*	—	19*	—	21*	—	21*	—	19
23.	—	10	—	7	—	19*	+	19*	—	21*	—	22*	—	20
24.	+	10	+	7n	—	20*	—	20*	+	22*	—	23*	—	21*
25.	+	10	+	7n	—	21*	—	21*	—	23*	—	24*	—	22*
26.	+	10	+	7n	—	22*	—	22*	+	23*	+	24*	—	23*
27.	+	10	+	7n	—	23*	—	23*	—	24*	—	25*	—	24*
28.	+	10	+	7n	—	24*	—	24*	+	24*	—	26*	—	25*
29.	+	10	+	7n	—	25*	—	25*	+	24*	—	27*	—	26*
30.	—	11	+	7n	+	25*	—	26*	—	25*	—	28*	—	27*
Per Cent Negative	37%		23%n		83%*		87%*		83%*		93%*		90%*	

+ = frequency of triad type is equal or greater than chance expectation
— = frequency of triad type is less than chance expectation
* = cumulative frequency of correct predictions is significant at .01 level for sign test
n = cumulative frequency of incorrect predictions is significant at .01 level for sign test

TABLE 11 / Results for Specific Hypotheses in the Adult Sample Triad Type

Group	210	Cum.	012	Cum.	111	Cum.	201	Cum.	120-b	Cum.	021-b	Cum.	030-b	Cum.
1.	+	0	−	1	−	1	−	1	+	0	−	1	−	1
2.	+	0	−	2	+	1	+	1	+	0	+	1	−	2
3.	+	0	+	2	−	2	−	2	−	1	−	2	−	3
4.	+	0	−	3	−	3	−	3	−	2	−	3	−	4
5.	−	1	+	3	−	4	−	4	−	3	−	4	−	5
6.	−	2	−	4	+	4	+	4	−	4	−	5	−	6
7.	+	2	−	5	−	5	−	5	−	5	−	6	+	6
8.	+	2	−	6	+	5	−	6	−	6	−	7	−	7
9.	+	2	−	7	−	6	−	7	−	7	−	8	−	8
10.	−	3	−	8	−	7	−	8	−	8	−	9	−	9
11.	+	3	−	9	+	7	−	9	−	9	−	10*	−	10*
12.	+	3	−	10	−	8	−	10	−	10	−	11*	−	11
13.	+	3	−	11	−	9	−	11	−	11	−	12*	−	12*
14.	+	3	+	11	−	10	−	12	−	12	−	13*	−	13*
15.	−	4	−	12	−	11	−	13*	+	12	−	14*	−	14*
16.	−	5	−	13	−	12	+	13	−	13	−	15*	−	15*
17.	+	5	−	14*	−	13	−	14*	−	14	−	16*	−	16*
18.	−	6	−	15*	−	14	−	15*	−	15	−	17*	−	17*
19.	−	7	−	16*	+	14	−	16*	−	16	−	18*	+	18*
20.	−	8	−	17*	+	14	−	17*	+	16	−	19*	−	19*
21.	+	8	+	17	+	14	−	18*	−	17	−	20*	−	20*
22.	+	8	−	18*	−	15	−	19*	+	17	−	21*	−	21*
23.	+	8	+	18	−	16	+	19	+	17	−	22*	+	21
24.	−	9	−	19*	+	16	+	19	+	17	−	23*	−	22*
25.	+	9	−	20*	−	17	−	20*	−	18	−	24*	−	23*
26.	−	10	+	20*	+	17	−	21*	−	19	−	25*	+	23
27.	+	10	−	21*	−	18	+	21	+	19	−	26*	−	24*
28.	+	10	+	21	+	18	−	22*	+	19	+	26	+	24
29.	−	11	+	21	−	19	−	23*	×	×	×	×	×	×
30.	+	11	+	21	−	20	+	23*	−	20	−	27	+	24*
Per Cent Negative		37%		70%		67%		77%*		69%		93%*		80%*

+ = frequency of triad type is equal or greater than chance expectation
− = frequency of triad type is less than chance expectation
* = cumulative frequency of correct predictions is significant at .01 level for sign test
× = both observed and expected frequencies are 0.0000 because of high symmetry of relationship

that of the seven separate predictions about triad types, five were correct (the types were rarer than the random graph prediction) and two were incorrect; and the entry in Column seven, "5," indicates that of the first five groups, all five showed majorities of correct predictions. The absence of asterisks in Columns four and seven indicates that these cumulative frequencies are not significant at the .01 level against the null hypothesis that half the predictions are correct.

The simplest prediction is that in most groups, most of the specific predictions will be correct. Column 7 of Tables 8 and 9 reveals that the claim has some merit. All thirty school room groups and twenty-five out of thirty adult groups (83 per cent) show majorities of correct predictions, although there is only one case, Group 22 in Table 8, where all seven are correct. This deviation from the 50 per cent success expected in random data becomes significant on the seventh group for the school sample and the tenth group among the adults. We infer that a significant majority of the 427 groups in the data pool have mostly correct predictions.

A second way to assess the model as a whole is in terms of the total deficit or surplus of non-permissible triads, Column 3 in the tables. In 83 per cent of the school groups and 73 per cent of the adult groups, there are deficits, as predicted. The former becomes significant at the .01 level on the tenth group and the latter becomes significant at the fourteenth group, although it wanders around the border of the critical region during the later groups in the series. We infer that a significant majority of the 427 groups in the data pool have deficits of non-permissible triads.

Both forms of the global hypothesis are confirmed, and in this limited operational sense we are led to agree with Homans that group after group will tend to form cliques and ranked levels on the basis of positive interpersonal relations.

We now know that the model, taken as a whole, does pretty well in its empirical tests. Next we ask whether each of its seven parts fares equally well. Tables 10 and 11 provide the necessary information.

A glance at the tables reveals enough asterisks to convey the impression that most of the individual predictions are successful, although we note one case (Type 0-1-2 in the school sample) where the hypothesis is rejected significantly. Table 12 summarizes the results in Tables 10 and 11.

We observe the following:

(a) Three hypotheses (0-2-1-b, 0-3-0-b, 2-0-1) are confirmed at the .01 level in both samples.
(b) Two hypotheses (1-2-0-b and 1-1-1) are confirmed at the .01 level in one sample and the .05 level in the other.
(c) One hypothesis (0-1-2) is confirmed at the .05 level in one sample and disconfirmed at the .01 level in the other.
(d) One hypothesis (2-1-0) tends toward disconfirmation in both samples, though it is not significant in either.

■ **TABLE 12 / Summary of Outcomes in Tables 10 and 11***

Outcome

	Disconfirmed		Neither	Confirmed	
Significance	.01	.05		.05	.01
M A N					
2 1 0			(A 37%) (S 37%)		
0 1 2		(S 23%)		(A 67%)	
1 1 1				(A 67%)	(S 83%)
2 0 1				(A 77%)	(S 87%)
1 2 0 *b*				(A 69%)	(S 83%)
0 2 1 *b*				(A 93%)	(S 93%)
0 3 0 *b*				(A 83%)	(S 90%)

* A = adult sample, S = school sample, figures in parentheses are the percentages of groups within the sample in which the hypothesis is confirmed.

Beyond the fact that the overall success of the model does not come from a minority of the triad types (five out of the seven hypotheses are supported at the .05 level in both samples), it is difficult to interpret the pattern in Table 12. The question is whether the less successful hypotheses (2-1-0 and 0-1-2) suggest meaningful defects in the model or whether we have merely been chastised by those gods who have decreed that sociological data shall never come out cleanly.

More soberly, since each specific hypothesis uses fewer observations than the global hypothesis, the specific predictions may be expected to show more internal variability than the overall tests. Such a probabilistic view would lead us to stress the distribution of the results — eight tests significant at the .01 level, three at the .05 level, and only three less successful — rather than to examine each prediction in isolation.

On the other hand, granted that it is *ex post facto*, there is a faint pattern in the results. Referring back to the proof of the graph theoretical model above, we remember that it is divided into three parts, part (a) about levels, part (b) about cliques within levels, and part (c) about order between levels. The three hypotheses about order between levels (1-2-0-b, 0-2-1-b, and 0-3-0-b) are all relatively successful; the single hypothesis about clique structures within levels (2-0-1) is nicely confirmed; and it is the three hypotheses dealing with levels per se which include our less fortunate results. We cannot infer that the level notion is to be rejected, for three of the six tests about it are significant at the .05 level, but it does seem to be a weaker part of the model.

Putting it another way, we may say that we have had some success in showing that *A* relationships tend toward a rank structure and some success in showing that *M* and *N* relations tend toward clusterability, but we have had more limited success in showing how these two structures are integrated to make a coherent whole.

In summary:

1. In both samples, the overall hypotheses of the model are supported so frequently that we infer most groups in the data pool show the predicted structural trends.
2. In both samples, three of the seven specific hypotheses are supported at the .01 level of significance and two at the .05 level.
3. Two of the seven specific hypotheses have equivocal or negative outcomes. Whether this is random variation or a substantive flaw in the model is unclear. If it is a substantive flaw, the weakness seems to lie not in the idea of ranking or the idea of cliques, but in the assumptions about how the ranking system and the clique system are articulated.

□ **RANDOM DATA**

We have concluded that a fairly large and heterogeneous collection of groups exhibits the structural trends we derived from *The Human Group*. Nevertheless, the confirmation is probabilistic; while most groups tend toward the structures implied by the model, none fitted the model perfectly. Hence, the validity of our probabilistic argument is crucial. Since the probability distribution of graph properties is not well studied, except for some properties of tournaments, we felt that it would be useful to buttress our case by a Monte Carlo analysis which might reveal any serious flaws in the reasoning. A thorough Monte Carlo analysis is a formidable task because one should run a large number of random

■ **TABLE 13 / Results in Data Samples and Two Samples of Thirty 20-Person Groups Simulated with Random Numbers**

		Data Samples		Simulated	
		School	Adult	I	II
No. of Groups		30	30	30	30
Percentage with negative indices		83%	73%	30%	40%
Percentage of groups with 4 or more hypotheses confirmed		100%	83%	50%	53%
Individual Hypotheses	*level*				
	<.01	5	3	1	
Confirmed	<.05		3		
	≥.05			3	3
	≥.05	1	1	3	3
Disconfirmed	<.05				
	<.01	1			1

groups varying in size and in *M-A-N* values. This was impractical for our small project, but for what it is worth, we did run two sets of thirty "groups" with data generated by random numbers. We set each at size 20, the median size for groups in the two samples, and set 15 per cent of the random "choices" as positive, again the median in the two data samples.

Table 13 summarizes the results.

Beginning with the index defined in Table 8, Column 3, we see that less than half the indices are negative in the simulated data, while 83 per cent and 73 per cent are negative in the actual data. (Incidentally, in the combined random number samples fifty-five out of sixty groups have indices with values between +.049 and −.049, and only three are less than −.049. This suggests that index values of −.050 or lower are worth considering seriously even though they appear small intuitively.)

Turning next to the number of hypotheses confirmed per group, we find the random data confirm four or more hypotheses in 50 per cent of the groups in Sample I and 53 per cent of the groups in Sample II compared with 100 per cent and 83 per cent in the two actual data samples.

Finally, considering the individual hypotheses, we find seven confirmations and seven disconfirmations in the random data, one confirmation and one disconfirmation significant at the .01 level; in contrast to 11 confirmations, all significant at the .05 level and three disconfirmations, one significant at the .01 level, for the real data. That in fourteen tests we get two differences significant at the .01 level in the random data gives some support to our previous notion that individual hypotheses have a lot more random fluctuation than the global hypotheses.

In sum, two sets of truly random data are a lot closer to our deduced expectations than are the real data we analyzed. The result is a double comfort. On the one hand, it suggests but does not prove that our probabilistic argument and the computer program are not grossly incorrect. On the other, it confirms our conclusion that the real data differ from those obtained from random graphs.

We conclude by repeating from our introduction: to the extent that our model is a plausible interpretation of Homans's ideas, our probabilistic reasoning is valid, and our 427 groups are representative, we believe our study provides favorable evidence for Homans's claim that if we examine voluntary interaction and sentiments in small groups, we will find two structures, differentiation into cliques and elaboration into ranks, and we will find them in group after group after group.

Chapter 11

The Effect of Weighted Links in Communication Networks

■ CHARLES H. HUBBELL

□ **A. STATEMENT OF THE PROBLEM**

A recurrent problem in behavioral science is the study of system structure and the effects of structure upon system behavior. Sociometry, for example, uses patterns of likes and dislikes to derive indices of social status and to identify cliques. Social anthropology analyzes the incidence of kinship ties in order to determine the boundaries of tribes and clans. Communication studies undertake to predict the effect of structural position upon the problem-solving behavior of group members.

Now the classical tradition in social-psychological analysis has been to treat the dyadic links in system structure as all-or-nothing relations — each link either exists or does not exist. It is possible, however, to conceive of these links as having differential *strengths:* influence flows more rapidly or in greater magnitude over one channel than over another.

Two structures which are topologically equivalent can thus differ radically as to the strengths which are assigned to their component linkages. And these differences can produce strong contrasts in the behaviors of the respective systems.

In a sociometric network, for example, an individual who receives a few strong choices will often emerge with higher status than someone receiving many weak choices. Or he may outrank someone with the same number and strength of choices received, because the *sources* of his choices are persons with higher status.

This paper explores some of the theoretical problems of differential linkage strengths, and reports on an empirical test of these implications — a laboratory study of group problem-solving in restricted communication networks. It will subsequently be suggested how the laboratory findings in the communication setting can be generalized to other empirical applications.

The analysis utilizes a linear input-output model, the usefulness of which has been demonstrated for economic systems (Leontief, 1941) and for migration fields (Lövgren, 1957). It is now proposed to apply that model to communication systems. If this can successfully be done, then the input-output model is established as a useful tool for all three of the "levels" which Levi-Strauss identified for "communication" (1953): communication of women, communication of goods and services, and communication of messages. The transmission, that is, of people, of energy, and of information.

How are weighted links operationalized? In a communication network, this is done by measuring the volume of message flow over the link. In laboratory experiments, these magnitudes can be controlled, by imposing them on the group. The sender is not permitted to transmit everything he knows, but only a prescribed fraction.

The group activity is a problem-solving task. Successful solution requires high "knowledgeability" on the part of the subject. It is hypothesized that a well-informed person will submit his answer sooner than a poorly-informed person will. These ideas are discussed in more detail below.

What are the *effects* of these weighted links? Position within the system structure affects the quality of information available to the member, and thereby affects the quality of information that he, in turn, can make available to others; that is, his status as a source of information (Shepard, 1954). And that system structure is now defined as a configuration of *weighted* links.

A member's information input is a function of

1. the strengths of weights of his incoming links, and
2. the quality of information possessed by his respective informants; i.e., how well informed they are.

These factors serve to define the individual's position in the group's communication structure, and his own "knowledgeability" is determined by that position. In a communication structure with weighted links, a person having a few strong contacts with knowledgeable informants can acquire and possess more information than someone receiving many messages from inferior sources. These relationships can be expressed in a precise mathematical form, as in the model discussed below.

We make a distinction between *messages* and *information*. The former are the vehicles for the latter. The information content of a message depends on the quality of information possessed by the sender; how well-informed he is. The *amount* of information in a message is a function of the length of the message *and* the quality of the message content.

The information content of the messages constitutes influence. This material possesses instrumental value for the subjects, in enabling them to approach their cooperative goal of severally achieving a correct answer to the problem. In accepting and using this information, they accept influence; and in passing on the best information that they can, they exert influence. If B, after receiving information from A, behaves differently than he would have in the absence of such information, then A has influenced B. Communication systems are thus one instance of the more general category of *influence* systems.

We distinguish between the amount of information to which member *i* has been *exposed* through incoming messages, say x_i, and the amount of information which he actually *possesses*, say s_i. Exposure is a *social* phenomenon, dependent upon his location in the system structure; possession is a *psychological* achievement, the result of his cognitive skill in interpreting the messages which he receives. The individual's ability to convert receipts into actual possession can be represented by an efficiency parameter k_i, with the functional relationship being

$$s_i^{(t+1)} = k_i x_i^{(t)} \tag{1}$$

This equation states that an individual's store of information at one time period is proportional to his exposure to information at the previous time period, the intervening time being required for the cognitive processing of his message inputs.

Information flows from still earlier time periods do not appear explicitly in equation (1), but we take account of their effect by including $x_i^{(t)}$, the individual's immediately prior information stock, as one of the components of his information exposure; in short, he has a memory. This serves, recursively, to include all of his prior information.

Individual efficiency k_i probably fluctuates over time as the person experiences spurts of insight, but for a first approximation it will suffice to ignore this refinement and treat k_i as having a fixed value for the individual. Both intra- and inter-individual differences in efficiency can be averaged out operationally by the use of large samples. Without loss of generality, we can let this common value be 1, and equation (1) becomes

$$s_i^{(t+1)} = x_i^{(t)} \tag{2}$$

For brevity, we refer to an individual's stock of information $s_i^{(t)}$ as his *status*, reflecting his competence as a source of information. The greater the value of $s_i^{(t)}$, the higher the standing of member *i* as an informant. This follows the usage of Shepard (1954), who points out that task competence and ability to provide task-relevant information to others, in a problem-solving group, are the measures of a member's status. Similar observations have been made by Blau (1955, 1964).

An individual's exposure to influence is the sum of his information inputs:

$$x_i^{(t)} = e_i^{(t)} + v_{i1}^{(t)} + v_{i2}^{(t)} + \cdots + v_{in}^{(t)} \tag{3}$$

where *n* is the number of persons in the network. Some of these inputs may, of course, be nil. The transmission of information as outputs and inputs gives rise to the "input-output" appellation for the model. The individual's inputs are of two types: *exogenous*, $e_i^{(t)}$, originating in the group's environment; and *endogenous*, $v_{ij}^{(t)}$, coming from members of the group. Included among the latter are the individual's self-inputs, $v_{ii}^{(t)}$.

The presence of exogenous inputs reflects the open-system character of the model. In the present experiment, the value of exogenous inputs is held constant over time, so we remove the superscript on e_i:

$$x^{(t)} = e_i + v_{i1}^{(t)} + v_{i2}^{(t)} + \cdots + v_{in}^{(t)} \qquad (4)$$

Each input $v_{ij}^{(t)}$ is the product of the status of the informant, $s_j^{(t)}$, and the strength of the connecting link, w_{ij}:

$$v_{ij}^{(t)} = w_{ij}s_j^{(t)} \qquad (5)$$

Substituting this into the previous equation, we have

$$x_i^{(t)} = e_i + w_{i1}s_1^{(t)} + w_{i2}s_2^{(t)} + \cdots + w_{in}s_n^{(t)} \qquad (6)$$

Substituting from (2) on the left side of (6), we have

$$s_i^{(t+1)} = e_i + w_{i1}s_1^{(t)} + w_{i2}s_2^{(t)} + \cdots + w_{in}s_n^{(t)} \qquad (7)$$

Substitution has eliminated $x_i^{(t)}$, relegating it mathematically to the status of an intervening variable. The resulting equation focuses on the social factor of system structure, rather than on the psychological factor of cognitive information processing. Individual differences in the latter are partialled out by empirical randomization in the assignment of subjects to network positions.

It is readily seen, from equation (7), that a person's own status is enhanced by heavy linkage weights w_{ij}, and by contacts with well-informed persons s_j.

There are n equations of the form (7), one for each member of the group. This entire set of scalar equations is equivalent to the single matrix equation

$$S^{(t+1)} = E + WS^{(t)} \qquad (8)$$

where E is the pattern of exogenous inputs to the respective members, $W = (w_{ij})$ is the $n \times n$ weight matrix which describes the linkage structure of the group, and $S^{(t)}$ is the group's profile of status scores. $S^{(t)}$ is also called the *state* of the system at time t; and $S^{(0)}$, in particular, is called the *initial state* of the system.

In the laboratory, $W = (w_{ij})$ is operationalized by controlling the volume of message flow over each link. The details are presented in Section E. Status $s_i^{(t)}$ is operationalized by answering order and also by questionnaire evaluations. It will be seen that the predictions of relative status hold up both within and across experimental networks.

Recursion on (8) generates a *sequence* of status profiles,

$$S^{(0)}, S^{(1)}, S^{(2)}, \ldots \rightarrow S \tag{9}$$

which converges to an *equilibrium* profile S; that is, one which reproduces itself when inserted in (8). It is accordingly written without superscript:

$$S = E + WS \tag{10}$$

with solution

$$S = (I - W)^{-1}E \tag{11}$$

In order for the solution (11) to exist, it is sufficient for the network represented by $W = (w_{ij})$ to be strongly connected (see Flament, 1963, p. 32), and for its row-sums w_i. to satisfy the inequality

$$\begin{aligned} w_i. &\leq 1 \\ (i &= 1, \ldots, n) \end{aligned} \tag{12}$$

with the strict inequality applying for at least one i.

These conditions are satisfied for the experiment reported here, in which every linkage weight is nonnegative. Where negative links exist, inequality (12) must be supplanted by

$$w_i.^* \leq 1 \tag{13}$$

where $w_i.^*$ is the row-sum of absolute values,

$$w_i.^* = |w_{i1}| + |w_{i2}| + \cdots + |w_{in}| \tag{14}$$

□ **C. THE GROUP TASK**

Each experimental group consisted of five subjects. Each member possessed some, but not all, of the information necessary to solve the problem. In order to reach his answer he was dependent upon his fellow members, and they, in turn, were dependent upon him, for information to solve the problem.

Sharing of information was restricted to written messages, with experimental control of the amount of message flow between each pair of members. The subjects interacted within a restricted communication network imposed by the experimenter. They were seated at a Bavelas-type apparatus (Figure 1), equipped with slots for the exchange of message cards within booths. Selected channels were blocked, to impose the topological network. Linkage weighting was achieved by imposing message quotas, described below.

■ **FIGURE 1.** Apparatus for Restricted Communications Networks.

The problem involved five abstract symbols — circle, square, star, triangle, and spiral. Each of these symbols was assigned beforehand, by the experimenter, to one of two classifications: *plus* or *minus*. An example is shown in Figure 2. These five symbols, together with their possible classifications, may

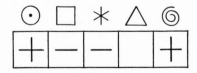

■ **FIGURE 2.** The Five Symbols and an Example of Their Classification.

be referred to as the *cognitive manifold* of the participants in this communication system. The group's task was to ascertain the proper classification for each of the five symbols.

At the beginning of the problem, each member received information about four of the five symbols. This information consisted of plusses and/or minuses, one for each symbol. For three of the symbols, this information was correct. For the fourth, it was incorrect. On the remaining fifth symbol, the member received no information at all. Thus each member's initial stock of information consisted of three correct items, one "counterfeit" item, and one blank, as in Figure 3.

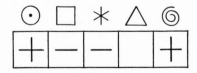

■ **FIGURE 3.** Example of a Classification Sheet.

Blanks and errors were distributed in such a way that every member drew his blank on a different symbol, and each member's error was assigned to a different symbol. This made for complete symmetry among the members, in the initial distribution of information. The amount and quality of initial information was the same for every member. The object, then, was for every member to learn what the correct assignments were for all five symbols.

The format for the message cards appears in Figure 4. The discretionary

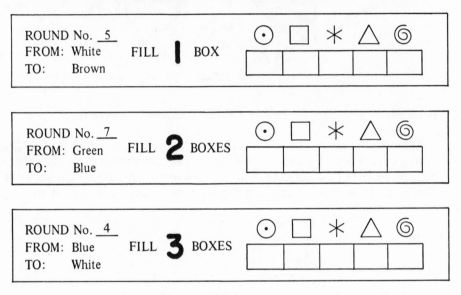

■ **FIGURE 4.** Message Cards, with Quotas.

part of message content consisted solely of plus and minus signs entered in the boxes under the symbols. Sender, receiver, and round number were already printed on the card. To write a message, the sender entered plus and/or minus signs in the appropriate boxes of the message form, no more than one to a symbol.

All messages were exchanged in unison, at the sound of a chime. Thus the circulation of information could be marked off into *rounds*. The sounding of the chime was actuated by the subjects themselves, in such a way that no one sent until everyone was ready to send.

Each box filled on a message card constituted one *message unit*. The sender was not allowed to use all five boxes on the message card. A restrictive quota was printed plainly on the face of the card, as in Figure 4, and the number of boxes filled on each card had to equal the quota exactly. Linkage strengths were controlled, accordingly, by experimental manipulation of these quotas. For any given channel within the group, the quota was held constant for every round and for every problem.

In addition to the messages from fellow members, each participant received a card from the environment — i.e., the experimenter — on every round, containing information about exactly one symbol (one message unit). The quality of this exogenous information was controlled, to approximate the average quality of the endogenous messages originating within the group.

Completion of a problem required the submission of separate answers from each of the group members. When a member felt that he had the answer, he signalled the experimenter privately, but continued to participate in the group's message exchanges. If he subsequently felt unsure about his answer, he could revoke it, and reinstate again whenever he was ready to do so. As soon as current answers were on hand from all five members, the task was terminated by the experimenter, and the correct answer was announced. No one was told how other members of the group had answered.

□ **D. EXPERIMENTAL CONDITIONS**

The topological version of the experimental network is diagrammed in Figure 5. The peripheral arrows in the diagram represent boundary inlets to the respective

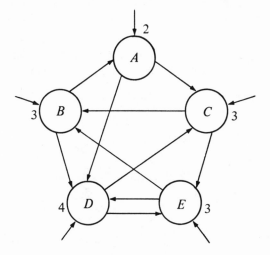

■ **FIGURE 5.** The Topological Network.
(The number appearing next to each node is its number of inlets.)

positions, for exogenous inputs. The number appearing next to each node is its number of inlets.

The topological network structure was invariant over the various experimental conditions. There was variation, however, in the pattern of linkage *strengths*. The three experimental conditions appear in Figures 6, 7, and 8. The number of lines in each arrow indicates the message quota for the corresponding link. Regardless of the experimental condition or position in the group, each member received exactly one message per round from the environment. The numeral appearing next to each node is the total number of message units received on each round, including the one unit furnished by the environment.

The networks were so chosen that all endogenous inlets at a given node had the same quota. In the *unbiased* network (Figure 6), this was two message units

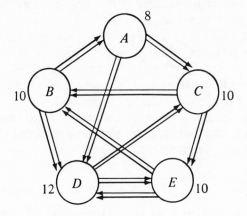

■ **FIGURE 6.** Unbiased Network.
The numeral appearing next to each node is the total number of message units which it receives on each round, including one unit from the environment and 5 units from itself.

for every node. In the biased conditions, it was one unit for some, and three units for others. The *majority bias* (Figure 7) is the condition in which the

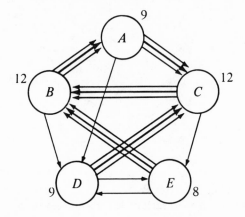

■ **FIGURE 7.** Majority Bias.
The numeral appearing next to each node is the total number of message units which it receives on each round, including one unit from the environment and 5 units from itself.

heavier inputs were distributed among three positions in the group (*A*, *B*, and *C*). For the *minority bias* (Figure 8), these were distributed between two members (*D* and *E*).

By holding the topological network invariant and varying the strengths of component linkages, it was possible to show how a member with a single heavy

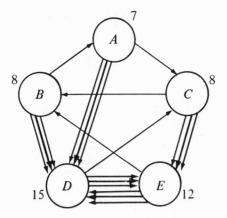

■ FIGURE 8. Minority Bias.
The numeral appearing next to each node is the total number of message units which it receives on each round, including one unit from the environment and 5 units from itself.

inlet could have his status elevated over that of a companion with several weak inlets.

Ten groups were run in each condition. All subjects in a given group were matched as closely as possible on intellectual ability, so that differences in problem-solving could be attributed to group structure, and not to personal ability. The experimental subjects were inmates of the Michigan Reformatory at Ionia, Michigan. All were males, ranging in age from 17 to 24 years. Considering the level of difficulty of the experimental task, an effort was made to secure subjects of adequate intellectual caliber. 150 subjects were used, in thirty groups of five men each. Each subject participated in exactly one group.

□ E. OPERATIONAL DEFINITIONS

Let q_{ij} be the message quota for the j-i link. Then i's total input of message units per round is given by

$$q_{i0} + (q_{i1} + q_{i2} + \cdots + q_{in}) = q_i. \tag{15}$$

where q_{i0} is the quota for i's exogenous link. The quotas q_{ij} for *intra*-system links can be arranged in a *quota matrix*, $Q = (q_{ij})$. These matrices are given in Table 1, for the three experimental conditions. Each q_{ij} shows how many message units i receives from j on each round. In the present experiment, we assume that q_{ii} is uniformly equal to 5, since the member is exposed to his own prior information on all five symbols (except for the first round, when his prior possession is only four symbols).

Equation (15) indicates the intensity of utilization of all incoming message channels. *Relative* intensity is determined by using the normalization

$$w_{ij} = \frac{q_{ij}}{q_{i\cdot}} \tag{16}$$

These are taken as the linkage weights.

If both sides of (15) are divided by $q_{i\cdot}$, we obtain

$$\frac{q_{i0}}{q_{i\cdot}} + \left(\frac{q_{i1}}{q_{i\cdot}} + \frac{q_{i2}}{q_{i\cdot}} + \cdots + \frac{q_{in}}{q_{i\cdot}}\right) = 1$$

Substituting into this from (16), we obtain

$$w_{i0} + (w_{i1} + w_{i2} + \cdots + w_{in}) = 1 \tag{17}$$

Thus an individual's inlet weights sum to 1; the recipient pools the content of his incoming messages, in an attempt to extract information from them.

Each quota matrix in Table 1 shows the message quotas for endogenous links.

■ **TABLE 1 /** Quota Matrices (q_{ij}) and Weight Matrices (w_{ij}) for the Three Experimental Conditions

	A	B	C	D	E	$q_{i\cdot}$		A	B	C	D	E
A	5	2	0	0	0	8		.625	.250	0	0	0
B	0	5	2	0	2	10		0	.500	.200	0	.200
C	2	0	5	2	0	10		.200	0	.500	.200	0
D	2	2	0	5	2	12		.167	.167	0	.417	.167
E	0	0	2	2	5	10		0	0	.200	.200	.500

Quota Matrix   Weight Matrix
Unbiased Condition

	A	B	C	D	E			A	B	C	D	E
A	5	3	0	0	0	9		.556	.333	0	0	0
B	0	5	3	0	3	12		0	.417	.250	0	.250
C	3	0	5	3	0	12		.250	0	.417	.250	0
D	1	1	0	5	1	9		.111	.111	0	.556	.111
E	0	0	1	1	5	8		0	0	.125	.125	.625

Quota Matrix   Weight Matrix
Majority Bias

	A	B	C	D	E			A	B	C	D	E
A	5	1	0	0	0	7		.714	.143	0	0	0
B	0	5	1	0	1	8		0	.625	.125	0	.125
C	1	0	5	1	0	8		.125	0	.625	.125	0
D	3	3	0	5	3	15		.200	.200	0	.333	.200
E	0	0	3	3	5	12		0	0	.250	.250	.417

Quota Matrix   Weight Matrix
Minority Bias

The marginal totals q_i. are the row-sums of these *plus* the exogenous quotas ($q_i \cdot = 1$), in each case. Table 1 also gives the corresponding weight matrices $W = (w_{ij})$, which are obtained from the respective quota matrices by the normalization (16).

The initial conditions $S^{(0)}$ and boundary conditions E were parameters, experimentally controlled in the form of information supplied to group members at the outset of each problem and during its course, respectively. The values of these were held constant across all groups, networks, individuals, and problems, subject only to randomization of specific information content.

Initial information $S^{(0)}$ covered four symbols for each member; we therefore set $s_i^{(0)} = 4$, for every member. The environment furnished information E on one symbol for each member on each round; we therefore set $e_i = 1$, throughout.

A member's status or influence level $s_i^{(t)}$ is coordinated to the quality of the information which he possesses on round t. This cannot be measured directly; for one thing, we can never tell whether he really "possesses" it yet. Indirect measures were used, therefore, as operational definitions of $s_i^{(t)}$, namely:

(a) finishing order in submitting correct answers; and
(b) questionnaire evaluation of an individual as a source of information, as judged by his fellow members.

These empirical measures are by-products of information quality, rather than quality itself.

Answering order — (a), above — was empirically determined on the basis of the round on which each member submitted his answer. All incorrect answers, however, were reckoned as tied for last place; the person who fixates on an incorrect answer doesn't really *possess* high quality information, even though it may have been made available to him in incoming messages — "exposure" x_i, in equation (1).

At the end of the laboratory session, each member filled out a questionnaire, certain items of which asked him to evaluate his respective informants as sources of information — (b), above. This furnished a separate measure of differential knowledgeability within the group.

☐ **F. HYPOTHESES**

The model assigns to each member, at each time period, an index which indicates how well-informed he should be, theoretically, at that point. Table 2 gives the magnitudes of these predicted scores for the Unbiased condition. These scores, for the successive time periods, are generated by the recursion formula (8). They have been rounded, at each step in the computation, to the nearest tenth. Finer discriminations would far exceed the fineness of the empirical data.

The columns of Table 2 are arranged in order of magnitude, rather than in

■ **TABLE 2 / Predicted Scores $s_i^{(t)}$ by Round Number t (Unbiased Condition)**

Round Number	Network Position:*	D	E	B	C	A
0		4.0	4.0	4.0	4.0	4.0
1		4.7	4.6	4.6	4.6	4.5
2		5.2	5.2	5.1	5.1	5.0
3		5.7	5.7	5.6	5.6	5.4
4		6.2	6.1	6.1	6.0	5.8
5		6.6	6.5	6.5	6.4	6.2
6		7.0	6.9	6.8	6.8	6.5
7		7.3	7.2	7.1	7.1	6.8
8		7.6	7.5	7.4	7.4	7.0
9		7.8	7.8	7.7	7.6	7.2
10		8.0	8.0	7.9	7.8	7.4
11		8.2	8.2	8.1	8.0	7.6
12		8.4	8.3	8.3	8.2	7.8
13		8.6	8.5	8.5	8.3	8.0
14		8.8	8.6	8.6	8.5	8.1
15		8.9	8.8	8.7	8.6	8.2
16		9.0	8.9	8.8	8.7	8.3
17		9.1	9.0	8.9	8.8	8.4
18		9.2	9.1	9.0	8.9	8.5
19		9.3	9.2	9.1	9.0	8.6
20		9.4	9.3	9.2	9.1	8.7
21		9.5	9.4	9.3	9.2	8.7
22		9.5	9.4	9.4	9.2	8.8
23		9.6	9.4	9.4	9.3	8.9
24		9.6	9.5	9.4	9.4	8.9
25		9.6	9.6	9.5	9.4	8.9
26		9.7	9.6	9.6	9.4	8.9
27	(equilibrium)	9.7	9.6	9.6	9.4	9.0

* Positions are listed from left to right in decreasing order of scores.

lexical order. Each column dominates those that stand to the right of it, in the sense that each entry in the dominating column is greater than or equal to the corresponding entry in the dominated column. Thus, adhering to this predicted rank order of network positions, the model predicts *D E B C A* as the status order for the five members in the Unbiased condition.

This rank order suggests two things — who will be most likely to answer next; and which member, in a paired comparison, will be perceived by his companions as more knowledgeable. The notion is that a better-informed member can and will state the problem solution sooner than a less well-informed person. The most likely person to answer on any given round, accordingly, is that person who is best informed among those who have not yet answered. A better-informed member should, moreover, be perceived as such, even subliminally, by his recipients.

Formally stated, then, the two hypotheses are

HYPOTHESIS 1a: In the *unbiased* condition, the *answering order* of the group members will be $D > E > B > C > A$.

HYPOTHESIS 1b: In the *unbiased* condition, the relative rank of group members, as indicated in *questionnaire ratings* by their companions, will be consistent with the order $D > E > B > C > A$.

To obtain data for Hypothesis 1b, the questionnaire asked for paired comparisons. Each subject was asked to compare his informants, as to their respective value as sources of information. Certain paired comparisons could never be made — member *A* vs. member *B*, for example — since there was no one who received messages from both members of the pair.

For the Majority-Bias condition, the equations of the model generate Table 3, from which the next two hypotheses are derived:

HYPOTHESIS 2a: In the *majority-bias* condition, the *answering order* of the group members will be $C = B > A > D > E$.

HYPOTHESIS 2b: In the *majority-bias* condition, the relative rank of group members, as indicated in *questionnaire ratings* by their companions, will be consistent with the order $C = B > A > D > E$.

The prediction of a tie for positions *C* and *B* rests on the fact that the predicted scores $s_i^{(t)}$ for the two positions are identical, except for the twenty-third round. Pretests indicated that groups would finish the problems by the fourteenth round at the latest, so there is nothing to differentiate *C* and *B*, here.

The hypotheses for the Minority-Bias condition were similarly derived, from Table 4. They are as follows:

HYPOTHESIS 3a: In the *minority-bias* condition, the *answering order* of the group members will be $E > D > B > C > A$.

HYPOTHESIS 3b: In the *minority-bias* condition, the relative rank of group members, as indicated in *questionnaire ratings* by their companions, will be consistent with the order $E > D > B > C > A$.

These last two hypotheses highlight the importance of treating the communication network as an interdependent system. In the Minority-Bias condition, *D* receives ten message units and *E* receives seven, per round. Casual inspection might suggest that the *quantitatively* greater input to *D* would enable him to outperform *E*. But thirty percent of *D*'s input is from *A*, who is extremely ill-informed, which depresses the average *quality* of *D*'s knowledge below that of *E*.

■ TABLE 3 / Predicted Scores $s_i^{(t)}$ by Round Number t
(Majority-Bias Condition)

Round Number	Network Position:*	C	B	A	D	E
0		4.0	4.0	4.0	4.0	4.0
1		4.7	4.7	4.6	4.6	4.5
2		5.3	5.3	5.1	5.1	5.0
3		5.8	5.8	5.6	5.5	5.4
4		6.2	6.2	6.0	5.9	5.8
5		6.6	6.6	6.4	6.3	6.1
6		6.9	6.9	6.8	6.6	6.4
7		7.2	7.2	7.1	6.9	6.7
8		7.5	7.5	7.3	7.2	7.0
9		7.8	7.8	7.6	7.4	7.2
10		8.0	8.0	7.8	7.6	7.4
11		8.2	8.2	8.0	7.8	7.6
12		8.4	8.4	8.2	8.0	7.8
13		8.6	8.6	8.4	8.2	7.9
14		8.7	8.7	8.5	8.3	8.0
15		8.8	8.8	8.6	8.4	8.1
16		8.9	8.9	8.7	8.5	8.2
17		9.0	9.0	8.8	8.6	8.3
18		9.1	9.1	8.9	8.7	8.4
19		9.2	9.2	9.0	8.8	8.5
20		9.3	9.3	9.1	8.9	8.6
21		9.4	9.4	9.2	8.9	8.7
22		9.4	9.4	9.2	9.0	8.7
23		9.5	9.4	9.2	9.0	8.7
24		9.5	9.5	9.2	9.0	8.8
25		9.5	9.5	9.3	9.1	8.8
26		9.6	9.5	9.3	9.1	8.8
27		9.6	9.6	9.3	9.1	8.8
28 (equilibrium)		9.6	9.6	9.4	9.1	8.8

* Positions are listed from left to right in decreasing order of scores.

The result is that E's performance is better than D's. The experimental confirmation of these two hypotheses (see below) emphasizes the discriminating power of the input-output model.

Three variations of the communication network were used in the laboratory experiment, and Hypotheses 1–3 predict the empirical outcomes for each of these conditions. Those outcomes can also be combined, to provide an overall test of the model's predictive power, as in the next two hypotheses:

HYPOTHESIS 4a: The algebraic model accurately predicts *answering order* for communication networks.

■ **TABLE 4 / Predicted Scores $s_i^{(t)}$ by Round Number t**
   (Minority-Bias Condition)

Round Number	Network Position:*	E	D	B	C	A
0		4.0	4.0	4.0	4.0	4.0
1		4.7	4.7	4.5	4.5	4.4
2		5.3	5.3	5.0	5.0	4.8
3		5.8	5.8	5.4	5.4	5.1
4		6.2	6.2	5.8	5.7	5.4
5		6.6	6.5	6.1	6.0	5.7
6		6.9	6.8	6.4	6.3	5.9
7		7.2	7.1	6.7	6.5	6.1
8		7.4	7.4	6.9	6.7	6.3
9		7.6	7.6	7.1	6.9	6.5
10		7.8	7.8	7.3	7.1	6.7
11		8.0	8.0	7.4	7.3	6.8
12		8.2	8.1	7.5	7.4	6.9
13		8.3	8.2	7.6	7.5	7.0
14		8.4	8.3	7.7	7.6	7.1
15		8.5	8.4	7.8	7.7	7.2
16		8.6	8.5	7.9	7.8	7.3
17		8.7	8.6	8.0	7.9	7.3
18		8.8	8.7	8.1	7.9	7.4
19		8.8	8.8	8.2	8.0	7.4
20		8.9	8.8	8.2	8.0	7.5
21		8.9	8.9	8.2	8.0	7.5
22		8.9	8.9	8.2	8.1	7.5
23	(equilibrium)	9.0	8.9	8.3	8.1	7.5

* Positions are listed from left to right, in decreasing order of scores.

HYPOTHESIS 4b: The algebraic model accurately predicts the outcome of the *questionnaire evaluations* in communication networks.

These hypotheses assert that if we know the weighted-link structure for any given network, then we can successfully predict the two types of outcomes for that network. For the tests of these hypotheses, accordingly, the outcomes for each network are compared against the predictions for that same network.

The foregoing hypotheses compare relative performance of network positions *within* experimental condition. A similar comparison can be made *across* conditions. For this prediction, the entries of Tables 2, 3, and 4 are aggregated into a single summary table. This is Table 5, which is truncated at the fourteenth round, since groups invariably finished each problem by then. As before, column-domination is from left to right, but reversals again appear over time. For certain pairs the direction of dominance is inconclusive, so that the entire

TABLE 5 / Predicted Scores $s_i^{(t)}$ by Round Number t, across All Experimental Conditions

Network Positions*
(abbreviations explained below)

Round Number	UnD	MaC	MaB	UnE	UnB	MiE	MiD	UnC	MaA	MaD	UnA	MaE	MiB	MiC	MiA
0	4.0	4.0	4.0	4.0	4.0	4.0	4.0	4.0	4.0	4.0	4.0	4.0	4.0	4.0	4.0
1	4.7	4.7	4.7	4.6	4.6	4.7	4.7	4.6	4.6	4.6	4.5	4.5	4.5	4.5	4.4
2	5.2	5.3	5.3	5.2	5.1	5.3	5.3	5.1	5.1	5.1	5.0	5.0	5.0	5.0	4.8
3	5.7	5.8	5.8	5.7	5.6	5.8	5.8	5.6	5.6	5.5	5.4	5.4	5.4	5.4	5.1
4	6.2	6.2	6.2	6.1	6.1	6.2	6.2	6.0	6.0	5.9	5.8	5.8	5.8	5.7	5.4
5	6.6	6.6	6.6	6.5	6.5	6.6	6.5	6.4	6.4	6.3	6.2	6.1	6.1	6.0	5.7
6	7.0	6.9	6.9	6.9	6.8	6.9	6.8	6.8	6.8	6.6	6.5	6.4	6.4	6.3	5.9
7	7.3	7.2	7.2	7.2	7.1	7.2	7.1	7.1	7.1	6.9	6.8	6.7	6.7	6.5	6.1
8	7.6	7.5	7.5	7.5	7.4	7.4	7.4	7.4	7.3	7.2	7.0	7.0	6.9	6.7	6.3
9	7.8	7.8	7.8	7.8	7.7	7.6	7.6	7.6	7.6	7.4	7.2	7.2	7.1	6.9	6.5
10	8.0	8.0	8.0	8.0	7.9	7.8	7.8	7.8	7.8	7.6	7.4	7.4	7.3	7.1	6.7
11	8.2	8.2	8.2	8.2	8.1	8.0	8.0	8.0	8.0	7.8	7.6	7.6	7.4	7.3	6.8
12	8.4	8.4	8.4	8.3	8.3	8.2	8.1	8.2	8.2	8.0	7.8	7.8	7.5	7.4	6.9
13	8.6	8.6	8.6	8.5	8.5	8.3	8.2	8.3	8.4	8.2	8.0	7.9	7.6	7.5	7.0
14	8.8	8.7	8.7	8.6	8.6	8.4	8.3	8.5	8.5	8.3	8.1	8.0	7.7	7.6	7.1

* Positions are arranged in generally decreasing order, from left to right. There are some reversals, over time (t).

NOTE: The respective networks are identified here by Un, unbiased; Ma, majority-bias; and Mi, minority bias. For example, UnD is position D in the unbiased network.

ensemble constitutes a partially-ordered set, as diagrammed in Figure 9. This

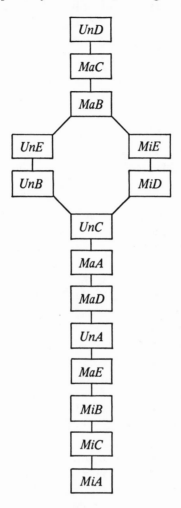

■ **FIGURE 9.** Predicted Rank Order of Network Positions.
SOURCE: Table 6. The respective networks are identified here as *Un*, unbiased; *Ma*; majority-bias; and *Mi*, minority-bias. For example, *UnD* is position *D* in the unbiased condition.

Rankings are transitive. The fifteen positions form a partially-ordered set, in which unranked pairs are predicted (for Hypothesis 4) as ties.

is the basis for the prediction embodied in Hypothesis 5. The unranked pairs are predicted as ties.

HYPOTHESIS 5: Comparing network positions across all experimental conditions, and using speed of problem solution as a criterion, the respective network positions will form a partially-ordered set, as diagrammed in Figure 9.

The empirical dependent variable for this hypothesis was the mean number of answering round, averaged over all individuals occupying the same structural position in different groups. This measure involves a departure from the pure rank-order principle, since rank comparisons cannot be made between individuals belonging to different groups; they do not participate in the same answering sequence.

☐ **G. THE STARVATION PHENOMENON**

The inferior performance of *MiD*, compared to *UnD*, reflects a *starvation* phenomenon. *MiD* has a greater message input than *UnD* (ten units per round, as against seven), yet member *D*'s performance is better in the Unbiased condition — both theoretically (Table 5 and Figure 9) and empirically (Table 7, below).

In the Minority-Bias condition, position *D* receives nearly half of the group's message flow, but this occurs at the expense of *A*, *B*, and *C*. The deprivation suffered by the latter members means that they are poorly informed, which affects adversely the quality of the messages which they transmit to others. This inferiority propagates through the network — a *system* effect — to impoverish all members of the group, including even the privileged *D*.

Thus position *D* either gains quality at the sacrifice of quantity, or vice versa. A similar assertion can be made for position *E*, which is closely associated with *D* in the communication network. It is only a conservative orientation which causes us to treat *UnE* and *MiE* as an inconclusive pair, in our theoretical predictions. In actuality, *UnE* outstrips *MiE* by the sixth round. It takes twenty-seven steps before either of these networks reaches equilibrium, and real-life communication systems, with their complex and ongoing tasks (cf. Shepard, 1954), probably approach equilibrium more closely than the present experimental situation does, with the fixed and finite cognitive manifold involved in its task. But even with these limitations, the superiority of *UnE* over *MiE* is empirically substantiated here (Table 7, below).

The comparison presented here suggests that the higher-ranking members of any system ultimately benefit from certain minimum standards for the welfare of all members. Robbing peasant Peter to pay princely Paul may be a shortsighted policy. The mathematical nature of the principle would make it worth investigating for influence systems of all types — whether the resources are wealth, power, prestige, or information. The benefits to the elite are indirect, of course. But persons of limited vision who consider only immediate, local advantage — a common tendency in our culture — may actually be shortchanging themselves.

☐ **H. EXPERIMENTAL RESULTS**

All of the hypotheses involve predictions of rank order among the various network positions. These are compared against the observed rank orders, and evaluated by nonparametric tests (Kendall's *tau*, 1948).

Hypotheses 1–4 can be tested in either of two ways, which may be called the "joint" and "several" approaches, respectively. In the "joint" approach, the rank orders observed in the several experimental groups are combined into a single composite ranking, which is then compared against the predicted rank order. In the "several" approach, each experimental group is compared separately against the predicted order.

For Hypotheses 1, 2, and 3, the composite rank order is constructed from the consensus of the several observations. In this process, individual departures from the consensus disappear from view. As a result, the composite rank order is better, on the average, than the separate rank orders from which it is developed. This is reflected, in Table 6, by the uniformly greater *tau* values for the composite case than for the case of separate observations. But the composite ranking is treated as a sample of size 1, while the separate observations constitute a sample of size 8 or 9. Thus the smaller *tau* values have a higher statistical significance, due to the larger sample size.

For Hypothesis 4, the "joint" approach used the composite rank orders for the respective experimental conditions, treating them as a sample of size 3. In the "several" approach, the observed rank order for each group was compared against the ranking predicted for its network, yielding a sample of 26 cases.

Answering order (Hypothesis 1a) permits the comparison of every possible pair of members, but questionnaire evaluation (Hypothesis 1b) does not. The questionnaire asked each participant to judge the knowledgeability of his respective informants, and certain comparisons were impossible (*B* versus *C*, for example), since no one received messages from both members of the pair. Thus Hypothesis 1a was able to predict a complete ranking of the five members, while Hypothesis 1b had to settle for a partial ordering, with uncompared dyads being treated as ties in the statistical test. Similarly for the contrasts between Hypotheses 2a and 2b, 3a and 3b.

The hypotheses are supported at the probability levels indicated in Table 6. The significance levels for questionnaire responses are characteristically lower than those for answering order. This is an acceptable state of affairs, since too much sensitivity on the part of the subjects would cause them to give more credence to message inputs from favored sources, thereby distorting the operational values of the weights w_{ij} on which the model's predictions are based.

The foregoing hypotheses compare relative performance of network positions *within* experimental condition. A similar comparison *across* conditions is made by Hypothesis 5. The empirical dependent variable for this hypothesis is the mean number of answering round, averaged over all individuals occupying the same structural position in different groups with the same network pattern. These data appear in Table 7.

The predicted rank order of network positions can be compared with the observed order by inserting the data of Table 7 in the partially-ordered set of Figure 9. Comparison of predicted with observed ranks discloses $17\frac{1}{2}$ reversals of prediction, as indicated in Table 8. (The fractional total is due to ties.)

■ **TABLE 6 / Experimental Results (Within-Condition)**

Answering Order		Test of Composite Observation*		Test of Separate Observations**	
Hypothesis 1a (Unbiased Condition)	$N = 8$	$\tau = .70$	$p = .073$	$\bar{\tau} = .20$	$p = .09$
Hypothesis 2a (Majority Bias)	$N = 9$	$\tau = .50$	$p = .173$	$\bar{\tau} = .26$	$p = .03$
Hypothesis 3a (Minority Bias)	$N = 9$	$\tau = .60$	$p = .117$	$\bar{\tau} = .34$	$p = .006$
Hypothesis 4a (All Conditions)	$N = 26$	$\tau = .60$	$p = .005$	$\bar{\tau} = .27$	$p = .0002$

Questionnaire Evaluations		Test of Composite Observation*		Test of Separate Observations†	
Hypothesis 1b (Unbiased Condition)	$N = 8$	$\tau = .33$	$p = .354$	$\bar{\tau} = .21$	$p = .084$
Hypothesis 2b (Majority Bias)	$N = 9$	$\tau = .67$	$p = .125$	$\bar{\tau} = .20$	$p = .078$
Hypothesis 3b (Minority Bias)	$N = 9$	$\tau = .67$	$p = .125$	$\bar{\tau} = .37$	$p = .005$
Hypothesis 4b (All Conditions)	$N = 26$	$\tau = .56$	$p = .012$	$\bar{\tau} = .26$	$p = .0009$

* For Hypotheses 1, 2, and 3, observations over the several groups were combined into a single composite rank order, which was then tested against the predicted order. For Hypothesis 4, these three composite orders were treated as a sample of three observations, against their respective predictions.

† The rank order observed in each group was compared separately against the predicted rank order for the corresponding network; the results were treated as a sample of size N.

■ **TABLE 7 / Mean Number of Observed Answering Round, for All Structural Positions**

UnE	5.73	*MaA*	6.20	*MaD*	6.67
UnD	5.81	*UnB*	6.29	*UnA*	7.35
MaB	5.93	*MiD*	6.35	*MiC*	7.41
MaC	6.19	*MaE*	6.59	*MiB*	7.70
UnC	6.19	*MiE*	6.61	*MiA*	9.26

NOTE: The respective networks are identified here as *Un*, unbiased; *Ma*, majority bias; and *Mi*, minority bias. For example, *UnE* is position *E* in the unbiased network.

The hypothesis is supported at the .05 level of significance, as shown in Table 8. Some of this support comes, of course, from pairs of positions within the same network structure, already invoked in support of Hypotheses 1–4. But if the analysis is confined to between-condition pairs, the significance level then rises to $p = .0002$; there are only $11\frac{1}{2}$ reversals among 75 position-pairs.

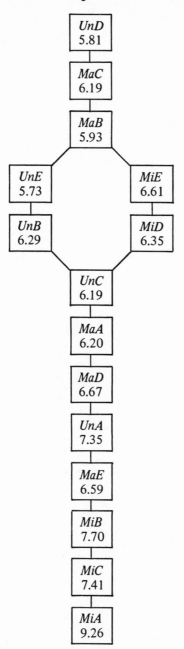

■ **FIGURE 10.** Cross-Condition Comparison of Predicted and Observed Answering Order.

The location of the respective boxes indicates their predicted rank order, in speed of answering. The number within each box is the mean number of the observed answering round, for the corresponding network position. The respective networks are identified here as *Un*, unbiased; *Ma*, majority-bias; and *Mi*, minority-bias. For example, *MiC* is position *C* in the minority-bias network.

■ TABLE 8 / Reversals of Predicted Rank

Predicted Lower Ranks	Predicted Higher Ranks (with Observed Mean Answering Round)														Row Sums
	UnD (5.81)	MaC (6.19)	MaB (5.93)	UnE (5.73)	UnB (6.29)	MiE (6.61)	MiD (6.35)	UnC (6.19)	MaA (6.20)	MaD (6.67)	UnA (7.35)	MaE (6.59)	MiB (7.70)	MiC (7.41)‡	
MaC (6.19)***	–														0
MaB (5.93)		1													1
UnE (5.73)	1	1	1												3
UnB (6.29)				–											0
MiE (6.61)				½*	½*										1
MiD (6.35)				½*	½*	1									2
UnC (6.19)		½†		–	1	1	1								3½
MaA (6.20)		–			1	1	1	–							3
MaD (6.67)								–	–						0
UnA (7.35)									–	–					0
MaE (6.59)						1				1	1				3
MiB (7.70)										–	–	–			0
MiC (7.41)										–	–	–	1		1
MiA (9.26)										–	–	–	–	–	0
Column Sums:	1	2½	1	1	3	4	2	0	0	1	1	0	1	0	17½ (Grand Total)

* Predicted as ties (partially-ordered set of Figure 9)

† Empirical tie

‡ The numbers in parentheses are the mean number of the observed answering round, for the respective network positions.   τ = .67   p < .05

An even better performance can be attributed to the model by taking account of two other factors in the laboratory situation — *reciprocation economy* and *input overload*. This section is devoted to a discussion of those factors and their effects.

Of the $17\frac{1}{2}$ reversals tabulated in Table 8, thirteen involve positions D and E of the respective networks. Now these two are the only positions which are linked in *both* directions. This bilateral contact, unlike unilateral ones, permits certain economies in communication. If D agrees with some of the content of E's latest message, for example, his reply can tacitly confirm the values for those particular symbols by overtly concentrating on others. The effect is to enhance the information capacity of the mutual D-E link. (Several subjects sensed the superior value of this channel, and commented on it afterwards.)

This *reciprocation economy*, or *mutuality bonus*, can be incorporated into the mathematical model. For purposes of illustration, let us interpret each box filled on a D-E or E-D card as being worth 1.5 message units, but retain the value of 1 message unit for each box filled on any other card. (The magnitude 1.5 is arbitrary, but will serve for purposes of illustration.)

This adjustment affects the D and E rows of the matrices in Table 1. The new rows for those matrices appear in Table 9. D and E now derive relatively more benefit from communications received from each other, since any such card now carries an implicit message, above its printed quota.

■ **TABLE 9 / D and E Rows of Quota and Weight Matrices,**
Adjusted for Mutuality Bonus

(The A, B, and C rows remain the same as in Table 1)

	A	B	C	D	E	q_i.	A	B	C	D	E
D	2	2	0	5	3	13	.154	.154	0	.385	.231
E	0	0	2	3	5	11	0	0	.182	.273	.455

Quota Matrix   Weight Matrix

Unbiased Condition

	A	B	C	D	E	q_i.	A	B	C	D	E
D	1	1	0	5	1.5	9.5	.105	.105	0	.526	.158
E	0	0	1	1.5	5	8.5	0	0	.118	.176	.588

Quota Matrix   Weight Matrix

Majority-Bias Condition

	A	B	C	D	E	q_i.	A	B	C	D	E
D	3	3	0	5	4.5	16.5	.182	.182	0	.303	.273
E	0	0	3	4.5	5	13.5	0	0	.222	.333	.370

Quota Matrix   Weight Matrix

Minority-Bias Condition

The weight matrices on the right-hand side of Table 9 are obtained, using the normalization (16), from the quota matrices on the left-hand side.

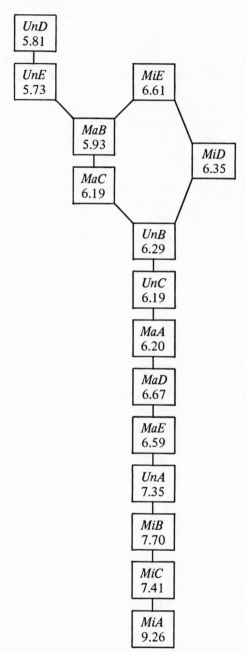

■ **FIGURE 11.** Predicted Rank Order of Network Positions, Adjusted for Mutuality Bonus.
SOURCE: Tables 10 and 7. The respective networks are identified here as *Un*, unbiased; *Ma*, majority-bias; and *Mi*, minority-bias. For example, *MiD* is position *D* in the minority-bias condition.

■ TABLE 10 / Predicted Scores $s_i^{(t)}$ by Round Number t, Adjusted for Mutuality Bonus

Network Positions*
(abbreviations explained below)

Round Number	UnD	UnE	MaB	MiE	MaC	MiD	UnB	UnC	MaA	MaD	MaE	UnA	MiB	MiC	MiA
0	4.0	4.0	4.0	4.0	4.0	4.0	4.0	4.0	4.0	4.0	4.0	4.0	4.0	4.0	4.0
1	4.7	4.6	4.7	4.7	4.7	4.8	4.6	4.6	4.6	4.6	4.5	4.5	4.5	4.5	4.4
2	5.3	5.2	5.3	5.3	5.3	5.4	5.1	5.1	5.1	5.1	5.0	5.0	5.0	5.0	4.8
3	5.8	5.7	5.8	5.9	5.8	5.9	5.6	5.6	5.6	5.6	5.5	5.4	5.4	5.4	5.1
4	6.2	6.2	6.2	6.4	6.2	6.3	6.1	6.0	6.0	6.0	5.9	5.8	5.8	5.8	5.4
5	6.6	6.6	6.6	6.8	6.6	6.7	6.5	6.4	6.4	6.4	6.3	6.2	6.2	6.1	5.7
6	7.0	7.0	7.0	7.1	7.0	7.0	6.9	6.8	6.8	6.7	6.6	6.5	6.5	6.4	6.0
7	7.4	7.3	7.3	7.4	7.3	7.3	7.2	7.1	7.1	7.0	6.9	6.8	6.8	6.6	6.2
8	7.7	7.6	7.6	7.6	7.6	7.6	7.5	7.4	7.4	7.3	7.2	7.1	7.0	6.8	6.4
9	8.0	7.9	7.9	7.9	7.8	7.8	7.8	7.6	7.6	7.6	7.4	7.3	7.2	7.0	6.6
10	8.2	8.2	8.1	8.1	8.1	8.0	8.0	7.9	7.9	7.8	7.6	7.5	7.4	7.2	6.7
11	8.4	8.4	8.3	8.3	8.3	8.2	8.2	8.1	8.1	8.0	7.8	7.7	7.5	7.3	6.8
12	8.6	8.6	8.5	8.4	8.5	8.3	8.4	8.3	8.3	8.2	8.0	7.9	7.6	7.4	6.9
13	8.8	8.8	8.7	8.5	8.7	8.4	8.6	8.5	8.4	8.3	8.2	8.0	7.7	7.5	7.0
14	9.0	8.9	8.9	8.6	8.8	8.5	8.8	8.6	8.6	8.5	8.3	8.2	7.8	7.6	7.1

* Positions are arranged in generally decreasing order, from left to right. There are some reversals over time (t).

NOTE: The respective networks are identified here by Un, unbiased; Ma, majority-bias; and Mi, minority-bias. For example, UnD is position D in the unbiased network pattern.

These revised weight matrices generate new score profiles for the respective groups. These are summarized in Table 10, which supplants Table 5. As before, column-dominance is roughly from left to right, although there are some inconclusive pairs. That dominance order generates the partially-ordered set of Figure 11, using Rounds 4–10, the rounds on which subjects usually submitted their answers.

The mutuality bonus for members D and E results in an enhancement of the predicted scores for those positions, as early as the third or fourth round. The increase in D's and E's scores then propagates to other network positions, to generate larger predicted scores for the other members as well. (This reflects the interdependent nature of the linked system.)

These coordinated increases do not change the predicted rank order of positions within the Unbiased and Minority-Bias networks. They do effect a change in the Majority-Bias network, however, causing B to rise from second to first place, above C. B benefits promptly from the increment to E's score, but C's improvement is delayed by inferior inputs from member A, whose position is the last to be reached by the propagating increments. (The differences involved here are minuscule, but the theory is sensitive to, and capitalizes on, those magnitudes.)

Intuitively, the reciprocity-bonus notion seems promising, but the gains are offset by losses. Comparing the theoretical predictions of Figure 11 with the empirically observed answering times, we discover $18\frac{1}{2}$ pairwise reversals (Table 11). This is one more reversal than for the original hypothesis (see Table 8), so that the application of the mutuality bonus has so far served only to worsen the yield.

Inspection of Table 11, however, reveals the Minority-Bias network as the principal source of the difficulty: thirteen of the $18\frac{1}{2}$ reversals involve positions MiD and MiE. One explanation of this situation would be as follows:

The actual reciprocity bonus rests, not on *our* recognition of mutuality, but on the participants' awareness of it. Unless they perceive the existence of their bilateral linkage, they cannot capitalize on it. Both the linkage and the awareness must be mutual, because the failure of either individual to take advantage of the economy will alert his partner to the fact that the bonus is not operative.

MiD and MiE, in particular, do not reap the benefits of mutuality. One possible way to account for this is the stress experienced under *input overload*. The sifting of conflicting reports, under pressure, is a stressful situation. MiD has the largest *message* input of any of the fifteen structural positions considered. Several subjects in this position complained afterward about the tremendous burden of paperwork. The subject is overwhelmed, and is unable to extract all the information contained in incoming messages. The flood of messages inundates the individual, impairing his performance and depressing it below the level otherwise to be expected. In other words, D's efficiency parameter k_D is lowered (cf. equation 1).

Moreover, MiD receives relatively poor information, since his informants are in the most disadvantageous positions. MiE is less likely to suffer from overload;

TABLE 11 / Reversals of Predicted Rank (Mutuality-Bonus Hypothesis)

Predicted Higher Ranks (with Observed Mean Answering Round)

Predicted Lower Ranks	UnD (5.81)	UnE (5.73)	MaB (5.93)	MiE (6.61)	MaC (6.19)	MiD (6.35)	UnB (6.29)	UnC (6.19)	MaA (6.20)	MaD (6.67)	MaE (6.59)	UnA (7.35)	MiB (7.70)	MiC (7.41)‡	Row Sums
UnE (5.73)‡	1														1
MaB (5.93)	–	–													0
MiE (6.61)	½*	½*	1												2
MaC (6.19)	–	–	–	1											1
MiD (6.35)	½*	½*	½*	1	½*										3
UnB (6.29)	–	–	–	1	–	1									2
UnC (6.19)	–	–	–	1	½†	1	1								3½
MaA (6.20)	–	–	–	1	–	1	1	–							3
MaD (6.67)	–	–	–	–	–	–	–	–	–						0
MaE (6.59)	–	–	–	1	–	–	–	–	–	1					2
UnA (7.35)	–	–	–	–	–	–	–	–	–	–	–				0
MiB (7.70)	–	–	–	–	–	–	–	–	–	–	–	–			0
MiC (7.41)	–	–	–	–	–	–	–	–	–	–	–	–	1		1
MiA (9.26)	–	–	–	–	–	–	–	–	–	–	–	–	–	–	0
Column Sums:	2	1	1½	6	1	3	2	0	0	1	0	0	1	0	18½
															(Grand Total)

* Predicted as ties (partially-ordered set of Figure 11)

† Empirical tie

‡ The numbers in parentheses are the mean number of the observed answering round, for the respective network positions. $\tau = .65$ $p < .05$

■ **TABLE 12** / **Predicted Scores $s_i^{(t)}$ by Round Number t, Adjusted for Mutuality Bonus and Input Overload**

Network Positions*
(abbreviations explained below)

Round Number	UnD	UnE	MaB	MaC	UnB	UnC	MaA	MiE	MiD	MaD	MaE	UnA	MiB	MiC	MiA
0	4.0	4.0	4.0	4.0	4.0	4.0	4.0	4.0	4.0	4.0	4.0	4.0	4.0	4.0	4.0
1	4.7	4.6	4.7	4.7	4.6	4.6	4.6	4.7	4.7	4.6	4.5	4.5	4.5	4.5	4.4
2	5.3	5.2	5.3	5.3	5.1	5.1	5.1	5.3	5.3	5.1	5.0	5.0	5.0	5.0	4.8
3	5.8	5.7	5.8	5.8	5.6	5.6	5.6	5.8	5.8	5.6	5.5	5.4	5.4	5.4	5.1
4	6.2	6.2	6.2	6.2	6.1	6.0	6.0	6.2	6.2	6.0	5.9	5.8	5.8	5.7	5.4
5	6.6	6.6	6.6	6.6	6.5	6.4	6.4	6.6	6.5	6.4	6.3	6.2	6.1	6.0	5.7
6	7.0	7.0	7.0	7.0	6.9	6.8	6.8	6.9	6.8	6.7	6.6	6.5	6.4	6.3	5.9
7	7.4	7.3	7.3	7.3	7.2	7.1	7.1	7.2	7.1	7.0	6.9	6.8	6.7	6.5	6.1
8	7.7	7.6	7.6	7.6	7.5	7.4	7.4	7.4	7.4	7.3	7.2	7.1	6.9	6.7	6.3
9	8.0	7.9	7.9	7.8	7.8	7.6	7.6	7.6	7.6	7.6	7.4	7.3	7.1	6.9	6.5
10	8.2	8.2	8.1	8.1	8.0	7.9	7.9	7.8	7.8	7.8	7.6	7.5	7.3	7.1	6.7
11	8.4	8.4	8.3	8.3	8.2	8.1	8.1	8.0	8.0	8.0	7.8	7.7	7.4	7.3	6.8
12	8.6	8.6	8.5	8.5	8.4	8.3	8.3	8.2	8.1	8.2	8.0	7.9	7.5	7.4	6.9
13	8.8	8.8	8.7	8.7	8.6	8.5	8.4	8.3	8.2	8.3	8.2	8.0	7.6	7.5	7.0
14	9.0	8.9	8.9	8.8	8.8	8.6	8.6	8.4	8.3	8.5	8.3	8.2	7.7	7.6	7.1

* Positions are arranged in generally decreasing order, from left to right. There are some reversals over time (t).

NOTE: The respective networks are identified here by *Un*, unbiased; *Ma*, majority-bias; and *Mi*, minority-bias. For example, *MaC* is position *C* in the majority-bias network pattern.

his volume of message input is no greater than MaB's or MaC's.

Parameters for the overload effect should be assessed empirically, of course. Lacking empirical measures, we might reason that input overload prevents MiD and MiE from benefitting from the mutuality bonus, and eliminate that bonus from the Minority-Bias condition. This would bring that network back to the original matrices of Table 1. Predicted scores for the participants in that network are then the original ones of Table 6, while the other two networks retain the mutuality bonus and utilize the adjusted score profiles of Table 10. The respective scores are set forth in Table 12.

This final choice of linkage weights produces the predictions and results diagrammed in Figure 12. The total number of reversals of prediction is reduced to $10\frac{1}{2}$ (see Table 13), and between-condition reversals to $5\frac{1}{2}$ (the latter all due to inconclusive pairs). The greatest magnitude for any pairwise reversal (that between MiB and MiC) is reduced to 0.29, a time lag of scarcely more than a quarter of a round, on the average.

The input-overload principle has been invoked here to withhold the reciprocity bonus from both MiD and MiE. It can be argued, however, that it is only position MiD that suffers from overload, with ten incoming messages per round; MiE's seven units being no greater than MaB's or MaC's.

This latter interpretation would lead us to use the D row, but not the E row, of the quota matrix for the Minority-Bias condition in Table 9; and correspondingly the D row, but not the E row, of the weight matrix. But the successive score profiles S thus generated for the Minority-Bias condition would produce no change in Figure 12 or Table 13, on which the revised hypothesis is based. Hence we can rest our case, as far as input overload is concerned.

To summarize this speculative analysis: In using the model, the initial assumption was that a recipient can cope with any amount of influence input and continue to function smoothly in his relay of output to others. It is empirically possible, however, for input overload to occur — the individual becomes overwhelmed with stimuli and breaks down. Where this occurs, it is a limitation on the domain of validity of the model, particularly of equation (6). This is comparable to the limitations of domain for a linear physical model, such as one representing an electrical network whose elements can melt under excessive temperatures, temperatures which can be generated by the system itself.

In a social system, the concrete limits of the domain are a function of the experience of the specific participants. A member of long standing, socialized to the activities and culture of the system, should have greater tolerance for pressure than a novice does. It should be possible to measure these limits, to some extent, in the laboratory or in field settings.

Further research should devote attention to the specification of parameters both for input overload and for reciprocation economy. In the meantime, reciprocation difficulties can be sidestepped operationally by the use of networks in which mutual links do not appear. But for most structures of any interest, that would call for networks with more than five members.

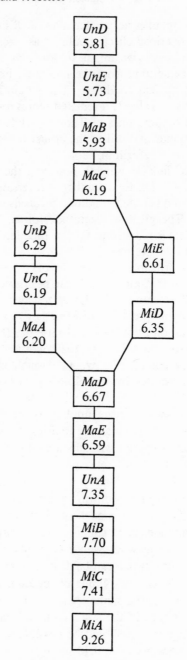

■ **FIGURE 12.** Predicted Rank Order of Network Positions, Adjusted for Mutuality Bonus and Input Overload.

SOURCE: Tables 12 and 7. The respective networks are identified here as *Un*, unbiased; *Ma*, majority-bias; and *Mi*, minority-bias. For example, *UnD* is position *D* in the unbiased condition.

■ TABLE 13 / Reversals of Predicted Rank (under hypothesis of Mutuality Bonus and Input Overload)

Predicted Higher Ranks (with Observed Mean Answering Round)

Predicted Lower Ranks	UnD (5.81)	UnE (5.73)	MaB (5.93)	MaC (6.19)	UnB (6.29)	UnC (6.19)	MaA (6.20)	MiE (6.61)	MiD (6.35)	MaD (6.67)	MaE (6.59)	UnA (7.35)	MiB (7.70)	MiC (7.41)†	Row Sums
UnE (5.73)‡	1														1
MaB (5.93)		–													0
MaC (6.19)		–	–												0
UnB (6.29)		–	–	½†	1										1½
UnC (6.19)		–	–	–	1										1
MaA (6.20)		–	–	–	½*	½*									1½
MiE (6.61)		–	–	–	½*	½*	1								2½
MiD (6.35)		–	–	–	–	–	–	–							0
MaD (6.67)		–	–	–	–	–	–	1	–						2
MaE (6.59)		–	–	–	–	–	–	1	–	–					0
UnA (7.35)		–	–	–	–	–	–	–	–	–	–				0
MiB (7.70)		–	–	–	–	–	–	–	–	1	–	–	–		1
MiC (7.41)		–	–	–	–	–	–	–	–	–	–	–	–	–	0
MiA (9.26)		–	–	–	–	–	–	–	–	–	–	–	–	–	0
Column Sums:	1	0	0	½	3	1	1	2	0	1	0	0	1	0	10½
															(Grand Total)

* Predicted as ties (partially-ordered set of Figure 12)
† Empirical tie
‡ The numbers in parentheses are the mean number of the observed answering round, for the respective network positions.

τ = .80   p = .02

□ **J. THE INTERACTION MULTIPLIER AND RESPONSE THRESHOLDS**

At the outset of the problem-solving task, each member's knowledgeability score is $s_i^{(0)} = 4.0$. As a result of successive message inputs from his companions and the environment, his store of information undergoes a progressive improvement in quality. So do his outgoing messages, thus propagating the improvement throughout the system.

The quality of each member's information improves through successive time periods, accomplishing a progressive reduction of his uncertainty. This progressive improvement enables a member's confidence to rise until it ultimately reaches a threshold level where he is willing to commit himself to a problem answer.

The progressive increase in predicted score levels appears in Tables 5, 10, and 12. This progressive improvement reflects the *multiplier effect* of open systems. It can be called an *interaction* multiplier, since sheer participation in an interactive system can raise an individual's performance level above the value of his initial score and/or boundary inputs.

The improvement is in the quality, rather than the quantity, of information. The cognitive manifold for the problem is fixed in size, consisting of five symbols and two conceivably possible values for each symbol (+ and −).

The average answering rounds for the various positions can be used to develop a numerical estimate of *answering threshold* — the score level at which individuals typically submit their correct answers. Tables 5 and 12 give predicted score levels (information quality), by network position, for successive rounds. The numbers of the rounds are, of course, integers. By interpolation, it is possible to obtain score levels corresponding to the (fractional) average answering rounds of Table 7. These interpolated scores are set forth in Table 14.

Inspection of Table 14 suggests 6.9, the average of the entries in the last column, as the motivational threshold for submitting answers. (There is individual variation, of course, around that threshold.)

What is the meaning of this 6.9 value? One possible interpretation is as follows: Each member's initial score has been assigned a value of $s_i^{(0)} = 4.0$, equal to the number of symbols on which he receives information at the outset of the problem. But this initial data is only three-fourths correct, since information about one of the symbols is deliberately false. If, accordingly, a 75% correction is applied to all predicted score levels, then the revised value of $s_i^{(0)}$ becomes 3.0, and the average answering threshold becomes 5.1. The latter would correspond to 100% certainty on all five (5) symbols, permitting the individual to commit himself to an answer.

Theoretically, a threshold of 6.7 ought to suffice, since that would reduce to 5.0 under the 75% correction. In other words, subjects should have answered about a round earlier than they did. This delay might stem from caution, with the average subject waiting for "supersaturation" before arriving at the conviction requisite to sending in his answer. The timing of one's *answer* is optional, but the perfectly-informed subject proceeds to disseminate completely accurate information to his companions in the mandatory message exchanges. To put it

■ TABLE 14 / Answering Threshold

Experimental Condition	Network Position	Mean Number of Answering Round*	Predicted Score at that point†
Unbiased	E	5.73	6.9
	D	5.81	6.9
	C	6.19	6.9
	B	6.29	7.0
	A	7.35	6.9
Majority Bias	B	5.93	7.0
	C	6.19	7.1
	A	6.20	6.9
	E	6.59	6.8
	D	6.67	6.9
Minority Bias	D	6.35	6.9
	E	6.61	7.1
	C	7.41	6.6
	B	7.70	6.8
	A	9.26	6.6

Mean: 6.9

* Actual answering rounds are integral numbers, by operational definition. Fractions appear here, due to averaging over many subjects and problems. See Table 7.

† These scores are obtained from Table 12, whose entries are the scores predicted for round numbers which are integers, by interpolation.

differently, the information which a subject possesses may actually be better than he thinks it is.

On the other hand, it may be that the subject does not actually "possess" the information yet; his message-interpreting efficiency may be below par — i.e., $k_i < 1$, in equation (1).

The conclusions drawn in this and the previous section are admittedly speculative in nature, but are suggestive for directions of further research.

□ K. COMPARISON WITH OTHER MODELS OF INFLUENCE NETWORKS

Before closing, it is of some interest to compare the present study with network-structure studies in the Bavelas tradition (e.g. Leavitt, 1951; Guetzkow & Simon, 1955; Shaw, 1954, 1956). These experiments employed accurate information. Recipients could assume that message content was true. Redundant messages added nothing to the individual's knowledge. In a communication system, only supporting or invalidating information counts; and corroboration provides no new information, in the Bavelas situation.

In real-life networks, however, participants welcome redundant messages for their value in reducing uncertainty and confirming earlier messages. Members will often go to considerable lengths to solicit duplication of earlier-received message content. The introduction of counterfeit information, in the present experiment, motivates subjects to behave this way, and prolongs their dependence on each other, thus maintaining the interdependence of the system over a protracted time interval.

The Bavelas model (1950) takes account, accordingly, of only the single shortest chain of links connecting each pair of positions; by contrast, all chains of all lengths are relevant in the weighted-link model presented here. The Bavelas model assumes, moreover, an unlimited channel capacity for each link in the network, with no restrictions on linkage strength; a property which is unrealistic for real-life communication systems. Finally, since the Bavelas model is based on a purely distance rationale, it would be difficult to coordinate it to structures with weighted links. In particular, it does not permit inter-network comparisons of positional effects. (On that last point, see also Flament, 1963, pp. 50–52.)

□ **L. SUMMARY AND CONCLUSIONS**

It is my contention that current treatments of system structure, in the behavioral sciences, are inadequate. A major purpose of the present paper is to show the greater predictive power of a weighted-link model. (By assigning equal weights to the links, structures with unweighted links can be subsumed as a special case under the more general weighted-link model.)

The laboratory experiment reported here demonstrates the power of the model, accounting for otherwise unexpected reversals in role performance, and even enabling comparisons between positions in different networks.

Experimental variance can result from the behavior of individual subjects (sampling errors) or from inadequacy of the model, or both. A number of simplifying assumptions, in the construction of the model, serve to increase the hazards of empirical proof; hazards which stem from the fact of system *structure*. The risk could be ameliorated by a detailed analysis of the performance of each individual subject. Relationships which hold up separately, at the micro level, may break down at the macro level due to cumulative slack in the empirical system. Since each individual's performance is so dependent upon the performance of others, the effect of a single substandard k_i can propagate socially through the system, as shown by equations (7) and (8).

The constant k_i is an efficiency parameter specific to individual i, here assumed to be constant over time, reflecting his characteristic sensitivity (to inputs) and caution (regarding output). Individual differences in the value of the efficiency parameter could then account for departures of observed answering order from the predicted status rank based on s_i.

The experimental data have been analyzed on a molar basis, however, not a molecular one. The model specifies the magnitudes and patterning of certain inputs to the system, and predicts the patterned output of the system as a whole, without reference to the details of internal behavior at each network position.

A molecular analysis, by contrast, would have traced the influence process in detail, observing the actual (empirical) information status of each subject at each point in time. In other words, the model predicts the dependent variable $S^{(t+1)}$ from $S^{(t)}$, which is *also* predicted. It does *not* insert empirical values for $x_i^{(t)}$ — which, in matrix form, would be $X^{(t)}$. The reference is to equations (1), (2), and (8).

Still another hazard for testing the model is the fact that "mean number of answering round" has drawbacks as an inter-group measure. It is all to the credit of the model that it predicts as well as it does, despite these several hazards.

In the experiment, the input-output model was applied to a controlled inter-action system in the laboratory. The method is equally applicable to free communication in natural settings. In such situations, q_{ij} is taken as the observed magnitude of communication between persons i and j. Linkage strengths are then operationalized by the normalization (16), permitting predictions of status by means of the model.

The mathematical model is applicable, at least in principle, to any type of influence system in which structural linkages can be differentially weighted. These include sociometry, with degrees of liking; dominance, with gradations of power; and cognitive processes, with degrees of association between ideas. Nothing in the model prevents its extension to structures which include negative links, and this is the next direction for the present program of research.

Weaver (1948) made a plea for scientists to engage in the study of organized complexity. The increasing use of matrix algebra provides us with a tool which can be devoted to that end. Greater mathematical sophistication on the part of present-day behavioral scientists thus enables us to attack problems which previously defied analysis. The success of the present model with communication networks suggests the possible fruitfulness of attempting similar investigations in the other areas mentioned just above. Successful research in these directions would help to establish wide generality for the model, for the analysis of system structure and behavior.

□ M. APPENDIX: A GENERALIZATION OF KENDALL'S *TAU*

Kendall's *tau* (1948) provides a method for testing the success of predictions about ranked data. If the prediction is good, there will be close agreement between the predicted and observed rank orders; and the extent of this agreement can be measured by the number of pair-reversals occurring between the two rankings. A *reversed pair* of items is one whose relative order is different in the two rankings. According to the null hypothesis, all possible rankings of the data are equally likely. If the number of reversals is sufficiently small, then, under the null hypothesis, the observed rank order will be a rare event, and hence statistically significant.

It is often possible, however, to make *several* observations of a predicted ranking. This calls for a test which permits comparison of the prediction against *several* observed rankings. This can be achieved by an extension of Kendall's method, which it is the purpose of this appendix to describe.

Let n be the number of items to be ranked, and let N be the number of observations of this ranking. Let r_k be the number of reversed pairs appearing in the kth observation, and let $\bar{r}$ be the mean number of reversals over all N observations.

Kendall's tables give, in effect, the sampling distribution of r_k. If we indicate the mean of this distribution by μ, and its variance by σ^2, then the sampling distribution of $\bar{r}$ will have mean μ and variance

$$\sigma_{\bar{r}}{}^2 = \frac{1}{N}\sigma^2.$$

With increasing n, the distribution of r_i tends rapidly to normality. By the Central Limit Theorem (Cramér, 1951, p. 214), an increase in N accelerates this tendency, for $\bar{r}$.

Where five items are ranked, the null hypothesis generates the following relative frequency distribution for r_k:

r_i	0	1	2	3	4	5	6	7	8	9	10
$f(r_i)$	1	4	9	15	20	22	20	15	9	4	1

The mean and variance of this distribution are $\mu = 5$ and $\sigma^2 = 25/6$. For eight observations on such a ranking, the sampling variance will be $\sigma_{\bar{r}}{}^2 = 25/48 = 0.52$, and for nine observations it will be $\sigma_{\bar{r}}{}^2 = 25/54 = 0.46$. The mean of the distribution, in either case, is five reversals.

The test procedure, then, is as follows. Each observation produces a ranking, which is compared with the predicted ranking and scored for the number of reversed pairs, r_k. The mean number of reversals for the entire sample, $\bar{r}$, is then used to compute a standard score,

$$z_N = \frac{\mu - \bar{r}}{\sigma_{\bar{r}}}.$$

The significance level of z_N is then obtained from a table of the normal distribution. Where the direction of the ranking is predicted, a one-tailed test is used.

Thus, for a sample of eight observations upon the ranking of five items,

$$z_8 = \frac{5 - \bar{r}}{.72}$$

and for a sample of nine observations,

$$z_9 = \frac{5 - \bar{r}}{.68}$$

Obviously, the average number of reversals per observation must be considerably less than 5 in order to attain statistical significance.

This test rests on the assumption of statistical independence. It is the separate observations of the ranking that are independent, not the items within a ranking. The sampling distribution is defined on this basis. Thus the distribution for r_k is for a sample of size $N = 1$.

The special case of tied ranks presents no difficulty for this test. If a given pair of items is tied in rank, in either or both of the predicted and observed rankings, then this is reckoned as *half* a reversal in computing $\bar{r}$ and the regular procedure is followed. These half-points necessitate interpolation in the underlying distribution of r_k, which is discrete, but this interpolation is accomplished automatically in computing z_N, which is continuous.

Kendall does not tabulate r, but a statistic S which is related to it. This is computed by counting $+1$ for every regular (unreversed) pair of items, and -1 for every reversed pair. Ties are scored 0. The relationship between S and r is given by

$$S = \tfrac{1}{2}n(n - 1) - 2r.$$

One feature of this is that the sampling distribution of S is centered upon a mean of zero.

Kendall's *tau* statistic is related to the number of reversals by the following formula:

$$\tau = 1 - \frac{4r}{n(n - 1)}$$

This is a correlation coefficient, whose values can range from $+1$ to -1. These extreme values correspond to the cases of no reversal and complete reversal, respectively. The *tau* statistic thus provides a convenient summary index of the degree of association between the observed and predicted rankings.

In the case of several observed rankings, treated here, it is a simple matter to compute the mean *tau* by the analogous formula

$$\bar{\tau} = 1 - \frac{4\bar{r}}{n(n - 1)}.$$

Where the ranking involved five items, this becomes $\tau = 1 - \dfrac{\bar{r}}{5}$.

□ **N. REFERENCES**

Bavelas, Alex, "Communication Patterns in Task-Oriented Groups," *Journal of the Acoustical Society of America*, Vol. 22 (1950), pp. 725–730.

Blau, Peter M., *The Dynamics of Bureaucracy* (Chicago: University of Chicago Press, 1955).

Blau, Peter M., *Exchange and Power in Social Life* (New York: John Wiley & Sons, 1964).

Cramér, Harald, *Mathematical Methods of Statistics* (Princeton: Princeton University Press, 1951).

Flament, Claude, *Applications of Graph Theory to Group Structure* (Englewood Cliffs: Prentice-Hall, 1963).

Guetzkow, Harold, and Herbert A. Simon, "The Impact of Certain Communication Nets upon Organization and Performance in Task Oriented Groups," *Management Science*, Vol. 1 (1955), pp. 233–250.

Kendall, Maurice G., *Rank Correlation Methods* (London: Charles Griffin, 1948).

Leavitt, Harold J., "Some Effects of Certain Communication Patterns on Group Performance," *Journal of Abnormal and Social Psychology*, Vol. 46 (1951), pp. 38–50.

Leontief, Wassily W., *The Structure of the American Economy, 1919–1929* (Cambridge: Harvard University Press, 1941).

Levi-Strauss, Claude, "Social Structure." In A. L. Kroeber, ed., *Anthropology Today* (Chicago: University of Chicago Press, 1953).

Lövgren, Esse, "Mutual Relations Between Migration Fields: A Circulation Analysis." In D. Hannerberg, T. Hägerstrand, & B. Odeving, eds., *Migration in Sweden: A Symposium* (Lund: C. W. K. Gleerup, 1957).

Shaw, Marvin E., "Some Effects of Unequal Distribution of Information upon Group Performance in Various Communication Nets," *Journal of Abnormal and Social Psychology*, Vol. 49 (1954), pp. 547–553.

Shaw, Marvin E., "Random versus Systematic Distribution of Information in Communication Nets," *Journal of Personality*, Vol. 25 (1956), pp. 59–69.

Shepard, Herbert A., "The Value System of a University Research Group," *American Sociological Review*, Vol. 19 (1954), pp. 456–462.

Weaver, Warren, "Science and Complexity," *American Scientist*, Vol. 36 (1948), pp. 536–544.

Chapter 12

Relations among Status, Power, and Economic Rewards in Simple and Complex Social Systems*

■ JAMES C. KIMBERLY

This chapter has two general purposes. One is to attempt to specify the basic ways in which ranks on different dimensions of stratification are equilibrated.[1]

* The author gratefully acknowledges support for work on this chapter from a Ford Foundation grant to the Graduate School of Business at Stanford University during the summer of 1964 and from a National Science Foundation grant to himself (GS-687) during the period from 1965 to 1968. The author is indebted to Morris Zelditch, Jr., Francesca Cancian, and Bo Anderson for reading and commenting on various earlier drafts of the chapter. He is also indebted to Joann R. Kolmes for a comment in a final examination relating certain modes of increasing system ranks to collective action to prevent replacement.

Two earlier versions of the chapter were read at annual meetings of the American Sociological Association. One was read in the theory section of the meetings at Miami Beach, Florida, in 1966. The other was read in a social stratification session of the meetings at Boston, Massachusetts, in 1968. The present version is a revision of the latter paper completed in January 1971.

[1] This problem is implicitly posed by Weber. See Max Weber, "Class, Status, and Party," in Max Weber, *From Max Weber: Essays in Sociology* (translated by H. H. Gerth and C. Wright Mills) (New York: Oxford University Press, 1958), pp. 180–195. It is developed by Benoit-Smullyan. See Benoit-Smullyan, "Status, Status Types, and Status Interrelations," *American Sociological Review*, 9 (April 1944), pp. 151–161. Since Benoit-Smullyan's paper was published, much work has been done on the problem. The author has attempted to relate some of the basic ideas in this work to the problem of equilibration of ranks on different *sub*dimensions of the status or prestige dimension. See James C. Kimberly, "A Theory of Status Equilibration," in Joseph Berger, Morris Zelditch, Jr., and Bo Anderson, editors, *Sociological Theories in Progress*, Vol. I (Boston: Houghton Mifflin, 1966), Chapter 9; Kimberly, "Status Inconsistency: A Reformulation of a Theoretical Problem," *Human Relations*, 20 (May 1967), pp. 171–179; and Kimberly and Paul V. Crosbie, "An Experimental T_st of a Reward-Cost Formulation of Status Inconsistency," *Journal of Experimental Social Psychology*, 4 (October 1967), pp. 399–415. This chapter is a logical extension of the author's work in that it deals with the problem of equilibration of ranks on different dimensions, as opposed to subdimensions of a single dimension, of stratification. For a recent review of the general problem of equilibration of ranks, see James C. Kimberly, "The Emergence and Stabilization of Stratification in Simple and Complex Social Systems," in Edward O. Laumann, editor, *Social Stratification: Research and Theory for the 1970s* (Indianapolis: Bobbs-Merrill, 1970), pp. 73–101, especially 83–96.

The other is to attempt to define *inter*system processes which have differential effects on the degree of *intra*system stratification.[2] Four such processes are identified. Three of these are power processes which involve threats by systems low in the intersystem stratification structure to disrupt productive processes at the intersystem level. The other is a competitive process which involves increases in productivity by systems low in the intersystem stratification structure. All of these processes are modes of increasing *system* ranks and, hence, are consequences of aspiration for high system ranks. The processes also involve equilibration of system ranks.

Before considering these two problems directly, certain basic concepts must be presented. We begin not with the dimensions of stratification, but rather with certain components of social systems and certain attributes of individuals which are related to the system components. Then we move to the dimensions of stratification, showing how they relate to the system components and individual attributes.

□ BASIC CONCEPTS

A social system has a *culture*, which consists of one or more goals and at least two kinds of norms. A *goal* denotes a desired state of affairs, whereas a *norm* denotes a prescription for behavior. *Task norms* define the system's productive structure or division of labor. Such norms encompass behavior which is related to the control and coordination of productive behavior as well as behavior which is directly productive. Another kind of norms is what, for lack of a better term, we shall refer to as *non-task norms*. These norms apply to all members of the system. By contrast, some task norms apply to certain members, and other task norms apply to certain other members, which is why they define the division of labor.[3] We identify only two types of non-task norms in this chapter. One we shall call *equality norms*, which define behavior that *every*

---

[2] This problem has not been well defined. Partially relevant is Simmel's idea that conflict leads to increased cohesion and centralization. See Lewis A. Coser's discussion in his *Functions of Social Conflict* (Glencoe, Ill.: Free Press, 1956), pp. 87–95. The author's ideas are generally in line with Coser's qualification of Simmel's idea that conflict and centralization tend to occur together. The author's thinking about the problem was originally stimulated by Merton's work on anomie, especially his ideas concerning the ways individuals may react to frustrated aspirations, and Bales's ideas concerning sources of strain in social systems, especially his ideas concerning the expansion and contraction of the stratification of groups as a consequence of attempts to deal alternately with external adaptation and internal integration. See Robert K. Merton, *Social Theory and Social Structure*, revised edition (Glencoe, Ill.: Free Press, 1957), Chapter 4, and Robert F. Bales, "Adaptative and Integrative Changes as Sources of Strain in Social Systems," in A. Paul Hare, Edgar F. Borgatta, and Robert F. Bales, editors, *Small Groups*, revised edition (New York: Knopf, 1965), pp. 127–131. A fuller discussion of Bales's ideas is found in his book, *Interaction Process Analysis* (Cambridge, Mass.: Addison-Wesley, 1950), Chapter 5.

[3] The distinction between task and non-task norms was suggested by Linton's concepts of specialities and universals. See Ralph Linton, *The Study of Man* (New York: Appleton-Century, 1936), pp. 272–273. The author has employed the distinction in earlier works under the labels of special and universal functions and norms. See Kimberly, "A Theory of Status Equilibration," pp. 214–216, and Kimberly, "Status Inconsistency," pp. 172–174.

system member owes to every other member. Courtesy norms are good examples.[4] The other type of non-task norms we shall call *representational norms*, which define how *every* system member should behave toward the members of one or more *other* systems. Norms concerning secrecy about *intra*system affairs are good examples.[5]

In addition to a culture, a social system has a *behavioral structure*.[6] This consists of all the behavior relevant to the norms contained in its culture. The distinction between norms and behavior permits the derivation of the concept of *conformity-deviance*.[7] We shall use the term *position* to refer to the set of task norms which define the individual's location in the system's productive structure. The individual's behavior relative to his position we shall refer to as *performance*, which may be good or poor depending upon where it falls on a conformity-deviance continuum.[8] Non-task norms do not define anything like a position because they apply to all individuals within the system. However, as in the case of position, behavior relative to these norms may fall at different places along a conformity-deviance continuum. Such behavior we shall refer to as *conformity to non-task norms*, or, in the case of a specific type of non-task norm, as conformity to whatever type of norm is involved. Such a reference will always be to a *degree* of conformity.

The perspective the above concepts constitute leads logically to a consideration of attributes of the individual which explain conformity-deviance. These are *skill* and *motivation*. Both account for the level of the individual's performance. However, motivation alone accounts for the level of his conformity to non-task norms. Skill cannot be a factor in such conformity because non-task norms apply to all system members and, hence, must be within the skill of all members.

□ **DIMENSIONS OF STRATIFICATION**

We can turn now to a consideration of the dimensions of stratification, taking up status first. We use the term *status* in the sense of evaluation in terms of superiority-inferiority or prestige. The concepts presented in the previous section lead to a conception of status as a set of different kinds of evaluations.

[4] Bales's concept of a solidarity structure might be said to be somewhat similar to the concept of equality norms. See Bales, *Interaction Process Analysis*, pp. 78–80.

[5] Blau's conception of basic norms is somewhat similar to the concept of representational norms. See Peter M. Blau, *The Dynamics of Bureaucracy*, revised edition (Chicago: University of Chicago Press, 1963), pp. 201–202.

[6] This is a widely accepted view. See, for example, George C. Homans, *The Human Group* (New York: Harcourt, Brace, and World, 1950), Chapter 5, especially pp. 121–127, and Robin M. Williams, Jr., *American Society*, 2nd edition (New York: Knopf, 1965), Chapter 3.

[7] In his early work, Homans attempted to account for the emergence of stratification primarily in terms of deviation from norms. However, he dealt principally with norms which apply to all members of a group. See his analysis of the stratification structure of the bank wiring room in *The Human Group*, Chapter 3, especially p. 79, and Chapter 6, especially pp. 138–144.

[8] The concepts of position and performance are similar to concepts used by Davis. See Kingsley Davis, *Human Society* (New York: Macmillan, 1949), pp. 89–91.

We stress the term "kinds" to prevent confusion between differences among evaluations of a *single* base of status and differences among evaluations of *several* bases of status. The former differences result from a lack of knowledge of the base of status in question and/or a low degree of consensus on criteria for evaluating it. The latter differences may result from these factors, but they also may result from the fact that the unit in question is objectively high on some bases of status and objectively low on others.

The system components of position, performance, and conformity to non-task norms, and the individual attributes of skill and motivation are, we think, universal bases of status.[9] Position, performance, skill, and motivation relevant to performance as a set appear to be evaluated often in terms of the availability of persons competent to fill the set, that is, in terms of replaceability of the position occupant.[10] The use of replaceability as a criterion of evaluation would account for the tendency for performance, skill, and motivation to be evaluated as well as position.[11]

The individual's position, performance, skill, and motivation relevant to performance shall be referred to as his *instrumental status*, and his conformity to equality and representational norms as his *non-instrumental status*. We do not include motivation relevant to conformity to equality and representational norms in non-instrumental status because, as indicated earlier, such conformity directly reflects such motivation.

The concepts of instrumental and non-instrumental status assume that people can in some way generalize from specific components to a more general status. When the specific components of a status are equilibrated, that is, aligned at a given height, this should not be difficult. When they are not, it seems likely that some average of the components is used.[12]

[9] For a similar view see Kingsley Davis and Wilbert E. Moore, "Some Principles of Stratification," *American Sociological Review*, 10 (April 1945), pp. 242–244. Conformity to non-task norms as a base of status is not explicitly dealt with by these authors. Its importance was suggested by Tumin's discussion of conscientiousness as a base of equality in social systems. See Melvin M. Tumin, "Rewards and Task Orientations," *American Sociological Review*, 20 (August 1955), pp. 419–423.

[10] Compare Davis and Moore's idea of scarcity of personnel and Schumpeter's discussion of evaluation of functions. See Davis and Moore, p. 244, and Joseph A. Schumpeter, *Imperialism and Social Classes* (New York: Augustus M. Kelley, 1951), pp. 205–206.

Emerson has argued that status depends upon availability of persons for positions. (He uses the term "role" in a way similar to that in which we use the term "position.") However, his argument differs from the present one in that he sees the emergence of status basically as an attempt to reduce power advantages among system members. See Richard M. Emerson, "Power-Dependence Relations," *American Sociological Review*, 27 (February 1962), pp. 31–41, especially p. 40.

[11] Compare Davis and Moore, pp. 242–244.

[12] Anderson has developed a model of information integration based on an averaging assumption, and it has received some empirical support. See Norman H. Anderson, "A Simple Model for Information Integration," in Robert P. Abelson, *et al.*, editors, *Theories of Cognitive Consistency* (Chicago: Rand McNally, 1968), pp. 731–743. In line with Anderson's work are findings by Himmelfarb and Senn and Berger and Fisek that persons apparently average indicators of social status. See Samuel Himmelfarb and David J. Senn, "Forming Impressions of Social Class," *Journal of Personality and Social Psychology*, 12: 1 (1969), pp. 38–51 and Joseph Berger and M. Hamit Fisek, "Consistent and Inconsistent Status Characteristics and the Determination of Power and Prestige Orders," *Sociometry*, 33 (September 1970), pp. 287–304.

Systems as well as individuals have statuses. If the instrumental statuses of individuals within the system are equilibrated, that is, if the components making up these statuses are aligned at a given height for each individual, they are probably simply averaged across individuals to arrive at an instrumental status for the system. If they are not equilibrated, the components are probably averaged first for each individual and then across individuals to arrive at an instrumental status for the system.

Do systems have non-instrumental statuses? Probably rarely, if at all. The non-task norms of a system are not likely to be known to the members of other systems, and it is, of course, these persons who evaluate the system.

Evaluation of systems implies the existence of a complex system. By a *complex system* we mean a system of systems. The systems within a complex system are related in terms of the means-end relations which obtain between their goals. For means-end relations to obtain between systems' goals, there must be a superordinate goal to which the systems' activities are directed. Thus, in addition to the means-end relations between systems' goals, the systems within a complex system are related also in the sense that the goal of each of them is a means to a superordinate goal.[13] Systems within a complex system shall be referred to as *simple* systems.

Let us consider power next. We use the term *power* in the sense of ability to control the actions of others. The power of a system member derives from the dependence of other system members upon him for attainment of the system goal. Such dependence stems from the division of task activities which are essential to attainment of the system goal among the members of the system. Once such activities are divided, members have equal *potential* power, because any member can prevent attainment of the goal by not performing his activities. Given this, how do we explain the fact that the *actual* power of system members is seldom, if ever, equal? The explanation appears to be that members are differentially replaceable. If a member threatens not to perform his activities, the other members will attempt to replace him, and his actual power will always depend upon how easy this is.[14]

As in the case of status, systems as well as individuals have power. It seems likely that a system's power is assessed in a manner similar to the way its status is assessed. The individual's bases of power are, of course, the same as his bases of status, namely, position, performance, skill, and motivation. If these are equilibrated, that is, aligned at a given height for each individual, the general power of each individual is probably simply averaged to arrive at the

---

[13] This conception of goal structure was suggested by Gouldner's discussion of rational systems. See Alvin W. Gouldner, "Organizational Analysis," in Robert K. Merton, Leonard Broom, and Leonard S. Cottrell, Jr., editors, *Sociology Today* (New York: Basic Books, 1959), pp. 400–428.

[14] These ideas were suggested by Thibaut and Kelley's and Emerson's conceptualizations of power in terms of dependence and Davis and Moore's idea of scarcity of personnel. See John W. Thibaut and Harold H. Kelley, *The Social Psychology of Groups* (New York: Wiley, 1959), Chapters 2 and 7, Emerson, and Davis and Moore, p. 244.

For empirical evidence concerning the effect of replaceability on power, see Harold L. Wilensky, *Intellectuals in Labor Unions* (Glencoe, Ill.: Free Press, 1956), Chapter 11, especially pp. 226–230

system's power. If the bases of power are not equilibrated, they are probably averaged first for each individual and then across individuals to arrive at the system's power.

Let us consider now the third and final dimension of stratification, namely, economic rewards. We use the term *economic rewards* in the sense of objects which are either potentially or actually useful to the individual in a material sense.[15] An important difference between economic rewards and status and power is that economic rewards are completely transferable, whereas status and power are not.[16] Both status and power, as we have indicated, are based in part on the attributes of skill and motivation, and these are at best only partially transferable from one individual to another through learning.[17]

As in the cases of both status and power, systems as well as individuals have economic rewards. It seems likely that such rewards are assessed in a manner similar to the ways a system's status and power are assessed. If the different kinds of rewards received by individuals are equilibrated, that is, aligned at a given height for each individual, the general levels of rewards for individuals are probably simply averaged across individuals to arrive at a value for the system. If the different kinds of rewards are not equilibrated, they are probably averaged first for each individual and then across individuals to arrive at a value for the system.

☐ PROCESSES OF RANK EQUILIBRATION

We can turn now to the first of the two general problems we wish to consider, namely, the question of the basic ways ranks on different dimensions of stratification are equilibrated. We begin at the individual level. In the previous section, we argued that instrumental status is often, and power is always, determined by how difficult it is to replace individuals, and that this varies with position and the levels of performance, skill, and motivation required. Given these arguments, we can say that instrumental status and power generally will be aligned.[18] Malalignment should occur only during periods when the productive requirements of the system increase expected levels of performance, skill, and motivation above those characteristic of available individuals or, conversely, when training processes increase levels of skill and motivation

---

[15] We do not intend to imply here that economic rewards have only material uses. In a later section, we shall consider some important implications of the symbolic aspects of economic rewards.

[16] Compare Talcott Parsons, "A Revised Analytical Approach to the Theory of Social Stratification," in Reinhard Bendix and Seymour M. Lipset, editors, *Class, Status, and Power* (Glencoe, Ill.: Free Press, 1953), pp. 94–95.

[17] In addition to being partially transferable because skill and motivation can be learned, status and power are also partially transferable because position can be ascribed and because position makes, at least temporarily, some contribution to status and power, even if the individual does not have the skill and motivation to perform the activities it entails.

[18] Compare George C. Homans, *Social Behavior* (New York: Harcourt, Brace, and World, 1961), Chapters 8 and 14, and Peter M. Blau, *Exchange and Power in Social Life* (New York: Wiley, 1964), Chapter 5.

characteristic of available individuals above expected levels based on the productive requirements of the system. Under these conditions, it seems likely that power will fluctuate while status will tend to remain at the level the *usual* demand for and supply of persons dictates. Our rationale for this is that it appears that persons generalize from demand and supply factors to the characteristics of positions and the attributes of their incumbents so that in time position characteristics and incumbents' attributes, for example, difficulty and skill, tend to constrain variation in status that variation in demand and supply factors might cause.[19]

Let us consider next how economic rewards are related to instrumental status and power. For simplicity, we shall assume that instrumental status and power are equilibrated as we have specified. Economic rewards should tend toward equilibration with instrumental status-power because such rewards tend to be viewed as rewards for performance in a position. The equilibration of instrumental status-power and economic rewards comes about, we think, through a justice-type process.[20]

Thus far, we have not dealt with the question of how non-instrumental status fits into the structure of stratification we are describing. It does not appear to fit neatly in the sense of varying systematically with the other bases of stratification, but this may be the concept's basic value. It may provide a way of understanding how equality exists in the midst of inequality. The bases of non-instrumental status are, it will be remembered, conformity to different types of non-task norms. Earlier, we defined two types of such norms: equality and representational norms. Clearly, conformity to such norms is a base of status. Is it also a base of power? Probably not. It is true that the members of a system are dependent in a sense on one another for expressions of equality and for proper representation of the system to other systems. However, failure to conform to these types of norms may be tolerated, especially when one occupies a difficult position.[21] Thus, it seems likely that status but not power will be conferred for conformity to these types of norms.[22]

The relations among status, power, and economic rewards specified thus far involve two assumptions. One is that evaluators have knowledge of the bases of stratification, that is, of position, performance, skill, motivation, conformity,

---

[19] This may be one reason why occupational evaluation is reasonably stable over fairly long periods of time in complex societies.

[20] For a general treatment of justice, see Homans, *Social Behavior*, Chapter 12.

[21] Compare Blau, *The Dynamics of Bureaucracy*, pp. 202–203.

[22] The rationale here is that only behavior which is viewed as essential can be a base of power.

We should point out here that the conception of representational norms used in this chapter is not intended to encompass every possible relation a member of one system may have with members of another system. There are probably representational-type norms, for example, those relating to negotiation in competition or conflict situations, which do not apply to all system members and, hence, which do require greater skill than that possessed by the least able system member. Conformity to these kinds of norms, or better, performance relative to them, probably is a base of power. We omit consideration of such norms in the interest of simplicity. We hope to incorporate them into the theory in the future.

and economic rewards. The other is that evaluators agree on criteria for evaluating these bases.

How would ranks on the dimensions of stratification be related if these assumptions were not true, that is, if there were a lack of knowledge and/or a lack of consensus on criteria of evaluation? We think that ranks still would tend to equilibration, but in a way quite different from the ways specified above. We suggest that when evaluators have little knowledge of the bases of stratification or when they do not agree on criteria for evaluating these bases, they tend to use the base which is best known and/or on which there is the most agreement on criteria of evaluation to assess bases which are only vaguely known or not consistently evaluated.[23] This type of equilibration is a result, we think, of the operation of a balance-type process.[24] Knowledge and consensus probably vary separately for bases of instrumental status-power, bases of non-instrumental status, and economic rewards because the members of systems probably weight these sets of bases differentially.[25]

The question of how the equilibration of ranks through a balance-type process may affect the averaging processes described earlier in connection with the problem of how system ranks are arrived at should be considered at this point. In order to average, an evaluator must have knowledge of the bases of stratification being averaged, and each of these must be consistently evaluated by other evaluators. As just indicated, it is when these conditions do not fully obtain that we suggest equilibration occurs through a balance-type process in which the best known and/or most consistently evaluated rank is used to assess other ranks. It seems likely that what happens under these conditions is that the averaging process occurs for the best known and/or most consistently evaluated rank, and then the other system ranks are assumed to be roughly the equal of the system rank arrived at by the averaging process.

□ **EFFECTS OF INCREASING SYSTEM RANKS ON STRATIFICATION OF SYSTEM MEMBERS**

The second general problem to consider is that of defining *inter*system processes which have differential effects on the degree of *intra*system stratification. As indicated earlier, these processes are modes of increasing *system* ranks and, hence, consequences of aspiration for high system ranks. They also involve equilibration of system ranks.

---

[23] Compare Parsons, p. 105.

[24] For a general theory relating balance processes to the assignment of ranks in the absence of knowledge of the bases of ranks, see Joseph Berger, Bernard P. Cohen, and Morris Zelditch, Jr., "Status Characteristics and Expectation States," in Berger, Zelditch, and Anderson, editors, *Sociological Theories in Progress*, Vol. I (Boston: Houghton Mifflin, 1966), Chapter 2.

[25] That the members of systems differentially weight what we have called bases of instrumental status-power and bases of non-instrumental status is suggested by Bales and Slater. See Robert F. Bales and Philip E. Slater, "Role Differentiation in Small Decision-Making Groups," in Talcott Parsons, *et al.*, *Family, Socialization, and Interaction Process* (Glencoe, Ill.: Free Press, 1955), pp. 290–292.

We suggested earlier that evaluators average across individuals to arrive at an instrumental status for the simple system. We indicated that a simple system rarely has a non-instrumental status because its non-task norms are not likely to be known to evaluators. We also suggested that a simple system's power and economic rewards are assessed in ways similar to the way in which its instrumental status is assessed.

In dealing with the present problem, we shall make two simplifying assumptions. First, we shall assume that a simple system's instrumental status and power are equilibrated and shall treat instrumental status and power as a single rank. Thus, we shall think of a simple system as having only two ranks: instrumental status-power and economic rewards. Second, we shall assume that its members uniformly aspire to high ranks for it.

For a simple system to increase its ranks above those resulting from its location within the productive structure of the complex system, it must have greater power than that which results from its location in that structure. That a simple system does have a base of power in addition to that which results from its location in the complex system's productive structure can be seen if we consider a basic difference between power at the simple and complex system levels.

An individual has power because he can frustrate, within the limits of the ability of the simple system to replace him, attainment of the simple system's goal. Similarly, a simple system has power because it can frustrate, within the limits of the complex system's ability to replace it, attainment of the complex system's goal. Now, there are two ways a complex system can replace the members of a simple system: individual by individual, or as a group. The latter is more difficult and more disruptive for the complex system. It is more difficult because it is harder to locate a group of replacements than it is to locate a single replacement. It is more disruptive because often it is possible to keep a simple system producing in the temporary absence of a position incumbent by reallocating the task activities which make up the vacant position among the incumbents of other positions. Thus, if the members of a simple system agree among themselves to withdraw *en masse* if one of their number is replaced, they have an additional base of power in that they have increased the difficulty of replacing them. Henceforth, we shall refer to this additional base of power as *collective action to prevent replacement*.

How can the members of a simple system use collective action to prevent replacement to increase their system's ranks. Is there any reason to believe they increase one rank before the other? Let us attempt to answer the last question first. Earlier we suggested that evaluators use the base of stratification which is best known and/or on which there is most agreement on criteria of evaluation to assess other bases of stratification when knowledge of the bases of stratification and/or consensus on criteria of evaluation of these bases is low. At the intersystem level, there is apt to be less knowledge and less consensus than there is at the intrasystem level. Given this, it seems likely that simple system members in attempting to increase their system's ranks will attempt to increase the rank which is clearest in terms of knowledge of its bases and/or consensus on criteria of evaluation of these bases, because this will increase, through the operation of the balance-type process described earlier, their system's other rank.[26]

Let us return now to the question of how the members of a simple system can use collective action to prevent replacement to increase their system's ranks. We distinguish three ways: system mobility, system merging, and increasing the system's share of economic rewards.

System mobility refers to movement of the entire membership of a simple system from a lower to a higher system. This would appear to be very rare because of the different ranges of skills that different simple systems require.

System merging refers to the merging of a lower simple system with a higher one. Essentially, this would appear to involve integration of two simple systems under a single leadership. Presumably the leaders of the lower simple system would be included in the leadership of the new simple system created by the merger. This would also appear to be fairly rare because it dilutes, through the averaging processes described earlier, the ranks of the higher simple system.

Increasing a simple system's share of economic rewards refers to obtaining a larger percentage of the economic rewards received by the complex system. We use the term "percentage" because it is probably the proportion, not the absolute amount, of economic rewards a simple system obtains that determines its rank on this dimension.

Mobility and merging differ from increasing economic rewards in respect to which rank is increased first. In mobility and merging, the instrumental status-power rank is increased first through movement to another system and through combination with another system. Economic reward ranks commensurate with the higher system and the new system then follows. In increasing economic rewards, the economic reward rank, of course, is increased first. A higher instrumental-status power rank then follows.

As indicated earlier, all three of these modes of increasing a simple system's ranks involve use of collective action to prevent replacement. The general process is probably as follows. The members of the simple system threaten to frustrate attainment of the complex system's goal by ceasing to produce unless mobility, a merger, or an increase in economic rewards is granted. This threat is backed up by an additional threat to withdraw *en masse* if any simple system member is replaced. The professionalization process provides examples of system mobility, at least in a limited sense, and system merging. The shifting of a large number of activities from a higher to a lower professional group is an instance of system mobility in a limited sense, and the acceptance of a previously unaccepted group into a professional association is an instance of system

---

[26] We assume that the attribution of a rank to a system or an individual usually leads to acquisition of the bases of that rank. For example, the attribution of power probably often leads to actual power. (Compare Berger, Cohen, and Zelditch, pp. 39–42.) Specification of the conditions under which this occurs and which it does not is an obvious extension of the theory.

Even when attribution of a rank does not lead to acquisition of its base, the mere belief by others that the unit possesses it can be rewarding.

merging. An industrial strike, of course, is usually an instance of increasing economic rewards.

A fourth way of increasing the ranks of a simple system is to increase productivity. In this mode, the instrumental status-power rank is increased first. This occurs because increasing productivity involves improving performance, and this is a base of instrumental status-power. Increasing productivity does *not* involve, of course, use of collective action to prevent replacement.

Having outlined the ways in which a simple system can increase its ranks, we can now consider the question of how these modes of increasing ranks may affect the stratification of individuals *within* the simple system. In attempting to answer this question, we postulate a process in which simple system members give additional weight to bases of instrumental status-power or non-instrumental status. We do not visualize this process as one in which weight is shifted from one of these sets of bases to another, but as one in which additional weight is introduced.[27]

All those modes of increasing the ranks of a simple system which require the use of threats to frustrate the attainment of the complex system goal and to withdraw *en masse* if any simple system member is replaced, namely, mobility, merging, and increasing economic rewards, should result in *decreases* in certain aspects of stratification of individuals within the simple system. Our reasoning is as follows. For the threats just mentioned to be effective, any dissension among the members concerning the threats must be kept secret. This requires giving additional weight to conformity to representational norms having to do with secrecy. Further, making the threats involves some risk of replacement of all members, and asking individual members to take this risk requires some kind of reward. We think this takes the form of giving additional weight to equality and, hence, to conformity to equality norms. Since both these types of norms apply to all members and are within the skill of all members, conformity to both types of norms should increase. This should *decrease* non-instrumental status differences among members.

If knowledge of the bases of stratification and consensus on criteria of evaluation of these bases are *high* within the simple system, this decrease should *not* affect instrumental status-power or economic reward differences among the members because non-instrumental status will be no clearer than any other rank and, thus, should not be used to assess instrumental status-power and economic rewards. However, if such knowledge and/or consensus is *low*, the decrease should lead to *decreases* in instrumental status-power and economic reward differences. This should occur because non-instrumental status differences, given the additional weight being placed on their bases, should be the clearest differences, and this should result in their being used to assess instrumental status-power and economic rewards.

---

[27] Bales postulates a process in which weight is shifted from one system structure to another. He does this, however, because he views the structures as conflicting. See Bales, "Adaptative and Integrative Changes as Sources of Strain in Social Systems."

The remaining mode of increasing the ranks of a simple system, namely, increasing productivity, should have just the opposite effect on stratification of individuals within the simple system. It should result in *increases* in certain aspects of stratification. Our reasoning is as follows. Increasing productivity involves giving additional weight to position, performance, skill, and motivation. We assume that the alignment of positions, and skills and motivations in productive structures is never perfect and often is quite imperfect. Put another way, positions are characterized by levels of difficulty, and skills and motivations tend to be *above and below* what the positions require.[28] Since malalignment of these factors decreases productivity, placing additional weight on productivity should result in improvement in the degree to which they are aligned, and, consequently, in increased productivity.[29] Since the skills and motivations of some members are above and those of others below their positions, increasing alignment of these factors should *increase* instrumental-status power differences among members.

If knowledge of the bases of stratification and consensus on criteria of evaluation of these bases are *high* within the simple system, this increase should *increase* economic reward differences among members because, under these conditions, instrumental status-power and economic rewards are related through a justice-type process. The increase should *not* affect non-instrumental status differences because, under these conditions, non-instrumental status is assessed independently of other ranks. However, if such knowledge and/or consensus is *low*, the increase should lead to an *increase* in both economic rewards and non-instrumental status differences. This should occur because instrumental status-power differences, given the additional weight being placed on their bases, should be the clearest differences, and this should result in their being used to assess both economic rewards and non-instrumental status.

□ SUMMARY: A MODEL OF RANK EQUILIBRATION PROCESSES AND EFFECTS OF INCREASING SYSTEM RANKS ON STRATIFICATION OF SYSTEM MEMBERS

In this section we shall attempt to make as clear as possible the logical structure of the theory presented in the previous sections. To do this, each major concept and proposition must be reviewed. Rationales for the hypotheses will be presented as the hypotheses are reviewed. Wherever a rationale is felt to be fairly complete in the sense of adequately explaining the phenomena in question, it is separately labelled as such. Wherever this is not felt to be the case, it is indicated by statements to the effect that the phenomena are viewed as occurring in a given way or that the rationale offered is simply a suggestion.

---

[28] The author's work on equilibration of ranks on different subdimensions of the status dimension deals with the consequences of these types of malalignment. See Kimberly, "A Theory of Status Equilibration"; Kimberly, "Status Inconsistency"; and Kimberly and Crosbie, "An Experimental Test of a Reward-Cost Formulation of Status Inconsistency."

[29] Compare Homans, *Social Behavior*, pp. 248–263.

Concepts: Ranks.

Status. Status is used in the sense of evaluation in terms of superiority-inferiority or prestige. Two general kinds of status are distinguished: instrumental and non-instrumental.

Instrumental. Instrumental status is defined as evaluation of the individual's position in the system's productive structure, his performance relative to his position, his motivation relative to performance, and his skill.

Non-instrumental. Non-instrumental status is defined as evaluation of the degree to which the individual conforms to non-task norms. Two such norms are defined: equality and representational.

Equality norms. Equality norms are defined as norms which specify behavior which every system member owes to every other. Courtesy norms are cited as examples.

Representational norms. Representational norms are defined as norms which specify behavior which every system member is expected to display toward the members of one or more other systems. Secrecy norms are cited as examples.

Power. Power is defined as the ability to control the behavior of others.

Economic rewards. Economic rewards are defined as objects which are actually or potentially useful to the individual in a material sense. Such rewards, unlike status and power, are completely transferable from one individual to another.

Hypotheses: Emergence of ranks.

Instrumental status and power. It is hypothesized that both instrumental status and power result from difficulty of replacing individuals. The more difficult an individual is to replace, the more instrumental status and power he has.

Rationale: That persons grant prestige and compliance to others in accordance with the degree to which they are dependent on them for the attainment of a system goal.

Economic rewards. The emergence of economic rewards is not treated explicitly, but it would seem that it is fundamentally related to dependence in the sense that instrumental status and power are. A basic difference, however, is that because the economic reward rank is completely transferable from individual to individual, it may result from a number of factors in addition to dependence. For example, it can be increased through physical force whereas prestige probably cannot.

System ranks. It is hypothesized that systems as well as individuals have ranks. These are viewed as being arrived at through averaging processes in which the instrumental status, power, and economic rewards of system members are separately averaged to arrive at instrumental status, power, and economic reward ranks for the system. It is suggested that systems probably do not have non-instrumental statuses because members of other systems are not likely to know the system's non-task norms.

Hypotheses: Equilibration of ranks. It is hypothesized that equilibration of an individual's ranks occurs in two different ways, depending on whether or not evaluators know the bases of stratification and agree on criteria of evaluation of these bases.

Under conditions of knowledge and agreement.

Instrumental status and power. It is hypothesized that when there is knowledge of the bases of stratification and agreement on criteria of evaluation of these bases, instrumental status and power are generally equilibrated.

Rationale: That instrumental status and power have the same bases.

It is suggested that conformity to the types of non-task norms distinguished in this chapter is not a base of power because a lack of such conformity probably is tolerated when one occupies a very difficult position.

Instrumental status-power and economic rewards. It is hypothesized that when there is knowledge of the bases of stratification and agreement on criteria of evaluation of these bases, instrumental status-power and economic rewards are equilibrated.

Rationale: That economic rewards are viewed as rewards for performance in a position and, hence, are equilibrated with instrumental status-power through a justice-type process.

Under conditions of a lack of knowledge and/or agreement. It is hypothesized that when there is a lack of knowledge of the bases of stratification and/or agreement on criteria of evaluation of these bases, equilibration of ranks of all kinds, *including non-instrumental status*, is effected by using the rank which is clearest in terms of knowledge and/or agreement to assess other ranks.

Rationale: That in the absence of knowledge and/or agreement, balance-type processes govern assignment of ranks.

System ranks. It is hypothesized that equilibration of a system's ranks occurs primarily through use of its clearest rank to assess other ranks.

Rationale: That there is likely to be a lack of knowledge and/or agreement on the part of members of other systems who are, of course, the system's evaluators. This probably stems largely from the amount of contact possible at the intersystem level.

Concepts: Systems.

Simple system. A simple system is not defined in a detailed way, but it is clear that we mean by the term a set of positions directed toward a goal which is a means to a superordinate goal of a larger system. In addition to positions, which consist of task norms, we include in the concept non-task norms. We also include all of the behavior of individuals relevant to positions and norms.

Complex system. A complex system is defined as a set of simple systems whose goals are means to its goal.

Concepts: Modes of increasing simple systems' ranks.

System mobility. System mobility is defined as the movement of the entire membership of a simple system from a lower to a higher system. The shifting of a large number of activities from one professional group to another is given as an example of limited system mobility.

System merging. System merging is defined as the merging of a lower simple system with a higher one. The acceptance of a previously unaccepted group into a professional society is given as an example.

Increasing economic rewards. Increasing economic rewards is defined as a simple system obtaining a larger percentage of the economic rewards accruing to the complex system. An industrial strike is given as an example.

It is suggested that all of these modes of increasing system ranks involve collective action to prevent replacement, that is, threats by the simple system to frustrate attainment of the complex system's goal unless the objective involved in the mode is granted and to withdraw *en masse* if any simple system member is replaced.

Increasing productivity. Increasing productivity is defined simply as improving performance. This mode of increasing system ranks, of course, does not involve the use of collective action to prevent replacement.

Hypotheses: Factors determining choice of modes of increasing system ranks. It is hypothesized that which of the modes of increasing system ranks is used is determined by which of the system's ranks is clearest in terms of knowledge of the bases of stratification and/or agreement concerning evaluation of these bases.

Rationale: Under the conditions of low knowledge and agreement that prevail at the intersystem level, equilibration of system ranks is governed by a balance-type process. Consequently, the simple system attempts to increase whichever of its ranks is clearest in terms of knowledge and/or agreement because this will increase, through the balance process, its other rank.

When instrumental status-power is clearest. It is hypothesized that when instrumental status-power is the clearest rank, system mobility, system merging, or increasing productivity is used to increase system ranks.[30]

Rationale: That all of these modes of increasing system ranks involve increasing the instrumental status-power rank first. System mobility does this through movement to a new system. System merging does it through combination with a more highly valued system. And finally, increasing productivity does it through bringing positions, skills, and motivations into better alignment and increasing performances.

When economic rewards is the clearest rank. It is hypothesized that when economic rewards is the clearest rank, increasing economic rewards is used to increase system ranks.

Rationale: That this mode of increasing system ranks involves increasing the economic reward rank first.

Hypotheses: Effects of different modes of increasing system ranks on stratification of system members.

System mobility, system merging, and increasing economic rewards. It is hypothesized that system mobility, system merging, and increasing economic

---

[30] In the present state of the theory, we are not able to specify the additional factors which determine which of these three modes will be used in a given instance. We hope to be able to specify such factors in the future.

rewards *decrease* non-instrumental status differences among individuals within the simple system.

Rationale: All of these modes of increasing system ranks involve threats to frustrate attainment of the complex system goal and to withdraw *en masse* if any simple system member is replaced. Such threats result in members placing greater weight on non-instrumental status. This comes about for two reasons. First, in order to make the threats effective, dissension among members concerning the threats must be kept secret. This leads to greater emphasis being given to conformity to representational norms having to do with secrecy. Second, members have subjected themselves to the possibility of replacement and must be rewarded for doing so. This is done by giving greater emphasis to conformity to equality norms. Since conformity to representational and equality norms requires no more skill than that possessed by the least able member, members become more equal with regard to conformity to the two types of norms and, thus, more equal on the non-instrumental status dimension.

Effects of decrease of non-instrumental status differences when knowledge and agreement are high within the simple system. It is hypothesized that when knowledge of bases of stratification and agreement on criteria of evaluation are high within the simple system, the decrease in non-instrumental status differences does not affect instrumental status-power and economic reward differences among members.

Rationale: That under conditions of high knowledge and agreement, non-instrumental status is not used to assess instrumental status-power and economic rewards. Put another way, equilibration does not occur through a balance-type process, and it is only when it does that non-instrumental status affects instrumental status-power and economic rewards.

Effects of decrease of non-instrumental status differences when knowledge and agreement are low within the simple system. It is hypothesized that when knowledge of bases of stratification and agreement on criteria of evaluation are low within the simple system, the decrease in non-instrumental status differences *decreases* instrumental status-power and economic reward differences among members.

Rationale: Under conditions of low knowledge and agreement, the clearest rank will be used to assess other ranks. This will be non-instrumental status because of the additional weight being given to it. Put another way, equilibration does occur through a balance-type process, and non-instrumental status is the rank about which equilibration takes place.

Increasing productivity. It is hypothesized that increasing productivity *increases* instrumental status-power differences among individuals within the simple system.

Rationale: Increasing productivity involves giving greater weight to the productive structure. Certain components of this structure — positions, and skills and motivations — probably are never perfectly aligned. Skills and motivations tend to be above and below what various positions require. Malalignment affects productivity negatively. Giving additional weight to productivity leads to improvement in alignment of the components, and consequently, to increased productivity. Since the skills and motivations of some members are above and those of others are below their positions, increasing alignment of these factors should increase instrumental status-power differences among members.

Effects of increase in instrumental status-power differences when knowledge and agreement are high within the simple system. It is hypothesized that when knowledge of bases of stratification and agreement on criteria of evaluation are high within the simple system, the increase in instrumental status-power differences among members results in an *increase* in economic reward differences among members.

Rationale: That under conditions of high knowledge and agreement, instrumental status-power and economic rewards are related through a justice-type process.

It is noted that the increase in instrumental status-power differences should not affect non-instrumental status because under the conditions of high knowledge and agreement, non-instrumental status is assessed independently of other ranks.

Effects of increase in instrumental status-power differences when knowledge and agreement are low within the simple system. It is hypothesized that when knowledge of bases of stratification and agreement on criteria of evaluation are low within the simple system, the increase in instrumental status-power differences results in *increases* in economic reward and non-instrumental status differences among members.

Rationale: Under conditions of low knowledge and agreement, the clearest rank will be used to assess other ranks. This will be instrumental status-power because of the additional weight being given to it. Put another way, equilibration takes place through a balance-type process, and instrumental status-power is the rank about which equilibration occurs.

Chapter 13

Models of
Intragenerational Mobility*

■ THOMAS F. MAYER

□ **ABSTRACT**

A review is made of existing mathematical models of intragenerational mobility. These models are of two general sorts: aggregate individual models and structural models. Next, the general theory of continuous time finite state Markov processes is discussed. Three continuous time Markov mobility models are presented. The birth and death process model assumes direct transitions can only occur between adjacent status categories. The exponential decline model assumes mobility rates decline monotonically with age. The absorbing state model contends persons become increasingly concentrated in mobility states from which no exit is possible. All three models are evaluated using empirical mobility data collected by Blau and Duncan. Unfortunately, the Blau and Duncan data do not satisfy the assumptions of the exponential decline or absorbing state models, and only tentative conclusions are possible. Seven major unsolved theoretical problems of mobility are defined: identification, structure, heterogeneity, non-stationarity, constraint, interdependence, and antecedence. Technical problems of mathematical analysis, details of the Blau and Duncan data, and estimation procedures are discussed in appendices.

□ **1. THE PROBLEM OF MOBILITY**

The phenomenon of social mobility has intrigued social scientists for at least two generations. Perhaps the most recent example of this fascination has been the popularity of social mobility as an object of rigorous formal analysis. The attraction which the mobility phenomenon exercises upon advocates of sociological rigor rests upon three considerations: First, social mobility is generally recognized as a process of great substantive importance. Consequently, rigorous analysis of social mobility is difficult to disregard on grounds of triviality or substantive vacuity. Second, the problem of explaining mobility is well formulated. This means several things: the main features of mobility process are well known and have been confirmed by a considerable number of independent studies; the ideas of class and status which undergird notions of mobility possess a reasonable degree of conceptual clarity; even more importantly, the widely accepted contingency table method of reporting empirical mobility data

* The author would like to thank Joseph Berger, J. Michael Coble, Otis Dudley Duncan, Joel Levine, J. Laurie Snell, and Morris Zelditch, Jr. for their help in preparing this paper.

provides a convenient handle on the basis of which rigorous analysis readily proceeds. A third source of the nexus existing between social mobility and rigorous analysis centers around the question of measurement. As this paper will amply reveal, even the best mobility data are not free of measurement problems. Nevertheless, the measurement difficulties confronting students of social mobility are of a lesser magnitude than those encountered in other sociological fields.

The search for rigorous methods of analyzing social mobility has assumed two forms. One tendency addresses itself primarily to the problem of causation. Workers in this tradition construct and test models of the causal relationships impinging on social mobility. By far the most impressive example of the causal approach is the path analytic methodology used by Blau and Duncan in *The American Occupational Structure*. The other tendency emphasizes the problem of representing mobility as a process occurring through time. Although any serious representation of mobility implies a causal pattern, the central concern of the second tendency is not inference of causality, but depiction of movement between social strata. The models discussed are examples of this second or representational approach.

Social mobility assumes several different guises: geographic and status mobility, horizontal and vertical mobility, intergenerational and intragenerational (or career) mobility, etc. This paper focuses on intragenerational, vertical, status mobility defined as the movements of an age cohort between hierarchically arranged status levels. This choice is predicated on several considerations. In the author's opinion, the social ramifications of vertical status mobility far exceed those of other mobility forms. Moreover, existing data on intergenerational mobility suffer from a number of methodological problems including the fact that they do not depict the actual experience of any real cohort.[1] These arguments have motivated the writer to concentrate on vertical, status, career mobility.

□ **2. THE MOBILITY MATRIX**

Before reviewing existing models of mobility, it is necessary to discuss the career contingency table better known as the intragenerational frequency matrix. This matrix is the starting point and central focus of almost all current mobility models. We shall explain the career contingency table and its various transformations by developing a fictitious example.

Suppose we sample 1,000 persons of similar age and obtain information which enables us to assess their status position at two points in time t_1 and t_2. Suppose, further, we define three general status levels high, medium, and low so that each person falls into exactly one of these levels at each point in time. We can then construct a three by three career contingency table which cross

---

[1] Otis Dudley Duncan: "Methodological Issues in the Analysis of Social Mobility," in Neil J. Smelser and Seymour M. Lipset (eds.), *Social Structure and Mobility in Economic Development*. Chicago: Aldine, 1966, Chapter 2.

classifies a person's status position at time t_1 against his status at time t_2. The cell entries in such a table indicate the number of persons in each particular cross-classification. Table 1 is a hypothetical career contingency table illustrating the example developed above.

■ **TABLE 1 / Hypothetical Career Contingency Table Illustrating Vertical, Status, Career Mobility between Time t_1 and Time t_2**

Status position at time t_1		Status position at time t_2			
		High	Medium	Low	Row marginals
	High	100	70	30	200
	Medium	100	250	50	400
	Low	50	150	200	400
Column marginals		250	470	280	$N = 1,000$

The size of the frequency matrix depends on the number of status categories specified. If the number of status categories defined at time t_1 equals the number defined at time t_2, the frequency matrix will be square.

Some models of mobility work directly with the career contingency table. Others, however, focus on the matrix of outflow proportions derived from the frequency matrix by an elementary procedure: to obtain the outflow matrix, one divides each cell of the frequency matrix by the appropriate row marginal. This procedure yields a matrix with non-negative elements and row sums equaling unity. A square matrix having these properties is called a stochastic matrix. The outflow matrix corresponding to the frequency matrix in Table 1 is given below.

■ **TABLE 2 / Hypothetical Outflow Proportion Matrix Illustrating Vertical, Status, Career Mobility between Time t_1 and Time t_2**

Status position at time t_1		Status position at time t_2			
		High	Medium	Low	Row proportion
	High	.500	.350	.150	.200
	Medium	.250	.625	.125	.400
	Low	.125	.375	.500	.400
Column proportion		.250	.470	.280	

The elements of the outflow table give the proportions of persons moving between the various status categories. More specifically, the element in row i and column j of the outflow table gives the proportion of persons occupying the status category corresponding to row i at time t_i who occupy the status category corresponding to column j at time t_2. For example, the element in the first row and second column of the matrix given in Table 2 (.350) states the proportion of persons occupying a high status position at t_1 who occupy a medium status position at t_2.

Sometimes the proportions given by the outflow matrix are interpreted as probabilities. This means the element in row i and column j is regarded as the probability a person in status category i at t_1 will be in status category j at t_2. When this probabilistic interpretation is made, the outflow table is typically called a transition matrix, and its elements referred to as transition probabilities.

All models considered in this paper postulate a finite set of hierarchically ordered status categories which we label $S_1, S_2, \ldots, S_n$. Define the random variable x_t as the status category occupied at time t. Using this notation

$$p(x_{t_2} = S_j \mid x_{t_1} = S_i) \qquad i, j = 1, \ldots, n \qquad (1)$$

indicates the probability a person occupying status category S_i at time t_1 will occupy category S_j at time t_2. In other words, (1) is a theoretical expression for the transition probability between S_i and S_j over the time interval between t_1 and t_2. Define $P(t_2 \mid t_1)$ as the matrix of probabilities given in (1) where i is the row index and j the column index. The outflow matrix between time t_1 and time t_2 — the derivation of which has been described above — furnishes an estimate of the theoretical probability matrix $P(t_2 \mid t_1)$.

By way of illustration consider the hypothetical study outlined earlier. Three status categories were specified: high, medium, and low. Let S_1 equal high status (H), let S_2 equal medium status (M), and let S_3 equal low status (L). The theoretical matrix $P(t_2 \mid t_1)$ would then have the form given in Table 3.

■ TABLE 3 / Theoretical Matrix $P(t_2 \mid t_1)$ under the Assumption of Three Status Categories: S_1 = High Status (H), S_2 = Medium Status (M), and S_3 = Low Status (L)

$P(t_2 \mid t_1) =$	$p(x_{t_2} = H \mid x_{t_1} = H)$	$p(x_{t_2} = M \mid x_{t_1} = H)$	$p(x_{t_2} = L \mid x_{t_1} = H)$
	$p(x_{t_2} = H \mid x_{t_1} = M)$	$p(x_{t_2} = M \mid x_{t_1} = M)$	$p(x_{t_2} = L \mid x_{t_1} = M)$
	$p(x_{t_2} = H \mid x_{t_1} = L)$	$p(x_{t_2} = M \mid x_{t_1} = L)$	$p(x_{t_2} = L \mid x_{t_1} = L)$

Moreover, the hypothetical outflow matrix stated in Table 2 provides an estimate of this theoretical matrix. For example, $p(x_{t_2} = M \mid x_{t_1} = H)$ equals the probability a person will be of medium status at t_2 given he was of high status at time t_1. The element in the first row and second column of Table 2 (.350) furnishes an estimate of this probability.

We are now in a position to review existing models of social mobility. We will distinguish two general categories: aggregate individual models and structural models. We will discuss each category separately and then make some comparisons between the two.

□ 3. AGGREGATE INDIVIDUAL MODELS OF MOBILITY: A CRITICAL REVIEW

Aggregate individual models of mobility treat the mobility process on the microsocial level. The essential regularities they postulate govern the way in which individuals move between social strata. The mobility behaviors of different persons are usually regarded as independent, and the mobility process as a whole is viewed as the aggregate of these individual patterns.

The mathematical nature of an aggregate individual model is not uniquely determined by this conceptual description, and in fact aggregate individual models of several different mathematical types exist. For the most part, however, aggregate individual models have been of two sorts: Markovian and Semi-Markovian. This being the case, we shall organize our discussion of aggregate individual mobility models around the Markovian–Semi-Markovian distinction.

A. Markovian Aggregate Individual Models

Markovian mobility models can be divided between those which treat time as a discrete variable and those which treat it as a continuous variable. Since most current Markovian models are of the former sort, and since the basic ideas of Markov theory are more easily grasped in the discrete case, we begin by discussing discrete time models.

As indicated in the previous section, we postulate a finite set of hierarchically ordered status categories labeled $s_1, \ldots, s_n$. We also define a set of random variables $\{x_t; t \geq 0\}$ which state the status category occupied at each point in time. A discrete time model only considers the mobility process at a countable set of time points which we designate $0, 1, 2, \ldots$. Usually these points demarcate equal time intervals, but this is not necessary. Thus, in the discrete case we are only concerned with the random variables $\{x_t; t = 0, 1, 2, \ldots\}$.

The basic principle which distinguishes Markov models asserts that the status category a person will occupy in the future depends only on the status category he occupies at present and not at all on the categories he has previously occupied. This is sometimes referred to as the principle of path independence. As an example of this property, consider three people with the following status histories.

	Time			
	0	1	2	3
Person I	High	High	High	Medium
Person II	Medium	Medium	Medium	Medium
Person III	Low	Low	Low	Medium

These people all have different status histories, but their status levels at the last time recorded (time 3) are identical. A Markov model would make identical predictions about their future behavior.

In formal terms the path independence principle can be defined as follows:

$$p(x_k = S_{i_k} \mid x_{k-1} = S_{i_{k-1}}, \ldots, x_1 = S_{i_1}) \tag{2}$$
$$= p(x_k = S_{i_k} \mid x_{k-1} = S_{i_{k-1}}). \quad k = 1, 2, \ldots$$

The path independence property makes possible a convenient notational simplification:

$$p(x_m = S_j \mid x_k = S_i) = p_{ij}(m, k), \quad \begin{matrix} i, j = 1, 2, \ldots, n \\ k = 0, 1, 2, \ldots \\ m = k + 1, k + 2, \ldots \end{matrix} \tag{3}$$

where n equals the number of status categories stipulated.

The earliest mobility model known to the author was the finite Markov chain model proposed independently by S. J. Prais[2] and by Blumen, Kogan, and McCarthy.[3] The Markov chain model adds stationarity and homogeneity assumptions to the path independence principle. Under the stationarity assumption the transition probabilities, $p_{ij}(m, k)$, depend only on the difference $m - k$ and not on the specific values of m and k. Thus we may write

$$p_{ij}(m, k) = p_{ij}(m - k). \quad \begin{matrix} i, j = 1, 2, \ldots, n \\ k = 0, 1, 2, \ldots \\ m = k + 1, k + 2, \ldots \end{matrix} \tag{4}$$

If stationarity holds, transition probabilities over a fixed time interval remain constant regardless where the interval occurs in the overall time sequence. It is conventional to write p_{ij} (1) simply as p_{ij}. The homogeneity assumption asserts that all persons have identical transition probabilities. According to the Markov chain model, the probability of transition from one status category to another over an interval of fixed length is independent of time and identical for all members of the mobility cohort.

To discuss the main properties of the finite Markov chain model it is convenient to use matrix notation. Define matrix P as

$$P = \{ p_{ij} \}_{i,j=1}^{n}. \tag{5}$$

Thus, P equals the theoretical transition matrix $P(t + 1 \mid t)$ discussed in the

[2] S. J. Prais: "Measuring Social Mobility," *Journal of the Royal Statistical Society*. Series A, 11B, 1955, pp. 55–66 and S. J. Prais: "The Formal Theory of Social Mobility," *Population Studies*. 9, 1955, pp. 72–81.

[3] I. Blumen, M. Kogan, and P. J. McCarthy: *The Industrial Mobility of Labor as a Probability Process*. Cornell Studies in Industrial Relations, Vol. VI, Cornell University, Ithaca, N. Y., 1955.

previous section. To estimate the number of persons in each status category at times 0, 1, 2, ...: define the random variable $N_k(i)$ as the number of persons in category S_i at time k and let the n dimensional random row vector N_k equal

$$N_k = [N_k(1), N_k(2), \ldots, N_k(n)]. \qquad k = 0, 1, 2, \qquad (6)$$

Vector N_k states the frequency distribution of persons over the various status categories at time k. Define the vector $E[N_k]$ as

$$E[N_k] = \{E[N_k(1)], E[N_k(2)], \ldots, E[N_k(n)]\}. \qquad k = 0, 1, 2, \ldots \qquad (7)$$

$E[N_k]$ gives the expected number of persons in each of the status categories at time k. Under the assumptions of the finite Markov chain model the following relationship holds:

$$E[N_k] = N_0 P^k. \qquad (8)$$

This expression asserts that the expected distribution of persons over status categories at time k equals the actual distribution at time zero multiplied by the kth power of the transition matrix.

The finite Markov chain model is characterized by the transition matrix P and the initial frequency distribution vector N_0. Formula (8) can be used to calculate the first moments of the status category sizes. Matrix P and vector N_0 also permit calculation of higher moments using a method suggested by John Pollard.[4]

Perhaps the most interesting aspect of the finite Markov chain model is its asymptotic behavior. If some power of the matrix P has only positive elements, a condition almost always satisfied if P is estimated from actual mobility data, then

$$\lim_{k \to \infty} P^k = Q \qquad (9)$$

where Q is a stochastic matrix all of whose rows are identical. This implies that a person's asymptotic status category is independent of his initial status category. The finite Markov chain thus suggests an asymptotic equality of opportunity.

To illustrate these asymptotic properties we consider the example developed in Section 2. Suppose P equals the matrix in Table 2. Note this matrix has only positive elements. Hence (9) applies, and the resulting Q matrix appears in Table 4. Each row of the matrix Q gives the unique stability vector of the matrix P. This means each row of Q equals the unique probability vector V such that

$$VP = V. \qquad (10)$$

Berger, Kemeney, and Snell have elaborated the finite Markov chain model

[4] John H. Pollard: "On the Use of the Direct Matrix Product in Analyzing Certain Stochastic Population Models," *Biometrika*. 53, 1966, pp. 397–415.

■ TABLE 4 / Q Matrix Corresponding to Transition Matrix Given in Table 2

.298	.490	.212
.298	.490	.212
.298	.490	.212

considerably.[5] These authors introduce the concept of mean first passage time between two status categories. The mean first passage time equals the average number of time units needed to move from one status category to the other. They suggest the matrix of mean first passage times furnishes insight into the proximity of various status categories.

Berger, Kemeney, and Snell have also pointed out the problem of "lumpability" which arises because a finite Markov chain model may no longer be a finite Markov chain if certain status categories are combined (lumped). They state conditions which make lumping permissible. In addition, these authors have proposed the notion of equal exchange and have formulated criteria under which equal exchange holds. A situation of equal exchange exists if for any two status categories S_i and S_j, the number of persons moving from S_i to S_j equals the number of persons moving from S_j to S_i.

The empirical performance of the Markov chain model has not been particularly impressive. When applied to concrete data, the model consistently overestimates the number of persons leaving their initial status category. The extent of overestimation increases with the length of the time interval considered. This specific failing has furnished the starting point for subsequent mobility models.

To cope with this difficulty Blumen, Kogan, and McCarthy proposed a modification of the homogeneity assumption.[6] A mobility cohort, they suggest, contains two subsets, movers and stayers. Movers behave exactly as suggested by the finite Markov chain model. Stayers, however, remain permanently fixed in their initial status level. Let s_i give the proportion of persons starting in status category S_i who are stayers, and let S be the diagonal matrix whose ith diagonal element is s_i. Define M as the stochastic transition matrix for movers, and let I be the nth order identity matrix (i.e. the diagonal matrix of order n with ones on the main diagonal and zeroes elsewhere). For the mover-stayer model, the analog to (8) is then

$$E[N_k] = N_0[S + (I - S)M^k]. \qquad k = 0, 1, 2, \ldots \qquad (11)$$

To grasp the meaning of (11) it may be useful to decompose the right side

[5] J. Berger and J. L. Snell: "On the Concept of Equal Exchange," *Behavioral Science.* 2, 1957, pp. 111–118 and J. Berger, J. G. Kemeny and J. L. Snell: "Applications [of Markov Chains] to Mobility Theory," pp. 191–200 in J. G. Kemeny and J. L. Snell: *Finite Markov Chains.* Princeton: Van Nostrand, 1960.
[6] Blumen, Kogan, and McCarthy: *op. cit.*, pp. 104–136.

of the expression into its constituent parts. $N_0 S$ is a row vector giving the number of stayers in each status category. $N_0(I - S)$ is a row vector giving the number of movers in each status category at time zero, while M^k equals the kth power of the transition matrix for movers. The term $N_0(I - S)M^k$ is exactly analogous to (8). Thus, (11) equals the fixed frequency distribution of stayers plus the initial distribution of movers transformed according to the kth power of the transition matrix.

The mover-stayer model poses considerably greater estimation problems than the finite Markov chain model. Blumen, Kogan, and McCarthy's analysis revealed the mover-stayer model mitigated but did not eliminate the difficulties associated with the earlier formulation. Using improved estimation procedures, Goodman was able to obtain a better fit with the mover-stayer model.[7] A definitive test of the mover-stayer formulation would require better time series mobility data than is currently available. The plausibility of the mover-stayer dichotomy is certainly open to question. Some critics regard this dichotomy as an artificial device for shoring up a fundamentally inadequate formulation; others view it as a gross understatement of the actual heterogeneity present in mobility cohorts. Whatever its shortcomings, the mover-stayer model has stimulated a number of fresh approaches to modeling mobility. At least two of the structural models discussed in the next section reveal the influence of the mover-stayer formulation.

Continuous time Markov mobility models do not differ fundamentally from their discrete counterparts. Such models consider all points in time after an arbitrarily designated starting point. Thus, they consider the random variable set $\{x_t; t \geq 0\}$. The path independence principle for continuous time Markov models is almost identical to (2) and may be stated as follows:

$$p(x_t = S_{i_t} \mid x_s = S_{i_s}, \ldots, x_r = S_{i_r}) \tag{12}$$
$$= p(x_t = S_{i_t} \mid x_s = S_{i_s}). \qquad t > s > \cdots > r \geq 0$$

This indicates that the probability of occupying a status category depends entirely on the last known status category occupied and not at all on the earlier history of the mobility process.

Blumen, Kogan, and McCarthy suggested the earliest continuous time model, which we will identify as the homogeneous decision point model.[8] Like the finite Markov chain formulation, this model makes stationarity and homogeneity assumptions. The homogeneous decision point model assumes that transitions between status categories are governed by a fixed stochastic matrix M. Such transitions, however, occur only at so-called "decision points" which are distributed over time according to a Poisson process with parameter λ. Let $z(t)$ be a random variable giving the number of decision points occurring in t time units. Then the assumption of a Poisson process with parameter λ implies

[7] Leo A. Goodman: "Statistical Methods for the Mover-Stayer Model," *Journal of the American Statistical Association.* December 1961, pp. 841–868.
[8] Blumen, Kogan, and McCarthy: *op. cit.*, pp. 137–161.

$$p[z(t) = k] = e^{-\lambda t} \frac{(\lambda t)^k}{k!} \qquad k = 0, 1, 2, \dots. \tag{13}$$

If $P(t)$ equals the transition matrix implied by the homogeneous decision point model over a time interval of length t, then

$$
\begin{aligned}
P(t) &= \sum_{k=0}^{\infty} p[z(t) = k] M^k \\
&= \sum_{k=0}^{\infty} \left[e^{-\lambda t} \frac{(\lambda t)^k}{k!} \right] M^k.
\end{aligned}
\tag{14}
$$

In principle, calculation of the theoretical transition matrix $P(t)$ only requires knowledge of the matrix M and rate λ.

The homogeneous decision point model is an analog of the finite Markov chain model in continuous time and suffers from all its defects. Bartholomew has suggested attacking these defects by relaxing the homogeneity assumption.[9] This, one should note, is exactly the strategy which in the discrete time situation led to the mover-stayer model. Specifically, Bartholomew assumes decision points occur at different rates for different persons. Let $P(t \mid \lambda)$ equal the transition matrix under the assumption that decision points occur at rate λ. In other words, $P(t \mid \lambda)$ equals the matrix given in (14). Let $F(\lambda)$ be the distribution function of the decision rate distribution. Then $P(t)$, the transition matrix implied by the nonhomogeneous decision point model over a time interval of length t, equals

$$
\begin{aligned}
P(t) &= \int_0^{\infty} P(t \mid \lambda)\, dF(\lambda) \\
&= \int_0^{\infty} \sum_{k=0}^{\infty} \left[e^{-\lambda t} \frac{(\lambda t)^k}{k!} \right] M^k \, dF(\lambda).
\end{aligned}
\tag{15}
$$

Bartholomew's model seems to mitigate some of the difficulties posed by the homogeneous decision point formulation. Unfortunately, a number of problems remain to be solved before this model becomes completely operational.

B. Semi-Markovian Aggregate Individual Models

Semi-Markovian models are variations of Markovian formulations.[10] The distinction between Markovian and Semi-Markovian models lies entirely in the

---

[9] David J. Bartholomew: *Stochastic Models for Social Processes*. London: John Wiley, 1967, pp. 27–34.

[10] For a mathematical treatment of Semi-Markov processes see Ronald Pyke: "Markov Renewal Processes: Definitions and Preliminary Properties," *Annals of Mathematical Statistics*. 32, 1961, pp. 1231–1242; and Ronald Pyke: "Markov Renewal Processes with Finitely Many States," *Annals of Mathematical Statistics*. 32, 1961, pp. 1243–1259.

principles governing duration of stay in each of the status categories $S_1, \ldots, S_n$. According to the discrete time Markov model, transitions between status states occur regularly at fixed intervals. These movements may be from a state to itself, but such an occurrence is considered a transition. Continuous time Markov models stipulate that duration of stay is subject to an exponential probability law, the parameter of which depends upon the status category occupied (Appendix A contains a demonstration of this assertion). In both cases duration of stay is independent of the next status category.

If one considers only transitions between status categories and not duration of stay in these categories, Semi-Markovian models are exactly like their Markovian counterparts. Define J_k as the random variable giving the status state occupied after the kth transition. For Semi-Markovian models, path independence holds in the following way:

$$p[J_k = S_{i_k} \mid J_{k-1} = S_{i_{k-1}}, \ldots, J_0 = S_{i_0}] \qquad (16)$$
$$= p[J_k = S_{i_k} \mid J_{k-1} = S_{i_{k-1}}]. \qquad k = 1, 2, \ldots$$

Thus, the status category occupied after the kth transition depends only on the category occupied after transition $k - 1$ and not on status categories previously occupied. Duration of stay in a particular status category, according to the Semi-Markov model, is an arbitrary positive random variable which may depend on both the state presently occupied and the state next entered. Moreover, if the sequence of status categories actually occupied is known, the lengths of stay in these categories are independent of each other.

To clarify the nature of the Semi-Markovian model it may be useful to describe how such a model might be simulated. For this purpose one requires a matrix of transition probabilities P, a set of positive valued random variables $\{x_{ij}\}_{i,j=1}^{n}$ (one corresponding to each ordered pair of status categories), and a set of probabilities $\{a_i\}_{i=1}^{n}$ which defines the initial distribution over the various status categories. To select an initial status category one samples from the distribution specified by $\{a_i\}$. Suppose S_i is the initial state thus obtained. One uses the transition matrix P to select the status category next entered. Suppose this category is S_j: to simulate the length of stay in the initial state s_i one now samples a value of the random variable x_{ij}. Next, one selects the status category entered after S_j, again using transition matrix P. If one assumes this category is S_k, length of stay in S_j is simulated by sampling a value of the random variable x_{jk}, and so forth.

Semi-Markovian mobility models involve more complicated mathematics than do Markovian models. As a consequence, few mobility models of this type have been developed, and those which do exist are rather special cases of the general Semi-Markovian formulation. It is likely, however, that Semi-Markovian models will assume greater importance in the near future.

Perhaps the most significant Semi-Markovian mobility model (of an aggregate individual nature) currently in the sociological literature is the Cornell Mobility Model developed by Robert McGinnis and his colleagues at Cornell

University.[11] The basic innovation of the Cornell Mobility Model is the "axiom of cumulative inertia" which asserts "the probability of remaining in any state [status category]... increases as a strict monotonic function of duration of prior residence in that state."[12] Thus, the longer a person remains in a status category, the smaller is the probability of his leaving. Duration of stay depends only on the category presently occupied and not on the subsequent status category.

For analytic purposes McGinnis redefines the state space of the Cornell Mobility Model converting it to an ordinary Markovian formulation. Specifically, he partitions each status category according to duration of stay therein. The resulting process can be treated by the usual algebraic methods.

Although the Cornell Mobility Model has several attractive features, it poses formidable estimation problems which have not yet been adequately solved. Computer simulation suggests the model has a long-run distribution independent of the initial distribution, but this conjecture remains unproven. As yet, the Cornell Mobility Model has not been applied to real data.

C. Critical Remarks

The most basic shortcoming of these models derives from the aggregate individual concept itself. According to this notion, each individual follows an essentially isolated career trajectory, mobility being simply the sum of these independent movements. Aggregate individual models inevitably neglect the interdependent aspects of the mobility process. They treat the distribution of status positions as the outcome of numerous independent transitions, not as a social constraint operative on the mobility process. Thus, the distribution of status positions appears as an essentially fortuitous reality rather than as a manifestation of underlying social or economic institutions.

Failure to deal with the interdependent and structurally constrained aspects of the mobility process might be termed the social inadequacy of aggregate individual models. Existing aggregate individual models might also be criticized from the opposite perspective: they do not permit sufficient variation in individual mobility behavior. Usually the probability law which governs individual mobility behavior depends only on the status category presently occupied, other social variables together with previous mobility experience being totally disregarded.

Lastly, existing aggregate individual models do not reflect the impact of social change on the mobility process. The parameters of these models remain

[11] Robert McGinnis: "A Stochastic Model of Social Mobility," *American Sociological Review*, October 1968, Vol. 33, N. 5, pp. 712–722; G. C. Myers, R. McGinnis, and G. Masnick: "The Duration of Residence Approach to a Dynamic Stochastic Model of Internal Migration: A Test of the Axiom of Cumulative Inertia," *Eugenics Quarterly*, 1967, Vol. 14, pp. 121–126; N. W. Henry, R. McGinnis, and H. W. Tegtmeyer: "A Finite Model of Mobility," Paper presented to the Population Association of America, annual meetings 1968; Robert McGinnis and John White: "Simulation Experiments on a Stochastic Attraction Model," Unpublished manuscript, 1967.
[12] McGinnis: *op. cit.*, p. 716.

stationary over time, and the predictions they generate approach an equilibrium level. Thus, presently available aggregate individual models portray static rather than dynamic social systems.

□ 4. STRUCTURAL MODELS OF MOBILITY: A CRITICAL REVIEW

Structural models, in contrast to aggregate individual mobility models, treat the mobility process on the macrosocial level: they assert the existence of structural constraints which limit individual mobility patterns. To date, the most important constraint which structural models have considered is that imposed by the distribution of available status positions. Individual mobility must produce results which conform to this distribution, and, consequently, the mobility behavior of different persons cannot be entirely independent. Future structural models will no doubt consider other social constraints in addition to those stemming from the overall status distribution.

The quasi-perfect mobility model developed successively by Harrison White and Leo Goodman was one of the first structural formulations.[13] Quasi-perfect mobility is best understood with reference to the notion of perfect mobility which applies if status destination is independent of status origin. When a frequency matrix $\{f_{ij}\}$ manifests perfect mobility, it is possible to define a set of row multipliers, R_i, and a set of column multipliers, C_j, so that each element of the frequency matrix equals the product of corresponding row and column multipliers. Thus,

$$f_{ij} = R_i C_j. \qquad i, j = 1, \ldots, n \qquad (17)$$

Empirical mobility matrices rarely manifest perfect mobility. The quasi-perfect mobility model was constructed as a more realistic alternative to the perfect mobility formulation which retained certain of the latter's characteristics.

According to Harrison White's version, quasi-perfect mobility exists if status origin has no effect on the status destination of persons abandoning their initial status position. If quasi-perfect mobility of this sort holds, it is possible to define row and column multipliers which generate all cells not on the main diagonal. Thus (17) must be modified in the following way:

$$f_{ij} = R_i C_j. \qquad i, j = 1, \ldots, n; i \neq j \qquad (18)$$

How can we assess whether an empirical mobility matrix manifests quasi-perfect mobility or not? For this purpose, White suggested a procedure which treats the row marginals, the column marginals, and the main diagonal of the empirical matrix as constraints, and assumes all allocations among the non-diagonal cells satisfying these constraints to be equally likely. The non-diagonal cell frequencies with the highest joint probability of occurrence are calculated,

[13] Harrison C. White: "Cause and Effect in Social Mobility Tables," *Behavioral Science*, Vol. 8, 1963, pp. 14–27; Leo A. Goodman: "On the Statistical Analysis of Mobility Tables," *American Journal of Sociology*. Vol. 70, pp. 564–585.

and these modal frequencies are compared with the frequencies actually observed. With only three status categories (i.e. a three by three mobility table) agreement between observed and expected frequencies was rather good. It declined rapidly, however, when more status categories were considered.

Leo Goodman modified White's formulation in several ways. First, he pointed out the theoretical distinction between treating the row and column marginals as constraints and failing to do so. Second, he generalized the quasi-perfect mobility concept so that any set of cells S, not simply those on the main diagonal, might act as constraints on the mobility process. Goodman's version of quasi-perfect mobility equation (18) has this form:

$$f_{ij} = R_i C_j. \qquad i, j = 1, \ldots, n; \ (i, j) \notin S \qquad (19)$$

Third, Goodman calculated expected rather than modal frequencies and compared these with empirical mobility data. Goodman's work injected greater generality, elegance, and simplicity into the quasi-perfect mobility model. It did not, however, alter the model's conceptual foundation or markedly improve its predictions. The quasi-perfect model remains today a seminal, if not entirely successful, attempt to depict the specifically sociological constraints operative on the mobility process.

The immobility decay model proposed by Joel Levine — following a suggestion by Frederick Mosteller — is related to the quasi-perfect mobility model.[14] The immobility decay model examines a mobility table using an analysis of variance paradigm which postulates row effects, column effects, and interaction effects. Row effects represent the impact of the origin status distribution on the mobility process, while column effects delineate the impact of the destination distribution. Origin and destination status distributions, argues Levine, are the outcome of non-sociological forces such as economic processes. The uniquely sociological dimension of mobility involves the interrelationships between status categories not attributable to exogenous factors. Levine identifies interaction effects as the distinctly sociological aspect of the mobility process.

The first step in constructing the immobility decay model involves defining a suitable measure of interaction. If rows and columns of a mobility table are multiplied by suitable constants, any desired set of row and column effects can be produced.[15] A satisfactory interaction measure should, therefore, remain invariant when rows and columns are multiplied by constants. The "odds ratio," defined as

[14] Joel H. Levine: *Measurement in the Study of Intergenerational Status Mobility.* Unpublished doctoral dissertation, Department of Social Relations, Harvard University, 1967; Frederick Mosteller: "Association and Estimation in Contingency Tables," *Journal of the American Statistical Association.* Vol. 63, N. 321, March 1968, pp. 1–28.

[15] W. Edwards Deming and Frederick F. Stephan: "On a Least Squares Adjustment of a Sampled Frequency Table when the Expected Marginal Totals are Known," *Annals of Mathematical Statistics.* 11, 1940, pp. 427–444.

$$O_{ij} = \frac{f_{ii} \cdot f_{jj}}{f_{ij} \cdot f_{ji}}, \qquad i, j = 1, \ldots, n; \, i \neq j \tag{20}$$

where $\{f_{ij}\}$ is the mobility frequency matrix, is such a measure. Note that

$$\frac{(R_i C_i f_{ii})(R_j C_j f_{jj})}{(R_i C_j f_{ij})(R_j C_i f_{ji})} = \frac{f_{ii} f_{jj}}{f_{ij} f_{ji}} = O_{ij},$$

which demonstrates the odds ratio is in fact invariant under multiplication by row and column constants.

A distinct odds ratio corresponds to each pair of status categories and points in time. It is appropriate to symbolize the odds ratio between status categories S_i and S_j over the time interval s, t as $O_{ij}(s, t)$. If no change of status category occurs, the odds ratio is infinite, while under perfect mobility it equals unity. With this relationship in mind Levine uses the odds ratio as a measure of status immobility.

According to the immobility decay model, the invariant aspects of mobility are best revealed by the odds ratio. For fixed status levels S_i and S_j the model asserts the odds ratio $O_{ij}(s, t)$ declines exponentially as a function of $t - s$. (Thus the name immobility decay model.) When tested against the Blumen, Kogan, and McCarthy data, the decay hypothesis was strongly confirmed, and there is reason to believe further exploration of the interaction methods proposed by Levine will prove fruitful.[16]

Nevertheless, the immobility decay model has some important limitations. Although Levine conceives it as a superior alternative to aggregate individual formulations, and particularly to Markovian models, it offers a substantially less complete picture of the mobility process than the latter. It is less useful, for example, in projecting future status distributions and does not permit calculation of transition likelihoods. Moreover, Markovian models also predict an odds ratio decay which under certain circumstances may closely parallel the exponential form Levine postulates.[17] Finally, the theoretical as opposed to the statistical justification for use of the odds ratio measure remains cloudy and requires further clarification.

The opportunity chain model developed by Harrison White is the most recent structural formulation known to the author.[18] The opportunity chain model postulates a system with a well-defined set of jobs classified among a set of status categories and called a "career frame." The model deals with flows of two kinds: flows of men between status categories and flows of jobs or opportunities opposite in direction to the flow of manpower. Consider the

---

[16] For further analysis of contingency tables using interaction methods see Leo A. Goodman: "How to Ransack Social Mobility Tables and Other Kinds of Cross-Classification Tables," *American Journal of Sociology*. 75, July 1969, pp. 1–40.

[17] The present author will discuss this in a future paper.

[18] Harrison C. White: "Control and Evolution of Aggregate Personnel: Flows of Men and Jobs," *Administrative Science Quarterly*. 14, March 1969, pp. 4–11 and Harrison C. White: *Opportunity Chains*. Cambridge, Mass.: Harvard University Press, 1970.

relationship between these two flows more closely. A person only moves from category S_j to category S_i if he leaves a job in the former status level and fills a job in the latter level. Thus, there has been a flow of manpower from S_j to S_i and a flow of opportunity in the opposite direction from S_i to S_j.

Let $J_i(t)$ be the number of jobs in category S_i at time t and let $N_i(t)$ be the number of persons in S_i at t $(i = 1, \ldots, n)$. Define

$$V_i(t) = J_i(t) - N_i(t). \qquad i = 1, \ldots, n \qquad (21)$$

Clearly $V_i(t)$ equals the number of vacant jobs in S_i at time t, and $V_i(t)$ is assumed to be non-negative. The opportunity chain model assumes the overall rate at which men move into the vacant jobs of category S_i is a constant v (independent of the status category considered) times the current number of vacant jobs $V_i(t)$. Secondly, the opportunity chain model assumes q_{ij}, the probability a vacancy moves from S_i to S_j given a transition out of S_i occurs, is constant over time. These two assumptions imply $vq_{ij}V_i(t)$ is the overall rate at which persons from stratum S_j fill vacant jobs in stratum S_i.

Consider the simplest kind of opportunity chain model which arises if neither men nor jobs ever leave the career frame considered. Such a closed career frame implies that

$$\sum_{j=1}^{n} q_{ij} = 1, \qquad i = 1, \ldots, n \qquad (22)$$

and that the number of jobs in each status category is constant over time

$$J_i(t) = J_i. \qquad i = 1, \ldots, n \qquad (23)$$

Under the assumption of a closed career frame, the following system of differential equations may be derived from the basic postulates of the opportunity chain model:

$$\frac{dN_i(t)}{dt} = v\left[V_i(t) - \sum_{k=1}^{n} V_k(t)q_{ki}\right]. \qquad i = 1, \ldots, n \qquad (24)$$

The first term on the right side of (24) gives the total rate at which persons are entering S_i to fill vacancies there, while the second term gives the total rate at which persons are leaving S_i to fill vacancies in other status categories.

If the number of jobs in each category is known and if the number of persons in each category at time zero is also known, then standard methods will suffice to solve for $N_i(t)$ and $V_i(t)$ using (21), (23), and (24).

The more realistic assumption of an open career frame permits persons to enter and leave the system and also permits jobs to be created and terminated. Equations (22) and (23) do not hold for an open career frame. The differential equations corresponding to an open career frame are a bit more complicated than those in (24), but the basic principles are the same. General solution of the equations produced by the assumption of an open career frame is quite difficult. Using certain simplifying assumptions, White is able to derive equilibrium values for $J_i(t)$, $N_i(t)$, and $V_i(t)$.

The opportunity chain model is particularly interesting as an attempt to reconcile the effect of social structure with the process of individual movement. The line of attack suggested by White permits the incorporation of many complexities which actually characterize stratification systems. It clearly deserves further development.

The limitations of the opportunity chain model derive from three sources: the shortcomings of the career frame concept, the difficulty in obtaining analytic solutions of the equations generated, and the problem of parameter estimation. The concept of career frame is most applicable to certain formal organizations (like the Episcopal churches studied by White) which preserve the integrity of specific occupational positions over time. The opportunity chain model seems most appropriate for describing mobility processes within such organizations. It is doubtful, however, whether the career frame notion can be applied to broader, less structured contexts. Thus, the utility of the opportunity chain model for the kind of mobility processes traditionally of most interest to sociologists is rather uncertain.

The more realistic versions of the opportunity chain model also pose greater mathematical difficulties. Simplifying assumptions are sometimes appropriate, and on other occasions numerical or analog methods can be used. However, a satisfactory mobility model must surely generate predictions other than simple equilibrium values. Lastly, it seems the data required to estimate the parameters of the opportunity chain model are difficult to collect and are unavailable in most ordinary mobility studies.

A number of common themes run through the literature on structural mobility models: one theme is a vigorous rejection of the atomistic conception implicit in aggregate individual formulations, a second is the search for the uniquely sociological component of mobility as opposed to those aspects which might be attributed to economic or social psychological processes, and yet a third theme centers around the determination to avoid mathematical gimmickry as a way of dodging essentially theoretical or conceptual issues.

Structural models have called attention to the fact that institutional mechanisms regulate the process of social mobility. Although existing structural models depict mechanisms which may not be actually operative, the theoretical importance of institutional controls on mobility can no longer be doubted. For all their conceptual ingenuity, however, structural models do not rival their aggregate individual counterparts in flexibility, ease of application, and ability to generate projections about the future. At the present juncture the central task of mathematical mobility theory is to synthesize the depiction of atomistic mobility behavior implicit in aggregate individual models with the sensitivity to social constraint and interdependency displayed by structural theories. White's opportunity chain model certainly represents one step in this direction. Perhaps the models considered below represent yet another.

□ 5. CONTINUOUS TIME MARKOV MODELS: GENERAL THEORY

The work discussed in the following sections constitutes a sociological theory in progress. A general theoretical framework is developed within which several models are constructed. These models simultaneously attempt to represent real mobility data and to eliminate certain conceptual difficulties associated with the previous formulations. On neither score are they entirely successful; they indicate, however, successive stages in an ongoing process of theory construction the current directions of which are described in the concluding section.

The basic theoretical orientation which permeates this paper is that of aggregate individual models. Subsequently, modifications of this orientation are made with the intention of incorporating certain features characteristic of the structural perspective. The aggregate individual orientation is a foundation, on the one hand because of its mathematical tractability and, on the other, because of a flexibility which permits incorporation of many constraints thought to be operative on career mobility.

More specifically, continuous time finite state Markov chains provide the theoretical framework we will use. Intragenerational mobility occurs continuously, and it seems natural to model it with a continuous time process. More importantly, however, the regularities governing the mobility process are easier to express and understand with concepts arising only in continuous time formulations. The basic rationale for the continuous time approach is the theoretical simplicity which results.

According to the path independence assumption for continuous time Markov chains stated in (12), the probability of occupying any particular status category depends entirely on the last known status category occupied. Most properties of continuous time Markov chains follow from the path independence assumption. Appendix A carries out a mathematical analysis of continuous time finite state Markov chains: here we present only the highlights of this analysis.

For our purposes, the main distinction between discrete and continuous time Markov models arises because the latter can be characterized by means of their instantaneous properties. We use transition rates rather than transition probabilities in working with continuous time models. A transition rate means a flow of persons between two status categories at a particular point in time. In mathematical terms, a transition rate is a derivative.

Let $p_{ij}(t, h)$ equal the probability a person occupies stratum S_j at time t given that he occupied stratum S_i at time h. In symbols,

$$p_{ij}(t, h) = p(x_t = S_j \mid x_h = S_i). \qquad \begin{array}{l} i, j = 1, \ldots, n \\ t > h \geq 0 \end{array} \tag{25}$$

The transition rate $a_{ij}(h)$ between S_i and S_j at time h equals the derivative of $p_{ij}(t, h)$ with respect to t evaluated at $t = h$. Thus

$$\lim_{t \to h} \frac{p_{ij}(t, h) - p_{ij}(h, h)}{t - h} = \left. \frac{\partial p_{ij}(t, h)}{\partial t} \right|^{t=h}$$

$$\equiv a_{ij}(h). \qquad \begin{array}{l} i, j = 1, \ldots n \\ h \geq 0 \end{array} \tag{26}$$

In general, we cannot be sure this derivative actually exists. The derivative always exists, however, if the continuous time Markov chain is stationary.

The reader will recall from earlier discussion that stationarity holds if the probability of a transition depends only on the length of the time interval between the two points considered. If stationarity holds, we may write, as in (4),

$$p_{ij}(t, h) = p_{ij}(t - h). \qquad i, j = 1, \ldots, n \qquad (27)$$
$$t > h \geq 0$$

Under this condition the transition rate between S_i and S_j equals

$$\lim_{t \to 0} \frac{p_{ij}(t) - p_{ij}(0)}{t} = \frac{dp_{ij}(t)}{dt}\bigg|^{t=0} \qquad (28)$$
$$= a_{ij}. \qquad i, j = 1, \ldots, n$$

Thus the transition rates of a stationary continuous time Markov chain are constant.

Let us consider the properties of transition rates for stationary Markov chains. It is easy to show that the following relationship holds:

$$a_{ij} \begin{cases} \geq 0 & \text{if } i \neq j \\ \leq 0 & \text{if } i = j \end{cases}. \qquad i, j = 1, \ldots, n \qquad (29)$$

To comprehend this relationship, recall that a_{ij} equals the rate at which $p_{ij}(t)$ is changing when $t = 0$. Moving from one stratum to another requires some time: over an interval of length zero no transitions can occur. Thus,

$$p_{ij}(0) = \begin{cases} 0 & \text{if } i \neq_e j \\ 1 & \text{if } i = j \end{cases}. \qquad i, j = 1, \ldots, n \qquad (30)$$

Since $p_{ij}(0)$ assumes its minimum possible value (zero) when $i \neq j$ and its maximum possible value (one) when $i = j$, it can only increase or remain stable in the former case and decrease or remain stable in the latter case. This explains the relationship stated in (29). Another way of stating this is the following: At the start of a time interval the only possible flow from S_i to S_j is a positive one which puts persons formerly in S_i into S_j if $i \neq j$ and a negative one by which the number of persons in S_j decreases if $i = j$.

A second important relationship involving the transition rates is the following:

$$-a_{ii} = \sum_{\substack{j=1 \\ j \neq 1}}^{n} a_{ij} \qquad i = 1, \ldots, n \qquad (31)$$

which clearly implies

$$\sum_{j=1}^{n} a_{ij} = 0. \qquad i = 1, \ldots, n \qquad (32)$$

This relationship reflects the fact that the status categories $S_1, \ldots, S_n$ are mutually exclusive and collectively exhaustive on the one hand, and that we are not permitting persons to enter or leave the system on the other. Thus, a person leaving one status category must enter another, while a person entering a status category must have departed from some category of the system. Since transition rates are negative for departures and positive for arrivals, and since the flow of arrivals from a given origin to all possible destinations must equal the flow of departures from the given origin, the rationale underlying (31) and (32) is apparent.

It is frequently convenient to array the transition rates in a matrix form. Define matrix A as

$$A \equiv \{a_{ij}\}_{i,j=1}^{n}. \tag{33}$$

A is sometimes called the infinitesimal generator of the continuous time stationary Markov chain. Equations (29), (31), and (32) reveal the main properties of matrix A. Equation (29) asserts the non-diagonal elements of A are non-negative while the diagonal elements are non-positive. Equation (32) implies the rows of A sum to zero. In fact, any matrix whose rows sum to zero and whose non-diagonal elements are non-negative can function as an infinitesimal generator.

The role of the infinitesimal generator in continuous time models parallels the role of the transition matrix in discrete Markov models. The infinitesimal generator together with the initial distribution provides a complete characterization of a continuous time stationary Markov model. Using the infinitesimal generator it is possible to calculate the transition probabilities predicted by the model over any time interval desired. This calculation is made by means of the following formula derived in Appendix A:

$$P(t) = \sum_{k=0}^{\infty} \frac{t^k}{k!} A^k. \tag{34}$$

The power series on the right converges for all square matrices A. (The summation, however, must usually be performed by computer.)

The problem of inferring the appropriate infinitesimal generator on the basis of the transition matrix $P(t)$ has no general solution. The most useful single formula is the following:

$$A = \frac{1}{t} \sum_{i=1}^{\infty} \frac{(-1)^{i-1}}{i} [P(t) - I]^i. \tag{35}$$

This expression has three drawbacks: First, it does not always converge. It will not converge, for example, if the matrix $P(t)$ is singular (i.e. the determinant of $P(t)$ equals zero). Second, even if it does converge, (35) may not provide the best estimate of the infinitesimal generator. Third, the formula does not enable us to place restrictions on the structure of the infinitesimal generator as we sometimes wish to do.

The failure of (35) to converge for all transition matrices $P(t)$ reflects the fact that not all such matrices can arise from a continuous time stationary Markov chain. The estimation problem and the problem of restrictions arise because several different infinitesimal generators may produce the same transition matrix.

It is possible to simulate a continuous time stationary Markov model on the basis of the initial distribution and the infinitesimal generator. Description of how such a simulation would be executed may clarify the nature of the continuous time model. We will exploit two aspects of the infinitesimal generator A. The random variable which equals length of stay in state S_i $(i = 1, \ldots, n)$ has an exponential distribution with parameter $|a_{ii}|$. When a transition out of S_i occurs, the process will move into S_j $(i \neq j)$ with probability $a_{ij}/|a_{ii}|$.

We can now construct sample careers in the following way: Sampling from the initial distribution assumed known determines an original status category. Let S_i indicate the stratum thus selected. To determine length of stay in S_i, sample from an exponential distribution with parameter $|a_{ii}|$. Next, select the status category entered after leaving S_i by sampling from the distribution

$$p_{ij} = \frac{a_{ij}}{|a_{ii}|} \cdot \qquad j = 1, \ldots, n; i \neq j$$

Let S_j be the state thus obtained. Determine length of stay in S_j by sampling from an exponential distribution with parameter $|a_{jj}|$. The stratum entered after leaving S_j is selected by sampling from the distribution

$$p_{jk} = \frac{a_{jk}}{|a_{jj}|} \cdot \qquad k = 1, \ldots, n; k \neq j$$

This procedure continues until the sum of the staying times obtained exceeds a previously designated career length.

The general discussion of the continuous time Markov model need not proceed further, as the results subsequently required have been discussed above. As indicated earlier, the continuous time Markov process provides a framework for theory construction. The mobility models we propose, though based on this framework, are not identical with it. One model restricts the set of permissible transitions. Another relaxes the stationarity assumption. The third redefines the state space. Future development of mobility theory along these lines will involve more extensive modifications of the basic continuous time model, some of which are mentioned in the final section.

Philosophy of science teaches us that theory construction should proceed by a method of successive approximation, each formulation striving to rectify the failings of its predecessors. The models presented below represent temporally successive attempts to construct an adequate model of mobility. They do not, however, represent a progression of success or improvement; each reflects a somewhat divergent conception of the mobility process. Collectively they indicate the variety of models conceivable within the continuous time Markovian framework.

□ **6. THE BIRTH AND DEATH PROCESS MOBILITY MODEL**

The first model of mobility we consider is the finite state birth and death process. This is a stationary continuous time Markovian model which arranges strata in a definite status order and permits direct transitions only between adjacent status categories. The birth and death process model is in some ways the continuous time analog of the discrete random walk. The rationale undergirding this model draws support from at least two sources.

First, almost all empirical studies of intragenerational mobility suggest that the extent of mobility between two social strata varies inversely with the status distance between them. Such an effect would arise if direct transitions could only occur between adjacent strata. Under these circumstances movements between non-adjacent strata could take place only after entering all intermediate strata. Hence, a constraint of the sort which characterizes the birth and death model might explain the observed relationship between status and mobility.

The second source from which the birth and death conception draws support is less conventional, but not less convincing. The folklore of modern American society talks about the ladder of success and treats upward mobility as a series of steps, each relatively small but which collectively can elevate a person far above his original station. Downward mobility is likewise regarded as a stepwise process although no comparable idiom exists for it. Assuming such collective images crystalize widespread folk wisdom, they lend additional credence to the birth and death formulation.

The constraints implied by the birth and death model appear most clearly in the infinitesimal generator of the process which assumes the following form:

$$a_{ij} \begin{cases} \geq 0 \text{ if } |i - j| = 1 \\ \leq 0 \text{ if } i = j \\ = 0 \text{ if } |i - j| > 1 \end{cases} \qquad i, j = 1, \ldots, n \qquad (36)$$

or written as a matrix,

$$A = \begin{cases} a_{11} & a_{12} & 0 & 0 & \ldots & 0 \\ a_{12} & a_{22} & a_{23} & 0 & \ldots & 0 \\ 0 & a_{32} & a_{33} & a_{34} & \ldots & 0 \\ \vdots & \vdots & & & & \\ 0 & 0 & \ldots & \ldots & a_{n,n-1} & a_{nn} \end{cases}. \qquad (37)$$

Any continuous time Markov model with such an infinitesimal generator is a finite state birth and death process.

The criteria appropriate for the evaluation of the birth and death process model differ from those relevant to the other models presented herein. That the birth and death model will not provide a completely satisfactory description of mobility is a foregone conclusion since stationary continuous time models with even more degrees of freedom do not furnish such a description. The important question is whether the performance of the birth and death model is significantly worse than that of continuous time models with less stringent constraints. If not, the stepwise movement of the birth and death model may indeed account for the bulk of career mobility.

Estimation of the infinitesimal generator is the main technical problem confronting the birth and death model. The estimation methods used are discussed in Appendix C. Once the infinitesimal generator has been estimated, (34) can be used to obtain transition probabilities over any time interval desired.

The birth and death process model was applied to career mobility data collected by Peter Blau and Otis Dudley Duncan on American men. Appendix B presents the empirical data used and discusses their general characteristics. Blau and Duncan obtained mobility data on four age cohorts (in March 1962): 25–34 years, 35–44 years, 45–54 years, and 55–64 years. The birth and death model was applied independently to the transition matrices of each cohort.

The author divided all persons into five status categories based on the Duncan status score of their occupation. These categories were the following: $S_1 =$ 80–96 (professionals), $S_2 = $ 60–79 (upper white collar — semi-professional), $S_3 = $ 40–59 (skilled manual and lower white collar), $S_4 = $ 20–39 (semi-skilled manual), $S_5 = $ 0–19 (unskilled manual). The labels given these categories are very approximate and are intended mainly to provide the reader with some notion of the occupations included in each stratum.

Application of formula (34) requires an estimate of t, the length of a cohort's presence in the labor force. To obtain t we assumed all persons entered the labor force at age 18 and treated the midpoint of the age interval defining a cohort as the age of all cohort members. Thus, 12, 22, 32, and 42 were the values of t assigned to the 25–34, 35–44, 45–54, and 55–64 cohorts respectively.[19] Table 5 presents the infinitesimal generator estimated for each cohort under the assumptions of the birth and death model. Table 6 gives the outflow percentages predicted with these generators.

Comparison between Table 6 and Table B1 of Appendix B indicates that the predictions of the birth and death model differ considerably from the Blau and Duncan data. Like several other Markovian formulations, the birth and death model consistently underestimates elements on the main diagonal. In fact, the bulk of the predictive error occurs in diagonal cells or cells immediately adjacent to them. This lends some support to the restrictions imposed by the birth and death model, but signifies the operation of other factors as well.

Comparison between the birth and death model and other continuous time models is equally important as comparison with empirical data. If no con-

---

[19] Although it is necessary to assign a single value of t for each cohort, this raises some serious problems. The actual ages at which cohort members enter the labor force may differ by as much as ten years. Since each cohort is defined by a ten year age interval, this means length of presence in the labor force may vary by up to twenty years among members of a single cohort. Moreover, persons entering the labor force at higher status levels are likely to enter at higher ages. Thus variance in length of presence is not only substantial, but is nonrandomly distributed among status levels. The Blau and Duncan age cohort data are much less homogeneous than would be desirable for testing continuous time models even when the synthetic cohort interpretation is avoided.

■ **TABLE 5 / Birth and Death Model Infinitesimal Generators for 25–34, 35–44, 45–54, and 55–64 Cohorts in that Order Using *t* = 12, 22, 32, and 42 Respectively**

−.0460 −.0320 −.0260 −.0220	.0460 .0320 .0260 .0220			
.0660 .0299 .0165 .0140	−.1398 −.0867 −.0584 −.0494	.0738 .0568 .0419 .0354		
	.1250 .1113 .0659 .0557	−.2230 −.1711 −.1064 −.0990	.0980 .0598 .0405 .0343	
		.1447 .0931 .0754 .0638	−.2195 −.1396 −.1037 −.0877	.0784 .0465 .0283 .0239
			.0683 .0490 .0273 .0231	−.0683 −.0490 −.0273 −.0231

straints are placed on the infinitesimal generator, the resulting model will reproduce the Blau and Duncan transition matrix exactly. This is because the number of free parameters equals the number of data points. If the constraints imposed by the birth and death model are relaxed one at a time, the degree of predictive improvement is very gradual at each step. On the other hand, the imposition of additional constraints over and above those entailed by the birth and death model sharply increases predictive error. Quite possibly, the birth and death formulation provides the optimum predictive power per parameter for any continuous time stationary Markov mobility model.

Examination of Table 6 reveals an important regularity. The entries in each cell decrease monotonically. The consistency of this trend suggests a reduction in overall mobility with advancing age. Such a reduction might result from non-homogeneity like that proposed by the mover-stayer model, a mechanism of the sort operative in the Cornell mobility model, or a non-stationarity in the mobility process itself. The exponential decline model discussed next pursues the latter possibility.

□ **7. THE EXPONENTIAL DECLINE MOBILITY MODEL**

If two existing Markovian formulations account for the decline of mobility

■ **TABLE 6** / **Outflow Percentages Predicted by Birth and Death Model for 25–34, 35–44, 45–54, and 55–64 Cohorts in that Order Using $t = 12, 22, 32,$ and 42 Respectively**

Status category of job in March 1962

		S_1	S_2	S_3	S_4	S_5
	S_1	67.5	23.4	6.6	1.9	0.5
		59.0	28.4	9.0	2.8	0.8
		51.9	31.7	12.0	3.5	0.9
		50.2	36.2	9.0	3.7	1.0
	S_2	33.6	37.7	18.1	7.6	2.9
		26.5	41.9	19.3	8.6	3.7
		20.2	42.8	23.9	9.4	3.7
		23.6	46.7	16.6	9.5	3.6
Status category of first job	S_3	16.1	30.7	26.3	16.8	10.1
		16.5	37.9	22.6	14.0	9.1
		12.0	37.7	27.5	14.1	8.7
		13.4	37.9	20.2	17.4	11.2
	S_4	6.9	19.1	24.8	24.2	25.0
		8.0	26.4	21.8	21.3	22.6
		6.4	27.4	26.2	19.1	20.8
		6.2	24.6	19.7	24.2	25.3
	S_5	1.6	6.6	13.6	22.9	55.4
		2.5	11.8	14.9	23.8	47.1
		1.7	10.5	15.7	20.1	52.1
		1.4	7.9	10.6	21.3	58.9

Identification of status categories

	Range of occupational status score	Approximate job description
S_1	80–96	Professional
S_2	60–79	Upper white collar — semi-professional
S_3	40–59	Skilled manual and lower white collar
S_4	20–39	Semi-skilled manual
S_5	0–19	Unskilled manual

with age, why is it necessary to construct a new Markov model for this purpose? The mover-stayer model, or any non-homogenous Markov model, cannot explain the kind of intragenerational mobility decline actually observed. For example, correlations of occupational prestige over a fixed time interval increase with the age of the cohort considered.[20] This result is not consistent with the

[20] Unpublished research of Robert W. Hodge and Angela Lane, Department of Sociology, University of Chicago.

mover-stayer model or other formulations based on simple non-homogeneity. Although the Cornell mobility model might in principle explain these correlations, its current shape does not permit application to empirical data. Hence, another Markovian formulation is by no means superfluous.

The exponential decline model relaxes the stationarity assumption. Specifically, it assumes all elements of the infinitesimal generator decline at a uniform exponential rate. Thus

$$a_{ij}(t) = a_{ij}e^{-ct} \qquad i, j = 1, 2, \ldots, n \tag{38}$$

or

$$A(t) = e^{-ct}A \tag{39}$$

where c is a scalar constant giving the rate of exponential decline. The uniform character of mobility decline implies that movements between strata become less frequent with advancing age, but given that a change of strata occurs, the probabilities of specific transitions remain fixed.

Under conditions of uniform exponential decline — or uniform change of any kind — transition probabilities can be calculated with slight modifications of the techniques used in the stationary case. Since all elements of $A(t)$ change at an identical rate, the exponential decline effect can be achieved by holding the infinitesimal generator constant at its initial value A and adjusting the time variable in an appropriate way. Because all instantaneous mobility rates change according to the exponential function e^{-ct}, the differential dt becomes $e^{-ct} dt$. Hence, the outcome of the non-stationary process governed by the infinitesimal generator $A(t)$ after s time units is equivalent to the outcome of the stationary process with generator A after

$$\int_0^s e^{-ct} dt = \frac{1 - e^{-cs}}{c} \tag{40}$$

time units. Substituting (40) for t in (34) yields

$$P(s) = \sum_{k=0}^{\infty} \left[\frac{A^k \left(\dfrac{1 - e^{-cs}}{c} \right)^k}{k!} \right], \tag{41}$$

which permits calculation of any desired transition probabilities.

The exponential decline model has parameters of two kinds: the initial instantaneous transition rates $\{a_{ij}\}$, and c, the rate of exponential decline. Estimation techniques are discussed in Appendix C.

A meaningful test of the exponential decline model requires time series mobility data. Unfortunately, no such data are currently available. As a substitute we will treat the Blau and Duncan mobility data as information about a single synthetic cohort at various stages of its occupation career. Such a synthetic cohort interpretation is fraught with difficulties, some of which are discussed in Appendix B. The four transition matrices presented in Table B1 will be regarded as the outflow percentages of the synthetic cohort after 12, 22, 32, and 42 years in the labor force respectively. The non-stationary infinitesimal generator estimated for the exponential decline model appears in Table 7, and the outflow percentages computed with this generator appear in Table 8.

■ TABLE 7 / Exponential Decline Model Infinitesimal Generator A(t)

−.0485	.0347	.0200	.0017	.0021
.0379	−.1116	.0524	.0152	.0061
.0196	.1138	−.2466	.0866	.0266
.0042	.0477	.1279	−.2969	.1171
.0000	.0065	.0397	.1249	−.1711

$\exp(.1494)t$

The exponential decline model achieves a substantially better fit to the Blau and Duncan data than did the birth and death model. In addition, the predictive errors of the former are not nearly as systematic as those of the latter. When applied to the synthetic cohort, the exponential decline model predicts a rapid reduction in mobility. Very few transitions between strata occur after the cohort has been in the labor force twelve years, and mobility virtually halts after twenty-two years. Although the swift mobility slowdown does not cause the model to deviate markedly from the observed outflow percentages, such a precipitous mobility decline is implausible and can be refuted by abundant evidence.

This excessive rate of decline is not, however, an intrinsic fault of the exponential decline model. The rate is easily reduced by lowering the value of c (which in the above case equals .1494). The relatively large estimate of c may simply reflect the inadequacies of the synthetic cohort as a representation of actual intragenerational mobility.

□ 8. THE ABSORBING STATE MOBILITY MODEL

The third continuous time mobility model we consider, the absorbing state model, also predicts a decline in mobility with age but offers a somewhat different rationale. This model redefines the state space by assigning two states to each status level. One is a transient state from which persons can move to other social strata. The other is an absorbing state in which persons entering become permanently fixed. An absorbing state can only be reached from the associated transient state, and all persons are assumed to be in transient states at the start of the mobility process. A diagram of the absorbing state model for the case of five strata appears in Figure 1.

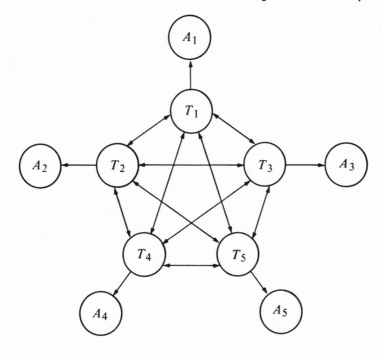

Notation:

(T_i) = transient state corresponding to strata S_i

(A_i) = absorbing state corresponding to strata S_i

→ = transition possibility

■ **FIGURE 1.** A Diagram of the Absorbing State Model for the Case of Five Strata

The absorbing state model explains the seeming decline of mobility with age by the progressive concentration of a cohort in absorbing as opposed to transient states. Also the absorbing state model permits more varied forms of non-stationarity than does the exponential decline formulation. The decline of all mobility rates need not be uniform. The infinitesimal generator of a five strata absorbing state model is a ten by ten matrix which is conveniently partitioned into four five by five matrices in the following way:

		transient states	absorbing states
$A =$	transient states {	B	C
	absorbing states {	O	O

Here B is a matrix with non-positive diagonal elements and non-negative elements elsewhere, C is a diagonal matrix, and O is a matrix of zeros.

In applying the absorbing state model we resort once more to a synthetic cohort interpretation of the Blau and Duncan data. The infinitesimal generator of an n strata model contains n^2 independent elements which must be estimated.

■ **TABLE 8** / **Outflow Percentages Predicted by Exponential Decline Model for 12, 22, 32, and 42 years in the Labor Force in that Order**

Status category of present job

		S_1	S_2	S_3	S_4	S_5
	S_1	74.1	14.6	7.2	2.3	1.8
		71.1	16.1	7.9	2.8	2.2
		70.4	16.5	8.0	2.9	2.2
		70.3	16.5	8.1	2.9	2.3
	S_2	14.7	60.4	14.1	6.5	4.4
		16.1	56.9	14.9	7.1	5.0
		16.4	56.2	15.0	7.3	5.2
		16.4	56.0	15.1	7.3	5.2
Status category of first job	S_3	9.1	29.5	35.0	15.6	10.9
		10.2	30.9	31.5	15.7	11.7
		10.5	31.1	30.9	15.7	11.9
		10.5	31.2	30.7	15.7	11.9
	S_4	4.7	19.2	22.8	30.6	22.8
		5.6	21.0	22.9	27.6	23.0
		5.8	21.4	22.9	27.0	23.0
		5.8	21.5	22.9	26.9	23.0
	S_5	2.1	10.3	16.1	24.0	47.6
		2.7	12.2	17.3	24.1	43.7
		2.9	12.6	17.5	24.1	42.9
		2.9	12.7	17.6	24.1	42.8

Identification of status categories

	Range of occupational status scores	Approximate job description
S_1	80–96	Professional
S_2	60–79	Upper white collar — semi-professional
S_3	40–59	Skilled manual and lower white collar
S_4	20–39	Semi-skilled manual
S_5	0–19	Unskilled manual

(Estimation techniques are discussed in the Appendix C.) Table 9 presents the infinitesimal generator computed for the absorbing state model. Table 10 gives the outflow percentages calculated with this generator.

■ **TABLE 9 / Estimated Infinitesimal Generator for the Absorbing State Model**

	T_1	T_2	T_3	T_4	T_5	A_1	A_2	A_3	A_4	A_5
T_1	$-.0364$	.0102	.0122	0	.0006	.0133	0	0	0	0
T_2	.0307	$-.1095$	.0304	.0116	0	0	.0367	0	0	0
T_3	.0098	.0544	$-.1417$	.0445	.0226	0	0	.0103	0	0
T_4	0	.0302	.0546	$-.1549$	.0622	0	0	0	.0078	0
T_5	0	0	.0338	.0627	$-.1125$	0	0	0	0	.0160
A_1	0	0	0	0	0	0	0	0	0	0
A_2	0	0	0	0	0	0	0	0	0	0
A_3	0	0	0	0	0	0	0	0	0	0
A_4	0	0	0	0	0	0	0	0	0	0
A_5	0	0	0	0	0	0	0	0	0	0

Unfortunately, the estimation procedure devised for the absorbing model requires several series which did not converge when applied to the synthetic cohort data. The infinitesimal generator presented in Table 9 was based entirely on the 25–34 cohort data. Consequently, the absorbing model accurately predicts synthetic cohort results at $t = 12$ but diverges progressively for larger values of t. Whether the convergence problem encountered here indicates an intrinsic failing of the estimation technique or an idiosyncrasy of the synthetic cohort results is not yet apparent.

The absorbing model predicts a somewhat less precipitous decrease in mobility than did the exponential decline formulation. This may, however, be an artifact of the estimation difficulties discussed above. Slow mobility decline is certainly not a necessary characteristic of the model.

According to the absorbing model, presence in a social stratum may signify presence in either the transient or the absorbing state corresponding to that stratum. We define the sojourning rate of a social stratum as the propensity to remain in the transient state associated with that stratum. On the other hand, a stratum's fixation rate is the rate of entry into its absorbing state. The concepts of sojourning and fixation rates suggest a typology of social strata. Sojourning and fixation refer respectively to the voluntaristic and non-voluntaristic aspects of social inertia. Sojourning implies inertia based on motivational inducements, while fixation suggests structurally enforced inertia. Dichotomizing and cross-classifying these notions yields the following typology:

Fixation Rates

		High	Low
Sojourn Rates	High	Retention Strata	Inducement Strata
	Low	Coercion Strata	Transitional Strata

Retention strata keep members both through motivational and structural devices; persons entering such strata are likely to remain. Conversely, transitional strata have very slight ability to retain members: they serve mainly as stepping stones between other strata. Coercion strata retain members by structural but not by motivational methods. They may, for example, constitute the highest status levels attainable by persons of a certain educational level. Inducement strata constrain persons by motivational factors. They sometimes establish a status floor beneath which a person need not sink. The absorbing state model may be useful not only as a representation of the mobility process, but also for the purpose of delineating the morphological structure of the stratification system.

In summarizing the continuous time models discussed above, it may be useful to compare the central ideas of each as they relate to mobility. The birth and death process model sought to assess the extent to which total mobility can be explained by stepwise movements up and down the status hierarchy. The results obtained with this model suggest much, but not all career mobility is explicable in this manner. The birth and death model might best be regarded as an effort to test a causal hypothesis rather than a proposed description of the mobility process as a whole.

The exponential decline model suggests the crucial aspect of intragenerational mobility is the process of aging which affects all transition possibilities in a uniform manner. This model depicts mobility as an aggregate individual process. A common pattern of mobility decline emerges because all persons undergo similar experiences with increasing age. Eventually an equilibrium is reached, not because various types of mobility transitions counterbalance one another, but because all mobility ceases. In fact, the equilibrium condition depends upon the rate of mobility decline and is usually not the same as that resulting when no decline occurs.

The absorbing state model views career mobility as a gradual realization of the consequences inherent in social structure. Here also an equilibrium condition is approached which permits no mobility. This equilibrium, however, arises as a realization of the potential inherent in the structure of the stratification system and is not, as with the exponential decline model, the result of changes occurring on the individual level.

■ TABLE 10 / Outflow Percentages Predicted by Absorbing State Model for 12, 22, 32, and 42 Years in the Labor Force in that Order

Status category of present job

		S_1	S_2	S_3	S_4	S_5
	S_1	79.5	9.5	7.4	2.0	1.6
		69.7	14.0	9.3	3.7	3.3
		63.4	17.3	10.0	4.7	4.6
		59.3	19.8	10.2	5.2	5.5
	S_2	19.3	57.8	12.6	6.6	3.7
		23.2	50.8	12.5	7.4	6.1
		24.0	49.9	11.7	7.3	7.1
		23.9	50.6	11.0	6.9	7.5
	S_3	10.2	26.1	34.2	15.9	13.6
		15.3	29.7	25.2	14.7	15.2
		18.0	31.5	22.4	13.0	15.1
		19.5	33.2	21.1	11.7	14.6
	S_4	4.9	19.3	20.9	31.4	23.5
		9.8	24.9	20.2	22.7	22.4
		13.3	28.1	18.5	19.4	20.7
		15.5	30.3	17.1	17.5	19.6
	S_5	2.5	10.1	18.2	22.4	46.7
		6.5	17.7	19.4	19.9	36.5
		10.1	22.2	18.2	17.0	32.6
		12.6	24.9	17.0	14.8	30.7

(left axis label: Status category of first job)

Identification of status categories

	Range of occupational status scores	Approximate job description
$S_1 = (T_1 + A_1)$	80–96	Professional
$S_2 = (T_2 + A_2)$	60–79	Upper white collar — semi-professional
$S_3 = (T_3 + A_3)$	40–59	Skilled manual and lower white collar
$S_4 = (T_4 + A_4)$	20–39	Semi-skilled manual
$S_5 = (T_5 + A_5)$	0–19	Unskilled manual

The conceptual distinctions between the exponential decline and absorbing models may seem abstruse and trivial. The future development of continuous time mobility models depends, however, on precisely these distinctions. If the notion undergirding the exponential model is accepted, future continuous time models will concentrate mainly on developing more complex forms of non-stationarity. If the idea behind the absorbing state model gains acceptance, future mobility models will proceed by elaborating the structure of the stratification system and then exploring the consequences of this structure.

□ **9. UNSOLVED PROBLEMS AND FUTURE DIRECTIONS**

The absence of adequate mobility data has been a serious handicap in constructing adequate models of career mobility. We have used synthetic cohort data mainly for the purpose of illustrating several alternative formulations. We do not suggest this artificial data provides a serious test of model adequacy except possibly in the case of the birth and death model. Procurement of adequate process data must be foremost on the agenda of any career mobility theorist.

Nevertheless, some progress has been made towards construction of a serviceable mobility theory. Although continuous models entail somewhat greater mathematical complexity than their discrete counterparts, they possess several important advantages which we now reiterate. The principles governing the mobility process are more likely to reveal themselves in instantaneous transition rates than in transition probabilities computed over some finite time interval which may reflect the outcome of several counteracting trends. Introduction of additional theoretical assumptions is often easier in continuous than in discrete time models. Moreover, the intrinsic character of intragenerational mobility suggests the use of continuous time formulations. Intragenerational mobility is well defined for any positive time interval and approaches zero as the interval considered contracts.

Mathematical complexity need not pose an insurmountable barrier to the further development of continuous time models: such models can be investigated by other than analytic methods. Earlier in this paper we gave intuitive descriptions of the Semi-Markov process and the continuous time stationary Markov chain. On the basis of these descriptions, appropriate model simulations could be constructed; in the future such simulations will furnish a central method for the investigation of mobility models. The complexity required for a realistic description of career mobility doubtless exceeds the capacities of traditional mathematical analysis.

The three models presented in this paper are all Markovian. The general Markovian assumption is considerably less restrictive than is sometimes supposed. A mobility model can be given a Markovian cast if an adequately descriptive state space exists such that transition probabilities depend only on the state presently occupied and the value of the time index. Whether future mobility models retain or reject the Markovian assumption is not of great moment: mobility theorists using analytic, as opposed to simulation, methods will require some such assumptions to render their models mathematically tractable. A more important consideration is whether future model builders will seek basic regularities in transition rates or in other aspects of the mobility process. Those models based upon postulated regularities in transition rates will inherit the Markovian tradition whether or not they use the path independence axiom.

In addition to developing a general conceptual framework, we have investigated two basic problems of mobility theory: the problem of structure and the problem of non-stationarity. The structure problem concerns the network of transitions permissible within the stratification system. The birth and death model attacked this problem indicating stationary transitions to adjacent strata alone were not sufficient to explain empirical mobility data. The exponential decline and absorbing models present two ways of dealing with the problem of age non-stationarity. Although the adequacy of these models remains uncertain, the strictly technical problems associated with them have been resolved sufficiently to permit routine application when appropriate mobility data becomes available.

Nevertheless, the task of developing a rigorous theory of intragenerational mobility has barely begun. We conclude this paper by taking stock of the major unsolved (or partially solved) problems of mobility theory and suggesting some possible lines of attack. Seven such problems will be discussed: identification, structure, heterogeneity, non-stationarity, constraint, interdependence, and antecedence.

Identification is the problem of determining the number and composition of social strata. This involves deciding which status positions should be combined in a single stratum and which should not. It may also entail imposing a rank order on the strata thus defined. In the past, identification of social strata has been accomplished in a rather opportunistic fashion, depending on the measures which happened to be available and on the partitions which rendered cell frequencies of transition matrices sufficiently large. An adequate theory must, however, identify the social strata suitable for the analysis of intragenerational mobility. This choice of strata should reveal as simply as possible the regularities operative in the career mobility process. The author is currently experimenting with latent structure analysis and smallest space analysis as methods of identifying appropriate strata sets. Ultimately, however, the problem of identification must be solved by a theory of career mobility rather than by generalized statistical routines.

The problem of structure involves determining the patterns of movement permissible between social strata and specifying the way in which particular strata function in the overall mobility process. The birth and death process model, for example, answered the problem of structure by permitting only transitions between adjacent status categories. Thus, each stratum functioned as a rung in a mobility ladder. At present we are searching for methods which do not require an *a priori* assumption about the nature of permissible movements between occupational strata. A satisfactory answer to the problem of structure must await a solution to the problem of identification.

The problem of heterogeneity arises because not all persons obey the same type of mobility process and, even if they do, the parameters of the process are not the same. The mover-stayer model attempts to cope with this problem, but it almost certainly understates the actual extent of heterogeneity.

It is not presently clear how to deal with the heterogeneity existent even in the most homogeneous sample. The author has taken two slightly different approaches to the heterogeneity problem: One approach partitions the population into a number of mobility classes, each of which obeys a distinct Markov chain. Although we have been able to establish a lower bound on the number of mobility classes, most technical problems associated with this multi-class Markov model remain unsolved.[21] The second approach operates within a continuous time framework. It assumes that the eigenvectors of the infinitesimal generator for the mobility process are constant over the entire population but that the eigenvalues are distributed in a probabilistic fashion. This second formulation is in a very early state of development.

The problem of non-stationarity is one of representing the changes which occur in the mobility process over time. Non-stationarity occurs in two forms: age non-stationarity and time non-stationarity. The nature of the non-stationarity problem is most easily comprehended through the concept of stationarity. Age stationarity exists if the transition rates of a cohort are unaffected by increasing age. Time stationarity exists if transition rates at each age remain fixed over time. Age stationarity implies that each cohort follows a stationary mobility process, but the mobility processes of different age cohorts need not be identical. Time stationarity asserts that all cohorts obey the same mobility process, which may be non-stationary. The problem of non-stationarity exists because neither age nor time stationarity characterizes the empirical mobility process. The exponential decline and absorbing state models are both attempts to deal with the problem of age non-stationarity. Future models must separate the effects of age and time non-stationarity and must develop more general methods for representing these phenomena.

The problem of constraint arises because exogenous conditions restrict the mobility process. Preeminent among these are the limitations imposed by population size, age distribution, occupational structure, and geographic distribution of the labor force. Solving the problem of constraint involves constructing models which represent the effects of these exogenous factors on the mobility process. In the case of career mobility the impact of occupational structure is particularly important. To deal with this issue, the author hopes to erect a model which combines basic Markovian notions with those of the quasi-perfect mobility model. One aim of this formulation is to provide better procedures for distinguishing structural mobility (i.e. mobility induced by changes in the occupational structure of society) from circulation mobility (i.e. mobility which would occur even if occupational structure remained constant). Another objective is to define and estimate "intrinsic" mobility rates which remain invariant under all sets of exogenous constraints.

The problem of interdependence is more subtle but not less important than the others discussed in this section. Most existing mobility models treat the career trajectories of different persons either as independent or as related exclusively through exogenous constraints on the mobility process. The career patterns of different persons may, however, be directly related. For example, the careers of some people may establish patterns which others then follow, or

---

[21] Thomas F. Mayer: "Multi-Class Markov Models and the Rank Criterion," unpublished mimeographed paper.

the upward mobility of one person may facilitate the upward mobility of his friends, etc. Representation of such occurrences and their impact on the mobility process defines the problem of interdependence. Future mobility models must move beyond the atomistic treatment of individuals and toward a conceptualization which reflects the interrelated aspects of mobility.

How does past mobility pattern affect future mobility? This is the problem of antecedence. Most Markov mobility models simply dismiss the problem of antecedence by assuming that past mobility history has no influence on future mobility over and above that exerted by present status category. The Cornell mobility model confronts the antecedence question by postulating a monotonic decline in transition probabilities with duration of tenure in a particular social stratum. Although this is a valid first approximation, the assumption of monotonic decline seems overly restrictive and not entirely plausible. An alternative hypothesis, which we are currently exploring, postulates a monotonic decline in downward mobility but a monotonic increase in upward mobility according to length of stay in present social stratum. Whatever assumption eventually proves appropriate, rigorous mobility theory must squarely confront the problem of antecedence.

Although the seven problems discussed above overlap considerably, each one has a distinctive focus. A truly satisfactory mobility theory must address itself to all seven. No such theory presently exists nor is likely to emerge in the immediate future. Nevertheless, the problems of identification, structure, heterogeneity, non-stationarity, constraint, interdependence, and antecedence suggest avenues by which an adequate theory might be approached. The solution of any one would surely constitute a milestone on the road toward scientific comprehension of the mobility process.

□ **APPENDIX A. MATHEMATICAL ANALYSIS**
OF THE CONTINUOUS TIME FINITE STATE
MARKOV CHAIN MOBILITY MODEL

We assume social mobility obeys a continuous time finite state Markov chain. Let $S_1, \ldots, S_n$ be the status categories which are the states of the model. Define $p_{ij}(t, h)$ as the probability the process occupies S_j at time t given that it was in S_i at time h. The assumption of path independence implies

$$p_{ij}(t, h) = \sum_{k=1}^{n} p_{ik}(s, h)p_{kj}(t, s). \qquad 0 \leq h < s < t \qquad \text{(A1)}$$

If no time has elapsed, no change of status can occur. We assume the probability functions $p_{ij}(t, h)$ are continuous as elapsed time approaches zero. This assumption means

$$\lim_{t \to h} p_{ij}(t, h) = \begin{cases} 0 & \text{if } i \neq j \\ 1 & \text{if } i = j \end{cases}. \qquad \text{(A2)}$$

Sometimes we will wish to make a stationarity assumption. Such an assumption asserts the function $p_{ij}(t, h)$ depends only on the time elapsed $t - h$ and not on the specific values of t and h. Thus we write

$$p_{ij}(t, h) = p_{ij}(t - h). \tag{A3}$$

If stationarity holds, it is possible to demonstrate the existence of the following limits[1]:

$$\lim_{t \to 0} \frac{p_{ij}(t) - p_{ij}(0)}{t} = \left. \frac{dp_{ij}(t)}{dt} \right|^{t=0} = a_{ij}. \qquad i, j = 1, \ldots, n \tag{A4}$$

It follows from (A2) and the definition of a probability function that

$$a_{ij} \begin{cases} \geq 0 & \text{if} \quad i \neq j \\ \leq 0 & \text{if} \quad i = j \end{cases}. \tag{A5}$$

The constants a_{ij} are sometimes called instantaneous transition rates. They give the rate at which the transition probability functions $p_{ij}(t)$ change when elapsed time equals zero ($t = 0$).

If stationarity does not hold, the limit in (A4) need not exist. If this limit does exist, it has the following form:

$$\lim_{t \to h} \frac{p_{ij}(t, h) - p_{ij}(h, h)}{t - h} = \left. \frac{\partial p_{ij}(t, h)}{\partial t} \right|^{t=h} = a_{ij}(h). \tag{A6}$$

When this limit exists, it follows from (A2) and the definition of a probability function that

$$a_{ij}(h) \begin{cases} \geq 0 & \text{if} \quad i \neq j \\ \leq 0 & \text{if} \quad i = j \end{cases}. \qquad h \geq 0 \tag{A7}$$

In the absence of stationarity, instantaneous transition rates, even when they exist, are not constant. We assume in what follows that stationarity does hold.

Using (A4), we obtain the following relationship among the instantaneous transition rates:

$$\sum_{j=1}^{n} p_{ij}(t) = 1$$

$$\sum_{\substack{j=1 \\ j \neq i}}^{n} p_{ij}(t) = 1 - p_{ii}(t)$$

$$\lim_{t \to 0} \sum_{\substack{j=1 \\ j \neq 1}}^{n} \frac{p_{ij}(t)}{t} = \lim_{t \to 0} \frac{1 - p_{ii}(t)}{t} \tag{A8}$$

$$\sum_{\substack{j=1 \\ j \neq i}}^{n} a_{ij} = -a_{ii}.$$

[1] Kai Lai Chung: *Markov Chains with Stationary Transition Probabilities.* Second Edition. New York: Springer-Verlag, 1967, pp. 128–139.

This result reminds us that the n status categories are mutually exclusive and collectively exhaustive. A person leaving one status category must enter another, and hence the exit rate $-a_{ii}$ must equal the sum of the entrance rates

$$\sum_{\substack{j=1 \\ j \neq i}}^{n} a_{ij}.$$

To operationalize the continuous time model we must derive a formula which enables us to calculate the transition probabilities $\{p_{ij}(t)\}$ for any desired value of t. We now obtain a functional relationship which enables us to calculate the transition probabilities $\{p_{ij}(t)\}$ in terms of the instantaneous transition rates.

(A1) implies,

$$\frac{p_{ij}(t+h) - p_{ij}(t)}{h} = \frac{\sum_{k=1}^{n} p_{ik}(t)p_{kj}(h) - p_{ij}(t)}{h}$$

$$= \sum_{\substack{k=1 \\ k \neq j}}^{n} \frac{p_{ik}(t)p_{kj}(h)}{h} + \frac{p_{ij}(t)[p_{jj}(h) - 1]}{h}.$$

Taking the limit on both sides as $h \to 0$ and using (A4),

$$\frac{dp_{ij}(t)}{dt} = \sum_{\substack{k=1 \\ k \neq j}}^{n} p_{ik}(t)a_{kj} + p_{ij}(t)a_{jj}$$

$$\frac{dp_{ij}(t)}{dt} = \sum_{k=1}^{n} p_{ik}(t)a_{kj}. \qquad i, j = 1, \ldots, n \tag{A9}$$

Here we have a set of first order linear differential equations with constant coefficients. The desired formula is obtained by solving these equations.

At this point it is convenient to adopt matrix notation. Define

$$P(t) = \{p_{ij}(t)\}_{i,j=1}^{n}$$

$$P^{(1)}(t) = \left\{\frac{dp_{ij}(t)}{dt}\right\}_{i,j=1}^{n}$$

$$P^{(k)}(t) = \left\{\frac{d^k p_{ij}(t)}{dt^k}\right\}_{i,j=1}^{n} \qquad k = 1, 2, \ldots$$

$$A = \{a_{ij}\}_{i,j=1}^{n}.$$

The matrix A is sometimes called the infinitesimal generator of the process. The equations in (A9) may now be written

$$P^{(1)}(t) = P(t) \cdot A. \tag{A10}$$

Let us successively differentiate (A10) on a term by term basis. Thus,

$$P^{(2)}(t) = P^{(1)}(t) \cdot A = P(t) \cdot A^2$$
$$P^{(3)}(t) = P^{(1)}(t) \cdot A^2 = P(t) \cdot A^3$$
$$\vdots$$
$$P^{(k)}(t) = P^{(1)}(t) \cdot A^{k-1} = P(t) \cdot A^k. \qquad k = 0, 1, \ldots \qquad \text{(A11)}$$

It follows from (A2) that $P(0)$ equals the identity matrix I. Consequently, setting t equal to zero in (A11) yields

$$P^{(k)}(0) = A^k. \qquad k = 0, 1, \ldots \qquad \text{(A12)}$$

We next expand the transition function $p_{ij}(t)$ in a MacLaurin series

$$p_{ij}(t) = \sum_{k=0}^{\infty} \frac{t^k}{k!} \left[\frac{d^k p_{ij}(t)}{dt^k} \right]^{t=0}. \qquad i, j = 1, \ldots, n \qquad \text{(A13)}$$

Writing this in matrix notation,

$$P(t) = \sum_{k=0}^{\infty} \frac{t^k}{k!} P^{(k)}(0). \qquad \text{(A14)}$$

Substituting (A12) in (A14),

$$P(t) = \sum_{k=0}^{\infty} \frac{t^k}{k!} A^k. \qquad \text{(A15)}$$

This is the desired formula which expresses the transition matrix $P(t)$ in terms of the infinitesimal generator A. Due to the similarity between the matrix series above and the MacLaurin expansion of the scalar function e^{at}, (A15) is sometimes written

$$P(t) = e^{At} = \sum_{k=0}^{\infty} \frac{t^k}{k!} A^k. \qquad \text{(A16)}$$

It will be useful to know the distributions of the random variables defining lengths of stay in the various status categories. Let $Z_i(t)$ give the probability of remaining in S_i t time units or longer. The path independence and stationarity assumptions imply

$$Z_i(t + h) = Z_i(t) \cdot Z_i(h)$$
$$\frac{Z_i(t + h) - Z_i(t)}{h} = Z_i(t) \left[\frac{Z_i(h) - 1}{h} \right].$$

Consider persons occupying S_i both at the beginning and at the end of a time interval: the smaller the time interval, the greater the likelihood these people will have remained in S_i throughout the period. In the limit, $Z_i(h)$ and $p_{ii}(h)$

are identical. Hence,

$$\lim_{h \to 0} \frac{Z_i(t+h) - Z_i(t)}{h} = Z_i(t) \lim_{h \to 0} \left[\frac{p_{ii}(h) - 1}{h} \right]$$

$$\frac{dZ_i(t)}{dt} = a_{ii} Z_i(t). \qquad \text{(A17)}$$

Solving this differential equation under the initial condition $Z_i(0) = 1$ yields

$$Z_i(t) = e^{a_{ii}t}. \qquad i = 1, \ldots, n \qquad \text{(A18)}$$

Thus length of stay in status category s_i is exponentially distributed with parameter $|a_{ii}|$.

We will sometimes want to estimate the infinitesimal generator A, given knowledge of the transition matrix $P(t)$. In other words, we will want to determine the matrix A such that (A16) is satisfied for given $P(t)$. To explain how such a calculation can be made we must introduce two new concepts: the concept of a matrix function and the concept of the values of a function on a matrix spectrum.

Suppose P is a square matrix of dimension n. The spectrum of matrix P is simply its set of eigenvalues. Let $\lambda_1, \ldots, \lambda_k$ be the set of all distinct values assumed by eigenvalues of P, and let $m_1, \ldots, m_k$ equal the number of eigenvalues with each of these values respectively. Consider the scalar function $f(x)$ and the numbers

$$f(\lambda_i), \; \frac{df(\lambda)}{d\lambda}\bigg|^{\lambda=\lambda_i}, \ldots, \; \frac{df^{m_i-1}(\lambda)}{d\lambda^{m_i-1}}\bigg|^{\lambda=\lambda_i}. \qquad i = 1, \ldots, k \qquad \text{(A19)}$$

These numbers are called the values of the function $f(x)$ on the spectrum of matrix P, and they are denoted

$$f(\Lambda_p).$$

Now consider the scalar function $h(x)$ which has the following power series representation:

$$h(x) = \sum_{i=0}^{\infty} c_i x^i. \qquad \text{(A21)}$$

The matrix function $h(P)$ is defined as

$$h(P) = \sum_{i=0}^{\infty} c_i P^i \qquad \text{(A22)}$$

whenever this series converges. The above series converges whenever the power series in (A21) converges for all eigenvalues of P.[2]

[2] F. R. Gantmacher: *The Theory of Matrices.* Vol. I. New York: Chelsea, 1959, p. 113.

We have already dealt with one matrix function, e^{At}. The previous paragraph together with the properties of the power series expansion for the exponential function imply e^{At} exists for all square matrices A. Consider the scalar function $\ln x$ with power series expansion:

$$\ln x = \sum_{i=1}^{\infty} \frac{(-1)^{i-1}}{i} (x - 1)^i. \qquad 0 < x \leq 2 \qquad \text{(A23)}$$

When it exists, the matrix function $\ln P$ equals

$$\ln P = \sum_{i=1}^{\infty} \frac{(-1)^{i-1}}{i} (P - I)^i. \qquad |\lambda_j - 1| < 1, j = 1, \ldots, k \quad \text{(A24)}$$

Clearly, this series does not converge for all square matrices P.

An important theorem of matrix theory holds that if the values of some function $g(x)$ on the spectrum of matrix P (i.e. the numbers $g(\Lambda p)$) all equal zero, then the matrix function $g(P)$ equals 0, the matrix all of whose elements are zero, whenever this matrix function exists.[3] Define $g(x)$ as

$$g(x) = \ln e^x - x.$$

This function and all its derivatives equal zero. Consequently, for square matrix Q

$$g(Q) = \ln e^Q - Q = 0 \qquad \text{(A25)}$$

whenever $g(Q)$ is defined. Set $Q = At$ and define

$$P(t) = e^{At}$$

as in (A16). Assuming the necessary convergence, (A24) and (A25) yield

$$A = \frac{1}{t} \sum_{i=1}^{\infty} \frac{(-1)^{i-1}}{i} [P(t) - I]^i. \qquad \text{(A26)}$$

This is the estimation formula required. It converges whenever $|\lambda_j - 1| < 1$ for all eigenvalues λ_j of transition matrix $P(t)$.

Coleman has suggested an iterative procedure with less stringent convergence requirements than (A26).[4] Rearranging (A15) yields

$$A = \frac{1}{t} \left[P(t) - I - \sum_{k=2}^{\infty} \frac{A^k t^k}{k!} \right]. \qquad \text{(A27)}$$

[3] *Ibid.* p. 113.
[4] James S. Coleman: *Introduction to Mathematical Sociology*. London: Free Press, 1964, pp. 177–182.

The Coleman procedure uses this expression iteratively to estimate the desired infinitesimal generator.

□ **APPENDIX B. INTRAGENERATIONAL MOBILITY DATA**

The data used in this paper came from a study entitled "Occupational Changes in a Generation" (O.C.G.) conducted jointly by Professors Peter M. Blau and Otis Dudley Duncan.[1] The United States Bureau of the Census collected the data in March 1962 as an adjunct to its monthly Current Population Survey. The O.C.G. study included about 20,700 males between the ages of 20 and 64 and obtained information on father's occupation, first job, and job in March 1962.

Each occupation was given a status score based on the mean education and mean income of its practitioners.[2] Actual status scores ranged from zero to 96, and on the basis of these the present author divided occupations into five strata defined by the following status score intervals: 0–19, 20–39, 40–59, 60–79, 80–96. The 0–19 status category includes carpenters, automobile mechanics, painters, truck drivers, gardeners, janitors, construction laborers, porters, and others. To give a rough idea of the occupations included in this category we label them unskilled manual. Clearly, this label is not entirely accurate.

The 20–39 category contains shipping clerks, welders, brick masons, plumbers, deliverymen, retail salesmen, and policemen, to mention a few. Occupations in this category are identified as semi-skilled manual. The 40–59 category includes electricians, telephone linemen, airplane mechanics, mail carriers, bookkeepers, clergymen, toolmakers, and funeral directors. We label these occupations skilled manual and lower white collar. The 60–79 category contains manufacturing foremen, wholesale and manufacturing salesmen, secretaries, draftsmen, salaried managers, teachers, accountants, and veterinarians. These occupations are considered upper white collar — semi-professional. Finally the 80–96 category includes professors, editors, engineers, bank managers, architects, lawyers, doctors, and postal officials. We call occupations in this category professional. (The empirical mobility matrices examined in this paper use this five-strata classification scheme.)

Intragenerational mobility matrices relating first job to present job were obtained for each of four male age cohorts: 25–34, 35–44, 45–54, and 55–64 (age refers to age in March 1962). Refinements of these matrices giving outflow percentages from first job to job in March 1962 appear in Table 2. These

[1] A full report of the O.C.G. study is given in Peter M. Blau and Otis Dudley Duncan: *The American Occupational Structure*. New York: John Wiley, 1967. The specific tables we use do not appear in this volume because Blau and Duncan have usually combined age cohorts for purposes of analysis. The author obtained these tables through the courtesy of Professor Duncan.

[2] For a full description of the status scoring system, see Otis Dudley Duncan: "A Socio-economic Index for All Occupations" in Albert J. Reiss, Jr., *et al.*, *Occupations and Social Status*. New York: Free Press, 1961, pp. 109–138. A brief description of the scoring procedure appears in Blau and Duncan: *op. cit.*, pp. 117–128.

outflow matrices are based on frequency tabulations which omit all persons of farm origin and were inflated to match independent estimates of U. S. population by age, sex, and color.

■ **TABLE B1 / Outflow Percentages from First Job to Job in March 1962 for Males 25–34, 35–44, 45–54, and 55–64 in March 1962 Given in that Order**

Status Score of Job in March 1962

		80–96	60–79	40–59	20–39	0–19
Status Score of First Job	80–96	79.7	10.0	7.4	1.2	1.7
		74.8	15.4	7.7	1.4	0.7
		68.6	17.9	8.1	3.2	2.2
		66.1	20.5	8.0	1.8	3.6
	60–79	20.1	57.4	12.4	6.5	3.6
		15.0	56.5	15.2	7.9	5.4
		12.2	56.9	21.7	4.4	4.8
		15.4	60.3	9.2	8.3	6.8
	40–59	10.8	26.3	33.8	15.6	13.5
		10.6	32.3	31.0	15.6	8.5
		8.0	33.1	33.6	13.2	12.1
		10.2	28.8	31.5	17.6	11.9
	20–39	4.2	20.9	20.5	32.2	23.1
		6.2	20.9	23.2	24.6	25.1
		5.7	20.1	25.7	29.2	19.3
		3.4	23.4	21.6	29.3	22.3
	0–19	2.2	10.8	18.0	22.1	46.9
		3.3	15.0	16.9	24.7	40.1
		2.0	10.6	18.5	26.5	42.4
		2.1	10.0	15.5	22.2	50.2

Although the matrices given in Table B1 represent the mobility patterns of four different age cohorts, we will sometimes interpret them as information about a single synthetic (i.e. hypothetical) cohort at various stages of its occupational career. Thus, the first matrix indicates net intragenerational mobility when the synthetic cohort ranges from 25 to 34 years of age, the second matrix represents net mobility when the cohort ranges from 35 to 44 years of age, and so forth.

The technical problems engendered by the synthetic cohort interpretation are legion. To regard it as an accurate rendering of intragenerational mobility implies age is the only factor differentiating the mobility patterns of various cohorts. The composition of the four age cohorts differs on variables such as religion, race, national origin, and regional distribution. Can we safely assume these variables utterly lacking in causal import? More importantly, the specific history of each cohort affects its mobility pattern significantly. The two younger age cohorts, for example, entered the labor force only after the Depression, yet this event permeated the occupational experience of the older cohorts.

Even more problematic is the fact that the synthetic cohort does not satisfy the Markovian assumption. The path independence assumption implies there should exist stochastic matrices transforming the 25–34 matrix into the 35–44 matrix, the 35–44 matrix into the 45–54 matrix, etc. In fact, however, the matrices accomplishing these transformations are not stochastic. Thus, we know immediately a Markovian model cannot achieve perfect fit with the synthetic cohort data.

In view of these difficulties why do we make the synthetic cohort interpretation? The absence of adequate time series data on intragenerational mobility is the most obvious and truthful answer. Other justifications also exist, however. The synthetic cohort interpretation does not distort all aspects of the intragenerational mobility process: it is particularly useful in examining the effects of age on mobility. Furthermore, this paper's main purpose is not analysis of mobility data but exposition of a theory about mobility. The synthetic cohort data, whatever its other failings, provides a convenient device for illustrating this theory.

□ APPENDIX C. ON ESTIMATION TECHNIQUES

We outline below the procedures used to estimate the infinitesimal generators of the birth and death, exponential decline, and absorbing state models. We shall use A and $\hat{A}$ to designate the true (or theoretic) and estimated infinitesimal generators respectively, while $P(t)$ and $\hat{P}(t)$ indicate true and observed transition probability matrices over the time interval $[0, t]$. We assume the existence of exactly n social strata and the availability of empirical transition matrices defined over several different time intervals.

1c Estimation Procedures for the Birth and Death Process Model

The technique used to estimate the infinitesimal generator of the birth and death model is a modification of a more general method which might be called the eigenvector method. Assume the true infinitesimal generator is diagonalizable (i.e. similar to a diagonal matrix). That is, assume there exist inverse matrices T and T^{-1} plus a diagonal matrix.

$$V = \begin{bmatrix} \lambda_1 & 0 & \cdots & 0 \\ 0 & \lambda_2 & \cdots & 0 \\ \vdots & & & \\ 0 & \cdots & \cdots & \lambda_n \end{bmatrix} \tag{C1}$$

such that

$$A = TVT^{-1}. \tag{C2}$$

It is not difficult to show that $\lambda_1, \lambda_2, \ldots, \lambda_n$ are eigenvalues of generator A, that the columns of T are right eigenvectors, and that the rows of T^{-1} are left eigenvectors. Moreover,

$$A^k = TV^kT^{-1}. \qquad k = 0, 1, 2, \ldots \tag{C3}$$

Using (C3),

$$
\begin{aligned}
P(t) &= \sum_{k=0}^{\infty} \frac{A^k t^k}{k!} \\
&= \sum_{k=0}^{\infty} \frac{TV^kT^{-1}t^k}{k!} \\
&= T\left[\sum_{k=0}^{\infty} \frac{V^k t^k}{k!}\right]T^{-1}
\end{aligned}
\tag{C4}
$$

$$
P(t) = T\begin{bmatrix}
\sum_{k=0}^{\infty} \frac{\lambda_1^k t^k}{k!} & 0 & \cdots & 0 \\
0 & \sum_{k=0}^{\infty} \frac{\lambda_2^k t^k}{k!} & \cdots & 0 \\
\vdots & & & \vdots \\
0 & \cdots & & \sum_{k=0}^{\infty} \frac{\lambda_n^k t^k}{k!}
\end{bmatrix}T^{-1}.
\tag{C5}
$$

By the MacLaurin series for the exponential function,

$$e^{\lambda t} = \sum_{k=0}^{\infty} \frac{\lambda^k t^k}{k!}. \tag{C6}$$

Hence,

$$
P(t) = T\begin{bmatrix}
e^{\lambda_1 t} & 0 & \cdots & 0 \\
0 & e^{\lambda_2 t} & \cdots & 0 \\
\vdots & & & \vdots \\
0 & 0 & \cdots & e^{\lambda_n t}
\end{bmatrix}T^{-1}.
\tag{C7}
$$

It is easy to see that $e^{\lambda_1 t}, e^{\lambda_2 t}, \ldots, e^{\lambda_n t}$ are the eigenvalues of $P(t)$ and that its eigenvectors are identical to those of A.

If A is diagonalizable, $P(t)$ will also be, and the eigenvalues of A are logarithmically related to the eigenvalues of $P(t)$. The diagonalizability of $P(t)$ does not, however, imply that of A. Nevertheless, if $\hat{P}(t)$ has positive eigenvalues and the following spectral representation

$$
\hat{P}(t) = T\begin{bmatrix}
\mu_1 & 0 & \cdots & \cdots & 0 \\
0 & \mu_2 & \cdots & \cdots & 0 \\
\vdots & & & & \vdots \\
0 & \cdots & & \cdots & \mu_n
\end{bmatrix}T^{-1}
\tag{C8}
$$

where $|\mu_k - 1| < 1$ $(k = 1, \ldots, n)$, a reasonable estimate of the infinitesimal generator would be

$$
\hat{A} = T \begin{bmatrix} \dfrac{\ln \mu_1}{t} & 0 & \cdots & \cdots & 0 \\ 0 & \dfrac{\ln \mu_2}{t} & \cdots & \cdots & 0 \\ \vdots & \vdots & & & \vdots \\ 0 & 0 & \cdots & & \dfrac{\ln \mu_2}{t} \end{bmatrix} T^{-1}. \tag{C9}
$$

Unfortunately, this is not a practical way of estimating the infinitesimal generator of the birth and death model. Deriving a complete set of eigenvalues and eigenvectors from the empirical matrix $\hat{P}(t)$ is not easily done, and several eigenvalues are almost certain to be complex. Moreover, the eigenvector technique does not constrain the estimated generator in the manner required by the birth and death model. A modification of this method does, however, yield a satisfactory estimate of A.

Assuming $P(t)$ is a regular stochastic matrix, the Frobenius theory of positive matrices implies $\mu = 1$ is the largest eigenvalue of $P(t)$, the multiplicity of this eigenvalue is one, and there exists an eigenvector V corresponding to $\mu = 1$ which is strictly positive. Thus, the eigenvector V is unique up to a multiplicative constant. If, on the other hand, A is diagonalizable, the argument above implies $\lambda = 0$ is an eigenvalue of A having multiplicity one, and V is an eigenvector corresponding to λ. Thus,

$$
VP(t) = V, \tag{C10}
$$

and

$$
VA = 0V = (0, \ldots, 0). \tag{C11}
$$

Let $V = (v_1, v_2, \ldots v_n)$ and recall that the infinitesimal generator of the birth and death model has the following form:

$$
A = \begin{bmatrix} a_{11} & a_{12} & 0 & 0 & \cdots & & 0 \\ a_{21} & a_{22} & a_{23} & 0 & \cdots & & 0 \\ 0 & a_{32} & a_{33} & a_{34} & \cdots & & \vdots \\ \vdots & & & & & & \\ 0 & & \cdots & & \cdots & a_{n,n-1} & a_{nn} \end{bmatrix} \tag{C12}
$$

where $a_{kk} = -(a_{k,k-1} + a_{k,k+1})$. Expanding (C11) yields the following set of equations:

$$
\begin{aligned}
a_{11}v_1 + a_{21}v_2 &= 0 \\
a_{k-1,k}v_{k-1} + a_{kk}v_k + a_{k+1,k}v_{k+1} &= 0 \quad k = 2, \ldots, n - 1 \quad \text{(C13)} \\
a_{n-1,n}v_{n-1} + a_{nn}v_n &= 0.
\end{aligned}
$$

The solution to the equations in (C13) is only unique up to a multiplicative constant. We eliminate this indeterminacy by requiring that the elements of V total one. A solution to these equations is

$$g_k = \frac{a_{12} \cdot a_{23} \ldots a_{k-1,k}}{a_{21} \cdot a_{32} \ldots a_{k,k-1}} . \qquad k = 1, \ldots, n \qquad \text{(C14)}$$

Clearly, every g_k is non-negative. Thus,

$$v_k = g_k \Big/ \sum_{j=1}^{n} g_j, \qquad k = 1, \ldots, n \qquad \text{(C15)}$$

and letting $n_k = v_{k-1}/v_k$,

$$n_k = \frac{v_{k-1}}{v_k} = \frac{g_{k-1}}{g_k} = \frac{a_{k,k-1}}{a_{k-1,k}} \qquad k = 2, \ldots, n \qquad \text{(C16)}$$

implying

$$a_{k,k-1} = n_k a_{k-1,k}. \qquad k = 2, \ldots, n \qquad \text{(C17)}$$

Using (C17), it is possible to eliminate all $a_{k,k-1}$ thus reducing the number of free parameters by $n - 1$. To do this, however, requires estimates of the n_k. Expression (C10) suggests an estimate of V can be obtained by solving the following matrix equation:

$$\hat{V}\hat{P}(t) = \hat{V}. \qquad \text{(C18)}$$

After obtaining $\hat{V}$, (C16) may be used to estimate the $\hat{n}_k$. We have now reduced the estimation problem to that of calculating the $a_{k,k+1}$.

A person leaving stratum S_k enters stratum S_{k+1} with a probability $a_{k,k+1}/|a_{kk}|$ and enters stratum S_{k-1} with probability $a_{k,k-1}/|a_{kk}|$. The ratio of these probabilities is $a_{k,k+1}/a_{k,k-1}$, and a rough approximation of this ratio is

$$\frac{a_{k,k+1}}{a_{k,k-1}} \sim \sum_{j=k+1}^{n} P_{kj}(t) \Big/ \sum_{j=1}^{k-1} P_{kj}. \; (t) \equiv f_k, \qquad k = 2, \ldots, n - 1 \qquad \text{(C19)}$$

Using (C17) and (C19),

$$\begin{aligned} a_{k,k+1} &\sim a_{k,k-1} f_k \\ a_{k,k+1} &\sim a_{k-1,k} \cdot n_k \cdot f_k. \end{aligned} \qquad k = 2, \ldots, n - 1 \qquad \text{(C20)}$$

Applying (C20) successively yields

$$\left\{ \begin{aligned} a_{k,k+1} &\sim a_{12} \prod_{j=2}^{k} n_j f_j \\ a_{k,k-1} &\sim a_{12} \prod_{j=2}^{k} n_j f_j / f_k \end{aligned} \right\} . \qquad k = 2, \ldots, n - 1 \qquad \text{(C21)}$$

The appropriate estimator for f_k is apparent from the definition in (C19). The expressions in (C21) eliminate all but one free parameter a_{12}. A value for this parameter can be found by a computer search procedure or with additional mobility data such as the proportion remaining in a given stratum throughout a fixed time interval.

2c Estimation Procedures for the Exponential Decline Model

The exponential decline model postulates a non-stationary infinitesimal generator $A(x)$ of the form

$$A(x) = e^{-cx}A. \tag{C22}$$

Hence, we must estimate the scalar c and the matrix A. Since

$$\int_0^t e^{-cx}\,dx = \frac{1 - e^{-ct}}{c}, \tag{C23}$$

expanding the non-stationary generator $A(x)$ over the interval $[0, t]$ is equivalent to expanding the stationary generator A over the interval $[0, (1 - e^{-ct})/c]$, and this is equivalent to expanding the stationary generator,

$$B_t \equiv \frac{1 - e^{-ct}}{ct} A, \tag{C24}$$

over the interval $[0, t]$.

Suppose we possess transition matrices $\hat{P}(u)$, $\hat{P}(v)$, $\hat{P}(w)$, $\ldots$. If the exponential decline model holds, then $\hat{A}_u$, $\hat{A}_v$, $\hat{A}_w$, $\ldots$ the stationary generators calculated for these transition matrices (with $t = u$, v, w, $\ldots$ respectively), should be estimates of B_u, B_v, B_w, $\ldots$. Formula (A26) of Appendix A can be used to estimate A_u, A_v, A_w, $\ldots$. If this series fails to converge, the iteration procedure based on (A27) may yield the desired estimates. We henceforth assume the estimates $\hat{A}_u$, $\hat{A}_v$, $\hat{A}_w$, $\ldots$ and thus $\hat{B}_u$, $\hat{B}_v$, $\hat{B}_w$, $\ldots$ are available.

It is evident from (C24) that $r(u, v)$, the ratio between corresponding elements of B_u and B_v, depends only on u and v and is identical for all such element pairs. In fact,

$$r(u, v) = \frac{u(1 - e^{-cv})}{v(1 - e^{-cu})}, \tag{C25}$$

and

$$c = \frac{1}{v}\ln\left[1 - \frac{v}{u}r(u, v)(1 - e^{-cu})\right]. \tag{C26}$$

An estimate of $r(u, v)$ can be obtained from $\hat{B}_u$ and $\hat{B}_v$. With this in hand (C26) can be used iteratively to obtain an estimate of c. Rearranging (C24) yields

$$A = \frac{ct}{1 - e^{-ct}} B_t. \tag{C27}$$

Since estimates of c and B_t are available, (C27) makes possible an estimate of generator A.

3c Estimation Procedures for the Absorbing State Model

If n social strata exist, the absorbing state model contains $2n$ states of which $T_1, T_2, \ldots, T_n$ are transient and $A_1, A_2, \ldots, A_n$ are absorbing. Define $Q(t)$ as the $2n \times 2n$ transition probability matrix defined on these states over the interval $[0, t]$. Our basic strategy is to estimate $Q(t)$ for some value of t and then to use the iterative procedure based on (A27), with suitable constraints, to obtain the infinitesimal generator of the absorbing state model.[1]

The definition of an absorbing state implies only transition probabilities of the form $q_{T_i,T_j}(t)$ or $q_{T_i,A_j}(t)$ or $q_{A_i,A_i}(t)$ can be non-zero. Transition probabilities of the latter kind always equal one. Moreover, if $P(t)$ is defined in the usual way,

$$P_{ij}(t) = \begin{cases} q_{T_i,T_j}(t) + q_{T_i,A_j}(t) & \text{if } i \neq j \\ 1 - \sum_{\substack{i=1 \\ i \neq j}}^{n} P_{ij}(t) & \text{if } i = j \end{cases} \cdot \qquad i, j = 1, \ldots, n \qquad \text{(C28)}$$

If we assume all persons are in transient states at time zero, then

$$P_{ii}(t) = q_{T_i,T_i}(t) + q_{T_i,A_i}(t). \qquad i = 1, \ldots, n \qquad \text{(C29)}$$

Estimates of $P_{ij}(t)$ are known to be available. Assuming all persons originate in transient states, (C28) and (C29) can be used to estimate the entire matrix $Q(t)$ provided we can approximate the quantities $q_{T_i,A_j}(t)$.

Suppose we have the transition matrices $\hat{P}(u)$, $\hat{P}(v)$, $\hat{P}(w)$, $\ldots$ where $u < v < w < \cdots$. Using (A26), calculate $\hat{A}_u$, the stationary generator for $\hat{P}(u)$. Expand $\hat{A}_u$ over the intervals $[0, v]$, $[0, w]$, $\ldots$ thus obtaining matrices $\hat{P}_u(v)$, $\hat{P}_u(w)$, $\ldots$ respectively. We assume

$$\hat{q}_{T_i,A_i}(v) - \hat{q}_{T_i,A_i}(u) = \hat{p}_{ii}(v) - \hat{p}_{u:ii}(v) \qquad \text{(C30)}$$

since if the absorbing state model holds, non-stationarity must result from progressive concentration in absorbing states. Define $f_i(x)$ as

$$f_i(x) \equiv \hat{q}_{T_i,A_i}(u) - \hat{q}_{T_i,A_i}(x). \qquad \text{(C31)}$$

Clearly, $f_i(u) = 0$, and $f_i(v)$, $f_i(w) \ldots$ are known from (C30). More importantly, $f_i(0) = \hat{q}_{T_iA_i}(u)$ since $\hat{q}_{T_iA_i}(0) = 0$.

We can extrapolate to $f_i(0)$ from the known values of $f_i(x)$ using the Gregory

---

[1] See James S. Coleman: *Introduction to Mathematical Sociology*. London: Free Press, 1964, pp. 177–182.

backwards formula, the general form of which is

$$f(x + \theta h) = f(x) + \theta \nabla f(x) + \frac{\theta(\theta + 1)}{2!} \nabla^2 f(x) + \cdots \qquad (C32)$$

where ∇^k indicates the kth backward difference.[2] Thus, we obtain $\hat{q}_{T_i, A_i}(u)$, and using (C31), we can also derive $\hat{q}_{T_i, A_i}(v)$, $\hat{q}_{T_i, A_i}(w)$, ...

We must still derive $\hat{q}_{T_i, A_j}(u)$ ($i \neq j$) before estimation of matrix $Q(u)$ is possible. This we do by assuming

$$\hat{q}_{T_i, A_j}(u) = \hat{p}_{ij}(u)\hat{q}_{T_j, A_j}(u). \qquad (C33)$$

The rationale behind (C33) is rather weak; however, the quantities involved are small. Using (C28) and the analytic properties of absorbing states, we can now estimate the entire matrix $Q(u)$ and then, through the Coleman iteration procedure, obtain the desired infinitesimal generator.[3]

---

[2] See Harold Jeffreys and Bertha Swirles Jeffreys: *Methods of Mathematical Physics* 3rd ed. rev., Cambridge, England: Cambridge Univ. Press, 1962, pp. 267–268.

[3] The Coleman iterative procedure based on (A27) only converged for one of the $Q(t)$ matrices estimated from the O.C.G. data. Consequently, the fit of the absorbing state model was rather poor.

Chapter 14

A Measure of Relative Balance for Social Structures

■ ROBERT Z. NORMAN & FRED S. ROBERTS

□ **ABSTRACT**

As an extension of the Heider and Cartwright-Harary theory of balance in social structures (signed digraphs), the need for a measure of relative balance which is derived from some plausible axioms is indicated. Such a measure should reflect the balance ordering, i.e., the relation: one social structure is more balanced than another. Axioms which such a measure should satisfy, developed in Norman-Roberts (1972), are presented. They give rise to a measure which determines the balance ordering uniquely up to certain parameters measuring the effect of "semicycles" of different lengths. The proof of this result, given in Norman-Roberts (1972), is outlined. Special values of the parameters are shown to give rise to measures previously suggested as plausible in the literature. Finally, the measure is applied to formalize certain distinctions made in the theory of distributive justice described in an earlier paper in this volume. The distributive justice distinctions lead, for the first time, to an example which demonstrates why, in measuring relative balance, it is not only convenient but necessary to allow different length semicycles to have different weights.

□ **1. SIGNED DIGRAPHS**

Many empirical relationships in the social sciences seem to have positive and negative evaluations. Thus, for example, the relations 'likes,' 'associates with,' 'chooses,' 'tells truth to,' all seem to have opposites: 'hates,' 'avoids,' 'rejects,' 'lies to,' etc.

A good model for a social structure with such positive and negative relationships, say a small group, is a signed digraph. A *digraph* (directed graph) consists of a finite set of points together with a set of directed lines joining some of the points. A *signed digraph* is a digraph in which a sign (+ or −) is associated with each (directed) line. Figure 1 shows two signed digraphs.

The points are thought of as elements of the structure, e.g., members of the small group or objects of concern to these people. If a line from x to y is positive (or negative), this indicates that the relationship between x and y is positive (or negative). The absence of a line between x and y is interpreted as either indifference or absence of the relationship in question. Much of the literature relevant to our topic has been restricted to the case of signed *graphs*, i.e., where the relationships (lines) are not directed, although in fact many such relationships are directed. The results for signed graphs all apply without much modification to the case of signed digraphs.

Much of the terminology about signed digraphs that we shall use has been introduced in the book by Harary, Norman, and Cartwright (1965). For our

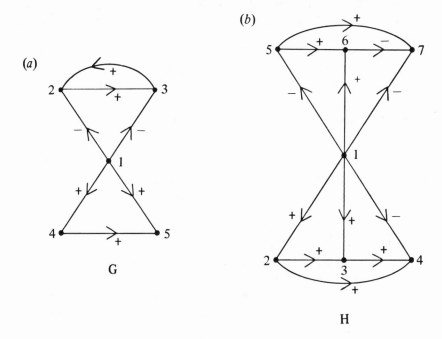

■ **FIGURE 1.** Two signed digraphs are shown. The points are represented by black dots, the directed lines by arrows. The sign of a directed line is indicated by a + or −.

purposes, the most important concept is that of a *semicycle*. A semicycle is obtained by starting at a given point in the digraph and following from point to point along lines of the digraph, disregarding direction of the arrows, making sure never to cross the same point twice, and finally returning to the original point. Two semicycles are considered the same if one is obtained from the other by changing the initial point or reversing the order of following the lines.

To give some examples, in the signed digraph G of Figure 1, the sequence of directed lines 12, 23, 13 defines a semicycle. This is the semicycle obtained by following from point 1 to 2, from 2 to 3 and from 3 to 1. We use the notation 13 rather than 31 to indicate that the third line used is directed from 1 to 3, though in this case we are following it from 3 to 1. The sequence of edges 13, 23, 12 also defines a semicycle, but this is considered the same semicycle as that given by 12, 23, 13 since it is obtained from the latter by reversing direction. (This semicycle is considered distinct from 12, 23, 13 by Berger et al. [1962]. The reader is referred to Taylor [1970, p. 55] for further discussion of this point.) The semicycle 23, 13, 12 is also considered the same as 12, 23, 13 since it is obtained from the latter by changing the initial point. On the other hand, the semicycle 12, 32, 13 is different from 12, 23, 13 since this uses the directed line 32 rather than the directed line 23. In the signed digraph H of Figure 1, the sequence 17, 67, 56, 15 gives a semicycle. The sequence 16, 67, 57, 15 gives a different semicycle, since it cannot be obtained from the former by change of direction or change of initial point. The sequence 67, 17, 12, 23, 13, 16 does not give a semicycle, since it uses the point 1 twice.

We shall say that the *length* of a semicycle is the number of lines in it. Thus, the semicycle 12, 23, 13 in G has length 3. We shall make some additional technical comments on the counting of semicycles in Section 6.2.

Finally, it should be remarked that in the theory of digraphs the word cycle has a more special meaning than semicycle (this is also mentioned in Section 6.2).

□ **2. HISTORICAL BACKGROUND**

The notion of "balance" of a social structure has occupied sociologists generally, and the theory of structural balance has recently been surveyed by Taylor (1970). This theory derives from Heider (1946), who described what he meant by balance by giving a series of examples and asserting that unbalanced social structures exhibit a certain tension resulting in a tendency to change in the direction of balance. Search for a precise definition of balance led to the formulation of such a notion for signed digraphs. Heider observed that of the four structures in Figure 2, the first and third are balanced while the second and fourth are unbalanced. (For a more detailed discussion of this example, the reader is referred to Harary, Norman, and Cartwright [1965]). In particular, the first and third semicycles in Figure 2 have an even number of negative lines while the remaining two semicycles have an odd number of negative lines.

This observation led Cartwright and Harary (1956) to generalize to longer semicycles, and to suggest that an arbitrary semicycle should be called *balanced*, or *positively balanced*, precisely if it has an even number of negative lines; and *unbalanced* or *negatively balanced* otherwise. Sometimes the words positive and negative are used instead of positively balanced and negatively balanced. Finally, Cartwright and Harary suggested calling a signed digraph *balanced* if each semicycle of it is balanced, and established several interesting criteria for balance. There is some empirical justification for the Cartwright-Harary definition.

To give some examples illustrating these definitions, in Figure 1, the semicycles 23, 34, 24 and 15, 57, 17 of the signed digraph H are balanced, i.e., positively balanced, while the semicycles 14, 34, 13 and 15, 56, 16 are negatively balanced. Thus, H is not balanced. On the other hand, the signed digraph G of Figure 1 is balanced.

This early mathematical work on balance was intriguing as far as it went, both mathematically and in terms of its applicability. But it seemed clear that very few social structures are balanced and that of the rest it makes sense to say that some are more balanced than others. Indeed, Heider's observation

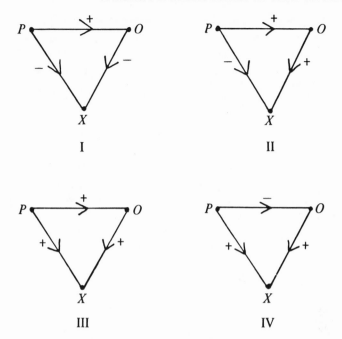

FIGURE 2. *One interpretation: P* is a person, *O* another person, and *X* an impersonal entity. The relationships shown are *P*'s evaluation of *O*, *P*'s evaluation of *X*, and *O*'s evaluation of *X*. According to Heider (1946), situations I and III are balanced, II and IV are not.

that a structure tends to change in the direction of balance calls for a measure of the extent to which one imbalanced structure is more balanced than another. Morissette (1958) speaks of "degrees" of balance and reformulates Heider's basic propositions about balance as follows:

PROPOSITION 1. The magnitude of forces toward balance is inversely related to the degree of balance of the system.

PROPOSITION 2. The magnitude of tension created by a system is inversely related to the degree of balance of that system.

Others have expressed much the same idea by asserting that an unbalanced structure tends to change in the direction of balance. It is unrealistic to think of this change as taking place in one step. Instead, the words "direction of balance" suggest that a structure should change by a sequence of steps which gradually increase the relative balance. To make these ideas precise, what is needed is not a definition of an absolute concept of balance but rather *a measure of relative balance — a way of deciding whether one structure is more balanced than another.*

Aware of the need for such a measure, Cartwright and Harary (1956) suggested as a first approximation to relative balance of a signed digraph the ratio of the number c^+ of balanced semicycles to the total number c of semicycles. Using this definition, the signed digraph H of Figure 1 has relative balance 3/7, because it has 6 positively balanced semicycles (12, 23, 13; 23, 34, 24; 16, 67, 17; 15, 57, 17; 12, 24, 34, 13; 15, 57, 67, 16) and 14 semicycles in all (the positive ones plus 13, 34, 14; 12, 24, 14; 15, 56, 16; 56, 67, 57; 12, 23, 34, 14; 13, 23, 24, 14; 15, 56, 67, 17; 16, 56, 57, 17). By way of comparison, if the sign of the directed line 14 in H is changed from $-$ to $+$, the new signed digraph H' (shown in Figure 3) has relative balance 5/7, for it has 10 positively balanced semicycles (12, 23, 13; 13, 34, 14; 12, 24, 14; 23, 34, 24; 16, 67, 17; 15, 57, 17; 12, 23, 34, 14; 12, 24, 34, 13; 13, 23, 24, 14; 15, 57, 67, 16) and 14 semicycles in all (the positive ones plus 15, 56, 16; 56, 67, 57; 15, 56, 67, 17; 16, 56, 57, 17). Thus, according to this measure, the new digraph is more balanced than the original one.

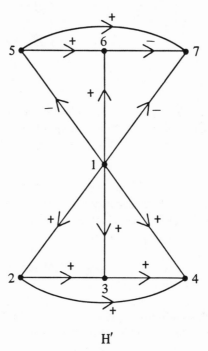

H'

■ **FIGURE 3.**

Using the Cartwright-Harary definition of balance, Morissette (1958) performed an early experiment which tended to confirm Heider's Propositions 1 and 2 as formulated above. Taylor (1970) surveys the empirical work which tests these propositions.

Harary (1955) also introduced the notion of limited balance (of order N). Namely, a signed digraph is said to be *N-balanced* if each semicycle of length at most N is balanced. It seems natural to speak of *relative N-balance* as well, and use as a measure the ratio of the number of balanced semicycles of length at most N to the number of semicycles of length at most N. (For a discussion of the psychological and sociological significance of limited balance, see Cartwright and Harary [1956].)

We first became interested in the problem of measuring relative balance when we became dissatisfied with the rather naive measure c^+/c. Our first informal idea was that semicycles of different length contribute differently to balance, with longer semicycles being relatively less important, an idea also mentioned by Flament (1963), by Cartwright and Harary (1956), and by Taylor (1970). Indeed, according to Taylor (p. 77), "the empirical utility of formalization [of the theory of balance] seems to rest, to a great degree, on a solution to" the problem of how to incorporate or measure differing effects of semicycles of differing length. We shall give an example below (see Section 9) which indicates why it is not only convenient but necessary to allow different weights for different length semicycles.

Our first idea was to use a measure of the form $\sum f(m)c_m{}^+ / \sum f(m)c_m$, where $c_m{}^+$ is the number of balanced semicycles of length m and c_m is the number of semicycles of length m, and $f(m)$ measures the importance of semicycles of length m.[1] In particular, it seemed appropriate to use for $f(m)$ values that decrease as m increases, such as $1/m$ or $1/m^2$ or $1/2^m$. (According to Taylor [1970, pp. 76 and 206ff], some evidence accumulated by Zajonc and Burnstein [1965] about the difficulty of learning and recalling longer semicycles suggests that longer semicycles will have less effect upon a person's tension than shorter ones.)

Returning to the signed digraph H of Figure 1, suppose we take $f(m) = 1/m$. Here, $c_3{}^+ = 4$, $c_4{}^+ = 2$, $c_3 = 8$, $c_4 = 6$, and so the new relative balance measure gives

$$\frac{(1/3)c_3{}^+ + (1/4)c_4{}^+}{(1/3)c_3 + (1/4)c_4} = \frac{(1/3)4 + (1/4)2}{(1/3)8 + (1/4)6} = 11/25.$$

The numbers $f(m)$ which appear in the measure are called parameters and are to be determined by the user of the measure. Together with the measure there must be a procedure for deciding, in a given situation, what parameters to use. We shall argue in Section 3 that there could be no satisfactory measure of relative balance not involving some parameters. In Section 7 we give the reader some guidance in choosing these parameters. The Cartwright-Harary measure is a special case of this general measure, and is obtained from it by taking $f(m) = 1$ for each m. We shall argue below (see Section 9) that there are many important distinctions which cannot be made with this choice of parameter. The relative N-balance measure above uses

$$f(m) = \begin{cases} 1 \text{ if } m \leq N \\ 0 \text{ otherwise.} \end{cases}$$

---

[1] Flament (1963) has a slightly different suggestion.

(Considerably different balance measures have been suggested, in particular the so-called line index. We refer the reader to Harary-Norman-Cartwright [1965], Harary [1959], and Flament [1963] for a discussion, and to Taylor [1970, pp. 60ff and 188ff] for a survey of such measures.)

While research was continuing on a measure of balance, a group of sociologists at the Stanford University Laboratory for Social Research was applying balance theory to the study of small groups and was interested in a balance measure to apply to their studies. (Cf. Berger, Zelditch, and Anderson [1966], Zelditch, Berger, and Cohen [1966], etc.) *In particular what was desired was a balance measure which was not ad hoc, but rather which could be derived from a simple set of assumptions or axioms.* The task of formulating such a set of axioms and mathematically deriving from them a balance measure led to the present research.

In formulating our axioms we were guided by the objective of deriving a balance measure which would tell us, given any two signed digraphs, which is more balanced. While the measure will assign numbers to them, it is not the actual numbers, but rather their relative size that is important. Thus, any two measures which give rise to the same order of balance are considered equivalent from our point of view. Indeed, the order of balance is the basic concept; the measure of balance should be viewed simply as a convenient means for determining this order. To our surprise, the axioms we listed led us back to our original idea of obtaining a measure of relative balance by differentially weighting different length semicycles, summing, and then taking ratios.[2]

In the following we begin, after several introductory remarks in Section 3, by presenting in Section 4 a set of axioms for balance. In Section 5 we discuss the proof, given in Norman-Roberts (1972), that the axioms uniquely determine the balance ordering, subject to the specification of certain parameters. In Section 6 we describe the measure and illustrate it with several examples. Section 7 discusses the parameters and remarks on how the parameters can be chosen. In Section 8 we indicate how the results of this paper can be applied to measure local balance rather than global balance. In Section 9 we apply the measure to formalize certain distinctions of the theory of distributive justice described in an earlier paper in this volume (Chapter 6). Finally, in the Appendix we discuss the problem of axiomatizing the balance ordering directly, rather than using the indirect approach applied in the earlier sections. We present a second axiomatization for the balance ordering which results in the same representation theorem for the measure of balance. The results in the Appendix are much more sophisticated mathematically, and we do not discuss them in any detail.

□ **3. SOME INTRODUCTORY REMARKS ON WHAT THE MEASURE DOES AND DOES NOT DO**

Our purpose is to define a measure of relative balance that is applicable to

---

[2] Of course, the final set of axioms as listed in this paper is somewhat different from our original list. But the changes (additions, deletions, and modifications) are all based on mathematical motivations arising from the proofs we constructed.

social structures. The wide collection of social structures to which our measure seems applicable consists of those which, in their abstract form, can be represented by signed digraphs. Signed digraphs have the advantage of being precisely defined, a quality essential to the axiomatic development of a measure. In applications it will thus be necessary to translate a given social situation into a signed digraph, and then to apply the measure of relative balance.

The significance of this translation procedure must not be overlooked. It is the task of the user of the measure to translate his social situation into a signed digraph. This translation procedure is illustrated by a specific example in Section 9. Given this signed digraph, our balance measure presents the user with a number which in some sense represents its degree of balance. This number in and of itself is not important. It is significant only when we are considering two or more structures where it is used to answer the question: which of the two structures is the more balanced? The numbers are simply used to determine the ordering, with the situation getting the higher number considered more balanced. Thus, if it should turn out that one structure has balance .55 and another .43, the measure tells us that the first is more balanced than the second. We would not say that the first is more and the second less than half balanced; nor would the difference .12 have any special significance.

The reverse procedure, that of assigning a sociological interpretation to a given signed digraph, can often lead to different plausible interpretations. Now of two given signed digraphs, one may be more balanced under one sociological interpretation and less balanced under another. This indicates that it will be impossible to assign a fixed number to measure the balance of a given signed digraph.

In conclusion, in order to be universally applicable, our measure of relative balance will have to involve some parameters whose value is to be determined beforehand by the user. In Section 7 we show how the user can determine the parameters arising in our measure before he applies it. This is accomplished by merely answering a few key questions relative to balance in his social situation. First, in the next section, we turn to the axioms for balance.

□ 4. THE AXIOMS

4.1. Distance Axioms

Our approach to obtaining the balance ordering is axiomatic, and is modeled after that of Kemeny and Snell (1962) in their attempt to obtain a consensus from the rankings among alternatives obtained from a group of experts. They first axiomatize a measure of distance between two rankings and then define a consensus ranking in terms of the distance measure. Similarly, instead of directly axiomatizing a measure of relative balance, we first axiomatize a measure of distance between two so-called "semicycle sequences" and from this determine the relative balance of the corresponding signed digraphs. We assume that the importance of a semicycle depends solely on its length, and that the relative weights for the lengths of semicycles depend on the particular interpretation of signed digraphs in the social setting. Once these relative weights are determined and fixed, our axioms determine the distance function and the balance ordering uniquely.

In measuring distance and balance it will be necessary to count the number of positive semicycles of each length in a signed digraph, starting with length 3. For the signed digraph of Figure 4 the sequence of numbers (2, 1, 0) represents the fact that there are 2 positive semicycles of length 3, one of length 4, and none of length 5. The sequence (1, 1, 1) counts the negative semicycles, for there is one for each of the lengths 3, 4, and 5.

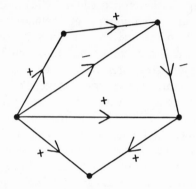

■ FIGURE 4.

This means of counting is fine as long as all the signed digraphs under discussion have the same maximum semicycle length. To compare signed digraphs of different maximum semicycle length we can conveniently represent the count of semicycles by tacking on additional zeros. Thus, if we need to compare the signed digraph of Figure 4 with one having a semicycle of length 6, we might represent positive and negative semicycle counts above by the sequences (2, 1, 0, 0) and (1, 1, 1, 0), since there are no semicycles of length 6. To avoid the multiplicity of representations it is convenient to think of these sequences as having infinitely many components, all but the first (finite) few being zero. Thus these two sequences would be (2, 1, 0, 0, . . .) and (1, 1, 1, 0, . . .), where the ellipsis is used to indicate infinitely many zeros from that point on. For practical purposes we will simply ignore the unneeded zeros.

To introduce some definitions, suppose G is a signed digraph. By its *positive semicycle sequence* we shall mean the infinite sequence $A = (a_3, a_4, \ldots, a_m, \ldots)$, where a_m is the number of (positively) balanced semicycles of length m in G. The entries in A of course are 0 from some point on. Similarly, if b_m is the number of negative semicycles of length m, then $B = (b_3, b_4, \ldots, b_m, \ldots)$ is the *negative semicycle sequence*. The pair (A, B) is the *semicycle sequence pair*, or the *semicycle pair* for short. In the following we shall develop a technique for determining the relative balance of two signed digraphs. The order of balance will be based entirely on the semicycle pair. (Some people allow the possibility of semicycles of length 2. The following discussion is easily modified to include these semicycles placing components a_2 and b_2 at the beginning of the appropriate semicycle sequences.)

In what follows, sequences will be denoted by capital letters A, B, C, ... and A will always be the sequence $(a_3, a_4, \ldots, a_m, \ldots)$, B the sequence $(b_3, b_4, \ldots, b_m, \ldots)$, etc. If A and B are sequences, $A + B$ is the sequence obtained by adding corresponding entries, i.e., the sequence $(a_3 + b_3, a_4 + b_4, \ldots, a_m + b_m, \ldots)$. If k is an integer, kA is the sequence obtained from A by multiplying each term by k, i.e., kA is the sequence $(ka_3, ka_4, \ldots, ka_m, \ldots)$. (These definitions are the usual ones for the arithmetic of vectors.)

All of our sequences will be *nonnegative*, i.e., each entry will be positive or zero. Two special examples of sequences are needed. One is called 0, and denotes the sequence all of whose entries are 0. The other has all but one of its entries 0, and the remaining entry is 1. More precisely, for each semicycle length m we denote by I_m the sequence $(a_3, a_4, \ldots, a_m, \ldots)$ in which $a_i = 0$ for $i \neq m$ and $a_m = 1$. Thus, $I_5 = (0, 0, 1, 0, \ldots)$. The sequence kI_m is the same as I_m except that k replaces 1. Thus, $kI_5 = (0, 0, k, 0, \ldots)$. In Figure 5, G has semicycle pair $(I_4, 5I_3)$ and H has semicycle pair (I_3, I_3). It should be mentioned that every pair of sequences (A, B) with either $A \neq 0$ or $B \neq 0$ is the semicycle pair of some signed digraph.

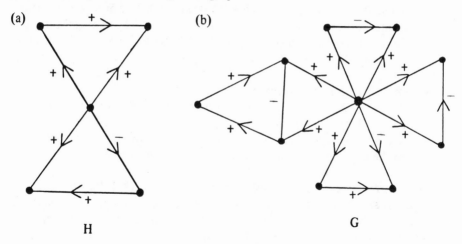

(a)   (b)

H   G

■ FIGURE 5. G has semicycle pair $(I^*, 5I_3)$. H has semicycle pair (I_3, I_3).

Our first objective is to find a distance measure d which assigns to each pair of nonnegative sequences A and B a real number $d(A, B)$ representing the distance from A to B. This distance function will be asked to satisfy certain axioms, motivated by the Kemeny-Snell (1962) axioms for distance between preference rankings. To introduce the axioms, we need to define the notion of one sequence being between two others. We use the Kemeny-Snell definition here, and say that if A, B, and C are sequences then B is *between* A and C if for all m, $a_m \leq b_m \leq c_m$ or $a_m \geq b_m \geq c_m$. We denote this $[A, B, C]$.

For example, if $A = (2, 1, 0)$, $B = (1, 4, 5)$ and $C = (0, 6, 5)$ then $[A, B, C]$.

Note that $a_3 \geq b_3 \geq c_3$ but $a_5 \leq b_5 \leq c_5$; the betweenness relations need not be in the same direction.

We shall assume that the measure d satisfies the following four axioms, which are identical to those given in Norman-Roberts (1972).

DISTANCE AXIOMS. Let A, B, C be sequences of nonnegative integers (zero from some point on).

AXIOM 1. *Nonnegativity:*
  $d(A, B) \geq 0$ and $d(A, B) > 0$ if $A \neq B$. In words, the distance from A to B is a nonnegative number, and the distance from A to B is positive if A is different from B.

AXIOM 2. *Symmetry:*
  $d(A, B) = d(B, A)$. In words, the distance from A to B is the same as the distance from B to A.

AXIOM 3. *Betweenness:*
  If $[A, B, C]$ then $d(A, C) = d(A, B) + d(B, C)$. In words, if B is between A and C, then the distance from A to C is obtained by adding the distance from A to B and the distance from B to C. In other words, if B is between A and C, then we can find the distance from A to C by going through B.

AXIOM 4. *Translation Invariance:*
  $d(A + C, B + C) = d(A, B)$. In words, if we add the same sequence C to each of A and B, i.e., replacing each component a_m of A by $a_m + c_m$ and b_m of B by $b_m + c_m$, then the distance from one of the new sequences to the other is the same as the distance from A to B.

To illustrate these axioms, suppose we take $A = (2, 1, 0)$, $B = (1, 4, 5)$, $C = (0, 6, 5)$. Moreover, suppose that distance is measured by taking the sum of the absolute values of the differences between the components; i.e., in symbols, suppose $d(A, B) = \sum |b_m - a_m|$, etc. Then $d(A, B) = |1 - 2| + |4 - 1| + |5 - 0| = 1 + 3 + 5 = 9$, $d(B, C) = 3$, $d(A, C) = 12$, $d(B, A) = 9$, $d(C, B) = 3$, $d(C, A) = 12$, $d(A, A) = 0$, $d(B, B) = 0$, $d(C, C) = 0$.

It is not hard to show that if distance is measured using this procedure, then Axioms 1–4 are satisfied. Indeed, the numbers we have calculated are all nonnegative, and positive if the sequences are different, illustrating Axiom 1. Axiom 2 seems to hold, since, for example, $d(A, B) = d(B, A)$ and $d(B, C) = d(C, B)$. To illustrate Axiom 3, note that $[A, B, C]$ holds, and we also have $d(A, C) = d(A, B) + d(B, C)$. Finally, to illustrate Axiom 4, note that

$$(A + C) = (2 + 0, 1 + 6, 0 + 5) = (2, 7, 5)$$
$$(B + C) = (1 + 0, 4 + 6, 5 + 5) = (1, 10, 10).$$

Then $d(A + C, B + C) = 1 + 3 + 5 = 9$, the same as $d(A, B)$.

The example just given illustrates the fact that if distance is defined by

$$d(A, B) = \sum_{m=3}^{\infty} |b_m - a_m|, \tag{1}$$

then all the axioms are satisfied. It turns out that any distance measure satisfying Axioms 1–4 is closely related to the distance measure (1). In fact, it can be shown (cf. Section 5) that if d is a distance measure satisfying these axioms, then there is a "weighting function" $f(m)$ so that d is given by

$$d(A, B) = \sum_{m=3}^{\infty} f(m) \cdot |b_m - a_m|. \tag{2}$$

The measure (1) is a special case of the measure (2), obtained by taking $f(m) = 1$ for each m.

> REMARK. There are properties of distance to which we are accustomed which are not stated in the axioms. For example, we usually assume $d(A, A) = 0$, i.e., that the distance from a point to itself is 0. We also usually assume the triangle inequality, i.e., $d(A, C) \le d(A, B) + d(B, C)$. In fact, these properties of distance follow from the four axioms stated above, and thus we do not need to state these additional properties as axioms.

4.2. Balance Axiom

Our study of balance will be restricted to the class of all signed digraphs having at least one semicycle. The notion of balance is ambiguous for signed digraphs with no semicycles,[3] so these signed digraphs are omitted from our discussion.

The purpose of our balance measure is to decide whether one signed digraph is more balanced than another. Our axiom for balance relates the order of balance to the distance measure. Since order can be conveniently determined through a numerical valued measure, this axiom is expressed in terms of a balance measure b, which assigns to each signed digraph (with at least one semicycle) a number $b(G)$. This measure b is not uniquely defined by the axiom; only the ordering it produces is unique. After stating the axiom and the uniqueness theorems for balance measures, we present a particularly convenient measure b that produces the right order.

The balance axiom we need, Axiom 5, relates the balance measure b to the distance measure d discussed in the previous section.

> AXIOM 5. Let G and H be signed digraphs with semicycle pairs (A, B) and (C, D) respectively. Then

---

[3] These signed digraphs have been called *vacuously balanced* by Cartwright and Harary (1956), who discuss some experimental work by Jordan (1953) which indicates that the vacuously balanced social structures have a degree of balance (more precisely, degree of "pleasantness") essentially neutrally located between the balanced and the unbalanced ones.

$$b(G) \leq b(H) \quad \text{if and only if} \quad \frac{d(A, 0)}{d(0, B)} \leq \frac{d(C, 0)}{d(0, D)},$$

where 0 is the semicycle sequence consisting entirely of zeros.

Axiom 5 allows us to determine the balance ordering from the distance measure. It says that relative balance is dependent only on the semicycle sequences, and in particular on how far the respective positive and negative semicycle sequences are from those of certain signed digraphs having no positive semicycles and others having no negative semicycles. Partly to motivate the use of the ratio here rather than, say, the difference, we note that we are assuming the following principle: if the distances from 0 of both the positive and negative semicycle sequences are doubled, then we would expect the balance to remain unchanged. Any two balance measures satisfying Axiom 5 are considered equivalent from our point of view, as they give rise to the same balance ordering. That is, if b and b' are two such measures, then for all G and H, $b(G) \leq b(H)$ if and only if $b'(G) \leq b'(H)$.

Axiom 5 differs from the balance axioms in Norman-Roberts (1972) in the sense that those are stated in terms of a balance order, while this one is stated in terms of the measure b. The difference is not significant.

Formally, it would be nice to derive a balance ordering strictly from axioms stated in terms of balance and not introduce the extra concept of distance. We outline such an approach in the Appendix. Our reason for using the distance axiomatization here was twofold. First, we were motivated by the Kemeny-Snell approach to preference rankings, which led to a unique measure. Second, and more important, we wanted to begin with some quite simple axioms and see where they led us. The problem of listing a more formally satisfying set of axioms came second.

□ 5. UNIQUENESS OF THE BALANCE MEASURE

The axioms discussed in Section 4 determine the balance ordering uniquely, subject to choice of parameters $f(m)$. This is proved in detail in Norman-Roberts (1972). The present section contains a discussion of the uniqueness theorems. The reader not interested in specifics about uniqueness should skip to Section 6.

The first step in the mathematical development in Norman-Roberts (1972) shows that Axioms 1–4 uniquely determine the distance measure up to choice of parameters $f(m)$. Precisely, as hinted in Section 4.1, one proves the following theorem.

THEOREM 1. *Uniqueness of Distance:*
For any given positive real numbers $f(3), f(4), \ldots, f(m), \ldots$, there is a unique distance measure d on the set of all sequences of nonnegative integers (zero from some point on) which satisfies Axioms 1–4 and has the property that for each semicycle length m, $d(0, I_m) = f(m)$. Specifically, if $A = (a_3, a_4, \ldots, a_m, \ldots)$ and $B = (b_3, b_4, \ldots, b_m, \ldots)$, then

$$d(A, B) = \sum_{m=3}^{\infty} f(m)|b_m - a_m|. \tag{3}$$

Thus, one interpretation of the number $f(m)$ is to consider it as the distance between the sequence 0 and the sequence I_m. We offer another interpretation below.

The determination of the balance ordering follows directly from Theorem 1. The following theorem states the main result.[4]

THEOREM 2. *Uniqueness of the Balance Ordering:*
Suppose that b is a balance measure which assigns a real number to each signed digraph with at least one semicycle. And suppose that there is a distance measure d satisfying Axioms 1–4 and related to b by Axiom 5. Then:
(a) There are positive numbers $f(3), f(4), \ldots, f(m), \ldots$ so that for any two signed digraphs G and H with semicycle pairs (A, B) and (C, D), respectively,

$$b(G) \le b(H) \longleftrightarrow \frac{\sum\limits_{m=3}^{\infty} f(m)a_m}{\sum\limits_{m=3}^{\infty} f(m)b_m} \le \frac{\sum\limits_{m=3}^{\infty} f(m)c_m}{\sum\limits_{m=3}^{\infty} f(m)d_m}, \tag{4}$$

where $A = (a_3, a_4, \ldots, a_m, \ldots)$, $B = (b_3, b_4, \ldots, b_m, \ldots)$, $C = (c_3, c_4, \ldots, c_m, \ldots)$ and $D = (d_3, d_4, \ldots, d_m, \ldots)$.
(b) If $f'(m)$ also satisfies (4), then there is a positive number q so that for all $m, f'(m) = qf(m)$.
(c) If b is a measure of balance satisfying (4), then there is a distance measure d satisfying Axioms 1–4 and related to b by Axiom 5.

As a consequence of Theorem 2, we see that the balance ordering is determined uniquely up to specification of parameters $f(m)$. In order to ascertain the relative balance of a signed digraph G with semicycle pair (A, B), we need only calculate the numbers

$$B(G) = \frac{\sum\limits_{m=3}^{\infty} f(m)a_m}{\sum\limits_{m=3}^{\infty} f(m)b_m}. \tag{5}$$

Now, if we take

$$b(G) = \frac{\sum\limits_{m=3}^{\infty} f(m)a_m}{\sum\limits_{m=3}^{\infty} f(m)(a_m + b_m)}, \tag{6}$$

[4] The precise formulation of this theorem differs from that in Norman-Roberts (1972), where the result is stated in terms of a quaternary relation L.

then

$$b(G) \leq b(H) \quad \text{if and only if} \quad B(G) \leq B(H).$$

Since any two measures of relative balance giving rise to the same balance ordering are considered equivalent, we may take (6) as the measure of relative balance. This has the advantage that each term in the denominator is the product of $f(m)$ by the number of semicycles of length m in the signed digraph. Thus, if one is studying the effect on balance of varying the assignment of signs to the lines of a fixed digraph, the denominator remains constant and the relative balance is determined by the size of the numerator alone. Another advantage of (6) is that the balance comes out as a number between 0 and 1.

Part (b) of Theorem 2 says that the parameters $f(m)$ are essentially unique, given the balance ordering. One can show that the parameters $f(m)$ can be interpreted directly in terms of the relative balance of some simple signed digraphs, and this gives us a simple way to determine the parameters in practice. In particular, one can prove (cf. Norman-Roberts [1972]) the following theorem.

THEOREM 3. Suppose b is a balance measure on the class of all signed digraphs having at least one semicycle, and suppose there is a distance measure d satisfying Axioms 1–4 and related to b by Axiom 5. Let H be the signed digraph consisting of one positive and one negative semicycle of length 3. For given positive integers k, ℓ and m, let G be a signed digraph with semicycle pair $(kI_m, \ell I_3)$, i.e., G has k positive semicycles of length m and ℓ negative semicycles of length 3. Then we may assume that $f(m)$ as described in (a) of Theorem 2 satisfies the following:

$$f(m) \leq \ell/k \quad \text{if} \quad b(G) \leq b(H)$$

and

$$f(m) \geq \ell/k \quad \text{if} \quad b(G) \geq b(H).$$

In this theorem, H might be thought of as a "half-balanced" signed digraph. To determine $f(m)$ we search for the smallest fraction ℓ/k we can find such that $b(G) \leq b(H)$. Then $f(m)$ is approximated by ℓ/k.

For example, as an application of this theorem, if G and H are as shown in Figure 6 and G is regarded as no more balanced than H, then $f(5) \leq 3/2$.

□ **6. THE BALANCE MEASURE**

6.1. Description of the Measure

There are many balance measures which are related by Axiom 5 to a distance measure d satisfying Axioms 1–4. For any such balance measure the balance ordering, of course, is completely determined. Any two such measures are

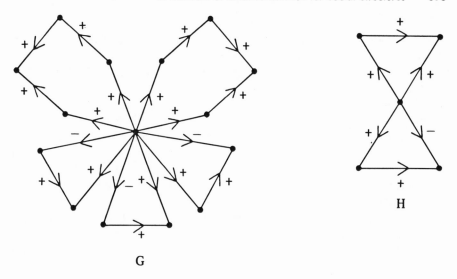

■ FIGURE 6. *G* has semicycle pair $(2I_5, 3I_3)$; *H* has semicycle pair (I_3, I_3).

regarded as equivalent from our point of view. In particular, a convenient measure which satisfies the axioms is given by

$$b(G) = \frac{\displaystyle\sum_{m=3}^{\infty} f(m)a_m}{\displaystyle\sum_{m=3}^{\infty} f(m)(a_m + b_m)}, \tag{7}$$

where *G* has semicycle pair (A, B).

For example, the signed digraph *H* shown in Figure 1 has semicycle pair $((4, 2), (4, 4))$ and the signed digraph *H'* shown in Figure 3 has semicycle pair $((6, 4), (2, 2))$. Thus, $b(H) = [4f(3) + 2f(4)]/[8f(3) + 6f(4)]$ and $b(H') = [6f(3) + 4f(4)]/[8f(3) + 6f(4)]$. If the parameters $f(m)$ are chosen to be $1/m$, for example, then we have $b(H) = 11/25$ and $b(H') = 18/25$, and we conclude that in this case *H* is less balanced than *H'*.

It is interesting to note that this measure *b* is exactly the measure $\sum f(m)c_m{}^+/\sum f(m)c_m$ discussed in Section 2. In particular, choice of $f(m) = 1$ for all *m* leads to the measure c^+/c suggested by Cartwright and Harary (1956). (Only the relative *N*-balance measure discussed in Section 2 must be redefined, since by Theorem 2, $f(m)$ is required to be positive. We simply take $f(m)$ to be 1 if $m \leq N$ and $f(m)$ arbitrarily small for $m > N$, where how small we take $f(m)$ depends on the length of the longest semicycle appearing in any of the signed digraphs under study. We shall denote the parameters for the relative *N*-balance measure by $f_N(m)$.)

6.2. A Remark on Counting Semicycles

A remark about the counting of positive and negative semicycles is in order. The signed digraph of Figure 7a has two semicycles: e_1, e_2, e_3, and e_1, e_2, e_4.[5] If there are lines going in both directions between two points (as from x_1 to x_3 and x_3 to x_1), and both lines have the same sign, then the signed digraph can be conveniently represented by drawing nondirected lines between such points, as shown in Figure 7b. In practice, in applications of balance theory, a signed digraph like this is sometimes considered to have only one (negative) semicycle rather than two. In general, if all the two-way relations can be represented by nondirected lines with signs, rather than dealing with the number of positive and negative semicycles, users of balance theory frequently count the number of positive and negative *cycles* in the signed *graph* obtained by omitting all arrows. A *cycle* here is defined analogously to a semicycle, i.e., as a sequence of nondirected lines starting from a given point and returning to it, and never going through a given point twice.

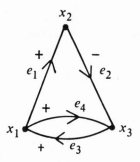

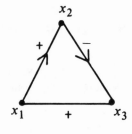

■ FIGURE 7a.   ■ FIGURE 7b.

Our balance ordering is based entirely on the semicycle pair. The discussion applies equally well to the situation where instead of the semicycle pair one is dealing with the sequence pair obtained by this modified method of counting semicycles. But it should be pointed out that the relative balance ordering obtained can vary considerably depending on the semicycle counting procedure used. It is up to the user to decide on one or the other.

Fortunately there are two important special cases where we can use either semicycle counting procedure and get the same results. One is the case where the digraph is asymmetric, i.e., where there are never lines in both directions between two points. The second important case arises when all the relationships are symmetric and symmetric pairs of lines have the same sign. Here we are dealing with a signed graph. (This situation might arise, for example, in the study of small groups, where each point of the group represents a person and each line a relationship such as 'associates with'.) Here, for any balance ordering obtained by a given choice of parameters $f(m)$ and with the strict semicycle counting procedure, there is a corresponding choice of parameters $f'(m)$ which

---

[5] It also has a semicycle e_3, e_4, but we are disregarding semicycles of length 2.

gives the same balance ordering under the modified semicycle counting procedure, which is simply the cycle counting procedure. That is, since there are 2^m semicycles in a given cycle of length m, one simply takes $f'(m) = 2^m f(m)$.

□ 7. THE PARAMETERS f(m)

In using the balance ordering defined by (7), it is first necessary to specify the function f, which is a measure of the effect of the length of a semicycle. In this section, we discuss the selection of an appropriate f.

The positivity of f alone is frequently sufficient to determine relative balance. Namely, in computing balance, it often will follow that

$$\sum f(m)a_m / \sum f(m)(a_m + b_m) > \sum f(m)c_m / \sum f(m)(c_m + d_m)$$

simply because $f(m) > 0$. In this case, the user of the measure need not select a particular f. The example given in Section 9 illustrates this point.

More often, it is possible to avoid specifying f exactly by just using several of its qualitative properties. For example, as we argued earlier, it is natural to assume that longer semicycles are not as important for balance (or imbalance) as shorter ones. Thus, we would expect that for all $m \geq n$, if G and H had semicycle pairs (I_m, I_n) and (I_3, I_3) respectively, then $b(G) \leq b(H)$. (G has one positive semicycle of length m and one negative semicycle of length n, and no other semicycles, while H has only two semicycles, each of length 3, one positive and one negative.) It follows that $f(m) \leq f(n)$ whenever $m \geq n$. Frequently this "monotone nonincreasing" property of the numbers $f(m)$ is sufficient to determine, on the basis of the formulas $\sum f(m)a_m / \sum f(m)(a_m + b_m)$, which of two signed digraphs is more balanced.

If these qualitative properties of f are not sufficient to answer questions of relative balance, the user will have to specify a particular parameter or class of parameters. If semicycles of different lengths are considered equally important, then the Cartwright-Harary f, i.e., $f(m) = 1$, for all m, will suffice. Or, the relative N-balance f, i.e., $f_N(m)$ as defined in Section 6.1, might be a natural modification of this. Otherwise, the user can still choose the parameters in a systematic way which we shall describe. It is important to indicate, lest there be any confusion, that the user must make such a choice only once during his study. From then on his f remains fixed.

In general, Theorem 3 allows us to describe a series of specific tests on f, a series of specific decisions as to which of two signed digraphs is more balanced, on the basis of which the user will be able to choose a particular f. This is easy enough to do if we limit ourselves to a short list of plausible f's, such as $1/m$, $1/m^2$, $1/2^m$, $3/m$, $3/m^2$, $3/2^m$, $1/(m-2)$, $1/(m-2)^2$, $1/2^{m-2}$, etc. Then Theorem 3 gives us simple tests to choose between any two of these. Such tests are summarized in Table 1.

The basic procedure in the use of Table 1 is the following. To choose between f and f', find the entry in the row marked f and the column marked f'. Let G be a signed digraph with semicycle pair shown as this entry. (Recall that

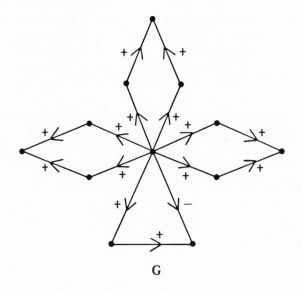

G

■ FIGURE 8.

$3I_4$ is the sequence $(0, 3, 0, 0 \ldots)$, $2I_3$ is the sequence $(2, 0, 0, \ldots)$, etc. Figure 8 shows a signed digraph with semicycle pair $(3I_4, I_3)$.) Let H be a signed digraph with semicycle pair (I_3, I_3). The user must decide whether or not $b(G) \leq b(H)$. If so, choose f rather than f'. If not, choose f'.

If two parameters f and f' share the same row or column, they are equivalent as far as the balance ordering is concerned. The choice between them is arbitrary. Thus, for example, the choice between $f(m) = 1/m$ and $f'(m) = 3/m$ can be made on purely computational grounds. Since it is often simplest to have $f(3) = 1$, the choice of f' will frequently be appropriate.

■ TABLE 1

f \\ f'	$1/(m-2)^2$	$1/2^m$ or $1/2^{m-2}$ or $3/2^m$	$1/(m-2)$	$1/m^2$ or $3/m^2$	$1/m$ or $3/m$
$1/(m-2)^2$		$3I_4, I_3$	$3I_4, I_3$	$2I_4, I_3$	$2I_4, I_3$
$1/2^m$ or $1/2^{m-2}$ or $3/2^m$			$4I_5, I_3$	$2I_4, I_3$	$2I_4, I_3$
$1/(m-2)$				$2I_4, I_3$	$2I_4, I_3$
$1/m^2$ or $3/m^2$					$3I_4, 2I_3$
$1/m$ or $3/m$					

Table 1 can be used another way, which is frequently more helpful if the user is starting out with no specific choice of f's in mind. Namely, he should first consider the signed digraph G with semicycle pair $(2I_4, I_3)$. On the basis of this signed digraph, the user can separate the measures into two classes, only one of which contains feasible f's. Namely, if $b(G) \le b(H)$, where H is a signed digraph with semicycle pair (I_3, I_3), then only the top three rows give feasible f's. Conversely, if $b(G) > b(H)$, then only the bottom two rows give feasible f's. Next, having limited the choice to either the top two rows or the bottom three, the reader can go to the table and easily make his selection.

The reader can easily extend Table 1 to other plausible parameters f, if he understands the simple principle on which the table was built. To illustrate, let us consider the choice between $\dfrac{1}{(m-2)}$ and $\dfrac{1}{(m-2)^2}$. Suppose G and H are the signed digraphs with semicycle pairs $(3I_4, I_3)$ and (I_3, I_3) respectively. Note that in both cases, $f(3) = 1$. Using Theorem 3, $b(G) \le b(H)$ implies $f(4) \le 1/3$. Thus $f(4) < 1/2$. But if $f(m) = 1/(m-2)$, then $f(4) = 1/2$. We conclude that we cannot have $f(m) = 1/(m-2)$. On the other hand, if $b(H) \le b(G)$, then we have $f(4) \ge 1/3$. Thus, $f(4) > 1/4 = 1/2^2$, and we conclude that $f(m)$ cannot be $1/(m-2)^2$.

□ **8. LOCAL BALANCE**

In practice we frequently have in the signed digraph G a distinguished point P. This might be true for example in small group studies where all the relations are evaluated from the point of view of a particular individual. In this case, a possibly more useful measure is the "local balance" at P, introduced by Harary (1955). Here, the procedure is the same as that described above, except that every time the word "semicycle" is mentioned, it should be replaced by the words "semicycle through P." Thus, let $a_{m,P} = $ the number of positively balanced semicycles of length m through P and let $b_{m,P} = $ the number of negatively balanced semicycles of length m through P. Then, following (7) of Section 6.1, the local balance at P, $b_P(G)$, is given by

$$\sum_{m=3}^{\infty} f(m)a_{m,P} \Big/ \sum_{m=3}^{\infty} f(m)[a_{m,P} + b_{m,P}].$$

To give an example, let us return to the signed digraph H of Figure 1 and calculate the local balance at the point 1. Here, the only positively balanced semicycles of length 3 through this point are 12, 23, 13; 16, 67, 17; and 15, 57, 17. Thus, $a_{3,1} = 3$. Similarly, $a_{4,1} = 2$, $b_{3,1} = 3$, $b_{4,1} = 4$, and all other $a_{m,1}$ and $b_{m,1}$ are 0. Thus, $b_1(H) = [3f(3) + 2f(4)]/[6f(3) + 6f(4)]$.

It also seems tempting to speak of different degrees of local balance. Thus, a second degree local balance measure at P might be obtained by some sort of (weighted) average of the local balance at points of distance at most one from P. Higher degree local balance measures might be obtained by taking points of distance at most N, for some N. (Taylor [1970, pp. 211ff] suggests measuring locality of a semicycle by measuring its distance to P.) All of these suggestions are ad hoc, and the whole concept of different degrees of local balance, if it turns out to be valuable, should probably be put on a firmer axiomatic foundation.

A much more difficult situation arises if we have no distinguished point P. It still may be useful to measure local balance. If the computations are not too involved, it may be useful to compute not only global balance, but also local balance at all the points (and possibly several degrees of local balance at each point). Investigation of all this data might reveal that a particular point is crucial.

A final question of considerable subtlety which is mentioned by Taylor (1970, p. 214) centers around how one weighs the effect of a long local semicycle (semicycle through P) versus that of a short nonlocal semicycle. Undoubtedly the answer will involve an understanding of the relation between the parameter $f(m)$ and an additional parameter measuring locality of a semicycle.

□ **9. AN APPLICATION
OF THE BALANCE ORDERING
TO THE DISTRIBUTIVE
JUSTICE PROCESS**

A concrete application will illustrate the use of the balance ordering derived above in a theoretical context, the theory of distributive justice.

The theory of distributive justice is concerned with the relations among certain actors' socially valued characteristics (hair color, sex, mechanical ability, etc.) and socially valued rewards (salaries, promotions, privileges, esteem of others, the key to the executive washroom, etc.).

The basic underlying idea in this theory is that an actor develops certain expectations about what his rewards or goal objects should be, based on comparisons with other actors. If there is a violation of expectation, the situation is called imbalanced. Tension is produced and there is some sort of pressure to change the situation.

The outlines of a theory of distributive justice are described in Berger, Zelditch, Anderson, and Cohen (1972) and in Zelditch, Berger and Cohen (1966). We shall briefly sketch this theory, but shall freely refer the reader to details in Berger et al. (1972) (Chapter 6 of this volume).

Basically, the situation deals with two actors, an individual person P, and another person, O. Both P and O *possess* certain *characteristics* in either high or low *states* (e.g., high or low "mechanical ability"). Moreover, both P and O possess certain *goal objects* in either high or low states (e.g., high or low "salary") and have *expectations* about achieving these goal objects. States of characteristics and goal objects may be *relevant* to each other. An element (the state of a characteristic or goal object) e_i is said to be relevant to another element e_j if whenever a person possesses e_i he expects to possess e_j.

The entire theory is developed from P's point of view, and his *evaluations* of states of characteristics and goal objects are based on a *referential structure* consisting of generalized persons (e.g., "typical skilled auto mechanics") with *similar* characteristics and goal objects. Although we shall not make explicit use of the referential structure (except in one place), the reader should understand that it is important in defining the evaluations we do use.

In the following, we shall illustrate how the balance measure derived earlier formalizes certain important distinctions made in distributive justice theory. In the process of analyzing one of these distinctions more deeply, we shall learn something about our balance measure, namely that it is not only convenient but necessary to allow different length semicycles to have different weights. To our knowledge, such a conclusion has not been theoretically derived before.

To begin the formalization, let us again denote by P and O the two actors and let P' be P considered as a referent for P's evaluation. Let us restrict our discussion to one characteristic and one goal object, with one state of each possessed by P and by O. As Berger et al. (1972) do, let us assume that P' and O each receive the evaluation accorded the states of their characteristics, with these evaluations of states of characteristics made in accordance with certain "spread of value" assumptions. Finally, let $GO(P)$ and $GO(O)$ denote the states of the goal objects possessed by P and O respectively. Note that $GO(P)$ and $GO(O)$ may be the same, if both P and O possess the same state of the goal object (such as high salary, for example).

We look at P', O, and the states of the goal objects, as do Berger et al., from the point of view of P, and assume that P evaluates the state of each goal object either positively or negatively. We assume that P is seen to possess $GO(P)$ and O to possess $GO(O)$, we indicate possession by introducing the lines $P'GO(P)$ and $OGO(O)$, and we assume that possession is a positive relationship. Thus we obtain a signed digraph G_1 as shown in Figure 9.

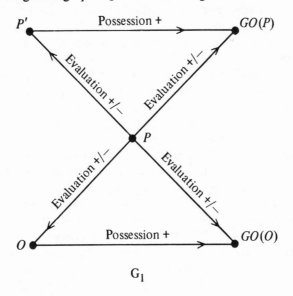

G_1

■ FIGURE 9.

Under the assumption that $f(m)$ is positive, we have calculated in Table 2, using (7) of Section 6.1, the relative balance measure $b(G_1)$ of G_1 for different choices of signs on the remaining lines: PP', $PGO(P)$, PO, $PGO(O)$. Cases 1, 4, 13, and 16 are called by Berger et al. cases of *justice*; Cases 6, 7, 10, and 11 are cases of *collective imbalance*; Cases 2, 3, 14, and 15 are cases of *other imbalance*, and the remaining cases are those of *self imbalance*.

■ TABLE 2   Relative Balance in 16 Cases of Distributive Justice

Cases	PP'	$PGO(P)$	PO	$PGO(O)$	$b(G_1)$	Description
1	+	+	+	+	1	Justice
2	+	+	+	−	1/2	Other Imbalance
3	+	+	−	+	1/2	Other Imbalance
4	+	+	−	−	1	Justice
5	+	−	+	+	1/2	Self Imbalance
6	+	−	+	−	0	Collective Imbalance
7	+	−	−	+	0	Collective Imbalance
8	+	−	−	−	1/2	Self Imbalance
9	−	+	+	+	1/2	Self Imbalance
10	−	+	+	−	0	Collective Imbalance
11	−	+	−	+	0	Collective Imbalance
12	−	+	−	−	1/2	Self Imbalance
13	−	−	+	+	1	Justice
14	−	−	+	−	1/2	Other Imbalance
15	−	−	−	+	1/2	Other Imbalance
16	−	−	−	−	1	Justice

Let us examine some of the distinctions which can be made. First, the balance ordering distinguishes just states from unjust states. The four cases of justice are exactly the ones receiving a relative balance of 1. For all other cases, relative balance is less than 1. The case of collective imbalance is distinguished from that of *individual imbalance* (self imbalance or other imbalance), since all the cases of collective imbalance receive a relative balance measure of 0, while all the cases of individual imbalance receive measure 1/2.

At this level of analysis, the order of balance does not make two other important distinctions of distributive justice theory. These are distinctions between self imbalance versus other imbalance and between *overreward* versus *underreward* (situations in which an actor possesses a goal object state which is too high versus those in which he possesses a goal object state which is too low). The self imbalance versus other imbalance distinction can be made by using the local balance at P', since $b_{P'}(G_1)$ is 1 in cases of other imbalance and 0 in cases of self imbalance. It is not clear that the over versus underreward distinction can be made on purely balance-theoretic grounds.

Interesting results can be obtained by considering the situation of collective imbalance in more detail. It is argued in Berger et al. (1972) that this situation has some elements of stability in it, since there is some chance of coalition behavior here. A balance-theoretic analysis of this observation is very revealing.

In a particular situation of collective imbalance, let us represent by a line the attraction or repulsion between P' and O and let us consider what sign (+ for attraction, − for repulsion) will be induced on this line. Let us assume that coalition will take place if and only if the two actors are attracted, and that the sign induced on this line will be that sign (if there is one) which makes the resultant signed digraph more balanced.[6] This accords with the general assumptions of balance theorists as outlined by Taylor (1970, pp. 85ff.).

There are four cases of collective imbalance: Cases 6, 7, 10, and 11 of Table 2. Let us consider the signed digraph G_2 of Figure 10 obtained from G_1 of Figure 9 by adding the line $P'O$. Let us denote by Case 6^+ the situation obtained from Case 6 where this line receives a positive evaluation, by 6^- the situation where it receives a negative evaluation. The cases 7^+, 7^-, 10^+, 10^-, 11^+, and 11^- have similar interpretations. We have calculated in Table 3 the numerator of the relative balance measure $b(G_2)$ in each of these cases. In each case the denominator is the same, so the numerator alone determines the balance ordering.

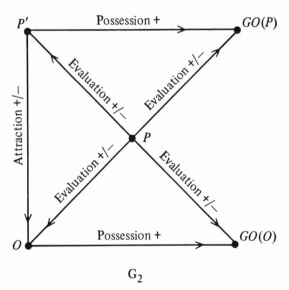

G_2

■ **FIGURE 10.**

Assuming that the parameter f is monotone nonincreasing, i.e., $f(m) \leq f(n)$ whenever $n \leq m$, we can now draw a number of substantive conclusions. The first one concerns our balance measure.

---

[6] It should be noted that this assumption implies that coalition behavior is explicable entirely by balance characteristics. We do not have to introduce any tendency or force which exists independently of balance forces. Such forces are called "cognitive biases" and are discussed in detail by Taylor (1970, pp. 120ff.).

CONCLUSION 1. *Differing Import of the Different Lengths of Semicycles:*
If there are situations of collective imbalance where coalition results, then semicycles of different lengths must in some cases have different weights.

To justify this conclusion, let us first assume that Case 6 is one where coalition occurs. It follows by our assumptions that 6^+ is better balanced than 6^-, so $f(3) + f(5) > 2f(4)$. Since $f(m)$ is monotone nonincreasing, we have $f(5) \leq f(4)$, which allows us to conclude that $f(3) > f(4)$. That is, semicycles of length 3 *must* carry more weight than those of length 4. The same conclusion follows if coalition occurs in Case 11. If coalition occurs in Case 7 or Case 10, however, we find that $f(3) + f(5) < 2f(4)$. Since $f(4) \leq f(3)$, we conclude that $f(4) > f(5)$. Here, semicycles of length 4 *must* carry more weight than those of length 5.

■ **TABLE 3** **Relative Balance of Attraction and Repulsion in Collective Imbalance Situations**

Case	Numerator of $b(G_2)$	Description
6^+	$f(3) + f(5)$	Both under
6^-	$2f(4)$	
7^+	$2f(4)$	Self under, other over
7^-	$f(3) + f(5)$	
10^+	$2f(4)$	Self over, other under
10^-	$f(3) + f(5)$	
11^+	$f(3) + f(5)$	Both over
11^-	$2f(4)$	

Another conclusion which follows from this analysis gives us a testable prediction concerning coalition formation. If coalition occurs in Case 6, it cannot occur in Case 7, since the former is the case if and only if $f(3) + f(5) > 2f(4)$, while the latter is the case if and only if $f(3) + f(5) < 2f(4)$. In fact, granting our assumptions, we have the following conclusion.

CONCLUSION 2. *Distinction among Different Cases of Collective Imbalance:*
One and only one of the following statements prevails:
  (i) In all collective imbalance situations, there is no coalition formation.
  (ii) Among collective imbalance situations, there is coalition formation only in the cases where self and other are both under or both over (Cases 6 and 11).
  (iii) Among collective imbalance situations, there is coalition formation only in the cases where exactly one actor is over and exactly one actor is under (Cases 7 and 10).

Moreover, (i), (ii), or (iii) prevails if and only if $f(3) + f(5)$ is respectively $=$, $>$, or $< 2f(4)$.

Intuitively, the most likely situation prevailing is (ii). By adding some additional information to the signed digraph and making some reasonable assumptions, we shall in fact be able to show that (ii) is the case.

To begin, we expand the signed digraph of Figure 9 by introducing explicitly the states of the characteristics seen to be possessed by P and O, labeled $C(P)$ and $C(O)$ respectively. We assume that $C(P)$ and $C(O)$ receive evaluations, which are indicated on the lines $PC(P)$ and $PC(O)$. As before, we shall assume that P' and O receive the evaluations accorded the states of their characteristics. Thus, the signs of the lines PP' and $PC(P)$ are the same, as are the signs of the lines PO and $PC(O)$.[7] The positive lines $P'C(P)$ and $OC(O)$ are added to indicate possession.

For the first time, we explicitly introduce information about relevance. (Relevance was introduced earlier if it is assumed that the evaluations we used were made according to the Berger et al. [1972] assumptions.) We assume relevance to be a positive relationship, and we draw a positive line from $C(P)$ to $GO(P)$ if $C(P)$ is relevant to $GO(P)$, and similarly for $C(O)$ and $GO(O)$. In our analysis, we shall assume that $C(P)$ is relevant to $GO(P)$ if and only if $C(P)$ and $GO(P)$ receive the same evaluation, and similarly for $C(O)$ and $GO(O)$. This follows from the Berger et al. assumptions about spread of value and relevance from the referential structure.[8]

---

[7] There are other plausible rules for determining evaluations for PP' and PO. For example, we might assume that these evaluations are determined a priori, and, perhaps, that P thinks highly of himself and not of O. Thus PP' is $+$ and PO is $-$ throughout. Under this assumption, the observed order of balance among cases of distributive justice turns out to be different from what it is under the assumption we use. In particular, as is plausible, Case 1 (both balanced high) is judged to be less balanced than Case 4 (self balanced high, other balanced low) and also less balanced than Cases 2, 3, 8 and 12 (individual imbalance with self balanced high or other balanced low). And one obtains quite different conclusions about coalition behavior in collective imbalance situations. It should also be remarked that there are some serious questions about assuming a priori evaluations. J. Berger (by personal communication) has pointed out that the distributive justice process may be inhibited if this occurs: "For example, if PP' is positive," it may be that "P is less likely to see a similarity between $C(P')$ and a negatively evaluated characteristic" in the referential structure. Or perhaps, under these conditions, spread of value doesn't occur in the way conceived in Berger et al. (1972).

[8] To see this, note that by the spread of relevance assumption, $C(O)$ will become relevant to $GO(O)$ only if there are states C_X and GO_Y in the referential structure so that C_X is associated with or relevant to GO_Y and $C(O)$, $GO(O)$ are similar to C_X, GO_Y respectively. Moreover, since the referential structure is balanced by the Berger et al. assumptions, it follows that C_X and GO_Y have the same evaluation. Thus by the spread of value assumption, so do $C(O)$ and $GO(O)$. Conversely, if $C(O)$ and $GO(O)$ have the same evaluation, it follows by the spread of value assumption that they are respectively similar to states C_X and GO_Y of the referential structure which have the same evaluation. It is tacitly assumed in Berger et al. (1972) that the referential structure, in addition to being balanced, unitary and differentiated, also is such that the positive (negative) state of a characteristic is associated with or relevant to the positive (negative) state of the goal object. It should be observed that the referential structure can be (vacuously) balanced without this occurring. But certainly there could be no distributive justice phenomenon if these characteristic and goal object states were irrelevant to each other. With the additional assumption of relevance, it follows that $C(O)$ becomes relevant to $GO(O)$, by the spread of relevance assumption. A similar discussion applies to $C(P)$ and $GO(P)$

We can summarize all the needed information in the signed digraph G_3 of Figure 11. The cases of distributive justice are now defined by the signs of the lines $PC(P)$, $PGO(P)$, $PC(O)$, $PGO(O)$. Figure 12 shows the signed digraph G_3 corresponding to these 16 cases, with the numbering corresponding to that in Table 4. In the last column of Table 4, we list the balance measure $b(G_3)$ for the signed digraph G_3 in each of these cases.

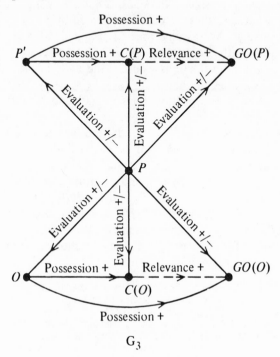

G_3

■ FIGURE 11.

It is not too hard to show that in fact the order of balance of these cases is completely determined without any assumptions about the parameter f except that it be positive. In particular, we find the cases ordered as before.

For suppose $a = [5f(3) + 3f(4)]/[6f(3) + 4f(4)]$ and $b = 2f(3)/[4f(3) + 2f(4)]$. Multiplying out, we see that $a > b$ if and only if

$$20f(3)^2 + 22f(3)f(4) + 6f(4)^2 > 12f(3)^2 + 8f(3)f(4).$$

This is true simply because f is positive, as can be seen by a term by term comparison.

Let us analyze coalition behavior in situations of collective imbalance using this more detailed signed digraph. Again, we do this by adding a line $P'O$

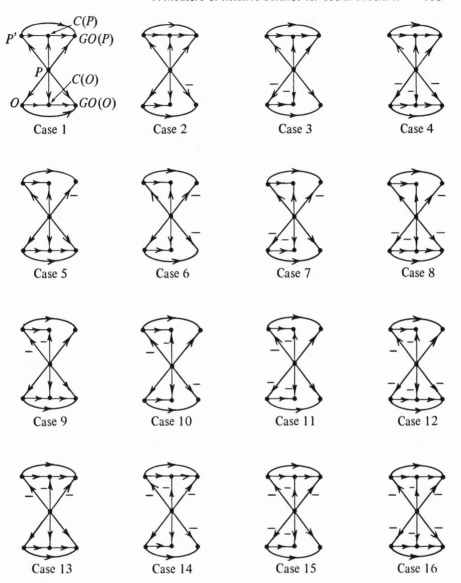

■ **FIGURE 12.** Signed digraph G_3 in 16 cases of distributive justice. (Lines without signs are +.)

and considering what sign will be induced on this line. The basic information is contained in the signed digraph G_4 of Figure 13. If the cases 6^+, 6^-, etc. are defined as before, we obtain the information shown in Table 5. We note

■ TABLE 4   Relative Balance in 16 Cases of Distributive Justice, with More Information Considered

Cases	$PC(P)$	$PGO(P)$	$PC(O)$	$PGO(O)$	$b(G_3)$
1	+	+	+	+	1
2	+	+	+	−	$\dfrac{5f(3) + 3f(4)}{6f(3) + 4f(4)}$
3	+	+	−	+	$\dfrac{5f(3) + 3f(4)}{6f(3) + 4f(4)}$
4	+	+	−	−	1
5	+	−	+	+	$\dfrac{5f(3) + 3f(4)}{6f(3) + 4f(4)}$
6	+	−	+	−	$\dfrac{2f(3)}{4f(3) + 2f(4)}$
7	+	−	−	+	$\dfrac{2f(3)}{4f(3) + 2f(4)}$
8	+	−	−	−	$\dfrac{5f(3) + 3f(4)}{6f(3) + 4f(4)}$
9	−	+	+	+	$\dfrac{5f(3) + 3f(4)}{6f(3) + 4f(4)}$
10	−	+	+	−	$\dfrac{2f(3)}{4f(3) + 2f(4)}$
11	−	+	−	+	$\dfrac{2f(3)}{4f(3) + 2f(4)}$
12	−	+	−	−	$\dfrac{5f(3) + 3f(4)}{6f(3) + 4f(4)}$
13	−	−	+	+	1
14	−	−	+	−	$\dfrac{5f(3) + 3f(4)}{6f(3) + 4f(4)}$
15	−	−	−	+	$\dfrac{5f(3) + 3f(4)}{6f(3) + 4f(4)}$
16	−	−	−	−	1

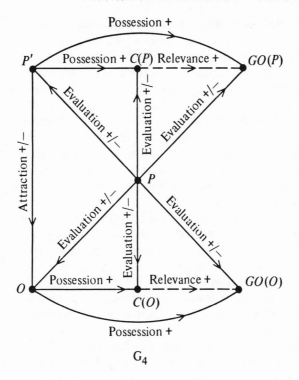

G_4

■ FIGURE 13.

that since f is positive, 6^+ is better balanced than 6^-. Thus we conclude that situation (ii) of Conclusion 2 holds.[9]

■ TABLE 5   **Relative Balance of Attraction and Repulsion in Collective Imbalance Situations, with More Information Considered**

Case	Numerator of $b(G_4)$	Description
6^+	$3f(3) + 2f(4) + 2f(5)$	Both under
6^-	$2f(3) + 2f(4) + 2f(5)$	
7^+	$2f(3) + 2f(4) + 2f(5)$	Self under, other over
7^-	$3f(3) + 2f(4) + 2f(5)$	
10^+	$2f(3) + 2f(4) + 2f(5)$	Self over, other under
10^-	$3f(3) + 2f(4) + 2f(5)$	
11^+	$3f(3) + 2f(4) + 2f(5)$	Both over
11^-	$2f(3) + 2f(4) + 2f(5)$	

[9] Note that if we assume a rule for assignment of the evaluations PP' and PO other than the one we have adopted, this conclusion need not follow. For example, if the a priori evaluations $PP' = +$ and $PO = -$ are used, then it is easy to show that coalition formation never takes place in cases of collective imbalance. This is not surprising, since P' and O receive opposite evaluations.

By the last part of Conclusion 2, it follows that $f(3) + f(5) > 2f(4)$, and, if f is monotone nonincreasing, this implies that $f(3) > f(4)$. That is, semicycles of length 3 are weighted more heavily than those of length 4. This is theoretical justification for the way semicycles are often weighted in practice.

To summarize, we have seen that a formalization of the distributive justice process using our measure of balance allows us to distinguish between cases of justice and injustice and between cases of collective imbalance and individual imbalance. Moreover, introducing the notion of local balance also allows us to distinguish between cases of self imbalance and other imbalance. The balance measure does not seem to be able to distinguish between cases of overreward and underreward, and it seems that this distinction might be due to extra–balance–theoretic forces.

Analysis of coalition behavior in a collective imbalance situation, in turn, tells us something about our balance measure. Namely, it shows that if the coalition behavior depends solely on forces of balance, and if there are situations of collective imbalance where coalition results, then semicycles of different lengths must in some cases have different weights. Next, using the balance measure, we obtain some testable conclusions about coalition formation. In particular, we see that if there is coalition formation in any collective imbalance situation, then it occurs exactly in those cases where self and other are both under or both over, or it occurs exactly in those cases where precisely one actor is over and one actor is under. More detailed analysis indicates that, under reasonable assumptions about determination of evaluations, coalition behavior can be expected to occur in exactly the both-under and both-over cases. This in turn implies that semicycles of length 3 must be weighted more heavily than semicycles of length 4.

□ APPENDIX: A DIFFERENT AXIOMATIZATION OF THE BALANCE ORDERING AND A CHARACTERIZATION OF EXTENSIVE RATIO SYSTEMS

From a formal point of view, it is somewhat unsatisfying to axiomatize the balance ordering by introducing the concept of distance. It would be nicer to state axioms purely in terms of the balance ordering. Our reasons for not doing this earlier were given at the end of Section 4.2.

Knowing now where the axioms of Section 4 have led us, namely to the representation (4) of Theorem 2, it is interesting and useful to list an alternative set of axioms, strictly in terms of balance ordering, which lead to the same balance measure.

Such a set of axioms was listed in Norman-Roberts (1972). To state them, let us begin by defining $\mathcal{S}$ to be the set of all infinite sequences of nonnegative integers with only finitely many nonzero terms. Suppose S is $\mathcal{S}$ less the sequence all of whose terms are zero.

Our axioms for balance will be stated in terms of the relation "is no more balanced than." We use the symbol $\leq$ to mean "is no more balanced than."

Thus $G \leq H$ is to be read "the signed digraph G is no more balanced than the signed digraph H." It is convenient to introduce one further abbreviation here. Suppose A, B, C, and D are sequences in S. Then the notation $L(A, B, C, D)$ will stand for the statement "a signed digraph G with semicycle pair (A, B) is no more balanced than a signed digraph H with semicycle pair (C, D)." (If there is no signed digraph G or H, $L(A, B, C, D)$ is assumed not to hold.) In terms of $\leq$, we have

$$G \leq H \quad \text{if and only if} \quad L(A, B, C, D).[10]$$

Thus, the relations $\leq$ and L are interchangeable, and each gives the balance ordering.

The appropriate axioms for the balance ordering are stated in terms of S and L. As suggested by (6) of Section 5, we want axioms which allow us to show that there are positive numbers $f(3), f(4), \ldots, f(m), \ldots$ so that

$$L(A, B, C, D) \longleftrightarrow \frac{\displaystyle\sum_{m=3}^{\infty} f(m)a_m}{\displaystyle\sum_{m=3}^{\infty} f(m)(a_m + b_m)} \leq \frac{\displaystyle\sum_{m=3}^{\infty} f(m)c_m}{\displaystyle\sum_{m=3}^{\infty} f(m)(c_m + d_m)}. \tag{8}$$

AXIOMS FOR THE BALANCE ORDERING. Let A, B, C, D, E, F, A', C' be members of S.

AXIOM 1. *Connectedness:*
$L(A, B, C, D)$ or $L(C, D, A, B)$. In words, if G and H are signed digraphs with semicycle pairs (A, B) and (C, D) respectively, then G is no more balanced than H or H is no more balanced than G.

AXIOM 2. *Transitivity:*
$L(A, B, C, D)$ & $L(C, D, E, F) \rightarrow L(A, B, E, F)$. In words, if G, H, K are signed digraphs with semicycle pairs (A, B), (C, D), (E, F) respectively, and if G is no more balanced than H and H is no more balanced than K, then G is no more balanced than K.

AXIOM 3. *Reversal Condition:*
$L(A, B, C, D) \rightarrow L(D, C, B, A)$.

AXIOM 4. *Quadruple Condition:*
$L(A, B, C, D) \rightarrow L(A, C, B, D)$.

AXIOM 5. *Highest Balance:*
$L(A, O, B, O)$ & $\sim L(C, O, A, B)$. In words, $L(A, O, B, O)$ says that any

---

[10] To be technically precise, we must note the following implicit assumption: the order of balance of two signed digraphs depends solely on their semicycle pairs.

signed digraph with no negative semicycles is no more balanced than any other. $\sim L(C, O, A, B)$ says that a signed digraph with no negative semicycles is always more balanced than one with some negative semicycles.

AXIOM 6. *Lowest Balance:*
$L(O, A, O, B)$ & $\sim L(A, B, O, C)$. This axiom is analogous to Axiom 5.

AXIOM 7. *Positivity:*
$\sim L(C, C, A, A + B)$. In words, if some negative semicycles are added to a signed digraph whose positive and negative semicycle sequences are identical, the new signed digraph is strictly less balanced than any signed digraph whose positive and negative semicycle sequences are identical.

AXIOM 8. *Additivity:*
$L(A, B, C, D)$ & $L(A', B, C', D) \rightarrow L(A + A', B, C + C', D)$.

AXIOM 9. *Density of Rationals:*
$\sim L(A, B, C, D) \rightarrow (\exists k, \ell > 0)[\sim L(A, B, kE, \ell E)$ & $\sim L(kE, \ell E, C, D)]$.
In words, suppose G and H are signed digraphs with semicycle pairs (A, B) and (C, D) respectively, and suppose H is less balanced than G. Then given any sequence E, for some k and ℓ, the signed digraph with semicycle pair $(kE, \ell E)$ is less balanced than G and more balanced than H. This means that the rational number k/ℓ is between the balance assigned to H and that assigned to G.

The basic result here, as proven in Norman-Roberts (1972, Theorem 7), is the following.

THEOREM 4. Axioms 1–9 are necessary and sufficient for there to be positive numbers $f(m)$ so that (8) holds for all A, B, C, D in $\mathcal{S}$ with either $A \neq 0$ or $B \neq 0$ and either $C \neq 0$ or $D \neq 0$.

This result is related to a large body of work in the theory of measurement, in particular to papers by Hölder (1901), Holman (1969), Luce (1965), Marley (1968), Roberts and Luce (1968), Scott (1964), Suppes (1951), and Suppes and Zinnes (1963). The reader is referred to Norman-Roberts (1972) for details of the connection with this earlier work.

□ REFERENCES

Berger, J., B. P. Cohen, J. L. Snell, and M. Zelditch, *Types of Formalization in Small Group Research*, Houghton Mifflin, Boston, 1962.
Berger, J., M. Zelditch, and B. Anderson, *Sociological Theories in Progress*, I, Houghton Mifflin, New York, 1966.

Berger, J., M. Zelditch, B. Anderson, and B. P. Cohen, "Structural Aspects of Distributive Justice, a Status Value Formulation," in J. Berger, M. Zelditch, B. Anderson (eds.), *Sociological Theories in Progress*, II, Houghton Mifflin, New York, 1972.

Cartwright, D., and F. Harary, "Structural Balance: A Generalization of Heider's Theory," *Psych. Rev., 63* (1956), 277–293.

Flament, C., *Applications of Graph Theory to Group Structure*, Prentice-Hall, Englewood Cliffs, N. J., 1963.

Harary, F., "On Local Balance and N-balance in Signed Graphs," *Michigan Math. J., 3* (1955), 37–41.

Harary, F., "On the Measurement of Structural Balance," *Behavioral Sci., 4* (1959), 316–323.

Harary, F., "On the Notion of Balance of a Signed Graph," *Michigan Math. J., 2* (1954), 143–146.

Harary, F., R. Z. Norman, and D. Cartwright, *Structural Models: An Introduction to the Theory of Directed Graphs*, Wiley, New York, 1965.

Heider, F., "Attitudes and Cognitive Organization," *J. Psych., 21* (1946), 107–112.

Hölder, O., "Die Axiome der Quantität und die Lehre von Mass," *Berichte der sächsischen Gesellschaft der Wissenschaften, Mathematisch-physische Klasse, 53* (1901), 1–64.

Holman, E. W., "Strong and Weak Extensive Measurement," *J. Math. Psych., 6* (1969), 286–293.

Jordan, N., "Behavioral Forces that are a Function of Attitudes and of Cognitive Organization," *Human Relations, 6* (1953) 273–287.

Kemeny J. G., and J. L. Snell, *Mathematical Models in the Social Sciences*, Chap. II, "Preference Rankings: An Axiomatic Approach," Blaisdell, New York, 1962.

Luce, R. D., "A 'Fundamental' Axiomatization of Multiplicative Power Relations Among Three Variables," *Philosophy of Science, 32* (1965), 301–309.

Marley, A. A. J., "An Alternative 'Fundamental' Axiomatization of Multiplicative Power Relations Among Three Variables," *Philosophy of Science, 35* (1968), 185–186.

Morissette, J. O., "An Experimental Study of the Theory of Structural Balance," *Human Relations, 11* (1958), 239–254.

Norman, R. Z., and F. S. Roberts, "A Derivation of a Measure of Relative Balance for Signed Digraphs and a Characterization of Extensive Ratio Systems," *Journal of Mathematical Psychology, 9* (1972), 66–91.

Roberts, F. S., and R. D. Luce, "Axiomatic Thermodynamics and Extensive Measurement," *Synthese, 18* (1968), 311–326.

Scott, D., "Measurement Structures and Linear Inequalities," *J. Math. Psych., 1* (1964), 233–247.

Suppes, P., "A Set of Independent Axioms for Extensive Qualities," *Portugaliae Mathematica, 10* (1951), 162–172.

Suppes, P., and J. L. Zinnes, "Basic Measurement Theory," in R. D. Luce, R. R. Bush, E. Galanter (eds.), *Handbook of Mathematical Psychology*, I, John Wiley & Sons, New York, 1963, 1–76.

Taylor, H. F., *Balance in Small Groups*, Van Nostrand Reinhold, New York, 1970.

Zajonc, R. B., and E. Burnstein, "Structural Balance, Reciprocity and Positivity as Sources of Cognitive Bias," *Journal of Personality, 33* (1965), 570–583.

Zelditch, M., J. Berger, and B. P. Cohen, "Stability of Organizational Status Structures," in J. Berger et al. (eds.) *Sociological Theories in Progress*, I [1966], 269–294.

Contributors

Bo Anderson took his Fil. Kand degree in sociology and philosophy at Uppsala University, Sweden, in 1952, and his Fil. lic degree in 1955. Thereafter he worked at the Board for Psychological Defense, Department of the Interior, Stockholm, Sweden, during 1956–1957. From 1957 to 1959, he held a fellowship at the Bureau of Applied Social Research, Columbia University. He then returned to Uppsala as Lecturer in Sociology, until 1961. He was Assistant Professor, Department of Sociology, at Stanford University from 1961, and has been Professor in the Department of Sociology, Michigan State University since 1967.

Professor Anderson has published a number of articles in English and in Swedish in professional journals and books. His major interests lie in the areas of theory and the sociology of politics. He has done research in Sweden, Mexico, and the United States, and has also lectured at the Universities of Helsinki, Finland, and Göteborg, Sweden.

Otomar Jan Bartos received his Ph.D. in sociology from Yale University in 1958, and did his postdoctoral work in mathematics and computer science at Harvard and Columbia Universities. He has taught at the University of Hawaii, Northwestern University, University of Pittsburgh and Dartmouth College. He is now Professor of Sociology at the University of Colorado. Among his publications are *Simple Models of Group Behavior* and *Process and Outcome of Negotiations* (scheduled to be published in 1973).

Joseph Berger received his bachelor's degree from Brooklyn College, and both his master's and Ph.D. from Harvard. After five years at Dartmouth College as Instructor and Assistant Professor of Sociology, Dr. Berger went to Stanford University. He is now Professor of Sociology and Director of the Laboratory for Social Research at Stanford.

Dr. Berger is co-author of *Types of Formalization in Small-Group Research*, and is co-editor of *Sociological Theories in Progress*, Vol. I.

Dr. Berger has had a long-standing research interest in both the developing and experimental testing of Expectation-States theories. He has also done research on status-value processes and, at an earlier date, research on mathematical models of occupational mobility.

393

Bruce C. Busching received his Ph.D. in 1969 from Stanford University. He is currently Assistant Professor of Sociology at the University of Virginia, where he pursues his interest in simple social systems.

Santo F. Camilleri is Professor of Sociology at Michigan State University. He received his Ph.D. in 1955 from the University of California at Los Angeles. He has taught at the University of Washington, Stanford University, and San Diego State College. His interests are in experimental social psychology, formal theory and research methods.

Bernard P. Cohen received his bachelor's degree from Harvard University, his master's from the University of Minnesota, and his Ph.D. from Harvard, the last in 1957. After two years as Lecturer in Social Relations at Harvard, he became Research Associate in the Computation Center at the Massachusetts Institute of Technology, then a Fellow of the Institute for Advanced Study there. In 1958 he moved to the University of California (Berkeley), and thence to Stanford University, where he is presently Chairman of the Department of Sociology.

Dr. Cohen is author of *Conflict and Conformity: A Probability Model and Its Application*, and co-author of *Types of Formalization in Small-Group Research*. His interests include studies of conformity and social influence, reference group behavior, and political behavior.

Thomas L. Conner took both his bachelor's degree and Ph.D. from Stanford University, and is presently Associate Professor in the Department of Sociology and in the Cooperation/Conflict Research Group of the Computer Institute for Social Science Research at Michigan State University.

He is currently doing research on mathematical models of interaction in small groups and simulation of hostile and friendly interaction between nation states.

James A. Davis received his bachelor's degree in journalism from Northwestern University in 1950, master's in sociology in 1952 from the University of Wisconsin, and his Ph.D. in sociology from Harvard University in 1955. He has served on the faculties of the Harvard School of Public Health, Yale University, University of Chicago, University of Washington, The Johns Hopkins University, and Dartmouth College. He is currently Professor of Sociology and Director, National Opinion Research Center, University of Chicago.

Dr. Davis has published research on models of relative deprivation, graph theory models of small groups, and nonparametric statistical methods. He is also senior author of several books based on national surveys of college and graduate students.

Sanford M. Dornbusch received his Ph.D. in sociology from the University of Chicago in 1952. At present he is Professor of Sociology at Stanford University. With various collaborators, he is currently engaged in the preparation of a series of monographs examining the exercise of and the response to authority in such varied contexts as academic departments within a university, nursing wards, and conventional and radical alternative schools.

Richard M. Emerson received his bachelor's degree from the University of Utah in 1950 and the Ph.D. from the University of Minnesota in 1955. He taught social psychology at the University of Cincinnati for nine years, where he also held a research position with the Department of Psychiatry. Since 1964 he has taught at the University of Washington, where he is now Professor of Sociology.

Dr. Emerson's research and writing has featured theory and experiments on social power. He is currently engaged in experimental studies of power and position in exchange networks, and field-historical studies of network structures. Those interests are reflected in the two chapters he contributes to this volume.

Thomas J. Fararo received his Ph.D. in sociology from Syracuse University in 1963. From 1964 to 1967, he studied pure and applied mathematics at Stanford University, and since 1967 he has been at the University of Pittsburgh.

After several years of empirical research activity in such areas as community decision-making structures and friendship networks, Dr. Fararo began working on theoretical problems using modern mathematical formalisms. His major aim since 1967 has been to construct mathematical frameworks which reflect sociological intuition and which allow the analyst to prove general theorems with sociological content. At present, Dr. Fararo is completing a forthcoming book which is an introduction to mathematical sociology.

Charles Hubbell received his M.S. in mathematics and his Ph.D. in social psychology at the University of Michigan. He is Lecturer in Sociology at San Fernando Valley State College, having previously taught at the University of Iowa and the University of California, Santa Barbara.

Dr. Hubbell is interested in mathematical models of social and psychic structures, treating structure as either a dependent variable, as in balance theory, or as an independent variable, as in input-output analysis. He is currently engaged in research on the effect of negative links in communication structures, and roll-call analysis of legislative voting. Another interest is the formalization of social theory, where he is working on an axiomization of *The Prince*, by Machiavelli.

James C. Kimberly received his bachelor's and master's degrees from Emory University and his Ph.D. from Duke. Dr. Kimberly taught at Stanford as Assistant Professor of Sociology from 1963 to 1968 and at Emory University as Associate Professor of Sociology from 1968 to 1971. Presently, he is Program Director for Sociology for the National Science Foundation.

Dr. Kimberly's published work focuses on the basic nature of social systems and stratification, the process by which stratification structures develop, the equilibration and disequilibration processes which occur within stratification structures, and the social psychology of stratification processes. He is presently engaged in work on a book on change in stratification structures.

Sherman Krupp received his Ph.D. in economics from the University of California, Berkeley, in 1961. Until 1965 he taught economics at the University of Pittsburgh, Florida State University, and Lehigh University. In 1965 he was appointed Professor of Sociology at Queens College, City University.

Professor Krupp has published articles in both economics and sociology. His main interest has been in the philosophy of the social sciences and in organizational theory. He is the author of *Pattern in Organization Analysis* and he has also edited and contributed to a collection of original essays in the methodology of economics, *The Structure of Economic Science*. Presently, he is expanding the argument of his contributed essay into a theoretical book on organizations.

James D. Laing is Associate Professor of Political Science and Sociology, School of Urban and Public Affairs, Carnegie-Mellon University. He received his B.S. in mechanical engineering from the University of Rochester in 1957 and his Ph.D. from Stanford University in 1967. Dr. Laing's research and publications are focused in three areas of inquiry: (1) evaluation processes and authority systems in formal organizations; (2) bargaining coalitions and payoff allocations in N-person sequential games; and (3) methods of prediction and analyses with quantitative data.

Samuel Leinhardt received his B.A., M.A., and Ph.D. (1968) degrees in sociology from the University of Chicago. He spent a postdoctoral year (1968–1969) as a Social Science Research Council Fellow in Mathematical Sociology at Harvard University. In 1969 he joined the faculty of Carnegie-Mellon University with joint appointments in the School of Urban and Public Affairs and the Graduate School of Industrial Administration where he is currently Associate Professor of Sociology.

Dr. Leinhardt is currently pursuing research in the sociology of health, the sociology of education, and the sociology of interpersonal sentiment. Common to each of these endeavors is the development of mathematical models to describe the structure of complex social systems and the utilization of empirical data to test the models' fidelity to reality.

Thomas F. Mayer received his Ph.D. in 1966 from Stanford University and presently has a joint appointment in the Department of Sociology and the Institute of Behavioral Science at the University of Colorado in Boulder. Dr. Mayer's interests center around the process of change as it occurs in macro-social structures. He is attempting to develop methodologies suitable for rigorous analysis of historically significant social processes. Dr. Mayer's present research concerns the adaptation of Fourier analysis and spectral theory for the purpose of studying social change.

Robert Z. Norman received his Ph.D. in mathematics from the University of Michigan in 1954, where he also served as a research assistant at the Research Center for Group Dynamics applying graph theory to problems in social networks. Since 1956 he has been teaching at Dartmouth where he is now Professor of Mathematics and Chairman of the Program in Mathematics and the Social Sciences. He is co-author with F. Harary and D. Cartwright of *Structural Models: An Introduction to the Theory of Directed Graphs*. His research interests combine graph theory and combinatorial mathematics with the development of models in sociology and psychology.

Richard Ofshe received his bachelor's and master's degrees in psychology and sociology from Queens College of the City University of New York and his Ph.D. from Stanford University in 1968. He joined the faculty at the University of California at Berkeley in 1967 as an Assistant Professor and was promoted to Associate Professor in 1971.

Dr. Ofshe's major research interests are in the areas of interpersonal behavior in small groups, attitude measurement, and utopian social design. His published books include *Utility and Choice in Social Interaction* and the *Sociology of the Possible*. A third book, *Interpersonal Behavior in Small Groups*, is scheduled for publication in 1972 and a fourth book, *Experimental Research Methods*, is nearing completion.

Fred S. Roberts received his Ph.D. in mathematics from Stanford University in 1968. He spent a semester as postdoctoral fellow in mathematical psychology in the Psychology Department at the University of Pennsylvania and then joined the Mathematics Department at the Rand Corporation in July 1968, where he remained until 1971. During the academic year 1971–72, he was a member of the Social Sciences Program at the Institute for Advanced Study, Princeton, New Jersey. Starting in 1972, he became an Associate Professor of Mathematics at Rutgers University.

Dr. Roberts' major interests have been mathematical models in psychology, sociology, and the environmental sciences. He has been especially interested in problems of graph theory, measurement theory, and ordered systems. His work has been concerned both with the applications of mathematics and with the influence of the social sciences on the development of new and potentially applicable mathematics.

W. Richard Scott received his Ph.D. in sociology from the University of Chicago. He is currently Professor of Sociology at Stanford University. He is a student of complex organizations, in particular those in which substantial numbers of professional employees are involved. He continues his interest in control systems in organizations and more recently has initiated a series of studies focused on the interrelations of technology or techniques of task performance and selected aspects of organizational structure.

Morris Zelditch, Jr. received his bachelor's degree from Oberlin College, and his Ph.D. from Harvard University. After five years as Instructor and Assistant

Professor of Sociology at Columbia University, he moved to Stanford University, where he was chairman of the Sociology Department from 1964 to 1968.

Dr. Zelditch is author of *A Basic Course in Sociological Statistics*, and co-author of *Types of Formalization in Small-Group Research*. His research includes the study of authority in experimentally created bureaucratic organizations and cross-cultural studies of role-differentiation in the family.

Index

Ability, 30, 31
Act, cost of, defined, 97
Actor: motivations of, 21; and utility assumptions, 22; and available responses, 23; and theory of social exchange, 24; in game situation, 28; in team behavior, 28–29; and frequency of actions, 40; stimulus generalization and differentiation, 43; behavioral repetoire of, 46; specific definition of, 61; category of, 83; collective, 85–86; characteristics of, 119, 126, 144; and status situation, 128–129; Galtung, 184, 194–211: Kimberly, 211–214
Adams, J. S., 90, 121, 122, 127
Additivity, 390
Alienation: during French 1968 revolt, x–xi, xiv; law of, xv
Alternatives, 60
Altruism, 61
American Occupational Structure, The (Blau and Duncan), 309
American Sociological Association, xvi
American Sociological Review, The, 231
American Soldier, The (Stouffer et al.), 89, 90
Anderson, B., 90, 183, 364, 378
Animal behavior, 42, 43, 49, 50
Anomic state, 123–124; in status situation, 145
Answering order: and bias conditions, 265; prediction of, 266
Antecedence, 343
Appraising right, 166
Approval, 31–32; of experimenter, 32; of partner, 35
Asch, S. E., 92
Ashby, W. R., 196
Aspiration, 21; educational, xii–xiii, xvi; levels of, 10, 28, 54, 55; loss of, 77; status, 84; for high system ranks, 298
Association, of elements, 129–130

Association relations, 140–141; and relevance relations, 141
Atkinson, John, 54n
Atkinson, R. C., 187, 188, 189
Attitude: formation, 88; evolution of, 90
Authority, 162–179; as authorized control, 164; link, 166, 167; relationship, 166, 167; comparison of concepts of, 168–170; and legitimacy, 168–169
Authority rights, 165–166; defined, 164; and negative evaluations, 168
Authority structure, xx; defined, 167
Authority system, 166–167; incompatability of, 163, 170–179; defined, 166; structural, 167, 171; and legitimacy, 168–169; unstable, 176–177
Autokinesis, and influence, 92
Avoidance, 24

Backman, Carl, 38
Balance: and exchange relations, 62, 66; measurement of, 63; and initiations, 66; state of, 67; Heider's theory of cognitive, 99; defined, 100; vacuous, 100; and status, 132–133, 141, 145; of local system, 136; type process, 298; measure of relative, 358–391; of a social structure, 360; theory of structural, 360; ordering, 365, 389–390; measure, 370–375, 379, 381, 388; uniqueness of ordering, 371; description of measure, 372–373; parameters of measure, 375–377; local, 377–378; ordering and distributive justice, 378–388; lowest, 390
Balancing processes, 68, 69, 86; and division of labor, 74; through withdrawal, 77; and power in unilateral monopoly, 80; and boundaries, 81
Bank Wiremen, behavior of, 219, 229

401

Homogeneous system, 208
Hughes, E. C., xviin; status ambiguity formulation of, 120–121
Hurewitz, Paul, 232
Hyman, H., xviiin, 88, 89

Justice: process, 120; formulation of problem, 120–122; in local system, 135–136, 137; in status situation, 141, 145; defined, 144; collective vs. individual, 145; cases of, 380

Identification, within social strata, 341
Imbalance: states of, 99, 100, 101; self vs. others, 144; degree of, 197; self, 380
Imbalance, collective, 380, 388; cases of, 381; distinction among cases of, 382–383; and coalition behavior, 384–387
Incompatibility: of authority system, 163, 170–171; sources of, 171–176; and contradiction, 172; and instability, 176–177; resolution of, 177–178; empirical studies, 178–179
Individual, generalized: characteristics of, 133; and goal objects, 133
Influence: acceptance of in decision-making, 30; of partner's decision, 35; operation of, 91; systems, 254
Initiation, 55–57, 59, 69, 84; in operant language, 45; timing of, 47–48; operationalizing the concept of, 49; and balance-imbalance, 66
Injustice: in status situations, 141; collective and individual, 142; definitions, 144
Input: exogenous and endogenous, 255, 259; overload, 275, 278–283
Input-output model, 252–253, 287
Instability: and incompatibility, 176–177; defined, 176; hypothesis predicting the presence of, 179
Interaction: social, 60; frequencies of, 218–219; multiplier, 284–285
Interdependence, as a source of incompatibility, 173
Interpersonal utility comparisons, 62
Intersystem: process, 292, 298; level, 299
Intrasystem: stratification, 292, 298; level, 299
Investigation, xii; historical, xi, xiv, xviii; generalizing, xi, xv; pure historically oriented, xvi
Investments, 126; and exchange formulation, 127
Israel, J., 144

Jackson, E. F., xviii, 185
James, John, 232
James, R., 92
Jaques, Elliot, measure of responsibility, 170
Jay, Phyllis, essay on Indian langur, 230
Jessor, Richard, 232
Judgment, 28

Kadushin, Charles, 81, 82, 83
Kelleher, Roger, 53n
Kelley, Harold H., 38, 41, 47, 49, 55n, 88, 89, 91, 113
Kemeney, J. G., 314, 315, 365, 367, 370
Kendall's *tau*, 270, 271; generalization of, 287–289
Kenkel W. F., xviii
Kimberly, J. C., 183, 184, 212; substatuses of theory of status equilibration of, 185; treatment of equilibration, 195; formulation of "the structure of status," 211; system, 213
Kimberly Actor, 211–214; functions of, 211
Kluckhohn, C., 186
Kogen, M., 313, 315, 316, 322
Kuhn, Alfred, 38, 41, 62

Lange, O., 196
Lantz, Donald L., 232
Lawrence, D., 144
Leavitt, Harold, 285
Lenski, G. E., xvii, xviii, 90, 120, 121
Leontief, Wassily, 252
Levine, Joel, 321, 322
LeVine, Robert A., 232
Levi-Strauss, Claude, 253
Lewin, Kurt, 23; field theory, 53
Liking: frequencies of, 219; degrees of, 287
Links, weighted: in communication networks, 252–290; strengths of, 253; control of strength, 258, 259; choice of weights, 281; operationalizing of, 287
Living, level of, 77
Local system: and referential structure, 135, 138; and status value, 135, 137, 138; balance and justice in, 136; characteristics and goal objects of, 137, 139; and association relations, 140
Losses, in decision-making theory, 23, 24
Lövgren, Esse, 253
Luce, R. D., 25, 27, 187, 214, 390; ranking postulate status of, 188, 189
Lyle, William H., 232

McCarthy, P. J., 313, 315, 316, 322
McFarland, D. D., 214
McGinnis, Robert, 318–319
McKersie, R. B., 5